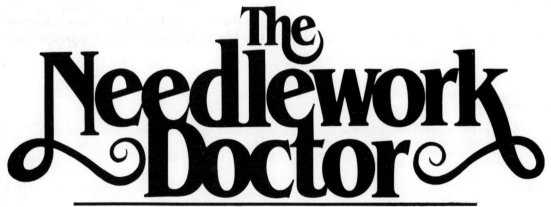

The Needlework Doctor

How to Solve Every Kind of Needlework Problem

Mary Kay Davis

Illustrations—ELIZABETH MEYER
Embroidery Consultant—BEATRICE FULTON KEEBER

Black-and-White Photography—JACK KAUSCH of Jack Kausch Photography
Color Photography—MASON PAWLAK of Boulevard Photographic, Inc.

A SPECTRUM BOOK

Prentice-Hall, Inc., Englewood Cliffs, N.J. 07632

Library of Congress Cataloging in Publication Data

Davis, Mary Kay.
　　The needlework doctor.
　　"A Spectrum Book."
　　Includes index.
　　1. Needlework.　I. Title.
TT751.D38　　1982　　　　746.4　　　　82–12331
ISBN 0–13–611087–8
ISBN 0–13–611079–7 (pbk.)

**This book is dedicated to
Penny, Betsy, and Matt Davis—
my three most satisfying projects.**

This book is available at a special discount when ordered
in large quantities. Contact Prentice-Hall, Inc., General Publishing
Division, Special Sales, Englewood Cliffs, N.J. 07632.

ISBN 0-13-611079-7

ISBN 0-13-611087-8 {PBK.}

Editorial/production supervision
　　and page layout by Inkwell
Interior design by Maria Carella
　　and Christine Gehring Wolf
Color insert design by Christine Gehring Wolf
Manufacturing buyer: Cathie Lenard
Cover design by Hal Siegel
Illustrated by Elizabeth Meyer
Embroidery consultant: Beatrice Fulton Keeber
Black-and-white photos by Jack Kausch,
　　Jack Kausch Photography
Color photography by Mason Pawlak,
　　Boulevard Photographic, Inc.

All anecdotes in this book are based in fact,
but names and places have been changed
to prevent identification of particular students and classes.

Prentice-Hall International, Inc., *London*
Prentice-Hall of Australia Pty. Limited, *Sydney*
Prentice-Hall Canada Inc., *Toronto*
Prentice-Hall of India Private Limited, *New Delhi*
Prentice-Hall of Japan, Inc., *Tokyo*
Prentice-Hall of Southeast Asia Pte. Ltd., *Singapore*
Whitehall Books Limited, Wellington, *New Zealand*
Editora Prentice-Hall do Brasil Ltda., *Rio de Janeiro*

Contents

Preface, vii
How to Use This Book, xi
Preventive Medicine, xiii

PREPARATION

 Education, 3
INTRODUCTION, 3
TEACHERS AND CLASSES, 4
PUBLICATIONS, 7 (Understanding Directions, 9)
GROUPS AND GUILDS, 12 (E.G.A., 13; N.S.C.A.E.,
    13; Valentine Museum 14)

 Kits, 15
INTRODUCTION, 15
ALL KITS, 17
NEEDLEPOINT, 20 (Stranded Yarn, 18, 20; Tapestry
    Yarn, 19, 21)
EMBROIDERY, 21 (Floss, 18; Twisted Threads, 19)

 Design and Color, 23
INTRODUCTION, 24
DESIGN, 25 (Theory, 25; Design Facts, 26; Design
    Balance Chart, 28)
COLOR, 28 (Vocabulary, 28; Theory, 29; Color
    Facts, 31; Using Color, 32)
TEXTURE, 32
FINAL YARN CHECK, 39

 Creative Problem Solving, 40
INTRODUCTION, 41
GAMES AND TECHNIQUES, 42 (Locating Problems,
    43; Identifying Problems, 43; Gathering
    Solutions, 44; Choosing Cure, 47)

PROCESS

 What to Buy and Where to Store It, 53
INTRODUCTION, 54
SHOPPING GUIDELINES, 54
NEEDLEPOINT SHOPPING, 56 (Yarn Volumes Chart, 57)
EMBROIDERY SHOPPING, 58 (Counted Thread
    Volumes Chart, 58; Embroidery Purchases, 59)
STORAGE, 59 (Canvas, 60; Cloth, 61; Threads, 62;
    Yarns, 64; Accessories, 66)

 Marking, Painting and Dyeing, 69
INTRODUCTION, 70
PAINT, 70 (Pens and Inks, 71; Pen Test, 71; Crayons,
    72; Dyes, 72)
COLOR BLEEDING, 77

 How to Start, 78
NEEDLEPOINT INTRODUCTION, 78 (Techniques,
    80; Tension, 84; Transferring Designs, 87;
    Changing Scale, 87)
EMBROIDERY INTRODUCTION, 89 (Hoops, 90;
    Techniques, 91; Transferring Designs, 94)

 Stitching Excellence and Mistake Survival, 96
UNIVERSAL EXCELLENCE, 97
NEEDLEPOINT EXCELLENCE, 98 (Surviving
    Mistakes, 102)
EMBROIDERY EXCELLENCE, 104 (Surviving
    Mistakes, 106; White Yarn Erasers, 106)

MATERIALS

 Canvas and Cloth, 109
CANVAS INTRODUCTION, 109 (Vocabulary, 110;
    Canvas Types, 110; Gauge, 110; Quality, 113;
    Denier Test, 114; Grain, 116)
CLOTH INTRODUCTION, 116 (Suitability, 117;
    Purchasing, 118; Weave, 119; Grain, 119)

 Woolen Yarn, 121
INTRODUCTION, 121 (Types, 123; Suitability, 125;
    Dyes, 126; Grain, 127; Techniques, 129)
YOU THE CONSUMER, 127

 Non-Woolen Threads, 131
INTRODUCTION, 131 (Vocabulary, 132)
PROTEIN (ANIMAL) FIBERS, 134

CELLULOSE (PLANT) AND MAN-MADE FIBERS, 135
PETROLEUM-BASED MAN-MADE FIBERS, 136
FIBER CHARACTERISTICS CHART, 137 (Fiber
    Identification Tests, 140)

 Accessories, 144
INTRODUCTION, 144 (Beeswax, 145; Chatelaine,
    145; Emery Ball, 146; Frames, 146; Hoops, 147;
    Lamps, 148; Magnifiers, 149; Measures, 150;
    Needles, 151; Needle Book, 152; Needle
    Gripper, 152; Needle Threader, 153; Pin
    Cushion, 153; Scissors, 153; Stitch Finders, 153;
    Thimble, 154; Trolly Needle, 154; Waterproof
    and Disappearing Marking Pens, 154; Yarn and
    Thread Organizers, 154)

COMPLETION

 Cleaning, Wet or Dry, 159
INTRODUCTION, 159
CLEANING CATEGORIES, 161 (Cleaning
    Compounds, 165; Dye Fast Test, 166)
NEEDLEPOINT CLEANING, 167
EMBROIDERY CLEANING, 171

 Blocking, 174
INTRODUCTION, 174
NEEDLEPOINT BLOCKING, 175 (Vocabulary, 175;
    Theory, 176; Materials, 178; Techniques, 179;
    Color Bleeding, 187)
EMBROIDERY BLOCKING, 190 (Materials, 191;
    Techniques, 190)

 Finishing, 193
INTRODUCTION, 193
THE ENLIGHTENED CONSUMER, 194 (Linings and
    Trims, 194; Interlinings and Other Stiffeners, 195;
    Stuffings, 196; Fabric Protection Sprays, 196;
    Glues, 197)
UNIVERSAL FINISHING TECHNIQUES, 197
EMBROIDERY FINISHING, 201
NEEDLEPOINT FINISHING, 202

 Framing, 207
INTRODUCTION, 207
CHOOSING THE FRAME, 209
UNIVERSAL FRAMING TECHNIQUES, 211
NEEDLEPOINT FRAMING, 215
EMBROIDERY FRAMING, 216

UNUSUAL PROJECTS **Wall Hangings, 223**
INTRODUCTION, 223 (Design, 224; Stitching, 225;
Finishing, 226; Display, 228; Cleaning, 230;
Preservation, 230)

 Upholstery, 231
INTRODUCTION, 232
RECYCLING OLD UPHOLSTERY, 232
NEW UPHOLSTERY, 233 (Design, 233; Stitching
Tips, 235; Professional Upholsterers, 237;
Cleaning, 238; Preservation, 238)

 Rugs, 240
INTRODUCTION, 241; (Materials, 242; Stitching
Tips, 244; Tack Frame, 244; Finishing, 246;
Cleaning, 250; Repairing, 251)

 Antique Needlework, 252
INTRODUCTION, 252
IDENTIFICATION, 253 (Needlepoint, 253; Dyes,
256; Embroidery, 257)
PRESERVATION, 258 (Cleaning, 258; Table of
Cleaning Techniques for Antique Needlework,
259; Re-Blocking, 260; Repairing, 262)
CONSERVATION, 263 (Safe Display, 265; Storage,
266)

Bibliography, 268
Glossary, 273
Appendix, 281
    (Evenweave Cloth/Canvas—Needle—Thread
    Chart, 281; Embroidery Cloth Facts Chart, 283;
    Woolen Facts Chart, 282; Non-Woolen Thread
    Facts Chart, 284; Canvas Conversion Chart, 285)
Index, 286

Preface

How do I clean it? What should I do if dyes run? Will something awful happen if I store it in a plastic bag? These and other practical questions are encountered every day by every stitcher. *The Needlepoint Doctor* has collected information from the worlds of science and industry to shed light on stitching problems. The answers collected form a medicine chest with remedies for all needleworkers, from beginner to super-star.

Learn how to wash purse flaps, pillow tops, and other previously considered "unwashables," without having to dismantle them. Discover what you can clean yourself and—just as important—what's beyond your capabilities. Then find how to locate a *good* dry cleaner.

Read how to judge needlepoint canvas quality, all by yourself. The Denier Test is the key, and it's located in Chapter 9.

The Doctor contains charts to fill out so that you finally can determine for yourself just how much yarn—or thread—you'll need for the whole project. No more being sold four ounces too much or, even worse, one ounce too little.

Don't let the big ones get away. Upholstery, wall hangings and rugs are undertakings that are perfectly possible for all motivated stitchers. *The Doctor* is where you learn how to design, stitch, finish, display, clean, and preserve such accomplishments.

How many yards are in your skein of yarn? How many colors does a thread manufacturer produce? What's it made of and how will it behave? Tables containing all these facts and many more are located in *The Doctor's* Appendix.

Your trunk may contain a tablecloth stitched by your grandmother or a pillow embroidered by your mother-in-law. Directions for cleaning, repairing and displaying such "antiques" are to be found in *The Doctor*. Discover what you can—and can't—do with them.

All types of needlework, from needlepoint to surface stitchery to counted-thread embroidery, are treated in *The Doctor's* clinic. Embroidery answers can often illuminate needlepoint problems, and vice versa.

Facts and directions are illustrated by more than 250 photographs and drawings. Not only can you read answers to your questions, you can see the techniques and examples discussed.

The Doctor was prepared after reviewing hundreds of questions sent by needlework guilds throughout the United States. The problems that they raised are all included here, plus many, many more. Every stitcher will need a remedy from this medicine chest at some time or other.

There's never been a needlework book like this before. Information that sheds light on stitchery problems has been gathered from the fields of dry cleaning, museum conservation, organic chemistry, optics, psychology, physics, physiology and textiles. Facts have been clearly organized so that you can quickly discover what to do and how to go about doing it. Preservation, display, cleaning and repair—topics most other books don't touch—are thoroughly discussed here. And fortunately The Doctor makes house calls.

ACKNOWLEDGMENTS

Perhaps somewhere there's a race of super stitchers who could have written a book of this scope unaided. I'm not one of them. From the beginning it was obvious that if *The Doctor* were to see the light of day, I would have to depend upon the knowledge, talent, and good will of many gifted individuals. I am enormously grateful to each of the following:

First thanks go to "the team" of Liza Meyer, Bea Keeber, Jack Kausch, and Mason Pawlak, who belie the old saw that creative people are difficult to work with. It would be hard to locate four more gifted individuals than these, and without exception they were always thoroughly professional and totally delightful.

I'm not sure mere thanks are sufficient for Jan Crites, who needlepointed an illustration long distance—from Oregon to Michigan. It arrived on time, flawless and in perfect shape.

Vivian White of the Embroiderers' Guild helped me develop the original concept for this book and added to the *Materials* section from her vast store of expertise.

Museum conservators have greatly assisted *The Doctor*. Mary Ballard of the Detroit Institute of Arts provided invaluable input. John Bertalan, former Conservator, and Nancy Bryk, Textile Curatorial Aide at Greenfield Village and Henry Ford Museum, were unfailing sources of information and assistance.

No book of this type could be compiled without the assistance of research librarians. I was fortunate to have two excellent groups at my disposal: Joan W. Gartland and her staff at Greenfield Village and Henry Ford Museum; and Lee Tuttle and her staff at the Baldwin Public Library in Birmingham, Michigan.

I greatly appreciate the generosity of John and Trudy Steel, and William and Emily Strain, who allowed me to photograph antique textiles from their collections for inclusion in this book.

The needlepoint rug photographed in Chapter 19 was designed and stitched by Stephanie Doane, who kindly allowed me to Stretch-Block and photograph it. The needlepoint articles which were photographed being cleaned in Chapter 13 were very kindly lent by Joanne Shaw and Mary Larson.

Information leading to Stretch-Block directions first reached me through Elizabeth Rawlins of the National Cathedral in Washington, D.C., for whom this needlepoint technique was originated. Special thanks go to Helen I. Giammattei, of Wilmington, Delaware, for providing information from her practical experience with this type of blocking.

Professionals from various industries and firms generously shared their knowledge with The Doctor. Sincere thanks go to Roger Bognar of The American Paper Institute; Dick Crandall of Boulevard Photographic; Jack Crease of Appleton Bros., Ltd.; Maggie Gerson of Paternayan Brothers, Inc.; Dr. Thomas Gilmore and Tim Shackleford of The Stearns and Foster Co.; Camille Harbeck, graphic artist; Dr. Willard H. Keeber of Exxon Chemical Americas; Margaret McCormick and Sally Frisch of The Chatelaine Shop, Trenton, Michigan; Ernest W. Oskin of Huron Plastics; Virginia Richards of Detroit Edison; Arnold H. Rosman of the Dry Cleaning Institute; Bernie Saks of Kent Upholstering; J.K. Southwick of Van Wyck Products Co., Inc.; Donald P. Tassone of The Procter and Gamble Company; Joan Toggitt of Joan Toggitt Ltd.; Harry D. Wesch of The Wesch Cleaners; and Wade Wetmore and Mary Plimpton of Crown Zellerbach Corporation.

Thanks also go to my editor, Mary Kennan of Spectrum Books, for her help, advice, and cooperation.

And finally there's my husband Michael. He edited the manuscript, found detours around obstacles, put up with less-than-gourmet meals and suffered through unfinished needlework hanging on his dining room walls. Somebody like me is lucky to be married to somebody like him.

GUILD GRATITUDE

There isn't time or room to thank all the individual needleworkers who shared their stitching problems with The Doctor. The names of their organizations and guilds are given below and my most sincere thanks go to each of them.

California: Humboldt, Santa Clara Valley; *Connecticut:* Connecticut River Valley; *District of Columbia:* Washington, D.C.; *Florida:* Biscayne, Goldcoast, Sarasota; *Georgia:* Georgia; *Hawaii:* Hawaii; *Illinois:* Central Illinois Stitchers, Wild Onion; *Indiana:* Indianapolis; *Kansas:* Sante Fe Trail; *Kentucky:* Stitchery Guild of Kentucky, Bluegrass; *Massachusetts:* Boston, Berkshire County; *Michigan:* Ann Arbor, Birmingham–Bloomfield, Birmingham Antique Study Group, Dearborn-Fairlane, Flint Needle Pushers, Greenfield Village and Henry Ford Museum classes, Kalamazoo,

Metropolitan Detroit, Mid-Michigan, Monguagon, Needlework and Textile Guide of Michigan, Rochester; *Minnesota:* Needlework Guild of Minnesota; *New Jersey:* Colonial West Jersey, Princeton; *New York:* Buffalo, Genesee Valley, Long Island, Manhattan, Mohawk; *Ohio:* Dayton, Needle Arts of Toledo, Preble County Extension Homemakers; *Pennsylvania:* Altoona, Philadelphia, Red Rose; *West Virginia:* Tri-Area; *Wisconsin:* Badger, Fox Valley, Madison Area; *Mexico:* Mexico City.

How To Use This Book

Two sorts of patients consult *The Needlework Doctor*. If you're a speedy stitcher, you want a fast diagnosis: long-winded explanations get in your way. But if you're an information seeker, you want full disclosure: fast answers seem superficial when you're trying to learn. Speedy or Seeker, this book has been written expressly for you.

Here's how it works: *The Needlepoint Doctor* is to be taken as needed. You don't swallow every pill in your medicine chest all at once! When a symptom pops up in your work, decide whether it's located in Preparation, Process, Materials or Completion. Look at the chapter heads in the Contents for your chosen section, and the list of topics that follow them. That's where your cure can be found.

Every chapter starts with an introduction that gives basic information for all Seekers (and any Speedys who feel so inclined). Questions appear and are numbered in the order in which they arise as the project grows.

Speedy answers are printed in **bold-faced type** for easy visibility. When you have a choice of several approaches, answers are separated by the word -*OR*-.

The treatment for one sickness can often cure another. When this happens, a cross-reference to the original problem's chapter and question numbers will appear in parentheses for "(Chapter 4, Q13)." If the reference is within the chapter you're reading, only the question number will appear.

All charts and tests located in another part of the book refer to exact page numbers so that finding them is easy.

Tables of information about specific brands of yarn, threads, canvas and cloth are numbered with Roman numerals (I-V) and located in the Appendix.

Consumerism is a large part of healthy stitchery. Which remedies will give you the best results for your money and time? Consumer information is identified by a "$".

If you want to build up your creative muscles, read Creative Problem-Solving (Chapter 4). It contains games that get you in touch with the gifts that lie untapped, just beneath your surface.

With stitchery as with sore feet, why settle for life with a bunion when radiant health can be found just ahead? The Doctor is in!

Preventive Medicine

It's easier to prevent problems than to cure them once they've turned into plagues. Here are some pitfalls for your needlework to avoid so that its glowing health—and your pride—can continue indefinitely.

Acids

As wood and its wood-pulp children, paper and cardboard, age they produce minute amounts of acids. In less than a year these acids start accumulating and affect any textile fibers that touch them. The first disease symptoms are brown spots and brittleness. They come from oxidation, the same process that toasts bread but moving at a much slower rate.

The best way to combat acid deterioration is to prevent fibers from touching wood, paper or cardboard. But that's easier said than done if you want needlework framed, stored or upholstered.

Cloth can be protected by inserting barriers of polyurethane varnish, shellac or aluminum foil between the fabric and wood products. The liquids seal wood surfaces and form barriers that acids can't cross. Aluminum foil also prevents acid penetration, but aluminum itself must be separated from textiles by another barrier layer, this time of cloth. Aluminum ages ungracefully and can mar needlework if it rubs against it.

Hint: Always wash the sizing from cloth before placing it next to needlework. Starch in sizing oxidizes and forms acids, which is what you're trying to prevent.

Cardboard and paper, including tissue paper, behave just as their mother wood does. If you store a valued sampler wrapped in regular tissue paper, you're inviting chicken pox into the kindergarten.

Acid-Free Paper Products

Fortunately paper and cardboard can be manufactured from cloth scraps or chemically neutralized wood pulp, both of which are acid-free. They cost more but they age beautifully.

Acid-free paper products should be used in the wise framing, display and storage of your needlework. They aren't widely available and you may have to hunt for them a bit. Here's where to look.

CARDBOARD

Picture framers who frame valuable prints or engravings use acid-free "rag board" or "museum board." These cardboards come in a variety of colors and are safe—with this one exception: Some cardboards are 100% acid-free. Their edges look solid all the way through. Others are made of cheaper, acid-producing cardboard with a sheet of acid-free paper glued on top and bottom. Their edges look like a sandwich. If you plan to wrap embroidery around cardboard, choose the solid kind or cloth will develop a thin layer of browning and crack where it touches the acid edge.

BOXES AND TISSUE PAPER

Librarians use boxes and tissue paper in the preservation of valuable books and papers. If you live near a major museum or library with an archivist, he or she may be able to let you buy acid-free materials directly. But almost any librarian will have a catalogue from a reputable supplier of acid-free paper products. Order what you want by mail.

Perhaps someday, in the best of all possible worlds, needlework shops will carry acid-free tissue paper and storage boxes. It will certainly help needlework—and needleworkers—age more gracefully.

Toilet Paper

Warning: Over the years the word coming down the grapevine has been that toilet paper is acid-free. Supposedly the United States government passed legislation regulating this. Unfortunately, *this is not true.*

The trade organization for the American paper industry has never heard of such legislation. Two of the largest paper manufacturers in the United States have never heard of acid-free toilet paper either. They don't produce it, don't know anyone who does, and believe that the cost to manufacture such a product would make it too expensive to compete in the market place.

Perhaps, somewhere, an acid-free toilet paper does exist. But the major brands that move in America's interstate commerce today are no more acid-free than the brown paper bags you carry them home in.

Plastics

Everything in today's world seems to be wrapped in plastic, and needlework is no exception. Horror stories have been told about problems with dyes and fabrics, but plastics have great value for needleworkers when wisely used.

The most confusing thing about plastics is that without a Ph.D. in organic chemistry, you have a hard time telling one from another. Here are some facts to help identify them.

Polyethylene is probably the most common plastic in your kitchen. It's semi-opaque, inexpensive, lighter than water and *very stable* (in fact it's in trouble with environmentalists over that point—acids, alkalies, and solvents can't break it down). Most plastic bags, waste baskets, garbage cans and some plastic wraps are made of polyethylene. Usually it has a "waxy" feel, although no grease spots will transfer to cloth.

Polyvinylchloride (PVC) is dense, heavier than water, and it needs the addition of a "plasticizer" to improve its flexibility. The plasticizer is the problem here because it can wash out or rub off and could leave spots on fabrics. An example is the PVC shower curtain that grows increasingly stiff as its plasticizers wash away.

Anything labeled "vinyl" is PVC and should be avoided for storing needlework. Saran-type films, plastic upholstery materials and artificial leathers are usually made of this plastic.

Polystyrene is a clear, rigid plastic that is heavier than water and is attacked by some solvents. Plastic boxes are often made of it. Such boxes won't stain your needlework, but don't let moth crystals, sprays, alcohols, or their fumes touch this plastic.

Nylon forms cook-and-serve bags for storing and heating frozen foods. Such bags are strong and safe for storing fibers.

How do you tell one of these from the other? Look for labels.

-OR-

Put the plastic into a full bathtub and see if it floats or sinks. Then check against the preceding list of characteristics to pinpoint your plastic.

Plastic Storage

Most plastics are safer for storing needlepoint than acid-producing paper products. They keep dust and water from cloth. If the plastic is opaque, it can eliminate penetration of sunlight and ultra-violet radiation. Plastics are cheap, easily available and, let's face it, many stitchers use them for textile storage. What risks are they taking?

Mold and mildew can develop on cotton and linen—if the bags or boxes are sealed. Plastic not only keeps water out, it also seals it in. As air temperatures cool, moisture trapped in air inside a sealed plastic container will form water droplets and dampen the cloth inside the container. Mold and mildew spores that exist everywhere start to sprout in the dark, humid atmosphere—and you've got problems.

But if bags and boxes are left open and not packed together so tightly that air can't circulate, mold and mildew have no more chance inside than outside. The difference is free movement of air, or "allowing the cloth to breathe."

Permanent textile storage should not utilize plastic containers of any kind. We just don't know enough about how plastics will affect textiles over the long haul. Use washed cloth bags, acid-free cardboard boxes, or wood with a barrier between the needlework and the container.

However, short-term storage of textiles in plastic for *less than a year* probably will do little harm if the cloth can breathe. Use new containers and consume what you're storing as quickly as you can.

There is a need for paper manufacturers to produce acid-free paper bags and boxes for textile storage. These would solve most of our storage problems and The Doctor would unhesitatingly prescribe them.

PREPARATION

To make a dream into a reality, you have to begin somewhere. In needlework, as in medicine, the best place to start is usually at the beginning. Information is what you need and you don't have to go to medical school to find it.

For the class-oriented student, many gifted teachers make their services available for nominal fees. Check adult education programs in your school system, community centers, local colleges, museums and needlework shops. In Chapter 1 you will learn how to evaluate and benefit from such teachers and classes.

For the "do-it-yourselfer," many magazines and books are available in which talented artists tell you how to duplicate their creations. Chapter 1 tells how to get the most information from such directions.

Once you've learned how to do it, the next question is "What will I do?" The simplest answer may be a needlework kit. Chapter 2 tells how to profit from a kit's advantages while protecting yourself from its drawbacks.

If striking out on your own is more your style, you'll need some information about color and design. Chapter 3 uncovers therapeutic facts about the colors you'll see and the designs you'll create.

And if your creation comes down with the ague, read Chapter 4 to find how to diagnose and cure it. Creative problem-solving is as useful to the needlework designer as aspirin is to the general practitioner, and it's a lot more fun!

Preparation is where your dreams still live protected in your thoughts, before they've developed liver spots or hang nails. It's any project's Golden Time.

1 Education

FIGURE 1-1

As a needlework teacher who writes, I've done a lot of thinking about communication. Clarification flows easiest between you and me when I can see the lost look in your eyes. But instant feedback isn't available in print. We writers pick the best words we can—and then pray that they'll carry the message.

Sometimes, of course, that message just doesn't get through. The most dramatic example I can remember came stamping into one of my beginning needlepoint classes in the hands of a frustrated kindergarten teacher named Estelle.

Estelle had read a long, detailed "authoritative" article on blocking in a national magazine. She'd bought all the paraphernalia and spent one whole weekend pulling and tugging and mashing her thumbs. By classtime, the needlepoint was still warped out of shape and, by now, so was Estelle.

Unfortunately, nowhere in the article's three pages of fine print was water ever mentioned. The dry canvas had fought Estelle every step of the way—and the canvas had won (until I irrigated it).

The moral of the story is worth taking to heart. No matter what "expert" advice you choose to follow, keep a grain of salt handy. If it doesn't make sense to you, it may not make sense—period. Get a second opinion.

INTRODUCTION

Needlework ideas and information are usually communicated in three ways: through classes, in print, and by talking with other stitchers.

The wise stitcher chooses her teachers and classes with care. Questions to ask and information to collect before selecting classes are listed in this chapter.

Newspapers, magazines, and books communicate through words, pictures, graphs, and diagrams. The informed stitcher benefits from some insight into these media.

Needlework guilds are groups of interested stitchers who meet regularly to learn and exchange information. Many local groups have banded together to form several national, non-profit guilds. Information on national guilds, what they offer, and how they are contacted is included in this chapter.

TEACHERS AND CLASSES

A "good" needlework teacher should possess two skills: **demonstrated stitching expertise** and the **ability to communicate** that knowledge to others. Many stitchers are gifted. Not all are able to convey their gifts effectively. You want both skills in your teacher.

Should I buy a book or take a class to learn needlework?

Different methods work well for different students. Remember baseball's pitching and catching: one is as important as the other. If you're not "catching" from one teaching method, you may not be at fault. Try a new variety of pitcher.

FIGURE 1-2

One advantage of a living, breathing teacher is that **instruction is customized** for you (Chapter 4, Introduction). Directions can be rephrased until you understand them thoroughly. Good teachers have a great store of helpful hints to make work easy and fun.

The advantages of **written directions** are that they're **available** at midnight, on Sunday, and wherever you happen to be. They're inexpensive, generally costing less than most classes, and they give you a wide selection of projects from which to choose.

In most classes, you only learn what the instructor's teaching that day. But if you have trouble with written directions, you'll probably need a knowledgeable human to bail you out.

FIGURE 1–3

$$\frac{60 \text{ minutes}}{50 \text{ students}} = 12 \text{ seconds per student}$$

⟨2⟩ How do I choose a good class?
By studying the work of its students.

Gather the following information from as many students who have completed the course as you can find.

- Are the projects attractive to you? Were they completed?
- Are most of the pieces well stitched—as far as you can determine—or are they dirty, lumpy or haphazard looking? You'll know the teacher by the work of the majority of the students (one muddle doesn't count).
- Was the class taught how to block and finish their projects? They may not choose to do so, but they should have been given the information.
- Was the student satisfied with the cost, classroom, lighting, class size, and the instructor?

Class size determines the amount of individual attention given to each student. All classes fall into two categories: "project" and "process."

The purpose of a project-class is to complete one piece of needlework. Such classes are usually well-controlled, with limited choices available to the student and few decisions required of them.

Project-classes benefit from general demonstrations and don't require great amounts of individual attention per student.

In process-classes, a student learns to create with color, stitches, or whatever medium is being studied. Creating means making decisions. Students should be given enough time and individual counseling to enable them to choose well. Such classes are best kept small.

 What about teacher credentials?

In an effort to maintain high levels of needlework education, such organizations as the Embroiderers' Guild of America, the National Standards Council of American Embroiderers, and the Valentine Museum in Richmond, Va., provide certification programs for needlework teachers.

Certification tells you that a teacher knows the material thoroughly and has been exposed to proven teaching techniques. It requires approximately one year of concentrated work in addition to an outlay of money.

While certification indicates competence, its lack does not automatically indicate inferiority. Many gifted teachers cannot afford the time, the cash, or both. You're still well-advised to choose your class by studying the work of former students.

 What about night classes?

They're fine if you can overcome **one problem: light.**

FIGURE 1–4

Artificial lighting, which is adequate for fifth-grade reading on a dull afternoon, is rarely good enough for stitching needlework after dark. And it's never good enough for choosing or matching colors. Examine classrooms carefully. If you're at all in the dark, bring a portable stitching lamp and an extension cord to class with you.

What should a student expect of a teacher?

Information, organization, punctuality, good use of time, fiscal responsibility (materials necessary for the class should not cost more than they would on the open market), speed in catching and curing your problems, imagination enough to rephrase information in as many ways as it takes to communicate it to you, and positive thinking.

What should a teacher expect of a student?

Punctuality, attention (this isn't the time to discuss last Saturday's cocktail party), fiscal responsibility (pay fees promptly so that class time isn't wasted on finances), homework (we all have crises, but what's coming next is based on what went before), no smoking during classes, input and questions, and a prompt exit. Teachers get tired too.

PUBLICATIONS

Written needlework information is published in three media: newspapers, magazines, and books. They are not alike.

Newspapers transmit comparatively little stitching information. What's there is usually in the form of a regular column written and distributed by a knowledgeable authority.

Most newspaper editors do not fancy themselves as stitchery expects and wouldn't be caught dead rewriting a needlework column. Whatever's in print is what the author submitted. You can pretty well trust a newspaper column if you can trust its writer. The only way to decide that is to try a few directions and see how they work.

FIGURE 1-5

Magazines are a different story. Needlework is only one of many departments competing for space in every issue. The amount of page space available in any month fluctuates with the fortunes of the advertising department, postal rates, competition from other departments, and various acts of God over which editors have no control.

Stitchery editors must be knowledgeable; they deal with many designers and writers whose work must be evaluated and occasionally even rewritten. Such editors have few breathing spaces between deadlines. Such time limitations usually prevent a writer from having the opportunity to recheck a magazine manuscript for accuracy after it's been edited or rewritten. Occasional inaccuracies will sneak into print. It remains for you, the reader, to study magazine directions carefully and, if they don't make sense, to check and double-check before committing time and money to the project. (Question 7.)

However, the frequent publication that makes magazine directions susceptible to error also allows them to be more adventurous than most books can afford to be. The leading edge of needlework's wave of the future appears on newsstands each month. Ideas that survive are refined, examined in depth and elaborated upon in the books that follow.

Needlework books give authors and designers the opportunity to double-check their manuscripts after they have been edited. Most ambiguities and mistakes are caught at this point.

Designs and information that will be of value to you both now and in the future are worth space on your bookshelves.

What can I do when I don't understand written directions?

Read them over more than once. (Chapter 15 Introduction). If that doesn't work, decide whether you're an eye, ear or muscle person (Chapter 4, Introduction) and try the following:

Go to the library and look up one or more books on the subject (example: needlepoint rugs). **Acquire more knowledge** about what you're going to undertake. When the same information comes to you through another author's words, it often becomes clear (Chapter 4, Introduction).

or

Read directions into a tape recorder and listen to them repeatedly. This often does the trick.

or

Find a needlework shop where **good quality classes are taught by those who work in the shop.** Purchase all materials here and cherish the employees. They'll help you decipher murky instructions and are available from nine to five.

Be aware that all needlework shops are not set up to provide this service. Do some preliminary telephoning before you set forth.

How can I make graphs easier to follow?

Don't panic over them. You may be getting in your own way. Study them slowly and carefully and, if they still don't communicate, try one or all of the following tricks.

Enlarge the graph at a photostatic shop (under "Blueprints" in your Yellow Pages). Ask for a "positive copy" or you'll get white lines instead of black. A grid of eight to ten lines per inch is comfortable (see Figure 1–7b).

Because of space limitations, published graphs are often reduced past the point where they can be seen easily by all eyes. Inflate them.

or

Photocopy the graph and color it as you would a coloring book, using crayons, pencils or pens. The addition of color often brings it to life (see Figure 1–6).

FIGURE 1–6

 9 **How do I keep from getting lost while following a graph?**

Try one or all of these tricks:

Use a pencil to **check off each stitch as you work it.** Eventually you won't need this prop because you'll know where you are, but it certainly bridges the gap until you get there.

or

Use two sheets of white paper to **block out everything above and below the line you're stitching.**

or

Place scissors, pencil or **needle pointing to the line** on the graph that you're stitching (see Figure 1–7a).

FIGURE 1-7a

or

Place a **ruler beneath the line** of the graph that you're stitching.

FIGURE 1-7b

or

Buy one of the many **magnetic graph-finders** on the market (Chapter 12, Q16).

or

Buy one of the **clear line-magnifiers** that enlarge the line you're following (Chapter 12, Q8).

 Should I follow written directions and graphs or stitch a prepared kit?
Kits are attractive because all decisions are made for you. But if these decisions don't fit your needs, you're better off working from written directions.
$ Purchasing raw materials and written directions is usually cheaper than buying a kit—sometimes dramatically so. The range of designs to choose from is much larger. Materials you purchase will probably be of higher quality than those kit manufacturers can afford to include. Color choices meet your needs perfectly. Size choice is yours and if you want to place that small medallion in the middle of a large chair seat, buy enough materials and sail ahead.

You can change the scale of needlepoint or counted thread embroidery by changing the gauge canvas or evenweave cloth it is worked on (see Canvas Conversion Chart, p. 285). Example: a pattern that could make a scatter rug on #5 canvas can make a doll house rug when worked in petit point.

GROUPS AND GUILDS

Guilds are great! You meet other stitchers on a regular basis for education, enrichment, and pure enjoyment. Costs are modest; benefits, huge; and you meet the most delightful people in town.

Local guilds come in all shapes and sizes, from small groups of fifteen to organizations with hundreds of members. Meetings can be held in mornings, afternoons or evenings; in homes, churches or museums. Often day and evening groups coexist within the same guild. Each group has its own personality. Visit all those available to you before deciding which one fits your needs.

If you're new in town, stitching groups can be located by asking needlework shop owners. They're often active members. Or write to the headquarters of national guilds to find the affiliates nearest you.

Visiting guild meetings is encouraged. To find out when and where to go, contact the group's Membership Chairperson. Ask if there's a guest fee (small) to defray refreshment costs. You'll be welcomed warmly.

Most local needlework guilds are affiliated with the Embroiderers' Guild of America (E.G.A) or National Standards Council of American Embroiderers (N.S.C.A.E.), but not all choose to do so. Some individual, local groups flourish handsomely. Don't overlook such a guild if one happens to be located nearby. They're usually very special.

There are also national organizations dedicated to the exploration of one specific needlework technique. Examples are the American Needlepoint Guild, and the Counted Thread Society of America. If you wish to contact such groups, their mailing addresses can be found in the Reference Department of your public library.

If you're orphaned—without any guilds nearby— don't despair. E.G.A. and N.S.C.A.E. welcome member-at-large who receive all national membership benefits. Of course you'll be missing local meetings—unless you can organize a new guild yourself.

E.G.A.

The Embroiderers' Guild of America, known as E.G.A., was founded in 1957 as an American Branch of the London Embroiderers' Guild. It became the Embroiderers' Guild of America in 1960 when it was issued tax exempt status by the federal government as a charitable and educational organization. Membership was 300 in 1961; by the late 1970s it was over 22,000.

E.G.A. has approximately 220 chapters in the 50 states, the District of Columbia and Mexico. It offers its members access to annual national and regional seminars, Biennial National Exhibitions, correspondence courses, teacher certification, Master Craftsman Awards, slide collections, lectures, exhibits and a quarterly magazine called *Needle Arts*.

For further information, write to The Embroiderers' Guild of America, Inc., 6 East 45 Street, New York, New York, 10017.

N.S.C.A.E.

The National Standards Council of American Embroiderers was founded in 1968. It is a tax exempt educational organization dedicated to maintaining and promoting high standards in the art of needlework. Membership numbers approximately 4,000.

N.S.C.A.E. has approximately 130 chapters nationwide. It offers its members access to two national seminars, held in the Fall and Spring of each year; the biennial Needle Expressions traveling exhibition; slide and book lending libraries; speakers' bureau; correspondence school; teacher certification; museum information service and a quarterly magazine called *The Flying Needle*.

For further information, write to National Standards Council of American Embroiderers, P.O. Box N578, Northfield, Illinois, 60093.

Valentine Museum

This museum, located in Richmond, Virginia, has an excellent collection of textiles, costumes and antique embroidery tools. It provides unusual opportunities for needleworkers.

Every Spring a National Assembly for Embroiderers is held at the Valentine. Workshops are given in the needle arts, history of textiles and restoration. The Valentine provides correspondence courses and teacher certification. It does not sponsor local guilds. Anyone is welcome to affiliate.

For further information, write to Director of Education, Valentine Museum, 1015 East Clay, Richmond, Virginia, 23219.

2 Kits

FIGURE 2-1

Needlework kits are like icebergs. They look beautifully simple on the surface, but who knows what problems lurk below?

My mother sent for a kit once. She tried stitching the thing, with depressing results. What was supposed to look like a wise owl began to resemble a dead duck. Mother whisked it to me for corrective surgery.

It took a week to stretch, smooth, and restitch that poor bird. Its kit was marginal at best. The manufacturer had skimped on yarn, the directions might as well have been written in Babylonian, and the canvas felt like cobweb.

The owl's death throes came when I started to block it. Whatever had been used to color the canvas wasn't waterproof. Black lines oozed through owl features as I stood helplessly by, watching the needlepoint self-destruct.

Those black lines wouldn't go away. Soap, bleach, scouring powder and ink eradicator failed to make a dent. Yarns got a bit frazzled in the process—and they weren't the only ones.

What was I going to tell Mother?

I finally took a deep breath and phoned. It turned out that Mother isn't really all that fond of owls. But there's this adorable mushroom pillow that would look darling in the den. She's sent for it and. . . .

I'm expecting a phone call any day now.

INTRODUCTION

Commercial needlework kits usually contain a piece of canvas or cloth with a design printed on it, appropriate yarns or threads, one needle, directions, a

15

pretty picture of the finished project, and a bag that holds it all together.

Designs can be transferred to canvas or cloth in three ways. The best quality kits are silk screened. This technique is faster than hand painting, but still requires a high degree of individual attention. You pay for good paints, personal supervision and limited volume.

Moderately priced kits often utilize hot wax transfers which are stamped on textiles by a special machine. Such transfers behave somewhat like decalcomanias and can be very attractive. An individual is present during stamping to run the machine, but not every piece is assessed for accuracy. Production volume can be large.

Inexpensive kits can be run off on a printing press, using textile inks. Individual attention is kept to a minimum and production volume can be tremendous.

The problem with all three processes is "registration." Are the straight lines of the design in line with threads of canvas or cloth (see Figure 2-2)? Can you stitch it as it's drawn?

FIGURE 2-2

16

The more individual attention paid to a kit, the more likelihood there is that everything will line up. All textile meshes do not come off a bolt absolutely square. Repositioning may be necessary and machines can't decide what and where to adjust.

Individual attention costs money. With kits, as with most consumer goods, you get what you pay for.

ALL NEEDLEWORK

 How do I choose a kit?

- Before purchasing what appeals to you, have salespersons check to see that all materials that should be included are present. Have them identify the fiber and type of yarn or thread in the kit.

- From the store's supply, choose the nearest match to your kit's major yarn or thread colors. For future reference, write down on your receipt the identification and dye lot numbers of these "nearly-matching" threads. Keep fibers and types the same. You'll need this information if you run short of yarn.

- Buy at least one more needle to match the kit's. Check to see that the design is printed straight on canvas or cloth. If it's crooked, choose another kit.

- Save the receipt.

FIGURE 2-3

Almost more important than "which kit" is "where did you buy it?" One of the most valuable commodities you purchase is future help, if and when you need it. This assistance is available when you shop at needlework departments or stores.

A kit may cost slightly more there than if you bought it at a discount hardware store. But when you need advice, hardware salesmen aren't going to be much help. **Shop where the price includes assistance-insurance.**

How can I determine a kit's limitations?

You can't, until you get it home. However, such limitations needn't keep you from being able to stitch it. Recognizing a kit's potential icebergs will help you to avoid them.

- **Is the printed design colorfast?** Test each color with a dye-fast test. If any dye comes off on the tissue, spray lightly and seal the design with Clear Krylon or other acrylic spray sealers. Stitch on a frame so that flexing won't crack and flake the spray.
- **Are yarns or threads colorfast?** Run a dye-fast test on all threads *before* stitching with them. If any dyes run, substitute "nearly-matching" equivalent (Q1) or try Thread Cure (Chapter 10, Q8).
- **How strong is needlepoint canvas?** Run a Denier Test, p. 114. If the count is less than four per thread, stitch needlepoint on a frame. Such canvas is susceptible to severe warping, and is too fragile to take the hard blocking that such warping will make necessary.

How can I understand graphs or directions?

Read Chapter 1, Q8. If the graph is coded with little symbols, it can look very confusing. **Color each symbol** with a different crayon, pen or colored pencil. It can make a great difference.

What do I do when I'm running out of thread?

The minute you suspect that this may be happening, STOP! **Do not stitch to the end of your thread supply.**

FLOSS OR STRANDED YARN

Find your receipt and note the dye lot number of "nearly matching" yarn or thread (Q1). Buy enough of this to complete the kit. Follow directions in Chapter 8, Q9.

PEARL COTTON OR TAPESTRY YARN

You have fewer choices here. **Buy the "nearly-matching" color** you chose and use it when you run out. There may be a clear line between old and new areas.

or

Buy a duplicate kit and use its yarns.

or

Write the manufacturer for more yarn. You may get it; and then again, you may not. In either case, it will take time.

As a rule, the better (more expensive) the kit, the more materials it contains. Nonetheless, in any kit, you should expect to get enough yarn to complete the project, but not enough to waste. Un-work mistakes carefully (Chapter 8, Q8). All threads must be re-used.

If this minimum amount of yarn or thread has not been included in your kit, write to the manufacturer and **complain!**

$ Return the kit to the store from whence it came and complain. Wise merchants stand behind their merchandise. (However, you are more likely to get satisfaction if you bought the kit at a needlework store than from a hardware dealer.)

 What do I do when I've lost my directions or thread or needle?
Return to your needlework store with receipt in hand. They'll find substitutes for what you've lost. Extra directions can be photocopied from those in a duplicate kit. "Nearly matching" threads can substitute for what is gone.

If you didn't buy the kit from such a store, you have two choices. Either buy a duplicate kit and use its materials. Or go to a needlework store anyway and throw yourself on their mercy. They may welcome an opportunity to win a new customer.

6 **What do I do about canvas peeking through my needlepoint?**

Stranded Yarn

Flatten yarn (Chapter 7, Q8).

or

Loosen tension. Yarn should sit on top of canvas, not be yanked into it (see Figure 2–4).

If neither of these improves the coverage, you need more yarn per needleful. Return to the needlework store and buy the "nearly matching" color you chose when you bought the kit (Q1). Restitch over completed work with a single strand of new yarn; then add one strand of new to each needleful of old yarn and continue stitching the unworked canvas.

FIGURE 2–4

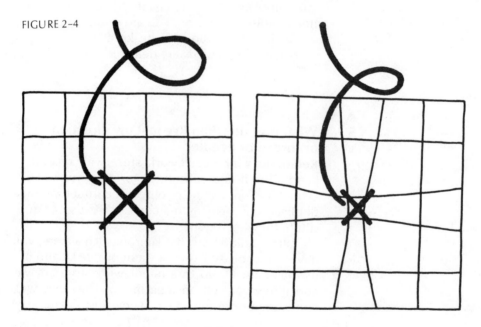

Tapestry Yarn

Loosen tension. If this doesn't cure the problem, buy a waterproof marking pen in the yarn's color (see Pen Test, p. 71). **Color unworked canvas** (see Figure 2–5) following directions in Chapter 6, Q1, 2. Continue stitching. This may leave a slight mark between old and new areas. If it is objectionable, you have no choice but to un-work all needlepoint, color the canvas, and start again.

FIGURE 2–5

 How do I block when there's not enough empty canvas on edges?
See Chapter 14, Q19. When canvas is of questionable size or quality (Chapter 9, Q2, 3), it's wise to work on a frame so that severe blocking can be avoided completely.

EMBROIDERY KITS

 How do I cover counted thread patterns printed unevenly on cloth?
This problem crops up most frequently on printed cross stitch samplers where markings are permanent. You have the choice of seeing printed marks beneath even stitches, or working stitches unevenly. Neither solution is elegant.

Purchase a piece of evenly woven cloth whose thread count per inch will allow your design to be worked in the scale it's drawn. Such cloth can be found in needlework and drapery fabric stores.

Example: If the kit has five *Cross Stitches* per inch, buy fabric with five, ten or twenty threads to the inch. On five, work each *Cross Stitch* over one thread; with ten, over two square threads; and on twenty, over four square threads.

Draw the kit's pattern on graph paper and proceed as if you had discovered it in a book or magazine. If inks or dyes have not penetrated through to the back of the kit's cloth, it can be re-used for uncounted surface stitchery.

 How do I avoid printed lines peeping through on crewel-work?
Pattern lines vary in thickness between kit brands.

- When filling shapes, pierce fabric with your needle along the *outer edge* of each line rather than down its middle.
- When working lines or stems, cover marks by choosing a thick stitch (example: *Chain* is thicker than *Stem*) or by working thinner stitches with enough thread per needleful to achieve complete coverage.

Superb kits are on the market. They make the work of talented designers available to any stitcher. Such kits are easy to buy, fun to stitch, and a joy to own. Buy good brands from reputable dealers and you should have happy stitching.

But do stay clear of sick owls!

3 Design and Color

I read recently about a dinner party given by a psychology professor for students in his Introductory Psych. course. As the group chatted politely in the living room, delicious aromas wafted past their noses. The menu smelled like roast beef and something tantalizing and garlicky. Every mouth was watering by the time dinner was served.

The students moved quickly toward the dining room—and stopped dead in their tracks on the threshold. Something was very, very wrong.

The mashed potatoes piled in their serving bowl looked deep grey, the roast beef appeared to be green, and the peas had somehow turned charcoal brown. Nobody knew what to do and then, one by one, they glanced at the professor. He was grinning delightedly.

Two students left the room abruptly. The rest, afraid of jeopardizing their grades, sat down to do battle. The food tasted delicious but they had trouble swallowing and, one by one, put down their forks.

Except for one boy. He had seconds of everything and was the life of the party. (It turned out later that he was color blind.)

Moral: Never underestimate the importance of color—in roast beef or in needlework.

FIGURE 3-1

23

INTRODUCTION

Over 500 years ago, the Renaissance architect Leone Battista Alberti wrote, "Beauty is . . . the harmony and concord of all the parts achieved in such a manner that nothing could be added or taken away or altered except for the worse."

When you produce your own needlework designs, you deal with the following elements:

> *Forms,* their shape, size, position and relative proportions.
>
> *Colors,* their value and intensity;
>
> *Textures,* their look and feel;
>
> *Organization* of the above; including movement, repetition, and contrast;
>
> *Your feelings* about all of the above.

FIGURE 3–2

How do I begin to design?
- Decide what you want to stitch.
- Think about where it will live when it's finished. The room in which a design will be displayed has great impact on how that design will look.
- Decide how large it will be.
- To guarantee that your finished project will be the right size and shape, draw an accurate outline that looks like an empty picture frame. Then do all your drawing and sketching on sheets of tracing paper placed over this "frame."

Where do I get ideas for designs?
Ask 753 designers and you'll get 753 different answers. Here are a few favorites:

- **Tracings.** Use tracing paper to trace shapes from existing designs. Cut and rearrange within your outline frame. Shapes can come from upholstery or slipcover material, greeting cards, magazines or a photograph of your house.
- **Patterns That Fit.** Select designs that are appropriate to the area where they'll live when they grow up. If you select motifs from the wood of a carved, Victorian chair, they will look at home worked in needlepoint on the chair's seat. Brass grillwork on a radiator cover could give you an idea for a Blackwork cushion that will live nearby.
- **Paper Dolls.** Cut out shapes—leaves, circles, corkscrews—and arrange them within the outline frame. When the positions please you, carefully place a sheet of tracing paper over them and trace. This tracing will be your design.
  The trick in this technique is not only to look at the shapes, but at the spaces between them. The in-between areas are called "negative spaces" and are as important to the design as your shapes. Be sure that both positive shapes and negative spaces are pleasingly arranged.
- **Torn Paper.** This is a great technique for designing abstractions. Cut or tear a sheet of paper into large and small fragments. Arrange

these within your outline frame, watching both positive and negative shapes. If you tear colored tissue paper, overlappings can give you ideas for color schemes.

Trace the finished design on tracing paper.

- **Household Objects.** Delightful patterns can develop if you arrange ordinary household belongings within your outline frame and trace them. Try paper clips, toothbrushes, clothespins, rubber bands, or cookie cutters. Let the shapes overlap if you want to.

- **Nature.** This is the most exciting, and the most difficult type of designing because it requires some degree of simplification. Cut a green pepper or a tomato in half and look at the pattern of its seeds and membranes. Look at tree bark, tire tracks in the snow or the patterns on sea shells. Sketch or, even easier, photograph. Cameras reduce three-dimensional objects to two dimensions, making your design job much easier.

    Eliminate fussy details and leave only what's important. Reread Alberti's definition of beauty that opened this chapter. This is your goal.

 How do I enlarge or reduce shapes for my design?
Read Chapter 7, Q13.

 How do I choose colors for my design?
Follow directions in Q11. Use your tracing as the design.

 What are therapeutic design facts?
- Forms, whether they're lines or shapes, have personalities (see Figure 3–3). Verticals are dramatic and strong. Horizontals are restful and weaker. Diagonals are emotional and produce movement within the design. They are weaker than verticals, but equal to horizontals. Curves add sensuous overtones to the personalities of verticals, horizontals and diagonals.
- Large shapes are stronger than small ones.

FIGURE 3-3

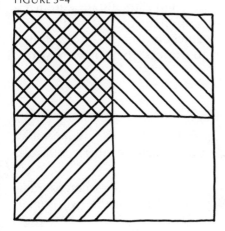

FIGURE 3-4

- Psychologically, the stronger half of a design is the top. The stronger side is the left. Therefore the psychologically strongest area of a composition is in its top, left quarter (see Figure 3-4). The weakest quarter is the lower right.
- Dark tones are stronger than light tints (for example, look at black print on white paper versus white print on black. The black letters are easier to read. (See Plate 6.)
- Colors that are warm, bright or contrasting (see Plate 4), are stronger than cool, dull, subtle shades (see Plate 5).
- Smooth or shiny surfaces are stronger than rough or dull ones.
- Stitching's texture slightly darkens the appearance of a thread's color as it adds shadows to it. On the other hand, shiny highlights lighten the appearance of a color and strengthen its impact.

6

How do I balance strengths and weaknesses?
The **"strong" elements in a composition are those that attract attention to themselves.** They form focuses for the viewer's scrutiny and should be balanced by "weaker" elements so that everything doesn't scream for attention at once (Table 3-1).

A weak shape can be strengthened by a strong color, texture, etc. **Balance weak with strong,** regardless of whether the strong element used is a color, form, texture or position in the design.

Similarities calm and unify. Contrasts excite and move. Remember to repeat similar shapes, similar overall textures and similar colors. But also pep them up with contrasts. You don't want pandemonium, but you don't want to be dull either.

As each element is added or subtracted, a design's total balance—like a scale's—will be upset and must be readjusted. This will happen over and over again during creation and is a large part of what "designing" is all about.

It's all a juggling act and there is never just one "right" answer. First and foremost, you must please yourself.

Table 3–1   Design Balance Chart

	Stronger	Weaker
Shapes	vertical	horizontal
		diagonal
	geometric	irregular
Size	large	small
Position	top	bottom
	right	left
Tone	dark	light
Color	red, yellow, orange	blue, violet
	bright	dull
	contrasting	subtle
Texture	smooth	rough
	shiny	dull

COLOR

Color is one of the most important elements any needleworker uses, whether the project is somebody else's kit or your own designed masterpiece. Colors define shapes, indicate distance from the viewer and—most important of all—set the emotional tone of the stitchery. This chapter will help you choose colors to express what you want said.

Vocabulary

- Primary Color (see Plate 2)—red, blue, yellow. Basic colors from which all other colors are made.
- Secondary Color (see Plate 3)—orange, green, violet. Colors formed by mixing two primary colors.

- Intermediate colors—red-orange, blue-green, etc. Colors formed by mixing a primary with a secondary color which contains that primary.
- Warm Colors (see Plate 4)—red, yellow, orange. Dominant, clear, appear to move toward you.
- Cool Colors (see Plate 5)—blue-green, blue, violet. Receding, soft, appear to move away from you.

The following words measure how much color is present.

- Hue—a more specific word for pure color on the spectrum (see Plate 1). Example: red.
- Value—relative darkness or lightness on a scale from black to white (see Figure I and Plate 11). Includes:

  Tints—hues mixed with white to lighten them ("pastels"). Example: pink is red mixed with white.

  Shades—darkened hues (sometimes mixed with black). Example: mahogany is red mixed with black (see Plate 11).
- Intensity—refers to the relative purity or dullness of a hue, and includes . . .

  Tones—grayed hues.

All tints or shades can be grayed, thus producing their own tones. The number of potential colors that can result is mind-boggling.

FIGURE 3-5

How do I see colors?

Eyes and light play a one-sided game of catch. **We can "see" only what light sources**—the sun, incandescent bulbs, fluorescent tubes—**pitch toward us** (see Figure 3-5).

Different light sources pitch differently. Black differs from white under all of them, but some colors seem to change when the light source changes. Such chameleons are called "metameric" colors.

To demonstrate this phenomenon, some dark night try looking at bluish-red yarn under flourescent lights in an otherwise darkened room. Quickly switch off the flourescents and turn on an incandescent light bulb. You'll be amazed at the change in the yarn's color. In sunlight, that yarn might appear to be still a third color.

8 How do colors interact?

Colors are slippery little devils. A red tomato looks one red under fluorescent light, another red in sunlight, and three different reds when sitting on white paper, or green, or black.

How a color "looks" is influenced, not only by the light in which we view it, but **by what other colors are nearby.** Pioneer work on the effects colors have on each other was done by Josef Albers at Yale and described in his book, *Interaction of Color.* This fascinating study has much to say to those of us who work with colored threads because Albers experimented with commercially available colored papers. He couldn't "mix in a dab of yellow, or just a touch of green" any more than we can. That luxury is for painters.

In his theory of "color subtraction," Albers states that when a small area of color is placed upon a large area of a different color, the hue and tone of the larger color will appear to be subtracted from the smaller color. This happens because few colors are pure. Almost all are mixtures of one color with bits of others. Painters recognize this when they mix pigments on their palettes.

For example: a grey pebble in your driveway appears simply grey, although it has overtones of many colors within it. But place that pebble on a large sheet of orange paper and it will look bluish. Its orange hue has been subtracted (see Plate 6).

Or place two identical pebbles on large sheets of paper, one black and the other white. One pebble will appear darker than the other because black subtracts dark tones and makes its stone look lighter. White, on the other hand, subtracts light tones and makes its pebble look darker (see Plate 6).

The subtraction theory has practical needlework applications.

- Since colors influence each other in a stitchery, they should be chosen at the same time and under the same light source.

- Also, since large color volumes affect smaller color volumes (but not vice versa), *color proportions* should be tested before purchasing yarns.
- Finally, if a stitchery is under way and color problems develop, the subtraction theory can often restore needlework to good health.

 ## What are therapeutic color facts?

- A color will appear lighter on a large, dark background (see Plate 6).
- A color will appear darker on a large, light background (see Plate 6).
- A color will appear purer on a large, greyed background.
- A color will appear grayed on a large background of its own, pure hue.
- A large, colored background will affect a small color strongly if the shape of the smaller color is irregular. It will affect the small color less if its shape is geometric. A circle is the least affected of all shapes.
- The more intense the background color, the more it will subtract itself from small colors placed upon it (see Plate 6).
- A color appears lighter when its area is large (remember this when you're choosing paint from paint chips). It appears darker when its area is small.
- Two colors can be made to look like one by the manipulation of their backgrounds. One color can be made to look like two by the same method.
- Background color can be manipulated to solve color problems within the design.

Beware of the color of white needlepoint canvas. Colors appear darker and more intense against a strong, white background than they'll look when a colored background is filled in. Crayon or paint an accurate sketch of the finished project before you choose yarns (Q11).

Select background yarn color when choosing yarns, but wait to purchase it until the design has progressed far enough to know if color problems are incubating. Many times, a slight change in the background color will cure the illness.

What about texture?

Texture is the character of a surface and is the most obvious difference between needlework and paintings.

There are two types of texture in needlework: *Stitch texture* appears to darken colors by casting shadows at every stitch intersection. The rougher the texture, the more shadows it will cast and the darker its color will appear. *Surface texture* depends upon the reflective quality of fibers used for stitching. For example, silk is more reflective than linen. The shinier the fiber, the smoother it appears and the more highlights it reflects.

Highlights lighten and as they grow stronger, tend to eliminate color. As a highlight intensifies, it moves color toward the pure white of sunlight. Shiny fibers appear lighter than dull fibers dyed the same color.

- To emphasize a fiber's shine, reduce its number of shadow-casting stitch intersections and use long, untextured stitches. A thread laid uninterrupted from side to side would shine best, although it would be a disaster in terms of wear.
- The more highlights and shadows an area of stitching contains, the more the eye is drawn to it and the stronger is its visual impact.

How can I create color combinations of my own?

The following suggestions are listed in order of increasing creativity. Plug in wherever you're comfortable.

Let a More Experienced Designer Assist You.

- Match colors to fabrics that you like. Textiles and yarns are colored with similar dyes and matching is easy because surface textures are similar.

Plate 2 (top left)
Primary colors

Plate 3 (bottom left)
Secondary colors

Plate 4 (top right)
Warm colors

Plate 5 (bottom right)
Cool colors

Plate 6 (left)
Color subtraction and tone
subtraction
Plate 7 (below left)
Disco
Designed and stitched by
 the author
Plate 8 (below right)
Family Tree
Designed and stitched by
 Bea Keeber

Plate 9 (left)
Oriental Poppy
Designed and stitched by Bea
Keeber

Plate 10 (below left)
Spring Bouquet
Designed and stitched by Bea
Keeber

Plate 11 (below right)
Tints, Tones, and T's
Designed and stitched by the
author

- Match colors to a painting, photograph or magazine illustration. Paints and photographic dyes are harder to match than textile dyes. Make allowances for the tendency of surface gloss to lighten color.

Hint: Keep tonal values of colors being substituted equal to those you're getting rid of. Example: Light blue should be replaced by light beige, not dark brown (see Figure 3-6).

FIGURE 3-6

Work with color combinations that are tried and true.

Hint: Use *unequal* volumes of these colors.

First make five copies of the Color Finder, Figure II, page 35. On one, cut out segments marked "A" and label the sheet "Complementary Colors." On the second sheet, cut out segments "B" and label it "Split Complement." Continue with all color combinations.

Place a cut finder over the Color Wheel, Figure 1. Push a straight pin through black dots in the center of both pages. Revolve each finder to discover one of the following color combinations:

- *Complementary Pair* (two colors)—*A:* A primary color plus the secondary color directly across the Color Wheel from it. (Example: red plus green.) Complements are the strongest possible combinations; intense and vibrant.
- *Split Complement* (three colors)—*B:* A color plus the colors on either side of its complement (Example: red, plus blue-green and yellow-green.) Not so strong as complementary colors; subtlety is possible.

33 *Design and Color*

Figure I

Figure II

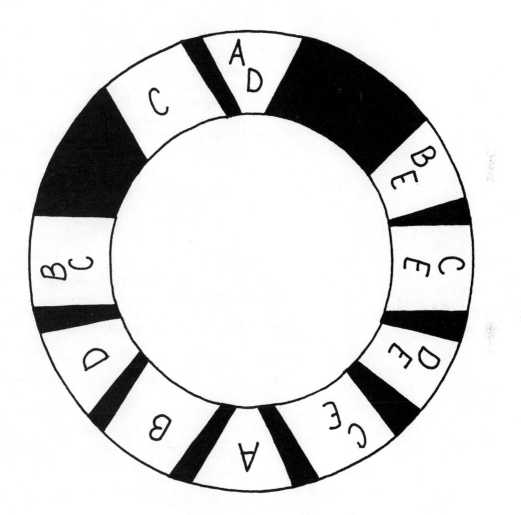

- *Double Split Complement* (four colors)—*C:* The colors on either side of two complementary colors (Example: red-violet, red-orange plus blue-green and yellow-green.) Can be subtle and fascinating, but must be carefully controlled. The more colors you juggle, the harder it gets.

- *Triad* (three colors)—*D:* Three colors evenly spaced around the Color Wheel (Example: red, blue, yellow.) Can be bright or as subtle as blue-violet, yellow-green and red-orange.

- *Analogous colors* (two to four)—*E:* Colors next to each other on the Color Wheel. Must include one primary color, but never two. (Example: the citrus colors of lime, lemon, orange and tangerine equal green, yellow, orange and red-orange.)

- *Monochromatic* (one color). A color scheme containing two or more variations of a single color (Example: peach, orange, brick). Always safe, but can be dull.

Start From Scratch

Collect as many color samples as you can from *one* of the following categories: crayons, paint chips; yarns; or scraps of colored paper, torn from magazines and kept as large as possible (see Figure 3–7).

- Make choices in daylight.
- Give yourself enough time. Color gels when it's ready.
- Lay out a neutral background to place colors against. Remember that backgrounds affect colors placed upon them, so avoid black and white; try a roll of brown wrapping paper or a medium grey blotter.
- Spread out color samples and begin mixing and matching.
- Discover a minimum of three—more is better—combinations that please you. Stand away from them and choose your favorite.

If you like bits of one and some of another, re-combine and see how it looks. There's no hard and fast rule to this. The first objective is to please yourself.

FIGURE 3-7

 Where should which colors go?
This question translates to which color should be in a large area and which in a small one and you'll need crayons to answer it. The following methods are of equal manageability, so choose whichever seems best for you.

Draw a coloring book outline around your design on a sheet of tracing paper. Use a black pen. **Trace or photocopy** the outline at least ten times. **Color** seven copies with crayons, placing different colors in different areas (see Figure 3-8).

FIGURE 3-8

FIGURE 3–9

Arrange colorings on walls, floor or table. Compare; **choose.** Either move to *final yarn check*

or

Decide which colored areas you like and blend these together on one of your blank copies. **Rearrange and refine** until you're satisfied. Run *final yarn check* (Q13), matching yarns to the sketch.

or

Trace separate elements, outlining each part of the design on a separate sheet of tracing paper. Use a black pen.

Copy each tracing two more times (total—three) on tracing paper and **color** each a different color. (Example: a basket could be brown, green, and yellow.)

Superimpose one sheet over another on a white background (see Figure 3–9). Assemble the whole design in one pile. Repeat with the other two piles of tracings.

Exchange colors from one pile to another until you get at least one total combination that pleases you. Staple it together so that your solution doesn't slip away.

Match yarn colors to tracings and run *final yarn check*.

How do I run a final yarn check?

This should be run *after* colors are chosen and *before* yarns are purchased.

- Obtain one strand of each yarn color you're thinking of using. Determine the volume of each color present in your colored sketch by making a graduated list of colors with the largest volume at the top and the smallest at the bottom.
- Cut several strips of cardboard, one-half inch by two inches. Wind yarn colors around cardboard strip according to your list. The smallest color will have three turns around the cardboard. Add three additional turns for each step up the list.
- Stabilize yarns with a piece of tape on the back. Cut away excess cardboard—you don't want its color entering into this.

If the colors please you, shop! BUT if you're not happy, wind the same colors around a second cardboard using the same numbers of turns in a different order. Wind the darkest next to the lightest, second-darkest next to second-lightest, and so on. Compare the two cardboards. If the second satisfies you, shop!

If you're still not happy, return to coloring and work out another combination. Your colors have malnutrition.

Yarn checks are a good and speedy indication of how happy you'll be with the color of the finished product.

FIGURE 3-10

4 Creative Problem-Solving

FIGURE 4-1

I first discovered creative problem-solving years ago when our daughter Penny was an exchange student in Acapulco. As a lovely Fall turned into an icy Winter, it became perfectly obvious that our parental duty was to visit our child.

Acapulco's harbor at sunset is incredibly beautiful. Inspiration hit with a blinding flash and a needlepoint masterpiece took off. It soared for about three square inches or, to be exact, until we stepped off the plane back home. As sleet hissed past our ears, Acapulco's inspiration stopped—cold.

But I am not one to desert a project. "Acapulco, Sunset" slogged on until I could have called it "Fruitcake" and nobody would have known the difference.

When one of my designs proves unruly, the pelican painting across from my dining room chair comes down and the problem canvas takes its place. Solutions often sprout between breakfast and supper.

But no solution attached itself to "Acapulco, Sunset." There it hung, month after month, attracting dust and looking like a moulting porcupine. My husband Mike began to get edgy.

Fortunately for our marriage, this was when I discovered the creative problem-solving books in the bibliography. "Acapulco, Sunset" became my guinea pig.

To my joy, some of the techniques worked. Once an illness was pinpointed, it was easy to cure, but for every problem that disappeared, two more seemed to pop up in its place.

Until the day finally dawned when no more problems sprouted. "Acapulco, Sunset" looked beautiful, as if I'd dashed it in off in a moment of flashing inspiration (instead of just beginning it that way).

Mike and the pelican are delighted.

INTRODUCTION

FIGURE 4–2

The most elegant solution to any problem is usually the simple one that gives the most effect for the least effort.

We gain most of our learning through one, two, or three of our senses. Sometimes we learn through our eyes by seeing designs, words, or visual aids. We learn through our ears when we hear directions or "talk our way through" exercises. We learn through feeling our muscles work. Some people need only to walk through a technique; when they're finished, they'll understand what's behind it.

Most of us use all three senses to reinforce learning, but one of the three usually dominates. This explains why one set of directions doesn't communicate to everybody. If you're oriented towards your ears, pretty pictures won't do much for you.

Do you remember names easily, but forget faces? If so, you learn through your ears. If you operate the other way around, you're an eye person. If walking through projects is your style, feeling muscles teaches you.

Problem-solving, like learning, needs a variety of approaches. Use the techniques that work for you, keeping in mind the following: muscular solutions, or "keep on doing it until it comes out right," take the most time. Visual solutions are the easiest to communicate in a book like this because needlework is a visual art and print is a visual medium. If you're an ear person, have directions read aloud to you. Read them into a tape recorder and play it back. You'll be amazed at how the words will begin to communicate.

The environment in which you solve problems is important. Try to be as undistracted as possible. The sky will not fall if you take the phone off the hook. Give yourself time; solutions often "arrive when they feel like it."

Use cheap, easy, quick materials for solving design problems; a large box of crayons, a pad of cheap newsprint, scissors, colored paper and an inexpensive pad of tracing paper (see Figure 4–3). These materials don't have to last through the ages. Their function is to clarify your thoughts so that you'll know what you want, and where you want to go with it.

41   *Creative Problem-Solving*

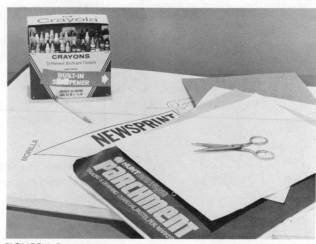

FIGURE 4–3

The most important item that you'll need for creative problem-solving is an open mind. Think about some of the clichés that we hear all the time: "Don't make mistakes." "Don't daydream." "Old ways are best ways." "There's a right way and a wrong way to do everything." "Problems are bad."

As a first lesson in creativity, ask yourself "Why?" to each of those statements. Then ask yourself what would happen if the opposite were true instead.

For example, take "Don't make mistakes." A large part of creativity is choice. The larger the group to choose from, the greater the potential for an elegant solution. Every answer can't win. Therefore, to arrive at the really elegant solution, you must dare to produce many losers in order to isolate the real winner. This is the basis of the "brainstorming" that keeps many ad agencies in business.

Or what about "problems are bad"? Problems are really opportunities in disguise—the bumps that jolt you off the path of follow-the-leader.

FIGURE 4–4

GAMES AND TECHNIQUES

Question: How do you eat an elephant?
Answer: One bite at a time.

There are as many ways to attack elephantine problems as there are people willing to bite into them. What follows is merely a starting point. Feel free to tailor these techniques to suit your needs as you move forward.

Difficulties are often encountered in isolating a particular problem because of our impatience to get on with the solving of it. Time spent correctly identifying stumbling blocks is time saved in the long run.

The purpose of the games that follow is to clarify your mind. What do you really like? How do you really want this stitchery to turn out? What techniques should you use to make it all happen?

The basic system can be summed up in the questions *Who? Where? What? How? Which? Why?* The answers to these questions solve problems in needlework.

The first thing to cope with is fear. Not many people are afraid of needlework—it's as unthreatening an occupation as you could find. But most of us are very afraid of making mistakes. "I flunked art in the fourth grade." "I can't draw a straight line." Begin the list of questions with this in mind.

 Who?
You and you, alone. Don't tell your friends about your project or gather outside opinions at this point. They're likely to do more harm than good.

 Where?
Locate the problem geographically (see Figure 4–5). Is it in the foreground (usually the focus), the midground, or the background? Is it in the upper right hand corner or the lower left? Keep in mind that obstacles rarely come singly. Identify one problem area and concentrate on cleaning that up. There will be time enough to cope with number two after number one is solved.

Write down the problem location on a sheet of paper.

What?
Define what's wrong with this area. Write your definition next to your location. If you can't put your finger on it, try one of the following games.

FIGURE 4–5

Adjective List

Write down a list of at least 50 adjectives and their opposites. The table above should get you started. Make two additional copies: One is for wishes, one is for reality, and one is to save for later.

On the "Wish List" (don't peek at the design), circle those words that most closely describe the way you'd like the needlework to look. On the second list (now you can look), circle those words that most closely describe the way you feel about the needlework *as it looks right now.*

Compare lists, underlining words that differ. Match each underlined word to whichever of the following categories it seems to fit (more than one category is O.K.): FORM, COLOR, TEXTURE, ORGANIZATION, FEELINGS. In the categories you've chosen lie your problem(s), and your solution(s).

or

Cross It Off

If you're comfortable with design theory, this takes much less time.

Look at the list of design categories—FORM, COLOR, TEXTURE, ORGANIZATION, FEELINGS. Analyze your stitchery, point by point. Cross off those areas on the list that you're happy with. The areas that remain on the list are where your problem lives.

How?
Gather ideas for problem solving. It's right to be wrong here.

Aim for quantity of ideas rather than quality.

Picture Perfect

Make 10 to 20 quick sketches of other ways the needlework could be arranged. Use newsprint and crayons. (Whatever drawing skills you have will be more than adequate for this.) Explore any or all of the following:

Table 4–1	Adjectives
big	little
rough	smooth
shiny	dull
bright	misty
dark	light
pointed	rounded
sharp	soft
regular	irregular
stable	moving
happy	sad
up	down
sparkling	drab
deep	high
tilted	straight
wet	dry
loose	tight
open	closed
calm	jittery
clear	confused
warm	cold
boiling	icy
hard	soft
noisy	quiet
sunny	shadowed
crisp	soggy
balanced	off-balance
direct	diffused
light	heavy
comfortable	painful
focused	vague
sandy	slimy
spicy	bland
clean	dirty
marching	retreating
thrusting	withdrawing
blowing	sucking
floating	struggling
sticky	slippery
liquid	solid
chewy	pasty
expanding	shrinking
exploded	compacted
swinging	still
fascinating	boring
ecstatic	depressed
nubbly	slick
dappled	solid
visible	invisible
solid	ghost
real	dream
geometric	irregular
brave	frightened
united	divided
attracting	repelling

FIGURE 4-6

- **Imagine the problem gone.** Eliminate it. Sketch. Could you substitute something else for it? Sketch. Any other ideas? Sketch, no matter how wacky.

- **Turn things upside down.** First the needlework: turn it on its side and then the other side, then upside down. Sketch. Turn yourself upside down and look at the needlework through your legs. Sketch what you saw. Turn the colors upside down. What would it look like if the apple were green and the leaves red? Sketch.

- **Turn things inside out.** Imagine how the needlework would look if you could see through to its back. Look at it in a mirror. Sketch. Put the background in the foreground and the foreground in the background. Sketch.

- **Flip.** Put the left on the right and vice versa. Reverse top and bottom. Sketch.

- **Change your focus.** Take the stitchery to another room, to the car, out under a tree, into the basement. Write down your impressions. Sketch. Imagine that the design is an oil painting, a color photo, a textile design, a centerfold in *Playboy*. How would it look? Sketch.

FIGURE 4-7

- **Daydream** a successful needlework in which this problem doesn't exist. Describe it in writing and analyze why it worked. Sketch how it looked.

- **Imagine** a version of the stitchery that would shock your grandmother, or one that's hysterically funny, or one that's naughty, or one that's unpleasant to you. Sketch them.

- **Pretend** that you're somebody else. Turn into Picasso, Mondrian, King Tut. Sketch.

- **Combine:** Take any two of your sketches and trace elements from each on tracing paper, producing a new sketch. Keep mixing and matching.

or

Verb List

Make a list of 50 verbs and their opposites like the Adjective List in *What?* Circle words that tell how the needlepoint *could be* fixed (see Figure 4–8).

Pair the circled words, making all possible combinations. On a separate file card for each pair, write a sentence describing the solution stimulated by the words. An example for "darken" and "comfort" might be, "Darken the tone of the foreground and reduce rough texture and color contrasts to a more soothing level."

FIGURE 4–8

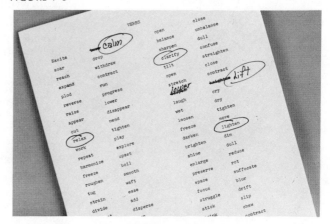

Eliminate pairs that don't fit the problem, but eliminate them slowly. The darndest combinations often contain the seeds of sensational solutions.

or

Research

Discover how this particular problem has been solved in the past. Study library books with illustrations of needlework, decorative arts or the fine arts. Describe and sketch each solution on a separate file card.

Be aware that somewhere between *What? and How?* you'll probably enter what I call the "messy" stage. This mess is dangerous because it's where many solutions wither. We're brought up to be nice and logical. A messy stage arrives when you stockpile seemingly unrelated facts that you'll need to manufacture your solution. Don't give up when you're almost home free. Mess comes just before "Eureka!"

 Which?
Choose the best solution.

Sketches

Place them along the wall, on the floor or atop the dining room table. You must be able to see them together (see Figure 4-9). Compare them. Eliminate those that are inappropriate after searching for the grain of genius that just might be lurking there.

Trace good parts of one sketch on tracing paper. Mix and match with good parts of another. Compare.

Continue tracing and refining until the Elegant Solution pleases you.

or

File Cards

Compare solutions on file cards. Eliminate carefully, adding new words and combinations that seem appropriate. Combine, eliminate and refine until you have chosen your solution.

FIGURE 4-9

FIGURE 4–10

This is the time to discuss *Serendipity*. Louis Pasteur said, "Chance favors the prepared mind" and he was right.

If your solution still isn't satisfactory, now's the time to ring in your subconscious. This is one of your most valuable tools and one in which many of us have very little faith.

The following are proven ways to stimulate subconscious solution-finding. They require saturating your mind with the problem's facts. You've already done that in *Which?* Subconscious solutions are not captured—they happen when you lease expect them. Relax and do something else.

Take a walk in a place full of all sorts of visual stimuli that have nothing to do with your problem. Avoid needlework stores. I get my best results from the 5 & 10 or hardware stores.

or

Sleep on it. Think about the problem just before you go to bed. Some creative souls get their inspirations just before they doze off. Others get them in the middle of the night. I have mine just as I'm waking. In any case, **have paper and pencil handy.** These flashes are pure gold, but they fade fast. **Write them down immediately,** for they may not pass your way again.

or

Put the stitchery where you can see it often during your everyday life. (This didn't work for "Acapulco, Sunset," but it has for other problem children). That perfect solution may hit you right in the middle of your corn flakes.

Of course none of these subconscious techniques is absolutely guaranteed, but the more confidence you have in your subconscious, the more reliably it will work for you. Solutions, when they arrive, are usually so brilliantly obvious that you can't believe you didn't see them before.

Now that you've covered the solution, fix the needlework. Some stitchers find problem-solving so fascinating that without self-discipline they'd never get on with fixing things. This is foolish because until you repair it, you can't move on to *Why?*

Why?

Evaluate the solution. Take the third and last copy of the Adjective List you made in *What?* Circle the words that describe the way you feel about the needlework now that it's finished.

Compare this list with your wish list. What did you do right? What did you do wrong? What have you learned that might help solve future design problems? Write it all down.

Why? is where learning takes place. Without evaluation, you can repeat the same mistakes over and over again. Keep records and consult them before the next problem-solving. Of course no two solutions are exactly the same, but the more you practice, the faster elegance appears.

Only if all of the above does not produce an acceptable solution would I ask for somebody else's criticism. Now, at least, you know what you like and what you want. The trouble with critiques is that, having asked for them, one tends to believe them. Sometimes outsiders can spot a problem immediately. More often they're just as confused as you are, only nobody realizes it.

Choose your critics carefully. Mine are a painter, an art teacher and a crewel embroiderer. Their areas of expertise give them different ways to view my work and I reciprocate with theirs.

Be prepared, however, to discount even the best of critics on occasion. You are the bottom line and you are the one who must be satisfied.

FIGURE 4-11

PROCESS

Stitchery dreams need many practical decisions before they turn into realities. Materials have to be gathered and the work has to be done. Information in this section will help you make such decisions quickly and correctly.

Consumer information is as important to embroidery and needlepoint as it is to grocery shopping. Where can you find the best quality for the lowest price? How do you judge quality when you see it? Chapter 5 tells you how and where to shop, and what to look for.

Once you have the materials, they must live somewhere. Wise storage can make the difference between excellent stitchery and work that looks so-so. Chapter 5 will tell you how to store materials, where to place them and what to enclose them in.

If you plan to paint a canvas, transfer a design to cloth or mark your needlepoint sampler's lines, Chapter 6 is for you. It gives the pros and cons of paints, pens, inks and dyes, and discusses the tools and techniques you'll need to use them.

Now is the time to start stitching. Chapter 7 takes you through beginning, from threading your needle to transferring your design to cloth or canvas. Even an experienced stitcher may pick up a trick or two here.

Chapter 8 tells you how to stitch excellently and when mistakes happen (as they do to all of us), how to fix things without making them worse. The one skill is as important as the other.

Process is where your dream becomes a reality while avoiding the aches and pains that litter its path. It's needlework's Maternity Ward.

5 What to Buy and Where to Store It

Early in my teaching career, I blithely told students to buy yarns anywhere. Their samplers needed enough citrus colors to cover a ten-inch square of canvas and "nobody could get into trouble with oranges and lemons." How wrong I was!

Delightful, quiet Leona returned to class with a shopping bag bulging twice as big as anybody else's. When her yarns came tumbling out, we all gasped.

A fast-talker had sold Leona armloads of wool dyed arsenic green, moldering orange, and bilious yellow. The colors fought like cats and dogs, and there was enough yarn to slipcover Mt. Rushmore.

Most needlework shops are not too enthusiastic about yarn returns once the wool has left the shop, and with good reason. What can they do with tidbits of dye lot #124 when they're currently selling lot #151? Leone was stuck with her wool-of-many colors.

After much pondering, we decided to use lots of brown as a peacemaker. This separated the feuding colors and actually made the sampler most attractive. Of course Leona had a bit of yarn left over. The last I heard, she was making a rug.

FIGURE 5-1

INTRODUCTION

Nothing is more frustrating than ending a needle-work project with leftover cloth or canvas for which you have no foreseeable need. Unless, perhaps, it's the vexation of getting well into a project and discovering that you don't have enough yarn to finish it. Either of these dilemmas can stem from the same source: letting somebody else decide how much material you will need.

Consumers travel a two-way street. The happiest journeys involve knowledgeable merchants and informed customers. Don't be one of those stitchers who starts a sale by asking, "I just don't know what colors to use—what would *you* suggest?" Taste is a very personal thing, and the shopkeeper should not be expected to know yours.

It's much better to do your own homework, deciding what you want, how to recognize its quality, and how much of it to buy. To help you make decisions, refer to this book as follows:

If you're interested in

- woolen yarn, read Chapter 10;
- embroidery flosses, linen, silk, cotton or rayon threads, or metallic fibers, read Chapter 11;
- cloth or canvas, read Chapter 9;
- needles, read Chapter 12;
- kits, read Chapter 2;
- marking pens, read Chapter 6
- paints and brushes, read Chapter 6.

SHOPPING

What guidelines should I use for shopping?

$ • **Be prepared to pay for materials of good quality.** Your time will be the same, whatever you stitch with, but the end results, appearance, and durability can vary greatly, depending on the materials you use.

$ • Call ahead to see which stores carry which materials and brands (Chapter 10, Q10). Ask if the shop carries a yarn or thread brand's "full color range." You'll have a wider field of colors to choose from if they do.

$ • Determine how the shop packages its wool. Do they sell it by the full skein (and is this measured by weight or yardage?), by partial skeins, or by individual strands?

    Note: one ounce is equal to 28 grams. Generally, the larger the package, the lower the unit price for each individual yarn strand.

• Shop from a list. This prevents confusion and impulse-buying with threads just as with groceries.

• Decide what volumes you need *before* you enter the store. Most salespeople are honest souls while they try their very best to please you. But let's face it, some people are better at math than others. It's better to do your computing yourself (Q4,5,6).

• Choose and match colors in natural light, not under artificial light. If this means that you have to carry the yarns to a window or outdoors, do so.

• Be sure that all yarns of one color are from the same dye lot. Have each color's dye lot number written on your receipt and SAVE THE RECEIPT. If you must purchase more yarn later, you'll know what to ask for.

• Buy three needles more than you think you'll need.

• You don't absolutely have to have additional accessories. Some may help you, but what's one stitcher's salvation is another's poison. Wait to buy a gadget until you're sure you need it (see Accessories, Chapter 12).

• If you live far from a well-stocked needlework shop, order by mail. Reputable mail order firms advertise in *The Flying Needle* (N.S.C.A.E.—see Guilds, Chapter 1), *Needle Arts* (E.G.A.—see Guilds, Chapter 1), and the better needlework magazines. Send for catalogs and comparison shop from them.

FIGURE 5-2

When next you're in your favorite store, regardless of where it's located, ask if they will serve you by mail. They'll probably be delighted to.

Needlepoint

2 **Which yarn colors should I choose?**
Read Chapter 3, Q11.

3 **How much canvas and cloth should I buy?**
$ Buy canvas and embroidery cloth **the size of your finished project** *plus* **four inches, lengthwise and widthwise.**

Don't accept needlepoint canvas with knots or flaws. Your knowledgeable shop owner will cut around them for you.

If you plan to frame or upholster the needlework, you may need extra cloth or canvas. Read "Framing," Chapter 16, Q14, or "Upholstery," Chapter 18, Introduction.

4 **How much needlepoint yarn should I buy?**
- **Fill in the Yarn Volumes Chart** (Table 5-1) after stitching a two-inch square with the yarn brand, canvas gauge, and background stitch you'll use for the project (see Figure 5-3).

FIGURE 5-3

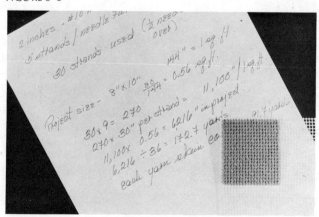

Table 5-1   Needlepoint Yarn Volumes Chart

Fill in the following numbers:

Number of yarn strands needed to stitch two square inches . . . (a)

Length of one yarn strand in inches . . . . (b)

Yards-per-skein of yarn brand
   (see Woolen Yarn Facts Chart, p. 282) . . . . (c)

Project length . . . . . . ✕ width . . . . . . = ... square inches   (d)

(d) . . . . . . ÷ 4 = ... (e)

(e) . . . . . . ✕ (a) . . . . . = ... (f)

(f) . . . . . . ✕ (b) . . . . . = ... (g)

(g) . . . . . . ÷ 36 = ... total yards yarn needed. . . . . (h)

Repeat for *each* color:

(h) . . . . . . ✕ color fraction . . . . . . = ... yards color . . . . (j)

(j) . . . . . . ÷ (c) . . . . . . = ... skeins color to buy.

Example:
(a) = 20
(b) = 30″
(c) = 190
project 12 inches ✕ 9 inches = 108 square inches (d)
108 ÷ 4 = 27 (e)
27 ✕ 20 = 540 (f)
540 ✕ 30 = 16,200 (g)
16,200 ÷ 36 = 450 (h)
450 ✕ ⅛ = 57 (j)
57 ÷ 190 = ⅓ skein—buy ½.)

- Divide the design into fractions (or percentages) of total area covered by each color (example: red—⅛, blue—¼, etc.). Be sure that all fractions add up to one. Do the best you can here and don't worry.

However, if mental math makes you nervous, you can calculate color fractions by putting a piece of 5–10 gauge canvas over a colored picture of the project. Write down a list of colors used. Go over the canvas, hole by hole, putting a check beside the *largest* color in each space. Count checks for each color, divide a color's answer by the total checks for all colors, and the answer will be each color's fraction. (Example: red got 68 checks. There were 540 checks altogether. 540 ÷ 68 = approximately ⅛.)

- When the answer contains a fraction (and even if it doesn't), buy the next larger number of skeins. And then buy one extra for the background color—just in case of emergency.
- Keep each color's dye lot numbers consistent and recorded.

 How do I decide how much thread to buy?
Fill in the Counted Thread Volumes chart (Table 5–2).

Be generous—remember that beginnings, endings and mistakes take thread, too.

Table 5–2 Counted Thread Volumes

Fill in the following numbers for *one* color:

Number of cloth mesh covered by color . . . . (a)

Length of one thread strand in inches . . . . (b)

Yards-per-skein of thread brand
   (see Non-Woolen Thread Facts Chart, p. 284)   (c)

Cloth gauge (number of threads per inch) . . . . (d)

Number of thread strands per needleful. . . . . (f)

a ÷ d = ... (e)

(e × 2 for blackwork or cross stitch)

e × f = ... (g)

g × b = ... (h)

h ÷ 36 = ... (j)

j ÷ c = number of skeins to buy.

Repeat for *each* color.

(Example:
(a) = 64
(b) = 20
(c) = 11
(d) = 10
(f) = 1
64 ÷ 10 = 6.4 (e)
6.4 × 2 = 12.8
12.8 × 1 = 12.8 (g)
12.8 × 20 = 256 (h)
256 ÷ 36 = 7 (j)
7 ÷ 11 = ¾ skein—buy 1.)

How do I decide how much embroidery yarn to buy?

$ For crewel and surface embroidery, there's no mathematical way to estimate your exact needs. The volume to buy is the volume you think you'll need, keeping the following facts in mind:

- Buy a known brand and be sure the shop has plenty of your dye lot on hand.
- See if the shop will accept unused skein returns and, if so, within what time framework. Buy what you think you'll use *within that time allotment.* Don't wait six months to get started.
- If worse comes to worst, a difference in dye lots between two separate flowers will probably never be noticed.
- Label any leftover yarns and flosses with brand name and dye lot number before storing (Q12, 14). This will be the beginning of an inventory that will be invaluable for future stitching.

STORAGE

As important as wise purchasing is careful storage of materials. Here are some practical and inexpensive ways to store the raw materials you'll gradually accumulate as you move further into the wonderful world of needlework.

Where should needlework materials be stored?
Store materials in an area that is **cool, dark, dry, dust-free and well ventilated.** A guestroom closet is an excellent choice; damp basements and hot attics are to be avoided.

Materials stored in strong light are subject to fading and sun rotting (or "sunburn"). If light is accompanied by heat, this deterioration accelerates (Chapter 16, Q1). Don't store materials in plastic if air can't move freely in and out of the bag (p. xv).

Most modern woolen yarn is effectively mothproofed at the factory. Unfortunately, carpet beetles and silver fish don't seem to know this—or care. Fumigate if you suspect such infestations.

Place loose covers of washed cloth or acid-free paper over stored materials to prevent dust and dirt from dropping on them.

How do I store the piece of canvas I'm working on?

Roll it around a cardboard tube from inside a roll of paper towels or waxed paper. Cover it with a plastic bag tied in place with a strand of yarn (see Figure 5-4).

FIGURE 5-4

Two perils to be avoided are dirt and creased canvas. Stitching bags are notorious for carrying everything from chocolate chip cookies to uncapped marking pens. Plastic protects the needlepoint from dirt, and the cardboard roll keeps it from being squashed by *Gone With the Wind*.

How do I store bulk canvas for future projects?

- If canvas pieces will lay flat, store them in a chest or drawer. If they're too large for flat storage, roll them over cloth-covered cardboard mailing tubes.

or

hang them from a hanger in a closet, using spring clothes pins or safety pins.

- If you have full-width sheets of canvas, roll them around a cloth-covered cardboard tube. The wider the tube's diameter, the flatter the canvas will be when it's unrolled. Cardboard

FIGURE 5-5

mailing tubes of various lengths are available at office supply stores. Tubes from rolls of wrapping paper also work if they're long enough.

Cover the canvas roll with washed cloth or acid-free paper, secured with string. If possible, store canvas rolls horizontally in a drawer or on a closet shelf.

An excellent storage idea, if you can find the space, is to attach an inexpensive curtain rod to some wall after inserting the rod through the center of your canvas roll (see Figure 5–5). Or use a spring-loaded curtain rod.

Less desirable, but more space-saving is vertical storage. Stand the covered roll in a laundry basket, clean waste basket or similar, tall container.

This has the drawback of possibly compressing the bottom edge which bears the roll's weight. Meshes near such an edge may be distorted.

How do I store embroidery while I'm working on it?

Take embroidery OUT of the hoop when you're not working on it. Cover loosely with a clean towel to keep stitchery clean.

To avoid creasing or crushing in your stitching bag, roll embroidery and towel around a cardboard tube from paper towels or waxed paper. Tie in place with a strand of yarn. If you store embroidery in a plastic bag, **do not** seal it closed (Preventive Medicine, p. xiii).

How do I store cloth for future embroidery?

Washable Cloth

Lay flat in a drawer or, next best, fold neatly and loosely. Cover with washed muslin, old sheets, or acid-free paper (Preventive Medicine, p. xiii).

Cloth That Must Be
Dry Cleaned

(satin, fabrics with sheen)
Roll loosely on a cardboard roll covered with washed cloth or acid-free paper. Cover fabric loosely (see Q9). Rolls avoid creases which can make permanent lines on fabrics with sheen.

 How do I store embroidery threads?

Group Storage

You'll need large (4×6 inch) index cards, or sheets of cardboard and a box to hold them (see Figure 5–6). Cut three or more shallow scallops from edges of cards, at top and bottom. Cut a half-inch slit to the right of each scallop. If card curls, use two together for added strength. Wind acid-free tissue paper between all scallops.

Wrap wools or threads loosely between scallops. Anchor ends by slipping them into slits. Label each thread with brand, color and dye lot.

FIGURE 5–6

Store yarns or threads of the same hue on the same cards. Store cards in a file box, shoe box, or other closed container.

The advantage of this method is that you can "pull" cards with threads you need, store the cards in your stitching bag until finished, and then re-file them without additional winding or fussing.

Individual Storage

Buy empty **35 mm. slide mounts** (no film in them) from a photography store. These look like an opened book (see Figure 5–7).

Fold the "book" and wrap with acid-free tissue paper. With the book's fold at bottom, wrap thread loosely around cardboard, leaving one-fourth inch at each side unwound. Anchor thread end by slipping between open corners of book.

Store in a slide storage tray. These have labels which can be used to identify brand and dye lots of each yarn and thread.

FIGURE 5–7

FIGURE 5–8

 How do I store wool skeins?
Store similar colors together. Don't lump everything in the bottom of your stitching bag. Try these organizing tricks.

Loosely knot each yarn color separately.

or

Loop each color over an embroidery hoop, plastic rings from 6-packs of frozen orange juices or beverages, or the handles of your stitching bag (let loose ends hang inside).

or

Store each color family in a separate plastic sandwich bag for not more than twelve months.

or

Make a needlework yarn carrier and slip each yarn's color beneath its own loop.

Yarn is always in danger from dirt, tangling, and stray fibers from other color wools. Store it, however organized, in a clean bag. Knot skeins *loosely,* and separate colors so that off-color fibers can't transfer from one skein to another.

FIGURE 5–9

How do I store leftover wool?
The method depends upon the yarn volume. Each dye lot and color family should be kept in its own unsealed, labeled, plastic bag. These directions presuppose a storage time of not more than one year. If you need longer storage, substitute bags made of washed cloth or acid-free paper.

- *Small yarn volumes.* Buy an inexpensive hanging **shoe bag.** Each color will live in its own pocket (see Figure 5–9). Hang from a closet rod or hook. This works beautifully until you've collected so much yarn that the pockets overflow. Then move on to:
- *Medium yarn volumes.* Buy a **shoe storage box** with compartments. These have a clear, plastic flap which zips open to give access to cubicles inside. Each color family will live in its own compartment, which should be plenty of space unless you're contemplating gigantic projects, in which case escalate to:
- *Large yarn volumes.* Obtain covered, **plastic shoe boxes** or, even larger, **plastic sweater boxes.** These stack nicely. If boxes are transparent, store them in the dark. If you can see through the sides, ultra-violet radiation can penetrate too (Chapter 16, Q1).

Replace plastic tops with rectangles of washed cloth held to boxes with strong rubber bands. This will let wool breathe and, at the same time, allow boxes to be stacked.

15 How can I store bulky frames and hoops?

Hang them from a closet rod on individual shower curtain rings (see Figure 5–10).

or

Hang them **over clothes hooks** on a closet wall.

or

Slip them **between books and bookends** on a shelf.

or

Hang them **over the necks of individual hangers** on a closet rod.

FIGURE 5–10

How do I store needles?
Dry.

- For needlepoint tapestry needles (blunt), use empty pill bottles or containers from spices or vitamins (see Figure 5–11). Don't mix different-sized needles in the same container unless you you enjoy figuring out which is which. Label containers.

- For embroidery needles (sharp), use the same kind of containers as for tapestry needles, but cover the bottoms with circles of felt or cotton balls to prevent dulling needle tips.

- A needlebook with flannel leaves is an old-fashioned idea that works just as well today as it did for grandmother. Label each page with a laundry or needlepoint marker. Put one type or size needle on each page to avoid confusion.

FIGURE 5–11

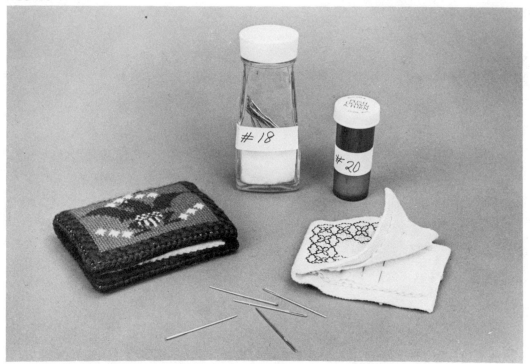

I'll never forget one winter night when I'd been stitching in bed and dozed off and dropped my needle. After opening one eye, I decided that it had probably fallen to the floor and could be retrieved in the morning.

"The morning" arrived at about 4 A.M. when my sleeping husband rose three feet in the air, blasting words I've never heard before. That needle hadn't fallen to the floor after all. We won't go into where it did end up.

I don't stitch in bed any more.

6 Marking, Painting, and Dyeing

FIGURE 6-1

My teaching career almost sank before it was launched. The first night of my first class at the Henry Ford Museum, I handed out lists of materials to buy. Hidden among the items was a highly recommended, yellow "waterproof" canvas marker which is no longer on the market.

Twenty students came to class the next week with twenty yellow markers. They drew sampler designs on canvases and some got a little off the track. When the evening was over, a lot of yellow had been spread around.

Six weeks passed quickly. The next-to-last class was Blocking Demonstration night, where I worked on a student's just-completed sampler. The pattern was the Maple Leaf, one of my favorites.

It was a gala evening until I thought I saw a hint of yellow on one blue leaf. Of course that was impossible (but I kept an eye on the leaf anyway). By the time all tacks were hammered there was no doubt—that sampler was coming down with jaundice.

Class *finally* ended and I dashed home, lemon in hand. After three hours of creative laundry, the truth was clear. Nothing was going to take the yellow out. Three lovely shades of French blue wool looked like mouldy Wonder Bread.

It had to be the pens. The manufacturer and I had a little confrontation which took them out of the needlepoint business, but there were still 19 samplers and one more class to live through. If only nothing got wet before I told them how to cope.

The moment of truth finally arrived. There weren't as many surprised gasps as I'd anticipated. The silence was explained when five yellowish samplers, all nicely blocked, emerged from five stitching bags.

I spent the following summer redoing six Maple Leaf samplers. I don't much care for the pattern any more.

INTRODUCTION

Marking or coloring canvas or cloth serves several purposes. It makes a ground fabric match its threads—in case stitching doesn't quite cover what's beneath. (In needlepoint this is called "grin through" and is no grinning matter.) Coloring lets a design look attractive before it's stitched. It acts as a permanent reminder of what the designer had in mind. It tells the stitcher where to switch colors.

Color can be applied to fibers in different ways. Each takes time. Decide whether coloring will be of enough benefit to you to justify the time necessary to do it.

Unwashed cloth and needlepoint canvas are stiffened and smoothed by the addition of sizing. Paint coats fibers and does not require sizing to be removed from them (see Figure 6–2). Dye, on the other hand, attaches itself directly to fibers. Dyes can have trouble penetrating sizing barriers.

Paint layers can flake off when cloth or canvas is vigorously flexed. Dye becomes part of the fiber and cannot be peeled off. Is your embroidery destined for a life of action or one of inactivity? Do you want to—or can you—remove sizing from your ground material? These answers will help you decide upon the right way to color your material.

Many artists outline designs first and then fill them in with color. Permanent marking pens, or a firm hand with India ink and steel pen points or fine brush are the recommended outlining methods.

 What are the pros and cons of each coloring medium?

Paints

Oil paint has an unlimited range of colors. It dissolves in turpentine or solvents that do not affect cloth or sizing. It is *very* slow drying, sometimes

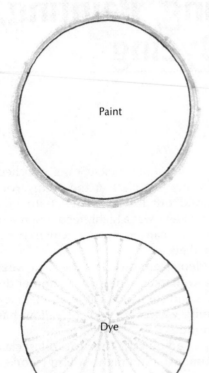

Paint

Dye

FIGURE 6–2

taking up to a week before it can be touched. It's permanent and waterproof when dry. Oil paints are inexpensive and widely available.

Acrylic paint has an unlimited color range. It dissolves in water, which can soften canvas and wrinkle cloth. It dries in several hours. It's permanent and waterproof when dry. Acrylics are inexpensive and widely available.

Fabric paints are really dyes. They're permanent and waterproof when applied according to package directions. Prang and Nazdar are two common brands which work best when sizing has been washed away. The color range is wide and can be mixed to make additional hues. Fabric paints dry quickly. Color is set by heat—usually ironing, an oven, or tumbling in a hot dryer. Prices and availability vary.

Pens and Inks

India ink is made of minute particles of carbon held in suspension in water by soap, borax, or a natural gum. It resists fading and is permanent and waterproof when dry. It is safe for cloth and threads. It comes in black only, is widely available and is inexpensive.

Fabric inks are dyes whose chemical compositions vary. Some can penetrate sizing on cloth or canvas and will adhere to fibers below. Others sit upon sizing and are soluble in any water which happens along. Dampness will carry their color wherever it penetrates and this "bleeding" marks needlework as well as fabric. Such inks are contained in "permanent" marking pens.

Permanent Pens come in a limited range of colors which do not mix well to produce additional hues. Their solvents do not wrinkle cloth, but may ooze into neighboring threads, diffusing and broadening lines. They dry almost immediately, are inexpensive and easily available.

Pen Test

Always test a new brand of a "permanent" marking pen on a scrap of your cloth or canvas. Dampen the scrap and rub vigorously for one minute with a white

71   *Marking, Painting, and Dyeing*

FIGURE 6-3

cloth. If ink does not transfer to the rubbing cloth, its marks will be permanent and waterproof when dry.

Washable Pattern Marking Pens produce marks that will dissolve in water once you've finished, *if* you follow directions exactly. Rinse *thoroughly* in cool water until line disappears. Wash with mild soap and cool water. Rinse completely. Do not heat, iron or expose markings to sunlight for long periods of time (Example: the beach), or they may become indelible.

These pens were developed for marking synthetic fabrics. Synthetic fibers look like smooth, glass threads (see Figure 6–3). Natural fibers such as cotton or wool have spongey structures. Ink hides in their minute holes and needs more than simple rinsing to remove it.

Crayons

Crayons (*Crayola* brand) come in a wide range of colors which can be mixed to produce additional hues. Crayon works best on flat, untextured, washed cloth. It is not recommended for canvas, where sizing is heavy and texture is rough. Color is set by ironing and becomes waterproof. Crayons are easily available and very inexpensive.

Dyes

Dyes are available in many forms and compositions. *Rit* brand dyes and natural colors derived from plant materials are not controllable enough to be used for painting cloth or canvas.

Procion dyes are chemical colors available in dry powders. These are dissolved in water much like Easter egg dyes. They can be mixed to form additional hues, which are painted on cloth or canvas like water colors. Heat sets color permanently. Sizing can prevent dye penetration and should be removed before coloring. Procion dyes are not universally available and may have to be ordered by mail. They are moderately expensive.

How do I paint on cloth or canvas?

Paint with a very dry brush (see Figure 6-4). Use as little solvent as possible (water with Acrylics or *Procion*; turpentine, or a fabric medium such as *Textine* by Grumbacher, with oils). Too much solvent causes fibers to spread and diffuse color. Remember that the rough texture of canvas wears away bristles on good brushes.

Do not clog canvas holes with paint. Use the least pigment that will color, carried in the least solvent that will spread it.

Hint: If you need large volumes of acrylic paint, mix it in a white plastic egg carton. You can close the top and keep the paint from drying out.

Hint: Coloring backgrounds is not necessary unless there will be a "grin through" problem.

FIGURE 6-4

What do I use to draw outlines on cloth or canvas?

- My favorite tool is a fine, steel "quill" pen point held in a pen holder and used with India Ink (see Figure 6-5). These materials are inexpensive; readily available in art supply stores, safe for all fibers, and produce a very thin line that is nonetheless easily visible. One disadvantage, if you're inexperienced with pens, is that sharp quill points can spatter if they catch on fabric—and once India ink is on a fabric, it's there for good.

FIGURE 6-5

- Washable pattern marking pens are discussed in Q1. When handled correctly, they will disappear after washing.
- Some permanent marking pens are dry while others are so juicy that inks spread color through surrounding fibers. *Many pens that are permanent on cloth are not permanent on canvas.*

Any pen that is not specifically formulated for needlepoint should be considered guilty until proven innocent. Run a "Pen Test," (p. 71) before using.

Do not use pencil on needlepoint canvas. Graphite lurks beneath canvas meshes waiting to attach itself to light-colored yarn as you stitch. I have a greenish sampler that started life buttercup yellow before pencil markings got to it.

If you already have bleedable inks or pencil marks on your project, spray it with crystal Krylon to seal it. Work in a frame to prevent spray from flaking off when flexed.

How do I mark lines on cloth or canvas?

Draw thin lines. The thicker the line becomes, the closer its color should be to the ground material. You may have to cover the line with white threads. Heavy, black or vivid markings will show through.

However, if this happens, correct as in Mistakes, Q5.

Drawing techniques on canvas are discussed in Chapter 7, Q3.

How can I cover mistakes if I've drawn wrong?

- On canvas, **use white acrylic artists' paint,** or "Liquid Paper" correction fluid used by typists. Dry before stitching. (I was dubious about these secretary's helpers until I tested them. They did not dissolve when washed, though thick areas did flake off when rubbed.)

- On cloth, there's nothing you can do unless you've used a pattern marking pen which will disappear when you wash it. If markings haven't penetrated to cloth's back, you can redraw and stitch on the reverse side.

How do I color with crayons and make them permanent?

Crayon marks look smoother on flat cloth than on needlepoint canvas (see Figure 6-6).

FIGURE 6-6

Work with sharpened crayons. Use Crayola's large box-with-a-sharpener. Wax from one color can soil the next crayon to be sharpened. "Clean" the sharpener after each use by giving the white crayon a few turns in it.

One color can be rubbed over another to produce a third, thus making possible a large range of hues. Wax has a visible texture which will soften when set, but won't disappear. Work evenly on a smooth surface, using constant pressure.

Crayon is **set by ironing,** adjusting the dry iron to the fiber being colored. Turn cloth upside down on a paper towel resting on an ironing board or padded surface. Press for 15 seconds.

7 **How do I paint with dyes on cloth or canvas?**
Remove starch sizing by washing. Iron flat. **Apply color** according to package directions and dry. **Set by heat**—either one hour in a hot oven or dryer, or by ironing on the fabric's back.

Fabric inks and paints, permanent pens and crayons all color with some form of dye (see Figure 6-7). Dyes often cannot penetrate sizing and fade when it is not removed.

FIGURE 6-7

Heat "sets" color by opening fiber pores and interior spaces so that dye can penetrate fibers thoroughly.

Use dyes only on fibers recommended by the manufacturer. One dye will not color all fibers equally well.

 What happens when coloring paints and dyes are cleaned?
If they are among the media listed in the introduction to this chapter, they are safe in plain water. Strong alkalies (detergents), strong acids (vinegar), and some spray chemicals (water repellants) can cause certain dyes to bleed. **Avoid such chemicals.** If they must be used, run Dye-Fast Test, p. 166 testing chemical in an inconspicuous area.

Hardened paint will not dissolve when washed, but flexing sometimes can flake it off.

Dry cleaning is generally safe for most dyes.

 How do I test dyes or paints for color-fastness?
Run Dye-Fast Test, p. 166 using cleaning solution. Repeat a separate test for each color present.

 What do I do when dyes are *not* colorfast?
Keep them away from water—washing, blocking, and sudden showers.

or

Keep rinsing until all dye is removed (Chapter 10, Q8).

If susceptible cloth or canvas has not yet been stitched, seal it by spraying with crystal Krylon or other acrylic spray. This is dangerous stuff to breathe and should be used only in a well-ventilated area or out-of-doors.

If cloth or canvas is partially stitched, don't let it get wet—ever. Work on a frame, be scrupulously clean, dry clean if soiled and avoid traditional blocking. A quick freshening (Chapter 14, Q10) is all that you can get away with safely.

FIGURE 6-8

7 How to Start

FIGURE 7-1

Perhaps a chapter on beginnings is the place to tell how I came to embroidery.

One day years ago, when my babies were somewhere between kindergarten and nursery school, I was invited to hear a lecture on embroidery. To be honest, I wasn't enraptured by the prospect, but any time spent with humans over the age of six was not to be sneezed at.

The slide-lecture full of beautiful creations began at 10 A.M. I didn't come up for air until lights went on again at 11:30. Where had this been all my life? How could I learn to do it all?

As soon as possible, I headed for the nearest needlework shop. It featured a large, beautiful kit picturing all sorts of vegetables. I bought it on the spot. (None of this "starting-out-small" for yours truly.)

Halfway through the kit, I met the cauliflower. It looked beautiful in the colored picture. It turned mouldy in my embroidery.

I never did conquer that cauliflower. It lurks in a drawer to this day. I *will* finish it some time. Or perhaps now that the babies are grown, I'll give it to one of them. Creativity should be shared, with or without cheese sauce.

NEEDLEPOINT INTRODUCTION

Before starting to stitch needlepoint, you'll need to know how much canvas to cut, what size needles to use, and how much yarn to stockpile.

Cut canvas the size of your project *plus* four extra inches, length and widthwise.

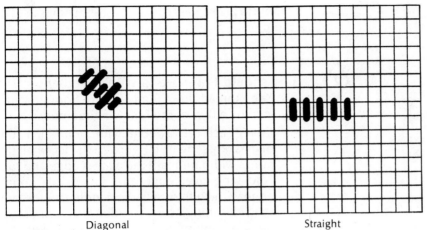

Diagonal   Straight

FIGURE 7-2

To find the right size tapestry needle or, with stranded yarn, how many strands to use per needleful, consult Table I in the Appendix (p. 281). To determine how much yarn you'll need to buy, look at the Needlepoint Yarn Volume Chart (p. 57).

Be aware that this number of strands will cover canvas if you're using *diagonal* stitches. When using *straight* stitches, add one more strand of wool per needleful (see Figure 7-2).

Now that you're equipped, keep the following truths in mind:

Do what you can to keep canvas threads from shifting. Precision of stitching depends upon precision of canvas meshes. All canvases start out in life with threads precisely aligned. Not all of them end up that way.

Each time you squash, mash or crumple, canvas will move out of alignment and the resulting needlepoint will look—and be—uneven.

As you stitch, count canvas threads, not holes. Visualize each stitch as a gift wrapping, enclosing its own particular number of threads.

  What should my first needlepoint project be? Any needlepoint that is appealing and easy. You should want to do it, but don't try to learn everything the first time at bat. Keep first projects small enough to finish while your initial enthusiasm lasts.

Examples are eyeglass cases, coasters, coin purses or a sampler.

How should I prepare to stitch needlepoint?

- Keep threads from unraveling or from snagging yarn by either of the following methods:
- Cover each canvas edge with a one-inch strip of masking tape (see Figure 7–3). Place half the tape's width beneath the canvas edge and rub. Fold tape over edge and rub. Scrub bound edge with knife or scissors handle to stick tape to itself through canvas holes (but don't scrub on the dining room table; I engraved #14 meshes on mine).

or

Fold one-inch twill tape (pre-shrunk) over edges and attach to canvas with your machine's zigzag or straight stitch. This is more permanent than masking tape, but takes longer.

FIGURE 7–3

- Separate individual yarn strands from skein by combing with fingers. If yarns are badly creased or crumpled, spray them with a light mist of water, lay straight and flat, and allow to dry before stitching.

 How do I mark on blank canvas?
Use a permanent pen (Chapter 6, Q1). **Draw between threads along a row of holes** (see Figure 7–4). Do not mark along a continuous thread. Each stitch wraps its own number of canvas threads. If markings lie along rows of holes, they divide one stitch's threads from those of its neighbor.

FIGURE 7–4

 How do I thread my needle?
It's easy once you understand the theory behind it. Here are three ways to do the job:

- *Crease and Squeeze.* Fold yarn over needle to achieve a sharp crease. Hide creased yarn be-

FIGURE 7-5

FIGURE 7-6

tween fat pads of your thumb and forefinger. Squeeze gently. You shouldn't be able to see the wool, but you can feel it.

Use the flat side of needle's eye as a wedge and slide needle between pads of your squeezing fingers (see Figure 7–5). The wool wants to decompress. The only space available is in the eye of the needle and that's where it will go.

Only two things can go wrong with this technique. If it's not working for you, check to see if you're peeking. If you can see it, you can't squeeze it.

or

Are you slipping the skinny side of the needle's eye between your fingers instead of the flat side?

- *Paper Folder.* Snip a paper oblong measuring one-inch by one-fourth inch. Fold in half lengthwise and hide yarn's end between folds. Insert narrow end of paper fold into needle's eye, folded corner first (see Figure 7–6). Thread the yarn with the paper.

- *Commercial Needle Threader.* These are inexpensive and found at notions counters and variety stores. Buy two or three. They tend to disappear at inconvenient moments.

Time Saver: Thread a different needle with each color you'll be using and keep them handy in a pincushion.

 Where should I begin stitching needlepoint?

- On a painted canvas, **work the design first and the background last.** Remember that traditionally, all Tent, Basketweave and Half-Cross stitches slant toward the upper right (though the sky won't fall if you're left-handed and slant toward the upper left).

- If you're stitching a graphed design on blank canvas, begin working as near the center of both as possible. Then everything that follows will be centered.

How do I anchor needlepoint yarn?

Use one of the following techniques (they all have the same goal—to **bury yarn ends on the back of canvas beneath completed stitching**):

- **Waste Knot on Empty Canvas.** Knot end of yarn. Point needle down, about two inches *along the row you plan to stitch.* Pull yarn to back, leaving knot on front. Return to Start and begin stitching (see Figure 7–7). As you approach knot, snip it off.

FIGURE 7-7

- **No Knot on Empty Canvas.** Place yarn in the same hole as waste knot, but don't bother knotting it.

  This is quicker than a waste knot and friction will keep yarn in place if you stitch immediately. If you anticipate delays, choose the knot.
- **Bury Yarn.** Hold end behind your work and bury as you stitch the empty canvas. This is my least favorite method since I seem to need three hands to make it work.

After canvas has been stitched, begin and end all yarns by running needle beneath one and one-half inches (almost one needle-length) of stitching on the back.

How do I stitch canvas?

- **Stab it.** Stitch in a two-motion, up-and-down action unless you are very experienced. This is called "stabbing." It takes longer than "sewing"

FIGURE 7-8

FIGURE 7-9

Flat

Twisted

FIGURE 7-10

(in and out in one motion) but regulates yarn and tension better.

- When you "sew" needlepoint, the needle applies leverage to each canvas intersection. If tension is not carefully controlled, stitches exert too much pressure, shoving canvas threads out of position (see Figure 7-8). You end with warped canvas.

  Point needle up through empty holes and down into holes containing yarn. This avoids splitting existing stitches.

- Two-Handed Method of Stitching (to be used with a frame). Place your "smart" hand (right if you're right-handed, otherwise left) beneath stretched canvas while the "dumb" hand is on top where eyes can help it. Pass needle from hand to hand, regulating tension and stitch placement as you go (see Figure 7-9). I know . . . it feels as if you're all thumbs at first but keep at it. Dexterity, confidence, and—best of all—speed will improve with practice.

8

What should I know about needlepoint tension?

- Regulate it by **allowing yarn to sit "fat" on top of canvas.**

  Yarn shouldn't be so tight that it shifts canvas threads, nor so loose that it loops.

- **Keep individual strands of yarn "flat."** They should lay side by side like railroad tracks instead of twisting like a candy cane (see Figure 7-10).

  An easy way to flatten wool is to run your needle up and down the yarn threaded in it. This combs and separates individual strands.

  When using Persian or persian-type wools, separate the three strands that form each yarn *before* threading needle. This makes yarn easier to flatten.

9

Should I use a frame for needlepoint?

I almost always work on a frame. Some stitchers avoid them like the plague. Read Chapter 12, Q4 for frame facts, and decide for yourself.

Large areas of diagonal stitches can warp unstretched canvas, but canvas can't move when it's stretched in all four directions. Stitching tension is kept even, which is an advantage for beginners.

If you use a roller frame, stretch its unrolled sides by lacing them to frame supports with string or pearl cotton (see Figure 7–11). Protect the rolls from becoming dirty when they're used as handles by using the waxed paper technique in Q11.

The larger the project, the more it will benefit from a frame.

FIGURE 7–11

How do I hold a frame?
Sit with frame in lap, leaning it against a table. This is easy and inexpensive, but you may develop neck muscle strain after working for several hours.

or

Sit at a table. **Clamp frame to table** with one or more "C" or "Stanley" clamps, protecting table's finish with several thicknesses of paper. This fastens the frame securely, but you're looking straight down and that angle strains neck muscles quickly.

or

Sit in an armchair, resting the frame on its arms. This is excellent if the frame's length and the chair's dimensions happen to match.

or

Use a "Fanny frame." This frame-holder is a C-shaped piece of wood. The top of the C clamps to your frame while the bottom wedges beneath you as you sit wherever you're comfortable. You can stitch for hours without muscle strain, but the frame has to be purchased and is not inexpensive (see Figure 7-9).

or

Use a floor frame. This is always ready for action and puts you in a comfortable working position, but it takes up floor space and is expensive.

How do I work on the center of a large, unframed canvas?

You must get the sides out of the way. Squashing, crumpling, and pleating are not the ways to do it.

Place unframed canvas on a sheet of waxed paper. **Roll** both around the cardboard tube from a roll of paper towels so that waxed paper covers roll (see Figure 7-12). Paper clip or pin the roll, top and bottom. Such a roll can serve as a handle and waxed paper will protect canvas from any dirt that might be lurking on your hands. Cut away paper from beneath area you'll be stitching.

When rolling needlepoint on a roller frame, protect rolls from dirt by basting plastic over canvas before rolling. You'll probably use such rolls for handles and, unprotected, they can become dirty.

FIGURE 7-12

How do I transfer a design from paper to canvas?

Employ any of the following lighting tricks, using a *waterproof* pen (Chapter 6, Q1).

Use **vertical light** sources available to you, taping design to a window, glass door wall or storm door with sunlight behind it. Tape canvas over design, centering carefully. Be sure that vertical and horizontal lines run parallel to canvas threads. The design will show through canvas meshes (see Figure 7–13).

Trace it with a waterproof marking pen. If design is hard to see, darken its main lines with a black pen. If you don't wish to mark on the pattern, trace its outlines on tracing paper and substitute for original design.

FIGURE 7–13

or

Make a horizontal light table. Separate leaves on your dining room table. Place a sheet of glass or clear plastic over the gap (don't cut yourself on sharp edges). Place unshaded lamp on floor beneath gap and tape design to glass, proceeding as directed in *vertical light.*

or

Use a glass coffee table in the same manner.

or

Rest a clean storm window on two saw horses and proceed as above.

How do I enlarge or shrink a design?

Use one of the following techniques:

Take design to a blueprint shop to **have it photostatted.** (Such firms are listed under "Blueprints," or "Photoenlarging" in your Yellow Pages.) Request a "positive image" in the dimensions you wish or you'll receive a blueprint. This is the easiest, but the most expensive answer to this question.

or

Borrow an **opaque projector** from a friendly teacher (this machine projects images on a wall or screen). Cut paper to the size you wish your design to be and tape it to a wall. Place design on projector, following manufacturer's directions. Move and focus the projector until the design fills the paper. Draw around the projection with a black pen. This outline becomes your design. Proceed as directed in Q12.

or

If the design is simple, sketch it on a small sheet of tracing paper. Enclose paper within a slide-blank, obtained from photographic stores. Project this "slide" with a **slide projector.** Focus and draw as with opaque projector.

or

Use a **pantograph.** This gadget is available at most art supply stores. It allows you to trace the original pattern while a pencil, attached to a complicated arm structure, simultaneously draws the pattern in the scale that you wish it to be. This is a little tricky to use and represents a moderate investment. If you plan to do much enlarging, it might be worth the time and money.

or

Draw blocks. Cover design with tracing paper, drawing a rectangular frame around the outside. Trace design within frame. Divide frame into identical rectangles larger than one inch per side, but of whatever size will completely fill the space. Blocks must be identical, but they need not be square (see Figure 7-14).

FIGURE 7-14

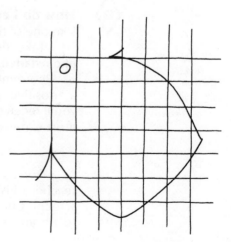

On a second sheet of paper, draw a new frame with whatever measurements you wish. Divide the new frame into as many rectangles as there were blocks in the old frame (Example: five East to West, and three North to South). Draw within each new block the section of the design that lived inside its corresponding old block. Outline new design with black pen and proceed as directed in Q12.

EMBROIDERY INTRODUCTION

Before beginning to stitch, you'll need to know how much cloth to cut, what size needles to use and how much thread to buy.

Pre-shrink materials only if the finished product will need frequent washings—Examples: table linens or clothing. Cut cloth the size of your project—Example: the size of the picture frame—*plus* at least four additional inches, length and widthwise.

If you plan to frame or upholster stitchery, you may need extra cloth. Read Chapter 18, Q3 or Chapter 16, Q14 before cutting.

To find the right type and size needle, consult Table I in the Appendix, and Chapter 12, Q10.

To determine how much thread you'll need, consult Chapter 5, Q4, 5, 6.

You'll need a hoop and, if you wish, a magnifying glass and thimble. Pros and cons of various accessories are to be found in Chapter 12.

- Now that you're equipped, keep the following facts in mind: The term "embroidery" includes crewel work and surface stitchery where stitches are placed as closely packed or widely spaced as you desire. It also included counted-thread techniques such as cross-stitch and blackwork, which depend upon absolute regularity for their effects. Techniques that help one category don't always assist the other. Where such a divergence occurs, directions will be labeled "crewel" or "counted thread."

FIGURE 7-15

- Position design so that it's "square" with the "straight of the grain" of your cloth. This means that warp threads (parallel to selvage) will run from top to bottom.
- **Always remove your hoop** when you stop stitching, even for "only a few minutes" (see Figure 7-15). Those minutes can stretch into months, by which time the hoop could have left indelible marks.
- If you mix washable threads with dry-clean-only cloth, or vice versa, you'll stitch a cleaning problem. Sometimes aesthetic reasons dictate such a mixture and the result should always be dry-cleaned. However, when you have a choice, pick cloth and thread that can be cleaned by the same method.

How do I begin embroidery?

- **Choose hoops with screw tighteners** (Chapter 12, Q5), not those with coil springs. Screws regulate tension better than springs. I prefer a hoop that takes care of its own support, leaving both hands free for stitching. Be aware that such hoops are more expensive than simple rings.

  If you plan to hold the hoop in your hands, choose a small one. Ideally, the thumb of your "holding" hand should almost be able to reach the center of the ring (see Figure 7-16). Then your holding hand can help your "stitching" hand guide its needle or manipulate its thread.

FIGURE 7-16

- **Tape hoop** by winding inner ring with one-inch twill tape (available in notion departments), anchored with tacking stitches. Outer ring will press embroidery cloth into tape padding, keeping cloth firm and reducing creasing.
- **Place cloth in hoop** by separating rings, placing inner ring flat on firm surface. Center motif over ring. Push outer ring down over cloth and inner ring, tightening screw adjustment moderately (see Figure 7-17). Pull fabric edges to draw cloth tight as a drum's head and finish tightening screw. Always be aware of the straight of the grain and don't stretch cloth crookedly.

FIGURE 7–17

As you stitch, cloth will work loose. Retighten when necessary. (When working with delicate fabrics, such as satins, read Chapter 8, Q14.)

 How do I hold a hoop?

- It depends on which type hoop you have. The most common method is to hold the hoop in one hand while stitching with the other. The smaller the hoop, the more help you can get from your "holding" hand (Q14).

- Simple rings can be attached to table tops by small "C" or "Stanley" clamps pressing hoop's screw-holder to table's edge (see Q10 to protect table). The ring will extend out in space and both hands will be freed for stitching (see Figure 7–18).

FIGURE 7–18

Place a scrap of cloth between clamp and fabric so that one won't stain the other.

Specialized hoops can stand on a table, on the floor, or wedge beneath you as you sit. When using both hands to stitch on such a supported frame, use two-handed method in Q7.

How do I stitch embroidery with wool?

- Be aware that **yarn has a direction** (Chapter 10, Q12). Cloth should stroke such needlefuls the "smooth" way, and help prevent scraped yarns.
- Work with yarn strands no longer than 15–18 inches.
- Do not loop yarn through the needle to make two strands from one. Since yarn has direction, looping guarantees that half will pass through cloth the wrong way. If you're short on wool, cut a strand in two and thread both halves correctly.

Where do I start stitching embroidery?

Crewel

Stitch **those areas first that eventually will appear to be covered** by other embroidery. If one leaf will look as if it's stitched beneath another, embroider the "lower" leaf first.

Counted Thread

Start with **the center of pattern in the middle of cloth.** Complete all embroidery within the hoop before moving to another area.

How do I anchor threads on my embroidery?
In any **firm way that avoids knots.** The following methods are representative:

Waste knot (Q6). Recommended for counted-thread.

or

Stabbed Stitch. Recommended for areas that will be covered by stitching.

Turn hoop over with cloth back facing you. Take a very small stitch, leaving one-half inch tail. Stab needle through this stitch (see Figure 7–19).

Turn hoop right side up. Check stab to see that thread is split. Stick needle through to the back *right next to* stabbed stitch. Embroider, covering stabbed stitch as you work.

FIGURE 7–19

or

Running Anchor. Recommended for long, linear stitches such as *Chain* and *Outline*.

Insert needle one-half inch from start along line to be stitched. Leave one-half inch tail on top. Make a series of tiny, running stitches aimed back towards the Start. Leave as little thread on top as possible. Stitch, piercing three or four "running stitches" as you cover them. Snip off tail as you approach it.

 How do I use my embroidery needle?

Work needle **in a two-motion, up and down manner** unless the stitch specifically needs a "sewing" technique. Most stitches do not. There should be no slack in your drumtaught hoop and no relaxed cloth for you to sew through. The looser the cloth, the more stitch-tension can pucker it.

When moving from one area of embroidery to another, **Do not drag threads** across the back. This can often be seen from the front and may cause puckering. Complete each area, cut its thread and begin anew in the next spot.

 How do I gauge tension?

Keep threads relaxed. Don't yank them too tightly (but don't let them sag either).

How do I fasten off Embroidery threads?
Whip through the undersides of five or six stitches, piercing them whenever possible.

How do I enlarge or reduce designs?
See Q13.

How do I transfer embroidery designs to cloth?

- **Light Method** (Q12). Tape cloth over design and trace with a "washable pattern-marking pen" sold at fabric stores.

    All lines will wash away when you block if you follow the directions *exactly* in Chapter 6, Q1.

- **Carbon Paper.** You'll need graphite paper (available at art supply stores—purchase by the sheet and not the roll) or less desirable dressmaker's carbon paper; masking tape; and a nut pick, blunt pencil, empty ball point pen or knitting needle.

    Make a sandwich of fabric taped to a flat surface, carbon paper (face down), and design on top, taped in place.

    Press *firmly* over the design's lines. Check after a few strokes to see if you're pressing hard enough to make clear lines.

    Dressmakers carbon smudges more than graphite paper. It can substitute if you stitch and store carefully. Smudges and lines may or may not wash out. Don't mark where you can't cover with embroidery.

- **Prick and Pounce.** This old-fashioned and time-tested method is taught in many embroidery books. It works but is messy, requires powdered charcoal, and leaves the paper pattern so perforated that it can fall apart.

- **Basting.** Although this method is not good for fine details, it is the only one that works for embroidering on piled fabrics, sweaters, or needlepoint.

    Trace pattern on tracing paper. Tack design to front of material, and baste over lines, right through paper, with a sewing thread differently colored from anything in your work.

Make stitches as small as possible.

Tear pattern from cloth, carefully pulling from side to side along basting perforations (see Figure 7–20). Embroider over bastings. If stitchery covers them, they needn't be removed but if you can see them, pull them out.

FIGURE 7–20

- **Commercial iron-on transfer patterns** are available. If you don't mind adhering to the size and shape of somebody else's inspiration, these are easy to apply and permanent. Follow directions exactly.

8 Excellence and Survival

Needlework shows are fascinating affairs. Years ago, whenever I envisioned stitchery judges (which wasn't very often), I thought of them as plump, pleasant ladies fluttering about planting blue ribbons. Then I was asked to judge a show and became enlightened.

The show was described as "open" which means that anybody may enter. Such shows attract large numbers of entries from all levels of skill.

We three judges gathered outside the exhibit hall to be given our final instructions. We were to assign points for composition, color, etc. and had three hours to finish the job.

The great doors swung open, showing us a vast auditorium divided into fifteen stitchery categories. Our 180 minutes divided by 15 gave us about 12 minutes per category if we didn't pause to scratch our heads or go to the ladies' room. A great truth flashed before my eyes—the name of this game was elimination.

Three magnifying glasses popped into view. We sank down on our knees, stretched up on our

FIGURE 8-1

toes and LOOKED, while pencils flew and points accumulated. At the end of three hours, the job was finished, although we felt as if we'd just completed the Boston Marathon.

We were just leaving as the audience came pouring in through those open doors. The last sound I heard as we turned a corner was a voice raised in furious indignation behind us, "Look at that ribbon! Why I could have done better in the third grade. Who judged this show, anyway?"

It was then that I learned the second great truth about judging shows: make a quick getaway.

NEEDLEWORK EXCELLENCE

The following tips apply to all needlework.

- **Don't use knots.** Anchor yarns or threads in the manner suggested for your type of needlework (Chapter 7, Q6, 18).

    Knots rub against fabric and provide a focus for wear. They can make visible lumps on the front of cloth. Other anchors are just as fast and much more desirable.

- **Stitch textures** show up best when worked with white or light colors (Chapter 3, Q10).

- **Good Housekeeping:** When you work with silk, fragile fibers or pale colors, protect the finished area by basting a patch over it. Use washed cloth, acid-free paper or plastic if the patch won't be there long. This prevents marring the stitchery with skin oils, dirt, or the friction of your hands.

    or

    Stitch areas farthest from your body first and work toward you. Your hands need never brush or rest on completed work.

- **Divide stranded yarns** by "combing" them with your fingers (Chapter 10, Q18).

- **Synthetic Fibers:** Man-made fibers are less forgiving than woolen yarns. Synthetics lack wool's spring structure. They will not expand or contract as easily and mistakes will show more.

- **Two-Needle-Switch** is a universal technique for when you run out of thread in the middle of a continuing stitch such as *Stem, Chain* or *Long-armed Cross*. Work until your old needle (#1) pulls thread to the back. Don't anchor it yet.

  Anchor new needle (#2) with a waste knot on the front about three needle-lengths ahead of where you stopped #1.

  Bring needle #2 up to top in the correct place for continuing stitching pattern. No break should be detectable from the front. Work at least three stitches with new yarn.

  Turn over and adjust tensions of old and new yarn ends so that transition looks even on the front. Snip off waste knot and anchor old and new yarns on the back.

NEEDLEPOINT EXCELLENCE

1 What is the "right" way of canvas grain?
"Grain" is straight when selvages run north to south. If you have no selvage on your canvas, see Chapter 9, Q1 for a technique to determine grain.

Canvas should be worked "cross grain" when it will be flexed after it is finished, or gravity will produce problems as it is used (see Chapter 17, Q2 and Chapter 18, Q3).

2 How do I keep from crumpling canvas?
Roll it (Chapter 7, Q11).

3 How do I store canvas while I'm working on it?
Wrap work in washed cloth while storing it, even for one night. A pillow case, tea towel or strip of sheeting will do nicely.

4 How do I handle my threads?
Here's a superb way to begin and end threads with any stitch *except Basketweave*. End old needleful by extending its yarn one and one-half inches ahead

along the line to be stitched next, bringing yarn up through canvas.

Begin new needleful by burying its end beneath just-completed work. New yarn will bury old yarn ends as it stitches over them. (Cut off old ends as you reach them.) Beginnings will not run behind the same area as endings, avoiding lumps. Yarns will consistently pull in one direction, keeping stitches precisely aligned.

 5 **What are some needlepoint-stitching tips?**

- In needlepoint, be as neat on the back of your work as you are on the front. Anchor yarns as you finish them.

- Keep yarn ends neatly clipped on the back. Avoid the "jelly fish" syndrome where they drip from the bottom, waiting to be caught by future stitches.

- Avoid long loops of yarn across canvas back when moving a color from one area to another. Either end the yarn and begin again, or bury the loop beneath finished stitching as it moves across the back.

  Long loops can be caught in future stitches. They may shorten during blocking, resulting in puckered canvas.

- Never store needles "stitched" through any part of the canvas that you plan to needlepoint. Prolonged tension on intersections can shift and stretch canvas threads. Future stitches over this area will be uneven.

- Flatten stranded yarns (Chapter 7, Q8) by allowing twisted strands to **unwind** as the needle hangs down like a pendulum.

or

Run needle up and down the yarn strands threaded in it.

or

Work each stitch over the tip of your index finger. Untwist any crossings as they appear by unrolling with your thumb (see Figure 8–2).

FIGURE 8-2

FIGURE 8-3

FIGURE 8-4

FIGURE 8-5

- As you stitch side-by-side areas of light and dark, or vividly colored yarns, complete light areas first whenever possible. Light wool picks up colored fibers as it passes through holes that already contain colored stitches. This can cause the light color to look dirty.

  If you must work light next to completed dark, ALWAYS stitch up in the empty holes and down in those containing dark stitches. Should wisps of color mar pale yarns, erase them, using *white yarn technique* (Q17).

- When a straight stitch meets a diagonal stitch, one must overlap the other or canvas threads will show through. Allow pattern stitches to overlap background stitches (see Figure 8-3).

- If your design is worked in *Continental* or small stitches, and you'd like a large stitch for the background, try this trick. Work a two-thread border around completed pattern, using *Continental* stitch and background-colored yarn. This prevents large and often loopy background stitches from overpowering the design and blurring its edges.

- Position large stitches in small areas by planning ahead. Complete as many full stitches as the area will hold. Fill in edges with "compensated" stitches (that portion of a stitch which will fit into what's left of the space—see Figure 8-4).

  Visualize a compensated stitch by using a piece of paper to block off the portion of the stitch's diagram that *you can't fit in.* Leave visible only what you can stitch and work it as you see it.

- Start background at the top, right corner (see Figure 8-5). Work across top until the design gets in the way. Thread a second needle and attach it to the side that's being "orphaned." Work both sides evenly, though they're now separated. When the design ends, finish second needle and complete background with original needle.

  By working background sides evenly, you avoid background stitch misalignments. *Do not drag yarn* across pattern back to work backgrounds from side to side. It wastes wool and can pucker finished needlepoint.

◇ 6
What if my needlepoint doesn't cover the canvas?

Flatten stranded yarn.

or

Loosen tension, letting yarn sit "fat" on canvas.

or

Add one more strand of yarn to each needleful.

If adding yarn proves to be the cure, you can beef up completed areas by restitching over them with a *single* yarn strand.

If tapestry yarn doesn't cover, paint the canvas so that it matches the yarn.

◇ 7
How do I work Basketweave excellently?

FIGURE 8–6

- **Stitch Basketweave along the grain of canvas** (Chapter 9, Q1). Make the first stitch in the upper, right corner of canvas. Study the two canvas intersections that will be covered by stitches #2 and #3.

  If a vertical thread is on top, cover the upper intersection first. If a horizontal thread is on top, cover the lower intersection first (see Figure 8–6).

  Work the rest of *Basketweave* in this order, remembering that interesections with horizontal threads on top look like stair steps. Climb Up Them (from bottom to top).

  Intersections with vertical threads on top look like greased poles. Slide Down Them (from top to bottom).

- Diagonal lines across light-colored *Basketweave* occur for many reasons. The worst offender is stitching two diagonal rows top to bottom, or bottom to top, instead of alternating directions. This produces a ridge that nothing can block out.

  As a precaution, never end a needleful at the very top or bottom of a row. As long as you're somewhere in the middle, you'll know which way to stitch when you pick up the work next week.

  Corroded needles or dirty hands can stain a strand of yarn which, when stitched, will give the appearance of a diagonal ridge.

Other types of ridges are harder to correct. Inconsistent stitch tension and inconsistent yarn thickness are the two culprits. Working *Basketweave* on a frame slows progress, but helps eliminate variations in tension.

When thick and thin yarns—Persian is a particular offender—produce ridges, separate individual strands before threading needle. Try to balance a thick strand within a thin, or medium strands together so that the total yarn thickness per needle is as consistent as you can make it.

- Begin and end *Basketweave* needlefuls by burying them on the back horizontally or vertically; *never* diagonally. Diagonal buryings add padding beneath stitches which can stretch them taut, forming a diagonal line of stitches under different tension from the rest. From the front, this will look like a ridge.

- Work consistently from the upper, right corner to the lower, left (Q5). Don't start backgrounds in various places, hoping to meet inconspicuously somewhere in the middle. It very rarely happens that way.

- After completing a painted, *Basketweave* canvas, hold it to a light or window to check for missing stitches. They'll show up as dots of light.

SURVIVING NEEDLEPOINT MISTAKES

How do I remove needlepoint errors?
Correcting mistakes is as important as proper stitching. If the flaw is **within the last eight stitches, unthread needle and remove each stitch in two motions,** front and back. This minimizes defuzzing wool. Pulling yarn backwards against its grain can "skinny" it and prevent good canvas coverage.

If the mistake is **beyond the last eight stitches, don't unstitch.** Slip needle beneath stitches on front and lift them away from canvas. **Cut** thread with sharp, pointed scissors (see Figure 8–7a). Pull out

FIGURE 8-7a

FIGURE 8-7b

cut stitches from back of canvas, not from front. Bury newly cut yarn ends beneath completed work using *paper-folder threading* technique (Chapter 7, Q4) and working needle *eye-first* into surrounding stitching (see Figure 8-7b).

Warning: These directions do not apply to **kits.** *Always* unstitch yarns in kits. You haven't enough to cut any away.

9 **What if I'm running out of needlepoint yarn?**
If you suspect this with stranded yarn, STOP STITCHING when you have about 40 strands of old yarn left. Buy more of the same dye lot (its number is on your receipt), or get the best match you can find (Chapter 2, Q1). Accept the fact that the match won't be perfect.

Thread the needle with one strand of new yarn and the rest of old. Complete five rows.

Thread the needle with two strands of new and the rest of old. Work five rows. Continue substituting one more strand of new after each five rows until new has completely replaced old in each needleful. This gradual change blurs the transition from one tone to another so that you may not even be able to spot where the switch took place.

EMBROIDERY
EXCELLENCE

 10 **Which is the "right" side of cloth?**
If it's not obvious, fold a corner of the back over the front. Look at both sides simultaneously in natural light (Chapter 9, Q17) and choose your favorite.

Twill (Chapter 9, Q19) should have its diagonal ridge on the front, running from top left to bottom right.

 11 **What is the straight of cloth grain?**
Selvages will run north to south (Chapter 9, Q19).

 12 **How can I be sure threads are dye-fast?**
Test them (Chapter 10, Q6).

 13 **How do I keep embroidery hoops from loosening?**
Wrap them (Chapter 7, Q14). Buy hoops with screw tighteners.

 14 **How do I prevent hoop marks?**
Don't leave embroidery stretched on its hoop. **When you leave it, loosen it.**

If you're stitching on satins, silks or delicate fabrics, place acid-free tissue paper over fabric. Insert cloth and paper into hoops. Tighten screw. Tear away paper from within ring, leaving paper padding between the hoops.

or

FIGURE 8-8

Place **a piece of washed cloth** beneath embroidery fabric. Machine baste them together in a circle one inch SMALLER than hoop's diameter, using a fine, ballpoint needle. Place basted cloths over bottom hoop, centering stitched circle.

Position top hoop over bottom. *Lift embroidery fabric over top hoop,* leaving washed cloth beneath it (see Figure 8–8). Top hoop is now sandwiched between two cloth layers.

Press hoops together, stretch bottom fabric, and tighten screw moderately. Slit bottom cloth and finish tightening. Both cloths are now stretched, but the bottom cloth is the only one in direct contact with hoops.

Cut away bottom cloth inside hoop to within one-half inch of bastings. Embroider. When finished, remove basting threads and bottom cloth will fall away.

How do I stitch with a magnifier?

$ Magnifiers come in all prices and degrees of complexity (Chapter 12, Q8). Choose one that fits your needs and pocketbook.

When embroidering under magnification, **work the first few stitches without the lens.** This establishes a size scale. Without this precaution, stitches may appear machine-like and too small to possess character.

What embroidery-stitching tips should I know?

- **Points:** When stitching around the tip of a leaf or other point, bring needle down at the point. Bring it up again, *almost* but not quite in the same hole, and work down the second side. Don't try to stitch around a point without stopping or you'll end with a curve.

  Exaggerate points slightly and they'll communicate sharply when seen from a distance.

- **Direction:** Stitch growing things as they grow. Work trees, flowers or fur out from the ground, the stem or the skin.

  When embroidering lines that represent fabric folds, stitch as the cloth would hang, from the top of the fold downward.

  Diagonal stitches are usually more graceful than horizontals or verticals. A curved leaf is most appropriately filled with diagonal stitches. A brick wall or house would be filled with straight stitches.

- **Knots:** Pull knot stitches (*Coral, Buttonhole*) in one consistent direction to "snug" the knots. If you pull them in all directions, they'll flop inconsistently.

FIGURE 8-9

- **Parallel, Filling Stitches** (Example: *Satin*): Begin in the center of the area to be filled (this is often the longest stitch). Work from middle to one side, completing one half (see Figure 8-9). Lay the loose thread of each additional stitch next to, and parallel with, its completed neighbor. Stab needle into pattern's line where the loose thread crosses it.

  Complete the shape by working its second half from the center out. Plan so that no cloth shows through stitches, yet don't pile one upon the other. Separate stitches should be able to be identified, yet be close enough to hide the fabric below.

- **Running Out Of Yarn:** This becomes a problem in a continuing stitch such as *Buttonhole* or *Chain*. Use the *two-needle-switch* described on page 98.

  Read Q9 for solutions to running out of yarn for the entire project.

SURVIVING EMBROIDERY MISTAKES

 How do I correct embroidery errors?
Cut them out CAREFULLY. Lift yarn on front away from cloth using a needle or crochet hook. Cut between yarn and cloth with sharp, pointed scissors. Remove cut yarn from back of embroidery. Do not try to unstitch by working your needle backwards into the embroidery. It very rarely works. Anchor cut ends.

Warning: Don't cut yarn from kits (Q8).

White Yarn Erasers

If colored fibers from yarns have "stained" embroidery cloth, cut white yarn into one-inch strands. Thread one into needle and pull through stitch's hole from back to front. Discard white yarn. Repeat with fresh yarns until they have attracted and removed colored fibers.

MATERIALS

The materials you use will determine, to a great extent, how successful your stitchery will be and how gracefully it will age. Some of the embroideries worked by the great needle artist Mariska Karasz were stitched with materials of less-than-superb quality. They've not weathered the intervening half-century well can be expected to get worse in the future—which is a great loss to all of us.

Chapter 9 will tell you about cloth and needle-point canvas: how to use it to best advantage, where to buy it, how to judge its quality and which types are best for your particular projects.

Woolen yarns are dissected in Chapter 10. You'll learn why they behave as they do, what you can—and cannot—expect of them and how to make them do the best possible job on your needlework.

Threads and yarns spun of non-woolen fibers are discussed in Chapter 11. What threads will perform best on your specific stitchery? How do the new man-made fibers behave? How can you tell one fiber from another if they're not labeled? The Fiber Characteristic Chart in this chapter will be of particular interest to all fiber consumers—and that means all of us.

Chapter 12 covers all the tools and trinkets that make stitching possible—and fun. Needles of all types are discussed, along with frames, the care and feeding of scissors, and the thimble controversy.

Time and money are two valuable assets that you invest in your needlework. Stitching hours stay the same, whatever you work with, but the quality of your materials can determine whether the patient flourishes—or flounders. Buy the best materials you can find at the lowest available price but don't substitute aspirin for penicillin. The invalid might not survive.

9 Canvas and Cloth

FIGURE 9–1

One afternoon, a friend named Karen was preparing to attend a workshop in Surface Stitchery. The group had been instructed to bring firm, white cloth stretched on a stretcher frame. Karen had pink cloth and green cloth and beige cloth; but she couldn't seem to come up with any white. And there was less than half an hour before everything began.

When the class started, Karen was safely settled in her seat, puffing quietly. The teacher immediately checked cloth and stretchers, and Karen's frame was chosen to demonstrate perfection. The unusual texture of her cloth was remarked upon. Other students looked green with envy.

When coffee break rolled around, the class gathered around Karen's frame. What on earth had she used? Where had she found it? How could they get some?

"No problem," she giggled. "All you have to do is find a baby." The cloth was a well-washed diaper belonging to her six-month-old son.

CANVAS INTRODUCTION

Needlepoint canvas is a durable, firmly woven textile in which holes between threads are larger than the threads themselves.

Fiber

Most of today's canvases are woven of cotton. Historically, canvas was made of linen. Linen canvases are still available today, with limited gauges and high prices.

Gauge

The number of vertical threads contained in one inch of canvas. Gauge number is usually listed after canvas type (Example: Mono 14, Double 18).

Canvas should be evenly woven so that the same number of threads run North to South as run east to west. This count is not so accurate, however, that you can use a ruler to find the number of threads you want. Always count.

$ Fine canvas gauges (over 24 per inch) are usually woven of silk, but occasionally nylon substitutes at a smaller price.

Vocabulary

- **Petit Point** is a general term for a canvas finer than 18 threads per inch.
- **Gross Point** is any canvas coarser than 18 threads per inch. These terms developed when both large and small *Cross* or *Continental* stitches were worked on the same double-thread canvas. The small stitches allowed more detail and were often used for stitching faces and hands, while gross point was used to depict clothing and scenery.
- **Quick Point** is a relatively new addition to canvaswork. Puffy yarns are stitched on large rug canvas to give speedy results with little detail.
- **Selvages** are the firmly woven edges of a fabric.
- **Denier** is a thread count which indicates canvas strength (Q3).
- **Warp** threads lie parallel to selvages.
- **Weft** threads lie at right angles to selvages.

Types of Canvas

What canvas types are available?

Mono has one thread per hole. There are two varieties, "floating" and "interlock" (see Figure 9–2).

FIGURE 9-2

Mono-floating canvas threads are woven over and under each other. They are round, strong, smooth, and easy to stitch and block. The canvas is widely available.

Mono-floating's disadvantages include mesh that slip out of position when manhandled or improperly stitched (Chapter 7, Q8, 9) and edges that will ravel if not bound.

Selvage test (to find straight of canvas grain). If mono-floating canvas doesn't have selvage attached, pull one thread from each side of a corner. One of the threads will be more corrugated than the other (see Figure 9-3). The crinklier thread is the warp and runs parallel to the selvage. Under most conditions, stitch so that it runs north to south unless stretch will be a problem (Chapter 17, Q2).

Mono-interlock's warp threads are knotted. The canvas doesn't ravel and can be cut into any shapes. Interlock is difficult to distort and curves cut from it can be clipped and machine sewn. It is widely available.

However, interlock has sharp sizing surfaces that scrape wool during stitching and afterwards, while the piece is in use. Woolen yarns wear faster when stitched on interlock than on floating canvas

FIGURE 9–3

(Chapter 10, Q13). Though interlock is difficult to distort, once it is out of shape, it's much harder to block straight. It is weaker than mono-floating or double.

On interlock canvas, the pairs of thin threads which form the knots lie parallel to the selvage. They should run from north to south.

Double (Duo)(Penelope) has two threads per hole. It is used where great strength is necessary, for *Half-Cross* stitches, or where *Petit Point* and *Gross Point* are to be worked on the same canvas. (Separate each double thread to place four little stitches in place of one large one.)

When double canvas is worked unframed, its paired threads tend to shift and it may become difficult to decide which hole the needle should enter. Mono-floating can produce the same results with less confusion—if you don't need strength or *Petit Point.*

One pair of double warp threads clings together like Siamese twins, parallel to the selvage. Weft threads run between selvages and are separated. Siamese twins should run north to south.

Plastic meshes are not formed of natural fibers. They don't warp or ravel and need no interfacing or blocking. The finished product can be washed safely.

But plastic canvases come in very limited gauges (5, 7, 10), whose meshes may not be square. Plastics are too stiff to be used for upholstery and most traditional needlepoint. Some brands have ridges which obscure straight stitches placed between them. (But if the same stitches are worked at right angles to ridges, the effect is excellent.) Plastic canvas is not recommended for heirlooms.

Cross Stitch (Waste) (Blue Line) is intended to be basted over cloth so that counted thread embroidery can be stitched over it. It is removed when the embroidery is completed. This is not needlepoint canvas. It can be recognized by a blue line woven every five threads (Q11).

Where can I buy canvases?

In needlework shops and departments, or through mail order houses. When shopping by mail, ask for a small sample so that you can determine the canvas's *Denier* (Q3).

$ Canvas is sold by the yard, by the fraction of a yard, and even by the inch according to the shopowner's system. Rolls vary from 24 to 54 inches wide (72 is possible but not widely available). Up to a yard, the more you buy, the cheaper canvas becomes per square inch. At a minimum, buy four extra inches, length and widthwise, beyond the dimensions of your project (Chapter 7, Introduction).

Canvas comes in white, often in tan and sometimes in colors. Tan and colors will not "grin" through dark stitching as noticeably as white canvas does, but their holes can be somewhat harder to see and stitch.

Don't buy canvas with knots or misweaves. A reputable shopowner will cut around these, for such flaws can mar the perfection of your stitching.

How do I determine canvas quality?

$ Canvas threads (not including plastic) are composed of a number of smaller "ply" threads twisted together and covered with sizing. **The more ply present** ("Denier" number) **the stronger is each thread of the canvas.**

FIGURE 9–4

Denier Test

Obtain one thread from canvas's edge. Strip off sizing with thumbnail, untwist ply threads and count (see Figure 9–4). The number of ply determines the Denier Number of your gauge and brand of canvas. The *Denier* test is an effective method for determining the strength of mono-floating canvas.

Double canvas, with two threads per hole, is stronger than comparably gauged mono-floating. Interlock is weaker than either. Its stiff, hard sizing undoubtedly helps reinforce ply threads, but abrasive coatings buried beneath stitchery still remain abrasive. Interlock is not recommended for upholstery, where it will be flexed; or for rugs or wall hangings where it will be stretch-blocked (Chapter 18, Q3; Chapter 19, Q1).

Interlock's wave is called "leno" and may be more familiar to you in marquisette curtains and thermal-weave blankets.

When mono-floating *Denier* sinks below four, keep shopping. A *Denier* of six is excellent.

4 **What gauge canvas should I buy?**
You can work a graphed design on any gauge canvas (see Figure 9–5). First **decide how large you want the finished product to be.**

FIGURE 9–5

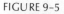

Count the number of threads needed to complete one row of the design (Example: 168). Divide the answer by the number of inches (12) you want it to measure. The answer (14) is the gauge canvas to buy.

Don't get hung up if the answer is 15½. Choose the nearest gauge and buy that. The difference will be unimportant, but keep in mind—

'Tis better to work on a gauge you can see,

Than strain eyes and muscles and temper, all three.

 **How big will my project be
if I switch from one canvas gauge to another?**
Consult the Canvas Conversion Chart in the Appendix to find out how many inches you'll gain or lose (see Figure 9–6).

FIGURE 9–6

 How should I cut canvas?
Cut canvas **along a row of holes.** Don't slice canvas threads running along sides. Use old, ratty scissors—canvas dulls sharp ones amazingly fast.

 How do I bind edges?
See Chapter 7, Q2.

Is there an up and down to my canvas?

Yes. It's called the "straight of the grain." **Place selvages (warp) running north to south.** If you have no selvage, see Selvage Test (p. 111) to discover grain.

Warning: Upholstery and wall hangings may need to be worked cross grain (see Chapter 18, Q3 and Chapter 17, Q2).

How can I count canvas threads easily?

Mono-floating canvas is woven of alternating vertical and horizontal threads. **Count only verticals (or horizontals) and multiply by two.**

or

Before starting, mark the center of one horizontal and one vertical size with a waterproof pen (Chapter 6, Q1). Work out from these centers, marking after every tenth thread along the two edges until you have a **"ruler"** on each side (see Figure 9–7). Use this ruler to speed counting.

FIGURE 9–7

How many strands of thread must I use to cover canvas?

Consult Table I in the Appendix, p. 281. It tells what types of threads cover which gauge canvas, and how many strands you'll need per needleful.

CLOTH INTRODUCTION

Cloth is a fine textile woven so that individual threads are larger than the holes between them.

Basic Rule: Let the embroidery fit the fabric.

- Cloth for Counted-Thread Embroidery should allow the comfortable passage of embroidery threads between cloth threads.
- Cloth for all stitchery should have enough substance and firmness to support the weight of embroidery threads once they're attached.

If either of these truths is disregarded, permanent "bubbles" can result as embroidery distorts the fabric's weave. Such bubbles will not block out.

Avoid unstable fabrics if embroidery stitches put pressure on cloth weave. Almost any stitches, other than straight darnings, are capable of exerting pressure if they're pulled tightly enough.

 What fabrics do certain techniques require?

- **Surface Stitcheries** (for example crewel work) can use any fabric that meets weave and weight requirements.

FIGURE 9–8

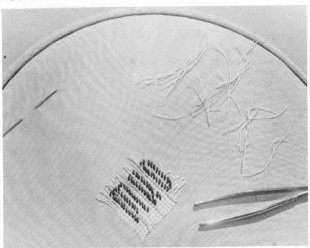

- **Counted-Thread Embroideries** (for example *Cross Stitch*): Warp threads woven north to south should equal weft running east to west. Measure and count long by two sides of a square inch. If answers differ by more than one thread, your design will be distorted.

If you want to work counted thread on a fabric whose weave cannot be counted, use "Waste Canvas" (Q1). Be sure to align it with straight of fabric's grain. Stitch counted-thread design over canvas using correctly sized crewel or chenille needle (Chapter 12, Q10). Spray finished stitchery with water. Pull individual canvas threads from beneath needlework until all canvas is removed (see Figure 9–8). Tweezers or long fingernails come in handy here.

Warning: Do not buy waste canvases manufactured from synthetic threads instead of cotton. Cotton fibers gain strength when wet and can be pulled from beneath stitchery, while wet synthetics will break, shred and make a mess. Identify fibers by the *Burn Test* (p. 140).

Where can I buy fabrics for embroidery?

Buy fabric in shops that sell dress goods, upholstery and decorating cloth, needlework supplies, or from mail order houses (Chapter 5, Q1).

Needlework shops carry fabrics especially woven for Counted-Thread Embroidery. Two widely available types are *Aida* (as in the opera!) with 11 or 14 threads per inch (#8 and #18 are manufactured, but they're harder to locate); and *Hardanger* with 22 threads per inch (Table II, Appendix).

Cotton satins and linen twill are safe choices for the surface stitcher.

FIGURE 9–9

How do I choose materials wisely?

Look at Embroidery Cloth Facts Chart, Table II in Appendix.

Make or obtain a fully colored sketch (including background) of your completed pattern (Chapter 3, Q11). **Take sketch with you as you shop.**

Choose cloth first. Match colors under natural light (Chapter 3, Q7). In a buying sequence, always make those choices first where you have the least selection. (It's easier to match threads to cloth than vice versa.)

How do I store fabrics safely?
Consult Chapter 5, Q11.

Are my cloth colors dye-fast?
Test them. Run Dye-Fast Test, Chapter 13, Q5.

Should I preshrink embroidery cloth?
Only if you have to. **Pre-shrink if the stitchery will be laundered frequently** (Examples: clothing or table linens). Cotton cloth can shrink up to 10% on the straight of the grain and sizing adds to a fabric's strength and stability. After sizing is washed out, most fabrics become softer and more easily distorted by stitching.

Does cloth have "right" and "wrong" sides?
Yes, but generally both embroider and wear equally well. Choose the side that pleases you most.

Should cloth be positioned in any particular direction?
Yes. Cloth has a "grain" that runs parallel to selvages. Ideally, **grain should run north to south** (Selvage Test). There will be less stretch in this direction.

Horizontal grain placement (cross-grain) is not calamitous if you don't plan to hang the needlework without support (Example: bell pull).

Fabric with its north-south direction running kitty-corner on the bias is a disaster looking for a place to happen. Avoid bias whenever possible. If you must stitch on it (Example: shirt yokes), back the piece with a stable lining.

What cloth weaves should I consider for embroidery?
You have three choices: Plain Weave, Twill or Satin.

Plain Weave has one "over" thread for every "under" thread. Its evenness is essential for counted thread. It seldom ravels badly; has a smooth, "bland" surface; is easy to wash and is inexpensive.

But Plain Weaves show wrinkles and dirt clearly and have low resistence to tearing.

Basketweave is a variation of *Plain Weave* in which two or more "over" threads cross an equal number of "under" threads. It makes large gauge *Counted-Thread* possible at the cost of increased shrinkage and ease of raveling.

Twill Weave has diagonal ridges formed on one side by long threads on the surface called "floats." It is durable, strong, has close texture, dirt-hiding ability and a forgiving nature toward mistakes.

But the texture of the cloth is noticeable, and it is expensive and more difficult to clean than *Plain Weave*.

Satin Weave has long "floats" on one side that produce high luster. It has beauty, sheen, dirty-shedding ability and a lack of texture.

However, it is extremely susceptible to abrasion and snagging, expensive, and is unforgiving when mistakes must be picked out.

"Satin" floats lie parallel to selvages; "sateen" floats run at right angles to them. When they're woven of the same fibers, "sateen" is the more durable, though the least glossy.

How do I clean embroidery?

In the best of all possible worlds, **embroidery cloth and threads should be able to be cleaned by the same method.** Wool yarns and cotton and linen cloth and threads can be washed carefully. Silks, rayons and woolen cloth should be dry-cleaned.

If you've mixed a washable with a dry-cleanable, the result should always be dry-cleaned.

For specific cleaning instructions, read Chapter 13.

What fibers should my cloth be woven of?

See Fiber Characteristics Chart, p. 137.

10 Woolen Yarn

FIGURE 10-1

One sunny morning while I was designing needlepoint cushions for a church chapel, the Altar Guild ladies came to visit. They mentioned a box of yarn that had been sitting in the closet for years. Could I use it?

Free yarn is not to be sniffed at and, after some hunting, we unearthed the box. It was jammed full of background wool left over from some long-ago project. The yarn was all one color and dye lot—and there were *fourteen pounds* of it! We could have upholstered the Washington Monument.

There was, however, one small problem. Although the yarn's amethyst color glowed brilliantly in sunlight, it died a horrible death inside the chapel. Light pouring through green stained glass made that particular shade of purple look as if Dracula had just left.

So—fourteen pounds of the finest needlepoint yarn went back into its closet. As we closed the door, one Altar Guild lady murmured, "They must have overbought a little."

INTRODUCTION

Woolen yarn is spun from the clipped, cleaned, and carded hair of mammals. Theoretically, any human or animal hair could be spun into yarn, and many types have been in different times and places. Today's commercial needlework yarns are spun from the wool of sheep.

Wool is formed of proteins extruded from hair follicles buried within the skin layer. Hair acts to

121

protect the skin by repelling water, trapping heat next to the body, and cushioning it against bumps. The functions it serves in Nature explain why wool behaves as it does in needlework.

Wool is elastic. It is composed of spring-like fibers which can contract and expand, making them forgiving of variations in stitch tension. Wool has natural protection against water-borne stains.

Scales layer down each woolen hair like shingles on a roof. Such scales can cling to each other. This is why yarns can be spun in almost any thickness. This also explains why wool felts. Woolen fibers are weak when dry and grow weaker when wet.

Before yarn can be spun, wool must be carded. Carding means brushing individual strands straight and parallel. Carded wool is weak and, under pressure, will separate. Woolen yarn's strength is produced by the twist given as it's spun. Yarns must retain their twist during stitching. If they untwist back into carded wool, they are weakened and easily broken.

Wool is among the easiest of fibers to dye.

All of a sheep's wool is not of the same quality. Fleece from the back and shoulders is usually much longer than that from the legs and tail. Yarns spun from long fibers are less likely to break when pulled through cloth or canvas, or to "pill" with use.

The difference between good embroidery yarns and those that are not-so-good is the difference between "worsted" and ordinary woolen yarn. All fleece is washed and carded before it is spun. Worsted has an additional step—combing—before spinning. This combing removes short fibers and causes long strands to lie straight and parallel.

Needlework worsteds have greater strength for less bulk than other woolen yarns and survive the abrasion of stitching better. The extra work that goes into their manufacture causes them to be more expensive but explains why stitching yarns look better than knitting wools after they're stitched.

Wool's disadvantages come from its protein nature. It is food for moths and insects, becomes brittle when heated, felts and shrinks during wet agitation, and weakens in water. It can cause allergic reactions in susceptible individuals.

FIGURE 10-2

What yarn types are available to me?

See Woolen Yarn Facts Chart, Table III in Appendix for brand information.

Tapestry yarn is not stranded (see Figure 10–3). One thick yarn is threaded through the needle and used to stitch needlepoint. It is too thick to use for most traditional embroidery.

FIGURE 10–3

Tapestry

Persian

Crewel

Advantages are that tapestry yarn doesn't need to be "flattened" (Chapter 7, Q8). It's easy to thread, strong, wears well and produces consistent, "pearl-like" *Continental* stitches.

But tapestry yarn can only cover #10–#12 gauge canvases. When yarn doesn't completely cover, "grin-through" is difficult to correct (Chapter 8, Q6).

Crewel yarn is a worsted composed of two loosely twisted woolen strands. It can be stitched with one or more yarn strands per needleful. This wool is used for both needlepoint and embroidery.

One advantage of using crewel yarn for needlepoint is that it can be used to cover any gauge canvas by varying the number of strands per needleful. Its springy resilience adjusts tension well. Many close shades allow "blending" or mixing of similar colors within the same needleful. Thinness makes it useful for stitching fine canvas gauges (like number 16). An ounce of crewel will cover more inches of canvas than an ounce of persian-type wool because persian yarn is thicker and has fewer yards per ounce.

But crewel yarn's loose twist makes it only

FIGURE 10-4

moderately resistant to rough treatment after the canvas is completed. Finished needlepoint can "pill" or become "hairy" with hard use. When crewel wool is used to stitch large canvas gauges (Example: number 10), for the increased number of strands per needleful can be bothersome to "flatten" and control. Individual yarn strands in long, straight stitches (such as Bargello) can become disarranged with wear.

For embroidery, crewel yarn has a wide color range, soft texture and springy resilience that make it an excellent thread. Crewel embroidery presumes its use.

Crewel yarn is less effective for counted-thread embroidery. Hairy wool fibers tend to blur lines (see Figure 10-4). Smoother threads such as silk, linen, or mercerized cotton are generally used for such needlework.

"**Persian**" or "Persian-type" needlepoint yarns do not usually come from Iran. The name is used to describe a loosely twisted worsted yarn composed of three, firmly-twisted individual threads. Such yarn can be stitched as is or separated into individual strands. It is used for both needlepoint and embroidery.

Persian wool can be used in needlepoint to cover any gauge canvas by varying the number of individual strands used per needleful. Its tight twist makes it resistant to rough wear. Thick, individual strands cover large gauge canvases with fewer strands per needleful than crewel wool. In long, straight stitches such as Bargello, Persian strands stay in place better than crewel yarn.

But Persian's color shades are not usually close enough to allow subtle "blending" of similar tones within the same needleful. Persian yarn is too thick to stitch fine canvas gauges smoothly. More ounces of Persian than of crewel are needed to cover a given canvas area.

Persian wool is excellent for surface stitchery. It wears well and many, vivid colors are available.

2 What about synthetic yarns?

Synthetic fibers have a glass-like microscopic structure. This makes them both more difficult to dye than wool and less elastic. (Elastic threads make varying stitch tensions look equal—they're forgiving.")

Synthetic yarns "pill" after the project is finished. They are available in fewer colors than wool. On the plus side, they are usually less expensive, are not susceptible to shrinking, felting or moth damage, and allergic souls are not susceptible to them.

3 How do I choose yarn colors?

Read Chapter 3, Q11 and Chapter 5, Q1.

4 Why can't I substitute other fibers for embroidery wools?

If you plan to enter competitions or leave stitcheries to your grandchildren, worsted yarns are the best wools for the job. They're also the most expensive.

The right thread for a needlework is usually the easiest to work with. It's strong, or resilient (or whatever you need it to be). Substitutes may work and they might last, but they're more likely to present you with problems you won't encounter if you use the "right" thread.

On the other hand, if you want to stitch, can't spend much and don't care if it lasts a hundred years, go ahead and substitute. Buy the inexpensive thread that seems to come closest to the best thread available for your project, and go to it.

FIGURE 10-5

What about dye lots?

They vary. Compute your needs carefully (Chapter 5, Q1). Purchase only one dye lot per color and write its number on the sales slip so you won't forget it. Try to purchase the same dye lot if you run short.

When you must substitute another dye lot, it probably won't make much difference if the different lots don't touch each other. Unfortunately, needlepoint backgrounds are where this crisis usually pops up and it *does* make a difference there.

Blur the transition from one lot to another by following directions in Chapter 8, Q9.

Are my yarn colors colorfast?

Probably, if they're manufactured in Northern Europe or the United States. If you're in doubt, run the quick *Colorfast Test* (Q7) on all colors.

Red, darks, and blacks are always suspect. Sometimes manufacturers saturate thread with dye to achieve deep color. If rinsing is not thorough, unattached dye can still remain loose to stain work during blocking.

How do I test threads for colorfastness?

Dampen a scrap of thread and lay on a damp, white facial tissue. Allow to dry (see Figure 10–6). If dye bleeds, try *Thread Cure* (Q8). If this doesn't solve the problem, substitute colorfast threads before you stitch—or never wet the embroidery.

FIGURE 10–6

What is a cure if threads bleed?

Soak the *unopened* skein in changes of tepid water until no more color escapes. Blot and dry flat, away from light and heat.

Where can I buy needlework yarn?

It's available in needlework stores, the needlework sections of department stores, some fabric shops, some knitting stores, and many craft shops (be careful of quality here—some craft shops sell excellent materials, but some do not). Check Yellow Pages under "Yarn" or "Needlepoint" to find specific listings in your area.

Needlework yarns are also sold by mail order. Many sources advertise in the publications of needlework guilds (Chapter 1).

How is yarn sold?

Yarn is sold **by weight or by yardage.** From there it can be divided into smaller volumes or single strands, depending upon the wishes of shopowners or manufacturers. See Woolen Yarn Facts Chart, Table III in Appendix, for information on specific brands.

The full number of yarn colors available in a brand is called its "Color Range." Some stores carry all available colors while others do not. The more colors available to you, the happier your choices will be.

FIGURE 10-7

How much yarn should I buy?

That's the $64,000 question. For crewel work, surface stitchery, counted-thread and needlepoint, read Chapter 5, Q4, 5, 6, and fill in the appropriate Volume Charts.

YARN TECHNIQUES

The purpose of all yarn techniques is to protect wool fibers from breakage or yarn from thinning.

Does needlework yarn have a top and bottom?

Yes. **Worsted yarns have a "grain"** or nap. They're spun in one direction and fibers lay on yarn like

FIGURE 10-8

feathers on a chicken. Wool should enter a needle's eye and cloth or canvas so that its "feathers" are stroked, not broken.

When worsted fibers are stroked correctly, they flatten like a fish's scales. Rub them the wrong way and they ruffle and break. The more broken fibers, the wispier yarn becomes and the less it covers.

Test yarn direction by **rubbing fingers down a vertical wool thread** (I do this best with my eyes closed). Reverse thread and stroke again (see Figure 10-8). One way should feel "hairier" than the other. Thread the bottom of the hairy direction into the needle's eye.

or

Rub wool beneath your nose or over your upper lip. This looks ridiculous, but works better than finger tips for many stitchers. Thread bottom of hairy direction.

You need to find grain direction only once for each bundle of yarn. All yarns within a cut skein will run in the same direction. Place a loose knot at the "threading" end of the skein or, with wound skeins, write on label, "thread newly cut (or still attached) end."

I must warn you here: Airplane seatmates, neighbors, or just about anybody who sees you wistfully stroking a strand of pink yarn with your eyes shut may think you a bit odd. But who cares about raised eyebrows when improved appearance and better yarn coverage are at stake?

◆13◆ How important is this wool direction?
If you're embroidering cloth, it's very important. Cloth is abrasive to yarn and becomes more so when you're pulling against yarn's nap (see Figure 10-9).

If you're needlepointing Interlock canvas, find the smooth direction. Interlock is abrasive (Chapter 9, Q1) and its yarn needs all the help it can get.

If you're working on mono-floating canvas, abrasion is less and yarn's direction becomes less important, but keep it consistent.

FIGURE 10-9

How many yarn strands should I use per needleful?
See Table I in Appendix.

Why do my yarn strands twist as I stitch?
Don't worry; if they are "S" twists, everybody's do it. (Chapter 11, Introduction). **The needle stays still in your fingers while yarn within it moves** with your stitching motion. Untwist regularly, using techniques described in Chapter 8, Q5.

Why do I have to use the "right" size needle?
Because **if you don't, you'll "skinny" your yarn** (Chapter 12, Q10). See Table I in Appendix.

How long should my yarn strands be?
For **needlepoint** (see Figure 10-10), yarn strands should be about **32 inches** when stitching mono-floating or double canvases. Use about 22 inches when stitching Interlock. The sharper the canvas, the shorter the yarn.

When stitching very fine canvases (16 or smaller), shorten yarn lengths even more. The more stitches a needleful makes, the more its yarn becomes worn and the shorter it should be.

For **embroidery,** cut yarn no longer than **15–18 inches.** Cloth is more abrasive than canvas, so embroidery yarns should be shorter than needlepoint yarns.

FIGURE 10–10

How do I keep a yarn skein from knotting when I remove individual strands?

Begin in center of cut skein and "comb" your fingers toward one end and then the other (see Figure 10–11). Safe storage (Chapter 5, Q13, 14) will prevent most tangles.

FIGURE 10-11

How do I store yarn?

Read Chapter 5, Q14.

11 Non-Woolen Threads

FIGURE 11-1

Some years ago, I bought a milk-white caftan in Morocco. It was heavily embroidered in turquoise and, even with a favorable rate of exchange, it cost a bundle.

I wore the caftan to rave notices. Everybody said that it looked sensational and I was blissful—until some clod spilled taco sauce on my right hip.

What one does with a hip full of taco sauce depends upon the fiber it's been spilled on. I retired to search for a fiber content label, hoping it would be bi-lingual since my French isn't up to translating laundry directions. I needn't have worried—there wasn't any label at all.

What fabric could it possibly have been? Would it dissolve if I washed it? What about sponging out the stain? Who knew? In desperation I sent the caftan to be dry-cleaned. It returned home slightly greyer than before, with a pale pink bloom on the right hip.

I still don't know what that caftan is made of, but I've appreciated America's textile-labeling laws ever since.

INTRODUCTION

Yarn, thread, and cloth are composed of textile fibers. Information about the nature of these fibers allows you, the consumer, to predict how any textile will behave—now and in the future. The more information you possess, the more you can tailor fiber purchases to meet the specific needs of your needlework.

Natural fibers come from animals (silk and wool) and from plants (cotton and linen). Man-made fibers—those not found in nature—are manufactured from wood or cellulose (rayon, viscose, acetate) and from petroleum (nylon, orlon, polyester). Each fiber-type has distinct advantages—along with some drawbacks. It pays the wise stitcher to know both the good and the bad about materials.

Certain words pop up constantly when discussing textiles:

- **Fiber**—a fine, thread-like filament.
- **Yarn**—a thick, elastic, hairy cord spun from individual fibers.
- **Thread**—a thin, firm, smooth cord spun from individual fibers.
- **Ply**—individual yarns (threads) twisted together to form a thicker yarn (thread) which is identified as "two-ply," "three-ply," and so on.
- **Blend**—yarn spun from two or more ply, each spun from a different fiber (Example: one ply of rayon twisted with one ply of cotton).
- **Mix**—yarn spun from a homogenous mixture of different fibers (Example: each ply is 50% rayon, 50% cotton).
- **Continuous filament**—extremely long fibers extruded from machines. *Nature* comes closest to producing a continuous fiber with silk, for which the "machine" is the silk worm. Continuous filaments do not need much twisting to be spun into thread (see Figure 11–2).
- **Staple fibers**—short fibers which *must* be twisted together to form yarns or threads. *Nature* produces them in many forms: cotton and wool are examples. Man-made, continuous fibers are often chopped up to produce staple characteristics such as softness and warmth.
- **Thread identification numbers**—vary with fibers and usually are unimportant except where they describe linen threads. In such linen I.D. numbers as *10/5,* the first number identifies the diameter of the ply (the thicker the ply, the lower the number) and the second number indicates how many plies are in the thread.

FIGURE 11-2

- **Twist**—holds staple fibers in place to form yarn. The greater the twist, the stronger the thread— up to the point where it kinks. From then on, further twisting weakens threads.

    Twists come in two forms: S and Z. These can be identified by matching thread's diagonal twist to the slant of the letters S or Z (see Figure 11-3). S and Z yarns of equal composition and twist have equal strength, but when used for embroidery, Z threads tend to become untwisted and weakened by right-handed stitching. They need more coddling than S yarns, which become more tightly twisted as they're stitched by right-handers.

FIGURE 11-3

Hint: Always check for *S* and *Z* twist before you buy threads. Most embroidery fibers sold in the U.S. are *S*'s but *Z*'s do exist. If you buy them, and you're right-handed, you'll have to fuss over them.

What threads are available for me to stitch with?

See Non-Woolen Thread Facts Chart, Table IV in Appendix. These are the major best-sellers, but keep your eyes open for newcomers to the market. They may have just what you're looking for and new types pop up all the time. Well-stocked mail-order houses are good sources for such threads. *When buying any thread you've never used before, always test colorfastness before stitching* (Chapter 10, Q7).

Protein (Animal) Fibers

Wool (Chapter 10) and **Silk**

Silks are usually imported from China, Japan, and France. They're beautiful to look at, challenging to stitch with, and available in many brands, in twists and in flosses. They are susceptible to abrasion and some silk dyes run in water. Therefore protect them during stitching and the life thereafter, and don't rinse, wash or perspire on them without first running a test for colorfastness (Chapter 10, Q7).

FIGURE 11–4

Carbohydrate (Vegetable) Fibers

COTTON

Embroidery Flosses are usually six-strand but you can adjust the number of strands used per needleful to the needs of your stitchery. They are usually colorfast but it's still wise to check.

Pearl Cottons are round, twisted threads of various diameters. They are made of mercerized cotton, have good sheen and are valuable for work under tension (for example, pulled thread). They are usually colorfast and hold their twist well during stitching.

Matte Cottons are loosely twisted threads with no sheen. They're soft, fairly thick and untwist easily during stitching.

Danish Flower Threads are imported from Denmark to work Counted-Thread embroidery. They're round, twisted threads with little sheen and only moderate strength. Some colors can run, so you will generally need to perform the *Bleeding Thread Cure* (Chapter 10, Q8) on unopened skeins.

LINEN

Linen threads come in thick and thin diameters. They're extremely strong, resist abrasion and have a soft gloss. Gauge thickness is discussed in the introduction to this chapter. They hold their twist very well during stitching and are usually colorfast.

Cellulose (Carbohydrate) Man-Made Fibers:

Rayon and Acetate

These two have lovely luster and beautiful dyes but can be extremely slippery to stitch. They're fragile and not always colorfast to light-fading or washing, so keep them clean and handle them gently. Check brand labels for fiber content (Q5).

Petroleum-Based Man-Made Fibers

Orlon and Nylon

These have only mediocre dyeability when compared with rayon and acetate. They're strong, comparatively inexpensive and have a tendency to pill during use. Check brand labels for fiber content (Q5).

 How many strands do I use per needleful?
Consult Table I in Appendix.

 What characteristics would a "perfect" fiber have?
See Fiber Characteristics Chart, Table 11–1. To begin with, **there's no such thing.** But if there were, it would dye easily, be inexpensive, attractive, strong when wet or dry, elastic (stretchy), resilient (bounce-back), and resistant to ultra-violet's bleaching and rotting.

It would resist acids; alkalies; oily soil; insects; mold and mildew; heat; pilling; wrinkling; shrinking; static electricity; abrasion; and the fading, bleeding and crocking (rubbing off) of dye.

Check any fiber you're investigating against this list to spot its shortcomings. These may not make any difference to your project. If so you've discovered the "perfect" fiber for your particular stitchery!

 What do these fiber characteristics have to do with my needlework?
See Fiber Characteristics Chart, Table 11–1. Some traits such as low price and good appearance speak for themselves. Of the remaining points, consider the following:

- *Low abrasion-resistance* can lead to thinning of thread or yarn while stitching and thinning of cloth or threads as the project wears while in use.

Table 11–1 Fiber Characteristic Chart

Fiber	Fiber Length Average	Appearance	Strength Dry	Strength Wet	Elasticity	Low Cost	Ease of Dyeing	Soil: Static Electricity	Soil: Oily Stains	Resists Light: Light Fade	Resists Light: Light Rot	Resists Chemicals: Acids	Resists Chemicals: Alkalies	Mildew	Pests: Insects	Heat	Wear & Tear: Abrasion (pilling)	Wear & Tear: Matting (resilience)	Wear & Tear: Shrinking
Natural																			
Cotton	¾″ – 1″	0	1	2	1	2	4	4	0	0	0	0	4	X	3	4	2	0	0
Mercerized Cotton		4	2	4	1	1	4	4	0	0	0	0	4	0	3	4	4	0	4
Linen	18″–20″	2	4	*	X	0	2	4	0	X	0	0	4	1	3	*	0	0	0
Silk	1300′–1400′	*	*	3	4	X	*	4	0	0	X	4	0	3	0	2	X	4	0
Wool	1″–20″	0	X	X	*	0	*	4	0	0	0	4	0	4	0	0	2	*	X
Man-Made Cellulose																			
Rayon	continuous filament	4	0	X	1	4	4	2	0	0	0	0	2	0	3	2	1	1	2
Viscose		4	2	0	2	4	4	2	0	0	0	0	4	0	3	3	1	1	2
Acetate		2	1	0	1	4	0	0	0	X	1	1	1	4	4	0	0	0	1
Petroleum																			
Acrylic		0	1	1	3	4	0	0	X	*	*	4	3	4	4	1	2	2	2
Nylon		4	*	*	4	4	0	0	0	0	0	X	4	4	4	3	*	4	4
Polyester		0	2	2	2	4	0	0	X	4	4	4	2	4	4	4	3	*	4
Metallics		4	0	0	0	0	0	4	4	2	4	4	2	4	4	0	0	4	4

KEY: 0—very poor
1—slightly
2—average
3—moderately
4—strongly
*—best in this category
X—worst in this category

- *Poor elasticity and resilience* means thread won't accommodate itself to variations in stitching tension. Stitches may not lie evenly. Fibers will mat down and won't bounce back after they're worn (these present no problems if you plan to frame the piece). Cloth won't close the holes made by picking out mistakes.

- *Static electrical charge* can attract air-borne soil and dirt suspended in wash water.

- *Attracts oily soil* means that food stains and the skin oils you deposit during stitching may be impossible to remove. Not recommended for table linens or clothing in direct contact with skin.

- *Susceptible to ultra-violet radiation* found in daylight or fluorescent lighting. Fibers can lose color or rot with "sunburn." Heat dramatically increases the speed of this deterioration. Susceptible needlework should be displayed away from windows and be lit only when necessary by incandescent bulbs (Chapter 20, Q6).

- *Susceptible to acids* means that the fiber cannot survive long contact with wood or wood products (Preventive Medicine).

- *Susceptible to alkalies,* which are usually encountered in soaps or detergents, means that washing with them is risky.

- *Attracts molds* means that these fibers must be stored clean, unstarched and dry (starch serves as an hors d'oeuvre for mildew, see Figure 11–5).

    The cellulose molecule is really a long chain of simple sugar molecules strung together like pearls. When the "string" is broken by acids or oxidation, individual sugar molecules remain. They provide food for molds, mildews and some insects.

- *Attracts insects* means that moths, carpet beetles, silverfish and cockroaches eat the proteins or carbohydrates in these fibers (see Figure 11–6).

- *Susceptibility to heat* indicates that such a fiber should be provided with good circulation of air. Threads displayed behind glass in direct sunlight can be subjected to dramatic shifts of temperature (Chapter 16, Q1). Fibers displayed

FIGURE 11–5

FIGURE 11–6

near heat sources and stored in hot attics deteriorate faster than those kept cool. Such deterioration doubles with every 10° rise in temperature.

- *Pilling* only happens to short, smooth, round fibers. As the fabric flexes, short fibers slip out of it (they have no kinks or projections to help hold them in place). As fibers project above the surface, they're bent or broken and snag each other, forming a "pill." This is anchored to the cloth by those fibers still working their way out. When they finally slip out or break, the pill falls away.

  The only way to combat pilling is to shave the fabric's surface with an electric razor, singe it with a candle, or refrain from flexing it in the first place.

- *Poor dyeability* foretells a limited color range and the possibility of future fading or bleeding. If dye has trouble penetrating a fiber, it often finds it convenient to leave.

- *Shrinkage* comes in two forms: relaxation and felting.

  "Relaxation shrinkage" can happen to any fabric woven with its warp threads under tension, as most cloth is. When such cloths are first washed, warp threads relax in the warm water and a small amount of one-time shrinkage takes place.

  "Felting shrinkage" happens when the scales on wool fibers expand and tangle in hot, wet, alkaline, churning environments. Such shrinkage precludes machine laundering of wool unless the threads are somehow stabilized (for example, a wool/nylon blend should not shrink).

Hint: Don't embroider jeans with wool unless you want smocked denims after they're washed.

 How do I know which fiber I'm buying?

- **Read the tag or label.** According to the Textile Fiber Products Identification Act of 1960 (enforced by the Federal Trade Commission), fiber manufac-

FIGURE 11-7

turers must include the following facts on tags or labels accompanying any fabric, yarn or thread:

1. The fiber or combination of fibers used in the item must be listed in order of predominance by weight.
2. The percentage (by weight) of each fiber present must be listed in decreasing order.
3. The name of the manufacturer must be listed.
4. If the item is imported, the name of the country where it was produced or processed must be indicated.

• **Check the brand name.** This can become confusing when various manufacturers call identical man-made fibers by different brand names. Here are some brands listed under their family (or "generic") names.

Rayon—Avril, Jetspun, Celanese, Bemberg
Viscose—Viscose
Acetate—Chromspun, Estron, Avisco, Arnel
Acrylic (Europeans call it Polyacrylic)—Orlon, Acrilan, Sayelle, Creslan
Nylon—Antron, Quiana, Caprolan
Polyester—Dacron, Kodel, Fortrell, Trevira
Metallic—Lurex, Lamé, Melora

• **Run identification tests:** *Burn Test.* This is the most widely used home test to identify fibers. Check your results against the Burn Test Chart, Table 11–2.

1. Obtain a small amount of thread, yarn or cloth, an ashtray, and a match or candle. Work in an area with little air movement. Light flame over, or in the ashtray.
2. Allow fiber to approach flame but not touch it (see Figure 11–8). Does it fuse, bend away from the fire, or does it not move at all?
3. Let the fiber burn. Does it burn quickly or slowly? With or without a flame? Does it melt?
4. Remove fiber from flame. Does it continue burning or self-extinguish? What does the smoke smell like?

FIGURE 11–8

Table 11–2

Table 11–2   Burn Test Chart

Fiber	As Thread Approaches Flame	In Flame	Remove Flame	Smell	Residue
Rayon (Viscose)	does not fuse does not move	burns rapidly with flame	creeping ember without flame	burning leaves or wood	little or no fluffy ash
Acetate	fuses does not move	melts and burns with a flame	continues to burn with melting	vinegar	irregular, black, brittle bead
Cotton	does not fuse does not move	burns rapidly with flame	continues to burn with or without flame	burning paper	small, fluffy grey ash
Linen	does not fuse does not move	burns rapidly with flame	continues to burn with or without flame	burning paper	small, fluffy grey ash
Wool	fuses, curls away from flame	burns slowly with flame	smoulders without flame, at times extinguishes	burning hair	lumpy, black, brittle ash that crumbles easily
Silk	fuses, curls away from flame	burns slowly with flame	smoulders, at times extinguishes	burning feathers	round, black, soft, brittle bead, crushes easily
Acrylic	fuses, does not move	burns rapidly with flame, melts	continues burning continues melting	acrid	irregular, black, hard, brittle residue
Polyester	fuses, shrinks from flame	burns slowly with flame, melts	usually self-extinguishing	"chemical"	round, black, hard, tough bead
Nylon	fuses, shrinks from flame	burns slowly, melts	usually self-extinguishing	boiling string beans	round, grey, hard, tough bead

5. Examine the burned residue when cool. Is it hard or soft, round or irregular, tough or crumbly? What color is it?

Wet-Dry Test. Used to distinguish rayon and viscose from cotton.

Break the thread in question when it's dry. Then wet it and break again. Which break took more effort?

Cotton is stronger wet than dry. Rayon and viscose are stronger dry than wet.

Broken-End Test. Distinguishes cotton from linen.

Break one thread and observe the broken ends under a magnifying glass. Cotton ends look like rounded brushes. Linen ends have tapered points.

6 What can I expect from mixtures of different fibers?

When different fibers are present in almost equal amounts (40–60%) in blends or mixes, they affect each other equally. As proportions change, the mixture increasingly resembles the characteristics of the larger-percentage fiber. Example: 70% polyester/30% cotton will behave more like pure polyester than a 50–50 mix of these fibers.

7 How can I tell look-alike fibers apart?

Fibers with sheen that could be confused with one another are rayon and acetate, mercerized cotton, nylon and silk. Rayon can be told from acetate by the *Burn Test* (Q5). Either can be identified from mercerized cotton by the *Wet-Dry Test* (Q5). Nylon and silk can be told from each other, and from all the rest, by the *Burn Test.*

Non-elastic fibers without sheen that could be confused are linen and cotton. Cotton fibers come from the seeds of a plant and are short. Linen fibers come from the stem of a plant and are long. When the *Broken-End Test* (Q5) is run, short cotton fibers fluff out and long linen fibers stretch to a point.

Elastic threads with a warm feel could be Nature's wool or man-made acrylic. Tell them apart by the *Burn Test.*

FIGURE 11–9

How do I know if my thread is colorfast?
Run the *Thread Colorfast Test* (and Cure) in Chapter 10, Q6, 7, 8.

How can I identify mixtures of different fibers in yarn or cloth?
In a Blend (see Introduction), separate individual ply with a sharp needle. Run *Burn Test* on each ply.

When each ply is composed of a mix of fibers, you can't identify them with home methods.

To test a fabric, fray two to four threads from warp, and an equal number from weft. Observe them, under magnification if necessary, to see if they're identical. Identify by the tests in Q5.

Why are some fibers more lustrous than others?
Fibers with a round cross-section give the highest sheen because light reflections are concentrated by their circular shapes. Folded cross-sections (clover-shaped, for example) give more subdued sheen because light bounces off several curved surfaces instead of just one. Man-made fibers can be extruded from nozzles equipped with different-shaped holes, thereby giving manufacturers control over the degree of their fiber's luster.

Can manufacturers vary their man-made fibers to produce qualities other than those listed here?
Yes and they do it all the time. Qualities discussed in this chapter are those that apply to man-made fibers in their simplest forms. If a manufacturer has added something special, that fact should be reflected on the fiber's label and, probably, on its price tag.

If you can find no indication that something new has been added, you're probably dealing with a generic fiber.

12 Accessories

FIGURE 12-1

I once had a lovely teaching assistant named Nancy. One evening, in the midst of demonstrating the pros and cons of stretcher strips, I was called to the phone and Nan had to take over.

As I hurried back after my call I heard waves of laughter exploding from the room. I yanked open the door to find Nan cowering in a folding chair, wrapped in plywood as if being attacked by a boa constrictor. The class was in hysterics.

Nan had been trying to demonstrate how to use my fanny frame—a contraption of flat boards and hinges that holds stitching frames in place and tucks neatly beneath me as I sit. It does this, that is, when its hinges are bent correctly. These weren't. Plywood jutted out in all directions, the frame reared skyward, and I suspect that part of Nan's derrière was being pinched by a naughty hinge. I rescued her as quickly as possible.

The class never did calm down that evening. Poor Nan didn't see anything funny in it all.

Moral: Choice of accessories is a very personal matter.

INTRODUCTION

One stitcher's balm can drive another needleworker to hives. There are many accessories on the market designed to smooth the way to stitching bliss. Only you can determine which of them is worth your money. And don't overdo it; it's possible to have so many accessories that it becomes difficult to find the stitching!

The following is an alphabetical list of needlework aids with their advantages and disadvantages. This list does not include accessories for stitchery display, such as trays, ice buckets, or paperweights. Only items directly related to the stitching *process* are listed.

Beeswax (1)
(See Figure 12-2)

Used when embroidering with fibers other than wool. Wax stiffens thread for threading into needles, makes unruly fibers behave, and smooths surfaces susceptible to ruffling and breaking. **Do not use with wool.**

Chatelaine (2)
(See Figure 12-2)

A ribbon hung around the neck to organize emery bag, small pin cushion, scissors, or other small accessories.

FIGURE 12-2

Emery Ball or Strawberry (3)
(See Figure 12–2)

Discoloration or rust on needles can transfer itself to needlework. A few passes through an emery ball will scour stains away.

Acids produced by the skins of some individuals discolor needles rapidly. Metal oxidation slows down a needle's penetration and a stitcher's speed. Emery balls are vital for such needleworkers.

Frames (4)
(See Figure 12–3, and read Chapter 7, Q7)

Many types are available to the needleworker. These are needed when stitches exert pull against cloth or canvas as in diagonal stitches, *Continental* Stitch, or pulled work.

Artists' stretcher strips (available in art supply stores). These wooden sides are sold in pairs, by the inch, to form opposite sides of a rectangular frame. Buy two sets; one for top and bottom and the other for left and right.

FIGURE 12–3

- *Advantages:* They're inexpensive, strong, allow four-way pull, are easily assembled, easy to attach to cloth or canvas, lightweight, can be taken apart and re-used, and the whole design can be seen at one glance.
- *Disadvantage:* They're bulky and can be awkward to stitch in public.

Roller frames are available in needlework shops and departments.

- *Advantages:* They need no assembly, are strong, lightweight, permit stitching of large needleworks, and can be carried and stitched in public.
- *Disadvantages:* They're moderately expensive, only allow two-way pull unless laced at sides, don't let you see entire design when it's rolled, can be awkward to attach to cloth or canvas, and can crush bulky stitches or fragile threads when rolling over them.

Disposable frames are for small stitcheries only. Cut two identical, mat-shaped frames from unused, butcher's meat trays or firm cardboard. Be sure that the window you cut is larger than the stitchery you plan to work. Sandwich cloth or canvas between frames and staple every inch, through the three layers, with a common desk stapler.

Hoops (5)
(See Figure 12–3)

These are needed when stitches exert pull against fabric, as in pulled work, crewel, large *Cross Stitches* over multiple threads.

In the following list, hoops are ranked according to how firmly they hold fabric taut. Winding an inner hoop with twill tape (Chapter 7, Q14) will raise any category two places on the list, which is arranged in order of *decreasing* efficiency. Types 1 through 6 possess screw tighteners:

1. Inner ring with extended lip which overlaps top of outer ring.
2. Side depth of an inch or more.
3. Ridge around center of inner ring (not at top, see #1).
4. Wood, no ridges or lips.
5. Plastic, no ridges or lips.
6. Metal, no ridges or lips.
7. Any of the above types with a spring tightener.

As for *size,* when a stand or fanny frame supports hoop, use one large enough to enclose the whole design. Large hoops are also used where fabric is delicate (Examples: satins, fragile finishes) or where cloth will be crushed by repositioning hoop (Chapter 8, Q14).

When embroidery is hand held use a hoop small enough for the "holding thumb" to reach the center (Chapter 6, Q12). Thread must be resilient enough to bounce back from hoop's crushing.

Hoop- or Frame-holders (6)

These come in many forms to free both hands for stitching (Chapter 7, Q15). The larger the holder, the more expensive it generally becomes.

Floor frames accommodate large stitcheries but take up space in a room. Table frames are more easily stored but need anchoring to prevent them from skidding around. Fanny frames are very comfortable to use but can be awkward to store. Try to borrow and use a frame-holder before you invest in one.

Hint: Be sure the holder can flip easily so that back of stitchery is accessible for anchoring and clipping threads.

Lamps (7)
(See Figure 12–4)

Lights come in many sizes, weights and prices, from large, expensive floor models with magnifying lenses to small, inexpensive, clip-on lights which focus on the needlework.

FIGURE 12-4

Eyestrain can be avoided by keeping the pool of light in which you work similar to the general light level in the surrounding room. Do not work under a spotlight in the dark. Eyes adjusting from dark-to-bright-to-dark will strain, and increase fatigue.

When traveling or attending workshops, pack a 100-watt bulb, an extension cord, and a small auxiliary lamp in your suitcase. No hotel room I've ever occupied (and very few guest rooms) had light adequate for stitching.

Magnifiers (8)
(See Figure 12-4)

Neck, table, and floor varieties assist *petit point,* silk work, some metal thread attachment, and any stitching where you feel that enlargement would be helpful. For how-to-use instructions, see Chapter 8, Q15.

Floor and table magnifying lenses are often encircled by fluorescent bulbs, adding light to magnification. These lamps are expensive but excellent for fine work. They tend to be fragile, heavy and not too easily portable.

Neck magnifiers are lightweight, inexpensive, portable and successful if you have an adequate source of good light. They do not enlarge as strongly as floor or table magnifiers.

Magnifying eye glasses are available at most 5 & 10's, and are used successfully by some stitchers. Magnifying lenses to add to your existing glasses (like clip-on sunglasses) are carried by some shops and mail order houses. Consult catalogs.

Bar magnifiers mark the area of a graph being worked and make it more visible. They are inexpensive and potentially helpful. Read Chapter 1, Q8, 9 for other solutions to the problem of small graphs.

Be aware that some individuals become seasick when they work with magnifying lenses for any period of time. If you can read without distress in a moving car, you're probably safe. But before investing a great deal of money on a magnifier, I'd try one out for a few hours.

Measures (9)
(See Figure 12–5)

Tape measures—easily carried, but not particularly accurate. Cloth or plastic can contract or expand, throwing measurements off.

Opaque Rulers—accurate, thick, rigid. Those marked with paint on the surface are susceptible to friction and, with time, can become illegible.

Transparent Plastic Rulers—thin, flexible, excellent for needlework. You can see through them to the work below, allowing it to be measured precisely. However heat warps plastic, so keep it away from boiling water, irons or the strove.

FIGURE 12–5

FIGURE 12-6

Needles (10)
(See Figure 12-6)

Choice is determined by type of needlework and weight of thread to be used. Graded by number—the higher the number, the smaller the needle.

The correct size sharp needle to use on cloth is the one that will open a hole large enough to pull threads through without de-fuzzing them *but* not a hole so large that the stitch can't fill it. You don't want either stripped threads or "holey" stitchery. Try an assortment of needles to find the one that meets the needs of your materials.

The correct size tapestry needle is the one that, when threaded, will not enlarge canvas or cloth meshes, but whose eye is large enough to hold threads without scraping fibers from them. Too small a needle-eye can "skinny" yarns unnecessarily. Determine what size *threaded* needle will begin to warp meshes and use the next smaller size.

EMBROIDERY
Use *sharp pointed* needles for crewel work or surface stitchery.

Crewel—short length, long eye—#3–#10.

Chenille—longest sharp commonly used in embroidery, very long eye—#13–#24. The same size as tapestry needle with identical numbering.

Beading—too fragile to stitch most fabrics. Use "betweens."

Betweens or *quilting*—very short with round eye—#1–#10. Useful for quilting or beading.

Darners—generally too long for most embroidery. For *counted-thread* on cloth or canvas, use *blunt pointed* needles.

Tapestry—medium length, long eye—#13–#26.

CURVED NEEDLES

These can be sharp or blunt. They are useful when you don't have access to back of needlework, especially when mending or repairing. Correct gauge is important. Sharp points can be blunted with an emery board or sand paper to simulate tapestry needles.

Sources other than needlework shops are rug repairers and friendly surgeons. Finding the right size curved needle may not be easy.

Needle Book (11)
(See Figure 12–6)

A small folder with a separate flannel page for each gauge and/or type needle. This is a good way to preserve, store and instantly locate the needle you need.

Needle Gripper (12)
(See Figure 12–6)

Occasionally needles need a firmer tug than can be provided by the average thumb and forefinger. To give additional traction, try small, uninflated balloons; strips of rubber cut from a jar-opener; or slices from the rough palm of an old rubber glove.

Needle Threader (13)
(See Figure 12-6)

This is a fine loop made of metal or wire designed to pass through a needle's eye, catch thread, and pull it back through the eye of the needle. It is inexpensive, small, and fragile. For large-eyed needles, a fine hairpin will do the trick. (Keep this in mind when stitching with children.) Threaders are very easy to lose—wear them around your neck or attached to a chatelaine. (For a no-cost paper substitute, see Chapter 7, Q4).

Pin Cushion (14)
(See Figure 12-2)

Thread a separate needle with every color you'll be using and store them on a pin cushion. A wrist type on the non-stitching arm is an inexpensive luxury.

Scissors (15)
(See Figure 12-2)

Shears can be dulled by cutting paper, canvas, or anything but thread and fabric. Even man-made fibers can dull sharp shears. Don't use embroidery scissors for any other job.

Sharp-pointed scissors are helpful when cutting out mistakes and working pulled thread or cut-work. In a pinch, manicure scissors can substitute.

Cutting canvas should be relegated to shears you don't love—it's a dull job.

Stitch Finders (16)

These are metal sheets coupled with magnetic strips to mark the row being stitched on a graph. For some less expensive alternatives, see Chapter 1, Q9.

Thimble (17)
(See Figure 12–2)

Available in ivory, mother of pearl, glass, horn and wood (usually antique), metal, china, plastic, and leather. Closed at the top or open at ends for long fingernails. Flat or rounded tops. Open or closed around finger sides.

Nothing is less agreed upon in stitchery than the necessity for thimbles. Those who use them couldn't stitch without them; those who don't, can't work with them.

Thimbles are needed when sharpness of a needle, or constant pressure of stitching makes a fingertip painful. Use one when you need one, but be sure it's correctly sized for your finger.

If you hate them but need one, try a leather thimble. It provides softness and flexibility along with protection.

Trolly Needle (18)

A combination of tapestry needle (blunt) and open-ended thimble to be used on the *non-stitching* index finger for laying and untwisting multiple threads before stitching with them. If flattening threads is your nightmare, this is the solution.

Waterproof and Disappearing Marking Pens (19)

See Chapter 6, Q1 for a discussion of marking pens safe for canvas. See Chapter 6, Q1 for information on pattern marking pens for cloth.

Yarn and Thread Organizers (20)

See Chapters 5, Q12, 13, 14.

FIGURE 12-7

I own a dandy little lamp that hangs around my neck and lights my stitching. I used to recommend it to classes before I met Dora.

Dora was, if nothing else, well-endowed. She entered our classroom like a frigate under full sail and made Dolly Parton look pre-adolescent. One night she asked to borrow my neck lamp.

Dora mumbled under her breath the rest of the evening. When asked what was wrong, she snapped, "I can't see a darned thing with this lamp." I hurried over to see what was wrong.

The lamp worked beautifully. The problem was that it pointed straight out into the room. Given Dora's topography, there was nowhere else it could shine. Her needlepoint lay in darkest shadow.

I decided not to explore this particular problem with the class. Dora had trouble with neck magnifiers too.

COMPLETION

Now that your dream has become a reality, what are you going to do with it? Professionals will clean and block and frame it for you—at a price—and many do very good work indeed. However any needleworker who has the determination and skill to carry a project through to this point, has what it takes to finish the job personally. All that's needed is the how-to information gathered together in this section.

Chapter 13 covers cleaning and dry cleaning, from the moment you finish the stitchery and decide that it's grubby, to how-to-cope when your boss spills shrimp dip on it. You'll learn what to do and, perhaps even more important, what not to do, along with the solutions and techniques to use.

Blocking, in one form or another, makes any stitchery look its best. But there are many blocking techniques. Chapter 14 tells you what methods to use for which purposes, and the easiest way to tailor blocking to your particular needlework.

"Finishing" means sewing and completing needlework, from purses and clothing to upholstery and curtains. Look in Chapter 15 for descriptions of techniques used in finishing, and learn how to turn that dream into a reality all by yourself.

Framing is easy, uncomplicated and can be done by anyone with access to one of the many do-it-yourself frame stores that are popping up everywhere. Chapter 16 tells you what to use, where to find it, how to assemble it, and which wall to hang it on.

Needlework is delightful, but there's more to projects than just stitching. Don't deprive yourself of the joy of mastering related skills. Saving and satisfactions will abound when you can proudly say, "I did it all myself."

13 Cleaning, Wet or Dry

FIGURE 13-1

When I first started stitching, my favorite colors were pure Marie Antoinette. There were lots of soft pastels, subtle color variations and acres of gold and white. The children were in cribs or playpens. It's interesting what has happened to my palette since.

When the kids began toddling, I moved in to my purple period. The tone was dark—just the shade to blend with grape jelly. (Grape was the cheapest flavor at the A&P and we spread a lot of it around.)

The kids advanced to grammar school and my favorite color jumped to middle green. It blended well with grass stains. (I never could keep those little sneakers off the furniture.)

Junior High arrived with stitcheries that were dark, dark, dark. Acres of teenaged arms and legs—always with food in hand—kept plopping down on my needlework. (Navy blue hides fudge stains very well.)

Now they're all in High School and I suspect a lipstick red period is about to dawn. (I plan to worry about this one.)

INTRODUCTION

Embroidery worked on linen or cotton cloth with colorfast linen or cotton threads is washed just as the unembroidered cloth would be. Woolen cloth stitched with woolen yarns must be dry cleaned, as you would any woolen garment. It's only when washables mix with dry cleanables in the same stitchery that cleaning problems surface.

Difficulties encountered when cleaning such needleworks arise because the stitcheries are "compound fabrics." They consist of a mesh of vegetable fibers (cotton or linen) covered with animal fibers (wool or silk). Animal fibers like one set of cleaning conditions; vegetable fibers prefer another. Solutions and techniques have to be chosen which won't clean one fiber at the expense of the other. This limits choices considerably.

"Cleaning" is defined here as the removal of soil by washing with water, or by dry-cleaning with solvents. Each method has its strengths and weaknesses. Wet washing usually gets fabrics cleaner but at an increased risk of damaging dyes or fibers.

When wool is wet, it loses much of its strength and becomes susceptible to shrinking, felting and dye-fading. Silk is not always colorfast and may run when washed. Cotton and linen gain strength when they are wet, but lose their smooth starch sizing (the hotter the water, the faster they go limp).

All of the above can be avoided by dry cleaning, but unless you have access to an excellent cleaner (Q10), your needlework may not get completely clean. Cleaning solvents that are not scrupulously filtered or re-distilled can deposit submicroscopic soil from previous jobs, leaving stitcheries dull and dingy. Once attached, such soil is difficult or impossible to remove.

Expert dry cleaning will be kind to fibers and colors, will not affect canvas sizing, and will use both laundering and dry cleaning techniques to remove stains that are beyond home-care capabilities. Never put stitcheries in a coin-operated dry cleaning machine, or let *anybody* press them.

Washing is a do-it-yourself project which depends upon detergents or soaps for its effectiveness. Some of these products are safe for needlework but most of them are not (Q4).

If you choose to wash, you'll need to be familiar with—and avoid—the following pitfalls.

Shrinking and Felting (Chapter 11, Q4).

Dye-Bleeding. Modern dyes produced in the U.S. and industrialized nations rarely run. Bleeding may occur in needlework stitched with yarns dyed in the last half of the 19th century, or with threads dyed more recently in nonindustrialized nations. See Dye-Fast Test, page 166.

Dye-Fading. Natural fibers are dyed with heat, water and agitation. These same conditions exist in washing where they can sometimes remove colors they put in.

Mechanical Damage. Threads of canvas, cloth or yarn rarely break when the needlework being washed is in good condition. If your stitchery shows sign of fading, browning or brittleness, or has thin and weakened spots when it's held up to a light, turn to Antique Needlwork, Chapter 20. You need special advice.

If all of the above has convinced you that you'll never clean anything again, read what can happen if you allow dirt and stains to move in permanently:

Deterioration of plant or animal fibers by chemicals produced as the stain oxidizes. You can't stop oxidation as long as the needlework lives in air.

or

Damage to some or all dyes from this same chemical oxidation.

or

Attraction of *insects*, molds and mildews to the spot. While these pests are usually attracted to the stain and not the fiber, they generally destroy both.

The most common sources of stitchery soil are airborne dirt and human beings. You deposit skin oils as you touch or stitch. Forced air heat from oil and coal furnaces puts more greasy soot into the air than gas or electric heat. Don't throw out your furnace for your needlework, but keep air filters clean. And hold the kids at arm's length when they're eating peanut butter and jelly.

CLEANING

Stitcheries containing silk or rayon (acetate) should *never* be washed. Silk colors may bleed and rayon will wrinkle. **Always dry clean.**

Needleworks stitched with mercerized pearl cottons or flosses on cotton or linen cloth or canvas can be laundered *if* their threads are colorfast. Test and rinse if necessary *before* stitching.

Stitcheries worked with woolen yarns on linen or cotton—cloth or canvas—cause the most headaches. Which type of aspirin you take depends upon the needlework's lifestyle. Your project will fit into one of the following four categories.

 What are cleaning categories?

Category 1

This category consists of needlework that **can be removed** (see Figure 13-2) and reblocked by traditional methods (Q6, 7 and Chapter 14). It helps to have a minimum of one inch of unstitched cloth or canvas surrounding stitchery on all sides, but this is not absolutely essential. Examples: pictures, tray or coaster inserts, slip seats for stools or chairs.

FIGURE 13-2

Category 2

In this category is needlework that is **permanently attached but still allows access to the back** of cloth or canvas. It can be reblocked, using special techniques (Q6, 7). Examples: purse flaps, pillow tops, tote bags, bell pulls, clothing such as skirt inserts or jacket yokes.

FIGURE 13-3

Category 3

This needlework is **permanently attached to something that blocks access to the back** of cloth or canvas. It cannot be reblocked (Q3). Examples: upholstery of large pieces of furniture, stitchery glued to anything, needlework backed with leather or vinyl, window valances or lambrequins.

Category 4

This category consists of needlepoint stitched on **plastic canvas** (Q6). Examples: Christmas tree ornaments, coasters, napkin rings.

How do I tell which fibers are in my stitchery?
To separate one from the other, use the Burn Test (p. 140), the Wet/Dry Break Test and the Broken End Test (p. 142).

Should I wash it or dry clean it?

Category 1

ALWAYS DRY CLEAN when needlework contains silk, rayon or acetate, or a fiber that you can't identify.

or

When a Dye-Fast Test (p. 166) using water comes out positive.

or

When the stain will not be removed by soap and water (Q5).

or

When needlework is fragile and brittle (Chapter 20, Introduction).
You can wash when you're dealing with color-fast wools, linens or cottons in good condition.

Category 2

ALWAYS DRY CLEAN when needlework is not badly soiled and is attached to a fabric that can be dry cleaned but will be damaged by water. Examples: pillows, bell pulls, some totes and purses. Do not dry clean leather or vinyl.

You can wash when needlework is stitched with colorfast threads and it's badly soiled.

or

When it is attached to leather or vinyl. Examples: purse flaps and belts.

Category 3

ONLY DRY CLEAN. Never wash these, because there's no way to remove soaps or detergents once you've applied them. They can attract future dirt and speed ungraceful aging of your stitchery. Furthermore, it's hard to clean all surfaces evenly when the surface to be cleaned is large. Other potential problems include wet needlework padding that can make stains, upholstery tacks that rust when wet, and water itself which stains woods and dissolves furniture glues.

Obviously this is not a do-it-yourself project. Let trained professionals dry clean these items for you; but be sure they use *clean* solvents and know what they're doing.

A word here about slipcovers (see Figure 13–4). They were created many years ago to take care of just this problem. If you can keep needlework furniture from becoming dirty in the first place, you're way ahead of the game.

FIGURE 13–4

Category 4

Always wash. Never dry clean because many plastics harden or dissolve in cleaning solvents. You have no idea which plastics recipe made your canvas, so play it safe.

Washing works like a charm and needs no blocking. Always remove all non-woolen trims ahead of time.

 What about soaps and detergents?

Brands that I've found to be safe and effective are Ivory Flakes in softened water, Liquid Ensure (The Stearns and Foster Co., Cincinnati, Ohio), or Liquid Woolite if you can't get either of the above.

Woolite has been blamed for some washing difficulties, though personally I have had no problems with it. It contains optical brighteners that yellow wool at three times its normal rate. You should be aware that the liquid form has a slightly different chemical composition from the powdered form. It is safer than most laundry detergents, but **follow directions to the letter** and rinse thoroughly.

Check other *mild* cleaning agents available to you to see if they dissolve and work in water no hotter than 90° F. Make sure that they do NOT contain oxygen bleaches or optical brighteners and that they do not make claims for getting your cottons snowy white. If they do, they're too strong for your needleworks.

Soaps are made from fats and lye or a strong alkali. They do not dissolve easily in cool water.

Wool can shrink or felt in temperatures over 100° F. By the time water is warm enough to dissolve most soaps, it's too hot to wash wool.

Detergents are combinations of chemicals which have soap's cleaning ability without its drawbacks. All detergents are not alike. They're tailor-made to meet specific needs.

Most detergents, formulated for cleaning cottons or dishes, are too strong for washing woolens. They also remove moth-proofing from yarns.

5   What's a dye-fast test?

If you have any suspicion that your yarns or threads may *not* be colorfast, take a few minutes to run the following tests before washing or blocking. These moments may save you hours of remorse. **Repeat the entire test with each color used.** You can test for two categories—colorfastness and dirt removal.

1. **Rub** color with a dry, white cloth (see Figure 13–5a).
   a. Does any dye rub off or "crock"? (This usually occurs with dark, saturated colors and indicates that all dye was not rinsed out after dying.)
      - If *yes*, dry clean the first time and run these tests again before washing thereafter.
      - If *no*, proceed to #2 "Blot."

2. **Blot.** Place a few drops of water on the color. Let sit one minute. Blot for one minute with folds of white tissue pressed between thumb and forefinger (see Figure 13–5b).
   a. Does any dirt come off on the tissue?
      - If *yes*, dirt is water soluble and can be removed by washing.
      - If *no*, test with Soap before deciding to dry clean.

FIGURE 13–5a

FIGURE 13–5b

b. Does any dye come off on the tissue?
- If *yes,* dry clean.
- If *no,* proceed to #3 "Soap."

3. **Soap.** Repeat #2 "Blot," substituting cleaning solution (in the dilution that you will use when washing) for water. After test, rinse area thoroughly, blot and dry.
   a. Does any dirt come off?
   - If *yes,* wash.
   - If *no,* test with #4 "Solvent."
   b. Does any dye come off?
   - If *yes,* dry clean.
   - If *no,* it can be safely washed.

4. **Solvent.** If you can obtain a little solvent before dry cleaning, repeat the #2 "Blot" test, substituting solvent for water.

If dirt won't loosen with water, soap or solvent, the needlework may not be cleanable. Consult an expert in textile conservation before trying anything more yourself. This is beyond your capabilities.

 How should I wash needlepoint?
The word "soap" is used here to mean any cleaning agent that satisfies the requirements in Q4.

Category 1a (Q1)

Needlepoint with a minimum of one inch unstitched canvas around all sides, should be washed as follows:

- Remove any backings, trims, and tape on edges. Dissolve soap in water, following package directions exactly. If you have hard water, soften with *Calgon,* following package directions.
- Keep water temperature between 80–90° F. This is very important. Wool can shrink and felt in water hotter than 100° F. If water cools too much, dirt can redeposit. Use a candy thermometer, check frequently, and keep boiling water and ice cubes handy to adjust temperatures quickly (see Figure 13–6a).

- Move needlepoint up and down *gently*. Don't wring, scrub or squeeze. Don't let needlepoint sit in wash water once it's clean; you'll give soil a chance to redeposit.
- *Rinse thoroughly.* You can allow each rinse to be a little cooler than the last. If you've used *Calgon,* keep using it until you reach the last rinse. Don't stop rinsing until you could drink the final water.
- Blot immediately with towels (see Figure 13–6b). Don't let needlepoint remain wet or rolled in a towel longer than necessary. Block at once (see Chapter 14). Dry horizontally, away from direct light or heat.

FIGURE 13–6a

FIGURE 13–6b

Category 1b

Needlepoint with little or no unstitched canvas around all sides (best when canvas is not very badly warped), can be washed as follows:

FIGURE 13-7

- Obtain a piece of #10 gauge plastic needlepoint canvas two inches larger than your needlepoint on all four sides. Mark centers of needlepoint sides, and of canvas sides. Lay needlepoint face up on plastic canvas, aligning center-sides.
- Match both sets of canvas threads and baste needlepoint to plastic canvas so that it lies perfectly straight and flat (see Figure 13-7).
- To help this straightening, spray with a light mist of water to relax canvas. Hold it in position with masking tape while basting.
- Baste with needle and thread, making small stitches over two mesh of plastic canvas and placing them one-quarter inch inside edge of needlepoint. Remove masking tape before washing.
- Wash as directed in 1a. Don't bend plastic canvas more than you have to. Rinse, blot and dry horizontally. No blocking is necessary. Remove plastic canvas when needlepoint is dry.

    As large needlepoint pieces dry, they may shrink and slightly curl plastic canvas. You can prevent this by thumbtacking plastic edges to a flat surface every three inches while needlepoint is still wet. Keep needlepoint facing up.

Category 2

Needlepoint permanently attached to leather or fabric that won't take washing but does allow access to the back of canvas, can be washed as follows:

- Buy a piece of #10 gauge plastic needlepoint canvas like that in Category 1b. Baste needlepoint to canvas through stitch line, or just inside it (see Figure 13-8a). Basting stitches should cover two plastic meshes. Spray with water if you need to relax canvas.
- Prepare a soap solution following package directions exactly. Be sure water temperature is between 80-90°F. and maintain it there with a warming tray, double boiler or thermos jug.

FIGURE 13–8a

FIGURE 13–8b

- Rest a piece of clean, metal, one-fourth inch "hardware cloth" (available at hardware stores) over sink. Place canvas on this mesh, face up.
- Use a new, small, flat sponge about three inches square. Squeeze soap solution through needlepoint into sink (see Figure 13–8b). Refill sponge with new, warm solution and repeat. Don't let canvas get too wet. Be careful when you get near edges that no solution goes beyond needlepoint. Continue until dirt has been flushed out of needlepoint, into sink.
- Rinse, using the same sponging technique, until all soap solution has been removed. Allow rinse waters to cool gradually. If you've washed in softened water, all rinses *except the last* should be softened too.
- Blot excess moisture from front and back with

towels. Wipe any moisture from leather or other non-textiles, which must be treated carefully. Leather hardens with moist heat and some leather dyes bleed in water. Wipe drops away the instant they land.

- Tack plastic canvas to a flat surface, needlework facing up, and dry horizontally away from direct light or heat. No blocking is necessary. Remove plastic canvas when needlepoint is dry.

Category 4

Woolen or mercerized cotton on plastic canvas, can be washed as follows:

- Remove backings, facings and trims. Prepare washing solution (Q4)
- Dunk needlepoint up and down in solution until it's clean. Rub spots lightly, but don't scrub hard.
- Rinse thoroughly until no trace of soap remains. Soften all rinses but the last if you softened wash water.
- Blot excess moisture with towel and dry away from direct light and heat. Blocking isn't necessary.

 How should I wash embroidery?

Category 1

If threads are colorfast (Q5) and your fabric doesn't require dry cleaning (Introduction):

- Wash in lukewarm water with mild soaps or detergents (Q4). Follow package directions.
- Gently agitate embroidery in soap solution, without wringing, squeezing or hard rubbing. *Do not* let stitchery soak after it is clean; quick in and quick out is the secret. A minute or two is usually all that's necessary.

- Rinse thoroughly until *all* soap has been removed. If you washed in water softened with *Calgon,* rinse with *Calgon* until the final rinsing. This process may seem lengthy, but keep at it until you'd be willing to drink the final rinse water. Soap left on an embroidery attracts dirt and oxidizes to an unpleasant brown color. You want to get it all out.
- Roll stitchery in a terry cloth towel, blot excess water and block immediately (Chapter 14). Do not leave embroidery sopping wet or rolled in a towel. Dry horizontally away from direct heat or light.

Category 2

Sponge embroidery as directed in Q6, Category 2, after basting it to plastic canvas.

8 ▷ How do I clean needlework stitched with metallic threads?

You must test them before cleaning. Some threads wash well in water and are damaged by dry cleaning solvents. Others behave just the opposite.

Snip off a sample of thread and soak in properly diluted cleaning solution. You'll soon know how it will behave.

FIGURE 13–9

9 ▷ When can I dry-clean needlework myself?

When soil is greasy, the spot is small, and the stain is fresh. Work in a well-ventilated room. Don't use dry cleaning fluids where you can't open windows or doors.

Start at the outside of the spot and work toward its center (see Figure 13–9). Follow directions on the container exactly. When finished, blot any excess cleaning fluid immediately.

Don't use gasoline. I know a woman who tried to dry clean curtains with gas—once. When the cleaning didn't move fast enough, she warmed the solution on a stove. She blew up the kitchen.

How do I locate a good professional dry cleaner?

As a general rule, **choose a plant where cleaning is done on the premises** rather than a substation where it's sent somewhere else.

or

Ask cleaners of oriental rugs. They have the same "compound fabric" problems as needlework. They may not want to handle your small items themselves, but they can recommend a knowledgeable cleaner for you.

or

Ask reputable dealers in antique textiles or oriental rugs for the name of the firm that does their cleaning.

or

Ask the curator in charge of a **museum textile collection** where its cleaning is done. Many museums do not have facilities to do their own cleaning jobs.

Do not depend upon a cleaner's advertising. This isn't the time to take advantage of a coupon or a sale.

What about spray moth proofing and water repellents?

Don't use them. Most commercial needlework yarns sold in the U.S. today are already mothproofed. Don't wash them in harsh detergents and they'll stay mothproofed.

Wool is naturally somewhat water repellant. It really doesn't need boosters.

Propellants and chemicals sprayed on needlework have been implicated in causing dyes, inks and paints to bleed. They haven't been around long enough for us to know if they will deteriorate fibers and dyes. Why take a chance?

14 Blocking

FIGURE 14-1

Some years ago, while designing illustrations for another book, I hit on a sensational quilt pattern variation. Colors were subtle, stitching was inventive and the total effect sang—on paper.

But the reality didn't turn out that way. Without a frame, my unusual stitching produced unusual results. Every stitch in every quarter was diagonal and pulled in the same direction. The needlepoint wasn't half finished when a slight ground swell appeared.

"Not to worry," I reassured myself, "It'll block right out."

Stitching was three-quarters through when the groundswell bloomed into a definite bump. It escalated quickly and as I finished the last needleful, I had what looked like half of Dolly Parton's bra. A family of squirrels could have set up housekeeping inside.

Those were the hardest blocking jobs I ever undertook (three of them to be exact). When it was all over, the canvas was more or less straight. It had its pictures taken for the book and then became a pillow on my living room couch.

I've spent the ensuing years watching that needlepoint reinflate. (It's nearly a C cup again.) I don't know about life after death, but there's certainly creeping after blocking.

INTRODUCTION

Blocking can be defined as the use of moist tension to enhance stitch appearance and straighten base fabric permanently.

174

Ask 524 stitchers the best way to accomplish this and you're likely to get 524 answers. Each of their techniques, however, would likely fall into one of three blocking categories: freshening, sizing-blocking, or stretch-blocking. The wise stitcher decides what he or she wants accomplished before choosing blocking methods. One technique doesn't cover all situations.

Needlepoint and embroidery present many similar blocking problems. Needlepoint is worked on tough canvas and its blocking is therefore the more challenging. But embroiderers might do well to read through "Needlepoint-Blocking," if only to be grateful for what they've been spared.

NEEDLEPOINT BLOCKING

Certain words pop up constantly when discussing blocking:

- **Canvas Border**—The two inches of unstitched canvas you left around your needlepoint (Chapter 5, Q3).
- **Canvas-Creep**—Not an unattractive needle-pointer, but one of the primary reasons for blocking. Once misshapen canvas is blocked to shape, it should stay that way. Any deviation from the blocked shape during use is known as "canvas-creep," and is caused by weakened sizing or stretched canvas.
- **Stiff-Mount**—Illustrated by stretched, firmly backed products such as framed pictures, brick covers and firmly interlined bags and purses; whose finishing reinforces blocking, eliminates flexing, and helps prevent canvas-creep.
- **Soft-Mount**—This technique is used to finish products that will be subjected to flexing when in use, such as soft pillows, upholstery, unstiffened purses, and bell pulls. Soft-mounts need strong blocking so that formerly misshapen canvas won't creep during future use.
- **Sizing**—Stiffening agent applied to canvas to help keep it in shape. Composed largely of starch.

- **Sizing-Block** (Q11)—The gentle, wet stretching of misshapen canvas to achieve correct shape without stretching canvas's warp threads (Q12). Future shape is maintained by re-stiffening of starch as it dries. Such a block is easy, though fragile. It should be reinforced by a stiff-mount to avoid canvas-creep. Sizing-block can be applied to any kind and quality of canvas. This is the technique to use if you must block to exact dimensions.
- **Stretch-Block** (Q12)—Severe stretching of misshapen canvas to remove stretch from individual warp threads. Future shape is maintained by removing all stretch from canvas. Once removed, stretch will not return. Can be soft-mounted without danger of canvas-creep.
  Stretch-block should only be used with good quality canvas (Chapter 9, Q3). Because canvas-stretch can vary, blocking to exact dimensions can be risky.
- **Freshening** (Q10)—The lifting and straightening of individual stitches usually accomplished by steaming (Chapter 12, Q4), which does not move underlying canvas. May be applied to any type and quality of canvas, except plastic, provided that it is not misshapen or dirty. Such canvases should be stiff-mounted.

Why should I block needlepoint?

Block needlepoint **to straigthen misshapen canvas**; to pull canvas away from stitching and allow stitches to sit on the surface; and to improve the appearance of any piece.

What are characteristics of canvas during blocking?

Canvas threads appear much **more corrugated in one direction** (warp) than they do in the other direction (weft) (Figure 9–3). This difference in thread appearance is used to identify direction of canvas "grain" (Chapter 9, Q8). Corrugations, formed during weaving, also explain canvas creep.

As sizing weakens or canvas is subjected to strain, corrugations of warp threads can flatten out like straightened coil springs. Once flattened, they won't bounce back to their former shape. This is why canvas creeps and why the stretch should be pulled out of the canvas before finishing objects that will be subjected to flexing or pressure (Q12).

How much a particular canvas will stretch may depend upon information that you, as consumer, may not have available. In general, though, be prepared for variations in the stretch of different canvases.

Most canvas is composed of cotton fibers that can stretch from three to seven percent during stretch-blocking.

- Mono-floating and double canvases stretch *parallel to selvages.* Cross-stretch between selvages is usually insignificant. Thus, a twelve-inch "square" pillow could stretch 5/16 to 3/4 inch more in one direction than in another.
- Interlock canvases stretch in *both* directions and to a greater degree than mono-floating.
- Linen canvas has less stretch than cotton.
- Both cotton and linen gain strength with water. It is safer to pull them into shape wet than dry.

3. What are characteristics of needlepoint yarns during blocking?

Wool is the most elastic fiber available. When wet, it loses strength but retains elasticity. As long as wool is supported by canvas, it will adjust itself beautifully to any stretch or shift in canvas shape.

Silk should not be blocked by water. Although it is very flexible, it is susceptible to water spotting and dye bleeding.

Cotton and linen yarns are inflexible, wet or dry. They won't adjust gracefully to extreme shifts in canvas shape. Needlepoint stitched primarily of cellulose fibers (pearl cottons, for example) should not be allowed to warp. If you don't work on a frame, avoid diagonal stitches. Straight and cross stitches will not warp canvases.

FIGURE 14-2

What size canvases can I block myself?

The smaller the canvas, the less pull you have to exert on it. A five-inch coaster pulled with ten pounds of pressure will have 2.0 psi (pounds-per-square-inch) stretching it. A ten-inch pillow under the same pressure will have 1.0 psi. The same ten pounds pulling on a fifty-inch rug will exert 0.2 psi, or not enough pressure to move it at all.

To put that fifty-inch rug under the same tension as that five-inch coaster, you'd have to exert one hundred pounds of pull. Here's where an upholsterer's blocking tool and stretch-blocking techniques come in handy (Q12).

The bigger they are, the harder they block.

What shape canvas can I block?

Keep canvas rectangular, no matter what shape you've needlepointed upon it. If canvas corners are square and blocked on a gridded board, your circle, heart, or vest will come out straight and true.

If you're working on a complex shape (for example, a vest), make a paper pattern *before* stitching and block so that needlepoint will fit the pattern *exactly*.

Should I wash needlepoint before I block it?

Only if it's dirty. Soap will remove more sizing than plain water will. However, if proper laundering procedures (Chapter 13, Q6) are followed, needlepoint is in much less danger from a good washing than it is from remaining dirty.

What materials will I need to block needlepoint?

- Tacks—non-rusting upholstery tacks

    or

    non-rusting staples (see Figure 14-3)
- Hammer—claw or tack

    or

    staple gun (desk staplers aren't strong enough).
- Pliers

FIGURE 14-3

or

> Upholsterers' stretching tool for stretch-blocking.

- Water in a clean spray bottle.
- Blocking Board—If you don't already have one, get a piece of ½-inch or ⅝-inch thick plywood, with square corners (no sink cutouts), larger than your needlework. One board can last your entire stitching career so get one large enough for any piece you're likely to work, but not so big that it's a storage headache.

Prepare the board by placing a square grid on it in one of the following ways. Both will protect needle-point from stains soaking through from the wood below.

Using permanent black marker or India Ink and a yardstick, draw lines across the board at one-inch intervals, parallel to edges. Cover the board with three coats of polyurethane varnish or shellac, allowing it to dry thoroughly between coats.

or

Wrap the wood smoothly with heavy duty aluminum foil. Buy enough new ½-inch gingham to cover board. The gingham must be at least 85% cotton; 100% cotton is best. (Pre-washed gingham won't work.) Cover board tautly. Miter corners and staple cloth every one-fourth inch to back of board being careful to position gingham lines so that they run parallel to board edges and at right angles to each other. Dip board in hot water, thoroughly wetting cotton, and allow it to dry horizontally. Relaxation shrinkage will shrink cotton cloth so that it fits the board like a second skin.

Should I block needlepoint face up or face down?

It depends upon what texture you want to achieve. **Block face up if you want texture maximized.** Block face down if you want texture minimized. The pressure of tacked canvas will press stitches flat.

The appearance of needlepoint texture is actually determined by the shadows cast by stitches and their intersections. Maximized shadows give the effect of rough texture; minimized shadows appear smoother (Chapter 3, Q10).

Can I block more than once?

Yes. If the first block doesn't get it absolutely straight, pull out the tacks and re-block after two hours. (It's much easier the second time.) Fibers will have softened and will be more elastic. Dry horizontally.

You can block as many times as you think necessary, bearing in mind that each addition of water washes away some canvas sizing.

How do I freshen needlepoint?

Use a steam iron. Either stretch canvas on a four-way stretcher or pin it face up on a flat ironing board, using non-rusting pins every quarter of an inch. Position steam iron one-fourth inch *over* canvas (see Figure 14–4). *Do not let the iron touch the needlepoint.* Steam thoroughly and allow to dry in place. Stitches will absorb steam and relax enough to lift and equalize.

or

Use steam in bathroom. Place needlepoint on a four-way stretcher upside down. Nothing should touch the stitchery. Run hot water in shower for 20–30 minutes. **Do not** put the needlepoint in the shower, but allow stitchery to remain in the steamy room, upside down, until dry. Gravity aids fluffing of stitches.

FIGURE 14-4

This technique works marvelously in tiled bathrooms. But watch out for wallpaper and paint.

The last time I tried it, I ran the hot water heater cold, shut off the shower and went to bed. Next morning, the needlepoint was beautiful, but strips of old paint hung from the ceiling like stalactites. I've utilized steam irons ever since.

 ### How do I sizing-block needlepoint?

This technique is excellent for blocking to exact measurement, but do not use it if your needlepoint will be soft-mounted (Introduction). Where the following directions say "tack," you may substitute non-rusting staples placed diagonally to canvas edges.

- Wet canvas thoroughly. Blot by rolling in a white terry cloth towel. Wool repels water at first, so check that it's evenly dampened before proceeding.
- Tack one corner down on gridded board. Place first tack at corner and one on each side, one quarter inch away. Position tacks at least one-half inch beyond needlepoint. Hammer only halfway in—you may want to pull them out before you're finished.
- Pull one side of canvas along grid until it's stretched to the dimensions you desire (see Figure 14-5a). Tack second corner of Side 1.

FIGURE 14–5a

FIGURE 14–5b

FIGURE 14–5c

182

Tack the center of Side 1 along the straight board-grid. Tack halfway between tacks. Continue halving spaces between tacks until they are one-fourth to one-half inch apart. There should be no scallops along the needlepoint edge.

- Tack the third corner, pulling Side 2 along the grid line until it's stretched to the dimensions you desire (see Figure 14–5b). Straighten and tack Side 2 as you did Side 1.
- Tack the fourth corner into place. (This will be the hard one and you may need an extra hand.) Straighten and tack Sides 3 and 4 along board's grid. If you have a paper pattern (Q5) now is the time to place it over the canvas and adjust the tacks until the needlepoint corresponds exactly.
- Allow the board to dry horizontally, far from windows, fluorescent lights, and heat sources. It should take more than 24 hours to dry (see Figure 14–5c).

Four-Way Stretcher Variation

Use the same stretcher you've stitched on. Dip stretcher and canvas in water, blot away excess, and dry horizontally, face up. If tacks and staples are originally placed one-fourth inch apart, this should do a successful job with no additional fuss.

> *Advantages:* You can stitch, wash, rinse and block on the same frame. This is the easiest method I know.
>
> *Disadvantages:* Canvas must be tacked or stapled taut and closely (every quarter inch) *before* stitching begins. You must stitch on the frame. Non-rusting tacks or staples are essential.

 How do I stretch-block needlepoint?

Materials

BLOCKING BOARD
Ideally, stretch-blocking is done on a piece of plywood or an artists' stretcher frame measuring two

inches longer and wider than the finished needle-point. (In such cases, all canvas borders can be pulled over wood edges and fastened to the sides.)

But it is not always practical to cut a separate board for each project. For this reason, stretchblocking technique will be described first for a board cut-to-size and then adapted for a more versatile, larger blocking board.

TOOLS

Upholsterers' **stretch tool** (also used by artists for stretching canvases) **or pliers** (which will do but be harder to work with). Find upholsterers' stretch tools in the Yellow Pages under "Upholsterers' Equipment and Supplies" or "Art Supplies."

TACKS OR STAPLES

These should be positioned at least one-half inch beyond finished needlepoint's edge. Again, pound tacks only halfway in, for you may want to reposition them before you're through. Where the following directions say "tack" you may substitute non-rusting staples placed diagonally to needlepoint edge.

Technique:
Board Cut-to-Size

- Soak the needlepoint in cool water for at least two hours. Drain and blot by rolling in white terry cloth.
- On a board cut to size, position canvas so that it's centered and raw canvas hangs over the edge of wood. Use steel tacks and a magnetic upholsterers' hammer to tack the first corner to the edge of the board. Use five tacks, one at the corner and two along each side placed a quarter inch apart (see Figure 14–6a).
- Use the stretch tool to pull toward you from this first tacked corner along the blocking board's grid. Fold canvas over wood and tack a second corner to the edge with five tacks. Tack remaining two corners, pulling hard.

FIGURE 14–6a

FIGURE 14–6b

- Use stretch tool to alternately straighten the two opposite sides (see Figure 14–6b). Tack every quarter inch, first on one side and then on the other, beginning at corners and working toward center. Stop when halfway to center. Repeat on two remaining sides, stopping when halfway to center.

- Finish tacking the centers of the first two sides; then do the last two. These last sides are likely to be more difficult and you may need help.

- Check needlepoint for straight sides and square corners. Although scallops should not develop, if they do, pull out the tacks and reposition.

- Dry horizontally away from daylight, fluorescent lighting or heat sources. Needlepoint should take from 24 to 48 hours to dry.

  If the surface wrinkles after blocking, wait two hours. Remove tacks, one side at a time, and pull until the wrinkles disappear. This is much easier than the first blocking, and some stretch can still be removed.

Technique:
Large Blocking Board

- When the cost of wood makes cutting-to-size impractical, use a large blocking board. Fold raw canvas border in half and machine sew along two sides that meet at a corner.

- Stretch and tack folded corner flat on board, tacking through all canvas layers. Pull and fasten the opposite side over blocking board's edge, following directions on Board Cut To Size (see Figure 14-7a).
- Repeat process with remaining two sides. Three corners will be tacked into edges and only the sewn corner will be flat on the board (see Figure 14-7b). This will eliminate canvas shredding along edges.

FIGURE 14-7a

FIGURE 14-7b

 What happens when canvas and yarn get soaking wet?

If water is cool, no soap is present, and there's no agitation of the canvas, the needlepoint is in no danger. Shrinking and felting are the symptoms to be avoided. Wool felts when agitated in alkaline solutions with heat over 100° F. Cotton or linen threads in canvases soaked for stretch-blocking actually gain strength in water.

 Will paints, pens, or dyes run when needlepoint is wet?
They will if they're water soluble. See Chapter 13, Q5 for Dye-Fast Test and Chapter 6 for information on paints and inks. *If you have the slightest suspicion that your colors are not fast, run tests.*

- Oil and acrylic paints are both insoluble in water *after* they've dried.
- Marking pen inks *will* run unless they are specifically formulated for needlepoint canvas. *Test pens before you believe their labels* (Chapter 6, Q1).

FIGURE 14-8

 What should I do if dyes run while I'm blocking needlepoint?
Don't let the canvas dry. Keep washing or rinsing in the *same* kind of solution you were using when you first noticed the color running (see Figure 14-8). Keep water temperature and amount of soap, if any, constant. You want to keep the color running until what's loose has been removed.

Change the solution frequently and replace immediately with another just like it. Eventually, this should remove all loose dye and prevent it from reattaching elsewhere. Enough dye will probably remain so that you won't miss the excess.

Do not change water temperature; add salt, vinegar, or ammonia; remove soap if you were using it or add soap if you didn't have any before. Any of these might cause dye to reattach itself in the wrong area instead of vanishing down the drain.

When the water is finally colorless, rinse, blot and block as if you'd never had a crisis. Dinner may be late, but the patient will have survived.

 Should I paint rabbit-skin glue, liquid latex, or other stiffeners on the back of needlepoint?
Such additives reinforce sizing-block and give stiffness to an unstretched canvas. Stiffeners have their

pros and cons. If you choose to use them, follow specified directions for your brand.

On the plus side, they hold warped canvas in place and are easy and inexpensive. However, they're irreversible, cannot be removed (except with needle nosed pliers and determination), and interfere with the soft, textile quality of the needlepoint.

My friend Marie once worked a large, expensive, and time-consuming wall hanging. She left it with a trusted shop-owner for blocking and mounting. The finished product was to be mailed to her and in due time it arrived. Marie unrolled it and almost had a stroke.

Somehow, nobody knows why, all the white in the design had turned a rotten pink. The shop-owner swore it hadn't been that way when she packed it. All we can imagine is that a sizing, painted on the hanging's back, had somehow or other changed the color. Marie was sick, but nothing if not determined.

She bought some needlenosed pliers and, for the last five years, has been picking out glued-down stitches, one by one. She's almost finished. In my book, that's True Grit!

 How can I straighten a crooked motif in the middle of an otherwise blocked canvas?

- Stretch-block it. If that doesn't straighten everything . . .
- Dampen the needlepoint. Pin it flat on a soft surface such as *Celotex* or an ironing board. Spray extra water on the crooked area. Push non-rusting pins around the motif, manipulating it straight (see Figure 14–9). Let the canvas dry before removing pins.

One disadvantage here is the possibility of making visible holes around the motiff as you enlarge some meshes and contract others. But try it; you can always reblock to remove the holes.

or

Paint rabbit-skin glue over the straightened motif to hold it in place.

FIGURE 14-9

What can I do with finished needlepoint that has "crept" over the years?

Check for brittleness, fading, or any signs of sun rot or oxidation. **If canvas is at all faded or brittle, live with it as is.**

If, however, it's as supple as new and the front is as bright as the back, wash using technique 1b, Chapter 13, Q6

or

reblock by the sizing-block method, working with the canvas wet, not dry, and being sure to dry horizontally.

What if I don't have one and one-half inches of unworked canvas around the border?

You're limited to sizing-block. Do not try to stretch-block.

Machine sew a border of twill tape one-fourth inch *inside* the edge of stitched needlepoint, or one-half inch inside the edge of raw canvas, if enough exists. Work two rows of zigzag or straight stitching, using a sharp machine needle.

Dampen canvas, pull *gently,* and tack through twill tape every quarter inch (see Figure 14–10).

FIGURE 14–10

EMBROIDERY BLOCKING

The main differences between embroidery cloth and needlepoint canvas are density of the fabric, and presence or absence of heavy sizing.

All embroideries are stretch-blocked flat (Q12). Embroidery cloth's more delicate structure makes the muscle-power needed to stretch-block canvas unnecessary—for which embroiderers should thank their lucky stars.

 What materials do I need to block embroidery?
You will need **non-rusting tacks,** a **gridded board,** and (perhaps) a **hammer.** The kind of board determines the kind of tacks.

Plywood suitable for blocking needlepoint (Q7) can also block embroidery and you'll need non-rusting upholstery tacks and a hammer.

Acoustical tiles or *celotex* wallboard covered with gingham as described in Q7 will be easier to work with and will accept non-rusting push pins or thumb tacks (see Figure 14–11). You can also forget your hammer with the softer boards.

FIGURE 14–11

 How do I block embroidery?
All tacks should be positioned one-half inch inside cloth edges.

- Remove any masking tape from fabric edges. Wash or dampen embroidery. Blot dry by rolling in white terry cloth and remove immediately for blocking.
- Stretch fabric lengthwise, holding embroidery at center, top, and bottom, with "right" side facing you. Tack at top center. Pull hard against top tack and tack center bottom (see Figure 14–12a). Your fingertips should smart a little.
- Stretch fabric crosswise. Tack center of one side, pull against tack, and tack center of second side. The center of your embroidery should be at the center of your board.
- Tack four corners, lining them up with center tacks along blocking board's grid.
- Continue stretching fabric from side to side and tacking in order shown in Diagram 14–12b. Use as many tacks as necessary to eliminate scallops. Be sure that fabric is straight and square when finished, with its grain (warp and weft threads) parallel to the board's grid.

FIGURE 14–12a

FIGURE 14–12b

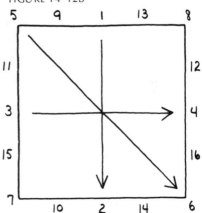

- If a tack is misplaced, remove it and reposition while fabric is still wet.

  If fabric still isn't flat and straight, wait an hour. Remove offending tacks and stretch more until all is perfect. The hour rest will not allow cloth to dry, but will soften it and allow further stretching to take place.

- Place blocking board flat, away from daylight, fluorescent lights, and heat sources. Allow 24 or more hours for complete drying.

This blocking procedure has variations, usually determined by the order in which tacks are inserted and the degree of dryness or wetness of the embroidered cloth. Linen and cotton are weaker dry than wet. Fragile fabrics should not be subjected to hard pulling in their dry state.

Can I steam-press embroidery?
Yes, but steam pressing is not as effective as blocking. It squashes embroidery and seldom adequately flattens small areas of ground cloth surrounded by stitching. If you must press, place embroidery face down on several thicknesses of terry cloth. Steam from edges toward the center. Use lots of steam. Pull cloth straight as you go and pin straight down through cloth edges, terry cloth, and into the ironing board itself. Place non-rusting pins every quarter of an inch. Allow cloth to dry in place.

What embroideries can't I block?
What you can't dampen you can't block. Silks, cloth woven of acetate or rayon, and elderly, fragile or unstable fabrics, should not be blocked (see Fiber Characteristics Chart, p. 137). Neither should any stitchery that contains a thread which is not colorfast.

When you are working with the above fibers, stitch on a four-way stretcher and never allow them to become dirty. Careful steaming can remove the few wrinkles that may result from this method.

15 Finishing

FIGURE 15-1

When I was young and unmarried, I started knitting a cable knit tennis sweater as a surprise for the great love of my life (I think his name was Steve). I had finished the front and part of the back by the time I was also finished with Steve, and the sweater moved to the back of the closet.

... Until I met George. George was everything that Steve was not (including a foot taller) and the sweater reappeared. Of course the knitting directions had to be changed a little. (Unravelling should have been the proper solution, but love wasn't *that* blind!) The first sleeve was well under way when George met a blonde, and that was that. Back to the closet.

And then along came Bill. He was perfection personified and out bounced the tennis sweater. Bill, however, was larger than his predecessors so I modified the directions—again.

That cable-knit sweater ended looking like a poorly crocheted afghan. Bill found it under his Christmas tree, just before we broke up in January.

All other things being equal, it's probably best to stick with one set of directions per project.

INTRODUCTION

This chapter will help make sense of the finishing directions that you already have. Very few stitchers take a project to the finishing stage without some idea of what it's going to be when it grows up. But problems can readily develop when your instructions seem to be written in Sanskrit.

So first the question is, "What's wrong with the directions?"

The most tempting answer is that the Stupid Author got them wrong. Honestly, this rarely happens. Incorrect instructions *have* been known to slip into print; but the greater majority—once understood—prove to be correct. The problem is that they don't communicate anything to *you*. Why?

Have you read them through from start to finish? The most common reason for communication gaps is that we joyously jump in with both feet before we know where we're going. *Chaos* sets in somewhere around paragraph 4.

Sit down with a cup of coffee and read through *all* the directions until they begin to make sense. This may take more than one reading, but give it a chance.

Then if you're still confused, try a few tricks. Do you learn best through your eyes, your ears, or by doing (Chapter 4, Introduction)? If ears are your key, read directions aloud into a tape recorder and play back (several times if necessary). You'll be amazed at how the words begin to communicate.

If you're an eye or muscle person, get some brown paper, scissors, and tape. Cut and manipulate paper as if it were stitchery, following directions, but taping instead of sewing (eliminate seam allowances). You can make your mistakes on expendable paper instead of irreplaceable needlework. This will eliminate the element of Panic, which may be preventing you from understanding the directions.

The problem with instructions is that they're usually written by experienced people. What seems elementary to Sherlock Holmes may not be included in his directions to the unfortunate Dr. Watson.

It often helps to have the same information pitched to you from another side of the ball park. Read on.

FIGURE 15-2

THE ENLIGHTENED CONSUMER

Linings and Trims

$ Purchase these before you choose yarns and threads. In any buying sequence, obtain first those items for which you have the *least* color choice. It's much easier to match yarn to lining than vice versa.

Linings should possess three virtues: They should be flexible enough to be turned under and attached neatly. They should match what they're lining in firmness and tightness of weave. They should be able to be cleaned by the same method as the needlework they protect.

Interlinings

Many types are available. Check to see that what you buy is of the correct stiffness, can be cleaned by the same process as your needlework, is non-stretchable if stitchery needs firm reinforcement (or stretchable if stitchery needs to conform to an irregular shape), and can be attached by a method compatible with the needlework. (Example: Don't use iron-on interlinings with plastic canvas or heat-sensitive acrylic yarns.)

Other Stiffeners
(see Figure 15–3)

Plastic canvas needs no interlining. It can be used for constructed needlework such as boxes, waste baskets, and book covers.

Wood is readily available, can be shaped and attached fairly easily, and is resilient and durable. But it's fairly expensive, stains when wet, releases acids as it ages (Preventive Medicine), and is heavy.

Cardboard is a wood product. It's widely available, inexpensive, and can be shaped and attached easily. But it bends and tears easily, dissolves when wet, releases acids as it ages (Preventive Medicine), and is heavy when used in large amounts.

FIGURE 15–3

Acrylic plastics are strong, chemically neutral, light-weight, durable and waterproof. But they're expensive, not always available, thick, brittle, and somewhat difficult to shape and attach.

Polyethylene Plastic (Examples: milk bottles, soft margarine containers) is inexpensive, chemically neutral, widely available, easy to cut, flexible, strong, lightweight, durable, waterproof and thin. But it is not rigid and it's hard to tell one plastic from another (Preventive Medicine).

Butcher's plastic meat trays (unused) are often free or *very* inexpensive, chemically neutral over a short term (hence not recommended for heirlooms), waterproof, easily available, lightweight, and can be shaped and attached easily. They're excellent for stuffing coasters and stiffening name tags. However they bend and crack easily, are weak and brittle, and break down chemically over the years.

Stuffings

Polyester fiber ("Dacron") is self-extinguishing when ignited, inexpensive, readily available, resilient, chemically neutral and waterproof. It has few drawbacks, but does mat slightly with much use.

Foam rubber (different brands will have slightly different characteristics) is firm, very resilient, waterproof and widely available. But it deteriorates with age, crumbling and releasing chemicals that damage fibers and/or dyes, it smoulders when ignited, and it's moderately expensive.

$ *Wool* and *down* are extremely expensive.

Cotton is inexpensive, waterproof, chemically neutral and widely available. But it mats, is highly flammable, non-resilient and subject to mildew when damp.

Fabric Protection Sprays

Some fabrics have stain repellents applied during manufacture. They usually cost more than similar, non-treated fabrics.

If you wish to spray a protection on stitchery, watch out for dyes, paints, and inks on the textile.

Propellants and/or solvents in such sprays can cause one or more of these coloring agents to bleed. Test *all* colors against the spray before applying it.

Place such treated stitcheries away from direct sunlight, heat, or fluorescent lights. Their long-term effect on sprayed dyes and fibers has not yet been determined.

Glues

Some types of construction call for glue as the preferred method of attachment. When its use is necessary, use a casein or milk-based glue. Hold needlework in place while drying, using clip clothespins, straight pins pushed through stitchery into a soft blocking board, or small, gold-colored safety pins (see Figure 15–4).

FIGURE 15–4

Hint: Waxed paper is excellent for protecting counter surfaces while gluing.

Try not to do anything irreversible to needlework, if you can avoid it. Once glue is applied, it's there forever. Sew whenever possible.

FINISHING TECHNIQUES FOR ALL NEEDLEWORK

How do I miter flat corners?

- Turn stitchery face down. Position flat stiffening (Introduction) over it, if any is used. Fold a

FIGURE 15-5

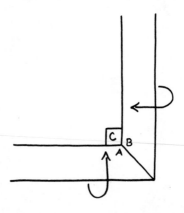

triangle (A-B-C) toward you and crease (AC should equal BC). (With needlepoint, the corner background stitch should *just* be visible from the back.)

- Fold A and B so that they touch C (see Figure 15-5). Crease. Stitch miter closed. When flat stiffening has a measurable thickness, place AB crease as far outside corner as the stiffening is thick. (Example: Mitering over ⅛-inch cardboard means placing first crease ⅛-inch outside cardboard corner.)

 How do I finish convex (outer) curves?

- Mark the curve line with basting or pencil on cloth, or waterproof marking pen on canvas. Machine baste two rows (one over the other) one-quarter inch *outside* curve line. Run a gathering thread through these machine stitchings (see Figure 15-6).
- Trim excess cloth from curve, three-fourths of an inch beyond the curve line.
- Pull gathering thread until fabric lies flat against back of curve. Press gathered bastings flat and hem in place. Cover with backing or lining (Chapter 17, Q7).

FIGURE 15-6

 How do I finish concave (inner) curves?

- Mark the curve line with basting or pencil on cloth; or waterproof marking pen on canvas.

FIGURE 15-7

Cut a facing of lining fabric as directed by pattern (making sure to include a seam allowance of one-half to three-fourths of an inch around the curve).

- Baste facing to stitchery along the curve line, with right sides together (see Figure 15-7). Trim seam allowances to between one-half and three-quarters of an inch (the thicker the cloth or canvas, the wider the allowance).

- Machine stitch around the curve line, using a sharp needle. Remove bastings. Slit canvas or cloth and facing to—but not through—the curve line.

- Turn the curve inside out (wrong sides together). Flatten needlework, spreading slits. Press.

- Top-stitch one-eighth inch inside curve to hold spread slits in place. Cover with lining (Chapter 17, Q7).

 How do I insert bias cording or commercial fringe?

- Make or buy the cording or fringe (directions are in basic sewing books). Baste along edge of needlework. Face cording (fringe) to center of fabric with raw edges facing outward (see Figure 15-8a).

FIGURE 15-8a

FIGURE 15–8b

- Baste second piece of fabric to stitchery, right sides together with cording (fringe) sandwiched between. The second basting should overlap the first.
- Machine stitch over basting lines. Cover all corners but leave side open where cording (fringe) ends meet. Remove bastings. Turn inside out. Insert stuffing or form being covered.
- Hand-stitch open side, allowing the cording (fringe) to form a large "X" where ends meet. Sew over center of 'X' (see Figure 15–8b). Trim away excess cording or fringe.

 5 **How do I cover edges without cording or fringe?**
Make lining slightly smaller than stitchery. When it's attached, stitchery will "roll over edges," making further edging unnecessary.

or

Stitch *Long-armed Cross, Binding Stitch, or Buttonhole* around needlework edge. Follow "roll over edges" directions above. Stitching will form the edge.

or

FIGURE 15–9

Crochet, macramé, braid or twist edgings from long strands of yarn which match or blend with stitchery colors. Sew over seams with small, invisible stitches (see Figure 15–9).

Directions for such edgings are included in books listed in Bibliography. Or simply braid yarn as you would a pigtail. Twists or braids require continuous strands of yarn from three to four times the length of the edging desired.

or

Do-It-Yourself **Fringe** is made by cutting pieces of yarn two and one-half times the depth of fringe desired. Fold one or more pieces in half. Pull loop through both sides of seam with a sharp crochet hook or large-eyed needle. Slip yarn ends through loop and pull closed. Position fringe regularly along seam, trimming even when completed.

How do I pad?

Place flat padding next to needlework back. Position interlining over padding. Cover with backing or lining (Chapter 17, Q7).

How do I interline?

Cut interlinings to fit the area *within* hemmed seam allowances (Chapter 19, Q10). Baste to back of stitchery. Cover with lining (Chapter 17, Q7).

Iron-on interlinings are easy and inexpensive but they won't allow your needlework to live to be an antique (Introduction). On embroideries with heavy stitching they sometimes fuse to the thread in spots, rather than to the cloth, producing peculiar-looking "bubbly" results.

CLOTH

How do I stitch embroidery?

With relaxed tension if the object is to be soft-mounted (Chapter 14, Definitions). Embroidery stitched tight on cloth under tension needs to be mounted under tension to remain flat. If your mounting will be soft, stay loose.

How do I hem cloth edges?

Complete stitching, block and miter corners. Turn cloth edges to the back and trim to between one-fourth and three-fourths of an inch (the thicker the material, the wider the seam allowance).

Fold raw edges under and attach seam allowances to back of stitchery with small, slanted, hemming stitches.

How do I line cloth?

Attach linings to embroidery following directions in Chapter 17, Q7. If you want to insert cording or commercial fringes while attaching linings, follow directions in Q4.

If embroidery should be backed to prevent distortion, follow directions in Chapter 20, Q4.

CANVAS

11 **How do I line canvas with raw edges?**
Read Chapter 17, Q7.

Conservation hint: Weave a few strands of each color yarn through back of needlepoint, to be there if future repairs call for them (Chapter 20, Q5).

12 **How do I double-stitch needlepoint?**
- Before stitching, draw a line five threads *inside* outer line. Stitch as usual up to this inner line (see Figure 15–10a). Don't compensate but work as close as you can get with whole stitches. This works particularly well on a frame.

FIGURE 15–10a

- Cut away excess canvas, five threads *beyond* outer line. Cut a square of five canvas threads from each corner (which will touch but not cut outer line corners).
- Fold canvas to back along outer line. Leave two canvas threads running along fold like railroad tracks (one inside the line, one outside it). Baste two canvas layers together, matching meshes.
- Complete stitching through both layers of canvas. "Railroad track" threads will remain unstitched (see Figure 15–10b).

FIGURE 15-10b

Note: Canvas worked double this way *cannot* be forcefully blocked. Therefore do all that you can (frames, gentle handling, straight stitches in place of diagonal) to keep canvas unwarped (see Figure 15–10c).

FIGURE 15-10c

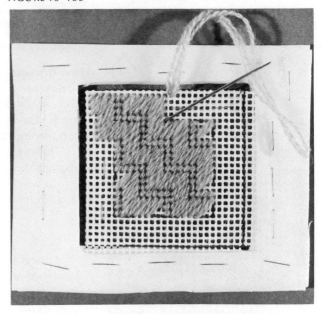

A gentle freshening (Chapter 14, Q10) can be of some help but won't correct severe distortion.

How do I line double-stitched needlepoint?

Fold under a seam allowance of one-fourth to three-eighths of an inch on lining. **Hem or whip to back of canvas,** leaving unstitched "railroad track" threads uncovered for subsequent construction (see Figure 15-11). You can stitch through both layers of holes along edge. Completely line all canvas segments *before* edging or attaching them to each other with *Long-armed-Cross, Gobelins,* or *Buttonhole* variations.

FIGURE 15-11

How do you join two pieces of canvas together?

Overlay raw edges by placing one piece of un-worked canvas upon another, matching five to eight threads. Baste together with large *Cross Stitches.* Stitch through both layers as if they were one.

This makes a good, strong junction, but if you're working *Continental* or *Basketweave* in a light color, the join will be subtly visible. Use a textured stitch or a medium to dark color and the join will disappear.

or

Splice raw edges. Unravel one-half to three-quarters of an inch on the double or mono-floating canvas piece to be attached. Use a crochet hook or large needle to pull each fringed thread through its corresponding hole in the other canvas (more than one thread can fit in a single hole if meshes are not of the same gauge—see Figure 15-12a).

FIGURE 15-12a

FIGURE 15–12b

Weave threads through the back of completed stitching or, if none is nearby, leave them on back to be caught by subsequent stitching (this can become a bit hairy). Baste both canvas layers together, matching meshes wherever possible. Stitch through both layers as if they were one.

Spliced joins are smoother and less noticeable than overlays and are equally strong. However, they're time-consuming.

or

Butt together double-stitched edges, side to side (Q12). Baste folded threads together with needle and thread *Cross Stitches,* matching mesh to mesh. Work stitchery over join as if it were not there (see Figure 15–12b).

This is the smoothest of the three joins, and is also the weakest. The slit is not backed by canvas and is held together only by yarn.

Matching two folded edges is like piling up drinking straws. They want to slip off each other and lodge in the holes between. Such a misalignment of canvas threads will be visible when stitched in light colors, so keep threads aligned by using *Cross-Stitch* bastings which tug in both directions, rather than straight or slanted bastings which will pull edges out of line. Or use a small, gold-colored safety pin every four to five threads to hold things together while you're working.

FIGURE 15–13

15 **How do you stabilize irregular canvas edges?**
If you're stitching a goldfish-shaped pillow, edges follow no predictable straight lines.

These are the situations in which interlock canvas "shines." Cut canvas, gather outer curves, clip inner curves and handle as you would cloth.

Floating canvas *will* fray. If you must use it, run a double line of machine stitching one thread beyond edge of finished needlepoint. Use a sharp machine needle and medium stitch. Squeeze a *thin* line of casein glue over machine stitching, being careful not to get any of the needlepoint (see Figure 15–13). Let glue dry. Baste, cut, clip and stitch *carefully,* keeping rumpling of canvas to a minimum.

FIGURE 15–14

How do I stitch and finish a ball or sphere?

- Find an atlas with a cut-orange-peel map of the world (see Figure 15–14). Trace and enlarge or shrink outline until its equator is slightly larger than the diameter of the sphere you're covering (styrofoam balls work well and are available in different sizes).

- Trace pattern on brown paper, cut and assemble with tape. Fuss with the pattern, trimming or adding to it until it forms a fairly respectable sphere. You don't need to insist on perfection at this stage, but seams should not gape. This step is the key, so allow enough time.

- Staple cloth or interlock canvas (14-gauge or finer) to a frame. Trace pattern lightly with pattern marking pen (Chapter 6, Q1). Add one-fourth-inch seam allowance to all curves, tapering where curves meet at equator. Stitch.

  Hint: Small, random, non-directional and allover stitching patterns work best for your first try. Horizontal stripes are also good.

- Cut out cloth or canvas, including seam allowances. Clip curves. Fold along tracing lines and baste seam allowances to needlework back.

- Whip all edges together inconspicuously. When globe is half-assembled, insert sphere. Continue assembly around inner ball.

- Dip assembled ball in water or spray well. (Dipping is preferable if the inner ball can stand the damp. Styrofoam can.) Blot and dry away from direct heat or light. Cloth and canvas will conform to the shape of the inner ball.

- Add hanging ribbons or any additional trims that you wish.

Such spheres can serve as World globes, Christmas tree ornaments, decorative balls for table accessories, or paper weights.

Half of such a globe, enlarged to correct size and cut at the equator, is a Juliet cap, beanie, or skull cap. Line with slightly smaller half-globe constructed of lining fabric. Trim equator edge.

16 Framing

FIGURE 16-1

I'm often asked to look at inherited needlework pictures. The stitcheries usually prove to be delightful, but their framing is generally dreadful. Most elderly needlework were mounted in the same sturdy way, one that unfortunately was all-too-common in the early part of this century. Here's how early framers earned their pay:

First find a slab of wood and make glue—a stew of cow hides and horses's hooves will do nicely. Slather goo on wood and push the needlework down into the mess until it's stiff as a corpse.

Then find a piece of glass and mash stitchery flat beneath it. Shove the whole sandwich into a girdle-tight frame whose back is sealed as snug as Fort Knox—in case a breath of fresh air might be tempted to sneak in.

Finally place the frame in the brightest possible sunlight so that everybody can *really see it.*

The results of such mountings are all-too-obvious today. Wool feels like Brillo and cloth is as brittle as burnt toast. What Grandma's dyes looked like back in '02 is anybody's guess—they haven't aged as gracefully as the lady herself. Stitchery-backs cannot be reached for study (which is just as well since, after all those years, wood and glue are probably all that's holding them together).

There's a lesson to be learned here: the glue pot is everybody's ticket to obscurity.

INTRODUCTION

There are five reasons to put needlework in a frame. The first is the most important: to protect it from dirt, wear and abrasion. But a frame also helps to focus the eye on the work's composition. It increases the visual size and importance of the needlework and serves as a transition between the stitchery and the wall behind it. And finally, framing can function as a problem-solver reinforcing important colors or shapes and helping to cure ailing compositions.

A frame ought to behave like a good actor's agent. It should allow what's being protected to be the star of the show. Don't let frames compete for attention.

Needlepoint and embroidery are framed similarly. The differences lie in the amount of tension needed to keep them from creeping out of shape, and the strength of materials used to accomplish this.

◆1◆ How do I protect my stitchery?

Framing has a great deal to do with the preservation of whatever's inside. It is unfortunate that, historically, many frames which were intended to protect stitcheries, have often contributed to their demise. Keep in mind the facts about acid-free papers in Preventive Medicine.

All textiles should live in equilibrium with the heat and humidity of air surrounding them. **Do not frame textiles in airtight containers that allow light to penetrate.** Sealed, glassed-in picture frames fit this description perfectly. Eliminate glass or, if such protection is necessary, cut holes in backings so that overheated air can escape. Be sure that holes in all backing layers line up with each other. Prevent the wall itself from restricting air-flow by attaching small, felt or cork spacers to the back of the frame.

You've heard that textiles have to "breathe." When framing needlework, this means coping with what is called the "greenhouse effect." Radiation and ultra-violet rays from the sun are able to penetrate clear glass or plastic. When they strike an object, they warm it, producing infra-red or heat rays. Infra-red can not pass through glass and gets trapped behind it.

The amount of air inside a sealed frame is very small and heats quickly. The higher the air temperature, the more moisture it can absorb from your needlework, dehydrating it. Every ten-degree rise in

FIGURE 16–2

temperature *doubles* the speed of oxidation. Fiber oxidation causes brittleness and "sun rot." Dye oxidation causes fading. You want to delay both of these as long as possible.

Where do I hang my needlework?

- **Hang stitcheries away from doors, fireplaces, and areas subject to rapid temperature changes** (Chapter 17, Q9). More dirt is deposited here than in more protected spots.

   Outer masonry walls with little or no insulation are notorious for "sweating" on their inner surfaces. If needlework is in direct contact with such a wall, it can become damp and susceptible to mildew.

- **Place framed stitcheries away from direct sunlight.** Don't light them with fluorescent picture-lamps or place them near grow-lights for plants.

   Daylight and fluorescent illumination are both rich in the ultra-violet rays that will eventually fade dyes and rot fibers. You can't completely eliminate such deterioration (unless you hang the picture in the dark); but you can certainly keep it in low gear with incandescent lighting and wise display.

FIGURE 16–3

How do I select a frame?

› Shape

When choosing a frame, keep in mind the therapeutic design facts listed in Chapter 3, Q9. Framing is an extension of your composition and the same rules apply to both.

   For example, vertical frames are more dynamic than restful, horizontal ones. Light green mats gently recede while bright orange ones charge toward you. There's no law that says that horizontal compositions have to live in horizontal frames. Place one in a larger, vertical frame and watch it acquire importance and dignity.

• Color

The colors of frames and fabric-covered mats should relate to colors within the stitchery. Be aware, however, that they will strengthen those identical colors within the needlework; so experiment with hues and tones or you may throw the whole composition off balance.

• Style

The more elaborate the needlework, the simpler the frame. Simple stitcheries can benefit from ornate frames.

The more dynamic the needlework, the stronger its frame must look to hold it all inside. You don't want your composition threatening to break out of its anemic-looking enclosure.

• Size

The smaller the needlework, the larger the frame you can choose. Very large stitcheries require comparatively inconspicuous frames.

• Proportions

Deep frames cast shadows. Shadows can dull or even obliterate stitchery texture (Chapter 3, Q10), and texture is the very element that distinguishes needleworks from other framed art. Let light reach stitches and define them.

What about do-it-yourself framing?
Anybody with ready-made frames or a tool bench and cheerful carpenter can make a frame. The only crucial element is straightness. Frames are, by definition, perfectly geometric objects. Everything inside had better be equally straight or needlework will seem to stagger drunkenly.

What materials will I need to frame my stitchery?

- A frame and a method for hanging it; mats, mounts and glass or sheet acrylic are optional.

- Mats make stitcheries appear larger and more important. They are good ways to bridge the gap between small needleworks and large frames.

- Traditionally most frames have been hung from screw eyes and wire attached to the frame back. New arrivals on the scene are gummed holders and sawtoothed metal plates. *Believe* weight restrictions when hanging any piece, and err, if you must, with too much rather than too little support.

- Acrylic is lighter in weight than glass. It scratches more easily and is more susceptible to heat (don't hang it over the stove), but it's easier to cut. It can break, but is generally safer to work with than glass. Both are equally guilty of admitting ultra-violet radiation.

When should I buy a frame?
Either before beginning or after completing the stitchery.

$ If you buy it before, you can stitch to fit, obtain the frame inexpensively, coordinate frame and stitchery colors, use frame to check straightness of blocking and mounting, and assemble final framing quickly.

If you buy it afterwards, you'll have the widest choice of frame styles available, and frame and mounting can be manipulated to solve design problems within the needlework. However, custom framing is *expensive!*

What should I look for when buying a frame?
Sturdiness, attractiveness, the right size rabbet edge, and a lip big enough to hide the stretcher, if you used one (see Figure 16–4).

Frames are designed to hold two types of art: thin prints of water colors and chunky, stretched canvases. A frame's rabbet edge should cover whatever's inside. Sometimes the same frame face will be available in two rabbet depths to cover both thick and thin.

FIGURE 16–4

What size frame should I buy?
Look for two sets of measurements: the outside dimensions and the size of the inner hole.

Outer dimensions should fit your taste, your wall, and be appropriate to your needlework (Q3). Inner dimensions of the hole are measured from lip to lip across the frame. This measurement should be one quarter of an inch less than the width or height of your finished needlework. Since the lip will hide an eighth of an inch of the stitchery's edge, you can see why blocking must be precise.

What's the difference between a mat and a mount?
A mat is a traditional divider between the frame and what's inside (see Figure 16–5). Thin cardboard mats don't work well with unglassed needleworks. Nothing holds them in place and, eventually, they curl or warp out of shape.

FIGURE 16–5

Stitchery mats must be firm enough to resist such buckling. Use flat, thin materials that can be shaped easily.

Such flat mats are held to the frame by squeezing between rabbet lip and needlework, or by gluing to the frame's lip before inserting stitchery.

Alternatives to stiff mats are appliquéd ones. Cloth can be sewed over canvas or cloth to bridge the gap between stitchery and frame edge. Try ribbons, calico, leather or velvets.

Hint: Gingham is delightful to look at but a pain to mat. Every line must exactly parallel the frame, and all wiggles show.

Mounts are three-dimensional frames-within-frames. They have molded faces and their sides fit inside the rabbet edges of outer frames. Mounts are usually shallower than outer frames, leading the eye down into the needlework inside.

Wooden mounts should be sealed wherever they touch needlework (Preventive Medicine).

 Do I need a mat?

Yes, if a frame is too large for the stitchery, if stretcher strip edges aren't covered by the frame's lips, if you want to make needlework look larger or more important, or if you want to change the needlework's basic shape (for example, mount a square stitchery in a round frame).

 How do I make a mat?

- Obtain a sheet of ¼-inch mat board, thin wood, white core board, acrylic sheet, ³/₁₆-inch *Upsom* board, mirror, or—if this isn't for the ages—a meat tray from the butcher's. Cut mat an eighth of an inch smaller than the measurement from one rabbet's edge to the other.

- Cut window inside mat one-fourth inch smaller than width and height of your needlework (see Figure 16–6). Use a sharp mat or *Exacto* knife, or a one-edged razor blade—carefully. Smooth edges if necessary.

FIGURE 16–6

How do I cover a mat with cloth?

- You'll need the cut mat; white, casein glue; cloth two inches longer and wider than mat; sharp scissors or knife (mat or *Exacto*); ruler and hard pencil.
- Place cloth (ironed if necessary) face down on waxed paper. Cover mat's front with a thin layer of glue, brushed evenly so that it doesn't puddle. Lightly press mat to cloth—glue side down. Center carefully and *don't* squash or glue will be forced through cloth to the front, leaving spots. Turn face up to check straightness of cloth grain. Dry face down under a weight.
- Trim away cloth flush with *outside* mat edge. Use pencil to draw lightly on wrong side of cloth through mat window. Lines should start at each corner and move inward at a 45° angle. Connect intersections with a straight line. Carefully cut cloth along lines, stopping one-fourth inch before you reach mat corners.
- Brush glue lightly over back of mat. Carefully fold cuts over inner window edges (see Figure 16–6). Press to glue (if necessary attach with masking tape until dry). Check edges for wrinkles and straighten cloth grain while glue is still wet. If corners aren't cut closely enough, trim *carefully* (you can always cut closer but can't reweave if you cut too far). Reinforce cut on back with a *little* glue (Chapter 15, Consumer Information). Dry right-side-up, under a weight.

How do I make a padded mat?

Cut padding (usually quilt batting) to fit mat. Cover with cloth as in Q12. Fold and glue outer and inner edges of cloth to *back* of mat only. Glued cloth holds padding in place.

How do I stiffen needlework for framing?

First block perfectly (Chapter 14), bearing in mind that the larger the needlework, the more pull will be exerted on it and the stronger its stiffening must be.

Where stitchery touches acid-producers (Preventive Medicine, p. xiii), seal all wood or cover cardboard with heavy-duty aluminum foil and re-cover with washed cloth. Miter corners neatly—you don't want lumps. Insert quilt batting between foil and cloth if you want to pad stitchery.

Needlepoint

Needlepoint can be stretched on artists' stretcher strips; or stiffener sheets of masonite, peg board or thin plywood, sealed or covered with aluminum foil and washed cloth.

STRETCHER STRIPS

Cut or buy stretcher strips three-eights of an inch smaller than the measurements between your frame's rabbet edges.

- Assemble stretcher following specific directions for your brand. Reinforce with flat "corner irons" (L-braces) or glue. Check squareness with a T-square or right angle.
- Center the stretcher over needlepoint. Canvas should be at least three inches longer and wider than stretcher. Mark centers of canvas and stretcher sides. Thumbtack canvas centers to stretcher centers.
- Remove top thumb tack. Fold canvas over stretcher and staple diagonally into its *side* (see Figure 16-7).

FIGURE 16-7

- Remove three remaining thumbtacks. Pull canvas from top staple to bottom center, using upholstery stretching tool or artists' canvas stretcher. Staple bottom center. Stretch and staple left and right sides.
- Staple two inches to left of top and bottom centers. Repeat two inches to right. Repeat along left and right sides. Continue stapling toward corners, pulling canvas taut and placing staples two inches apart into stretcher sides.
- Fold excess canvas at corner into triangle. Crease. Fold to short end of frame and staple in place. Trim excess canvas flush with back of stretcher.

Embroidery

Embroidery stiffeners can be ¼-inch *Upsom* board, white surfaced coreboard, *Celotex,* ceiling tiles or heavy cardboard. Cut them three-eights of an inch smaller than frame measurements between rabbet edges (Preventive Medicine).

- Finish all stitchery sides with one-half inch hems. Mark centers of four sides on stiffener and on needlework. Match centers and temporarily attach needlework to stiffener with pins or tacks pushed into stiffener's sides (see Figure 16–8).

FIGURE 16–8

- Remove top and bottom pins. Lace top center to bottom center tautly, sewing one-fourth to three-eighths inch inside hemmed edges through both layers of fold. Pull tight, knot and cut thread.

- Remove side pins and lace side centers. Check appearance of stitchery's front and adjust lacings if necessary. Miter corners.

- Use long thread to begin lacing from the right of top center to the right of bottom center, working toward right corners. All stitches should be one-fourth to three-eighths inch apart. Work through both layers of fold with equal tension. Knot and cut at corner.

- Use new thread to lace left side. Knot and cut. Turn stiffener a quarter turn. Lace left half and then right half. Check appearance of stitchery's front and adjust lacings if necessary. Check against frame, if you have one, to make alignment perfect.

    Advantages to this method are that you've done nothing irreversible. All material still remains on the back in case you want to reblock or sew it into a pillow. Laces will contract and expand with atmospheric conditions, in equilibrium with the stitchery.

What about "press-on" mounting boards?

These are stiffeners with a sticky surface that holds needlework in place while it's being framed. They're *not* for heirlooms, at least not yet. However they work and they're easy to use.

    Such "press-on" boards are more expensive than traditional methods. Furthermore, their sticky chemicals will probably break down sometime in the future, doing unpredictable kinds of damage to fibers or to dyes.

How do I assemble a frame?

- Place frame upside down on a soft surface (see Figure 16–9a). Insert glass or acrylic if you wish (Q1). Cut glass one-eighth inch smaller than frame and be sure it's clean on side next to embroidery. Place one-fourth to one-half inch

FIGURE 16-9a

spacers (small pieces of cloth-covered card-board or wood) along center edges between glass and whatever layer comes next to prevent layers from touching.

Avoid non-glare glass like the plague. It's more expensive than plain glass and, unless needlework is pressed tight against it, will blur and distort what you're displaying.

Remember to let air reach stitchery, through the back if necessary (Q1).

FIGURE 16-9b

- If you wish, insert mat or mount, face down into frame's rabbet.

- Place stretched or stiffened needlework so that it touches only protected wood or cardboard. Hold in place with half inch headless brads pressed into rabbet every four inches (see Figure 16-9b). Press brads with side of pliers and be careful not to shove so hard that you go through the frame into your thumb.

- Cover the back—unless glass is used—to keep insects out. Cut brown wrapping paper one inch larger than frame in all directions. Wet thoroughly and drain. Place thin line of casein glue along back of frame. Press damp paper over glue. Smooth and allow to dry. Paper will shrink and straighten beautifully (see Figure 16-9c). Trim excess paper, using one-edged razor blade or a mat knife.

FIGURE 16-9c

If glass was used, cut holes in all backings so that overheated air can escape. Separate frame back from wall with small foam or cork spacers glued to frame back.

17 › What if my rabbet edge is the same depth as my stretcher frame?

You're lucky! Attach the frame with four to eight 'I' shaped pieces of flat metal called "plates." "Turn buttons" are similar metal clips, available from framers. Screw metal into frame back and pivot the other side over the stretcher to hold it firm. Do not screw into stretcher—it would probably split.

18 › What if my rabbet edge is deeper than my stretcher frame?

Attach with **"offset" (or mirror) clips** which come in various sizes. Find those which will fit your measurements. Screw into back of frame, letting clips project behind stretcher to hold it (see Figure 16-10).

Should dimensions not fit any clip that's available to you, choose one that's a little too small. Raise it by placing one or more sheets of cardboard or wood beneath the clip until the right fit is achieved. Screw into frame's back.

FIGURE 16-10

19 › What if my rabbet edge is shallower than my stretcher frame?

This is the worst-looking solution of the three. Attach with **offset clips,** following the directions in Q18 (see Figure 16-11). The protruding stretcher can be made less obvious by painting it with black paint before hanging.

FIGURE 16-11

All three stretcher mountings have in common easy access. Frames can be removed and replaced by a simple twist of metal clips.

 How do I hang a heavy frame?

Any frame containing glass is considered to be "heavy." Attach small screw eyes to both bottom corners of frame (see Figure 16–12). Attach two screw eyes along each side, about two-thirds of the way up. Attach wire by firmly attaching to bottom screw eye, running it through side eyes above, across to second set of side eyes, and down to second bottom eye where wire is twisted and attached. This method supports heavy weights and holds the frame together.

Nail picture hangers chosen for Correct Load Capacity into wall if load is light, and into studs if load is heavy. If in doubt, hang picture from two hooks—it will hang straighter and be safer than with one.

FIGURE 16–12

 What about needlework trays?

They're frames used horizontally and therefore are subjected to different stresses from frames hung on a wall. Corners should be reinforced. When glass or acrylic is used to protect the stitched insert, seal to tray frame so that spilled liquids won't ooze over the edge and stain stitchery.

Use clear silicone sealant—available from plumbing or hardware stores. It remains flexible, is water repellent, and should *never* be allowed to touch embroidery. Otherwise, all facts pertaining to strong frames apply to trays.

UNUSUAL
PROJECTS

Stitching large needle projects is like eating arti-
chokes: time-consuming, lots of work, and not for
everybody. Large projects take persistence and plenty
of space, time, and materials. They're not the place
for the average, garden-variety beginner to start.
Discouragement is too easy to come by.

But if you're determined to conquer Mt. Ever-
est, nothing less will do. In Chapter 17 you'll dis-
cover the whys and wherefores of wall hangings.
You'll learn to design, stitch, line and mount them;
and where they should—and shouldn't—hang.

Upholstery has always fascinated needleworkers.
If your dream is a crewel-worked Chippendale sofa,
Chapter 18 will be for you. Specific subjects include
designing right on the furniture, choosing and getting
good results from an upholsterer, and learning which
stitches will—and won't—wear well on your wing
chair.

Needlepoint rugs present their own special
questions and Chapter 19 gives the answers. You'll
learn how to stitch large rugs on small frames, how
to block so that canvas creep won't come to call,
and how to assemble all those little pieces so that
the final rug is perfect.

The preservation of Great Aunt Bertha's samp-
ler, or Mother's ottoman cover, can be a delightful
experience and a labor of love—or it can be the
worst mess you ever got yourself into. Chapter 20
tells you what to do to antique textiles and, per-
haps more important, what you can't do to them.
You'll learn how to clean, repair, support, and dis-
play your treasures from the past.

Large and unusual projects present large and
unusual challenges, and they give gigantic satisfac-
tions. Open heart surgery and needlepoint rugs are

not everybody's cups of tea, but for those with the dream—and the determination—there's nothing to equal them.

17 Wall Hangings

FIGURE 17-1

One of my favorite students, Sarah, was from the state of Maine and proud of it. One long-ago summer she'd bought a needlepoint kit for a bell pull featuring pine trees and the Portland Lighthouse, and she couldn't wait to get started.

Unfortunately Sarah had yet to discover the blessings of *Basketweave*. *Continental* stitching progressed resolutely, with every stitch yanked nice and tight.

By the time the Portland Light came to class, it was hanging at an impossible angle. Colors were bright and design was delightful, but it looked the proof of the law of gravity's repeal.

That bell pull became our class's blocking project—if it could come straight, anything could. We blocked and reblocked and interlined and put weights in the bottom.

I wouldn't say that it ended up absolutely vertical, but at least now it's recognizable as a bell pull. It lives in Sarah's front hall to this day—a New England version of the Leaning Tower of Pisa.

INTRODUCTION

A piece of needlework hung on a wall within a frame is a picture. The same needlework displayed on the same wall without its frame is called a "wall hanging." Hangings can be stitched using any and all types of needlework: Examples are bell pulls, valances, banners and curtains.

Wall hangings should be lined for protection against gravity, damp and dirty walls, and, with curtains, valances and lambrequins, the ultra-violet rays

223

of the sun. Linings also hide needlework backs—which is usually a blessing for everyone concerned.

Hangings can be mounted in two ways: loose or stretched. Examples of loose mounts are curtains, banners and bell pulls. They drape softly, supported only from the top.

Stretched needleworks are supported on two or four sides over a rigid frame. Hangings stretched to their fullest dimensions give the effect of unframed pictures. Examples are folding screens, lambrequins and valances.

Sunlight and gravity pose more threats to wall hangings than flexing, friction and wear do. These stitcheries usually hang parallel to windows and are exposed to large volumes of sunlight which accelerates ultra-violet fading and rotting (Chapter 20, Q6). Vertical display also produces sagging as vertical threads stretch over long periods of time. Wise choices of materials, display areas, and lining and finishing techniques can delay fading and sagging, though they cannot totally prevent them.

FIGURE 17-2

 How do I design a wall hanging?
Follow directions in Chapter 3. The basic problems and processes are the same as for any needlework project—only the size is different.

Hint: Before buying anything, take your design to a photostat firm (located under "Blue Prints" in the Yellow Pages) and have them make an *exact size* copy of the proposed hanging. Color it and tape to the wall where it will live (see Figure 17–2).

Coexist with the design for a while. Large wall hangings dramatically change the feel of a room in ways that are hard to predict. Be sure that you'll be happy with the finished product before you invest time and money in it.

 How much of which materials should I buy?
Buy three extra inches of cloth or canvas on all four sides of hanging.

Cloth stretches most from selvage to selvage. Canvas stretches parallel to its selvages. Whenever possible, position your hanging's cloth with selvages running north to south, and canvas with selvages running east to west. Gravity will have less slack to pull on, and less sagging will develop over the years.

How much thread or yarn you'll need depends on your type of needlework. Fill out Volume Chart for Needlepoint. Fill out Volume Chart on for Counted Thread. Follow directions on for Embroidery.

③ Now that I have the design, how do I transfer it to cloth or canvas?

Follow directions in Chapter 7, Q12, 23. This project is no different from something smaller—there's just more of it. Try using the light table arrangement that puts glass over a slit in the dining room table.

④ How do I stitch it?

You'll have no problem with embroidery. **Put cloth in hoops** as directed in Chapter 7, Q14 and stitch. The larger the hanging, the more it's likely to get soiled, so be as careful as you can. Pillow cases are good protectors between stitching sessions.

With **needlepoint, wall hangings should be worked on a frame** so that Canvas Creep and gravity won't pull things out of shape in years to come.

If the project's not too big, you can stretch it on a large stretcher frame. This becomes impractical when the hanging is so wide that you can't comfortably stitch its middle.

FIGURE 17-3

At this point, work on a Tack Frame as illustrated in Chapter 19, Q7. Be sure (after you've started) to include one and one-half inches of completed needlepoint within the frame every time you move to a new area.

Roller frames are less effective than Tack Frames for stitching large wall hangings. They only provide two-way stretch, and rolling flattens stitch texture while producing uneven pull on the canvas yet to be stitched.

Hint: Loop leftover yarn from each dye lot through stitchery's back after blocking, and before lining. This will come in mighty handy if repairs ever need to be made.

Now that it's stitched, how do I block it?

With needlepoint, follow directions for blocking one-piece rugs in Chapter 19, Q8. With embroidery, follow directions in Chapter 14, Q21.

How do I sew panels together?

- If they're needlepoint, attach them to each other following directions in Chapter 15, Q14.
- If they're embroidery, sew them by hand or by machine. Press seam open. If you use a machine, be sure that its feed dogs move top and bottom layers equally, or your seam will wrinkle. Stitch all seams in the same direction (for example, from top to bottom).

Be aware that seams are the weakest parts of a wall hanging and the most susceptible to sagging. Check them often, and promptly repair any slits.

What lining should I use and how should I attach it?

An acceptable **lining should be of approximately the same density and weight as the stitchery.** (In other words, don't line needlepoint with organdy.) It must be cleanable by the method you will use for the hanging. If it will be washed, it should be preshrunk. It ought to be woven from a fiber that resists moisture and dirt especially if it will be hung on a masonry or outside wall. If it's to be hung at a window its fiber should be resistant to ultra-violet rotting (see Fiber Characteristic Chart, p. 137).

All canvas and cloth selvages should be cut off before lining. Casings for rods are machine stitched to linings *before* linings are attached to hangings.

Embroidery

- Finish bottom edge of wall hanging.
- Cut lining three inches narrower and two inches longer than hanging (see Figure 17–4). With right sides facing, center lining over needlework with top edges together. Place a strip of

FIGURE 17-4

buckram or pellon along top edge. Machine stitch along top edge, through the three layers, leaving one-half inch seam allowance.

- Turn lining and hanging so that wrong sides are together and press top seam. Turn under one-quarter inch along wall hanging's sides and press. Fold hanging to back and loosely tack to lining by hand. Make stitches inconspicuous.

- Turn up lining hem at bottom until fold is one-half inch above hanging's finished edge. Stitch hem, which will not be attached to needlework, at bottom edge.

  If hanging is loosely woven or liable to sag, this is the time to attach lining to it over its entire back for reinforcement. Directions are found in Chapter 20, Q4.

Needlepoint

- Trim excess canvas and hem sides, following directions in Chapter 19, Q10.

- Cut lining one inch wider and three inches longer than the finished wall hanging. Machine-stitch to top, turn, press and turn under lining sides. Tack to hanging by hand, making stitches inconspicuous and at least an inch apart. Continue lining process, following directions for embroidery above.

How do I hang it?

Loose Hanging

Machine-sew casing of twill tape, lining material or unbleached muslin to lining before attaching it as directed in Q7. Insert a rod through casing (see Figure 17–5a). Hang rods or dowels from wall brackets mounted beyond hanging's sides, or attach decorative cords or chains which can hang straight down from two points above, or in a triangle from one point.

FIGURE 17–5a

Attach finials, glue buttons or tack tassels to rod ends if you wish further decoration.

or

Pin loops of ribbon, tape or cloth—bottoms up—along top seam between lining and hanging (see Figure 17–5b). Stitch. Turn, complete lining and remove pins. **Insert decorative bar through loops** and hang as directed in "Casing."

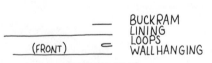

BUCKRAM
LINING
LOOPS
(FRONT)   WALLHANGING

FIGURE 17–5b

or

Hand-sew the "soft" side of Velcro strip to wall hanging top. Staple the "rough" half to a wooden strip. **Attach Velcro** halves and hang strip as directed in "Casing."

The entire weight of a loose wall hanging is supported by its top. **Distribute weight as evenly as possible by having many points of attachment,** not just a few (see Figure 17–5c). Avoid tacks, nails, staples and other sharp attachments which can do great damage—quickly.

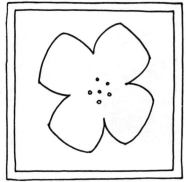

FIGURE 17-5c

Stretched Hanging

Obtain a piece of plywood or strong artists' stretcher frame one inch taller and wider than the wall hanging. Neatly wrap wood with washed cloth (old sheets are good), colored to blend with hanging and the wall behind it. Miter cloth corners neatly and fasten to back of wood with staples or rust-proof upholstery tacks.

Center and staple "rough" halves of two Velcro strips cut the width of the hanging, at top and bottom of wood. Hand stitch "soft" halves to top and bottom of wall hanging. Attach Velcro halves, stretching and supporting wall hanging. Velcro can also be attached to sides if necessary. Hang as you would a heavy picture (Chapter 16, Q20).

Be sure that the distance between Velcro strips is identical on wood and wall hanging. If placement of strips on wood stretches hanging too taut, it will be subjected to severe strain—and probably be damaged. If they don't stretch hanging enough, it will sag.

or

Hand stitch wall hanging to pre-shrunk neutral-colored linen or other firmly woven cloth. Match straight of both grains. Turn cloth over, wrong side up, and center plywood or stretcher frame over it. Wrap wood in cloth, keeping straight of cloth's grain parallel to straight wooden edges. Carefully miter corners. Staple cloth to back of wood. Hand stitch a lining over back of wood if you wish, though this is purely cosmetic. Hang as you would a picture.

FIGURE 17-6

For a padded look, insert polyester quilt batting between cloth and wood before wrapping. This gives a softer feel to the display.

9 **How can I preserve my wall hanging now that it's done?**

- **Don't hang it directly across from a window** if you can possibly avoid it. If you must use such a wall, consider shades or drawn curtains when no one is in the room.
- Keep the hanging away from active fireplaces, radiators and air conditioners where dirt is attracted (see Figure 17–6). Place where it won't rub against window sills, chair rails or furniture.
- Don't hang in narrow passages where people will brush against it. If the hanging's placed behind furniture, keep it high enough, or far enough behind, so that heads with hair oils and hair sprays won't lean against it.
- When you're away from home for long periods, cover the hanging with a sheet so that light can't reach it. Old fashioned dust covers weren't such a bad idea.

10 **How do I clean my wall hanging?**
Vacuum once a month through nylon or fiberglass screening as directed in Chapter 20, Q1. Wall hangings are exposed to dust, nicotine and wood smoke, cooking fats and dirt from walls and windows. Vacuum the back as well as the front, for that's where insects hide and lay their eggs. Read Chapter 20, Q1 for further cleaning directions.

11 **If moths attack or rips develop, what should I do?**
Read Chapter 20 for specific remedies for specific ills. If you've looped excess yarns through the hanging's back as recommended in Q4, you'll have the right yarn and dye lots to do a perfect repair job. Otherwise buy the best equivalents you can find, both in color and yarn thickness.

If yarns don't quite match, and they probably won't, read Chapter 19, Q13.

18 Upholstery

FIGURE 18-1

A friend of Mother's spent years stitching crewel upholstery for a Chippendale wing chair. It was one of those projects that seemed destined to last through The Ages.

But even The Ages come to an end and the chair was finished. I was sixteen at the time and was invited to a grownup dinner party celebrating the Event. Mother even allowed me to wear lipstick and (slightly) high heels; I felt like an adult!

The party began with cocktails, which I wasn't allowed to drink, and conversation, which I didn't understand. Being an adult obviously wasn't all it was cracked up to be. I concentrated on trying to keep my stomach from growling.

The buffet was served—finally. I wobbled into the dining room on my high heels, piled a plate sky high, and tried to balance the food and me simultaneously.

The juggling act worked until I hit the living room. There my quivering tomato aspic started to glide, flew into a half gainer and landed smack on the seat of the crewel armchair. It slid to a halt in the middle of a Jacobean leaf, oozing red around the edges. I stood petrified.

Our hostess appeared faster than I'd ever seen a grownup move. In no time at all, aspic was scooped up, seat was out of chair, and the whole party was squeezed into the bathroom discussing various cleaning methods. Nobody looked at me. Nobody talked to me. I wanted to die.

I have no memory of how, or even if, that crewel was cleaned. I can only recall seeing the chair once more—long after I was safely married. There seemed to be a lot more leaves on its seat than I remembered.

FIGURE 18-2

INTRODUCTION

The most common mistake needleworkers make when stitching upholstery is to make the piece too small (see Figure 18–2). A knife-edged cushion, to appear ten inches square, should contain one and one-half inches for the "crown" of the stuffing. Such stitchery needs to be worked approximately eleven and one-half inches square to achieve the appearance of ten inches.

Upholstered furniture needs a border of one and a half inches of additional fabric around each cloth segment, regardless of whether it's worked needlepoint or embroidered cloth. A little waste has to be allowed or the upholsterer will labor under handicaps that can affect the final appearance of your needlework.

OLD UPHOLSTERY

Recycling

Canvas and cloth tend to deteriorate before woolen threads do. They become brittle, dehydrated, and unable to absorb the water that formerly made them strong. They usually need support to keep from breaking.

Many of cellulose's long, molecular chains will oxidize over the years and break into simple sugar molecules. Some of these sugars actually dissolve in water. If extreme crispness indicates advanced oxidation, **do not wet** the fabric or it may disintegrate.

It is difficult and often impossible to remove old needlework from furniture, clean and block it, and return it to its former place. Slight shrinking or shifting will prevent edges and corners from realigning. Two solutions are possible.

If needlework has aesthetic, historic or emotional importance, remove it from furniture, clean and perhaps block it—keeping in mind its state of preservation—and frame it using techniques in Chapter 20, Q6. Such display will allow the needlework to be enjoyed while protecting it from flexing, abrasion and further wear.

Most upholstery workshops are busy places. If you want that piece of needlework saved, remove it yourself at home. Heirlooms have been thrown out because somebody didn't know, or forgot, that you wanted them saved.

or

FIGURE 18-3

If this upholstery is important to its piece of furniture, turn the whole thing upside down. Remove webbing, springs and stuffing *from the bottom* (see Figure 18-3). Leave the needlework in place. Back it by hand, using techniques in Chapter 20, Q4. Stuff the interior with good quality foam padding and replace webbing. The padding will adjust to needlework's contours and will allow the furniture to be sat upon. However, a word of . . .

Warning: If needlework is so fragile that this technique is advisable, it's too delicate for everyday use. The piece is FOR SHOW ONLY.

NEW UPHOLSTERY

① How do I design?

Upholstered Furniture

Cut brown wrapping or white shelf paper to fit pattern, and tape to the piece of furniture. Trim to fit approximately. Follow directions in Chapter 3, sketching overall designs on paper cover, and positioning them appropriately. Work out details on separate sheets of tracing paper. Color paper pattern with crayons to judge color placement and the overall effect.

Transfer designs to cloth or canvas, using techniques in Chapter 7, Q12, 23. Insert details from tracing paper wherever they fit into overall design.

Blocked Cushions and Pillows

FIGURE 18-4

It's better to stitch top and sides in one cross-shaped piece (see Figure 18-4) than to join tops and edges with cording, which wears, soils and can shift noticeably.

Borders are best positioned slightly inside edges and corners. If needlework stretches or shifts during upholstery, such a border won't be swallowed up in the seam allowance.

 ## How do I make a pattern for upholstered furniture?

- **Don't if you're not trained.** Have the upholsterer you'll be using cut and fit the entire job on your ground fabric, if you'll stitch embroidery, or on unbleached muslin or old sheets if you're needlepointing. The upholsterer should mark seam lines on embroidery fabric with chalk—which you will overbaste with thread before it brushes away. Muslin or sheeting for needlepoint can be marked with anything permanent since its function is to communicate and not to decorate.

    The top of each piece should be clearly marked so that you and the upholsterer both know which end is up. It's vital to be consistent and to agree with such markings.

    Although you must be prepared to pay such an upholsterer for his labor, a good pattern will make your work much easier and your finished product worth all the effort.

FIGURE 18-5

- An alternative to cloth patterns is to remove present upholstery and use it as a guide. As you cut, add one and a half inches for seam allowances. The advantages are time and money saved. The disadvantage is that nude furniture is out of action until you've finished the needlework.

What materials and stitches should I use?

- **Cloth** should be firmly woven of fibers that do not attract soil (Fiber Characteristics Chart, p. 137). It need not be pre-washed or shrunk. Do not use knitted fabrics.
- **Canvas** gauges normally used run from double's 10/20 to mono-floating's 18. Interlock canvas is not recommended for upholstery because its abrasive texture wears yarns prematurely. Mono-floating 14 is a good gauge to try if you're in doubt. **Buy the best quality canvas available** (Chapter 9, Q3).
- Overall **canvas direction** should be determined by the shape of the furniture to be covered. Floating canvas stretches more parallel to selvages than it does from side to side. Since you want the least stretch possible, canvas should be positioned whenever possible with its stretchiest direction running across the furniture's *shortest* dimension (see Figure 18–6).

  Example: a camelback sofa would have all canvas selvages running from top to bottom; a tall, wing chair would have them running from side to side.

  Once overall canvas direction has been determined, *all* canvas pieces should be positioned the same way.
- **Stitches** chosen for any area of upholstery should be appropriate to the amount of abrasion that area will receive. On arms, seats, and backs, avoid long stitches (*Gobelins*, long *Satin*), loose stitches (*Flat*, laid work), and highly textured stitches (*Double Straight Cross, French Knots*). Use these on sides, reverse, and skirts where they won't be rubbed.

FIGURE 18–6

- **Threads** and fibers should be chosen for their dry strength, resilience, resistance to abrasion, and resistance to soil. Check the Fiber Characteristics Chart.

 How do I stitch upholstery?

Embroidery

Read Chapter 7, Q17. **Pad inner hoops** to reduce creasing and release hoop tension each time you stop stitching. Keep the embroidery clean by using a clean cloth "holder" between hoop and hand.

Needlepoint

Work on a frame if at all possible. *Canvas-creep* can cause future distortion and should be avoided. Work stitches from an empty hole to a hole containing yarn, as directed in Chapter 7, Q7. This will insure that you have as much yarn on the canvas back as you have on the front—a necessity for good wearability.

 How do I block?

Embroidery

Follow directions in Chapter 14, Q21. Be sure that all vertical and horizontal cloth threads lie parallel to the grid on your blocking board.

Needlepoint

Follow directions for Stretch-Blocking in Chapter 14, Q12. Check against upholsterer's pattern before allowing canvas to dry.

In both cases, now is the time to put samples of all yarn and thread colors away in a safe place to be used for (Heaven forbid!) repairs.

What should I know about upholstering?

- Upholsterers may not want needlework blocked before they apply it, or they may want to block it themselves, or they may want you to block it. Determine which method will be used and what it will cost before committing yourself.

  Unblocked needlework is soaked and applied wet to furniture. If put on correctly, it dries straight in place. In such cases it's absolutely essential that *all* dyes, inks and paints be proved *waterproof* (Chapter 6, Q1).

- Upholsterers stitch, staple, or glue seams. You should insist on stitching.

- Staples and tacks for *edges* should be sharp. Not all brands are (see Figure 18–7). Blunt staples can snag embroidery threads and pull them out of shape. This wouldn't make much difference with a polypropylene plaid job, but it will with yours. Specify *sharp*.

- Keep the use of glue as minimal as possible. A little will be necessary. As some glues age, they can release chemicals which will deteriorate fibers and dyes before their time.

FIGURE 18-7

How do I locate a good upholsterer?

- Visit local needlework guilds and ask everybody you meet. Local patterns of excellence, and avoidance, will emerge.

- **Visit the workshop.** Ask to see needlework in progress if possible. Check on upholstering tips listed in Q6. Ask for references whose work has been in the same medium (crewel, needlepoint) as yours. Arrange to see these pieces and talk with their owners. If the upholsterer has never worked on a project like yours, keep on hunting.

- Gauge the upholsterers' responses to you (see Figure 18–8). Do they act as if you're a bubblehead trying to tell them how to run their job? Exit quickly. They should appreciate the time and effort you'll be putting into this project and work *with* you to achieve perfection.

FIGURE 18-8

All of this checking will take time, but so will your needlework. Careful and meticulous craftspeople *do* exist; it's well worth your efforts to locate one.

8 How do I preserve my needlework upholstery?

- Place it away from working fireplaces, radiators, and air conditioners, all of which attract dirt. **Keep it out of direct sunlight,** never positioning it in front of a window. Draw shades or curtains when the room isn't in use.
- Don't spray water repellents, do-it-yourself dry cleaners or other non-removable chemicals on needlework. Don't let it rub against woodwork, walls, or other furniture.
- When you're away from home for long periods, cover it with a sheet to keep dust and sunlight away. Keep the cat off, if at all possible.

9 How do I clean my needlework upholstery?

Follow directions in Chapter 13. **Move quickly**—the sooner you conquer stains, the less chance they have of moving in permanently.

First blot up liquid spills *immediately* and then sponge them with clear water only. Blot with a terry towel weighted with a book (see Figure 18–9). Leave for three to four hours. If stains don't disappear with this treatment, GET A PROFESSIONAL. The job is beyond your abilities.

FIGURE 18–9

Vacuum often through nylon or fiberglass screening as directed in Chapter 20, Q1. Most of your soil will come from air-borne dust.

Try to keep dogs, cats, unwashed kids and the newspaper off this particular furniture. Newspaper ink rubs off and is murder to remove.

10 How do I repair cuts or bruises to my upholstery?

Take express yarn or thread that you stored away when this project was finished and use it to follow directions in Chapter 20 for reconstructing your particular type of damage.

If no threads were put aside, purchase the nearest you can find to what was used in the original.

FIGURE 18-10

11 **Can I spray with soil-repellent sprays?**

These sprays repel liquids, not dirt, and are capable of doing a great deal more harm than good (Chapter 13, Q11). They should not be used on your needlework, with one exception: embroidered dining room chair seats that have been tested for colorfastness to the particular brand of spray you'll be using. No yarn covers the ground cloth, and it's probably in more danger from gravy and French dressing than it is from the spray.

19 Rugs

FIGURE 19-1

Long ago I volunteered to stitch one segment of a "magnificent" needlepoint rug destined to be auctioned for charity by a group I belonged to. Since we were all hooked on stitching, the rug seemed an inspired idea . . .

until painted canvases were handed out. Scenes were of the area we lived in, worked like old Delft tiles, in six tones of soft blue and white. It was instantly obvious that you couldn't tell Delft Blue paint #4 from Blue #6 and as for #5, forget it! Twenty of us squared our shoulders, squinted our eyes and set forth to do battle.

And battle it was! I grew to hate that thing with a loathing I didn't know I was capable of, but—eventually—it crept to an end. I handed it in with Hallelujahs!

My canvas had been worked on a frame and might have had a misplaced blue or two, but at least it was square. Others that I spotted were not so fortunate. Whoever was destined to straighten them up was in for a headache.

The shop assistant who got stuck with the job had never blocked anything remotely like it. Since no two segments were the same shape, blocking them became a nightmare and joining them was even worse. Ultimately the whole six-by-eight-foot rug had to be blocked again.

Nobody knew where to do it. Ping pong tables weren't big enough. Hardwood floors were too pretty. Finally the head honcho found a small storage closet with a beaten up floor and the blocker was ordered to stretch the rug there. Where she was to stand while accomplishing this miracle was never made clear. So she stapled, and yanked, and slogged over wet needlepoint, and bashed her toes. Finally she quit.

The last I saw that rug it was on a wall at auction with its straight lines rippling like ocean waves. That was years ago. It must look like a typhoon by now.

INTRODUCTION

A rug is meant to be placed horizontally on a floor. If hung vertically on a wall, the same piece of needlework is subjected to different stresses, and is called a "wall hanging" (Chapter 17).

In any rug, irregularities or high points tend to get more wear than even surfaces. These are the first places to catch dirty feet as they descend. Be aware of future peaks and valleys in a rug's contour as you contemplate its design. They'll determine how well it will wear.

Embroidered Rugs

Embroidered rugs should be worked on firmly woven linen or cotton. Burlap, composed of jute fibers, is weak to begin with and grows weaker when exposed to sunlight and moisture. It's not recommended for good needlework since the seeds of its destruction already exist within it.

One of the most successful rug embroidery stitches is *Chain*, worked with heavy yarns; but such rugs are not stitched often. Although embroidered rugs are beautiful, they don't have a consistent layer of hard-wearing wool covering the base fabric and don't hold up well in use. Such stitcheries are better treated as wall hangings, and admired for their beauty, than walked on and ground under our heels.

Needlepoint Rugs

These fall into three categories: One-piece rugs stitched on a continuous canvas, strip rugs worked on two or more long canvas pieces, and segment

FIGURE 19-2

rugs worked on four or more canvas rectangles that will be joined to form the rug (see Figure 19-2). Seams are weak points and, by and large, the more pieces in a rug, the less durable it will be.

One-piece rugs are the strongest type since they have no seams. They're bulky to stitch and can be *very* difficult to block. Maximum width of a one-piece rug is dictated by the width of canvas available, usually not over 54 inches.

Strip rugs are joined on their long sides and are less durable than one-piece rugs because of the seams. A long seam down the interior of a pattern can be difficult to incorporate into the design because it usually forms a textured ridge. However, strip rugs allow you to achieve widths beyond 54 inches. They too can be difficult to block.

Segment rugs are the easiest category to stitch and block, and the most fragile. Each segment is lightweight, and comparatively small (usually the size of a large pillow). Since all segments must mesh exactly, distortion of canvas should be avoided or perfectly blocked. When segment rugs are stitched by different individuals, they should be worked on identical frames. Otherwise, individual tensions can make exact blocking extremely difficult. All canvas segments must have selvages positioned in the same direction (Chapter 9, Q8).

 What yarns and canvas are best for rugs?

Yarns

Wool is most successful. Cotton has low elasticity and resilience, and will mat. Rayon should be avoided. Man-made yarns vary in resilience and pill when abraded (Fiber Characteristics Chart, p. 137).

Check yarn type against the gauge of canvas to be used (see Table I in the Appendix). Explore the possibilities of stranded Persian, tapestry and rug yarns.

Canvas

Use the best quality canvas available to you (Chapter 9, Q3). Mono-floating and double (Penelope) are to be preferred over Interlock, whose sharp edges can abrade yarns from the inside as the rug wears.

Canvas gauges normally used vary from #5 to #10.

Since rugs are supported horizontally on floors, they're not subjected to flexing or gravitational pull. Well-blocked and backed canvases will not sag or creep (Q8).

◇2 How do I design a rug?

Follow directions in Chapter 3, sketching and coloring until you're satisfied.

Hint: **Be sure to color backgrounds.** The combination of white paper and white canvas can exert diabolical influence over the colors that you choose (see Chapter 3, Q8).

Mark final sketch with number and letter grids like the coordinates found on road maps. Mark canvas with identical grids so that Section F-8 will be the same on the canvas as on the diagram (see Figure 19–3).

If stitches other than *Basketweave* are being used, draw stitch diagrams on graph paper so that you know how they will mesh and exactly where they will go. Don't be afraid; the whole rug needn't be graphed. If all roses are identical, graph just one.

Be sure that borders fit perfectly and that your design can fit comfortably inside such borders.

FIGURE 19–3

◇3 How much yarn should I buy?

Follow directions in Chapter 5, Q4, filling in Needlepoint Yarn Volumes chart.

◇4 How much canvas should I buy?

For one-piece and strip rugs, purchase canvas to equal the **size of the finished rug plus three inches** around all sides of each strip. For **segmented rugs, two inches on each side** of all segments will do. Rug canvas gauges are discussed in Chapter 9, Q4.

5 **What stitches should I use on a rug?**
Those that are **small, tight, smooth and will wear well** without attracting dirt or snagging. *Basketweave, Long-Armed Cross* and *Brick* over two threads work well. Long, loopy, rough stitches such as *Bargello, Double Straight Cross* and *Diagonal* are not recommended for rugs that aspire to a long life.

6 **How do I transfer a design to canvas?**
If the pattern is graphed, pattern transfer isn't necessary. Simply **draw grid coordinates** (Q2) and stitch what's inside area F-8 on the diagram within F-8 on the canvas.

If the design is ungraphed, draw it full scale on white shelf paper. Copy on canvas using one of the "Light" methods for pattern transfer described in Chapter 7, Q12.

7 **How do I stitch a rug?**
With patience. **The problem to be avoided is canvas warping.** The larger the rug, the more difficult it is to block successfully and the wiser you are to prevent warping in the first place. The easiest way to accomplish this on segmented rugs is to work each panel on the same, or an identical, frame.

On one-piece or strip rugs, warping becomes even more of a problem. In such cases, a tack frame is helpful.

Tack Frame

(see Figure 19–4a)

MATERIALS

- two pairs of artists' stretcher strips no smaller than 12 inches and no longer than 24
- one-inch headless brads
- four "flat corner irons" (L-shaped) and screws
- four flat "plates" (I-shaped) and screws
- four "corner braces" (three-dimensional right angles) and screws
- ruler, pencil, hammer, wood glue

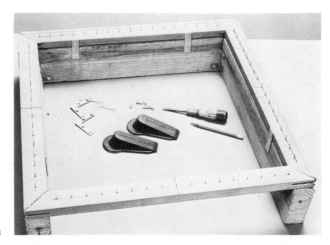

FIGURE 19–4a

- three pieces of unwarped 2 × 4 lumber, cut so that they make a three-sided box, with one long side open and *inside* edges flush with the inside of the stretcher frame.

METHOD

- Assemble stretcher strips into frame. Glue corners and reinforce the bottom of each corner with a flat corner-iron. On top, draw a line lengthwise down the center of each side. Start in the middle and mark each line at one inch intervals. Nail a headless brad into each inch-mark, so that it extends one-fourth to three-eighths of an inch above the wood. Turn frame bottom up.

- Center a narrow edge of each 2 × 4 piece on the bottom of its appropriate side. Glue flush with frame's *inside* edge and brace until dry. Sand rough edges. Reinforce by screwing flat plates to inner frame edges and 2 × 4s, and corner braces where 2 × 4s meet.

  If you plan to leave canvas on the tack frame for any time, seal frame with polyurethane varnish or shellac.

- This forms a box with one long, open side into which your hands can fit. Place the tack frame on an adjustable ironing board or card table. Push brads through canvas holes, along straight rows, stretching gently. Since all gauges have a hole every inch, this frame will hold all types and sizes of canvas (see Figure 19–4b).

FIGURE 19–4b

245 *Rugs*

- Stitch through unbraced front, turning Tack Frame over whenever necessary for attaching and snipping off yarns. If frame would be more comfortable tilted toward you, tape two rubber door stoppers beneath short sides or rest Frame's back on a book.
- When canvas must be moved to an unstitched area, gently pull it off brads and reposition. *Include one and one-half inches of completed needlepoint within tack frame each time you move.* This prevents ridges where one stretched area meets another. Brads will slip between stitches along a row of holes.

Many stitchers prefer to work rugs unstretched. However, I've noticed that such canvases can rapidly become misshapen and, though originally blocked straight, may suffer from severe canvas-creep in their later years.

 How should I block a rug?
Any time you can bend canvas over the edge of a blocking board and tack into its side, the job is easier and the block is more firmly held in place (see Figure 19–5a). This is why a frame of 2 × 4s or piece of plywood, two inches longer and wider than the finished rug, works better than a larger, flat surface.

- Block rug *segments* following directions in Chapter 14, Q12, blocking to *exact* dimensions (ideally, on the same board).
- Join segments together, following rules in Q9. Then re-block rug as a whole. This final blocking will take a large wooden area such as a floor that you're going to refinish anyway, an old ping pong table or—best of all—an exactly-sized frame made of 2 × 4s (see Figure 19–5b).
- Stretch rug to its original, pre-stitching size (or as near as you can come to it) following procedure in Chapter 14, Q12.

One-piece and *strip* rugs are first soaked in a bathtub or cool water overnight. Drain in empty tub for an hour or more. Place on blocking surface,

FIGURE 19-5a   Designed and stitched by Stephanie Doane.

FIGURE 19-5b

stretch and tack or staple from corners to center-sides following directions in Chapter 14, Q12.

Join strips and reblock strip rugs as a whole, following directions for segment rugs.

If canvas is badly out of shape, do the best you can and, after six to eight hours, remove tacks—one side at a time—and re-pull. This is nowhere near as hard as the first time around and, after re-tacking, usually gains you more straightening and one to two extra inches. Now let rug dry thoroughly, horizontally, before removing from blocking surface.

All this is hard work. However, problems arise when stretch is *not* pulled out of rugs, to return at some later date as canvas-creep.

How do I join segments and strips?

Hem or bind edges following directions in Q10. Then turn under and sew folds together with heavy thread following directions in Chapter 15, Q14. If thread proves noticeable, it can be covered by yarn stitched to match needlepoint.

FIGURE 19-6

or

Stitch together two raw canvas threads ("railroad tracks") along each edge (four threads total) using the *Long-Armed Cross,* the *Greek Cross* or the *Binding* stitch (see Figure 19-6). This forms an attractive seam with two drawbacks; it's weak because no heavy thread underlies it, and it may extend above the rug's surface, inviting dirt and wear.

or

Overlap two layers of canvas (eight threads wide) while stitching, and work through them both. This must be done before blocking and leaves a subtly raised band which becomes invisible if yarn colors are medium to dark in tone.

 How do I finish a rug?
First loosely weave a number of leftover strands of each color yarn through canvas back (see Figure 19-7). If repairs ever become necessary, the right wool will be available to make them (Chapter 20, Q5).

FIGURE 19-7

FIGURE 19-8

Hemming

Miter corners (Chapter 15, Q1), press and tack miter in place. Fold raw canvas along edges and hem to back of rug, folding on completed stitching so that edge looks worked (see Figure 19-8). Use heavy-duty or carpet thread.

or

Trim excess canvas to one-half inch. Stitch **rug binding** over raw canvas next to needlepoint with the rug lying right side up. Fold binding to back and hem to rug's back, mitering corners. Curl stitching over edges so that they look finished.

or

Fold canvas at edge of needlepoint, leaving two raw threads ("railroad tracks") along each fold. Miter corners and hem excess canvas to back. Work *Long Armed Cross* along edges.

Backing (Interlining)

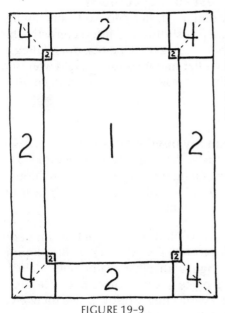

Raised portions of rugs wear first. Your hemmed rug has one layer of canvas in the middle, two layers on the sides and four layers at mitered corners (see Figure 19–9). This situation needs to be equalized before the rug is lined.

- Obtain a pre-shrunk (old or new) summer blanket from which to cut a piece the shape of the one-layer area. Trim so that it fits around any miters. Tack in place over the rug's back, along edges, and wherever a small stitch won't show in the center (eight to ten center-stitches are enough).
- Cut a second blanket piece to cover the one- and two-layer portions of rug. Tack in place along edges and eight to ten times in center. Only miters can now be seen from the back and the rug should be of even thickness.

FIGURE 19–9

Lining

Take firmly woven, pre-shrunk cotton or linen and fold under a one-half inch seam allowance. Hand stitch to rug back at needlepoint edge. Lining should cover all backings and allow *no* raw canvas to show at edges or corners.

If you plan to use a rug pad beneath—and this is advisable—attach wide strips of elastic diagonally across corners. Obtain a rug pad two to four inches smaller than rug, length and widthwise. Slip pad beneath elastic like a photograph in an album and it will stay in place.

Edge Trims

Fringe can be looped through rug edges. Tassels made of the rug's yarn can be attached to sides or corners. Consult finishing or macramé books for such trim directions.

How do I correct curling corners?

If the needlepoint is stretch-blocked, and linings and backings are pre-shrunk and fitted correctly, this shouldn't happen. However if it does, open lining at corners, **tack in a flat metal curtain weight** wrapped in washed cloth, and resew the lining (letting it out if it's too tight).

How do I clean my needlework rug?

Vacuum religiously. Place a bound piece of fiberglass or nylon screening over rug and vacuum through it (Chapter 20, Q1). This will keep the machine from sucking up loose yarn ends.

- If liquids are spilled, go into action *immediately*. DO NOT LET STAINS DRY. Blot liquid, gently sponge with clear water until stain is gone, and place a terry towel over the area, weighting it with a heavy book. Leave for twelve hours before uncovering.
- If this doesn't remove the stain, take off backings and linings, wash as directed in Chapter 13, re-block, and re-finish. This is probably the gentlest and most effective cleaning possible, though it's time consuming. Try it in your bathtub.
- Otherwise, take the rug to the best dry cleaner you can find and specify that you want clean dry-cleaning fluid (Chapter 13, Introduction).

Avoid spray cleaners, rent-it steam cleaners or liquids advertised for wall-to-wall carpenting. They leave their chemicals in permanent contact with needle-point, and can attract dirt and speed fading. Don't put it on if you can't rinse it out!

 How do I repair my rug?
- Read Chapter 20 for specific problems and their solutions. If you've woven wool through the needlepoint's back (Q10), you have the materials at hand to do a perfect job. If there's no wool there, buy the best match you can find. Both color and wool thickness should match, but they probably won't. When in doubt, go slightly darker rather than lighter, greener rather than pinker, and thinner rather than thicker. The whole idea is to make the rug look cleaner and fresher than the patch.
- When holes are the problem, repair canvas by applying a canvas patch (Chapter 20, Q5), and then stitching it to match. *Do not* whip hole edges together. Edges are just one degree more intact than the hole and you'll be subjecting them to great tension. Whipping simply enlarges holes.

 How do I cope with carpet beetles?
Most damage to rugs and church kneelers comes not from humans above but from bugs below. These gnawing devils don't advertise their presence, so you have to check. Every month, pick up the rug, vacuum its back and inspect it closely. If any damage has occurred, don't try home remedies. **Call an exterminator immediately.** The problem may be further reaching than you suspect.

The best remedy for carpet beetles is catching them early. Then repair specific damage as directed in Chapter 20.

FIGURE 19–10

20 Antique Needlework

FIGURE 20-1

My childhood memories of needlepoint are dreary because Mother was always working on the same ottoman cover. She obviously hated the thing, which was perfectly understandable once you saw it.

The background was dingy black tapestry wool. Flowers in the center, prestitched when purchased, appeared embalmed. Colors were bilious, drawing was bad, and the posies looked like last year's fungus.

Why Mother ever bought the thing is beyond me. She only worked on it when she was furious with Father, or with the three of us kids, or with the world in general. Fortunately for everybody concerned, those days were rare. But occasionally we'd run into the living room to find Mother yanking away at black tapestry wool with an equally black look on her face. We'd change course as fast as possible.

The ottoman cover never was finished and I suspect that it awaits me somewhere in the future like a moth-eaten sword of Damocles. Currently, when the subject of my needlework comes up, Mother just shakes her head and says, "You must take after your Father's side of the family."

INTRODUCTION

Needlework doesn't have to be one hundred years old to be called "antique." For our purposes, "antique" will mean any stitchery that needs special handling because of its fragile condition. The first commandment when working with old textiles is, "Thou shalt not do anything irreversible." You should

FIGURE 20-2

always be able to remove your repair if a better way to fix things comes along.

There are two ways to approach repair and display of old textiles. "Restoration" aims to return the stitchery to its original appearance. This usually requires the addition of non-original material. "Conservation" puts needlework in the most stable condition possible *without adding to it*. Which is more "honest"? Should you present only original fibers, complete with holes and battle scars? Or should you try to make the needlework look as it did when it was new? Only you can decide which path to take.

NEEDLEPOINT

The majority of old needlepoint emerging from attics falls into one of two categories: In the younger variety, probably stitched during the first half of the twentieth century, the background would have been worked on a canvas whose design was pre-stitched when purchased (see Figure 20-3a). Twentieth-century background-work is usually easy to identify. Turn it over. The back of background stitching is generally very regular. Lines of stitching lie parallel to each other. Design stitching often proceeds in all directions at once (see Figure 20-3b). This is only to be expected on canvases worked in different times and places by different individuals.

FIGURE 20-3a

FIGURE 20-3b

FIGURE 20-4a
Berlin Work book cover
from Collection of Greenfield Village
and the Henry Ford Museum

Nineteenth-century Berlin Work is the more complicated of the two categories (see Figure 20–4a). Designs were stitched on blank canvases, using special wools and sometimes silks. The stitcher worked from printed, graphed designs. Many gauges, qualities, and types of canvas and yarn were used at different times and places. The craze for this canvas work swept America during the years between 1830 and the end of the century. Some of what was worked remains with us today. How can you identify and preserve it?

Identification

Berlin Work is recognized by how it looks. When it shows humans or buildings, how are they dressed (see Figure 20–4c)? Figures or structures could not have been stitched *before* their clothes, or architectural styles, became fashionable.

What style of furniture or frame is the needlepoint attached to? Furniture was rarely upholstered with old cloth (though it may have been recovered since with more modern needlework). If the chair is Victorian, its needlepoint is unlikely to be Revolutionary.

American flags were often included in early designs. How many stars are on the flag? This usually dates textiles with some accuracy until 1875 when Betsy Ross and 1775 became fashionable again. Before the Centennial, poor Betsy was simply out of style.

FIGURE 20–4b

FIGURE 20–4c   Berlin Work figures from Collections of Greenfield Village and the Henry Ford Museum.

255

If the needlework includes beads, chenille, fringe, tassels or mixtures of wools and silks, it's probably Berlin Work. Eclecticism, or a-bit-of-this-with-a-bit-of-that, was a Victorian delight.

Look for dates, names or identifying labels on the stitchery or the wood to which it's attached. Woolen canvas work stitched between 1830 and 1880 is probably Berlin Work.

Dyes

The central problem with all of this nineteenth century canvaswork is the dyes used to color yarns. Before 1856, all dyes came from animal or vegetable matter and their colors were usually water-fast. In 1856, Sir William Perkin of England invented an artificial, chemical dye and named it "mauve." More "aniline" dyes were discovered during the 1860s and 70s.

Early aniline dyes were bright, comparatively easy to use, able to duplicate colors, and reasonably cheap. They immediately became immensely popular; but they weren't perfect by a long shot. Many bled in water, some bled when stitched with damp hands, and a few even bled when the weather turned humid. They were very susceptible to sun fading, and they still are. Washing and displaying such canvases are undertakings as risky today as they were a hundred years ago.

In working with Berlin Work, recognize what you *can't* cope with. Antique textiles do not forgive mistakes. Follow directions in this chapter exactly and, if you choose to experiment, pray as you go. You'll need all the Divine intervention you can get.

Fortunately, twentieth-century background-work has less finicky dyes. Handle carefully according to directions and you should have little trouble.

But what if your canvas doesn't seem to fit either category? Don't restore it yourself. Consult textile authorities in museums, college home economics departments, or magazines featuring antique textiles. A clear photograph often can communicate when your stitchery can't travel. You must identify what you have before you can know what to do with it.

FIGURE 20-5a Cross Stitch sampler dated 1770 from Collections of Greenfield Village and the Henry Ford Museum.

Embroidery

The majority of nineteenth-century stitcheries emerging from our bags and boxes are Cross Stitch, darning or other types of samplers (see Figure 20-5a); or elaborate creations worked primarily with and on silk (see Figures 20-5b and 20-5c). These stitcheries were intended to display the needle skills (very salable on the 1800s' marriage market) of the females who worked them. They were displayed proudly in the front parlor and given the greatest of care at the time they were worked.

FIGURE 20-5b
Mourning picture dated 1805
from collection of the author.

FIGURE 20-5c
Mid-19th century chenille Biblical
scene from the collection of
John S. Steel.

What's happened to them since is anybody's guess, but they're likely to have been framed once, even if they're not now. In all likelihood, they've been subjected to extreme "greenhouse" effects (Chapter 16, Q1) and will be well-oxidized.

Do not ever try to wash them yourself. Not only can dyes run (some almost certainly will if the embroidery's post-Civil War), but the ground fabric may partially dissolve in the wash water (Chapter 18, Recycling).

If the piece is worked on or with silks, don't even touch it more than you have to. Some late nineteenth-century silks were heavily "weighted" with metallic salts during the dyeing process to give them added weight and body. Over the years, these salts have made such silks stiff and dry. They cannot take washing, flexing or much activity of any kind. Examples of weighted silks are to be found on most Victorian "Crazy Quilts." They've dried up and blown away.

Live with your nineteenth-century silk embroideries as they are or pay an expert in textile conservation to restore them for you. This is *not* a job for amateurs.

Stitcheries worked in our century are more likely to be dye-fast, though *always* check before wetting (Chapter 13, Q5). Also identify natural fibers (Chapter 11, Q5) and the physical condition of the piece before doing anything to it. If it's dry, brown or full of holes, **do not use any of the following methods!**

However, if the condition is good, colors won't run and fibers can be washed (silk *can't*), wash gently following directions in Chapter 13, Q6, Category #2.

 How do I clean antique needlework?
Ideally, soil should be removed before stitcheries are repaired or displayed. Dirt gets in the way of further techniques, but clean carefully. If the piece measures much over fourteen inches in any direction, don't try to clean it yourself. The bigger they are, the more problems they present. Consult a textile conservator (Introduction).

How you clean depends upon the fibers present (see Table 20–1). Identify them with the Burn Test, p. 140. Silks should *never* be home cleaned. To

Table 20–1   Table of Cleaning Techniques for Antique Needlework

Fiber Content	Vacuum	May Be Washed	May Be Dry Cleaned	Consult Textile Conservator
Wool	x	x	x	
Wool and Beads	x*	x*		
Wool and Metal Threads	x			x
Wool and Silk	x		x	
Silk	x			x
Silk and Beads	x*			x
Silk and Metal Threads				x
Unidentified Fibers	x			x

*Be sure beads are *firmly* attached (Q1).

determine which cleaning process is best for your particular stitchery, consult Table of Cleaning Techniques For Antique Needlework.

Vacuuming

All antique needlework can be vacuumed (with the possible exception of beaded pieces where threads that hold the beads in place are weakened—see Table 20-1). In many cases, it's the only home cleaning method that should be tried. Vacuum both front and back whenever possible using the following method.

FIGURE 20–6

- Obtain one square foot of fiberglass or nylon window screening from your hardware store. Cover all sharp edges with tape.
- Vacuum with machine's flexible cleaning nozzle after placing screen *firmly* over stitchery. Hold vacuum nozzle almost, but not quite, touching screen (see Figure 20-6). If machine has an adjustment for decreasing vacuum suction, lower it. You want to remove loose dirt without sucking up yarns and threads.
- Keep repositioning screen and vacuuming through it until entire front has been cleaned. Repeat on back if possible.

Cleaning When One Side is Accessible

If you're coping with old upholstery or glued needle-work, home cleaning measures are limited to va-cuuming. Anything further should be left to an expert unless stitchery can be safely removed for cleaning and then be reattached.

Cleaning When Both Sides Are Accessible

- Vacuum both sides, using square of screen. Identify yarn and ground fibers with Burn Test. If silk is present, Stop and consult an expert.
- If no silk is present, run a Dye-Fast Test with water on *all* colors (p. 166). If no dyes bleed, wash using techniques in Chapter 13, Q6, Cate-gory #2.
- If dyes bleed in water, run a Dye-Fast Test with dry cleaning fluid on *all* colors (Chapter 13, Q5). Your dry cleaner will do this for you.
- If no dyes bleed, obtain a piece of new, stiff needlepoint canvas (any gauge finer than #10) extending one inch beyond needlework on all four sides. Center the stitchery and baste edges to canvas using stitches no longer than one-half inch. Dry clean flat, employing a skilled pro-fessional (Chapter 13, Q10). Do not allow the needlework to be pressed.
- If dyes bleed in dry cleaning fluid, **do not clean.** Either live with the needlework as it is, or pay a textile conservator to clean it for you.

 How do I block antique needlepoint?
If you've washed using Technique #2 (Chapter 13, Q6), there's no need to. Be sure that dyes, fibers and the physical shape of the stitchery are up to the stress of this technique (see "Embroidery").

Steam Method

- Obtain a steam iron and ironing board. If you cover the board with clean, checked gingham, precise blocking will be easier.
- Pre-heat iron so that steam is being emitted. Place iron over, *but not touching* the needle-point. Steam until the canvas feels warm but not wet. Quickly straighten with your hands, pulling *gently*. Check edges against gingham lines. Repeat steaming as often as necessary.
- Hold straightened needlepoint in place by pinning straight down through its edges into the board's pad. Use brass or non-rusting pins (see Figure 20–7). Allow to dry before unpinning.

FIGURE 20–7

In cases of badly warped needlepoint, it may be necessary to repeat this process several times, moving the canvas slowly toward the square. This is easier on stitchery than yanking it into shape the first time. Be aware that badly misshapen canvases will probably never again be absolutely straight, but you can certainly shape things up to some extent.

 How do I flatten clean-but-crumpled embroidery?

Don't iron it! You can produce the same results on cotton or linen with less danger if you **smooth.**

- First test all colors with Dye-Fast Test (p. **166**). Obtain a piece of sparkling clean and rinsed glass, larger than the embroidery. Spray it with a light mist of water.

- Lay the embroidery face up, flat on the damp glass, and gently smooth out wrinkles with fingers. If glass is put over a sheet of graph paper, you can use its lines to check straightness of warp and weft threads.
- Spray cloth lightly if you need a *little* more moisture. Work air bubbles out.
- Let flattened embroidery dry horizontally on glass, away from light and heat. It will peel away from the glass flat and smoothed.

 How do I keep needlework from re-warping or wrinkling?

Straightening **antique needlework benefits from backing** to protect it and keep it in shape. Use the following method.

Backing Technique

- Obtain stranded embroidery floss in colors to match your stitchery. You'll need a piece of washed, pre-shrunk and ironed, all-cotton cloth measuring two inches beyond the antique in all directions. Indian Head, unbleached muslin, or Kettle Cloth are good choices for needlepoint. Match linings to the weight and density of thinner embroidery fabrics.
- Place blocked or straightened needlework face down. Center backing over it, basting together along needlework's edges. Stretch backed stitchery face down on a stretcher frame with non-rusting thumbtacks pushed through the *backing fabric only.*
- Attach backing to embroidery from behind by making long, diagonal stitches held in place by *tiny* backstitches through both layers. Work in a zigzag pattern as diagrammed in Figure 20-8, using two strands of embroidery floss for needlepoint and one strand for lighter-weight embroideries. Place diagonal stitches two to three inches apart. Stagger adjacent rows so that stitches won't produce a "quilted" texture.

FIGURE 20-8

- Match color of the floss to the area of stitchery being backed. You don't want the backstitches noticeable from the front, and may have to change colors as you progress. Do not use knots. Attach and end threads by backstitching them several times along the backing's edge.
- Remove needlework from frame and turn under backing's seam allowance. Tack folds down inside needlework's edges. Line if backing will be visible.

 How can I repair antique needlework?

Consider these words of wisdom from *Caring for Textiles* by Finch and Putnam: "Be prepared for all sorts of odd stitching in the original and fall in with them, whatever private thoughts you may have about the technique of the person who did the embroidery in the first place."

RESTORATION

- Clean needlework as well as you can (Q1), getting rid of moth eggs and mildew spores as well as dirt. Back it but do not turn under backing's seam allowance yet.
- Stretch backed stitchery face up on stretcher frame with non-rusting thumbtacks pushed through *backing fabric only.*
- Restitch and repair through *both* layers, the original and the backing layer. Use a pointed crewel needle.

How to Replace Missing Wool

- When bugs have eaten every yarn in sight, restitch—matching color and wool thickness as nearly as possible. I use Appleton English Crewel yarns. They are finely stranded and come in a wide range of colors that blend with old dyes. Use as many strands as are necessary to obtain yarn thickness desired.

- When you can't match a color perfectly, go *very slightly* darker and/or greener than the original. It's better that the stitchery look cleaner than the patch, than vice versa.

  When the same dark color is missing throughout the needlework, it is not because you have discriminating moths. Iron salts were often used when dying dark shades, and over the years, these salts have disintegrated that particular color wool. Any color remnants are still in the process of disintegrating. Remove them before restitching.

FIGURE 20–9

How to Repair Burns and Holes in Cloth or Canvas

- Do not sew edges together (Chapter 19, Q13).
- Obtain new cloth or canvas that matches the gauge and thread thickness of the original. Unstitch yarn for approximately one-fourth inch around the hole. Anchor loose ends on back.
- Cut a new patch, one-half inch larger than the hole, length and widthwise. Center patch to back of stitchery, aligning warp and weft threads. Baste in place (see Figure 20–9).
- Re-stitch with a crewel needle, covering patch, original material and backing. Don't split needlepoint canvas threads. Begin and end yarns with backstitches in the backing fabric only. Knots are not advised.

How to Repair Slits

Slits are indications that cloth or canvas has been weakened by oxidation or mildew. Patching can cause stresses that will produce more slits.

- Back very carefully. Restitch over lips of slit if necessary, but sometimes careful backing will draw edges together so that the slit becomes unnoticeable.
- Display and store this treasure with care. It is endangered.

CONSERVATION

The following measures can lengthen the life of needlework which shows signs of wear, but has not yet developed slits or holes.

Cover stitchery with a layer of fine, pre-washed polyester chiffon or georgette in a soft color that will blend with the needlework's background.

The fabric is translucent and will allow stitchery to show through. Don't use nylon net for this purpose. It's too sharp and can cut elderly fibers.

Use such upholstery as little as possible. Each flexing will shorten its life expectancy. Keep it away from direct heat, cold, bright sun and fluorescent lighting.

 How should I display antique needlework?

- Loose cushion or pillow covers will last longer if they are framed and enjoyed as pictures (Chapter 18, Recycling).

- Flexing brittle fabrics can snap microscopic fibers. This damage is cumulative and will eventually result in the disintegration of the textile. Don't use such stitcheries where they will have to move if you want to preserve them.

- Don't seal antique fabrics behind glass in airtight picture frames. If you need glass for protection, don't let it touch the needlework. Cut air holes in the frame's backings and attach small spacers to hold the frame away from the wall, allowing air to move freely. Read about the "greenhouse effect" (Chapter 16, Q1).

- Keep fragile fabrics in moderately humidifed air. If your sinuses and skin are shriveling, it's too dry for your stitcheries.

  Hot air absorbs more water than cold air. It sucks this moisture from the objects it surrounds—you, your plants, furnishings, or anything damper than it is. Textile fibers need a certain moisture content to remain flexible. Without it, they eventually dehydrate and become brittle.

- Place antique needlework away from fireplaces, registers, radiators, air conditioners, windows, air intakes and doors.

Quick temperature changes build up static electricity. Dirt particles are magnetically attracted to such areas and more soil is deposited around them than in the stable areas between.

- Don't allow raw wood or wood products to come in direct contact with elderly needlework (**see** Preventive Medicine). Keep such stitcheries out of direct sunlight and away from prolonged exposure to fluorescent lights. Use incandescent bulbs for illumination and cover stitcheries with a sheet or dust cover when you're away on vacation. Draw window shades when the room is not being used.

  Ultra-violet radiation is the most dangerous enemy of old textiles. It attacks them in two ways. One wavelength causes fading. Another wavelength causes a rotting sometimes known as "sunburn." Most fluorescent bulbs emit large amounts of both wavelengths.

- Keep antique textiles free of dust (Chapter 5, Q7). Dirt and dust particles are sharp and cut textile fibers as they move against them. Vacuuming helps remove this hazard. Even verticle hangings need to be vacuumed periodically.

- Allow fragile needlework, whenever possible, to rest in the dark for a time equal to its display in the light. Mine lives six months on stage and six months off.

  Light, heat and dirt are a textile's worst enemies. Cool, clean darkness helps slow them down.

How do I store antique needlework?

- Clean, rolled or flat, and cool and dry. Ideally, keep in the dark and allow air to circulate. Don't pile or overcrowd storage areas.

- Don't use plastic bags for longterm storage (**see** Preventive Medicine). They trap moisture, can eliminate light and will form a perfect breeding ground for mildew. Use clean, washed sheets, pillow cases or bags of unbleached muslin.

- Keep insects out. Use one-and-one-half ounces of paradichlorobenzene (widely available in

FIGURE 20-10

moth crystals—read contents on labels) per cubic yard of storage. Here's how to calculate it:

Measure your closet or chest. Multiply its length in feet by its width and then multiply the answer by its height. Divide the answer by six (see Figure 20–10). That's the number of ounces of paradichlorobenzene to buy. Replace it twice a year and don't let it touch needlework.

The chest or closet to be mothproofed should be kept closed and as airtight as possible. These crystals form a gas which can be dangerous to humans if breathed in large quantities over a long time (a whiff or two won't hurt you). Keep gas away from plastics—it melts some of them.

- Don't spray mothproofing on antique stitcheries. Old dyes can be damaged by modern chemical sprays. And don't depend on moth balls. They're only effective if your aim is good enough to hit the moth.

FIGURE 20-11

Finch and Putnam put it nicely in *Caring for Textiles: The Egyptian tombs ... had conditions very favourable for the safekeeping of textiles, namely, cool and dark with an even temperature and humidity and unpolluted air. Apart from the occasional graverobber, the textiles would have been undisturbed ...*

Sorry, but when it comes to graverobbers, you're on your own.

Bibliography

Practical Needlework

NEEDLEPOINT

Christenson, Jo Ippolito. *The Needlepoint Book.* Englewood Cliffs, N.J.: Prentice-Hall, Inc., 1976.

Davis, Mary Kay and Helen Giammattei. *Needlepoint From America's Great Quilt Designs.* New York: Workman Publishing Company, Inc., 1974.

———. *More Needlepoint From America's Great Quilt Designs.* New York: Workman Publishing Company, Inc., 1977.

Hanley, Hope, *New Methods in Needlepoint. New York: Charles Scribner's Sons, 1966.*

Knox, Gerald, ed. Better Homes and Gardens Needlepoint. Des Moines, Iowa: Meredith Corporation, 1978.

McMillan, Posy. *The Pursuit of Excellence.* 5401 Northcrest Road, Fort Worth, Texas 76107, 1975.

Rhodes, Mary. *Needlepoint.* London: Octopus Books Ltd., 1974.

COUNTED-THREAD

Cornelius, Rosemary, Peg Doffek, and Sue Hardy. *Exploring Blackwork.* Box 273, Ellington, Conn. 06029, 1975.

D.M.C. Library. *Assisi Embroideries.* 107 Trumbull St., Elizabeth, N.J. 07206, 1970.

Zimmerman, Jane D. *Blackwork Embroidery Patterns.* 2609 Ivy Drive #12, Oakland, Calif. 94606, 1975.

SURFACE STITCHERY

Alfers, Betty. *Creative Crewel.* New York: Grosset and Dunlap, Inc., 1970.

Davis, Mildred. *The Art of Crewel Embroidery.* New York: Crown Publishers, Inc., 1962.

Enthoven, Jacqueline. *Stitchery for Children.* New York: Van Nostrand Reinhold Co., 1968.

———. *The Stitches of Creative Embroidery.* New York: Van Nostrand Reinhold Co., 1964.

Francini, Audrey. *Crewel Embroidery.* New York: Van Nostrand Reinhold Co., 1979.

Wilson, Erica. *The Craft of Crewel Embroidery.* New York: Charles Scribner's Sons, 1971.

Textiles

Appleman, Naomi. *Threads and Yarns, Book I.* Nyack, N.Y.: The Crafts Gallery, Ltd., 1978.

Emery, Irene. *The Primary Structures of Fabrics.* Washington, D.C.: The Textile Museum, 1966.

Hall, A.J. *The Standard Book of Textiles.* New York: Chemical Publishing Co., Inc., 1965.

Joseph, Marjory L. *Essentials of Textiles.* New York: Holt, Rinehart and Winston, 1976.

Lyle, Dorothy Siegert. *Modern Textiles.* New York: John Wiley and Sons, Inc., 1976.

Wingate, Isabel B. *Textile Fabrics and Their Selection* (7th ed.), Englewood Cliffs, N.J.: Prentice-Hall, Inc., 1970.

Design and Color

Albers, Josef, *Interaction of Color.* New Haven: Yale University Press, 1963.

Birren, Faber. *Principles of Color.* New York: Van Nostrand Reinhold Co., 1969.

Garrett, Lillian. *Visual Design: A Problem-Solving Approach.* Huntington, N.Y.: Robert E. Krieger Publishing Company, 1978.

G.T.E. Sylvania. *Color Is How You Light It.* Danvers, Mass.: Sylvania Lighting Center.

Griffith, Thomas. *A Practical Guide for Beginning Painters.* Englewood Cliffs, N.J.: Prentice-Hall, Inc., 1981.

Howard, Constance. *Embroidery and Colour.* New York: Van Nostrand Reinhold Co., 1976.

Itten, Johannes. *The Elements of Color.* New York: Van Nostrand Reinhold Co., 1970.

Munsell, Albert H. *A Grammar of Color.* New York: Van Nostrand Reinhold Co., 1969.

Termini, Maria. *Silk Screening.* Englewood Cliffs, N.J.: Prentice-Hall, Inc., 1978.

Roth, Laszlo. *Package Design.* Englewood Cliffs, N.J.: Prentice-Hall, Inc., 1981.

Creative Problem-Solving

Adams, James L. *Conceptual Blockbusting.* New York: W. W. Norton and Company, 1976.

de Bono, Edward. *New Think.* New York: Basic Books, Inc., 1968.

Koberg, Don and Jim Bagnall. *The Universal Traveler.* Los Altos, Calif.: William Kaufmann, Inc., 1976.

McKim, Robert H. *Experiences in Visual Thinking* (2nd ed.). Monterey, Calif.: Brooks/Cole Publishing Company, 1980.

Finishing Techniques

Giammattei, Helen. "Blocking Church Kneelers," *Needle Arts,* Vol. X, No. 4 (Summer, 1979), 12.

Ireys, Katherine. *Finishing and Mounting Your Needlepoint Pieces.* New York: Thomas Y. Crowell Company, 1973.

Picken, Mary Brooks. *Singer Sewing Book.* New York: Grosset and Dunlap, 1954.

Young, Joan. *Miracles With The Binding Stitch.* Young at Heart, 1518 Spruce Dr., Kalamazoo, Mich., 1976.

Framing

Duren, Lista. *Frame It*. Boston: Houghton Mifflin Company, 1976.

Heydenryk, Henry. *The Right Frame*. New York: James H. Heiniman, Inc., 1964.

Sunset Books and Sunset Magazine Editors. *Picture Framing and Wall Display*. Menlo Park, Calif.: Lane Publishing Co., 1980.

Toscano, Eamon. *Step by Step Framing*. New York: Golden Press, 1971.

Large Projects

Lane, Maggie. *Chinese Rugs Designed for Needlepoint*. New York: Charles Scribners Sons, 1975.

Meilach, Dona Z. *Making Contemporary Rugs and Wall Hangings*. New York: Abelard-Schuman Ltd., 1970.

Znamierowski, Nell. *Step-By-Step Rugmaking*. New York: Golden Press, 1972.

Textile Preservation

Bird, C.L. *The Theory and Practice of Wool Dyeing*. 4th ed. Bradford, Yorkshire: Society of Dyers and Colorists, 1972, 190–92.

Finch, Karen and Greta Putnam, *Caring for Textiles*. New York, N.Y.: Watson-Guptill Publications, 1977.

Leene, J.E., ed. *Textile Conservation*. London: The Butterworth Group, 1972.

———, et al. "Artificial Aging of Yarns in Presence as Well as in Absence of Light and Under Different Atmospheric Conditions," Condensed Final Report. Washington, D.C.: ICOM, 1965.

History of Needlework

Anonymous. *The Ladies' Work Table Book.* Philadelphia: T. B. Peterson and Brothers, ca. 1850.

Hanley, Hope. *Needlepoint In America.* New York: Weathervane Books, 1969.

Hughes, Sherle. *English Domestic Needlework.* London: Abbey Fine Arts, 1960.

Morris, Barbara M. *Victorian Embroidery.* New York: Universe Books, 1970.

Whiting, Gertrude. *Old Time Tools and Toys of Needlework.* New York: Dover Publications, Inc., 1971.

Glossary

Abrasion   wearing away by rubbing.

Acid-free   neutralized paper products that do not produce acids when oxidized.

Acids   liquids whose pH is beneath 7.0. Examples are vinegar, lemon juice, hydrochloric acid.

Acrylic paint   artists' pigments held in suspension with acrylic (plastic) resins.

Alkalies   liquids whose pH is over 7.0. Examples are strong soaps and ammonia.

Aniline dyes   artificial dyes composed of chemicals; not naturally produced.

Background work   describes needlepoint canvases sold with designs pre-stitched and backgrounds left to be filled by customers.

Basketweave (needlepoint)   small, diagonal stitch covering one canvas intersection; worked on the diagonal.

Basketweave (weaving)   variation of plain weave in which two or more warp threads cross an equal number of weft threads.

Baste   to attach to cloth with long, straight stitches.

Bell pull   narrow, vertical band of embroidery formerly attached to servants' bell.

Berlin Work   19th century canvas designs worked in *Tent* or *Cross Stitch* from a colored graph. Usually wool, occasionally silk.

Bias   the diagonal direction of a fabric.

Bind   to cover, as, for example, covering rough canvas edges with a masking tape fold.

Bleeding (dye)   color running when fiber is wet.

Blend   yarn twisted of ply, each of which is composed of a different fiber.

Blocking	the process of straightening needlework to its pre-stitched size and shape by means of wetting and stretching.
Blue-Line Canvas (Waste, Cross Stitch)	lightweight canvas designed to be basted on plain cloth so that counted-thread designs can be stitched over it.
Burlap	a cloth woven of jute fibers.
Canvas	durable textile woven so that holes between threads equal or surpass the diameter of threads themselves. See *cloth.*
Canvas border	the two (or more)-inch frame of unstitched canvas left around needlepoint for blocking and finishing.
Canvas creep	the slow return of an insufficiently blocked canvas to its pre-blocked shape.
Canvas embroidery	see *needlepoint.*
Carbohydrate	any plant-produced, neutral compound composed of carbon, hydrogen, and oxygen. Examples are sugars, starches, and cellulose.
Carded	brushed.
Casing	a ribbon-shaped strip of cloth sewn on a larger fabric to hold a stiff rod or hanger.
Cellulose	a plant carbohydrate; the chief component of stems and woody plant parts.
Chatelaine	a ribbon hanging around the neck bearing such items as scissors, pin-cushion, emery bag, and needle case.
Chenille needle	a sharp needle, with the same size eye and gauge number as a tapestry needle.
Cloth	a fine textile woven so that individual threads are thicker than the holes between them. See *canvas.*
Complementary colors	those opposite each other on a color wheel. Optically they exhibit simultaneous contrast.
Concave	a hollow curve biting into the surface.
Conservation	the keeping of a needlework in safe and stable condition; preservation. See *restoration.*
Convex	an arched curve that protrudes from a surface.
Counted-Thread	techniques that depend upon counting individual threads of the base fabric. Examples: cross-stitch, needlepoint.
Crewel yarn	a loosely-twisted, two-ply worsted yarn.
Crewel Work	surface stitchery worked with crewel wools on cotton or linen.
Crocking	the removal of dry dye when cloth is rubbed.

Cross grain	at right angles to straight of grain; with cloth, from selvage to selvage.
Cross-Stitch canvas	see *blue-line*.
Crown	the amount of extra fabric needed to accommodate stuffing.
Darning	see *Pattern Darning*.
Decalcomania	paper bearing a transfer picture or design.
Denier	the number of ply per thread.
Diagonal Stitch	a stitch that physically covers an intersection of two canvas or cloth threads. See *straight stitch*.
Double (Duo, Penelope) canvas	canvas having two threads per hole.
Double-stitched needlepoint	worked through both layers of a folded edge.
Duo canvas	see *double*.
Dye-fast	color will not bleed in water.
Dye-lot number	the identification number of a quantity of yarn or thread colored by the manufacturer in one particular process and therefore identical.
Elastic	capable of stretching.
Embroidery	decoration of cloth with fibers and stitches. See *needlepoint*.
Even-weave cloth	cloth in which the number of warp threads equals the number of weft threads in a square inch.
Fading	weakening or alteration of a color as a result of ultra-violet oxidation or dye's solubility in water.
Felt	dense, unwoven, matted wool.
Felting	the process of tangling individual scales along a woolen fiber as a result of heat, moisture, alkalinity and agitation.
Fiber	a thread-like structure capable of being spun and woven. See *Staple* and *Filament*.
Filament	a long, thread-like fiber extruded through a nozzle. See *Staple*.
Flattened yarn	individual yarn strands laying parallel to each other.
Floats	long threads on a cloth surface.
Floss	untwisted embroidery fibers. See *twist*.
Fluorescent tube	emits rays in the blue-green-violet end of the spectrum. Also emits invisible, short, ultraviolet wavelengths.
Freshening	a light blocking of needlepoint with little or no pressure. See *sizing-block* and *stretch-block*.

Gauge (canvas or cloth)	the number of threads in a linear inch. The higher the number, the finer the weave.
Gauge (needle)	the diameter and length of a needle. The higher the number, the finer the needle.
Grain (yarn)	direction in which individual fibers lie smoothly. Also called "nap."
Greenhouse effect	heat buildup within an enclosure, caused by short wavelength ultra-violet rays passing through a transparent barrier and producing heat, which generates long wavelength infra-red rays that are trapped inside the enclosure.
Grin Through	needlepoint canvas insufficiently covered by yarn.
Gross Point	Counted-Cross or Tent stitched worked on a gauge larger than 18 threads per inch. See *petit point*.
Hanks	see *skeins*.
Hardware cloth	open, square grid of metal wires generally used as a base for plaster.
Hem	a folded cloth border; also, as a verb, to fold and sew down a cloth border.
Hue	pure color in a spectrum.
Infra-red	invisible, long light waves located beyond red in the spectrum. Perceived as heat. See *ultra-violet*.
Incandescent bulb	light bulb with a glowing filament which produces visible light in the red-orange-yellow end of the spectrum. Also produces some infra-red. See *fluorescent*.
India ink	minute particles of carbon held in suspension in water with soap, borax, or a natural gum.
Interlining	stiffening inserted between cloth and its lining.
Intersection (canvas)	point where two cloth or canvas threads cross.
Leno	weaving process used to make Interlock canvas, marquisette and thermal blankets.
Lining	cloth covering and protecting the back of needlework.
Lip	portion of a frame extending from the side of the rabbet inward, over the object being framed.
Liquid latex	non-skid solution painted on the backs of some rugs.
Mat	border inserted between a picture frame and the object framed. See *mount*.
Matte	without luster or gloss. Even, dull texture.

Mercerization	process of soaking cotton in sodium hydroxide to make it stronger, more lustrous and more receptive to dyes.
Mesh	an open grid; example: needlepoint canvas.
Metameric colors	colors that appear different under different light sources.
Miter	a fold that evenly divides a corner's right angle.
Mix (fabric)	thread or yarn spun from individual ply, all produced from a homogeneous mixture of fibers.
Mono-floating (canvas)	woven needlepoint canvas with one thread per hole, smooth sizing, and an over-and-under rippling texture; frays easily.
Mono-interlock canvas	knotted, Leno-weave needlepoint canvas with one hole per thread, rough sizing and a flat, even texture. Will not fray easily.
Mount	smaller, wooden frame within a picture frame. See *mat*.
Nap	see *grain*.
Needleful	the quantity of individual strands threaded in a needle at one time.
Needlepoint	decoration of canvas with fibers and stitches. Also called "canvas embroidery." See *embroidery*.
Needlework	decoration of any fabric with stitched fibers.
Oil paint	artists' pigments held in linseed oil suspension.
Oxidation	combining with oxygen in air to produce changes in color or consistency of a fiber.
Panel	one section of a larger needlework.
Pattern Darning	type of embroidery where fibers are slipped between cloth's warp and weft. Does not produce tension on cloth.
Pearl (perle)	type of twisted, mercerized cotton embroidery thread available in several thicknesses.
Penelope canvas	see *double*.
Permanent pen	contains dyes that penetrate sizing to color textile fibers beneath.
Persian yarn	a loose, three-ply yarn composed of firmly twisted, two-ply worsted.
Petit Point	Counted-Cross or Continental Stitches worked on a gauge smaller than 18 threads per inch.
Pill	ball of tangled fibers on the surface of a textile.
Plain weave	one over-thread for every under-thread. See *even-weave*.

Ply	individual fiber strands spun together into a yarn or thread.
Polystyrene	a hard, dense, clear plastic, heavier than water.
Polyurethane	a flexible, semi-opaque plastic, lighter than water.
Polyvinylchloride	a heavy, strong, dense plastic, heavier than water.
Preservation	see *conservation.*
Primary colors	red, blue, yellow.
Protein	any animal-produced compound containing amino acids. Contains nitrogen, carbon, hydrogen, oxygen, and often sulfur.
Quick Point	needlepoint stitched on large-gauge canvas.
Rabbet	the sides of a frame surrounding its inner hole.
Rabbit skin	glue-like sizing painted on the back of some needlepoint canvas to stiffen them.
Raw edge	see *canvas border.*
Registration (kits)	alignment of canvas or cloth threads with the straight lines in a painted or drawn design.
Relaxation shrinkage	slight, one-time shrinking taking place when a new fabric is wet for the first time.
Resilient	bounces back to original shape after stretching.
Restoration	the return of a textile to its original appearance. See *conservation.*
Roller frame	needlework frame designed to stretch large stitcheries so that they can be rolled compactly, exposing only the area being stitched.
Sateen	cloth with long floats on one side, running at right angles to selvages.
Satin	cloth with long floats on one side, running parallel to selvages; smooth, lustrous texture.
Scale	relative size or proportion.
Secondary colors	green, orange, violet.
Segment rugs	composed of four or more smaller sections, joined together.
Selvage	the tightly-woven edge of a fabric.
Sewing motion	in and out passage of needle in one motion. See *stabbing.*
Shade	a hue darkened usually with black; example: red plus black equals mahogany.
Sheen	luster.
Shrink	to become smaller after becoming wet.

Simultaneous contrast	tendency of a color to intensify the color opposite it on the color wheel (complement).
Sizing-block	blocking of needlepoint and embroidery under moderate pressure. See *freshening* and *stretch-block.*
Sizings	fabric finishes composed mostly of starch. Stiffens and smooths cloth.
Skein	quantity of yarn or thread wound on a reel. Usually contains a standard weight or yardage.
Soft-mount	unstretched, unbacked, loose, or padded finishing, as, for example, that of a pillow. See *stiff-mount.*
Solvent	liquid capable of dissolving something.
Spin	to twist staple fibers into a thread or yarn.
Splice	to join by lapping two ends together.
Stabbing	moving needle in and out of canvas or cloth in two motions. See *sewing.*
Staple fiber	a fiber of short length, usually not over one and one-half inches. See *filament.*
Stiff mount	stretched, supported finishing; example: framed needlework. See *soft mount.*
Straight grain	the direction of cloth or canvas parallel to selvages.
Straight stitch	one that lies parallel to cloth or canvas threads but does not physically cover their intersections. See *diagonal stitch.*
Strand	one individual ply from a divisible yarn or thread.
Stretch-block	blocking of needlepoint under hard pressure; removes stretch from canvas. See *freshening* and *sizing-block.*
Stretcher (stretcher strips)	two pair of wooden strips that join at corners to form a frame on which to tack needlework for stitching.
Surface Stitchery	decoration of a fabric's surface with stitched fibers; usually a freely worked embroidery. See *counted-thread.*
Tack Frame	make-it-yourself needlepoint frame to stretch small areas of large canvases while they're being stitched.
Tapestry yarn	thick, unstranded wool that covers #10-gauge needlepoint canvas.
Tension (stitching)	pull exerted by thread or yarn on cloth or canvas.
Texture	character of a surface.
Thread	thin, firm, smooth cord. See *yarn.*
Thread (canvas)	one strand of heavily sized fibers composing an evenly woven, open mesh.

Threads	generic name for all types of spun fibers, including yarns.
Tint	hue lightened with white; example: pink.
Tone	greyed hue. Relative darkness or lightness on a scale from black to white.
Twill	cloth with diagonal ridges on one side.
Twill tape	firm tape for attachment when strength is important.
Twist	diagonal slant given to a thread in spinning; Direction can be that of 'S' or 'Z'. See *Floss*.
Ultra-violet	invisible, short light rays located beyond violet in the spectrum; fades and rots textiles. See *infra-red*.
Unstable fabric	one with too few threads or too loose a structure to achieve dimensional stability. Unless backed, liable to stretch or warp out of shape.
Warp (n.)	threads strung on a loom under tension, through which weft threads move; parallels selvages. See *weft*.
Warp (v.)	to move or shift out of position.
Waste canvas	see *blue-line*.
Weave (n.)	structure of fabric.
Weave (v.)	stitching threads over and under existing threads.
Weft	threads woven through warp at right angles to selvage.
Worsted	thin, strong yarn spun of long, parallel woolen fibers.
Yarn	thick, elastic, hairy cord. See *thread*.

Appendix

Table I   Evenweave Cloth/Canvas-Needle-Thread Chart

Cloth and Canvas Gauge	Needle Gauge (tapestry or chenille)	Thread Fiber	Type	Individual Strands per Needleful
#5	#13	Wool	Rug	1
			Tapestry	2
			Persian	8 single
#7	#14	Wool	Rug	1
			Persian	4 single
#10	#16	Wool	Tapestry	1
			Persian	3 single (1 3-ply)
			Crewel	5
		Cotton	#1 pearl	1
#12	#18	Wool	Persian	2 single
			Crewel	4
			Medici	6
		Cotton	floss	12 (2 6-ply)
			#3 pearl	1
			matte	1
		Silk	Au ver a soie (French)	6
			La Paleta (Mexican)	5
		Nylon	Veloura	1
		Linen	10/5	1
#14	#18	Wool	Persian	2 single
			Crewel	3
			Medici	5
		Cotton	floss	9 single
			#3 pearl	1
		Silk	Au ver a soie (French)	5
			La Paleta (Mexican)	4
		Rayon	Bella Donna	1
			Ostara	1
		Linen	10/2	1
#16	#20	Wool	Persian	1 single
			Crewel	2
			Medici	4
			Orchidee	1
		Cotton	floss	7 single
			#5 pearl	1

Cloth and Canvas Gauge	Needle Gauge (tapestry or chenille)	Thread Fiber	Type	Individual Strands per Needleful
		Silk	Au ver a soie (French)	4
			La Paleta (Mexican)	3
#18	#22	Wool	Persian	1
			Crewel	2
			Medici	3
			Orchidee	1
		Cotton	floss	6 (1 6-ply)
			#5 pearl	1
			#8 pearl	2
			Danish Flower Thread	3
		Silk	Au ver a soie (French)	3
			La Paleta (Mexican)	2
			Zwicky	6 single
		Linen	20/2	1
			16/2	1
		Rayon	Marlitt	4
#20	#22	Wool	Crewel	1
			Medici	2
		Cotton	floss	4 single
		Silk	Au ver a soie (French)	2
			La Paleta (Mexican)	1
			Zwicky	5 single
		Linen	20/2	1
#24	#24	Wool	Medici	1
		Cotton	floss	3 single
		Silk	Au ver a soie (French)	1
			Zwicky	3 single
#30	#26	Cotton	floss	2 single
		Silk	Zwicky	2 single
#40	#10 crewel	Cotton	floss	1 single
		Silk	Zwicky	1 single

In the Evenweave Cloth/Canvas-Needle-Thread Chart, the number of strands to be used per needleful is based upon the Tent Stitch. Begin with the number of strands recommended and adjust to the needs of your stitches and your tension.

Table II Embroidery Cloth Facts Chart

Identifying Name	Fiber Content	Evenweave Gauge	Not Evenweave
Aida	100% linen	8	
Cork		19	
Elsa Williams		20–21	
Hardanger		20,22,25,26,28	
Conemara		25	
Dublin		25	
Kerry		25	
Belfast		30	
Shannon			X
twill			X
Demo	100% cotton	2	
Domino		6	
Aida		8, 18	
Filet (Scandinavian)		8	
Marley		8½	
Hardida		11, 22	

Ainring		18	
Congress		18, 24	
Davos		18	
Hardanger		22	
Britta		27	
Gerda		27	
Linda		27	
Donau			X
embroidery satin			X
twill			X
Java	100% wool	18	
Danish		36	
Novara	100% polyacrylic	14	
Alba		14	
Monza		14	
Gardasee		14	
Terni		14	
Florina	100% viscose	14	
Teramo		25	
Rimini	52% cotton/	25	
Modena	48% viscose	25	
Lugano		25	
Teramo		26	
Cesena			
Klosters	40% cotton/ 60% rayon	7	
Floba	30% linen/ 70% viscose	18	

Table III Woolen Yarn Facts Chart

Yarn Brands	Number of Colors	Yards per Skein (weight in ounces)	Comparison of Yarn Diameters (1 strand will cover Gauge #____)	Number of Strands Yarn Can Be Divided Into
Appleton English crewel—hank skein	380	195 (⅞) 30	#20	1
Elsa Williams Crewel	130	30	#20	1
Medici	100	500 (1¾)	3 on #18	1
Paterna Crewel	252	30	# 20	1
Colbert 6 Persian (DMC 484)	222	5.4	#16	3
Paternayan Persian	343	120 (1)	#16	3
Nantucket	140	7.5	#18	1
Appleton English Tapestry	380	15	#10	1
Elsa Williams Tapestry	138	40	#10	1
Lane Colbert Tapestry (DMC 486)	430	8.8	#10	1
Orchidee Tapestry	300	11	#18	4

Table IV   Non-Woolen Thread Facts Chart

Thread Brand	Fiber	Yards	Packaging	Comparison of Thread Diameters (number of strands needed to cover canvas gauge #___)	Number of Strands Thread can Be Divided Into	Number of Colors
Danish Flower Thread	matte cotton twist	30	skein	3 strands on #18	1	90
DMC Matte Cotton		11	skein	1 strand on #12	4	213
DMC Pearl Cotton #3	mercerized cotton twist	16.4	skein	1 strand on #14	1	160
#5		27.3	skein	1 strand on #18	1	234
#8		95	skein	2 strands on #18	1	152
DMC Embroidery Floss	mercerized cotton floss	8.7	skein	6 strands on #18	6	328
Fawcett 20/2	linen twist	15	skein	1 strand on #18	1	33
10/2		15	skein	1 strand on #14	1	33
10/5		15	skein	1 strand on #12	1	33
Swedish 16/2		10	skein	1 strand on #18	1	123
Au Ver a Soie (French)	silk twist	1¼	single strand	3 strands on #18	7	500
Kanagawa (Japanese)		8	card	3 strands on #18	1	200
La Paleta (Mexican)		32	spool	2 strands on #18	1	126
Zwicky	silk floss	4.4	skein	6 strands on #18	6	156
Bella Donna	rayon twist	25	skein	1 strand on #14	1	56
Ostara	viscose rayon twist	24	skein	1 strand on #14	1	62
Marlitt	rayon floss	11	skein	4 strands on #18	4	109
Veloura	nylon flocked ribbon	10	skein	1 strand on #12	1	33

Table V Canvas Conversion Chart

Use this chart to determine the amount of canvas needed for a design when changing the gauge of the canvas.

If, for example, you want to switch from #14 to #10: On #14 canvas, a design measures 11″. Row A is #14 gauge. Row B is #10 gauge. Multiply the number in the square where Row A and Row B intersect by the design's dimensions on #14 canvas. The answer will be its size when stretched on #10 canvas— 11″ × 1.4″ or slightly over 15″.

A. Known Gauge	B. Desired Gauge					
	5	10	12	14	16	18
5	1.0	0.5	0.4	0.35	0.3	0.27
10	2.0	1.0	0.8	0.7	0.6	0.5
12	2.4	1.2	1.0	0.9	0.8	0.7
14	2.8	1.4	1.2	1.0	0.9	0.8
16	3.2	1.6	1.3	1.1	1.0	0.9
18	3.6	1.8	1.5	1.3	1.1	1.0

Reproduced from *More Needlework from America's Great Quilt Designs* by Mary Kay Davis and Helen Giammattei by permission of Workman Publishing Co., New York. 1977 Mary Kay Davis & Helen Giammattei.

Index

Abrasion, 136–137, 273 (see Pilling)
Accessories, 55, 144
Acid-free paper products, 273
barriers, xiii; boxes, xiv; cardboard, xiv, 195; museum board, xiv; purchasing, xiv; ragboard, xiv; tissue paper, xiv; toilet paper, xiv
Acetate, 135, 137, 140–141, 142
cleaning, 161, 163
Acids, 77, 137–138, 273
Acrylic, 137, 141 (see also Orlon, Plastic)
paint, 71, 273
Alberti, Leone Battista, 24
Albers, Josef, 30
Alkalies, 77, 137–138, 273
Analogous colors, 36
Aniline dyes, 36
Antique canvaswork:
background work, 253, 273; backing, 262–263; Berlin Work, 255–256, 273; blocking, 260–261; cleaning, 258–260; conservation, 253; display, 265–266; identification, 255–256; preservation, 253; repairs, 263–264; storage, 266–267
Antique embroideries:
backing, 262–263; cleaning, 258–260; condition, 257–258; display, 265–266; repairs, 263–264; smoothing, 261–262; storage, 266–267
Antique needlework:
conservation, 253, 265–266; definition, 252; storage, 266–267; Table of Cleaning Techniques for Antique Needlework, 259

Background work, 253 (see Antique canvaswork)
Backing, 249, 262–263 (see Interlining)
Ball, stitching, 206
Banners, 224
Basketweave, 120, 273 (see Cloth)
Basketweave stitch, 101–102, 273
check for missing stitches, 102; preventing diagonal lines, 101; stitching with canvas grain, 101
Beeswax, 145
Bell pulls, 224, 273
Berlin Work, 255–256 (see Antique canvaswork)
Bias (see Cloth grain)
Bleeding (see Dyes)
Blocking:
antique needlework, 260–262; definition, 174, 274; embroidery: board preparation, 190; materials, 190; techniques, 190–192
needlepoint:
board preparation, 179–180, 183–184; materials, 178–179, 184
rugs, 246–247; techniques: board cut-to-size, 184–185; four-way stretcher variation, 183; freshening, 180–181; large blocking board, 185–186; sizing-block, 181–183; stretchblock, 183–186
upholstery, 236; vocabulary, 175–176, 274; wall hangings, 226
Books, 4, 8
Borders:
cushion, 234; rugs, 243
Boxes, acid-free, xiv
Broken End Test, 142 (see Fiber identification tests)

Burn Test, 140, 142 (see Fiber identification tests)
Burn Test Chart, 141

Canvas:
border, 56, 175, 274; colors of, 113; counting threads, 116; creep, 175, 176–177, 189, 274
rugs, 246, 274
definition, 109, 274; direction, 116, 224–225, 235; edges (see Canvas border)
butt, 205; covering, 80; double-stitched, 202–204; missing, 189; overlaying, 204; splicing, 204–205; stabilizing, 205
fibers, 109; gauge, 110
Canvas Conversion Chart, 286; changing, 115; determining, 114–115
grain (see also Canvas direction, Selvage Test)
determining, 116; stitching Basketweave with, 101
purchasing, 56, 113
imperfections, 113
quality, 113–114
denier, 110, 113; Denier Test, 114
size to cut, 78; storage: bulk, 60–61; individual canvases, 60, 98
stretch, 177, 224–225, 235; techniques:
cutting, 115; marking, 81; transferring designs to, 87
types:
Cross Stitch, 113, 118; double, 112; duo, 112; mono-floating, 111; mono-interlock, 111–112; penelope, 112; plastic, 112–113; waste, 113, 118
warping, 85
Carbon paper, 94
Cardboard, xiv, 195
boxes, xiv
Carbohydrate fibers (see Fiber, natural)
Cellulose, 135, 137–138, 232, 274
Chatelaine, 145, 274
Charts:
Burn Test, 141; Canvas Conversion, 286; Counted Thread Volumes, 58; Design Balance, 28; Embroidery Cloth Facts, 283; Evenweave Cloth/Canvas-Needle-Thread, 281–282; Fiber Characteristics, 137; Needlepoint Yarn Volumes, 57; Non-Woolen Threads Facts, 285; Table of Cleaning Techniques for Antique Needlework, 259; Woolen Yarn Facts, 284
Classes:
choosing, 5; cost, 7; night, 6–7
Cleaning solutions:
attract soil, 164, 250–251; brands, 165; detergents, 165; optimum temperature, 165; soaps, 165; sprays, 239, 250
Cloth:
appropriate to embroidery, 116–118; choosing, 118; definition, 116, 274; direction, 224–225; dyes, 119; fibers, 143; front, 104, 119; gauge, 114–115; grain: bias, 119, 273; cross-grain, 119, 275; straight, 90, 104, 279
pre-shrinking, 89, 119; purchasing, 56, 118; size to cut, 89; stretch, 224–225; storage, 61–62
dry-cleanable, 62; washable, 61

transferring designs to, 94–95; warping, 117; weaves:
basketweave, 120; plain, 119–120; sateen, 120; satin, 120; twill, 104, 120
Color:
combinations, 32–36
analogous, 36; complementary, 33, 274; double split complement, 36; monochromatic, 36; split complement, 33; triad, 36
definition, 28; effect on texture, 97; facts, 31; Final Yarn Check, 39; interaction of, 30; matching, 55
nearly-matching yarn colors, 17, 264
perception, 29; placement, 37–38; vocabulary, 28–29
Colorfast Test, 126 (see also Dyes)
Compensated stitches, 100
Complement, 33, 274 (see Color)
Complaint procedures, 19
Compound fabrics, 159–160
Concave curves, finishing, 198–199
Conservation:
antique needlework, 265–266; definition, 253, 274
Convex curves, finishing, 198
Cording:
drawbacks, 233; techniques, 199–200
Corners:
mitered, 197–198; rug, curling, 250
Cotton:
cleaning, 162; description, 137, 141–142; dye lots, 126; embroidered threads, 135; mercerized, 135, 137, 142, 277; stuffing, 196
Counted thread embroidery (see also Embroidery)
beginning, 92–94; blocking, 190–192; cleaning, 120, 159–161, 171–172; cloth, 117–118
Embroidery Cloth Facts Chart, 283; evenweave, 275; Evenweave Cloth/Canvas-Needle-Thread Chart, 281–282
definition, 274; framing, 207–208; graphs, easy reading, 9–11; hoops, 90–92, 147–148; magnifiers, 105, 149–150; mistakes, correcting, 106; needles, 151–152; scale, changing, 11–12, 286; stitching techniques, 89–90, 92–94, 97; threads, 135
Counted Thread Volumes Chart, 58; Non-Woolen Thread Facts Chart, 285
Crayons, 72, 75–76
setting color, 75–76
Crewel and surface stitchery (see also Embroidery)
beginning, 92–94; blocking, 190–192; cleaning:
antique, 258–260; new, 120, 159–161, 171–172
cloth, 116–120
Embroidery Cloth Facts Chart, 283
definition, 274, 279; designs, enlarging or reducing, 87–89
transferring to cloth, 94–95
framing, 207–208, 216–217; hoops, 90–91, 104–105, 147–148; magnifiers, 105, 149–150; mistakes, correcting, 106; needles, 151; stitching techniques, 89–90, 97–98, 105–106
Crewel yarn and threads, 123–124, 134–135, 274 (see also Yarn)

how much to buy, 59; Non-Woolen Thread Facts Chart, 285
Cross Stitch canvas, 113, 118, 275
Curtains, 223–224
Cushions:
  borders, 234; cleaning, 162, 164; cording, 199–200, 233; stuffings, 196

Denier, 110, 275 (see also Canvas)
  denier number, 113; Denier Test, 114
Design:
  Balance Chart, 28; beginning, 25; enlarging or reducing, 87–89; facts, 26–27; idea sources, 25–26; rugs, 243–244; transfer: to canvas, 87; to cloth, 94–95; iron-on, 95; light methods of, 87, 94
  upholstery, 233–234; wall hangings, 224–225
Directions:
  lost, 19; understanding, 9, 193–194
Displaying:
  antique needlework, 265–266; pictures, 209; upholstery, 238; wall hangings, 230
Double-stitched canvas edge, 202–204, 248, 249, 275
Double split complement, 36 (see Color)
Dry-cleaning, 160, 172–173
  do-it-yourself, 160, 172; drawbacks, 160; professional, 164, 173
Duo canvas, 112, 275 (see Canvas)
Dye-Fast Test, 126, 166–167
Dye lot, information, 17, 126
  number, 55, 275
Dyes (see also Paints, textile, Wool dyes)
  aniline, 256; antique, 256; bleeding, 126, 160, 273
    cure, completed needlework, 77, 187; cure, unused thread, 126
  brands, 72; Colorfast Test, 126, 166–167; fading, 138, 161, 209, 266 (see also Ultraviolet radiation); heat setting, 76, 77

Emery ball, 146
Embroiderers Guild of America (E.G.A.), 13 (see also Guilds)
Embroidery (see also Counted thread; and Crewel and surface stitchery)
  beginning, 25, 92; blocking, 190–192; cloth, 116–120
    appropriate, 117; Embroidery Cloth Facts Chart, 283; transferring designs to, 94–95
  cleaning, 90, 120, 159–161, 171–172; definition, 89, 275; designs, 25–28
    transferring, 94–95
  mistake removal, 106; needles, 151–152; patterns, unevenly printed, 21; stitching techniques, 92–94; 97–98, 105–106; storage: bulk cloth, 61–62; individual embroideries, 61
Evenweave cloth (see Counted thread embroidery)

Fabric protection sprays, 173, 196–197, 238–239
Fading, 137–138, 266, 275
Fanny frames, 148
Felting, 139, 160, 275
Fiber:
  blends, 132; brand names, 140; Characteristic Chart, 137; continuous filament, 132, 275; definition, 275; identification, 139–142
    cloth fibers, 143
  identification tests, 140–142
    Broken End, 142; Burn, 140–142; Burn Test Chart, 141; Wet-Dry, 142
  man-made:
    cellulose, 132, 135, 137–138, 232; petroleum-based, 132, 136, 137
  mixtures, 142; natural, animal (protein), 132, 134, 137, 278

vegetable (carbohydrate), 132, 135, 137, 274
  staple, 132; vocabulary, 132–134
Filament, continuous, 132 (see also Fiber, staple)
Final Yarn Check, 39 (see also Color)
Floating, mono, canvas, 111 (see also Interlock canvas)
Floor frames, 148
Floss, 135, 275, 281–282, 285
Four-way stretcher variation, 183 (see Blocking)
Frames, canvas:
  function, 84–85; holders, 148; storage, 66; types:
    disposable, 147; roller, 147; stretcher strips, 146–147
  using, 85–86
Frames, picture:
  anatomy of, 211; assembly, 217–219; choosing, 207–208, 209–210; color, 210; function, 207–208; hanging, 211, 220; materials for, 211; mounting, embroidery, 216–217
    needlepoint, 215–216
  purchasing, 211–212; shape, 209; size, 210, 212
Freshening, 180–181, 275 (see Blocking)
Fringe, 199–200, 250

Gauge, 110, 114–115, 276
Glue, 197
  rabbit skin, 187–188
Glossary, 273
Grain:
  Basketweave, stitched with, 101; canvas, 98, 116, 176
    Selvage Test, 111
  cloth, 90, 104, 119; yarn, wool, 92, 127–128, 276
Graphs, easy reading, 9–11
  graph finders, magnetic, 11
Greenhouse effect, 208–209, 265, 276 (see also Heat damage; and Ultraviolet radiation)
"Grin through," canvas cures, 20–21, 70, 73, 276
Gross point, 110, 276
Guilds, needlework, 6, 12–14
  E.G.A., 13; N.S.C.A.E., 13; Valentine Museum, 14

Heat damage, 137, 138–139, 208–209, 265
Highlights, 32 (see Texture)
Hoop or frame holders, 148
Hoops:
  choosing, 90, 147–148; preventing marks, 104–105; size, 90, 148; storage, 66; taping, 90; types, 147–148; using, 90–92

Inks, textile, 71 (see also Pens)
  India, 70, 71, 73, 276
Insect damage, 59, 137–138, 161, 230, 251, 263
Interlock, mono, canvas, 111–112, 128, 205, 235, 243 (see also Floating canvas)
Interlining, 195, 276
  antique needlework, 262–263; attaching, 201; purchasing, 195; rug, 249

Kits:
  contents, 15–16; cost, 11; covering embroidery outlines, 21–22; limitations, 18
    insufficient materials, 18–19
  patterns, how applied, 16–17; purchasing, 17

Lamps, 148–149
Learning, 41–42
Leno weave, 114, 276 (see Interlock canvas)
Light method of design transfer, 87, 94
Light rotting, 137–138 (see also Fading)
Linen:
  canvas, 109; cleaning, 162; cloth, 283; description, 135, 137, 141–142; thread, 177, 285
    identification numbers, 132

Lining:
  antique needlework, 263; canvas, 202; cloth, 201; definition, 276; double-stitched canvas edge, 204; purchasing, 194–195; rug, 249; wall hanging, 223–224, 226–227
Liquid latex, 187, 276

Magazine articles, 4, 7–8
Magnifiers, 11, 149–150
  using, 105
Mat, picture, 211–214, 276
  making, 213–214
    cloth covered, 214; padded, 214; plain, 213
  materials, 213–214
Matching colors, 55
Matting, fiber, 137–138
Measuring tape and rulers, 150
Meat trays, butchers', 147, 196, 213
Mercerized cotton (see Cotton)
Metallic threads, 137
  cleaning, 172
Mildew and mold, xvi, 137–138, 161, 263
Mistakes, correcting:
  hiding mismarkings, 75; removing stitches:
    embroidery, 106; needlepoint, 102–103, 106
Mitered corners, 197–198, 277
Mold (see Mildew and mold)
Monochromatic colors, 36
Mono canvas (see Canvas)
  -floating, 111, 276; -interlock, 111–112
Moth proofing spray, 173, 267
Mount, 212–213, 277
Museum board, xiv

National Standards Council of American Embroiderers (N.S.C.A.E.), 13 (see also Guilds)
Nearly-matching yarn colors, 17, 20, 103
Needle:
  book, 152; gripper, 152; threader, 153 (see also Paper folder); trolly needle, 154
Needlepoint:
  backgrounds, 100; beginning, 82; blocking, 175–189; canvas (see Canvas)
    Evenweave Cloth/Canvas-Needle-Thread Chart, 281–282
  cleaning, 167–171
    antique, 258–260; rugs, 250–251; upholstery, 163–164, 238; wall hangings, 230
  definition, 277; designs, enlarging or reducing, 87–89
    transferring to canvas, 87
  double-stitched edge, 202–204, 248, 249 (see also "Railroad Tracks"); dyes, running, 126, 160
    cures, 126, 187
  first project, 79; framing, 215–216; frames, 84–86, 146–147; mistakes, correcting, 102–103, 106; needles, 151–152; scale, changing, 11–12, 286; stitching techniques, 83–86, 99–102; yarn, 92, 123–130 (see also Yarn; and Wool)
    Needlepoint Yarn Volumes Chart, 57; Woolen Yarn Facts Chart, 284
Needles, 151–152
  curved, 152; determining size, 151; storage, 67, 99; threading, 81–82
Newspaper columns, 4, 7
Nylon, 136–137, 140–142

Opaque projector, 87–88
Orlon, 136, 140 (see also Acrylic)
Oxidation damage, 161, 208–209, 232, 258, 277 (see also Greenhouse effect, Heat damage, Ultraviolet radiation)

Paper products, acid-free, xiii–xiv
Paper folder, 82

Paints:
acrylic, 71, 273; oil, 70–71, 277;
textile, 71–77 (see also Dyes)
application, 73, 76; bleeding,
cure, 77, 187; cleaning, 77;
color fastness, 77
Pantograph, 88
Pasteur, Louis, 48
Paradichlorobenzene, 266–267
Pencil, 74
Pens:
permanent marking, 71, 74, 87,
187; quill, 73; safety test, 71–72;
washable pattern marking, 72,
94
Penelope canvas, 112, 277 (see
Canvas)
Persian yarn, 124–125 (see Yarn)
Petit point, 110, 277
Photostat, 9, 87
Pilling, 124, 125, 137, 139, 277
Pillows (see Cushions)
Pin cushion, 153
Plastic canvas, 112–113
aid to dry-cleaning antique
needlework, 260; aid to washing
needlepoint, 169–171; cleaning
needlepoint worked on, 163,
171
Plastic:
acrylic, 196; identification, xv;
storage in, xv–xvi, 266
Ply, 132, 278 (see also Fiber)
Polyester, 137, 140–141
Preservation (see Conservation,
Repair and restoration)
Problem solving:
How? 44–47
picture perfect, 44–45; re-
search, 46–47; verb list, 46
subconscious, 48; What? 43–44
adjective list, 44; cross it off,
44
Where? 43; Which? 47–48
file cards, 47; sketches, 47
Who? 43; Why? 49
Protein fibers (see Fiber, natural)
PVC, xv (see Plastic)

Rabbet, 211, 218–219, 278
Rabbit skin, 187–188, 278
Rag board, xiv
"Railroad Tracks," 202, 204, 248,
249 (see Needlepoint,
double-stitched edge)
Rayon, 135, 137
cleaning, 161, 163
Registration, pattern, 16, 278
Repair and restoration:
antique needlework, 263–264;
definition, 253, 278; rugs, 251;
upholstery, 238; wall hangings,
230
Roller frames, 147, 278 (see
Frames, canvas)
Rug:
backing, 249; blocking, 246–247;
borders, 243; cleaning, 250–251;
corners, curling, 250; design,
243, 244; embroidered, 241;
hemming, 248–249; joining segments, 247–248; lining, 249–
250; materials for, 242–243; repairs, 251; stitching, 244–246;
tack frame, 244–246; types,
241–242
Running out of thread, cure:
embroidery, 106; needlepoint,
103; two-needle switch, 98

Samplers, 257
Sateen, 120, 278
Satin, 120, 278
Scale, changing, 11–12, 278
Canvas Conversion Chart, 286
Scissors, 153
Selvage, 98, 104, 111, 224–225,
235, 278 (see also Grain)
Selvage Test, 111
Sew stitching, 83–84, 278 (see
also Stab stitching)
Shopping guidelines, 54–56
Shrinking, 119, 137
felting, 139; pre-shrinking, 89;
relaxation, 139

Silk:
antique, care, 257–258; blocking,
177; cleaning, 161, 163; descrip-
tion, 132, 134, 137, 141–142;
dye running, 160; protection
while stitching, 97
Sizing, xiii, 70, 76, 175, 279
Sizing-block, 176, 181–183, 279
(see also Stretch-block)
Slide projector, 88
Soaps, 165 (see Cleaning solutions)
Soft-mount, 175, 279 (see also
Stiff-mount)
Split complement, 33 (see Color)
Sprays, cleaning, 238, 250
mothproofing, 173, 267; water
repellent, 173, 196–197, 238–
239
Stab stitching, 83–84, 279 (see
also Sew stitching)
Staple fiber, 132, 279 (see also
Filament, continuous)
Static electricity, 137, 138, 265–
266
Stiffeners, 195–196
Stiff-mount, 175, 276 (see also
Soft-mount)
Storage:
canvas, 60–61; cloth, 61–62;
conditions, 59, 267; frames and
hoops, 66; needles, 67; in plas-
tic, xv–xvi, 266; threads, 62–63;
yarns, 64–66
Stranded yarn, 20, 97, 123–125,
279
flattening, 20, 84, 99
Strawberry, emery, 146
Stretch-block, 176, 183–186, 279
(see also Sizing-block)
Stretch, canvas, 176–177, 224–
225, 235, 279
cloth, 224–225
Stretch tool (see Upholsterers'
stretch tool)
Stretcher strips, 145–147 (see
Frames, canvas)
Students, evaluation of work, 5–6
responsibilities, 7
Stuffing, 196
attaching, 201
S twist, 122, 129, 133–134
Subconscious, 48
Surface stitchery (see Crewel and
surface stitchery)
Synthetic fibers, 125, 132–143
unforgiving, 97

Table frames, 148
Tack frame, 244–246, 279
Tapestry yarn, 19, 21, 123, 279
Teachers, 5–7
advantages of, 5; certification, 6;
evaluation, 5–6; responsibilities,
7
Tension, 20, 21, 279
embroidery, 93; needlepoint, 84
Textile Fiber Products Identification Act, 139–140
Texture:
definition, 24, 32, 279; effect of
color on, 97; highlights, 32; luster,
143; stitch, 32; surface, 32
Thimbles, 154
Threads (see also Yarn)
brands, 55, 135, 285; color
matching, 17, 55; definition,
132, 279–280; dye bleeding,
cures, 77, 126, 187; dye-fast
tests, 126, 166–167; purchasing,
55–59
for crewel and surface stitchery, 59; Non-Woolen Thread
Facts Chart, 285; Counted
Thread Volumes Chart, 58
running out of, cure, 98, 103,
106; storage, 62–63; synthetic,
135–143; types:
floss, 135, 275, 281–282, 285;
twisted, 133–134, 135
Tissue paper, xiv
Toilet paper, xiv
Transfers, iron-on, 95
Trays, 220
Triad, 36 (see Color)

Twill, 104, 120, 280
twill tape, 189, 228, 280
Two-handed stitching, 84 (see
Needlepoint)
Two-needle switch, 98

Ultraviolet radiation, xv, 138, 208–
209, 223–224, 238, 266,
280 (see also Heat damage;
and Greenhouse effect)
Upholstery:
blocking, 236; cleaning, 163,
172, 238–239; designing, 233–
234; preservation, 238; professional, 237–238; recycling old,
232–233; repairs, 238; stitches,
235; threads, 236
Upholsterers' pattern, 234–235
stretch tool, 184–185

Vacuuming, screen, 259–260
Valences, 223–224
Valentine Museum, 14 (see also
Guilds)

Wall hangings:
blocking, 226; cleaning, 230;
design, 224–225; display, 230;
lining, 223–224, 226–227; materials, 224–225; mounting:
loose, 224, 228; stretched,
224, 229–230
repairs, 230; stitching, 225
Warp, 110, 176–177, 280 (see also
Selvage)
Washing, 160–165
embroidery, 171–172; needlepoint, 167–171
Waste knot, 83, 98
Waste canvas, 113, 118, 280
Waterproof pens (see Pens)
Water repellent sprays, 173, 196–
197, 238–239
Weft, 110, 176–177, 280 (see also
Warp)
Wet-dry Test, 142 (see Fiber identification tests)
White yarn erasers, 110, 106
Wood, acid-producing, xiii
protective barriers against, xiii
Wool (see also Yarn, Worsted)
carding, 122; cleaning, 162–171;
description, 121–122, 137, 141–
142, 177; dyes (see also Dyes)
bleeding, cures, 126, 187;
Colorfast Test, 126
dye lots, 126; felting, 139, 160;
grain of, 92, 127–128; shrinkage,
139; spun, 122; storage, 64–66,
173, 266–267
Woolen Yarn Facts Chart, 284
Worsted, 122, 123, 124, 280

Yarn (see also Threads; and Wool)
buying, 55; color matching, 17,
18–19, 55; coverage, 20–21;
definition, 132, 280; dye lots,
126; grain of, 92, 127–128;
length for stitching, 92, 129; purchasing, 55, 56–59, 127
Needlepoint Yarn Volumes
Chart, 57; Woolen Yarn Facts
Chart, 284
running out of, cure, 98, 103,
106; storage, 64–66; stranded:
flattening, 20, 84, 99; separating strands, 81, 130; strands
per needleful, 79
synthetic, 125; twist, 122; types:
crewel, 123–124; persian,
124–125; tapestry, 19, 21, 123

Z twist, 122, 133–134

MP6N

THE JOFFREY BALLET

ROBERT JOFFREY
AND THE MAKING OF
AN AMERICAN DANCE COMPANY

SASHA ANAWALT

SCRIBNER

SCRIBNER
1230 Avenue of the Americas
New York, NY 10020

DESIGNED BY ERICH HOBBING

Set in Sabon

Manufactured in the United States of America

1 3 5 7 9 10 8 6 4 2

Library of Congress Cataloging-in-Publication Data

Anawalt, Sasha, 1956–
The Joffrey Ballet : Robert Joffrey and the making
of an American dance company / Sasha Anawalt.
p. cm.
Includes bibliographical references and index.
(alk. paper)
1. Joffrey Ballet—History. 2. Joffrey, Robert. 3. Ballet dancers—United States—
Biography. 4. Choreographers—United States—Biography. I. Title.
GV1786.J65A53 1996
796'.8'0973—dc20   96-32454
CIP

ISBN 0-684-19724-3

Cover photo by Jack Mitchell
(Left to right) Nels Jorgensen, Robert Joffrey, and Paul Sutherland

To
William Bernard Anawalt
Katharine de Lancey Anawalt
Thomas Cunningham Anawalt
Lucy Spalding Anawalt

Contents

Author's Note   9

A Joffrey Ballet: *Astarte*   11

PART ONE: BREAKING GROUND

1. The Chili Recipe   17

2. Finding Ballet   23

3. Gerald Arpino   31

4. Coming-of-Age   41

5. New York, New York   55

6. Dancer to Choreographer   67

7. In Good Company   75

8. Adversity   83

PART TWO: CORNERSTONE

9. Six Dancers and a Station Wagon   97

10. Quarrying the Repertoire   113

11. The Models   125

12. Rebekah Harkness Kean   141

13. Ambassadors   153

14. Treachery at Watch Hill   163

15. President Kennedy and the USSR   175

16. The Split   187

CONTENTS

PART THREE: THRESHOLD

17. The Nation's Closet   199
18. City Center Joffrey Ballet   209
19. Image   223
20. The Green Table   231
21. Astarte   241
22. The Dance Spirit   251
23. Crossing Over   267
24. Muses   291

PART FOUR: HOME

25. The Ashes   309
26. Los Angeles   325
27. Sacrifices   337
28. The Nutcracker   347
Afterword   355
Notes   365
Bibliography   387
Chronology of Works   391
Acknowledgments   441
Index   443

Author's Note

"Girls, come on, Fonteyn and Nureyev in *Romeo and Juliet*. We've got to go," my mother said, while showing us how to stuff our pajamas into our snowsuits so that we looked presentable enough for the Metropolitan Opera House. We would stay for the first part, then dash back to our apartment. With our nightclothes already on, my sister and I could jump into bed and get enough sleep for school the next day. In my family, going to the ballet was an adventure.

Our dinner table conversations revolved around dance. My parents wanted to know what we thought about different performances, and the reasons behind our opinions. My mother started to write about dance. My father, a painter, started to concentrate more on figure work.

I saw my first Joffrey Ballet performance in 1966. There were as many, if not more, trips to the New York City Ballet and American Ballet Theatre and the Royal Ballet and Martha Graham. We lived near Jacob's Pillow Dance Festival in the summers and saw everything, embracing director Ted Shawn's approach that a balance of ballet, modern, and ethnic forms provided the best diet for anyone interested in movement. It was a sensibility not altogether different from Robert Joffrey's.

When I became a critic at the *Los Angeles Herald Examiner* at the end of 1983, I thought it was absolutely wrong that the Joffrey Ballet's history had not been recorded in a book. Flashing through my mind, almost as vividly as if I had seen them yesterday, appeared Lisa Bradley and Maximiliano Zomosa and Robert Blankshine and Gary Chryst and Rebecca Wright and Christian Holder and Francesca Corkle. They were some of the Joffrey dancers who made me see and made the act of seeing be something important and vital. They enchanted me. W. H. Auden said, "The state of enchantment is one of certainty. When enchanted, we neither believe nor doubt nor deny: we *know*, even if, as in the case of a false enchantment, our knowledge is self-deception."

I knew. But I was curious to know why. Why did Joffrey create the company he did? In order to answer the question it became imperative to

9

examine his childhood, his early training, and his formative years. His roots and heritage are largely undocumented.

Joffrey cared about his image. He had an effective publicity machine. I doubted the versions the public knew. He fascinated me, and I was determined to know him better. I had interviewed him formally twice. I have never been to his residence. Although I have had cooperation on this book from Gerald Arpino, Rima Corben, and Edith D'Addario of the Joffrey Ballet and School, I have generously been left alone to dig. I made my own path to him.

I then asked how. How did Joffrey and Arpino, with no connections, no money, get started and keep the company running for more than forty years? They were first-generation Americans—ballet professionals, but also entrepreneurs—and I had a hunch that in learning about them I would begin to see something about the history of American performing arts.

I went to St. Paul's School in Concord, New Hampshire, for high school in 1971, and Rochelle Zide, an ex–Joffrey dancer, was on the faculty. I took her ballet class, in part, because I had studied ballet at American Ballet Theatre and at Margaret Craske's school in the Village and I missed the regular discipline. I relocated to Los Angeles in 1980; the Joffrey Ballet moved there into the Dorothy Chandler Pavilion three years later. By then I was a dance critic. It seemed no matter where I went, there was the Joffrey.

When I decided to write this book, I had to go home many times to New York to do research. In my old bedroom, I opened the door to my closet. There were stacks of Joffrey programs that my mother had saved. Not only programs, but souvenir brochures and newspaper clippings and press releases. I couldn't help feeling that this book had been waiting for me to write it.

This is a personal exercise and an adventure. It is about *knowing*. It is about discovering the distinction between false and real enchantment. A master teacher, Robert Joffrey had a sure instinct for both.

Auden continues his explanation saying, "When we are truly enchanted we desire nothing for ourselves, only that the enchanting object or person shall continue to exist. When we are falsely enchanted, we desire either to possess the enchanting being or be possessed by it." I wrote this book so that Joffrey and the performances he made happen will fade less quickly and so that everyone can take a look.

A Joffrey Ballet:
Astarte

Let's look at a ballet, a Joffrey ballet, one of the few he choreographed in his lifetime and probably the ballet that is most closely associated in the popular mind with the company: *Astarte*. Astarte was the ancient Babylonian goddess of fertility. She was a sex goddess.

It's 1967. You enter the City Center theater at West Fifty-fifth Street. The building used to be a Mecca Temple for the Ancient Order of the Nobles of the Mystic Shrine and was rescued from demolition. It feels like a temple inside. Gold is on the ceiling, there is a feeling of mosaics and Arabian influence, onion spires, a faraway land. The scruffy red velvet seats are uncomfortable, too close together, placed too low, not right for dance, but amiable, cozy with diminished grandeur. The audience: women with their hair in a Jackie Kennedy flip; mothers with cat glasses; a few old ladies with their old-lady friends; no children; young men sporting long sideburns. One or two people wear turtlenecks and Nehru jackets. More than a few have long hair. There are also men in white shirts, pin-striped suits, and ties, whose average age looks to be about thirty-two. They've all come to the theater, many perhaps expecting to see something akin to a tutu, a pas de deux in the classical fashion, a love duet with elite appeal.

In the orchestra pit: a rock band. The music begins and it's loud. (Joffrey sometimes rehearsed the ballet to Iron Butterfly's "Inna-Gadda-Da-Vida," but he doesn't use that song in the ballet.) The original score by Crome Syrcus drew inspiration from Country Joe and the Fish, Moby Grape, as well as Iron Butterfly. It is constructed to match the thirty-minute running time of a one-thousand-foot reel of film. The sensation is acid rock, blasting, twisting, pulling you through sound as if you had fallen into a black hole and then reached back and took the hole with you. A weird place to be. Strange land for an evening at the ballet. A rock concert when you didn't ask for one.

Lights. Mild audience abuse: two follow spots rake the audience. A piercing bright strobe light flashes you right in the face. The curtain rises.

11

The stage is bombarded by color film images projected on a billowing, stretchy white cloth. The environment is kinetic, rigged like a sailboat where mainsail, spinnaker, and jib are combined. The scenery breathes. The four different film images of the same dancers whipping up the play of their bodies against one another at a discothèque seem to inhabit space. The impression is of an extensive, active hologram.

The film: a woman's figure fills the screen. She looks as if her entire body has been tattooed with paisley psychedelic designs, swirling peacock eyes, flower blossoms, every inch colored in. Every contour is emphasized by Day-Glo colors brought to life under black light. She's been graffitied. Objectified. The film splits her like a prism and we see the same image of her many times.

She is Astarte. Onstage: she is a real woman, dancer Trinette Singleton, who has risen from a fetal curl to a frozen stance. We see her fine features, aristocratic eyebrows, hair parted in the middle, and a mark on her forehead: a lotus blossom outlined in dark pencil. Her lips are red and beneath her eyes are black dots. She stares at us, beyond us, perhaps toward a man in the audience. Come on, come on, come on, the fibers in her body are alert and wanting to say, come on, come on, come on.

In the audience stands dancer Maximiliano Zomosa (on opening night the Joffrey Ballet people positioned him behind Clive Barnes, critic for the *New York Times,* intentionally, and Zomosa by accident put his hand on Barnes's shoulder as he pushed himself to his feet). Zomosa wears a yellow-brown corduroy suit, blue work shirt, and paisley tie. His sideburns are sharp triangles. Think of pyramids in Egypt. He is tall and lean. He has dark, sullen eyes and bronzed skin. As if summoned toward the stage, he moves with slow, sustained steps. After climbing the stairs, he strips to his briefs, folds the clothes neatly, and approaches Astarte. He scans his opened hand in front of the goddess's glazed eyes. She does not blink. She is in a trance. He takes her, manipulates her reverentially, not violently. There are arabesques and pirouettes and balances. This sex goddess wears pointe shoes. The kinetic environment behind them pulsates; the womb is their space. He forgets himself, seduces the goddess, bending her head backward, stealing a kiss, stealing her lotus (the tattoo on her forehead, the symbol). In bliss, he somersaults as though gravity no longer holds him captive.

The film shifts to black-and-white. Two giant images of the dancers' faces, Singleton and Zomosa, are projected side by side, alienated, separated. The images slide into darkness.

Astarte takes her revenge. She banishes the man to the outside world. Simultaneously the kinetic environment flies, floats into space, to reveal the workmanlike brick walls of the City Center backstage area, bare and bereft.

Zomosa exits through a door at the rear of the stage and onto the street. The single, sombre black-and-white film shows him walking, still undressed, past the taxicabs and cars, past the theater. Pedestrians look in the doorway at the audience looking at him, them, and the film. The muted roar of the traffic enhances the final surge of music. The ballet ends, and half a year later it graces the cover of *Time.*

PART ONE

BREAKING GROUND

CHAPTER 1

The Chili Recipe

Part of the myth of Robert Joffrey is that he was destiny's child. Joffrey himself liked to believe that he could have been born anywhere, to any parents, and would still have created one of America's finest ballet companies. He projected the image that dance chose him. Embarrassed by his parents and their working-class background, he refused in his youth to let even his closest friends into his family's three-room Seattle apartment. In New York City, where he lived all of his professional life, photographs of Joseph and Mary Joffrey and their relations were fastidiously hidden and shown only under pressure from trustworthy colleagues.

When presented with indisputable evidence that he had indeed come from a set of very real circumstances, Joffrey sometimes conjured up stories that exploded the so-called facts into bits of mysterious nonsense. One explained why his official documents said he was born on December 24, 1928, when he had told everyone the year was 1930. He said that he had had an older brother who was stillborn in 1928, and Joseph Joffrey, his father—a devout Muslim who believed that the firstborn male was the most significant—had finessed the records so they would reflect the next son, Robert, as having been born in that year. This unorthodox action permitted his father to bestow his fullest affections on Robert as the eldest. It also provided Joffrey a convenient justification that could correct his father's rewrite and show that he was two years younger than he actually was—not an atypical practice for a theater professional.

Although Joffrey's explanation seemed implausible, it was possible. There were stories about other Middle Eastern and Central Asian immigrant families in America at the time who had passed on the deceased eldest brother's birth certificate to the next son. Robert Joffrey was most *probably* born on December 24, 1928. His birth certificate and school records substantiate that date. A search at the Bureau of Vital Statistics in Seattle for other siblings' birth certificates turned up nothing, a search that Joffrey himself would undoubtedly have delighted in causing.

He embraced privacy as an article of faith. Whenever Joffrey failed to produce an explanation about his origins, he would change the subject.

17

Throughout his life, he withdrew from scrutiny and confrontation. While he believed that all people were fundamentally good, he did not much savor the company of others. His social graces were so ingrained, however, that he could not allow himself to be anything less than charming in public; and his buoyant nature made it all but impossible for him to persuade most that he was secretly a mild misanthrope, who longed not to be diverted from his work. His desire for isolation perhaps conflicted too strongly with his ambitions as an artistic director, and his ambitions prevailed. He was a master at repression and a master of his will.

The restraints he placed on himself also applied, although in somewhat looser fashion, to his dance company. Many writers who desired to learn the facts and then publish unofficial Joffrey Ballet histories in book form were met with a fierce, polite resistance. Joffrey would sidestep and procrastinate and then steer them in other directions. He hired in-house historians and publicists to construct the company's image according to his wishes.

Robert Joffrey lived for the dance; his life was based on action, moving forward, evaporating in present time without the intrinsic need to stop and look back. He was a ballet classicist by principle, and in ballet, the story is told through the body. On the stage, idealism and illusion hold an absolute, unsentimental power. Dancers are trained from a young age to alter and enhance their natural human postures—to become unreal. They slim down close to the bone, learn to turn out their legs at the hip, lift their spines, and stretch away from themselves, freeing their bodies from their bodies, as it were, to communicate ideas and emotions. The hard physical truth, the effort, is masked. Joffrey may have been persuaded by his art that it was not important for people to know why they were seeing what they were seeing—the magic was impenetrable. Dance in its impermanence held no one responsible for certainty. It took no prisoners, and the artistic director, masterminding the onstage actions, was obligated to remain an invisible force, an enigma.

But under a cool and direct light, both Joffrey and his dance company prevail in a scrutable reality where many of the conjectures, if they are not true, are at least credible. He spent almost twenty years in Seattle with Joseph and Mary, his parents, and when their backgrounds are examined, a dynamic chronicle emerges, buttressed by traditions and a moral conscience, that has everything to do with who Robert Joffrey is and what his vision for American ballet became.

Dollha Anver Bey Jaffa Khan, or Doulat Khan,[1] as he was known before his name was anglicized to Joseph Joffrey, was born on October 11, 1886,[2] in Hazara, Afghanistan,[3] where his father was the ruling khan of a village. He was a Pakhtun, the largest ethnic group in Afghanistan and the second-largest ethnic group in modern Pakistan. For centuries, the

Pakhtuns had withstood invasions by conquerors scheming to gain control of the Khyber Pass, gateway between Afghanistan and India. By the turn of the century, the long-standing struggle for freedom had taken its toll on Pakhtun society. From the nomads in their black-wool geodesic tents to the intelligentsia in their adobelike structures, the Pakhtuns saw outside civilization to be an unforgiving march in opposition to their humanity. Violence often fractured internal family structures and pitted brother against brother, creating the backdrop for the world in which Dollha grew up.[4] It was an understanding of Robert Joffrey's that Dollha's father was murdered by Dollha's uncle in an act of revenge, or *badal*. Although surviving family members cannot corroborate the fratricide, the story had been repeated so often it became part of the family history.

In a speech given by one of Dollha's brothers, Aurang Shah, in California in 1957, on the occasion of Pakhtunistan Day,[5] he described what life was like in a Pakhtun village at the time of the Mogul and British onslaughts:

> *When a man left his lookout post near his home, his wife took over his gun. . . . He bought Springfields from America, for they were considered the best. Men who could not afford guns were handy with swords and captured rifles and ammunition from the British. Small children carried food to their fathers. Signals from neighbors told if friend or foe was near. Dogs were trained to bring food, water, and ammunition to the outposts and return home with the rifles of the dead or mortally wounded—to lunge directly at the throats of the enemy.*[6]

By 1910, the fatherless boys had matured into bright, eager men. They attended a liberal school opened by Abdul Ghaffar Khan, a spiritual teacher in their district. Their contemporary, Abdul Ghaffar Khan and his precepts and convictions forever influenced the brothers.

Ghaffar Khan became known as the Gandhi of the Frontier. He found persuasive relevance in the belief that before God all people were equal: men and women, servant and khan. To him, honor lay in forgiveness; "Man is a Muslim who never hurts anyone by word or deed," he said, quoting Prophet Muhammad.[7] On a grassroots level, Ghaffar Khan inspired many Pakhtuns to embrace Islamic laws of morality, to return good for evil, and ultimately, to pressure the British for social and political reforms through passive resistance. Joffrey's father and his uncles forged a lifelong friendship with Ghaffar Khan that bridged to America.

In 1916, their mother pressured her patriotic sons into emigrating to the United States. She hoped that they would acquire a Western education and experience the justice and freedom that had been idealized by Ghaffar Khan. Dollha and Aurang were the first of the family to leave. Their destination was Seattle, for no apparent reason other than that the next freighter leaving China was headed to the Pacific Northwest. Naim Shah, Aurang's son and Robert Joffrey's younger cousin, recounting stories told to them by their fathers, stated:

"They came on a freighter, leaving from either Karachi or Bombay, that went via Manila in the Philippines to China. They took the Pacific route. Bob [Joffrey] confirmed that our grandmother sent them because there was opportunity in America. She sent them off with a sack of gold. I asked about the gold. 'Was it in nuggets?' 'Oh, be quiet,' they said. We were growled at. Bob's father and mine were secretive. They'd talk about the past if they wanted to, but it wasn't information you'd get by sitting around on a Sunday afternoon and saying, 'Gee, where'd you come from?' I think it's because they'd had one harsh life over there and they wanted to leave most of it behind."[8]

First arriving in Canada, the two men then crossed the border into Washington and immediately went to work in the Seattle area sawmills. They spoke only Pakhto and Urdu, yet within the year had emerged as entrepreneurs, forming their own business, selling chili out of pushcarts on the streets. Their recipe was an original: a chicken-and-beef-based chili loaded with Mexican and Central Asian spices and ripe olives that apparently pleased the locals' newfound taste for hot and exotic food. Somewhere along the line, the chili became so popular that they sold the recipe.

With the money, which is said to have come from a large food corporation (possibly Gebhardt or Hormel), Dollha and Aurang went their separate ways. Dollha remained in Seattle and, in 1922, opened a restaurant, the Rainbow Chili Parlor. Aurang moved south to Petaluma, California, where he attended high school to learn English. He eventually achieved the goal he had set for himself in Afghanistan, graduating with a medical degree from Tufts University and an MA in public health from Harvard University. Following these accomplishments, he moved to Sacramento, California, married a Lutheran, started a family of four, and founded the Azad Pakhtunistan Association of America—determined to sustain the Pakhtuns' ambition to win their freedom as a distinct sovereign state. Both he and Dollha kept the chili recipe folded in their wallets at all times to remind them of what had been the key to their success in the new land.

After Aurang left him, Dollha concentrated on running his restaurant. He was never as politically inclined as his brother, with whom he stayed in constant touch, and unlike Aurang, who was known for saying, "I am not a Muslim. I am a Harvard graduate,"[9] Dollha upheld many Islamic principles and considered himself a Muslim. Five times a day, he turned toward Mecca and knelt on a prayer rug, reciting verses from the Koran, but he also took certain steps toward assimilation. He readily called himself Joseph and wore three-piece suits and Stetson hats. As an observant Muslim, he did not drink, and yet he served alcohol regularly to his patrons. Joseph was an astute and sociable being, driven by a strong sense of hospitality. The Rainbow Chili Parlor's tavern suited him well. By thrusting him into conversations with his clientele, bartending taught him English. The tasks that bored him fell to his employees, including Marie Gallette, who had, in 1920, emigrated from Lucca in northern Italy with two of her brothers.

Marie Gallette was a nurse and amateur concert violinist who had spent her youth touring from city to Italian city, performing in the local cafés. She liked to boast that music was perhaps her inheritance due to geography because her hometown was also the birthplace of Puccini, but when she became a teenager, her prime ambition was to leave home. She and her brothers had judiciously saved their money for the dream of finding greater prosperity in America. "My mother was so thrilled to come to America," said Robert Joffrey. "She was determined to go to school and become an American citizen. She was devoted to America and said she'd never go back to Europe. My father was the opposite. He loved America, but he never gave up his Afghanistan citizenship. So there was a strong contrast between the two."[10]

Marie Gallette had fluffy nut-brown hair and pale, creamy skin; she was plump, wore little hats, and liked the occasional cigarette. Joseph hired Mary, as she came to be called, to wait on tables and run the cash register. At twenty-six, she was quick and observant, and although at times stubborn and temperamental, she let nothing distract her from her work. She revered, above all, the virtue of steadfast loyalty, and for that reason Joseph trusted her and came to see her as a most appropriate mate.

In 1922, Mary and Joseph were married. Conventional love, however, seems to have played little part in their union; they were estranged almost from the start and were known to quarrel, to sleep in separate beds, and to disregard each other's presence. Robert Joffrey, as an adult, told a friend that he believed his father had married Mary only because it had saved him the cashier's salary from the restaurant payroll.[11]

Others felt she was picked by Joseph simply because he wanted children: "She was really only used to produce Robert and then was never touched again," said one early Joffrey friend.[12] Another contributed: "Mary worked for Joseph. They had Bob. That was the whole reason for them to meet."[13]

The striking differences between Joseph's and Mary's cultural backgrounds alone might have caused their mutual alienation. Mary was a Catholic from Italy and while she did not regularly attend Mass, the rosary beads were a familiar sight in her hands. Although Joseph said that he "respected people for being dedicated to their beliefs"[14]—an attitude that is in keeping with the Koran—the jump for him to a full acceptance of Mary's Christianity might have been more difficult than he had anticipated. They also shared no common language; her English was just as spotty as his, and acquaintances noticed that they had serious trouble communicating.

"It was difficult for Mary," said Gerald Arpino, who first met the Joffrey family in 1945. He lived with Robert Joffrey for forty-three years, approximately three of them in the same house with the Joffreys in Seattle. He continued, "She was a phenomenal woman in her own right and, I think, frustrated by her own brilliance. She could have continued being a concert violinist. She had great intellect, but was frustrated by her marriage situation and was not able to cope. She surrendered to it."[15]

Mary and Joseph's more obvious differences, however, may appear minor in the face of the difficult time they had starting a family. Sticking to her principles of marital devotion, working long hours for Joseph, stifling any thought of divorce, Mary seemed unable to carry a child to term. In this regard, she, a "high-strung and neurotic"[16] Catholic, felt a deep sense of failure. Then, finally, after several miscarriages and six years of struggle, on Christmas Eve in 1928 at Seattle General Hospital, Mary gave birth to a son. They named him Anver[17] and apparently took no notice of the coincidence between their event and the one of the more famous Mary and Joseph that had happened a day later nearly two thousand years before. Joffrey reached his twenties before he himself realized the parallel. It played into his predestination paradigm, but otherwise he ignored the tenuous similarity, though he always loved Christmas and expended maximum effort in its celebration.

His parents took him home from the hospital to their downtown apartment in the Windsor Hotel and immediately bestowed upon him the formal American appellation Robert, preferring to call him Bobby. Although they did not know it, Bobby would be their only child, and on one thing they were in total agreement. He was their reason for living.

CHAPTER 2

Finding Ballet

The Great Depression struck the year after Bobby's birth. His parents managed to sustain their business; and, in fact, the failing economy may have been the least of their problems. Of more immediate concern was the physical condition of their son. His legs were bowed and his feet turned in, which Mary and Joseph were told could lead to problems in his hips and jeopardize his ability to walk normally. To correct the distortions, casts were put on his feet. So she could give more attention to Bobby, Mary turned over her restaurant accounting work to Henrietta Williams, and although it would not seem significant then, two and a half years later Williams would become the aunt of Richard Bernard Englund. He was to be the first close friend to share Bobby's love for ballet.

When Bobby's ordeal with the casts ended, his legs were still noticeably bowed, but the potential hip problem seemed to have been averted and Mary returned to work, taking Bobby along with her. Once Bobby started kindergarten, he would join his mother at the restaurant after school, where she gave him small tasks to do, such as arranging napkins and putting olives on the salads.

Bobby attended the Bailey Gatzert School on Twelfth South and Weller Streets in Chinatown. The school was an unusual choice because it was not in his district. Fewer than thirty-five non-Asians were in the student body; the majority were Japanese. Bobby wanted desperately to be seen by others as fitting in. "I wanted to be accepted. I didn't want to be unique at that point," he said.[1] He wanted the chance to find out what being an American meant, and to him that entailed attending a school where the student body reflected Seattle's population, approximately 80 percent of which had been born in America and were white. He asked to be transferred to another public school, and Joseph and Mary did what he wanted. In 1936, he attended Summit Elementary.

Joseph decided that inside the home his son would learn some of the Pakhtun traditions. His highest priority was for Bobby to speak Pakhto and to be familiar with Islamic precepts and orthodox Muslim practices. He tried but failed. To Joseph's utter consternation, Bobby, even at this early age, resisted him. Although he didn't articulate it as succinctly as he would later on, Bobby told his father that he was an American and that he was not like him. Perhaps because Joseph was accustomed to pampering Bobby as a sickly child, he let him get away with the impudence, but a line had been drawn between them that would never go away and would repeatedly be tested. "There was always conflict in their household," said one of Joffrey's childhood friends, as Joffrey did not understand then that being Muslim and American were not mutually exclusive. "His father wanted him to be Muslim and he wanted to be American. It was never any other way. But his father loved him—and admired him."[2]

For his ability at a young age to force his parents into yielding to his wishes, Bobby earned the incalculable respect of his younger cousins on the family's Afghan side. "What surprised me in a sense was that Bob was so American rather than Afghan," said Naim Shah. At gatherings the other children "seemed to be putting on acts" for their parents. They were subdued and obedient. Bobby wasn't exactly a rebel; his manners were formal and his temperament sweet and ebullient, but he made it clear to Shah that he "didn't perform for anybody." Said Shah, "He was his own person."[3]

Bobby and his father were not at complete odds; they both liked having fun too much, and having lost his own father to fratricide, Joseph had paid a price for family infighting that he cared not to repeat. Every Sunday until Bobby was eleven years old, Joseph took him to the zoo in Woodland Park. The animals fascinated them both, prompting Joseph to buy Bobby two rabbits (Peachie and Snowball) and a German shepherd (Goldie). The pets were a disaster, however, because Bobby was desperately allergic to them. At age eight, he was diagnosed as an asthmatic.

Joffrey always maintained that he started taking ballet because his pediatrician told him that exercise would help his asthma. "When I danced, the wheezing stopped," he said.[4] But it seems much more likely that the doctor suggested exercise not for the asthma, but for the bowed legs. "I think Bob took ballet primarily to strengthen his frame, his structural frame—even more than asthma," said Gerald Arpino.[5]

During the early 1930s, medical authorities were of the opinion that exercise *contributed* to respiratory problems, and the more common advice was to have their patients desist from physical activities.[6] In later life, when he became a professional dancer, Joffrey would probably not have wanted to call attention to his bowlegs, and so, he might have preferred to tell the story that he came to ballet because he was an asthmatic. It was not a complete stretch of the truth.

Whatever the circumstances, Joseph's first reaction to the doctor's recommendation was to enroll Bobby in boxing lessons. There is something deliberately macho about his choice that points the way to the facts: Bobby Joffrey was small. In adulthood he measured five feet four inches. As an eight-year-old, he was puny for his age. His parents were also small and somewhat chubby. The profile was in the genes. Maybe Joseph worried about Bobby being teased and picked on, maybe he thought boxing would teach him self-defense and pride. Boxing would be Joffrey's first exposure to instructed physical movement.

During this time a gentleman named Marcus Khan arrived in Seattle from the old country. Although he may not have been related, Marcus was hailed as Joseph's older brother and Bobby called him Uncle Marcus Joffrey. He would live with the Joffreys on and off during Bobby's childhood. He was dapper, suave, and roguish because he broke whatever rules there were to break. In photographs Marcus suggests the elegant movie star Omar Sharif, with flirtatious, mischievous eyes, a noble chin, and a cosmopolitan aura. Marcus was six years Joseph's senior and had his own ideas about how Bobby should be raised. He would often take Bobby out of school and steal him off to a double feature or the theater. He would also take him to the ballet. They became boon companions. "Poor Mary, Marcus drove her to distraction," Arpino lamented. "He was a terror. A real terror."[7]

People who remembered Marcus Joffrey, including his nephew Naim Shah, believe that he was homosexual. "The sexual activities of adults within the family were private," Shah said, "but not exactly hidden." He felt Bobby was able to sever the umbilical cord earlier than many children because he had the security of Marcus, who paid for whatever Bobby wanted when his parents wouldn't or couldn't, and who listened to him with genuine interest. "You have to get away from the family," Joffrey once told Shah when they were talking about the central role Marcus had played in Joffrey's life, and he was passing down the wisdom to Shah that Marcus had given him. "You have to get away from that controlling influence."[8] Marcus was Joffrey's role model, said Shah.

On one of their hooky outings, Uncle Marcus took Bobby with him to see the new Greta Garbo film *Camille*. The sight of Garbo, her posture, her clothes, her atmosphere, her voice, her phrasing, everything about her—"the way she dances with her face," Joffrey said[9]—moved him to see everything else in his world as unimportant. He particularly loved the line when she, waiting to be driven to the theater in her carriage, says, "Of course I order too many flowers and too many hats and too many everything, but I want them." In later years Bobby would be accused of indulging in similar extravagances. He became infatuated and began collecting every memento he could find relating to Garbo.

Fred Astaire and Gene Kelly soon shared the prime spot with Garbo. Bobby dreamed of being like Astaire and Kelly, tapping his way to fame, glamour, and Hollywood. He talked his parents into letting him quit boxing and take up tap dancing. They didn't have to look far to find

Dorothy Culper's Dancing School. Said Joffrey, "It was a little studio where you had everything, which was typical. Tap, ballroom, you name it. And it was above my father's restaurant, so I would run up there and have my classes and it would keep me out of mischief. Very convenient. I liked it, but I really didn't study ballet. I studied theatrical dancing, musical-comedy dancing."[10]

Uncle Marcus agreed to pay for the lessons. In 1938, the Joffreys moved to 1520 Boren Street and into the first house that they owned. They relocated their restaurant to the same block and changed its name to the Italian Tavern. There Bobby found a way to earn his own money to help pay for Dorothy Culper's classes: the curtained booths that lined the restaurant's walls could be transformed into makeshift theaters. Taking advantage of this setup, Bobby began performing his first choreography. Creating costumes from clothes that had been left unclaimed at the cleaner's next door, he viewed it as his particular challenge to invent dances appropriate to the borrowed attire.[11] He would then burst out from behind a booth's curtains and entertain the tavern's clientele with an improvisation:

"I would get money—I had a little tambourine and I'd dance, much to my father's horror. And I'd make quite a lot of money, which I always hoarded and kept. And I'd also get theater tickets, because the restaurant was near the theater and the artists ate there and tickets were often given to my father."[12]

Miss Culper instantly seized upon Bobby's flair for movement and concocted showbiz musical routines for him and a girl in his class named Patty. In 1939, she entered the duo in a contest that was headlined by Veloz and Yolanda, a leading exhibition ballroom team of the period. Bobby and his partner won the first prize: a $500 war bond. "I was in a tuxedo and she was in a little gown. It was a Fred Astaire–Ginger Rogers number," he said. "I think we got the prize because we were the youngest who had ever participated. We did a tango and probably looked like two little dolls."[13]

Bobby seemed unstoppable. Years later, when asked, "How long have you wanted a ballet company?" Bobby responded, "Since I was nine years old."[14] Everywhere he went, he danced. One afternoon in fifth grade at Summit Elementary, after weeks of rain, when the physical education teacher had run out of ideas for indoor sports activities, Bobby offered to teach them all how to polka. "I taught the boys and girls and we polkaed around the room," he said. "I was always planning. In school I would do little plays and direct them and make people do things and decorate. For Christmas, I always decorated the schoolroom and put on productions."[15] If by nine he knew what he wanted to do with his life, then by eleven he was already well on his way.

By 1939, Bobby had outgrown Dorothy Culper. He left her for a teacher whose reputation for being strict and professional had reached him. Bobby thought Ivan Novikoff could raise him to the standard of Fred Astaire as a tap dancer, but little by little Novikoff pushed him toward ballet. "I immediately became mesmerized and very wrapped up in the physicality of ballet," Joffrey recalled.[16]

Instead of Bobby conquering tap, Novikoff and ballet conquered him. He started taking a private lesson with Novikoff every day (also paid for by Uncle Marcus). Novikoff said he would never forget his newest pupil's determination, adding, "Bobby's elevation was brilliant, but he was bowlegged and too short. I told him he should never dance. He should not appear in front of people except to take a bow, because they will criticize him."[17]

Only months after having been introduced to ballet instruction, Bobby found himself on January 20, 1940, in Michel Fokine's haunting carnival-time masterpiece, *Petrouchka,* with Léonide Massine, Alicia Markova, and André Eglevsky, some of the most legendary artists of the day. Novikoff had signed him up to be a supernumerary (which meant a nondancing role) in Ballet Russe de Monte Carlo's matinée program at the Moore Theatre. The job paid fifty cents and was his first experience on the professional stage. Massine performed the title role of the sawdust-filled puppet in love with the Ballerina and murdered by the jealous Blackamoor.

For Joffrey it was a wonderful and overwhelming experience: "Massine pulled me offstage with him, when Petrouchka sneaks off at the end of the fourth scene, when he's dead. He grabbed me and a little girl, pulled us into the wings, and then shoved us back onstage. My devotion to *Petrouchka* started then. . . . And the Ballet Russe sometimes allowed us to take company class, if we stayed in the background. We'd also sneak in and watch rehearsals. It was thrilling.[18]

"I remember Massine dancing so brilliantly, and he became my idol. I thought he was wonderful. And his career—he was a choreographer, then he was a director—all of that sort of made me want to do things."[19]

Joffrey saw his own image in Massine. And, when they had reason to work together in 1969, Massine implied to Tatiana Massine, his daughter and assistant, that he saw himself in Joffrey.

After *Petrouchka,* Bobby confided to Novikoff that he wanted someday to have his own ballet company, and he vowed to include *Petrouchka* in the repertoire. He also told Novikoff that he wanted to choreograph what was integral to many ballet company repertoires: "I wanted to do a snowflake ballet down a ramp." In 1962, when recalling this conversation with Novikoff to Walter Terry of the *New York Herald Tribune,* Joffrey clearly viewed the snowflake ballet as one of the seeds that became the Joffrey Ballet. "It was a terribly corny idea—but look what it snowballed into!" he exclaimed.[20]

The experience of his first *Petrouchka* was soon matched by a Ballets Jooss performance on February 24, 1940, of *The Green Table* at the Moore Theatre. Choreographed by Kurt Jooss in his native Germany after World War I, *The Green Table* is a harrowing satire on war. Jooss had originally portrayed the central figure of Death; dressed in a gray leotard marked with black representations of human bones, Death strides in square, thunderous jolts like the Four Horsemen of the Apocalypse and entraps the innocents. He waltzes a young woman to her grave and mows down victims with an imaginary scythe. The ballet ends as the diplomatic Gentlemen in Black negotiate for another war at a table that is covered with regulation green baize. The German Expressionist choreography is precise, grounded, and morally intoned.

Recalling the day he saw the Jooss masterpiece,* Joffrey wrote:

> *I still remember vividly the flashing white gloves of the diplomats and Death's inexorable stomping, gathering in his victims. The sharp head movements the dancers made struck me as very different from the classical technique I was studying, but although the choreography was clearly "modern," some of the dancing looked so high on the half-toe that the dancers seemed almost to be on* pointe. *These details were etched in my mind in what must have been an exceptionally powerful performance....*
>
> *I carried the memory of that childhood performance of* The Green Table *with me like a talisman through my own early years in dance, until in 1966 I felt it was time to ask Jooss if my company might perform his work.*[21]

Bobby did not miss a single dance attraction that came to Seattle, and through Novikoff, he appeared in the Ballet Russe productions of both Fokine's harem bacchanal *Schéhérazade* and Alexandra Fedorova's two-act staging of Lev Ivanov's nineteenth-century classic, *The Nutcracker*. In *Schéhérazade*, as one of the servants, Bobby said he leapt onto the stage and, carrying a tray, sailed across and back again. As the Gondola Boy in *The Nutcracker*, he said he rode out on a gondola with Alexandra Danilova as the Sugar Plum Fairy, and when she stepped off to greet Igor Youskevitch, her cavalier, he made gestures with a feather. His memory for *The Nutcracker* might have been playing tricks, however, because Frederic Franklin, who danced in both and also staged both productions, said there wasn't a tray-carrying servant in *Schéhérazade* or a Gondola Boy in *The Nutcracker*.

Regardless of the details, there was little doubt that Bobby's adventures

---

*The cast Robert Joffrey saw in *The Green Table* included Rudolph Pescht (Death); Ernst Uthoff (Standard-Bearer); Hans Gansert (Old Soldier); Elsa Kahl (Woman); Lola Botka (Old Mother); Henry Schwarz (Young Soldier); Noelle de Mosa (Young Girl); and Hans Zullig (Profiteer). Ulla Soederbaum was in the corps.

both on and off the stage with Ballet Russe de Monte Carlo were formative. After many performances, Novikoff and Beuhal Kirberger, his wife
and professional colleague, entertained Massine, Danilova, and Nathalie
Krassovska in their home. Bobby was invited, too. Their conversation was
mostly in English because Kirberger was their hostess and she did not
speak Russian. In front of the roaring fire, Novikoff said, they talked
about his plans to develop an American Ballet Russe. "Bobby stole all my
ideas," he said in 1992, at age ninety-two, with tongue in cheek.[22]

Novikoff seemed to have exclusive claim in Seattle to Ballet Russe de
Monte Carlo in that whenever extra bodies were needed, Novikoff's students were the ones solicited by Jean B. Cerrone of Ballet Russe. Bobby's
acquaintance with Cerrone would later prove important, but another
consequence of Novikoff's attachment to Ballet Russe was that serious-
minded ballet students were drawn to him. Richard Englund, a blond-
haired and athletic boy, took class at Novikoff's for a brief time when
Bobby was there, and a friendship between them rapidly developed.
Bobby and Richard swapped dance anecdotes like some of their school
pals probably traded baseball cards. Their friendship would last throughout their lives with varying degrees of intensity.

Around this time, Bobby began spending his pocket money on dance
books and frequenting the public library to consume ballet and art
books. "I felt very lonely. There was hardly anyone I could talk to," he
said. "There was no community of dancers. I was an odd person because
I was a dancer."[23] Lillian Moore's *Artists of the Dance* was his first book
and it ignited an obsession with Vaslav Nijinsky, who by most reports
grew to be only five feet four inches and against whom Bobby confidently measured himself. Said Joffrey, "Practically the only books in the
library were on Nijinsky and Pavlova. And because I was a male dancer
and of similar stature to Nijinsky, I felt very close to him."[24]

Bobby's attention to the male roles in classical ballet sharpened as his
interest in Nijinsky increased. In January 1941 he saw the Ballet Russe
production of Fokine's famous, ethereal *Les Sylphides,* choreographed
for nineteen women costumed in long white tutus and for one male poet
to the romantic music of Frédéric Chopin, and remarked, "[I was] very
disappointed that the man had nothing to do."[25] The realization that men
were shunted to the background in traditional classical ballets—that they
were generally used as partners to ballerinas, in which case they were
supposed to be essentially invisible—had dawned on him. He honed his
critical skills, he started having opinions. He preferred works that used a
balanced male-to-female ratio, works that gave the leading man a purpose beyond carrying the ballerina from pose to pose.

Counted among such works were Fokine's intoxicating, lyric pas de
deux *Le Spectre de la rose* and the opulent *Schéhérazade,* and Nijinsky's

sensual *L'Après-midi d'un faune*—ballets that had been introduced during Diaghilev's Ballets Russes' Paris seasons between 1910 and 1912 with Nijinsky in the leads. Each had contributed to Diaghilev's burgeoning reputation as one of the great impresarios of the twentieth century and, through Nijinsky's spectacular performances, dignified the public's perception of male dancers as consequential artists in their own right. Whenever Ballet Russe de Monte Carlo performed the Diaghilev repertoire, Bobby made it a point to watch intently as Frederic Franklin, George Zoritch, and Igor Youskevitch, the new generation of male virtuosos, took over the roles that Nijinsky had originated. Bobby was determined that one day he, too, would dance them.

His fixation on the Diaghilev period would resurface again and again. By the late 1960s, he had told numerous people that Serge Diaghilev was his role model, and many of his associates would later confidently proclaim that he was Diaghilev reincarnated. It was a lofty boast given that Diaghilev had virtually defined and shaped ballet in the twentieth century through his masterful collaborative enterprises that brought together such young modernists as Erik Satie with Léonide Massine and Pablo Picasso, or Igor Stravinsky with Nijinsky and Nicholas Roerich. What tends to be forgotten in the rush to forge links between Diaghilev and Joffrey is the part Nijinsky played. Bobby came to Diaghilev through Nijinsky.

Despite his grandiose comparisons to one of the greatest male dancers who ever lived, Bobby had not been born with the best body for ballet. He had to struggle to transform his physical instrument into a workable machine. His appearance was odd: narrow, defined runner's calves exploding into the massive thighs of a pugilist and tapering into the slim hips of a swimmer. His small head rested on top of a preternaturally long neck. His shoulders sloped and his hands were once described as "hammy."[26]

If Joffrey wanted to remake himself, he had to rely on supreme self-discipline and the perceptive ability of his teachers. Bobby had grown up in a place where all things were possible. Immigrant parents from different worlds joined together by hard work and a good chili recipe helped their particular American dream edge toward reality. They bestowed upon Bobby the virtue of hope.

CHAPTER 3

Gerald Arpino

By the end of 1940, world war was hastening the Great Depression into retreat and President Roosevelt held a "fireside chat" over the radio in which he said the country was gearing for battle. The United States would become the "arsenal for democracy," he declared. On March 11, 1941, the Lend-Lease Act was signed into law, enabling America to lend tanks, warplanes, and ships that could be returned "in kind" after the war. When, on June 24, Germany invaded Russia, Roosevelt invoked the Lend-Lease Act and promised immediate aid to Russia. In another four years, the decision would quite circuitously have a major impact on Bobby Joffrey.

Novikoff arranged to support the war effort by sending his students to perform for bond rallies at the local military camps. These weekend excursions to such places as the Bremerton Naval Yard were Bobby's first exposure to a public that was not necessarily interested in ballet; a general public, some of whose members he feared might recognize him.

He had kept his ballet classes absolutely separate from his academic life. He had told no one at Edmond S. Meany Junior High what he did after school. "I was going to give up dancing because I was very interested in school at that point, and I was very attracted to a girl whom I used to see on the bus; she lived near where I took ballet," he said. "We were beginning to have games and dances [at parties after school], and it was that dangerous period [adolescence]. I didn't tell anyone at school that I was dancing. So I had to live two lives."[1]

After one bond rally performance, Bobby was approached by Catherine Spedden, his art teacher from Edmond S. Meany, who had been in the audience. Surprised, she said she hadn't realized the seventh-grader danced. "Oh, yes," he replied, "I do that as a sort of hobby."[2] Spedden looked kindly upon Bobby because he was her most outstanding pupil. Out of the three hundred who took her class for fifty minutes every day, he was the one whose work had attracted her attention. "He was also sociable, outgoing, and smart," she elaborated.[3]

The next year, in eighth grade, Spedden and her young student had built a solid friendship, mainly because Bobby had begun staying after school with a chum of his named Hugo Scarsheim. They came ostensibly to work further on their projects and help Spedden clean up, but she could tell that Bobby's true purpose was to talk. "He seemed restless and agitated," she recalled. "It was right at that time that he was debating about making art his life's work. He went back and forth, weighing the pros and cons between becoming a painter and becoming a dancer."[4]

Spedden thought Bobby had every right to consider a profession in the fine arts as a painter or collagist a realistic possibility. He was good at painting and drawing, original and creative, approaching her assignments from unexpected angles, but she kept her opinions to herself, recognizing that here was someone who was focused beyond his years and unequivocal about the conflict. She told him that she didn't want to be blamed for having unduly influenced him. Then one day Bobby bounded in, brown eyes "snapping with excitement," she recalled.[5] He announced he was going to be a dancer and that he was basing his decision on the theory that he could incorporate art into ballet, but not so easily the reverse.

Soon after sharing this epiphany with Spedden, he told the rest of the school by signing up for the annual Edmond S. Meany talent show as a solo ballet artist. Meg Greenfield, now a columnist for the *Washington Post* and *Newsweek,* was a student one grade below Bobby. She recalled his auspicious debut before his peers:

> *Bobby ballaydanced, as we put it in those days—balletdanced, can you believe it? I mean a boy? There is no way I can fully explain to you what an act of courage and conviction this entailed in that place at that time, but I will try. . . .*
>
> *My most treasured memory of him will always be at a school assembly in seventh grade, one of those assemblies where different students performed in a kind of variety show. At these gatherings someone might recite the Gettysburg Address to lend the thing class, but feats like yo-yo tricks and magic and hokey show biz routines were, as I recall, the basic fare. Vividly I can see Bobby . . . in tights, at about [fourteen] years of age, dancing gracefully in a small space on the stage and accompanied at the piano by a large, buxom woman wearing a suit and vast high-crowned hat. . . . She played intently, stealing the odd glance at him. He danced, absorbed, seeming to be someplace else. We poked and giggled. . . . If we'd had the word, we would have called him a "wimp." As it was, we called him a "sissy."[6]*

Bobby thereafter attacked ballet with a fervent energy and commitment. Through Novikoff, he began teaching. His classes were held on Saturdays in Tacoma, where Novikoff was increasing the number of his

School of Russian American Ballet satellites.* Bobby was familiar with Novikoff's version of the fundamentals, which sometimes leaned in the direction of the unscrupulous. Novikoff was known, for example, to encourage girls at the age of five or six to dance on pointe, in toe shoes, which was far too young and could expose children to permanent injury.†
Because of his commercialism, he came to be regarded as somewhat of a charlatan by people from competing ballet schools. Joffrey later told friends that he thought it was odd that Novikoff had used him to teach when he was only an inexperienced teenager, but he welcomed the opportunity.

Novikoff also required Bobby to perform frequently with Novikoff Festival Ballet, a junior amateur company that had a repertoire of twenty works. Publicity photographs for the troupe show Bobby Joffrey dressed in Russian folk-dance costume (white, high-collared cotton shirt with embroidered trim, dark cummerbund, baggy pants,‡ and boots), squatting low and kicking out one leg—just like the *trepak* variation in *The Nutcracker*. Another reveals a brooding classical portrait typically nineteenth century and Romantic: Bobby wears the standard dark tights and a full-sleeved Byronic shirt; he glances over one extended arm, the other hand interlaced in the fingers of a pensive, kneeling ballerina, who looks more like a debutante in flowing skirts of pale tulle. Bobby's perfectionism and intensity can already be spotted, and whether or not Novikoff's productions were commendable, they were stage experience—exactly what every aspiring danseur desires.

Novikoff was proud; he had molded Bobby from raw and difficult material. The next step was an audition with the Ballet Russe de Monte Carlo.

In 1944, Novikoff scheduled an audition with Alexandra Danilova and Frederic Franklin. Joffrey was fifteen and had reached his full adult height of five feet four inches. Beuhal Kirberger, Novikoff's wife, described the nerve-racking moment: "Mr. Novikoff took Bobby out on the stage to have him warm up holding the back of a chair. But he was frozen scared. . . . We got Bobby free of that chair, and Danilova worked with him. They liked him."[7]

The story was told somewhat differently, and with some inconsisten-

---

*By 1946, Novikoff was in charge of three dance studios bearing his name, in Bellingham, Tacoma, and Seattle. His advertisement read, "Correct fundamentals insure future success." He later spread into Salem, Oregon, and Walla Walla, Washington.

†Novikoff mended his ways over the years and raised the minimum age to twelve for letting girls begin pointe work.

‡Joffrey kept this very pair of pants, and when the time came for him to stage his own production of *The Nutcracker* in 1987, he asked designer John David Ridge to copy the pants for the ballet's second-act Russian variation.

cies, by Joffrey. According to him, he ran away from home, taking a cross-country bus trip on his own to New York to audition for Frederic Franklin, ballet master of Ballet Russe de Monte Carlo. Franklin invited him to join the troupe, but Bobby's parents "put their foot down"[8] because he had not yet graduated from high school.

Neither Franklin nor Danilova remembered ever formally auditioning Bobby, and no contract with him can be found in the Sergei Denham manuscripts and correspondences now housed in the Dance Collection at the New York Public Library for the Performing Arts. What Franklin did recall is a visit, around 1946, to the Seattle studio of Mary Ann Wells, who would become Bobby's next teacher. Wells had told him and Danilova (whose nickname is Choura) that she had a promising student and "we agreed to take a look." Said Franklin, "The promising student was Bob. We thought the class was very nice. As a matter of fact, Choura couldn't remember his name, and she said [in her broken Russian-English], 'You know, he looks like Western Union boy.' That's exactly what Choura said. And then years later she said, 'Frederic, you'll never believe. Western Union boy have company!' That was Bob Joffrey."[9]

But all that was in the future. Ahead for Bobby in Seattle was the grim prospect of having to stay there. Then, on September 7, 1945, the USS *Poughkeepsie,* sent by the Coast Guard to be handed over to the Russians as part of Roosevelt's Lend-Lease Act, anchored in Puget Sound. On board was a twenty-two-year-old first pharmacist's mate named Gerald Arpino. He had dark, tousled hair and vibrant, fluid eyes. There was also sadness to Jerry, as he was called, an ache to his line, his posture, that he fell into whenever he thought no one was looking. But the performer in him felt it was his duty to keep everyone on the USS *Poughkeepsie* laughing and full of hope. He was the crew's pet.

Jerry had joined the U.S. Coast Guard Reserve at the end of 1942, thwarting his mother, who had protested at length. He had dropped out of college, thus extinguishing the possibility of a medical career, and volunteered for the Coast Guard because several of his buddies had implored him to come along and he could not resist the patriotic call. He was seeking adventure beyond Staten Island, where he had been born Gennaro Peter Arpino* on January 14, 1923. Jerry was the ninth and final child in the Arpino family (one died at birth), and his siblings (five sisters, two brothers) always called him Baby. Their father, Luigi Arpino, who was originally from Vico Equense on the Bay of Naples, had estab-

*When he attended Sacred Heart parochial school in West Brighton on Staten Island, Arpino said the nuns had trouble pronouncing *Gennaro* and called him Gerald instead. He was nicknamed Jerry (which is the way he spells it). *Arthur* is the name given to him at his confirmation making his full appellation Gennaro Peter Arthur Arpino.

lished profitable beauty salons all over Staten Island. He owned grey-hound racing dogs and enough real estate on the island to be recognized as a man of some importance. "They almost thought he was the mayor," said Jerry's sister Jeannie Arpino.[10] But when the Depression came, Luigi lost practically everything and became despondent. He died of a heart attack when Jerry was only seven.

Jerry grew up feeling responsible for his mother's care. Starting at age eleven, he delivered the *Staten Island Advance* and mowed neighbor-hood lawns. With the money he saved, he bought Anna her first washing machine. Much later, he would purchase the family's first refrigerator and a new house at 297 Pelton Avenue on the "right" side of West Brighton's tracks.

Jerry had graduated from high school with honors; he was planning on becoming a doctor. Although naturally athletic, he was known as a book-worm. "If you wanted Jerry, you had to look in the dining room," said Jean-nie. "He'd sit there by the hour at the table beneath the Tiffany lamp, reading his book. He always had a book. 'Don't you ever put that book down?' I'd say."[11] Between raising money to help support his family and studying his academic texts, he hadn't had the time or the inclination to learn about the arts. "We were your typical Italian family," said Jerry; "we danced a lot at home, but not ballet of course. My sisters were champion black-bottom dancers and ballroom dancers . . . and my brothers were macho types, into riding horses, playing football, and racing cars."[12]

In the Coast Guard, because he was noticeably more lithe than any of the other sailors, Jerry had been given some tricky and painful jobs that required the use of his innate agility. He was the one chosen to swim to the victims' rescue when a nearby Allied freighter was torpedoed at night. "The whole sea was awash with red lights," he recalled. "And every red light was attached to the life jacket of someone. They put me in a rubber outfit and I swam out. I saw many dead bodies. Many red lights. I saved many a life that way."*

Jerry also watched for German submarines from the crow's nest of the *Escanaba,* a fifty-six-foot Coast Guard cutter onto which a hundred men were packed. "When it would tip, you could scoop the water up in your hand," he said. "Into the crow's nest at night under the stars, I'd take my rosary and say my Hail Marys, never really realizing the danger we were in. One time I sounded the alarm for submarines, and it was a whale. Another time [not on his watch] we hit an iceberg and had to return to the States."[13]

---

*Arpino saved people's lives, but he also quite literally saved a pair of red lights that is kept in the attic of his family's house in Staten Island. He told his sisters never to throw them away.

The *Escanaba* was repaired in Boston Harbor, and Jerry took the opportunity to have some minor surgery performed at a local hospital. But the *Escanaba* was seaworthy well before Jerry, and although he begged to be allowed to return to service, he was left behind. Three days later the ship hit a mine that killed everyone, including his best friend, George Aridas.

A first-generation American Catholic born to parents who had emigrated from Italy at separate times, Jerry's dramatic experiences in the Coast Guard increased his already fervent belief in God. He felt certain he had been saved for some larger purpose that he did not yet comprehend. His close brushes with death were also turning his only surviving parent, Anna Santanastasio Arpino, into a chronically nervous wreck. Arpino began to think it best not to keep telling her where he was stationed. But he developed a secret communication system with his beloved sisters Jeannie and Ninette that could be used in letters between them to let them know—without the Coast Guard having to censor and without Anna being aware—where he was and how he was faring.

When Anna Arpino learned through her daughters that her son was on his way to Seattle, she suggested to him that he look up her old friend Mary Joffrey. Mary and she had first met when Mary had visited Anna's hometown in Italy for a violin performance. They had stayed in touch all these years. Anna told Jerry that Mary had a son named Bobby, who was about six years younger than he. She suggested that Mary and Bobby might be good to him, show him around Seattle, and give him a home-cooked Italian meal.

When Jerry touched port in the fall of 1945, he phoned the Joffreys, who welcomed him warmly and suggested that he look up Bobby at Ivan Novikoff's ballet school. Arpino was not prepared for what happened next. He had never seen a ballet and certainly never taken a ballet class. Still wearing his seaman's uniform, Jerry walked into Novikoff's studio:

> *I decided to go down to meet the Joffreys' son never knowing I was meeting my destiny. Novikoff told me Bobby was taking a ballet class.*
>
> *"Ballet class?" I said.*
>
> *"Yes," he said. I had never experienced this.*
>
> *Novikoff looked at me and said, "Take off your pea coat, your sailor jumper. Off."*
>
> *I did it automatically. He started pressing me down with his hands on my shoulders. I did not know what was going on. He was speaking with a Russian accent.*
>
> *"Pleeeyay, pleeeyay [plié]," he said, pushing his hands on me and forcing me to bend my knees. "You have good heeps [hips]. Good, good heeps. You must, must dance."*

"I didn't come down here to dance." I said to him. "I don't know what you are doing. Who are you? Where is Bobby?"

He said, "Bobby is in class."

So I went and saw Bobby in class. And that was it. It was love at first sight.[14]

Jerry started taking ballet classes as regularly as he could with Ivan Novikoff. Because he was a beginner, he was placed in with the youngest children. Far from being humiliated, Jerry reveled, saying, "This new world of ballet fascinated me."[15] He arranged for his Coast Guard mates to help him go AWOL as much as possible so that he could increase the number of classes per week. He was trying, against the odds, he realized, to catch up to sixteen-year-old Bobby, with whom he had become fast friends.

Jerry and Bob told everyone they were cousins; they were inseparable and they became lovers. They were coming of age in the forties when homosexuality was socially unacceptable and was regarded, far more than ballet, as something to hide. The culture on a popular level was intolerant and unreceptive to the idea of male love as anything other than a mental illness and violation of nature. Incredibly, against such a backdrop, a wholesome attitude of acceptance seems to have prevailed in the Joffrey household. Naim Shah, Bob's younger cousin, observed that while Mary and Joseph never discussed their son's sexuality with other family members, they seemed to have known exactly who he was, and after a time, they were not ashamed. Before Jerry showed up, Mary tried in vain to prevent Bob from making male friends at Novikoff's studio. But Richard Englund was the nephew of the Joffreys' friend and colleague, and he could therefore hardly be dismissed. And Jerry was absorbed into the family "like a second son."[16]

If Bob had difficulties at home, it was because his parents' marriage was rough-edged and acrimonious. Jerry recalled the almost constant smell of Mary's fried chicken wafting through the small house as she cooked Bob's favorite food as a way of bribing him into spending more time there. "Bob's parents were not easy for him. They were so much older and different," said Jerry. "But Dad Joffrey I loved. He was heroic. I just adored him."[17] Almost every day, Joseph Joffrey blessed his son and Jerry. Then he'd dip his hands into his pockets and gather some coins that he'd drop into their hands.

Perhaps because his father was badgering him about the poor financial prospects of a professional dance career,* and perhaps because he was

---

*In 1942, a corps de ballet member was paid a minimum of $41.50 per performance week and a minimum of $20 for rehearsal weeks. ("What AGMA Means to Dancers," *Dance Magazine,* June 1953.)

falling in love with Jerry and was having to face his homosexuality, Bob became adept at secrets. "He could be a very good liar," said his friend Garth Rogers, who along with others noticed Bob struggling with a meticulous division of self.[18]

"He would have made a wonderful diplomat," his mother said of him, because he knew how to make people feel good and to get what he wanted by keeping everyone guessing. "Image was so important to Bob," added Rogers. By 1945, Bob was an experienced dance student accustomed to looking in the mirror and seeing reality in reverse, and so he could adjust to his own flip-sided truth. "He lived in a simultaneous dream world with his reality," Rogers continued. "And he started believing his place. . . . He was just wonderfully naïve."[19]

There is a photograph of Bob and Jerry on a boat taken at this time. Bob sits on top of a suspended dinghy, and Jerry is leaning against him, resting his arms on each of Bob's legs. They look absolutely, blissfully happy, windswept, and invigorated. Bob carried the photo with him and propped it near his makeup table in every theater in later years. Remembering these halcyon days in 1994, Arpino said:

"At first, you know—young, passionate. We all go through those phases of our sexuality. But it became more than that. We grew. We became entwined in each other's desires to build and see what American dance was about.

"I think it's one of the greatest friendships that has ever developed between two young men. Our company is born of our relationship. Without one or the other of us, I don't think it would have been manifested. The company grew out of a great love for each other. A love that became Platonic and was allowed to grow."[20]

Soon after Jerry arrived in Seattle, both he and Bob decided that it was time to graduate from Ivan Novikoff. Roena Meykar, a ballet student whom Bob admired, had left Novikoff earlier to study with Mary Ann Wells, and she urged Bob to follow suit. Richard Englund had also started studying with Wells, whose School of Dance had a well-deserved reputation for producing professional dancers.

When Joffrey and Arpino met Wells, this is what they saw: She wore flowing, tailor-made lavender culottes; she crisscrossed her hair in braids on the crown of her head and stuck little hand-decorated combs in them; she wore eyeglasses and was helpless without them. Her body was implausibly round for a ballet teacher.

Mary Ann Wells was an independent, a self-starter, a perfectionist, an original, a from-the-ground-up teacher who prized little more than finding, encouraging, and preserving her students' individuality and creative impulses. She trained beginners to beat drums, triangles, bells, and sticks and to generate their own walking-running-jumping rhythms that evolved into improvisational dances. Only when a student possessed a solid foundation in rhythm and free movement would she impose the academic discipline of classical ballet. She was an idiosyncratic teacher and an American, and she was about as far removed from the traditional Russian approach—the teacher smoking a cigarette, carrying a stick, rapping students on their behinds, and calling for the exaggerated repetition of sixty-four grands battements* to the front, side, and back—as one could get. There was no one with whom to compare her in Seattle.

In 1945, Joffrey and Arpino enrolled in Wells's school and appeared in her production of *Rumpelstiltskin*. "I knew there had to be more to dance than just the physicality of it, which was involving me so much. And Miss Wells, I think, fed my artistic soul," said Joffrey. "Her approach to dance was in a very wide scope."[21]

Wells became the most influential person in Robert Joffrey's artistic development. By leading him away from rote learning and stale ballet themes, she would profoundly influence his dance philosophy, his sense of beauty, his criteria for teaching. Throughout his life he credited only Wells with giving him the tools necessary to build a company, to choreograph ballets, to hire dancers, to arrange repertory, and to spot talent.

---

*A beating movement in which the extended leg is raised as high as possible, then is lowered, usually into first or fifth position.

CHAPTER 4

Coming-of-Age

Mary Ann Wells called him Robert because she considered him an adult. To almost everyone else he was Bob, a high school junior with a strong interest in ballet. Arpino, who was still in the Coast Guard, was initially viewed by Wells as the court jester to Joffrey's king. They came attached, that was clear, but their training and experience were vastly different. Joffrey had the potential to become a professional; Arpino had much to prove before Wells would accept him.

Contrary to the impression given by Wells's free-spirited philosophy, she was an exceptionally strict woman. She enforced discipline to the point of traumatizing some pupils. To her, dance was a moral matter; good ethics bred good dancing. "Do you want to be a dancer? Then you must be scrupulous and attentive to the details," she would often gently admonish. Then, according to one of her former students who adored her, she might finish such a lecture with: "You must come to class and you must not be distracted by anything; otherwise, please leave."[1]

Although she emboldened students to trust their intuition and be resourceful, she expected logic in the dance phrases they created in the choreography portion of her class. Rules and craft lead to liberation, she argued, and not the reverse. To some, this approach inhibited their creativity. To others, Joffrey and Arpino among them, the perfectionism and strong work ethic awakened sleeping talents. Both young men's minds expanded under Wells. But, partly because they arrived at her studio at different stages in their development, she produced in them radically different results.

Joffrey jumped right into Wells's elite professional classes, sometimes taking two a day. He also became her assistant for the children's classes that she taught in the evenings—a position that was regarded by some of Wells's longtime students as the surest sign of her approval. Others took her choice of Joffrey for the assistantship to mean that she thought of him as being a teacher, instead of a dancer. "And he was a marvelous teacher," said William Weslow, who was later invited to join the New York City Ballet.[2]

Joffrey himself may have been thinking the same thing. Wells made it clear that she was concerned about Joffrey's height, that his likelihood of getting into a classical company was not very good, because most ballerinas would tower over him. But Wells was never one to be negative or obdurate, not closing the door on a student with as much enthusiasm and passion as Joffrey. She believed that as long as a dancer possessed these attributes, then magic was possible. Explained Joffrey:

"Miss Wells felt you could change your body if you wanted to, depending on how you worked on it. The dance is illusion and so you must have in your mind an idea of what you want to look like and then try to achieve that. Her classes were never dry. She would instill in you phrases, images, to get the quality behind the movement. And what images [they were]."[3]

Wells's approach was called visualization. The images she called out to her students might be as mundane or simple as "Sing with your feet" or "Imagine the floor is a bed of hot coals" or "The puppet master is pulling your strings taut." These were elaborated upon by Wells with more metaphysical proclamations, such as, "Wake up the dead space! Send your energy through the rest of your body." Or, "Consider that your heart is not only a beating thing, it is eternity."[4] Joffrey gained through her method an awareness that the body has focal points, or "inner eyes,"[5] and that if a dancer is alert and clear about how to see with them, the audience sees what the dancer ordains—in Joffrey's case, someone tall. Visualization unearthed rich soil for the foundation of the Joffrey Ballet.

Early on, he took Wells into his confidence, disclosing that he wanted to direct his own ballet troupe someday. She replied, "Learn to dance first, Robert."[6]

Her defining characteristic was her nonelitism. She also had an agenda. She was a classical ballet instructor who had studied modern dance with Martha Graham, May O'Donnell, and Gertrude Shurr. For her, any dance form, be it Spanish flamenco or preclassic or Jaques-Dalcroze Eurhythmics or ballroom, could be applied to ballet. In the late thirties and forties, when Wells was first implementing such a pedagogical proposition, she was recognized as a trailbreaker. "It's been our priority in America to have a wonderful, rich, eclectic vocabulary of dance. Mary Ann Wells was a product of the current that was running through the country," said Coby Larsen, an early Wells student. "She had a pioneer spirit in dance. She was a forerunner to what we became."[7]

Wells's aim was to guide her students toward discovering and building something called American ballet. She saw in Robert Joffrey an ideal crusader for her cause. The next years would tell. Knowing that he was dead serious about his ambition to direct a company, what did she teach him? Who were her teachers?

Wells was born on June 7, 1894, in Appleton, Wisconsin. Her story intersects with the story of the emergence of modern dance in America. Her mother was a dancer and her paternal uncle, Boyd Wells, was a concert pianist of some international reputation. She was an only child; her father seemed not to have played an important role in her life. As a young girl, she recalled having two ambitions: "My first choice for a career was acting. I wanted to be the world's greatest actress. Failing that, I would have wanted to be the world's greatest pianist."[8]

Perhaps Wells appreciated Joffrey because she, like he, knew at such a young age the greatness that she wished to attain in the arts and acted upon it. By her late teens, Wells was occasionally performing with a stock theater troupe in Minneapolis. Her family by then had moved to Chicago, and it was here that Wells was introduced to ballet, taking lessons from the legendary Adolph Bolm, a former soloist with the Maryinsky Theatre in St. Petersburg. He had managed Anna Pavlova's first European tours in 1908 and 1909, then joined Diaghilev's Ballets Russes and was the company's leading character dancer. Bolm had come with Diaghilev's troupe on its first and second American tours, after which he remained to found his own company, Les Ballets Intimes.

Wells gained most of her knowledge of classical ballet from Bolm, but she also took classes from Hazel Sharp, who authored and illustrated a book on technique. Finally, Wells traveled to New York to study with Luigi Albertieri, who had been the great Enrico Cecchetti's favored pupil in Italy.

In the fall of 1916—which by poetic coincidence was the same year that Joseph Joffrey and Aurang Shah emigrated from Afghanistan—Wells moved to Seattle at the invitation of Nellie Cornish, director and founder of the Cornish School of Music. "Through the performances of Anna Pavlova, ballet had become the dream of young America. Youngsters wanted to get on their toes, to wear diaphanous 'tutus,' " Cornish wrote in her autobiography, explaining that she had decided to branch out from the music curriculum, hire Wells, and establish a dance department to capitalize on Americans' growing fervor for ballet.[9]

In the beginning, Wells seemed a kindred spirit to Isadora Duncan. She produced numerous recitals at Cornish, creating pantomime ballets in Grecian tunics by the side of reflecting ponds and huntress dances under the trees. Her impetus was to fortify and enlarge the dance department to a national dimension; for three consecutive summers she brought in Bolm as a guest teacher; she also presented him in performances. In 1923, she claimed about three hundred dance students under her jurisdiction at Cornish. She had by this time given up thoughts of a professional dance career and had married A. Forest King, a spice and gourmet-food salesman. King persuaded her to break out on her own, and in 1923, Wells opened a school at 165 Bell Street in a former Ford motorcar showroom, remembered by many for the large grate on the floor that trapped the incautious bare toes of some of America's soon-to-be-accomplished dancers.*

During the summers when her school was closed, Wells went on extended trips to New York, Los Angeles, and the San Francisco area looking for new ideas and guest teachers. When she was in her forties, she traveled to Bennington College in Vermont, and every single one of her future students—most significantly Joffrey and Arpino—would be touched by her experience there.

Bennington School of the Dance was where Martha Graham and some of her colleagues worked during the summer and, not incidentally, provided a haven for themselves as modern dance practitioners that was far removed from the New York ballet advocates who renounced them for not respecting the traditional canons of beauty, for allowing emotion to determine form, and for not possessing a gestural alphabet. Wells entered Bennington in 1938 and instantly aroused both curiosity and enmity. She was a blatant ballet dancer, seen by some as a traitor to her clan and by others as a spy who had foolishly dared cross the line of fire. She made no attempts to hide her classical background, none. "She was in her own world," said May O'Donnell, a Graham company member. O'Donnell befriended Wells as soon as she could because she admired her sense of adventure and the remarkable impression she first made. "Mary Ann was just like a big kid," said O'Donnell. "To her, the world was an exciting place. She was intrigued with the possibilities of modern dance, and she wanted to acquaint her students with its potential."[10]

---

*By the time Joffrey and Arpino showed up to take class with Wells in 1945, she had already graduated a number of artists who had gone on to impressive careers. Margaret Petit (Leslie Caron's mother) had become a favored musical-comedy star of the twenties; Marc Platt had been a soloist with Ballet Russe de Monte Carlo and was on Broadway in the original cast of *Oklahoma!* and later, he became director of ballet at Radio City Music Hall; Louise Kloepper had worked with Hanya Holm; Frank Hobi was or would become a member of Ballet Theatre, Ballet Russe de Monte Carlo, and the New York City Ballet, and the director of the Royal Winnipeg Ballet; Coby Larsen was in Paris at the Lido, and later she would become a Rockette at Radio City Music Hall; Mary Heater was a member of Ballet Theatre; and Tommy Rall was dancing in films and was headed for Ballet Theatre.

From her studio until the day she retired in 1958 came many others aside from Joffrey, Arpino, and Weslow, including Françoise Martinet of the Joffrey Ballet; Richard Englund of the National Ballet of Canada, Birmingham Civic Ballet, and American Ballet Theatre, and director of Joffrey II; Martin Buckner of the Washington Ballet; Roena Meykar, who went into the entertainment field; Blair Hollenbeck, who danced in Paris and directed a school in Amsterdam; Ann Needham, Willard Nagel, and Erik Cooper, who danced and sang on Broadway.

Wells's summer at Bennington was actually not her first encounter with Graham, though it was the crystallizing one. Beginning in 1930, Graham had come for several consecutive summers to Seattle to teach at the Cornish School, after visiting her family in Santa Barbara, California. Wells had taken Graham's courses. And so, by the time she arrived in Bennington, she was well on her way to integrating the classical discipline with the modern to produce what could legitimately be called American ballet.

"Ballet was a European art. Its roots were in France and Russia, and Miss Wells saw how it could become American," said Françoise Martinet, who was for many years a Wells protégée and who became an early Joffrey Ballet member. "She grafted modern dance technique onto ballet. She played with the forms. She crossbred and crossed over before there were even words to describe what it was she was doing."[11]

Wells indirectly furnished Joffrey with the complete program for structuring the Joffrey Ballet: she oriented him in an esthetic philosophy; and she, a lady of some means, also taught him how to suppress his immigrant background, how to dress and behave like an American gentleman.

Wells began having Joffrey and Arpino to tea with her at Frederick and Nelsons, a fine downtown department store, where she maintained an account. After tea, Joffrey would often linger with her to shop. Arpino hadn't the patience for such matters and later remarked, "I never knew what she thought of me. All her focus was on Bob."[12]

From Wells, Joffrey learned to distinguish fine fabrics from poor-quality substitutes. He learned how to appreciate the different ways fabrics move and absorb color and light. He acquired a taste for expensive handmade articles. His eye became cultivated under her guidance. In short order, he grew to trust Wells as an arbiter of style and etiquette. "I wouldn't say he was closer to Mary Ann than he was to his parents," cautioned Diane Lembo, a Seattle colleague who was perhaps Joffrey's most beloved female companion. "But his awareness of everything esthetic came from her."[13]

By the end of 1945, he had practically moved in with the Kings, spending most of his time at the studio and at their house. He left Broadway High School early each day because Wells had arranged for him to be excused in time for her afternoon class. "The early dismissal was very unusual," said Joffrey. "But because Miss Wells was so powerful as a figure in the city, because so many wealthy people sent their children to her for social dancing lessons, she was able to get it for me. She didn't say, 'You have to do it.' She said, 'It's your choice,' and by November, I realized the daily class was more important than high school." Arpino helped him over some of the initial hurdles by doing Joffrey's homework and substituting for him entirely in his private French tutorials with Madame

Corot. Wells piled onto Joffrey more books to read, chiefly Tamara Karsavina's *Theatre Street* and, later, *The Borzoi Book of Ballets*. These texts fed what some of his friends labeled his "classical complex"; it seemed he couldn't get enough of ballerinas and danseurs from the past, and one time, after rereading *Book of Ballets,* he told Wells, "I made a whole cast of *The Sleeping Beauty* with Alonso dancing and Ulanova and Fonteyn. I put each of the famous ballerinas of the time in the roles and they could alternate doing the roles. Then Toscanini was going to conduct. *Sleeping Beauty* was always to me a fascinating ballet."[14] *The Sleeping Beauty* evolved into a yardstick: as a director, he checked to see if his dancers were at any given year ready and sufficiently skilled to perform this Petipa ballet (music by Tchaikovsky) that is generally considered the touchstone of the late-nineteenth-century classical repertoire. The company, so far, has never performed it.

Eventually, Joffrey seemed not to have time for high school. Records from the Archives and Records Management Center for the Seattle Public Schools indicate that he dropped out in the middle of his junior year, 1945–46. He received no further report cards from Broadway High School after December 1945, and although his father once told a Seattle journalist that his son had graduated from Garfield High, records cannot be found to substantiate the transfer to Garfield. Joffrey's friends, including Arpino, think that he "must have" graduated, but none can remember a ceremony.

By Joffrey's own admission, his whole life at this point swirled around dance and Mary Ann Wells.[15] "Miss Wells was like a balm, a salve," said one of his friends. "That a person could be so good and so kind and create a home [for him]—he didn't really have a home environment that he was thrilled with. And, when he went to Miss Wells, it was a real escape. She totally changed his life in terms of having a philosophy toward living. Not just for dance. She taught him that your body is your temple, which he had never thought before, and that temple has to be respected in every way, in terms of its presentation and in terms of what you put inside it. That you should eat extremely well, and in an environment that is also beautiful. Bob loved to eat in a lovely restaurant if he could, rather than just run into a diner."[16]

Wells perceived the body as living architecture, and she was determined to understand human articulation in geometrical terms through the body and in combination with her notions of static and dynamic symmetry. "I began to see that many of the classic ballet positions—the arabesque, the attitude, etc.—were symmetrical, but quite static," she wrote in *Dance Magazine.* "The five positions of the arms . . . were codified. The beauty of their design was basic, but they could be explored and extended into patterns of much greater force."[17]

One consequence of her conviction that ballet had not been fully "explored and extended" was that in true maverick fashion she rearranged the classic system for her purposes. In her classes, the French terms were seldom heard. A *grand jeté* was called a "big jump," dancing *en pointe* was always "on toe," and so forth. Wells reasoned that if they heard English, then they would be more apt to think and dance American, and she reinforced her theory by incorporating Martha Graham's floor exercises into the daily class. These exercises were done while sitting, kneeling, or lying down. And they had certain advantages for the dancer: on the floor gravity doesn't tug on the bones and muscles in the same way it does when the body is upright.

From either supine or sitting positions, Wells made her students aware of their spines. She discussed placement: aligning the hips directly under the shoulders, and the knees, shins, ankles, and toes functioning in concert without bearing weight. Wells was one of the first ballet (as opposed to modern) teachers to address body alignment.

In addition, Wells enforced Isadora Duncan's notion that the dancer's power came from the solar plexus, or the nerve center right where the lowest ribs join and cover both the heart and the pit of the stomach. Wells believed that a dancer's expression improved with an uplifted back, freeing the arms as natural extensions of the torso. She was obsessive about arms and hands; every finger must harmonize with the body's total form. "The wrists and hands are the dancer's speech. They give quality to each movement," she averred.[18] "Most of the angry emotions or negative emotions—fear and anxiety—are expressed with the angles of the body. Most of the level, positive things are expressed with a circle of the body."[19]

Wells, too, often added her own inflections to the standard classical steps. For example, the pure classical *tendu*—which is the extension of the foot in contact with the floor, leg turned out and heel lifted—she twisted, so that the dancer rotated the leg in and then out before reaching a full extension of the foot. In her hands, then, the straight-lined *tendu* sometimes evolved into a spiral.[20]

In the interests of versatility and providing for her students' professional futures, Wells brought in Elisa Cansino (the aunt of screen actress Rita Hayworth) to teach flamenco and Spanish dance. "I decided that of all the national dances, Spanish was the most sophisticated and most useful to a student in developing an attractive stance and presence," Wells said.[21] Since she had studied dance composition with Louis Horst at Bennington, she offered instruction to her students in the same. Joffrey and Arpino learned the structure of the gavotte, the saraband, and the galliard.

These extra classes were given after four o'clock strictly to those who were intent on a dance career. Joffrey often did not leave the studio until ten at night. He remembered practicing his castanets in a brown paper bag on the bus to Cansino's class. By 1945, Joffrey's world was curiously contained—Wells had moved her studio to the same building occupied by Joseph Joffrey's Pine Street Tavern. Wells's studio was one flight up from the Tavern, and she liked to caution the students taking Cansino's Spanish class with their heeled shoes and boots, "Don't stamp too hard or we'll wake the drunks."[22]

Wells had a sense of humor, but she was mostly of a solemn mind, and her students knew about the precepts of her religion, the I AM. A sect and an outgrowth of the indigenous North American religions (such as Mormonism) that flourished in the western United States, the I AM had been started by Guy W. Ballard, who in 1930 received instructions from Saint Germain, a spiritualist materializing to him in a vision on Mount Shasta in California.* The underlying tenets for the I AM are close to Christianity; in fact, Jesus is one of their Ascended Masters. Wells didn't force her spiritual beliefs on people, but she let it be known that the I AM was important to her and her husband. Students were invited, as far as curiosity and need drew them, to find out more. Joffrey and Arpino remained on the periphery, but many of the I AM's almost superstitious habits and larger concepts (including visualization) became integral to their life and behavior. It is, in fact, virtually impossible to separate Joffrey from the I AM, even though he was never a devotee.

There was a strange edge to Wells, the tolerant in conjunction with the narrow, the romantic with the absolutist, the brilliant mixed in with perversity. Joffrey's adulation for Wells caused him to emulate her. She was a vegetarian, he tried to be one. When she refused to allow anyone to wear red in her school because of her I AM understanding that red destroyed spiritual harmony, he swore off the color and never wore it again. He was seventeen years old and testing everything to find out who he was. He did, however, stop short of embracing her politics. Some have said that she was a member of the John Birch Society, and many have said that she was patriotic to the point of being a right wing zealot. She was pro–Senator Joseph McCarthy in the fifties and proclaimed her vehement stance against Communism.

Both Joffrey and Arpino sidestepped the archconservative beliefs of Wells and drew more from such spiritual concepts of the I AM as:

- *Positive living.* The individual becomes whatever he expresses. His words and sentiments can reel back and infect his life. He must complete the sentence "I am . . ." with a positive statement, guard his emotions, and

---

*The Saint Germain Foundation still existed in 1996, and there were I AM sanctuaries around the country, as well as a Saint Germain Press in Schaumburg, Illinois.

control his condemnation of others. If not, he will be reincarnated as the person he reviled and mocked. The notion that one's words can "infect" one's life became very important to the way Joffrey handled his death.[*]

- *Light and the "etheric" counterpart.* People are surrounded by an aura, a glow of radiant light that vibrates through the ether and records their activity for eternity. Saint Germain is pictured suffused in exploding layers of gold, pink, and violet light. Red and black are destructive colors and are never worn by I AM members; costumes in these colors rarely appeared on the Joffrey stage, and never in a Joffrey or Arpino ballet. Many Arpino works are about light, either using the word *light* in the title or involving the lighting design as a major component in the ballet.

- *Visualization and secrecy.* The individual's ambitions, ideals, and desires will be manifested provided he does not speak of them to anyone else. He must cultivate the habit of meditation, seeing his plan in a state of perfection. Joffrey applied these concepts to the "vision" he had of his ballet company. Seeing the Joffrey Ballet whole in his mind, he attained it almost through sheer will. A deeply secretive person by nature, Joffrey also meditated.

- *America.* Saint Germain designated America as the next nation to carry his Light. He said that its people are heralds to the new Golden Age, embodying the potential of humankind. Arpino was the more openly patriotic of the two men, but Americanism was central to Joffrey's character. From the start, Joffrey described his company as a "vision of American dance."

On June 11, 1946, Arpino was discharged from the Coast Guard, having completed his four years of service with distinction. He moved in with the Joffrey family to live, taking over the entire third floor of their new home at 1010 East Lynn Street in a district far more upscale than their previous downtown quarters on Boren Street. Joffrey was on the second floor in a suite of small rooms that included a study, a sleeping porch, and a bedroom.[†] His parents were across the hall in their bed-

---

[*]It is interesting to note similarities between certain elements of these beliefs to Ghaffar Khan's interpretation of the Prophet Muhammad's instructions in the Koran. Joffrey's inability to make quick decisions was regarded as his Achilles' heel. He once said that he procrastinated not because he couldn't make up his mind, but because he always tried the positive approach, which often meant offending the fewest number of people—a process that frequently took longer. "If eighty percent of the idea was bad, but twenty was gold, Bob would wrestle in his soul to find out how to salvage the gold," said a general director of the company. Also, he had perhaps inherited through his father an understanding about time that was in conflict with the value and importance that most Westerners place on deadlines and time.

[†]This configuration was exactly the same as Joffrey had in the house he lived in the longest in New York, at 180 MacDougal Street in Greenwich Village.

rooms. Joffrey's maternal uncle Jo-Jo lived in the basement, and Uncle Marcus sometimes occupied another guest room. The house teemed with people. Large and square with beautiful, hand-crafted, well-proportioned dark wood molding, banisters, and cabinetry, it was a lesson in good taste; everywhere one looked, the eye could be pleased.

Joffrey needed a plausible front to hide his homosexuality at school and he had maintained one. Ballet class, though, was another matter: he could relax, safe in the knowledge that he and Arpino were not novelties. When one of their colleagues mentioned his suspicions about the pair to Wells, she replied, "They're human beings and that's the way some people are. Overlook it. They go together and they're very friendly and they love each other. And that's the case."[23] Wells's tolerance and compassion for homosexuals may be remarkable in light of some of her conservative views, but she was humane and not naïve. Her principal concern was building dancers and choreographers. She knew that her task would be lighter if they were comfortable and secure in their personal lives.

The thought of choreographing was extremely atypical for most ballet students, but not in Wells's class. At the end of each week, she invited one student to complete a combination that she had given only in part, and another to supply the arm movement for a combination that she had given in whole, but minus the arms. Then she would quiz them: Was the exercise dominantly from the Enrico Cecchetti or Agrippina Vaganova system?* By turning the tables on them, Wells taught her students both how to teach and how to create. Joffrey explained, "We'd have to tell her why the arms went that way. The class was very creative. . . . And then she would comment on the combinations we'd made up and say, 'You know, perhaps the way you put the movements together is interesting, but is it really a good exercise? Have you put too much into the exercise?' "[24]

Wells suspected early on that Arpino was a choreographer, but his dancing was coming along beautifully as well. Joffrey later observed that "Jerry had a wonderful soft plié like a cat. You never could hear him. . . . He had a good feeling for the dynamics of movement; a good sense of urgency and power. Everything moved from his torso. You'd say he was a natural."[25] Arpino began to appear more regularly at the Kings' house on equal footing with Joffrey. The Kings' soirées were the toast of Seattle's cultural elite. Into their home traipsed Imogen Cunningham, Morris Graves, Carmelita Maracci, Katherine Dunham, Carmen Amaya, Marc

---

*The Cecchetti method emphasizes a clean technique and line, with simple (not embellished) port de bras, and ninety-degree leg extensions. The Vaganova system is lyrical and somewhat stylized, stressing big extensions, arched backs, and *épaulement* at the expense of fast footwork.

Tobey, May O'Donnell, and Gertrude Shurr. And one evening, not long before Joffrey and Arpino were included in her circle, Wells hosted a dinner for Antony Tudor, the eminent choreographer newly installed at Ballet Theatre, and for Hugh Laing, the principal male interpreter of his works. Wells suggested Tudor listen to her recording of Richard Strauss's *Burleske* for Piano and Orchestra; in 1943, Tudor created *Dim Lustre*, to the same music.

At these parties Joffrey and Arpino often stuck close to Alexandra Danilova, whenever she was present, and besieged her with questions.* Danilova fondly recalled these episodes, saying in her Russian English, "These boys, they were so enthusiastic. They always stay a very long time, and at four o'clock at night, I always used to say, 'Now, come on, boys, go home. Go home. I have to dance.' "[26]

In June of 1947, acting on Wells's admonishment—"I will not finish you off, you must study with someone who has danced"[27]—Joffrey ventured east to Manhattan, enrolling for the summer session in the School of American Ballet, which was affiliated with George Balanchine and Lincoln Kirstein's company, which would become known a little more than a year later as the New York City Ballet.† A Georgian and the last in-house choreographer for Diaghilev's Ballets Russes, Balanchine came to the United States in 1933 at Kirstein's invitation and together they launched an academy that was the first in America to support a large faculty that existed for the purpose of training dancers for a single choreographer—Balanchine—whose company's esthetic and philosophical foundation sprang from his rigorous creative impulse. Even though he was from Russia, Balanchine was building an American ballet company. He was most interested in using the qualities of American dancers, and his choreographic style was deeply influenced by their, to quote Kirstein, "angelic unconcern toward emotion." His ballets defined neoclassicism; they relied on pure, undecorative movements that were the abstractions of musical text (Stravinsky, Tchaikovsky, and Mozart were among his favorites). He is regarded as one of the geniuses of the twentieth century, a choreographer who articulated to perfection the spirit and energy and imaginative life of the modern American.

When the course was over, Joffrey rushed back home, apparently to the surprise and consternation of Wells, who had expected him to remain in New York. "I did very well at the School of American Ballet and was put in the advanced class," he said. "But I felt I learned more with Miss

---

*Danilova and Frederic Franklin were frequent guest teachers at the Mary Ann Wells School of Dance, during the time that Joffrey and Arpino were there.

†During the previous summer, Joffrey and Arpino studied in Los Angeles with Carmelita Maracci and Maria Bekefi.

Wells."[28] She agreed to let Joffrey stay with her another year on the condition that he spend the time preparing for a graduation concert. He was to choreograph a full evening of solos, choose his own music, hire an accompanist, design the costumes and sets, rent the theater, get the tickets printed, and see to it that the recital was properly advertised.

On June 23, 1948, Robert Joffrey presented a "Program of Original Dance Compositions," financed by his parents, at the Woman's Century Club Theatre,* and he dedicated the evening to Wells. His program reflected her stance that ballet can tolerate many different stylistic approaches; it also signaled the formal beginning of his trademark eclecticism. Joffrey juxtaposed work against work; no two pieces were alike. Opening with *Vestris Suite,* to the music of André Grétry, he appeared onstage in a white powdered wig and a gold lamé costume. The piece was a sampling of French dances popular in the seventeenth century (*Rigaudon, Minuet, Tambourin*) and was based on Joffrey's interpretations of lithographs of Auguste Vestris, the acclaimed eighteenth-century virtuoso of the Paris Opéra, who, like himself, loved to leap through the air and dazzle the audience with bravura feats.

In contrast with the *Vestris* there followed *Two Studies: Obsession and Dedication,* a work synthesizing ballet with modern dance and accompanied by a Paul Hindemith score. Joffrey recalled it as "groveling around in bare feet looking for something lost"[29] and said that for inspiration he had looked at pictures of cave drawings in art books. Wells had implored Joffrey to try making a modern dance work, in part because she suspected that his performing future was in modern and not in ballet. Perhaps this explains her fancy for *Two Studies.* She liked it so much that she had, in fact, presented Joffrey in it earlier at her school's annual concert on June 6.

Next came *Punch,* a pantomime ballet to an excerpt from Prokofiev's *Romeo and Juliet,* which was notable because Arpino was also in it. Complying with Wells's mandate that the evening was for solo work, Arpino did not move a muscle. He was dressed as Judy with a pointed, green satin hat and slumped on a chair. "In an amorous mood [Punch] finds Judy unresponsive," read the program note.

Joffrey's favorite piece was the next: a romantic *Suite of Waltzes* to Franz Schubert in a "sort of Sylphide costume" that strung together everything he was technically capable of doing in ballet. He challenged himself—"I used every trick in the book."[30] His mother rushed backstage at intermission with tears streaming down her face, alarmed by his exhaustion and worried about his asthma. He was drenched with sweat; his heart was pounding; his chest was rapidly rising and falling, and she

*In 1996, the theater still stood, but as a movie house called the Harvard Exit Theatre.

implored him, "You must give up dancing."[31] He ignored her and went back onstage after the intermission for more. "Of course, I killed myself," he said. "I had spent six months working on the concert. I was very obsessed."[32]

A *Slavonic Folk Dance* (music by Béla Bartók) followed, and the only piece on the program by Wells, a Spanish *Malagueña*. The evening concluded with *24 Hour Liberty*, about an American sailor on shore leave, which was inspired by Gene Kelly and Fred Astaire movies, and Arpino's Coast Guard experience. The music for *24 Hour Liberty* was by Robert Russell Bennett—a jazzy Americana score for violin and piano. The entire program had live music, and the audience left the theater bedazzled. Joffrey received his first review from Maxine Cushing Gray in the internationally distributed *Dance News*:

> [Robert] Joffrey gave a seven-part program of original dance compositions with all choreography except one number and all costumes designed by him. The program was tasteful, well projected, strongly creative; his technique is soundly built and offers clean beats, good balance and astonishing extension à la seconde. He has acquired that fine sense of style and period in movement, costuming and music which frequently marks the work of Wells's pupils.[33]

By the time Gray's write-up appeared, Joffrey and Arpino had packed their bags and left for New York and the School of American Ballet's 1948 summer session. "Miss Wells always said you must find your own way," said Joffrey. "Do whatever makes it work for you."[34]

CHAPTER 5

New York, New York

Gerald Arpino recalled his mother's reaction in 1948 when he returned to Staten Island and told her that he had chosen dance for his profession: "She thought I'd gone off the deep end. She didn't understand anything about dance. Her idea was for me to have a house down the street so she could take care of all my children. And that, to her, was living."[1]

Arpino and Joffrey had already witnessed the panic that such news could bring to parents of males in the 1940s. Unlike the Joffreys, who had grown accustomed to the idea, Anna Arpino was hearing it for the first time. Her son had not told her what he had been doing in Seattle, and he did not want to explain himself now. Anna cried and begged him to reconsider, and when such theatrics failed, she appealed to Monsignor Rizzo and Father Tobin, the priests from the Church of the Sacred Heart.

Father Tobin was as good as family to the Arpinos; he ate dinner with them regularly and was one of the many "strays" (so called by the Arpino children) to whom Anna had opened her doors over the years. He had heard Anna's confessions and knew that when her youngest was in the Coast Guard during the war, she had made a bargain with God: if He let Jerry return home safely, she would let her son do whatever he wanted.

Father Tobin met with Arpino for an hour in a separate room, then brought son and mother together for a final confrontation.

"Annie, you're not going to get through to him," Father Tobin said. "So let it go."

"But I can't."

"I'll do anything for you, Mama, anything," said Jerry. "But this you can't take away from me."[2]

Father Tobin shot her a half-smile as if to argue, "You made a deal"— and Anna was soon teaching herself to knit dancers' leg warmers in various shades of I AM–approved purple. Said Arpino, "The rest of the family thought ballet was esoteric, and my brothers thought it was effeminate. . . . But my mother said to them, 'Look. You like to drive cars. You like to bowl. He likes to do what he calls ballet. I don't know what it is, but he likes to do it. Each of you is like a piece of wood, and when that wood burns, each of you gives off a different kind of smoke. He wants to dance, and that's fine with me.' "3

The stubborn arguments between mother and son soon ebbed. The household, which included Jeannie and Ninette, Arpino's two closest sisters, began to revolve around making the aspiring performers comfortable: homemade lasagna in the oven when they returned from the city; nightly poker games arranged for Anna and Bobby, who couldn't seem to get enough of cards; impromptu dancing exhibitions and charades—the most memorable of which was Bobby dressed in a Davy Crockett hat, goggles, an inverted rabbit-skin coat lining, and size 15 boots (that had been sent by his mother, whom they remorselessly kidded for having "already forgotten" her son's size), clasping a vacuum cleaner and clomping down the stairs. Bobby—and he was called Bobby by the Arpinos, who were under his strictest orders not to leak the nickname to Manhattan—made them laugh.

There were several ongoing puerile gags between him and Anna that suggest how tied he felt to her: Joffrey would lock Anna into the cellar whenever she went downstairs to jar the preserves; he would trap her while she slept in her rocking chair by running around and around it with her yarn; and he used to tie her nightgowns into knots and stuff them back inside her bureau. These antics won over Mama Arpino, who seemed to understand him. She saw how Bobby operated and she delighted in him, but often her pleasure was equal to her son's despair over the bold, conniving shenanigans that he pulled. Explained Gerald Arpino: "Napoleon and Diaghilev were Bob's idols. He had a Napoleonic complex. Bob was the beautiful, quiet [person], but he could twist you around his finger. He had all of us. He was a con artist from way back . . . I mean my mother used to say of Robert Joffrey—she adored him and we'd be sitting there and I'd get all emotional, etc. And Bob would be just as cool as a cucumber. She'd say, 'You know, Jerry, what's wrong with you?' She'd hold my hand. 'Look at Bobby. He could boil you in ice water.' She knew him well."4

Beneath the towering Norwegian maple trees on Pelton Avenue, the key to the Arpino household was love, a baroque, effusive, loquacious love. Compared to the Joffreys' home, where affection seems to have been bestowed for a price and with the inexorable stain of guilt, this was liberation. Under the Arpinos' influence, Joffrey became the child he never was: relaxed and silly and irresponsible. His and Arpino's plan was to reside at 297 Pelton Avenue until they could afford a Manhattan apartment. Joffrey's father had given him the money set aside for his college education so that he could attend the School of American Ballet. The gift represented a huge vote of confidence from Joseph Joffrey. His son had been accepted into Pratt Institute, the school of design and architecture in Brooklyn, but at the last minute he had turned the opportunity down.* "That was a very great blow to [my father]," said Joffrey, "when I didn't want to go to university."[5]

In July 1948, the two-month summer session at the School of American Ballet (SAB) began, and Joffrey and Arpino went daily from Staten Island to the city by ferry. Fortunately for him, classes were offered that summer at SAB with Merce Cunningham, a modern dancer and choreographer who had studied at the Cornish School and had been a member of Martha Graham's company. With Cunningham, Joffrey no longer felt the loss of the Wells curriculum that was drawn from various sources.

"Merce used to teach a modern class once a week and I never missed it," he said. With the "war" between ballet and modern exponents still raging, Joffrey followed Wells's example and did not take sides. "I think I'm the only one who took that class loving it. A lot of people didn't like it. I looked forward to it. I wrote down the combinations. I wrote down everything Merce said."[6]

On occasion, Balanchine himself taught class. Joffrey remembered one of them: "I was pleased because I had done a number of turns. And Mr. Balanchine came over and said, 'Bigger cross fourth, big deep, cross your legs. The end is the most important shape, that's what we remember.' He said nothing about my turns."[7] But his principal teachers at SAB were Anatole Oboukhoff and Pierre Vladimiroff. They had both graduated from the Imperial Ballet Academy in St. Petersburg and had danced with the Imperial Ballet of the Maryinsky Theater. Both had also partnered Anna Pavlova.

When Joffrey showed up in their classes, men were still scarce in ballet, and he intrigued them, particularly Oboukhoff, "a strong, even harsh teacher who frequently behaved as if he were training big cats, horses, or poodles rather than adolescent bipeds."[8] Oboukhoff passed out Life Savers to students who accomplished his combinations with conscientious artistry, and Arpino recalled that Joffrey received Life Savers on a regular basis, whereas he himself was never similarly rewarded.

In some classes Joffrey's dominant competitor was Edward Villella, seven years his junior. (Joffrey shaved two years off on his SAB enrollment form, and because he looked much younger than his twenty years, he was able to take classes with a teenage group.) Villella and he shared certain attributes, but Villella went on to become one of America's foremost premiers danseurs with Balanchine's New York City Ballet. Celebrated for his athleticism and stupendous elevation, he was instrumental in changing the popular perception that ballet was for sissies. There was

---

*Pratt Institute was a fully accredited college that awarded bachelor degrees while continuing to give certificate courses in specific arts disciplines.

a time when Villella and Joffrey were on a par, equal but not the same, as Villella remembered:

"He was the person akin to me because we were both not tall. We were also both people who could jump. My passion was to jump, and I had a soul mate with Bob. Bob had a great, wonderful, pixie enthusiasm about not only the dancing part of it, but the whole genre, the whole form, and that was delightful to be in the presence of. . . . He didn't have the perfect esthetic line for classical dancing. He also had very, very muscular thighs. He didn't have this pristine, long, elegant, purely classical demeanor. But he had facility. He could do tricks. But I think it was reasonably evident that he was not first dancer, premier danseur, potential. I think he knew that."[9]

Joffrey had read how Pavlova had private lessons with Cecchetti, and in Seattle, it had been his custom to have private lessons with Wells. These were habits he wanted to continue in New York. At the time, Alexandra Fedorova was the private instructor of choice. Fedorova had emigrated from Riga, Latvia, in 1937 and had become the Petipa and Ivanov authority in America. She had staged the popular one-act version of Ivanov's *Nutcracker* and the first whole third act of *Swan Lake* (called *The Magic Swan*) for Denham's Ballet Russe, as well as the *Paquita* pas des deux for Erik Bruhn and Nora Kaye. She was married to Michel Fokine's brother, Alexander, and was the mother of Léon Fokine, also a reputable teacher in America. As a former member of the Imperial Ballet and Diaghilev's Ballets Russes, Fedorova knew Vaslav Nijinsky well and had seen him perform on many occasions. Joffrey viewed her as the source who would give him the chance to learn Nijinsky's roles—and she did not disappoint. They met three times a week.

Through Fedorova he learned *Le Spectre de la rose*, variations from *The Nutcracker*, and the pas de trois from *Le Pavillon d'Armide*, the ballet that had caused such a rapturous sensation when presented on Diaghilev's first program in Paris in 1909. He also learned from Fedorova more about how to compensate for his diminutive stature. Nijinsky's dancing was about "illusion," she said—and hearing the similarity of terms to what he had already been taught by Wells about visualization, he plied Fedorova for more. "Nijinsky created illusion by breaking down movement into isolated parts, mastering each, and then recombining," he said, remembering Fedorova's observations. "He always practiced. But he didn't practice the way most dancers did at that time, by phrases or a coda step. Nijinsky would take the individual steps, be it *jeté battu* or a turn *en attitude*, and he would practice that sequence over and over again. He had the concentration to break things down and perfect them. Not of the whole, but of the individual. Much like a pianist."[10] A perfectionist, Joffrey modeled his work habits after Nijinsky's.

Having appeared briefly in Fokine's *Petrouchka* and in Fedorova's staging of *The Nutcracker* with Denham's Ballet Russe de Monte Carlo in Seattle, Joffrey shared a small measure of common ground with the Russians who were now his pedagogues. The door to their inner sanctum was slightly ajar, and Joffrey made clear that he was determined to step inside. "He was full of his own importance," commented one SAB teacher, conceding, "which is important for an artist." He would repay the debt to these ballets someday as a director, but for the time being, he had not given up the idea of performing. These were his prime dancing years.

Wells flew into New York and introduced Joffrey and Arpino to her longtime friend Gertrude Shurr. Shurr had recently published the first comprehensive textbook on modern dance and was teaching beginning modern for May O'Donnell. Her classes would prepare some of the students to join the newly founded May O'Donnell and Company. "I want you to take care of these boys. I want them to study with you," Wells said to her friend.[11]

Shurr gave them the once-over in class. "Jerry was so beautiful you could hardly take your eyes off him. He danced fabulously. He should have been a modern dancer because he's an actor. He felt the things. And when he was lyric, he wasn't afraid to show joyousness.

"But Bob, he was so tremendous as a technician. So generous. So advanced balletically. His attitude was so wonderful. He could do anything you asked him to do, and no matter what he did or what anybody did next to him, they just couldn't compare with him."[12]

By September 1949, Shurr and O'Donnell had moved into the same building as Ballet Theatre—on West Fifty-sixth Street between Sixth and Seventh Avenues. Joffrey was already integral to their enterprise, sometimes teaching O'Donnell's company class. The proximity to Ballet Theatre also proved advantageous, because one day Samuel Lurie, a member of the Ballet Theatre press department, poked his head into Joffrey's class and, excited by what he saw, recommended to Ballet Theatre co-director Lucia Chase that Joffrey be hired to teach the Saturday-morning children's classes. Chase, who had previously heard Joffrey's praises sung by Shurr, engaged the young man.*

O'Donnell had afforded Joffrey the chance to teach because she was fascinated by his complete lack of fear; he seemed so confident that modern dance would not ruin his ballet technique. "I'd ask him to jump and

---

*The classes Joffrey gave at May O'Donnell's and Ballet Theatre did not represent his first teaching jobs in New York. He had previously taught children's dance classes in Brooklyn and at the Gramercy School of Music and Dance on Fourteenth Street. Arpino taught at Gramercy as well, and John Wilson was his accompanist. Joffrey and Wilson eventually became acquainted, and Wilson became Joffrey's musical adviser and a charter Joffrey Ballet member.

fall to the floor, he'd fall to the floor," she said. "For a ballet person that was unusual. He had a sense of the excitement."[13]

Throughout this period of balancing Fedorova, O'Donnell, and teaching at Ballet Theatre, Joffrey continued his lessons at SAB. One afternoon Gordon Hamilton, ballet master and principal dancer with Roland Petit's Ballets de Paris, observed Joffrey during an SAB class. Afterward he encouraged him to audition for Petit. Les Ballets de Paris was performing at the Winter Garden Theater on Broadway and was several days into its first American engagement, competing simultaneously with the American debut of Sadler's Wells Ballet from Britain. Sadler's Wells was performing at the Metropolitan Opera House, where audiences were for the first time experiencing the full-length *Sleeping Beauty* and falling under Margot Fonteyn's thrall. They were also seeing Moira Shearer live; the heroine of the groundbreaking 1948 film *The Red Shoes*, Shearer had been clasped to the hearts of many Americans. A new wave of balletomanes was building.

Foremost on Gordon Hamilton's mind was that one of their male soloists had been injured. Petit needed to find a replacement in New York, somebody who could learn as many as three ballets in a day *and* look as though he was familiar with Petit's style. The small company of eighteen dancers accentuated eroticism. Dramatic, or *demi-caractère*, danseurs—intelligent practitioners of flamboyant pantomime—they worked in a style that, in the words of *Dance News*, was consistent with "what is generally accepted as typical French theatre: emotional, vivacious, at times exciting, at all times concerning itself with the great passion called love."[14]

Joffrey showed up at the Ballets de Paris's cattle call. "Two hundred boys auditioned," he said. "Three of us were finally picked—Jerry, myself, and another boy—then I got the job. I made lots of money. I was paid a great deal because I was a union member and the others weren't."[15]

Petit hired him on a soloist contract that, following the New York run, would take him on the company's eleven-week tour to other major American and Canadian cities. Although he had initially expected only to be dancing minor roles, Gordon Hamilton sustained a leg injury, and Joffrey inherited his principal parts as the Hunchback in *Le Rendez-vous* and the Bandit Leader in *Carmen*. The only American male in the troupe as well as the youngest, Joffrey performed a solo in Petit's *L'Oeuf à la coque* (*The Boiled Egg*)—"a mad fantasy about a big kitchen in Hell"—and rejoiced in dancing beside the company's stars, Renée "Zizi" Jeanmaire and Colette Marchand. He spoke two lessons' worth of French (Arpino having substituted for him at the rest of Mme. Corot's tutorials), and his inability to communicate presented a grave challenge. He seemed to other company members hopelessly reserved and more than a bit naïve.

Joffrey stayed with Les Ballets de Paris until the conclusion of the New York season in mid-December 1949, when he broke his contract. There was strong intimation that his excuse was the language barrier, but his asthma was acting up. "He was very ill and having such a hard time," said Gertrude Shurr.[16] The Ballets de Paris had given an unprecedented 118 performances at the Winter Garden, a grueling four-month schedule that must have drained Joffrey's energy. He also did not want to leave New York because of O'Donnell and Shurr and Ballet Theatre and the promises they held. "And," he said pointedly, "seeing that little company [Ballets de Paris] made me want to have a little company."[17]

He had by now permanently left SAB, and once free of Les Ballets de Paris, he resumed rehearsing for O'Donnell's troupe and picked up teaching an extra class at Ballet Theatre. Erik Bruhn and Violette Verdy were among the first to attend his class, and their star magnetism drew many, many more to discover him.

In September 1950, Elizabeth Goode Rockwell, director of the dance department at the High School of Performing Arts, hired Joffrey as a ballet instructor. Only two years old, the school had been founded as an independent division of the New York City Board of Education's Metropolitan Vocational High School. It operated out of a run-down building on West Forty-sixth Street. The students had to audition; they were an elite, possessing strong stage-career ambitions. Joffrey was one of the earliest, and at twenty-one, one of the youngest, dance faculty members, who included Ann Hutchinson and Lillian Moore, author of *Artists of the Dance,* the first ballet book he had owned. Taking his class was none other than Edward Villella, age fourteen.

At the end of the 1950–1951 school year, the dance department put on a workshop recital of choreography by faculty and students that gave the high school's seniors a chance to shine. For the program, Joffrey created a spirited pas de deux called *Hide and Seek* for Villella and Electa Arenal. The music was a piano improvisation by Betty J. Walberg and an original score, *Adagio,* by Ray Green (May O'Donnell's husband). Villella was only a freshman, but an exception was made for him because his technical facility was peerless—and there were some prodigious talents at Performing Arts with whom to compare him: Arthur Mitchell, who later joined the New York City Ballet and eventually founded Dance Theatre of Harlem, and John Leech (Jonathan Watts), who also later created important roles in Balanchine's works at the New York City Ballet.

Villella said the experience was "very significant" to him because it was the first time he had danced a pas de deux before the public. "I remember one very tricky move," he said, "and that was to do a double air turn and, coming out of it, to touch Electa's hand. She was in a *piqué arabesque* [on pointe with one leg extended high behind her]. It was obviously something I'd never done before, but it worked and I felt very pleased about that."[18]

A photograph of Villella and Arenal in *Hide and Seek* was reprinted in the September issue of *Dance Magazine,* and the caption mentioned Joffrey as the choreographer. But aside from the good publicity, Joffrey's principal gain from *Hide and Seek* was the realization that the Performing Arts students were willing to experiment with him on the creation of his ballets. They were pristine, unestablished, and eager. He promptly formed a happy friendship with Jonathan Watts, who inspired much of his early work.

By the time Joffrey had entered Petit's Ballets de Paris, he and Arpino had saved enough money to tackle the city and rent a Gramercy Park walk-up apartment. After 1949, Joffrey and Arpino were no longer sexually involved. They understood that each man was free to develop new partnerships. Their emotional commitment to each other, however, was inviolate. They treated each other in many respects like a traditional husband and wife. They still shared a bedroom (and would continue to do so for another fifteen years) and Joffrey would not consider severing the bond with Arpino, who shouldered the domestic responsibility for almost all their cooking, grocery shopping, and house cleaning.

Then, in February 1951, Arpino was cast as a swing dancer in *Bless You All,* a Broadway musical with score by Harold Rome and choreography by Valerie Bettis; it featured Bettis and starred Pearl Bailey. As a swing dancer, Arpino would replace anyone who was unable to dance on a given night (he was quickly elevated to a permanent soloist role). A month later, he won a solo part in *Annie Get Your Gun* at the Paper Mill Playhouse in New Jersey. Reflecting their improved circumstances, he and Joffrey relocated to a small studio on Seventeenth Street, later inviting Jonathan Watts along as a roommate. Watts and Joffrey had become lovers; the apartment arrangement made sense. But because Watts was almost five years younger than Joffrey and still one of Joffrey's High School of Performing Arts students, he and Joffrey felt certain such a relationship would not meet with administration or faculty approval, and so they hid it. Such would became the pattern for Joffrey: he always had Arpino, plus usually one principal lover whom he felt not at liberty to disclose, and many one-night sex partners.

"Bob was my teacher, so we were sneaking around," Watts said. "It would have been absolutely verboten for a teacher to be living with a pupil. Bob would say, 'Now we must not go up on the BMT subway together to school.' So we used to take separate trains."[19]

On the other hand, Watts had also been studying with Gertrude Shurr and had recently been inducted into May O'Donnell's company together with Joffrey. In that regard, they were on equal footing. Their attachment was charged. "When I became involved with Bob, he was highly sexual," said Watts more than forty years later. "Jerry and he were not romantically involved with each other then, but I believed them to have a perfect relationship the way married couples perhaps become better friends than they are lovers. This was their powerful bond. They balanced each other well and gave me a stable familial experience that changed my life."[20]

Watts, Joffrey, and Arpino spent almost every weekend on Staten Island with Mama Arpino and the sisters. They were fed nine-course Italian meals around a large oak table in the tiny blue dining room. Richard Englund also sometimes accompanied them. Watts projected himself as an exile from a family split by divorce, and as was the pattern for years to follow with many Joffrey dancers, he compensated for some of the lack of stability in his childhood years by finding it in the Arpino household, as well as in Joffrey and Arpino's New York abodes. Wherever Joffrey and Arpino lived seemed to exude a community feeling—"what's yours is mine, what's mine is yours"—of safe harbor and comfort and "homemade cookies and tea," said one dancer.[21] Clearly, Joffrey and Arpino had a weakness for waifs.

Among the dancers who flocked to Joffrey and Arpino early on, some were out-of-towners, some had left their parents at a young age, some had escaped from homes broken by divorce, alcoholism, or death. For most, the nurturing ambience Joffrey and Arpino offered was irresistible. Dancers were provided a place to spend the holidays, to retreat from cranky landlords, and talk about their favorite subject: ballet. Those who found Joffrey's and Arpino's parental attitude unprofessional or demeaning usually left the dance group.

On March 1, 1951, Joffrey and Watts made their debut with May O'Donnell and Company at the New England Conservatory of Music in Boston. The performance was well received, and O'Donnell began preparing for their New York premiere. Arpino, who was still studying with O'Donnell and Shurr, could not yet swell the ranks of O'Donnell's troupe because of his commitment to *Annie Get Your Gun*. Then in May 1951, he was asked to replace a dancer in Nana Gollner and Paul Petroff's Ballet Russe Company—and for the first time he found himself in white tights, doing classical roles. Within six years, Arpino had perfected his classical technique enough to partner Nana Gollner, a former prima ballerina with the Original Ballet Russe.

The small troupe of twelve departed for a four-month tour of South and Central America. On tour, Arpino befriended dancer Lillian Wellein, who was eighteen years old and traveling with her mother, the company's wardrobe supervisor. In time, Wellein would be instrumental to

Robert Joffrey's choreography, and her mother and Arpino's would hatch a devious friendship. Many thought that Arpino and Wellein were romantically involved because Arpino frequently called her his "girl-friend," possibly in the effort to placate his mother, who by 1955 had seemingly realized that her son was not heterosexual.

"Suddenly I noticed my mother was getting very friendly with Mrs. Arpino," wrote Lillian Wellein. "They telephoned one another more than often. I started to pay attention to their conversations, and it dawned on me that Mrs. Arpino was none too happy with the friendship between Bob and Jerry and wanted to find a way to use me to come between them.

"Bob loved to give parties, and his Christmas ones were always a delight. One night, as Mother and I were leaving a party, Bob took me aside and said, 'You would not go against me, would you?' I answered, 'After what you have done for me, how could I—*never!*' I realized then somehow he had heard about the mothers' plot."[22]

Following the O'Donnell concert in Boston, Joffrey informed Shurr that he was considering forming a ballet troupe. Mary Ann Wells had drilled it into him that a beginning choreographer should use students and not seasoned professionals as "guinea pigs." He obeyed her advice, which was: "To get dancers to move the way you want, you have to train them the way you want, and that means use your own students."[23] He established a choreographer's workshop at the High School of Performing Arts, in part so that he could build his own company. His $46-a-week salary went a long way toward paying him, in effect, to become a director.

From the high school's workshop, he handpicked dancers he thought understood him. He also scouted outside the school, and those whom he tapped were then invited to take evening ballet classes and rehearse with him in a small garret studio that he rented on West Eighth Street. This elite corps grew to think of itself not only as the nucleus for what became the Joffrey Ballet, but as *the* first Joffrey company. Many of its members would mark the Joffrey Ballet's beginnings from the fall of 1951 and declare its inaugural performance to be January 13, 1952. Joffrey did not share their view; he felt the group performed too irregularly to assume a formal identity. He also realized that some of the dancers were still high school students and that the turnover rate was too great to legitimize them as members of a true ensemble.

At the time, he did not know that many of the dancers would stick, and the company would, in fact, evolve out of this nucleus. Among its ranks until 1956 were Saint Amant, Electa Arenal, Gerald Arpino, Roberta Bernard, Jacqueline Cecil, Judith Chazin, Eric Creel, Diana Dear, Joseph Edwards, Carol Frishman, Barbara Ann Gray, Janet Greschler, Jacquetta Kieth, Marie Kolin, Mary Linero, Michael Lland,

Barbara Lucchi, Tania Makaroff, Françoise Martinet, Anthony Mordente, Shirley Neger, Brunilda Ruiz, Lolita San Miguel, Judy Schlein, Baird Searles, Michael Sears, Dana Sosa, Deidre Stone, Beatrice Tompkins, Jonathan Watts, Lillian Wellein, John Wilson, and Violetta Yon.

Its members were soon aware that Joffrey was the only instructor they had ever known who made them believe that despite their liabilities—too short, too tall, too round, too angular, too old—they could dance. Roberta Bernard assumed the position of Joffrey's administrator and ballet mistress; her story laid out the general picture:

"I came from a background of Russian training, but it did not fit my body rhythms and my sensibilities. . . . It wasn't until Bob came along that I was able to work the way my body was comfortable as an American body—that my muscles responded to my inner psyche. Then I could emerge. I was never a great dancer. I don't even know if I was a good dancer, but I never could have been part of that group without Bob's training. He knew how to capitalize on the flair, the style, the strengths, of each individual dancer—even if the dancer didn't fit the mold. Bob didn't look for everybody to have the same dynamic. He was happy with diversity."[24]

Right from the start Joffrey's company was generated out of a kind of wonderful hope: the hope to change what was self-evident and make people who, like himself, did not "fit their bodies" accommodate and conquer a strict and hierarchical classical system by asserting spirit over form through energy, constant drill, and individualized attention. Perhaps, somehow, there might be a clear space for a New York ballet company fostered by an American with a bipolar viewpoint, one that combined ballet and modern techniques in the repertory. Americans had formed their own ballet companies before: Dorothy Alexander in 1929, Willam Christensen in 1933, Josephine and Hermene Schwarz in 1937, Ruth Page with Bentley Stone in 1938, and Catherine Littlefield the same year. But none had rooted them in New York, the world's dance capital, and their ambitions were less grandiose than Joffrey's. He envisioned his company as a major force that would continue to enlarge upon ballet as a popular American entertainment, striding into the arena as a newcomer alongside the veteran heroes: the Ballet Russe de Monte Carlo, American Ballet Theatre, the New York City Ballet, Sadler's Wells Theatre Ballet, the Bolshoi Ballet, and the Royal Danish Ballet. "I thought it was impossible," said Alexandra Danilova, echoing many people's response to Joffrey's proposition.[25] He would have to fight for dignity on his own terms, and he would find his greatest sympathizers in the modern-dance camp.

In the winter of 1951, Joffrey rallied to a call from Trudy Goth, director of the Choreographers' Workshop, a nonprofit cooperative organization that sponsored performances at the 92nd Street Young Men's and Young Women's Hebrew Association's Theresa L. Kaufmann Auditorium, the Humphrey-Weidman Studio Theatre, and other loft locales. Goth was always on alert for untried choreographers who were seeking the opportunity to have their works performed on a real stage before a paying public. She invited Joffrey to audition, and he responded with a polished sketch for a two-act treatment of a Greek myth, *Persephone*. Arpino danced the part of Pluto, Wellein was Persephone, and Deidre Stone took on Demeter. The groups of Companions and Lost Souls consisted of Joffrey's favorite Performing Arts students. The original score was by flutist Robert Silverman, a colleague at Performing Arts and Jerome Robbins's cousin. Gertrude Handy executed the costumes (assisted by Wellein's mother) and Read Arnow the scenery.

Joffrey made every effort to present himself before Goth in the most professional light. A product of the art form's steady development and not a fad, he worked out of his background and constructed a piece that fused elements from the classical lexicon with those from modern. There were broken angles and odd rhythms; ankles were sometimes flexed in pointe shoes, wrists were bent to ninety degrees, palms were splayed, and the dancers executed contractions and spiral falls. Joffrey had assembled neophytes who were willing to admit there was more than one system, while also attempting to reach for something different in ballet. Goth slated them on her next program, scheduled for January 13, 1952, at the 92nd Street YM–YWHA on the Upper East Side—and then Joffrey's work began in earnest.

Gathering his musicians and dancers in the Eighth Street studio, he rehearsed them every night. One of the musicians remembered that a half-broken skylight sometimes sent drifts of snow onto the floor. The snow engendered a bleak and gloomy atmosphere that seemed mystically appropriate for the "king of winters, the infernal Pluto," the André Gide line on which Joffrey based the ballet.

While the musicians shivered on their stools, huddled into a dry corner, the dancers often scrambled to swab the melted snow so they would not slip and fall. "It really looked like the last act of *La Bohème*," said Marvin Schofer, the pianist. "Bob was unknown. Jerry was unknown. They were paying for this out of their piggy banks"—as far as the public and critics were concerned, "there was no company."[26] It was all about to happen.

CHAPTER 6

Dancer to Choreographer

By the ballet's premiere on January 13, 1952, Joffrey's experiments with *Persephone* were tentative and insufficiently developed. The only critic to review the concert, Doris Hering of *Dance Magazine,* found on first impression that *Persephone* was predictable, ambitious, and "competent if relatively uninspired." While leaving reason to believe that the work might gain impact with certain cast changes, Hering accurately described the ballet as a "mythological pageant in the vein of Balanchine's *Orpheus.*"[1]

Very often Joffrey's secret resource was the appropriation of existing materials. He favored the methodology of a collage artist; he used found elements and arranged them to form a new whole. Robbing outright was considered a virtue, provided the choreographer's objective was to develop the material and not merely to plagiarize. The little steals—the I-hope-nobody-notices—could bring an artist down, but at this point in his choreographic evolution, Joffrey was new at creating dances. He didn't have a systematic procedure, and he might never have one. He did not know.

But he was surprisingly open about *Persephone,* explaining that if he was robbing, then his hand was on the goods made by Martha Graham—at least that was where he had consciously placed it. "When I first came to New York, Martha Graham impressed me perhaps more than any other person," he said. "I just had never seen theater-dance the way she did it. Isadora Bennett was her press agent, and she used to sneak me in [to the theater] all the time. She'd give me a seat and say, 'Applaud. That's a critic's seat. I want you to applaud.' I'd say, 'Of course, I'll applaud.' "[2]

In *Persephone,* Joffrey explored dynamic volume—weight in space, seeing the body as existing not only on the frontal plane presented to the audience, but on the planes above, below, and around the figure. He was concerned with mass almost to the exclusion of line, asking rhetorically: What happens to a ballet dancer's shape and meaning when she embraces, rather than defies, gravity?

Besides Hering's review, Joffrey's debut prompted a curious assertion in *The Dancing Times,* a British publication, that Joffrey was "one of the most promising of the younger choreographers." Although the column was unsigned, it could be that critic P. W. Manchester of New York's *Dance News* had whispered into the ear of *Dancing Times* to encourage the bold claim. Manchester was managing editor of *Dance News* in New York and a recent émigré from London, and in her opinion, *Persephone*'s second act was cause for genuine excitement.

"Joffrey got absolutely the essence of what the Greeks thought about life after death," she said many years later in 1993, when asked about her thoughts on *Persephone* and her overt stance as Joffrey's champion. "There is no heaven or hell to the Greeks, you just go on living the way you were in real life except that you've got no possibility of changing anything. It was the one wonderful part of that ballet in which all of these people were dead and wandering about as they'd been in life, but with no power. The rest of *Persephone* wasn't particularly good. But that one scene made me think there was great talent there."[3]

The favorable word on Joffrey, and on Arpino as his principal dancer, began to spread. Joffrey and Arpino never missed a Dance Laboratory lecture at the 92nd Street Y by critic Walter Terry. Said Terry, "Bob and Jerry, with these enormous dark eyes, sat in the front row for every single talk and lecture-demonstration, lapping up backgrounds in dance so that intellectually they were as lively as they were in terms of actual performing and choreography."[4] They saw every performance possible, no matter the stature or discipline of the artist. Said Alexander Ewing, "Bob would sit through a five-hour Chinese opera and come out beaming, when the rest of the audience had walked out before intermissions. He always could find something to gain from what he saw."[5] Joffrey trumpeted himself as a regular at Kamin Dance Book Shop and Gallery; his bookshelves were the envy of dance librarians. His private files, crammed with hundreds of clipped articles and ballet-company advertisements from national and international publications, were the anguish of his roommates. He and Arpino also devoured recordings and scores. Said Marvin Schofer, "There was never a time when music wasn't going on in their apartment."[6]

The New York debut of May O'Donnell and Company took place on April 6, 1952. The only piece on the program in which O'Donnell herself did not appear was *Dance Sonata*, the evening's opener for her thirteen-member ensemble. Despite his harrowing schedule, Joffrey "always showed a keen and eager interest," said O'Donnell.[7] He had the discipline to forget about everything outside her four studio walls. For *Dance Sonata*, she designated him leader of the men (Gerald Arpino, Roy Graves, Jonathan Watts, and Arthur Yahiro); Nancy Lang was leader of the women.

Forty years later, O'Donnell said of Joffrey and Arpino and the era in which they worked with her:

> At the time of the early fifties, when Bob and Jerry worked with me, the modern dance was still an oddity to most people. When asked to describe it, one said that it was not ballet, jazz, Spanish, oriental, etc. It was still a pioneering venture and had little or no financial support. Dancers worked for love with the belief and the dedication that it was a vital and important expression that came out of the American spirit. To present a concert was difficult and a sure financial loss—there were no salaries for the dancers and they did not expect any.
>
> Bob and Jerry's technical skill and interest gave me the opportunity to experiment and expand the movement range of a work. . . . Bob was quiet, considerate, and worked with sensitive, concentrated power. . . . I knew that Bob's commitment to dance was his life.[8]

John Martin singled out Joffrey and Lang as "brilliant dancers" in his *New York Times* review and subsequently raved about the entire company in his end-of-the-season wrap, writing that "not in many a year has so able, so beautifully trained and so admirably directed a group made its appearance on the scene."[9] Reviews in *Dance News* and *Dance Magazine* reiterated the sentiment and mentioned Joffrey. "Wherever he was on stage, that was the center of the stage," explained P. W. Manchester.[10]

"I was a perfectionist as a dancer," Joffrey would later say. "I was the type of person who, if I was going to dance, I had to prepare myself the whole evening—I had to concentrate on myself only."[11]

Seventeen days after the O'Donnell company performance, Joffrey presented a scene from his new work *Teenage Scaramouche,* on a program at the Brooklyn Museum performed by High School of Performing Arts students. During this spring season he taught at Performing Arts and Ballet Theatre and at his own studio on West Eighth Street; rehearsed with May O'Donnell every night; and choreographed his own work whenever he could fit it in. As musical adviser and friend John Wilson observed, "Bob worked so hard and slept so soundly during this time that he had to have the telephone company call him every morning. I said, 'This is very expensive!' He said, 'I know, but I'll never get up without it. My mother used to wake me up with an elephant gun, but she's not here.' "[12]

Teenage Scaramouche was not the most complicated ballet for Joffrey to assemble because it had in effect been done before. Mary Ann Wells had presented a ballet that she had choreographed called *Teenage Scaramouche* at her students' spring recital in 1948. Both Joffrey and Arpino had danced in it; Joffrey was Scaramouche, "a braggart and a swaggerer" drawn from Italian comedy. The program notes for both Wells's recital and Joffrey's New York presentation read verbatim: "This modern Scara-mouche finds himself unpopular and takes solace in daydreaming and wishful thinking."

Had Joffrey stolen a whole ballet? Being derivative of Balanchine and Graham was one thing, but taking someone else's work—someone who might never know—was another. Joffrey's *Teenage Scaramouche* was structured around the talent he had at Performing Arts and, importantly, around an original score he had commissioned from John Strauss for piano, trumpet, flute, and viola. His chief desire as a choreographer was to collaborate, to generate a ballet with the cooperation and input from his composer, his designers, his scenarist. He had borrowed from Mary Ann Wells the ballet's plot, but not her music. It was around this time that his colleagues began to hear him say that Serge Diaghilev was his role model.

"The thing with Bob and those ballets—he was approaching the way he knew Diaghilev, or he thought Diaghilev, had approached ballet," said Watts, who was the original Scaramouche in Joffrey's version. "So, you had the entire ballet—every aspect of that ballet was being created together as a collaboration. That was part of the excitement of doing it. He was trying to re-create the way Diaghilev approached ballet. And Bob was at his best when he was collaborating."[13]

Joffrey came to the rehearsals fully prepared, having worked out movements beforehand. Wearing his routine uniform of a white, short-sleeved cotton shirt and dark pants, he snapped his fingers and slapped his thigh to the music's beat. Radiating his upturned smile, sweetened by a natural overbite, he impressed many as a sure-minded taskmaster.

Judy Schlein, an early Joffrey dancer, described his approach: "He worked everything out of you. But he was right there moving, placing and pushing, right with you. His energy was boundless. He didn't have to mock or berate or put any of us down. That was not his manner at all. From the shrug of his shoulder, we knew what he wanted. We were devoted. We used to rehearse sometimes until four in the morn-ing. He had no conception of dancers' endurance level. Nor did we."[14]

Dancing for Joffrey at the beginning was described as a "thrill," the thrill of being directed to an outrageous destination where the students could dance, dance, dance, and have everyone in the audience suspend disbelief. He radiated an honest view of life as fun and immediate; his discerning mind was compelled by the spirit of ceaseless inquiry. "But at the same time he created a distance between himself and us," said his assistant Roberta Bernard. "He was not interested in being friends or wasting time socially talking. You had tremendous respect for him."[15]

Persephone had resonated elsewhere in the dance world. In the spring of 1952, Trudy Goth asked him to present the two-act ballet in a new collaborative enterprise planned for July between the Choreographers' Workshop and Jacob's Pillow Dance Festival. Situated on one hundred and fifty acres of farmland in western Massachusetts, the Pillow was America's first summer dance festival. The festival was founded in 1933 and, except for three individual seasons, was from then until his death directed by Ted Shawn, who had established Jacob's Pillow as the base for his Men Dancers. It was the sine qua non of dance. Scarcely an artist of international merit had not been honored by an invitation to perform inside the first American theater built exclusively for dance. To reach the Pillow was to be anointed. Shawn had seen *Persephone* and wanted it, and Joffrey was honored. Shawn also selected three other works from the Choreographers' Workshop 1951–52 season. One of them was by Richard Englund, Joffrey's oldest friend, who had by this time transferred from Harvard University as an undergraduate to the dance program at Juilliard School of Music in New York. Goth arranged for what amounted to a "best of" program to be transported north for two performances.

Walter Terry, writing dance criticism for the *New York Herald Tribune,* attended the July 4 engagement at the Pillow and scripted a lengthy, fervent review that picked up on Joffrey's intention to explore further the integration of ballet and modern dance idioms that had been initiated about fifteen years before in Eugene Loring's *Billy the Kid,* Agnes de Mille's *Rodeo,* Catherine Littlefield's *Barn Dance,* and Ruth Page's *Frankie and Johnnie.* The aim was to have traditional ballet emerge from real life, at the same time telling a traditional story. "A difficult assignment," Terry remarked, adding, "There are flaws to his work. It is overlong, it postures occasionally, it borrows from Balanchine's style and its closing passages do not build as well as they might. But these youthful slips in no way obscure the genuine power, the very real beauty of a theater piece which clearly heralds the developing skills of a sensitive young artist."[16]

P. W. Manchester also traveled the distance to see the program, and one consequence of her and Terry's dedicated efforts to review Joffrey is that he forged friendships with them both. Just as he collected postcards, art books, and antiques, Joffrey collected dance historians. He had already attached himself to Lillian Moore, the former Balanchine dancer who was on the Performing Arts faculty. Manchester and Terry were also authorities on ballet history, and he wanted to pump them for information. But there was more to it than that. By becoming friends with dance critics and writers, he was constructing a network that he deemed absolutely necessary for anyone who even thought about trying to make a ballet company in New York. He was scripting his own lineage, and he found that these two people needed him as much as he needed them. They eagerly exerted an influence.

When first introduced to Manchester, Joffrey came prepared with a dozen red roses and, offering them, said, "Tell me everything you know." Manchester had been Marie Rambert's personal secretary in England during World War II and the assistant company manager of Ballet Rambert. She had written a book on Ninette de Valois's company, *Vic-Wells: A Ballet Progress* (1942). She had seen de Valois raise her troupe from Vic-Wells to Sadler's Wells (and it would become the Royal Ballet in 1956); her experience of the birth of British ballet was firsthand. "Of course he was milking me," she said.[17]

With Walter Terry, Joffrey invited a certain kind of hazard. Terry was known to play favorites with dancers and choreographers and to craft entire reviews in the *Tribune* around his so-called pets. His reputation over time suffered as a result, but when Joffrey met him, Terry was in his prime, facing off against John Martin of the *New York Times*.

New York's dance community in the 1950s lived, breathed, and trained along a section of Fifty-sixth Street between Sixth Avenue and Broadway known as the Ballet Belt, and sometimes jokingly called the dance belt. Everybody ran into everybody on the sidewalk on their way to and from class, rehearsal, and performance. Dance was still a relatively new art form in America; it hadn't been until 1927, for example, that editors at the *New York Times* had even considered the need for a bona fide critic to cover dance. By the 1950s, there were many more writers and dancers and related artists, and they often collided inside this bounded, tiny sphere. Sometimes their relationships veered into illicit territory: Terry and Joffrey had a brief affair toward the decade's end.

But in late 1952, Joffrey began spending Sunday afternoons with Manchester and Terry, sometimes up at Lillian Moore's parents' house in the Connecticut countryside. "Lillian loved Bob," said Manchester. "She loved his perfectionism and appreciated his depth of knowledge."[18] Moore represented ballet's old guard—devoted to the study of Romantic ballet, an erudite, somewhat colorless, proud woman. Ultimately Moore worked the most closely with Joffrey; she served as his guardian angel, the eyes behind his head during the difficult times when his company would sway toward extinction.

On November 26, 1952, *Scaramouche** was performed for the first time by Joffrey's nucleus group. He had tightened the work structurally, many of the dancers were professional, and the effort he put into editing and polishing the work for this Trudy Goth Choreographers' Workshop program paid off. Louis Horst, who was considered to be the finest dance accompanist of his time and who was Martha Graham's musical adviser,

---

*This was the ballet's new and final title.

enthusiastically praised John Strauss's score in *Dance Observer*, then wrote: "Mr. Joffrey is showing unmistakable evidences of becoming one of our most promising young ballet choreographers. . . .Gerald Arpino, as A Hero, was excellent."[19]

Three months later, on February 17, 1953, another new Joffrey work with the curious name of *Umpateedle*—"a long-short alternation of rhythm popular in Tin Pan Alley music," according to the program note—had its premiere at the Brooklyn High School for Homemaking. The piece was for his Performing Arts students and introduced Anthony Mordente in an exhilarating, athletic solo that would bring down the house. Watts would also become known for the ballet. John Strauss again composed the score, one that was filled with staccato rhythms "against the classical grain." The against-the-grain theme was echoed by Read Arnow in the costumes, because the girls' tutus were cut on a bias at the hemline so that they were shorter above one leg than above the other.

With the addition of *Umpateedle,* a connecting thread among Joffrey's three ballets became visible: his imagination served the male. Possibly spurred on by his emotional attachments to Arpino and Watts, he invented roles for them. He was attracted to masculine beauty; it moved and inspired him. Said Watts:

"Bob had experienced Balanchine's point of view that ballet was woman from his days as a student at SAB. It was probably important to him not to be a servant to that. He saw the beauty of male dancing *and* female dancing. As men, we were not given preference by Bob. We were equal in importance to the women."[20]

Joffrey's equal treatment of the sexes effectively downgraded the ballerina's traditional role. In this regard, he was more closely related to his colleagues in modern dance. Still, could anything of a sexual, psychological, or personal nature be read into the way he asked Arpino and Watts to move, and in the kinds of roles he crafted for them?

"I never felt anything but artistic fervor from Bob in the studio," said Watts. "Snapping his fingers . . . his hyper way of going into his own little world. Choreography can often be motivated by a physical draw to a dancer, but I never felt that with Bob. There was no confusion when you were in the studio with him. There was no confusion when you were in bed with him. Those two worlds were separate.

"As a choreographer and teacher, what is meaningful to consider about Bob is that he often isolated the male figure"—extricating him from the demands of partnering in order to let him fly solo—"he understood the male form, and he wanted it to be seen."[21]

Joffrey excavated territory for men—perhaps out of compassion for the career that for him was limited, more probably because he was genuinely excited by male virtuosity, beginning imaginatively with Nijinsky, and culminating in the fortuitous circumstances of having such outstanding talents as Villella, Watts, and Mordente intersect his path. He was one of the first teachers in America to conduct all-male classes. "His men were the strongest," said student Brunilda Ruiz, "because he knew their bodies were different from women's. It was like he had X-ray vision, and he'd give corrections that provided them the best placement, knowing exactly what to tell the boys to do."[22]

Arpino had come to ballet too late ever to possess the technical facility for bravura feats. Joffrey called him "my dramatic dancer," suggesting that he compartmentalized; Watts was his technician, his instinctively classical stylist. But for Arpino and Watts, to be a choreographer's muse was everything a dancer dreams of being, and Joffrey and May O'Donnell enabled them to fill the role.

In April 1953, the Bethsabee de Rothschild Foundation sponsored the American Dance Festival, a two-week season on Broadway at the Alvin Theatre. The festival assembled a generous cross-section of modern dance companies (seventeen works by eight choreographers) that "proved once and for all that the modern dance is indeed a valid artistic concept."[23] O'Donnell's company was one of the participants, and Joffrey, Watts, and Arpino performed in her *Dance Sonata*.

At one of the festival performances, Joffrey suddenly fell to the ground in agony. He could not get up and had to crawl offstage on his hands and knees. The doctor told him that he had badly and perhaps irreparably torn a ligament in his calf. Only twenty-four years old, he focused on steeling his patience, on decanting opportunity out of the apparent crisis. He applied some of the I AM precepts, and when his doctor informed him that his dancing career must prematurely end, he surrendered without regret or anguish. "By then his desire to choreograph had overtaken his desire to dance," explained Watts.[24] Twenty years later, Joffrey—who, in the positive spirit of the I AM, never wanted to harbor bad feelings about his past or to remind people that he had sustained an injury—presented somewhat different reasons for giving up dancing. He said, "I was the kind of dancer who couldn't hold down a full-time job and have aspirations to form a company. Something had to give, and it was more compelling to form a company."[25]

Joffrey immediately started looking for a place to open a school. "The school was to provide dancers for a company," he said. "Because I had heard everywhere that you had to have a school before a company."[26]

CHAPTER 7

In Good Company

In the middle of 1953, Joffrey and Arpino founded the American Ballet Center* at 430 Sixth Avenue in a converted necktie factory called the Dome, former headquarters of the American Communist Party, in Manhattan's Greenwich Village. Mom-and-pop businesses spilled onto many of the Village's tree-lined streets, which were organized with a whimsical cartographical logic based on the cow paths of the city's agricultural days. In a sense, confusion was the area's exclusion mechanism. Straight-and-narrow people who liked their architectural structures uniformly sized, their corners exact, and all their streets on a predictable grid were probably happier uptown.

In 1953, high-ceilinged apartments and renovated industrial buildings were still available for rent at inexpensive prices. When Joffrey, Arpino, Watts, and their grand piano moved into the new work space on one of the Village's few busy commercial avenues—joining Doris Humphrey, Merce Cunningham, Louis Horst, Edith Stephen, and John Butler, who had studios on different floors—they transported their personal belongings with them and called a spare room in the back home. "It was a communal affair, and we all helped each other," said Arpino. "It was the way we survived. We communicated and took interest in each other's art. I remember the time we gave our studio to Lotte Lenya free of charge to rehearse *Threepenny Opera*. We had no grants, no scholarships. We were independent artists who provided for each other."[1]

The American Ballet Center opened by offering a single afternoon class taught by Joffrey. His instruction was "highly experimental and innovative," said Watts. "Bob was burning with ideas" that he explored in his teaching as preludes to choreographing ballets.[2] Within the next months, Joffrey would begin teaching a two-hour pointe class for the

---

*In 1967, Joffrey disclosed to critic Clive Barnes that the reason he had named his school the American Ballet Center was that he thought ABC would be an unforgettable acronym. He was wrong. His school has always been better known as the Joffrey Ballet School and is listed both ways in the New York City telephone directory.

girls, and Lillian Moore would offer classes on the pirouette. Arpino eventually convinced Joffrey to let him teach three adult beginner and children's classes. He posted a sign depicting Pavlova and a pair of toe shoes, and the uninitiated came from blocks around, which contributed significantly to Joffrey and Arpino's income. Arpino also collected students' payments, answered the phone, demolished and rebuilt the walls—"When we ripped down our walls, we found Communist slogans and neckties with naked girls on them."[3] The same person who as a boy mowed lawns, delivered newspapers, and got straight A's in school was in his new element at the American Ballet Center.

By 1953, it was being reported that whereas previously most ballet organizations had operated at a deficit, it now seemed that some companies were paying their way from the box office. It seemed for the first time *possible* for some in ballet to make enough money to live. "The unprecedented 12-week season of New York City Ballet, the highly successful tours of Ballet Theatre and other dance groups this year prove the point . . . [that] ballet has emerged from its former restricted position of entertainment for balletomanes only," wrote the assistant secretary of the American Guild of Musical Artists (AGMA), a labor union for ballet and modern dancers and opera singers, in *Dance Magazine*. "We look to the day when a money-losing ballet company will be a thing of the past so that the issue will never again be raised."[4]

Although Joffrey did not consider that he had a real company yet, he was asked back to Jacob's Pillow Dance Festival on July 10, 1953, to present *Scaramouche* and *Umpateedle*. A full year went by before his next assignment: the annual April in Paris Ball at the Waldorf-Astoria Hotel. Joffrey recreated the court of Versailles for the gala benefit that used his and Ballet Theatre's students, and in which Victor Borge was cast as Louis XIV. The ball provided Joffrey with his first chance to choreograph for Ballet Theatre's codirector Lucia Chase.

On April 27, 1954, Chase presented the first Ballet Theatre Workshop at Kaufmann Auditorium at the 92nd Street Y. Joffrey had the privilege of being represented on her program with *Umpateedle*. Beatrice Tompkins was now among his troupe's members. A quixotic brunette with a fantastic flair for buoyant, theatrical work, Tompkins had danced for Balanchine for fifteen years, but she was not fitting in as well there as she had in the past and so she had retired. Joffrey admired her and offered her a place; Tompkins would, in time, profoundly affect his enterprise.

On May 29, 1954, the Robert Joffrey Ballet had its official debut. The performance at the 92nd Street Y belonged to him and him alone. In those days one could not simply rent the Y's Kaufmann Auditorium. One had to meet the approval of Doris Humphrey, who, since 1948, had directed the YM–YWHA dance program and who was on the committee in charge of bookings. Humphrey came to Joffrey's studio to see if he was worthy. Of her criteria, the dance press had previously written, "The committee nods to nobody but the genuine talent, without prejudice and without partisanship."[5] Agnes de Mille, Valerie Bettis, Paul Draper, Martha Graham, Carmelita Maracci, and Iva Kitchell had given their own programs in the past and consecrated Kaufmann Auditorium as a recital theater "without peer."

The 92nd Street Y was viewed almost exclusively as the mecca for modern dance. Few ballet choreographers had attempted to set foot on its hallowed ground, but Joffrey was from the very beginning regarded as an exception. "He's one of us," had opined Gertrude Shurr.[6] Like the moderns, he used his name in the company's title.

Joffrey may have been on the modern dance track in many respects, but there was a critical difference between him and O'Donnell or Humphrey, Limón, Graham, and Cunningham. Joffrey was from the start a commercial artist. He aimed for a broad public—a broad, as contrasted with mass, audience. "He was never doing mandarin art for twelve people in a loft," remarked his musician and friend Marvin Schofer.[7]

For the troupe's debut at Kaufmann, Joffrey created *Pas des Déesses* (Dance of the Goddesses). The ballet was intended to appeal to the mainstream, and forty years after its premiere, *Pas des Déesses* is still being performed. The ballet was to be a vivification of old-fashioned gentility, manners, and grace, and into it Joffrey willed all that was good, radiant, and clean in his soul, evoking an image that would stick to the company like honey. The image included the ballerinas' hairdo—parted down the middle, swept over the ears into a low bun in true Romantic fashion—which, somewhat modified, converted into a Joffrey ballerinas' trademark during the 1960s and 1970s.

Pas des Déesses was inspired by A. E. Chalon's famous lithograph of Arthur Saint-Léon, Marie Taglioni, Lucile Grahn, and Fanny Cerrito in Jules Perrot's 1846 production of *The Judgment of Paris*—three prima ballerinas of the nineteenth century competing for Saint-Léon's and the public's favor. The ballerinas were each terpsichorean paragons, but manifesting somewhat different qualities and strengths. For elevation: Taglioni, who introduced the fashion of the white, midcalf-length tutu and was among the first ever to dance on pointe. For uninhibited style: Grahn, a feisty dancer of Danish origin. For turns and adagio: Cerrito, who was in real life married to Saint-Léon.

Joffrey's challenge was to produce a period piece that illuminated these ballerinas' distinctive characteristics, working with his dancers, who were largely unschooled in the Romantic esthetic. *Pas des Déesses* tested his principles: "The best style is no style," he had said.[8] And "learn

the classical technique—then forget it."[9] He wanted his dancers to liber-
ate themselves from the academic rules and regulations they had learned
in class and serve the choreographer. He was interested in commitment
over textbook perfection. *Pas des Déesses* would ask the most of them as
individuals.

"I made the ballet really for the dancers I had," he said.[10] Personality
was a by-product, not an aim; a given that came from inside out and not
the reverse. He chose Lillian Wellein for Taglioni, Barbara Ann Gray for
Grahn, Jacquetta Kieth for Cerrito, and Jonathan Watts for Saint-Léon.*
Of her work with Joffrey on creating Taglioni, Wellein remembered,
"He, too, was an asthmatic, and so he realized my breathing capacity was
bad. He choreographed the ballet to allow me seconds to catch it again. I
really appreciated this thought for my health."[11]

The real genesis for *Pas des Déesses* had actually been a combination of
proddings from Lillian Moore, who was an absolute fanatic about
Romantic ballet, and from P. W. Manchester, who had come to Joffrey
with the idea of his employing the charming, ebullient music of John
Field. An Irish composer largely unknown in the United States, Field had
lived in the nineteenth century, and his most famous claim was perhaps
that his piano nocturnes had influenced Chopin. Manchester felt that
Joffrey had variously been using music that was not "tuneful" enough,
music that wasn't "structured" and "classical" and, therefore, "suitable"
for ballet. She wanted to effect a major change in his esthetic. "I thought
he should try his hand at something which is not a modern score," she
said. "But it should be that strong nineteenth-century beat."[12]

At the *Pas des Déesses* premiere on May 29, 1954, the critics blithely
sloughed off the work as too stereotypical, saying that it resembled most
obviously Keith Lester's reconstruction of Jules Perrot's well-known *Pas de
Quatre,* the version that Ballet Theatre had frequently performed, as
well as Anton Dolin's arrangement of the same. Doris Hering in *Dance Magazine* commented that "one could sense the care with which Mr. Joffrey had
pored over old Romantic lithographs to capture every nuance. . . . While
the piece lacked acuity of viewpoint, it had a winsome fidelity to the mood
of the time."[13] Walter Terry in the *New York Herald Tribune* liked the ballet better; "freshly inventive," he said.[14] Manchester, recognizing a conflict
of interest, abstained from writing a review.

The new work that fired the critics' imaginations was *Le Bal Masqué.*
It marked another departure for Joffrey, who for the first time was using
voice in his productions. John Wilson as a blind man sang the Poulenc
Cantata for Baritone and Chamber Orchestra. After *Le Bal Masqué,* Jof-

---

*Although Joffrey created the Saint-Léon role for Watts, Michael Lland danced the
premiere.

frey would continue to integrate song or spoken text into his ballets, including *Pierrot Lunaire* (1955), *Kaleidoscope* (1955), *Within Four Walls* (1956), *Astarte* (1967), *Remembrances* (1973), and *Postcards* (1980).

The critics categorically burst forth with enthusiasm for *Le Bal Masqué,* praising Joffrey's "tumultuous depiction of the borderland between reality and the unreal—a land where the blind have sight and the seeing do not." Hering (whose words those were) also rejoiced that "at long last," Beatrice Tompkins, as a tigerish blind woman, "had a role worthy of her considerable dramatic authority."[15] Walter Terry appreciated that "elements of the macabre, hints of evil, thrusts of passion, suggested clearly that Mr. Joffrey could work in areas other than those concerned with sweetness, graciousness or youthful joy."[16]

If *Pas des Déesses* had swept his consciousness into a bright and glorious light, then *Le Bal Masqué* had diverted his inner eye toward gray and threatening clouds. He loved the balance between sun and darkness because it reflected an earnest search for truth. But as the next eight years would prove, the feel-good, pleasant, and bouncy route of theatrical entertainment had more audience appeal than his dance-drama abstractions, such as *Le Bal Masqué,* and he would be forced to compromise the balance to stay afloat. Not until 1962 would he be able to restore an erotic, malevolent, or morbid tone to the repertory, but by then the company was established. One thing was constant with Joffrey: the company's existence came first. If he had to compromise, he had to compromise—as long as the company endured and his standards of presentation remained above reproach.

With the conclusion of the Robert Joffrey Ballet Concert, the press affirmed his group as a bona fide company, which to Joffrey's thinking it still was not. A company, for him, worked toward more than one performance a year—which was an insupportable existence, even though a necessary one for many modern dance troupes at the time. A ballet company meant institution, a regular and predictable association with an audience. Moreover, the dancers, designers, composers, and musicians had to be paid.

When the summer arrived, still keeping their studio in the Village, Joffrey and Arpino cleared out of the city and headed for Seattle, where Joffrey choreographed outdoor musical-theater productions of *The Student Prince, Carousel,* and *Oklahoma!* for the Green Lake Aqua Theater. A movement was underfoot in Seattle to form a civic ballet out of the seventy dancers at the Aqua Theater. Maxine Cushing Gray, respected editor of the local magazine *Argus,* had promoted the idea nationally in *Dance News,* and the concept appealed to Joffrey. He did not forget it, but neither was he tempted. Gray was pushing for him as the logical choice to direct such an entity.

With the arrival of fall, Joffrey and Arpino returned to Manhattan, intending to present another recital of original works. Joffrey made two new ballets: *Pierrot Lunaire* for Jonathan Watts, with music by Arnold Schoenberg, and *Harpsichord Concerto in B Minor,* music by Manuel de Falla. At one rehearsal, George Balanchine and Lincoln Kirstein paid the group a visit. Some of Joffrey's dancers called it an "audition" for Balanchine. It seems that Balanchine; his wife, Tanaquil LeClercq; Nicholas Magallanes; and Roy Tobias had attended the premiere of *Le Bal Masqué,* ostensibly to support their friend and colleague Beatrice Tompkins, and they had been impressed by the whole program. Balanchine and Kirstein were curious about Joffrey, and they were particularly interested in his student Jonathan Watts.

After the audition, they were "very encouraging," said Joffrey, and they indicated that they had liked *Pierrot Lunaire*. Then, Joffrey added, "Mr. Kirstein said, 'What can I do to help?' And I said, 'I really need five hundred dollars—a loan of five hundred dollars to pay the orchestra.' He was very gracious, and Mr. Balanchine told me to continue choreographing and to work. Years later, when I went to pay the debt back, Betty Cage [their general manager] said, 'Oh, no, no, that was a gift.' "[17]

Although Kirstein later acknowledged that he "doubted if there was much interest" on Balanchine's part in Joffrey,[18] Balanchine showed great kindness toward Joffrey over the years, granting him permission to perform eight of his works without having to pay royalties, lending him costumes, releasing his dancers to guest with the Joffrey Ballet, trading ballet masters, and recommending the Joffrey for the vacancy at City Center when the New York City Ballet relocated to Lincoln Center. Kirstein, too, kept in contact with Joffrey and his executive team, providing occasional counsel.

Soon after the "audition," Balanchine extended an invitation to Joffrey's leading classical dancer, student, lover, and muse, Jonathan Watts, to join the New York City Ballet. Watts accepted on the condition that he could perform *Pierrot Lunaire* for Joffrey's concert.* It was one of Joffrey's great early moments to see his student leave for the professional world. Watts's departure was not without negative repercussions, however. It virtually terminated Joffrey's output of serious-minded ballets in the traditional classical idiom, leaving him to wait for Brunilda Ruiz to mature, and for such dancers as Lisa Bradley, Lone Isaksen, Lawrence Rhodes, and Paul Sutherland to come along in another seven years. For them Joffrey would produce *Gamelan*.

On March 24, 1955, Joffrey offered the "Evening of Original Ballets"

---

*When Watts joined the New York City Ballet, he also ended the affair with Joffrey and moved out of the American Ballet Center's back room that they shared.

at Kaufmann Auditorium. The new, experimental pieces suggested that Joffrey was finally escaping from the shadow of giants. Whereas *Persephone* had reminded people of Balanchine's *Orpheus,* and *Pas des Déesses* of Jules Perrot's *Pas de Quatre,* and *Le Bal Masqué* of the "modishly decadent" works by Roland Petit, Joffrey was seen in this concert to be standing on his own feet. Critics pointed to *Pierrot Lunaire* as proof. An "unremittingly poetic" ballet, said Hering; Joffrey allowed himself "free rein in the portrayal of moonstruck characters seeking their destinies, and finding their doom."[19] The dancers wore cobwebby, transparent gray costumes as they sleepwalked in choral patterns that swelled dramatically and then slowly dissipated. At the climax, a young girl was passed among three men and then borne away by one of them.

Deborah Jowitt, a young, modern-dance student of Harriet Ann Gray's, and later dance critic for the *Village Voice,* was in the audience that night. Recalling in 1992 the concert in 1955, she said:

"I remember one image: I see this crowd of men in gray, but it could have been eight men. Jonathan as Pierrot was dressed just like them. And there was absolutely this sense that here was a choreographer.

"Joffrey's dancers didn't have that distant look that sometimes ballet dancers have. They seemed very fresh and very not-grand-or-glamorous, but just like young people who happened to have these slender, elegant limbs. Some of the dancers were extremely elegant.

"I thought, he's got wonderful dancers. He must be a very good teacher. . . . I went to Joffrey and started taking classes sometime after."[20]

Pierrot Lunaire was performed only that once. Accompanied by a speaker-singer performing all twenty-one songs in the Arnold Schoenberg cycle, the work was deemed musically too complex ever to be performed again—and furthermore, Watts had gone. As for the de Falla *Harpsichord Concerto in B Minor* on the same program, it suffered the same fate. But it was dropped by Joffrey probably because it was not very good. "[*Harpsichord Concerto*] seemed to me a mistake from first to last," wrote Manchester, "there was nothing in the choreography, nor in the way it was danced, that convinced me Joffrey really knew anything of the [Spanish] technique."[21]

Then, in late April of 1955, Joffrey received an amazing invitation from Marie Rambert to come to England and stage *Persephone* and *Pas des Déesses* for Ballet Rambert. Not only would he have his first major experience as a choreographer working with professional dancers, but he had also been invited by Rambert and her husband, Ashley Dukes, to spend the two-month duration as a guest in their house. Joffrey was delighted to have the opportunity to live with the woman who had assisted Nijinsky during the creation of his *Sacre du printemps,* the 1913 collaboration with Igor Stravinsky and Nicholas Roerich. He immediately accepted the invitation. P. W. Manchester had orchestrated the plan, having recommended Joffrey to Rambert without his knowing it. "Mim [Rambert] wanted to do something new and have a young American choreographer," she said. "I suggested Bob Joffrey. She'd never seen his work, but she took my advice—I said, nobody will get anywhere if people label him the next Balanchine; I think Bob had it more in him to be an American Ashton. Mim believed in me and knew I wouldn't give her a bum steer, so to speak."[22]

News of Joffrey's work had apparently preceded him across the Atlantic through a variety of sources. Lillian Moore had spoken highly of Joffrey to her influential friends, and David Vaughan, a young British dancer and choreographer, had been in New York for the "Evening of Original Ballets" and reported unfavorably that Joffrey was a "clever, eclectic and fashionable" choreographer who like so many others "needs to find a style." But Vaughan had also defined him as "the most well known" of the rising generation of younger American choreographers,[23] and his compatriots' curiosity was piqued. Said Clive Barnes, who at the time was assistant editor of *Dance and Dancers* in London, "I'd been told he was the most incredible thing to emerge in American ballet since Balanchine. . . . We expected him to be like Jerome Robbins [choreographer of the ballet *Fancy Free* and the musical *High Button Shoes*.]"[24]

Joffrey applied for his visa and purchased a steamship ticket, but in a sudden turn of events the American government would not let him go. It seemed he still owed money to a bank, and until he paid it off, he was stuck in New York. Hearing of his difficulties, Alice M. Bingham, assistant to Ben Sommers, president of Capezio, Inc., stepped in and promised to take full responsibility for his finances while he was gone. She was his first steadfast sponsor and he never forgot her generosity. Every Christmas Eve thereafter, she had the honor at his lavish parties of blowing a hunting horn to mark the transition from his birthday into Christmas.

Joffrey scheduled his departure for May 4. He was only the second American, after Bentley Stone, to have been invited by Rambert, and she, the midwife of British ballet, was a legend. In the not-so-distant past Rambert had guided the first steps of Frederick Ashton and encouraged Antony Tudor, who had choreographed his masterpieces *Lilac Garden* and *Dark Elegies* for her company. Her daunting celebrity and flair for fostering momentous choreographic talent no doubt weighed on his mind. He set sail on the *Queen Elizabeth* out of New York for his first trip to Europe, feeling "unprepared for the whole adventure."[25]

CHAPTER 8

Adversity

An emissary of Marie Rambert's escorted Joffrey to the studios. Time did not permit him to wash or change his clothes. Suitcases in tow, he was introduced to Rambert, who was about to teach a company class; she clasped his hand and said, "I hear you teach. Go ahead then, teach the class."

Joffrey was beginning to see that Rambert's reputation for a slightly sadistic manner was perhaps well deserved. But her eyes truly sparkled. He knew that he was her guest, but he was also her pupil. He stammered, "What?"

"I want you to teach. This is how you will get to know the dancers."

"Now?"

"Right now."[1]

After having traveled for a week without pause, Joffrey taught as best he could, and he made a fine first impression. "He was a little, bright, sprightly, thin youngster, and he kind of bounced along," observed Beryl Goldwyn, one of the most eloquent Giselles of her generation.[2]

Rambert's company was small, and it toured for fourteen or fifteen weeks a year throughout Britain. In 1955, at the age of sixty-seven, Rambert still presided over her dancers. She herself had never really been a dancer. She was a student of and a teaching assistant to Emile Jaques-Dalcroze in Geneva; Serge Diaghilev selected her to teach eurhythmics to his Russian dancers. There she befriended the lonely Nijinsky and performed in the corps of Diaghilev's Ballets Russes. She had studied classical technique under Enrico Cecchetti. While she was not known as a dancer, and opinions varied greatly about her ability as a teacher, her instinct for spotting top-rank potential and for knowing how to bring it into fruition was unerring. "If Marie Rambert had not existed, British ballet would have had to invent her"—a remark so broadly accepted that no one knows who first said it.

When Joffrey encountered her, she was in agile form and professed to him, as was her custom, that a good cartwheel still cleared her brain. He was also well aware that her warmth and ebullient wit were no less integral to her nature than the terrifying tantrums she threw. At work, her demand for professionalism was unremitting; she was strict and outspoken. "I don't go to choreographers," she had once said, "I wait for them to come to me, and then I discourage them for quite a while."[3]

Despite the apparent ruthlessness of some of Rambert's methods—locking artists into the studio until their work was done, for example—she often produced brilliant results. Her intellectual power and obstinate eye brought forth talents in others that would otherwise have remained dormant. Her most notable alumnus was Frederick Ashton, the only choreographer whom Rambert said she did not have to steamroll into fruition. In 1926, she had recognized that the movements coming from him, although he was only a beginning pupil, were instinctively superior to the choreography he was supposed to be following. She recommended he take over the project at hand and he ultimately created *The Scarlet Scissors: A Tragedy of Fashion* for the Rambert dancers. The ballet is recognized as the first genuine English ballet, and although critical response to it was only halfhearted, Rambert knew from that moment she could form a permanent classical troupe around Ashton's promise.

Joffrey never wrote an autobiography, but his life can be read in his company's repertoire—the time he spent living with Rambert and working with her company gave his "book" much of its final shape and tone. It was Rambert who completed the picture of Nijinsky for him; it was Rambert finally who, by her opposition to his choreographic impulses, incited him to launch his own professional troupe, one that would ultimately house the largest collection of Ashton's ballets outside the Royal Ballet.

More than any other contemporary director who did not descend directly from Diaghilev, Joffrey would accept responsibility for being a protector of twentieth-century repertoire. He fixed on preservation as fundamental to the artistic director's role, not when he was in England in 1955, but later, beginning in 1969, when he used the Joffrey Ballet to save many post-1910 masterpieces from oblivion. Interestingly, many of the reasons for his messianic ballet reconstructions related to episodes drawn from his youth. Joffrey's rescues were not the cool efforts of an impartial archaeologist. With the Ashton stagings that started with *Façade* in 1969, for example, Joffrey bore a fondness for the choreographer and his work, in part because he himself had spent time with Rambert, and he incorporated Ashton into the Joffrey Ballet's repertoire partly because he recognized that there was a link between him and Ashton through Rambert—just as he later revived Léonide Massine's choreography partly out of honor to his childhood days in Seattle, where he had met Massine during *Petrouchka,* the first ballet in which he had performed.

Joffrey's days with Rambert marked a turning point, and he spent as many as he could with her in her comfortable Camden Hill house. There Rambert would spout stories about Nijinsky, recounting how she had assisted him in the creation of *Le Sacre du printemps*. She seemed infatuated with Nijinsky. "Her eyes would light and she'd become a different person," said Joffrey, describing Rambert's response whenever the conversation drifted to *Sacre*.[4] On such occasions, Rambert would often take out her original *Sacre* score, on which she had scribbled explicit notes, mostly in Polish, about the steps, gestures, and motivations in Nijinsky's choreography. She made Joffrey crave to see the ballet.

In contrast to her jovial social conduct at home, Rambert in the studio was on the attack, voicing dissatisfaction with certain concepts in Joffrey's *Persephone*. He had come prepared with a recording of the Robert Silverman score and a film of the ballet to give Rambert a sneak preview before Roberta Bernard, his efficient red-haired assistant and dancer, arrived from New York and rehearsals began in earnest. This advance viewing, however, also opened the window for Rambert to advocate changes. With "her terrifyingly naked intelligence unshielded by the hypocritical decencies of politeness," she told him exactly what she thought.[5]

"What's all that squeaking noise in the background?" she asked, objecting to Silverman's spare, dissonant score. "*Persephone* is a great classical story line. You must use some great composer. Vivaldi! Naturally, use Vivaldi." She gave him *The Seasons* (after all, the story of Persephone was the Greek explanation of the seasons) and commanded, "Pick!" This came from someone who had been among the first to work with Stravinsky's *Sacre du printemps*. Joffrey was shocked by her narrow-minded reaction to what he thought was a magnificent piece of original music by Silverman. Reluctantly, he chose two movements of the Vivaldi; he felt compromised.

Then Rambert sent Joffrey to London's Slade School of Art to track down a student who would create the ballet's scenic elements. He returned with a structural model made out of wire. "It looks just like Noguchi!" thought Joffrey, pleased.*

But when he showed the mock-up to Rambert, she bluntly asked, "What's all that coat hanger?"

"These are trees in the Underworld," he replied. "We're going to move them and make them go like turnstiles in the subway; move them and walk around and underneath them."

"It's hideous. Put that set away. You can't have that set." And Rambert

---

*Isamu Noguchi had provided the costumes and décor for Balanchine's *Orpheus*, which is the ballet that many people had thought of when they saw *Persephone* in New York.

promptly hired Harri Wich, an Australian designer, who, said Joffrey, "did wonderful big asparagus for the Underworld, much to my dismay."[6]

Worse, in rehearsal Joffrey encountered resistance from the dancers, who had never worked with modern dance technique. "I'm not sure what they thought I was doing," he said. "But the Graham technique was a challenge to them and a challenge to me to interest them in it."[7] Rambert's members had possibly seen Martha Graham's company the year before, when eleven of her works had been presented in London, but they had never held their arms at obscure angles, had never contracted their torsos, had never squirmed on the floor—actions that were essential to *Persephone*. In the end, he had to settle for an approximation. There was not time to refine *Persephone* because the company was also learning Kenneth MacMillan's new piece, *Laiderette*, as well as Joffrey's *Pas des Déesses*.

Joffrey returned to America before his ballets had their London premieres on June 28, 1955, at the distinguished Sadler's Wells Theatre. He had commitments back home in Seattle to choreograph the summer musicals for the Aqua Theater. Perhaps to nobody's surprise, *Persephone* was resoundingly trounced by the critics. Wrote Cyril Beaumont: "Mr. Joffrey's musical sense sometimes falters, certain movements being unrelated. His choreography shows the influence of other minds and he needs to achieve a greater unity and harmony."[8] Said Mary Clarke: "Great hopes were placed on Robert Joffrey. . . . On the evidence of these two ballets he would seem to have a genuine and original talent for creating movement but almost no sense of theatre."[9] Suggestions were made about how his future could be spent: "If Mr. Joffrey would spend a few hard years working with a ballet company and learning to please a tough and possibly hostile audience, he might do much."[10]

Pas des Déesses, on the other hand, was an unqualified success with the audiences, whose standing ovations caused every writer to remark upon them. In their reviews, the critics seemed to breathe a sigh of relief. "Nearly a total success," wrote A. V. Coton.[11] "Simple, charming, evocative," said Richard Buckle.

Rambert decided to keep this "most successful novelty"[12] of her season in the repertoire for another five years. She even took *Pas des Déesses* on the company's 1957 tour to China, making it the first ballet by an American to be seen behind the Iron Curtain.

The adversity Joffrey had experienced at the hands of Rambert redoubled his commitment to launching his own company; he said:

> *I wanted one thing [with Rambert's production of* Persephone*] and I received something else. And I think that one has to learn to be dogmatic in their own choices, even if they're wrong. One has to be secure enough to take the challenges. . . .*

I don't think I felt the thumb of Rambert. I think I felt the thumb of inexperience on me. I had to realize that a choreographer has to instill in a dancer the desire to work on a ballet with you. It's different having dedicated followers as opposed to professional dancers. . . . And somehow [in England] I didn't have enough experience to explain to the dancers or to force them or to beat them or to manipulate them into achieving those distortions that I wanted.

. . . After seeing the Ballet Rambert, what I really wanted was my own company, to do what I wanted, to work the way I wanted to work and do the ballets I wanted to do. I wanted something different.[13]

. . . I wasn't so lofty as to think I was going to change ballet. But somehow I was driven, and I felt there was a need for something different from what I was seeing.[14]

For someone of a generally temperate disposition, Joffrey affirmed these sentiments with startling passion during a public interview conducted by Clive Barnes in 1985 as part of a series on American dance presented at the New York Public Library for the Performing Arts. Joffrey and Barnes were by then old acquaintances, having first met when Joffrey was with Rambert. They were about the same age; Barnes was at the time of their introduction an editor of *Dance and Dancers* in London (he would later become the cheif dance critic for the *New York Times,* and later still the *New York Post*). "Rambert wanted me to meet Joffrey," Barnes said. "She had no doubt that he was a real talent, and she wanted me to see for myself."[15]

Until the 1985 interview with Barnes, Joffrey had never heard that Rambert thought he had talent. In fact, he was certain she felt the opposite. He reported that when he returned from Ballet Rambert, Manchester had felt that by recommending him to Rambert she had "done them both a disservice."[16]

Seattle was Joffrey's first destination upon returning to the States. He arrived there too late to fulfill his obligation to stage Irving Berlin's *Annie Get Your Gun,* and so Arpino had taken over. This production is of some historical value, as it was Arpino's first choreographic attempt. "Gerald Arpino's choreography and the dancers added a great deal of color," wrote John Voorhees of the *Seattle Post-Intelligencer,* praising two of the numbers and adding, " 'The Sun in the Morning' choreography, however, looked more Las Vegas nightclub than anything."[17] The implications of Voorhees's concluding remark—what about Arpino's taste? is he selling it?—would recur in reviews by many other critics in future decades.

Joffrey choreographed the next Aqua Theater production, *High Button Shoes,* before heading back to New York with Arpino and several young Seattle dancers. The entourage of professional hopefuls included

Diane Lembo, his favorite female companion, who would weave in and out of his life as someone ultimately more important to the man than to dance. A former Cornish School student and the daughter of an Italian tailor, Lembo danced for Joffrey in the next project he was offered: an original "fairy tale" opera, *Griffelkin*, by Lukas Foss, with a libretto by Alastair Reid. It had been commissioned by NBC-TV Opera Theater.

Intended for young audiences, *Griffelkin*, directed by Kirk Browning, detailed the journey of a ten-year-old devil who receives the birthday gift of a trip from hell to the human world. He wreaks havoc, behaves abominably, and uses his magic elixir to bring stone statues to life and make stuffed toys dance. In the end, he cannot refrain from becoming entangled in human love and commits a good act, which banishes him from hell forever and transforms him into an ordinary mortal boy.

In *Griffelkin*, none of the singers appeared in physical form on the small television screen; the dancers were the only visible performers. *Griffelkin* allowed Joffrey to experiment further with the integration of song and dance—which had become his consuming interest, perhaps partly because choreographing to words allowed him to lean on explicit imagery and was, therefore, easier—and to test himself within a new medium that promised the broadest public he had yet known. The *New York Times* heralded the *Griffelkin* premiere on November 6, 1955, as "another substantial contribution to television" and called Joffrey's staging "admirable."[18]

But for Joffrey, *Griffelkin*'s true importance was that it changed the direction of his nascent company. After *Griffelkin*, in one of his first interviews about the formation of his troupe, he said, "I want to do the choreography for a Broadway show, and I really feel the singers should have training as dancers and vice versa. It's the direction musical comedy must take. My group [referring to his ballet company] will be a start in that direction."[19]

Apparently, the Green Lake Aqua Theater productions and *Griffelkin* had influenced Joffrey to conceive a ballet troupe, the Robert Joffrey Theatre Dancers, that would incorporate song.

Before he had gone to work with Rambert, Joffrey had begun to negotiate a deal with a representative from Concert Associates* who had been in the audience at the 92nd Street Y for Joffrey's *Pierrot Lunaire* and *Harpsichord Concerto in B Minor* on March 24, 1955. He had approached Joffrey immediately after with an offer to send five of his dancers on the road.[20] Joffrey had talked him into six dancers, then left

---

*Concert Associates was a division of Columbia Artists Management, Inc., that booked one-night stands to presold audiences on a Community Concerts Series.

the country for Ballet Rambert with negotiations remaining at the hand-shake stage. Then, in the spring of 1956, William Judd, a manager from Columbia Artists Management, Inc. (CAMI), Concert Associates' parent company, introduced himself to Joffrey, announcing that he was hunting for a chamber ballet troupe that could tour the southern states. Although the actual scenario is impossible to verify because memories are dim and so many behind-the-scenes people are dead, Joffrey's former colleague Marvin Schofer, who also worked for CAMI for seven years in the late 1980s, thinks that the inception of the Robert Joffrey Theatre Dancers probably went something like this:

"Columbia Artists has a hand in creating things to fill a market. So that if Columbia needs a string quartet, they go looking for a string quartet. What would very likely happen is that a manager at Columbia with an interest in dance might have gone to Bob [Joffrey] and said, 'We need a small company that is highly portable, that can do one-night stands, and can do some classical repertoire, but also has a very popular sparkle and flair to it. We can book a two-to-three-month tour and we can sell that. We have a market for that. That's called Community Concerts. Could you put together a company for that?'

"And Bob Joffrey says, 'Yes, of course, I can do that.' Now, if the man-ager—Bill Judd—said, 'Would you do the pas de deux from *Swan Lake*?' Bob would probably say, 'No, because it won't be good enough. But what I will give you is *Pas des Déesses*, which will have all the same stuff in it and everybody will go crazy. Trust me.'

"Judd, being very savvy, will say, 'Fine. We want this to be very pop-hit ballet, pop-hit oriented, which means we need pretty girls and good-looking boys and we need tutus. . . . You've danced on Broadway. Your star dancer, Jerry Arpino, has danced in revues—I mean that's really hoofing in the traditional way. And you've done television. You can pro-duce for a commercial audience.'

"Bob," concluded Schofer, "was perfectly poised at that point to cre-ate just the kind of company—it was a little designer company that could fit in a station wagon and tour on the Community Concerts Series."[21]

Hard evidence underscores the plausibility of Schofer's fabricated script. "I was told by Columbia Concerts, 'We need this kind of ballet, you've got to do this.' I wouldn't do *Sylphides* or *Swan Lake*," said Jof-frey. "I said that I would create something for the situation or find some-thing."[22] Joffrey oriented his company that spring in 1956 around a five-week Columbia Artists tour and around Arpino, his "dramatic dancer," for whom he made *Within Four Walls*. He cast the rest of his ensemble explicitly for *Pas des Déesses*, scouting for dancers who pos-sessed versatile stylistic sensibilities and minds open enough to to realize his vision; he said of his ideal dancer:

"If you're doing *Swan Lake,* you have to have girls all the same height. I don't want to have that. I want to have variety. Different heights affect the way you move, the quality of movement—a bigger person always moves differently, even though rhythmically they may be the same [as a smaller person], their thrust, their accent, is different because there's more to dance with—or less to dance with.

"And I think that because we [as Americans] don't have a tradition, we can break tradition. We are free to do whatever we feel or want . . . we were willing to accept anything, and I think that is one of our great freedoms—choice."[23]

He hired Glen Tetley for the role of Saint-Léon in *Pas des Déesses,* Beatrice Tompkins for Taglioni (and to be ballet mistress), Brunilda Ruiz as Cerrito, and Dianne Consoer as Grahn. The sixth dancer was his old friend and music adviser John Wilson, who would also play the piano. With the exception of Tetley, they had danced with Joffrey before.

Glen Tetley embodied Joffrey's will to exercise his right as an American to change ballet's traditional definitions. For example, Joffrey turned to Bill Judd during the company's audition to pick repertoire for the tour and introduced Tetley as "my danseur noble, my classical dancer." But Tetley's background was equal parts ballet and modern dance, which would make him by definition not a danseur noble. He had served in the U.S. Navy during World War II and had for a time studied at Columbia University's College of Physicians and Surgeons. When he met Joffrey, he was an experienced professional who had performed in Hanya Holm's choreography for *Kiss Me Kate* and *Out of This World;* in Gian Carlo Menotti's televised opera, *Amahl and the Night Visitors;* and in Pauline Koner's modern dance company. At twenty-nine, Tetley wasn't at all sure whether he wanted to help establish the Robert Joffrey Theatre Dancers. He was not convinced that it would be a "mature enough" experience.[24] Shedding light on the troupe's inception, Tetley explained his reservations:

> I remember Bob talking to each of us individually to discuss the concept of the company. Bea [Tompkins] came out of his office completely shattered. I could see that she was in tears, and I said, "What's the matter?" She said, "Bob asked me how old I was and I told him. And he said to me—he was shocked—he said, 'Don't you ever tell anyone how old you are. Never.' "
>
> Bob wanted to present the company as almost a teenage company. We were instructed to act almost like teenagers. I was in my twenties, but even when I was a teenager, I wasn't a teenager. I was out in the world earning my own living when I was thirteen. I resented the teenage concept of the company. That did bother me. I sort of tried to rationalize it to myself.
>
> But Bea and I had become instant friends. She had a sophistication and

was a very complex person, even a little, at times, neurotic. We had a joint sense of humor about things, and it was Bea who wanted me to be there and that's one of the reasons I decided to join.[25]

Interestingly, Tetley found that Joffrey was "tremendously insecure" throughout rehearsals. The apparent lack of self-confidence struck Tetley as inconsistent with Joffrey as a teacher. When Joffrey choreographed, said Tetley, "You could feel a resistance, and unless you stood there and were a tool and did what he had given you, it upset him."[26]

Jonathan Watts—still a close friend of Joffrey's at the time, although not involved with these particular rehearsals—said he had noticed that when Joffrey returned from Ballet Rambert, "something had gone out of him."[27] The rush of ideas, the facility in designing steps and movement phrases, had vanished. Watts believed that the fiasco with *Persephone* at Ballet Rambert and Rambert's perceived disappointment had damaged Joffrey's self-esteem, derailed his imagination, and by introducing the dreaded self-doubt had actually caused him to cease thinking of himself as a choreographer and to begin positioning himself exclusively as an artistic director.

Joffrey, as with most other American ballet directors, had not come out of an institution. Mary Ann Wells was not the Maryinsky; she was a classroom in Seattle and a recital in the spring. When insecure, Joffrey fell back on his own taste, his instincts, groping his way toward the unknown, marching forward by faith, not by imitation, and yet he was aware that "blindness" was perhaps his greatest advantage. He did not know what he was making, but, by 1956, the creation of his company was more important to him than his choreography. He figured it was only a matter of time before the troupe danced other people's work—but he had to have a troupe.

"We were told, 'Give it up. You'll never make it. You are pursuing an impossible dream,' " said Arpino. "The advantage Bob had was that he was a phenomenal dancer and teacher and diplomat."[28] Joffrey no longer identified himself as a choreographer first.

With the summer of 1956 fast upon him, Joffrey returned with Arpino and Watts to Seattle to stage *Call Me Madam* and *The King and I* for the Aqua Theater and to teach at the Cornish School.* He had also been commissioned by Alexandra Danilova to create a ballet for her to present

---

*Joffrey might have been noticeably insecure about choreographing, but the time prior to the troupe's first tour was his most prolific ever. On May 7, 1956, he contributed a new piece, *Workout,* with music by Robert McBride, to the Ballet Theatre Workshop's presentation of "Four Premieres" at the Phoenix Theatre. Arpino danced a leading role, and many of the ingenues they had brought with them from Seattle were also used. "A youth-on a South American tour, but the work was never made, because by the first of October he needed a complete company ready to tour the South, and he hadn't the time for extra assignments.

Back in New York, Joffrey's colleagues continued their preparations. Gloria Gustafson had been persuaded to donate her red-and-white Chevrolet station wagon for the six dancers' transportation on their twenty-three one-night stands. Nina Gustafson, Gloria's mother, had agreed to give Joffrey $5,000 to help pay for the women's toe shoes (two pairs each week), the dancers' costumes (purchased in part from Bloomingdale's and partly borrowed out of Gustafson's attic in Indiana), and one of the dancers' salaries ($100 weekly after transportation expenses; Columbia Artists agreed to cover only five dancers).

Joffrey flew back from Seattle at the end of August and resumed working on the three new ballets: *Kaleidoscope, Within Four Walls,* and *Le Bal.* Both *Kaleidoscope* and *Within Four Walls* incorporated the dancers' voices. Dianne Consoer captured some of the excitement in letters she wrote to her parents:

Our four ballets are shaping up pretty well now, although Joffrey is still choreographing the Gershwin number [Kaleidoscope]. *. . . I have two singing lines but I just yell the words since I can't carry a tune. This work is more musical comedy style. . . . He told me I must not get discouraged. He mentioned that I have a certain sincerity and love of dancing which comes through but is not recognized as easily as some of the flashier dancers around here. He said if I love it enough I should do all I can to succeed. . . .*

Joffrey's first love is the concert and his own group. He played hooky from the theatre today so he could work with us. He told them he had hay fever. He really suffers terribly with it. . . . Poor Joffrey has so many expenses. I think he will lose money this first year of the tour.

The agent, Miss Lauren [from CAMI], is coming to see the numbers this Sunday. She is a bit put out that she hasn't seen us before this time. . . . This company really is a wonderful chance to dance a lot and it's so much better than being in the corps of a big company.[29]

---

ful display-dance, by turns puckish and tender," said *Dance Magazine* of *Workout.* The ballet was performed only once again, which was later that summer in Seattle's Seward Park amphitheater.

On the same Ballet Theatre program, Joffrey also offered *Pas des Déesses,* entrusting it to one of the most illustrious casts possible in America at the time: Lupe Serrano, Ruth Ann Koesun, Sonia Arova, and Erik Bruhn. Tetley had taught them the ballet and introduced an edge of satire that most critics found positively choice. Within the next month, Lucia Chase of Ballet Theatre officially acquired *Pas des Déesses* for her company's repertoire and scheduled it for performance during the upcoming fall and winter tours through the United States and Europe.

The dancers held garage sales to raise more funds; and they drew an eclectic group of supporters. One such person, who found the feisty company irresistible, was Alex Ewing. The younger son of Lucia Chase, co–artistic director of Ballet Theatre, Ewing had attended the best New York City schools and had graduated from Yale University. Living with his wife on East Fifty-fifth Street, he was a former newspaper reporter turned novelist.

One fall day, Ewing mentioned to dancer Erik Bruhn, who was his mother's premier danseur noble at Ballet Theatre, that he missed the company of other people now that he was writing at home. Bruhn, who had become a regular both in Joffrey's Ballet Theatre classes and in Joffrey and Arpino's home for informal dinner parties at night, suggested that Ewing offer Joffrey his services as a business manager. Ewing had heard of Joffrey because so many of the Ballet Theatre teachers had complained to his mother that Joffrey was "stealing" their pupils. He was curious to see the "thief" in the Village. Here is his impression filtered from more than two decades of eventual association with the troupe:

> Joffrey had taken the Ballet Russe and turned it upside down. Ballet Russe had older dancers with a lot of experience, but these kids were really young and very inexperienced and they danced very well. It was a grassroots company and it had that early New York Mets attitude. Like the Mets, the company is based on belief—that you've just got to believe in it. You've got to have this faith and this energy like tough, street-guy kids. They're young and they don't have a lot, but they believe in what they are doing.
>
> I felt that Joffrey brought [ballet] down off an imperial pedestal, down into the stadium. The whole thing was practically out of Greenwich Village. It was not out of St. Petersburg. It was not even out of the upper reaches of New York. It was kid stuff. Very good. It really was. And that's why it was the Mets. It wasn't Mickey Mantle. It was a collection of people that had been put together and suddenly they jelled and they did beautiful things, but nobody that wasn't a ballet fanatic could name you five dancers in the company. The company had its own identity.
>
> They did not go beyond the New York City Ballet and Ballet Theatre and Ballet Russe, because those companies were there before—like the New York Yankees or the Boston Red Sox. . . . But Joffrey was a different atmosphere. It was an atmosphere without stars and without known ballets. And that was quite new.[30]

Ewing said his mother was "horrified" when he decamped to the Joffrey studio because he still held his position as executive secretary of the Ballet Theatre Foundation, and he did much of the administrative and publicity work for the Ballet Theatre Workshops at the Phoenix Theatre. His mother feared that he would become interested in the artistic end of

Ballet Theatre, and worse, that he would become interested in any competition. To many outside observers, Ewing's presence at the Joffrey Ballet signaled that the company was a renegade and that, therefore, something exciting might be happening for ballet.

PART TWO

CORNERSTONE

CHAPTER 9

Six Dancers
and a Station Wagon

On October 1, 1956, six dancers assembled on the sidewalk outside American Ballet Center. After loading a U-Haul trailer with theater lights, a tape player, some props, and their personal luggage, they hung their costumes on a rack in the back of the station wagon and said good-bye to Joffrey, Nina Gustafson, and Thelma, the waitress from Peake's Food Shop, who was their neighborhood champion and who had, against Joffrey's repeated wishes, regularly sneaked them extra helpings of meat and slices of pie. Their destination: Frostburg, Maryland, a strip-mining coal town in the westernmost part of the state, nestled amidst the pageantry of the Allegheny Mountains and lightly blanketed by the brick buildings of State Teachers College, a humble cradle for a ballet company world debut.

Joffrey stayed behind to teach at Ballet Theatre and to keep his school running. Along with the rest of the dance faculty, he had recently resigned from the High School of Performing Arts when it was apparent the administration was not going to provide increased salaries and improved benefits. The loss of income, paltry though it was, hit him when he could least afford it. His fee from Columbia Artists—$600 to $2,000 per performance, depending on where the troupe danced, with Columbia getting a 20 percent commission—did not cover the company's costs. Income from Joffrey's American Ballet Center together with Nina Gustafson's contribution made up the difference. The school was an expanding enterprise, but only because Joffrey was teaching there.

His company, on the other hand, was less of a sure thing. The contract with Columbia Artists covered only two tours, one during the October–November period in the South, and the other in the Midwest and Canada from January to May 1957. After that, who knew what would happen? Much as he yearned to accompany the six dancers on their maiden voyage, he could not justify his absence for two other reasons: he had been hired to choreograph Stella Adler's staging of Kurt Weill's *Johnny Johnson* at Carnegie Hall Playhouse (for a premiere on October 21), and on a purely practical note, there wasn't any room for him in the station wagon.

The red-and-white Chevrolet contained three rows of seats and was driven by the stage manager, Raymond Duffy. Almost at once the mop-haired, extroverted Duffy proved to be an inappropriate person to take the helm. He drove on the wrong side of the road, ignored stop signs, and allowed the U-Haul to swing from side to side, sweeping the high-ways clear of nearby motorists. Tires burst. Nerves frayed. Arpino recalled that he woke up en route to find Duffy cruising down the middle of a golf course. Within two weeks the dancers were on the phone to Jof-frey saying, "It's either him or us."[1] But Duffy, an experienced theater professional who had recently assisted Sarah Caldwell on her Boston Opera productions, had his practical uses and would have to be tolerated until December, said Joffrey.

When the troupe descended on Frostburg, Duffy located the theater, set the lights,* cued the tape recorder, made certain the piano for *Pas des Déesses* was tuned and that the floor was stageworthy. If it was not, he prevailed upon the dancers to help him coat the surface with rosin or Coca-Cola, which gummed the floor and prevented the women from slipping during performance. Or sometimes, to the horror of an onlook-ing auditorium janitor, Duffy would remove the treacherous veneer of shellac by scrubbing the boards with lye and water.

Beatrice Tompkins was in charge of the artistic presentation. Capable, efficient, droll, and wise, she wore natty wool knit skirt-suits and short black gloves to receptions and smoked cigarettes with an aristocratic air. She was Joffrey's eyes and mind on the tour. As the ballet mistress, she daily gave the dancers a strict classical barre that fine-tuned and warmed them up to perform. Their average distance between concerts would be 250 miles; that meant six to seven hours trapped in a sedentary position. They were always stiff when they disembarked.

Time permitting, the company rehearsed all four ballets before the performance—and they rehearsed them "full-out," meaning as though for an audience. Each theater's stage was different, some no bigger than the average living room, completely unequipped for ballet, with no wing

---

*The lightning designs had been executed in New York by Thomas Skelton. Joffrey had strong feelings about lighting and was careful to choose someone in whom he placed absolute trust. "Dance is poetic. It is special, and it needs lights. They create the illusion, they say the body is illuminated," he said. "I never believed in heavy sets. I always felt that in dance, so much more is light, especially because in the beginning the size of our stages varied." (Joffrey to Lois Draegin, January 8, 1985.)

space and a ceiling so low that the women, when lifted, disappeared into the curtains above. The next night they might encounter a high school auditorium or gymnasium large enough to accommodate a marching band. Tompkins adapted the ballets accordingly—modified the lifts, eliminated a jump here and there—and gave the impression that the ballet had been made to order for that space.

The dancers were otherwise on their own, responsible for applying their makeup, ironing their costumes prior to each concert, and washing them out after most—a task that was sometimes accomplished by standing in the hotel showers with the tutus and tights still on, throwing laundry detergent over themselves, and then drying the pieces out the next day in the car's interior. The dancers also pulled the theater curtains; and John Wilson jumped into the orchestra pit after the second ballet to play the piano for *Pas des Déesses*. He had done the arrangement for the ballet, having selected various pieces of John Field's music and stitched them together for Joffrey.

Joffrey had said that he would rather have one live musician for one ballet than taped music for the entire program; he wanted the audiences to immerse themselves completely in the theatrical experience. "I felt that a performance should be magical. No matter how small it is, I felt that when you went to it, you should see something special," he said. "It's not homemade. It's theater. You must have that. You're asking people to pay money, you want to give them fantasy, magic. You want to take them from their daily lives."[2]

The dancers were in complete accord. "The six of us were determined to keep up a very high level," said Glen Tetley. "No matter where we danced, we tried our best, as if the most educated and scrupulous eyes were upon us."[3]

Although they were supposed to behave "almost" as teenagers, the average age of the company members was, in fact, twenty-eight and a half years old. Three had served in World War II; one, Beatrice Tompkins, was a widow; and three were college graduates: Tetley from Franklin and Marshall College in Pennsylvania; John Wilson from Pomona College in southern California; Dianne Consoer from Mount Holyoke College in Massachusetts.

Consoer was blond and cool, her dancing described by a reviewer as "ribbons and moonlight," words that were thrown back at her by the others as a tease. Consoer's distant appeal was compared to Greta Garbo's, making her the first in a succession of Joffrey's dancers to resemble his movie idol. Consoer possessed a similar tactile sensuality, her delicacy reading as strength, her gestures calibrating the infinite sentiments of her heart.

Youngest was Brunilda Ruiz, age twenty. From Puerto Rico, she had moved to New York and discovered Joffrey at Performing Arts. Ruiz was almost purely Joffrey trained. Passionate about dancing, refined and meticulous, she aimed for the squeaky-clean perfect pose, without sacrificing the rhythmic dynamism, the pulse behind the gesture. She "dances right in the heart of the music," wrote one journalist.[4]

Ruiz and Wilson were in love and, by December, would be married. On the next tour in 1957, Ruiz would dance through her fifth month of pregnancy, and their newborn daughter would come with them on tours after that. It was often said that the Joffrey company was a family, and for good reason: Joffrey was not only the best man at Ruiz and Wilson's wedding, but he stood in for Ruiz's father and gave her away. He would reenact this parental role for Consoer and Jonathan Watts, who would also get married. Many of the company's members spent Thanksgiving, Christmas, and Easter together with Joffrey and Arpino. Dancing was for most of them their refuge; the stage, the company, the Greenwich Village loft, their sometime home.

Nine years older than Ruiz, John Wilson was tall and gangly and not at all a classical technician. Wilson brought to the troupe a seemingly infinite resource of games and mischief. His timing was superb both as a teller of jokes and stories offstage and as the company pianist onstage. As a dancer, he instinctively experimented with the standard ballet vocabulary until it spoke to him on his terms. He played with whatever material was thrown his way, and his inventiveness often translated into the other dancers' entertainment. He taught them to sing rounds, catches, and glees, and to improvise lyrics on their own. He would dress up and disguise himself, one time appearing in drag, whereupon, to the riotous delight of the other five, he convinced a gullible theater administrator that he was the Robert Joffrey Theatre Dancers' esteemed patroness.

Gerald Arpino was a dancer just like the rest and not given preferential treatment because of his longtime association with Joffrey. None of the dancers thought of him as cofounding the company with Joffrey, and at the time Joffrey and Arpino did not define his contribution as such, either. Arpino's fellow dancers saw that he worked hard and set goals for himself, frequently lingering on the stage long after the performance was over, trying to perfect a double *saut de basque* by the end of the season.

Dubbed by them, affectionately, Arpinsky the poor man's Nijinsky, Arpino was supposedly like Nijinsky because he could land from a jump without making a sound. He had an inaccurate sense of musical timing, though, which the others attempted to salvage by whispering the counts into his ear and then shoving him onto the stage when it was his time to enter. A fun-loving, spontaneous person, he was also prone to solemn moods; he withdrew and slept the instant he settled into the station wagon (perhaps exhausted from having to pretend he was a teenager when he was actually thirty-three),* but onstage, he was transformed.

The audiences went wild over Arpino's dancing, which was magnanimous, unabashed, dramatic, and energetic. It helped that he was handsome. The company was no-star, all-star—everyone a soloist and equal—yet there was something of the hero to Arpino, something special that set him apart.

Then there was Glen Tetley, who for ninety-two performances, practically in a row, would dance the Arthur Saint-Léon role of the poet in *Pas des Déesses*. The ballet was so arduous in its demands for partnering the three women that Erik Bruhn and Scott Douglas, who were dancing it for Ballet Theatre on tour the same year, had announced that they would not, could not, perform in any other ballet on the same program. Tetley, on the other hand, would perform three additional ballets every night. His stamina was fantastic, and although he was not a classicist, he had presence and evident mental grasp—the elegance of an artist who knew himself well.

Real teenagers might have mishandled the challenges of night-after-night adjustments and lacked the discipline it took to perform at peak in four physically demanding ballets. The dancers were establishing the foundations that would support Joffrey's vision. Nearly every trademark Joffrey Ballet esthetic can be traced back to those early Columbia Artists tours: the emphasis on youth, the eclectic repertoire, the democratic, all-star, no-star system, the fearless playing to the popular, rather than intellectually elite, crowd. Joffrey's ultimate plan could not be realized unless the first dancers were selflessly obedient.

He did not have to worry about filling the house or attracting an audience from town to rural town because his concerts were already pre-sold through the Community Concerts Series. He created ballets to suit the needs of Columbia Artists officials. He did not chafe, but rather yielded to the demands of the marketplace. And he still presented a quality product. Joffrey Ballet's survival from its inception depended on a tactical

---

*Arpino never told anyone about his adventures in the Coast Guard or the four medals he had earned. Such tales would have raised doubts about how old he said he was (twenty-eight). That chapter of his life was shut. He also dyed his hair black. His father had gone prematurely gray at age eighteen and Arpino had inherited the genetic disposition. Within the next two decades he would begin wearing a toupee. "There are only three things I won't talk about," Arpino once said, "sex, money, and my personal toiletries." His family had maintained the Arpino beauty salons on Staten Island after their father died in 1930, and the family prided itself on its mastery of hair color, manicures, and general beauty tips—all aimed at hiding one's age. When an Arpino was asked his or her age directly, the response was likely to be, "How much do you weigh?" The family was "too Christian" to lie and artful enough to figure out how to make the questioner commit that crime first, if it was to be committed.

understanding of what the audience wanted. In this regard he was not that different from such ballet directors as Kirstein and Balanchine at the New York City Ballet, Chase and Oliver Smith at Ballet Theatre, and Ruth Page at Chicago Opera Ballet—all of whom relied on income from the box office—but they were also heavily reliant upon unearned income donated by themselves and other patrons with the same passionate feelings about ballet and vested interests in seeing the art form grow on home turf.

Joffrey's company was for profit , but because his partner for the venture was Columbia Artists, it was more of a business rather than less. The box office drove the troupe, and this has resulted in the company's being particularly susceptible to the trends of fashion, economy, and celebrity, which has in turn meant that the company has reflected the society and times in which it danced.

In 1956, with World War II and the Korean War over, materialism dominated Americans' sense of purpose; they bought cars and settled down in the suburbs and had children; they were mesmerized and scandalized by Elvis Presley and transfixed by television's paragons of familial bliss, Ozzie and Harriet Nelson. With more discretionary money, energy, and time on their hands than had ever before been experienced by a majority of America's population, Americans thought about how they wanted to be entertained. "Across the nation there arose a demand for cultural activity beyond what had existed before the new affluence"—beyond motion pictures, radio, and television—"and that pressure gave impetus to the decentralization and proliferation of the arts that began in the 1950s," wrote Bradley G. Morison and Julie Gordon Dalgleish, cultural historians. "More activity called 'art' was made accessible to more people in more places than ever before in a phenomenon widely labeled a 'cultural boom.' "[5]

The passionate surge of interest in the arts was not motivated by improved financial circumstances alone. Following World War II, Americans were temperamentally primed, eager and confident enough to stop seeing themselves through European eyes and to attempt to secure their own cultural identity.[6] In ballet, a French form with Italian influences and Russian accents, self-conscious Americanization had begun as early as 1936 on Broadway with Balanchine's creation of *Slaughter on Tenth Avenue,* a ballet set within Richard Rodgers's musical *On Your Toes.* And the same year, Kirstein had formed Ballet Caravan, which according to him was "in microcosm, a permanent laboratory for classic dancing by, with and for Americans."[7] Asking, What is American identity in dance? Ballet Caravan endured for only three and a half years, but the principles of its repertoire of American-theme ballets, conceived, choreographed, scored, and designed by Americans, laid essential groundwork for what became the New York City Ballet and, by proxy, for the philosophy that many American classicists thereafter embraced.

In theoretical pursuit of American style, Lincoln Kirstein wrote his famous "Blast at Ballet" in 1938. Although Joffrey's curiosity and fervor about the American character seemed more persuasively evangelical than intellectual, he clearly owed a debt to Kirstein. It was as though Kirstein had authored the Declaration of Independence for American ballet, and no company was untouched by it. Kirstein wrote:

> The American style will not imitate the Russian, but instead be its equivalent for our time and place.
>
> . . . American style springs or should spring from our training and environment, which was not an Imperial School or a Parisian imitation of it. Ours is a style bred from basketball courts, track and swimming meets and junior proms. Our style springs from the personal atmosphere of recognizable American types as exemplified by the behavior of movie stars like Ginger Rogers, Carole Lombard, or the late Jean Harlow. It is frank, open and friendly. It can be funny without seeming arch, and serious without seeming pained. . . . The Russians keep their audience at arm's length. We almost invite ours to dance with us.[8]

But Kirstein's Ballet Caravan had come too early: his American audiences and even the artists he involved were not prepared to support the magnitude of his project. They didn't get it. For Joffrey, however, Ballet Caravan as well as Ted Shawn's Men Dancers had cleared paths that twenty years later allowed his troupe to scamper along as a vaguely familiar commodity. Shawn and his Men Dancers had spent seven years, beginning in 1933, performing one-night-stands across the country with the express purpose of destroying public prejudice against dancing by men. Joffrey benefitted from Kirstein's and Shawn's agendas and acknowledged that his troupe did not spring out of its own genius. His company was from the modern dance tradition, performing ballet and, critically, it was sponsored by a commercial organization. The Robert Joffrey Theatre Dancers was designed, to a degree, for market success.

When Joffrey toured in 1956, he found that Americans craved American entertainment and culture, and that they wanted to apply their minds to understanding the discrete qualities of Americanness. They wanted to back the product with their pocketbooks, too, and to witness the construction of modern American civilization by participating in it.

Middle-class prosperity in the 1950s gave rise to increasing numbers of ballet schools and students. Many ballet aspirants' parents had been enchanted by Anna Pavlova, some by Ted Shawn and Ruth St. Denis, some by Ballet Caravan, and some by the Ballet Russe de Monte Carlo on tour (just as Joffrey had been as a young boy); some had seen the 1948 movie *The Red Shoes,* and others, ballet on television's *Ed Sullivan Show.*

When the company had its premiere in Frostburg at Compton Auditorium at ten o'clock in the morning on October 2, six hundred people were in the audience. The college held a reception afterward and several guests breathlessly told the dancers that they "loved us on tippy toe";[9] the dancers passed around pointe shoes for them to examine.

As would happen for the next few years, the audience frequently referred to ballet as "precision dancing" or as the "Russian ballet." Even though Joffrey clearly was not Russian, in much of the provincial public's imagination ballet still automatically implied fluffy white swan tutus, glittering tiaras, imperial majesty, and glamorous Russian names splashed across marquees. Ballet was alien, exotic, and elitist—Russian.

But this image, which had been changing since about 1936, was continuing to change, and Joffrey would play a significant role in America's evolving cultural education. He would do it, in part, by hitching himself mostly to the pioneering accomplishments of Ballet Russe de Monte Carlo before him. He never forgot that he was not introducing ballet to places and people who had never seen it. Chances were the Russians had been there first, and Joffrey just made sure that he not only followed but that he extended Ballet Russe de Monte Carlo's territory.

In the 1955–56 season, concurrently with Joffrey Ballet's inaugural tour, there was a minor dance explosion. The Ballet Russe de Monte Carlo appeared in ninety-five cities across the United States (most of the dancers in the company were by then American). The Royal Danish Ballet had also come to the States; as the only company in the world in which the men were more important than the women, the Royal Danish Ballet's fall tour would ripple throughout the world of American dance. Ballet Theatre and Chicago Opera Ballet stormed parts of the country. Perhaps most germane to Joffrey history, for the first time ever a regional ballet festival bloomed from American soil, proving that ballet could grow outside New York.

The Southeastern Regional Ballet Festival, organized and held in Atlanta, Georgia, by Dorothy Alexander, brought unprecedented recognition to eight local ballet groups—one of which, Atlanta Civic Ballet, directed by Alexander, had been in existence for twenty-seven years. After the April 1956 event in Atlanta, regional associations were soon developed in the Northeast, Southwest, Pacific, and mid-states, calling national attention to the growing number of nonprofessional troupes that frequently did excellent work.

Robert Joffrey Theatre Dancers was, in a sense, a regional ballet company from New York City that performed everywhere but in Manhattan.

Smaller than any of the established major troupes of forty dancers or more, it could penetrate remote communities, far from the well-traveled highways. In 1956, when the call was for big-city entertainment on a chamber scale, Joffrey answered with *Le Bal, Within Four Walls, Kaleido-scope,* and *Pas des Déesses.*

"We found that if we did not perform *Pas des Déesses*," said one dancer, "we did not hook our audience. That's what they thought ballet was—the girls in those pretty pastel tutus and toe shoes. We could do anything after *Pas des Déesses* and they loved it. But they had to see that ballet."[10]

The rest of Joffrey's repertory opened the door to an alternative vision. The program typically began with *Le Bal,* a zesty and plotless ballet of diver-tissements to music by Emmanuel Chabrier. Joffrey employed his standby pseudo-Spanish movement idiom for it and, calling the dancers Guests, painted a romantic, old-style ballroom atmosphere. The women wore tiaras and carried fans; black lace veiled their bosoms, and their calf-length skirts were multilayered crinoline fantasies trimmed with ribbon. The men wore ruffled white shirts, dark vests, and pants. But the ballet was not as straightforward as it might seem. Joffrey poked fun at a number of "party ballet" clichés: Tompkins, a natural wit and a dancer-actor, was at one point carried onstage by the three cavaliers, who pretended to propel her forward as if she were in a gondola. Allusions were made to Balanchine's *La Valse* and *Bourrée Fantasque* and to the famous Rose Adagio of *The Sleeping Beauty*—references that suggested Joffrey was winking at anyone in the audience who might know as much as he about ballet.

Anyone who did caught on immediately to *Within Four Walls,* Jof-frey's dramatic work for Arpino with an original score by John Wilson incorporating little-known melodies by Stephen Foster. In the central role of a Young Man imprisoned by his conscience and destined for a wretched prearranged marriage, Arpino lashed out in a state of dementia and strangled his rival (Glen Tetley) for the love of another lady (Brunilda Ruiz). Joffrey's work was derivative—a cross between Agnes de Mille's *Fall River Legend* (1948), based on the true story of Lizzie Bor-den, who killed her father and stepmother with an ax, and Antony Tudor's *Lilac Garden* (1936), vivifying the psychological anguish of lovers constrained by social codes. *Within Four Walls* was the first of many ballets, however, in which Arpino would portray the misfit, the crazed outsider, the different one, and when he himself started to chore-ograph in 1961, this figure would repeatedly surface. He learned through the tours what captured an audience's attention: flashing jumps, inflated emotions, exaggerated lines, and accelerated paces.

The program's finale was *Kaleidoscope,* a frothy, neoclassical production that bubbled with vitality and enthusiasm and featured the dancers singing George Gershwin songs. "I got permission to do Gershwin, which was very unusual in 1956, and the dancers all sang," said Joffrey.[11] *Kaleidoscope* was exactly the pop-hit number that Columbia Artists sought. The dancers returned home to New York on November 7, 1956, and, although they had not been reviewed in the newspapers, were elated by a profound sense of the tour's success and by a mutual respect for their work.

They had danced in such places as Yazoo City, Mississippi; Cullowhee, North Carolina; and Normal, Alabama. They had performed at a black college where they were visited by choreographer John Butler's mother, who wrote ahead to Tetley and said, "Honey, somebody messed up because you aren't playing the white folks' school, you're playing the black school. I'm coming, but none of my so-called friends are coming."[12]

They had performed in ramshackle old movie theaters with WHITE and COLORED written above separate entrances, and one of the dancers, who had never seen such things in the North, said, "Oh, isn't that amazing, you can see a black-and-white movie if you go through this door, and a movie in color, if you go through that one."

They had witnessed the searing depth of prejudice, which they tried to do something about by relocating themselves to different hotels if African-Americans were not allowed in the ones in which the company was booked. Thus they caused segregated hotels to lose money.

They had been pursued by a nest of hornets during one performance and were repeatedly stung, until Brunilda Ruiz fell and had to be carried off as the curtain closed.

They'd been awakened by cows poking their heads through their motel windows.

They had donned their costumes in more biology classrooms than most of them had been in as high school students. "We left notes about the body parts that we approved or didn't approve of on blackboards where teachers had drawn diagrams for their kids to copy," said Arpino.[13]

He and Bea Tompkins had vaulted over a diner counter to boil three-and-a-half-minute eggs to Ruiz's specifications when a frustrated chef had come screaming out of the kitchen saying that he didn't know how to make three and one-half boiled eggs. "How do you make half an egg?" he declared, peering at them in panic.

They took these stories back with them to New York.

By tour's end, the company's cornerstone had been laid; the dancers were consolidated as a small troupe, eclectic in style, operating on a shoestring budget. Whatever skirmishes flared up among them were usually snuffed out within minutes. The red-and-white Chevrolet station wagon sputtered to the Arpino front lawn on Pelton Avenue, where it conked out as if on cue, remaining there, said the Arpino sisters, until plants were growing through the seats and the Joffrey Ballet was a name.

The dancers summarily bid adieu to Duffy, the driver. Then, in January, Joffrey rented a fancy coral-colored limousine from impresario Sol Hurok. It had four rows of seats; and on one side of the car, above the windows, Joffrey's dancers in a moment of vandalistic revelry scrawled, "Through these portals pass the tiredest dancers in the world." And on the other side, Dante's famous *Lasciate ogni speranza, voi ch'entrate* ("Abandon all hope, ye who enter"). In the capable hands of Jack Harpman, their twenty-year-old stage manager and Duffy replacement, they headed back onto the blue highways for more.*

On January 22, 1957, the company performed in Chicago, the largest city on its itinerary, and Joffrey flew out for the occasion. Had it not been for a blizzard on the same day, the diminutive Eighth Street Theatre might have been packed. But approximately fifty people, including two critics, Ann Barzel and Glenna Syse, managed to battle their way through the waist-deep snowdrifts.†

"If you were dreary and disappointed with the recent Ballet Russe de Monte Carlo visit, this is just the tonic required," wrote Syse in the *Chicago Sun-Times*. "Naturally, this young group has not the ripe mellow stature that comes with experience and extensive bookings. But it has rewarding flashes of poise and brilliance that cannot be overlooked. And all of the nine dancers kept their chins up and feet flying in spite of some obvious hazards—notably a tinny piano that apparently was minus pedals, and a small stage."[14]

Barzel, a seasoned writer, made a few pointed remarks about *Within Four Walls,*‡ referring to it as "Fall River Garden," and regretted that not

---

*Harpman constructed a boxlike structure that he called a coffin to fit on the limousine's rooftop luggage rack and carry the scenery and dancers' suitcases. The coffin weighed two thousand pounds, and although Harpman had been assured by the engineer who had built the car in Detroit that the limousine would hold up under the coffin's weight, plus the weight of ten people inside with the costumes and lighting equipment, after losing all four wheels at separate times and avoiding a near-fatal collision with a truck, the limousine had to be junked on April 6, 1957, midtour.

The dancers and Harpman then divided into two sedans. In one of them went the older generation: Harpman, Tompkins, Arpino, Consoer, and Tetley, who screeched to a halt at every antique shop. In the other, the youngsters: Ruiz, Wilson, Martinet, and Helenka Devon, who christened the troupe the Joffrey Jets.

†Both Joffrey and Arpino would repeatedly tell the story that the two critics who had come to the Chicago premiere were Barzel and Claudia Cassidy. This was told even in 1995, when the Joffrey Ballet became a Chicago resident, because Arpino wanted to demonstrate that from the beginning Chicago has been important to the company. But it seems likely that Joffrey and Arpino did not remember correctly.

‡Joffrey dropped *Within Four Walls* after the tour and became friends with Barzel, who would become one of his stalwart supporters; and Chicago would become the most consistent large-city stop on Joffrey tours, and its permanent home in July 1995.

all the ballets were as good as *Le Bal.* She also pounded home the firm opinion that Joffrey was enormously gifted and that his choreographic attributes—"freshness, intellect, taste"[15]—were equally apt for describing the dancers' performance.

Syse's and Barzel's reviews were only the second reviews the company had received, and the strength of them gave Columbia Artists the publicity support necessary to book the Robert Joffrey Theatre Dancers on a longer tour the next year, one that was geographically better organized. In the 1956–57 season, when few people knew what the Joffrey Theatre Dancers was, Columbia Artists had been forced to accept dates wherever communities showed the slightest interest in having a chamber ballet ensemble. In consequence, the troupe's itinerary made no sense.

Shortly after the Chicago engagement, for example, Jack Harpman drove the dancers north to Canada. He returned to the United States via Greenwich, Connecticut, where they performed. Then, over the course of two days, he drove 607 miles to Johnson City, Tennessee, where they danced in the morning, before packing up for Cookeville, Tennessee, 220 miles away, for another performance the next day, and then on to Greensboro, North Carolina, 400 miles away, for another concert the day after that.

The traveling on highways, which in those days were typically two-lane asphalt ribbons that closely resembled our contemporary back roads, was brutal, but could not begin to compare with the chaotic state of the theaters and the apathetic mind-set of the janitors they found when they arrived. Few of these places had ever before played host to ballet, and they were unprepared, despite Harpman's forewarning. Columbia Artists had sent out contracts and forms in advance, requesting information on stage dimensions, floor construction, and lighting equipment. Harpman had also enclosed an itemized list of the company's simple needs (a tuned piano in the orchestra pit, some makeup tables, running water, and a coatrack for costumes). Still, Harpman's list included more than almost anyone else on the Community Concerts Series artists roster seemed to be asking. Among the artists who shared the series with Joffrey were the Dupar Opera, the Irish Festival Singers, the Corelli Ensemble, mezzo-soprano Risë Stevens, and violinist Mischa Elman. They had relatively easy setups; Harpman wanted, and needed, more for the Joffrey, which had more bookings than any of the others.

"I came in raising holy hell. I was trying to protect the dancers and Bob Joffrey's reputation," Harpman noted later. "But Columbia Artists' only concern seemed to be getting their commission. They did not make sure that the theaters lived up to the letter of the contract." After one particularly frustrating incident, when a theater janitor had refused to tune the piano and move it off the stage in order to make room for the dancers ("If it's good enough for the Dupar Opera," he had shouted at Harpman, "it's good enough for you"), Harpman fired off an outraged telegram to Bill Judd at Columbia Artists. Judd responded to Harpman, "Do the best you can with the circumstances,"[16] then immediately telephoned Joffrey and insisted he get rid of Harpman by the next tour. Joffrey recognized beyond doubt that in Harpman he had the best possible stage manager. Harpman had grown up in Hollywood; he had played the neighborhood bully in a dozen *Our Gang* movies, and he had worked behind the scenes at the 92nd Street YM–YWHA for Trudy Goth. He was theater-smart, courageous, enterprising, and professional—willing to put his job on the line to ensure that the dancers and ballets were seen as they should be. Joffrey pacified Judd and held on to Harpman for the next ten years.

Among the dancers, it was generally agreed that without Harpman there might not have been a Joffrey troupe. With him, they never missed a performance. The company was sometimes late, but it always showed up.

In 1957, Joffrey added three dancers to the newly titled Robert Joffrey Theatre Ballet: Françoise Martinet, Ivan Allen, and Helenka Devon (whose name Joffrey changed from Helen Detloff). The charter members' salaries were increased $10, giving them a weekly paycheck of $110. By contrast, the new members were paid $86—a significantly lower amount because Joffrey had realized he could increase the company's size by paying new members less. He maintained this business practice for many more years: as the company's reputation grew, so did the number of dancers who wanted to join the troupe. He did not have to lure them with sensible salaries.

Ivan Allen apparently heeded the limousine's scribbled warning from Dante about abandoning all hope and, a week into the tour, left the company, complaining of the chilly air that streamed through the limousine's window and down his neck. Fortunately, Joffrey was on the tour with them; the first few stops were close enough to home for him to come and go independently. Allen had been hired specifically to dance the then obscure pas de deux from *The Sleeping Beauty*'s Vision scene, staged by Anatole Vilzak and taught to the company by Ludmila Shollar. Now Joffrey would teach Arpino the role with Devon as his partner.

But another disaster had struck prior to Allen's departure. In the middle of *Le Bal*, Beatrice Tompkins had torn a calf muscle and was unable to complete the performance. The next night, Françoise Martinet stepped into Tompkins's roles, after minimal coaching by Joffrey.

Martinet had already performed with Joffrey in New York and Seattle, and she would become his company's perpetual godsend. Born in Fez, French Morocco, she had emigrated to Seattle as a young girl and studied ballet with Mary Ann Wells. With her short pixie haircut, heronlike neck, sweet eyes, and lithe elegance, Martinet was a dead ringer for Audrey Hepburn in *Roman Holiday*. She kept a diary, and in the week after Tompkins's accident, she learned *Le Bal* and the part of Taglioni in *Pas des Déesses* by rehearsing in restaurants, gas stations, and every conceivable pit stop, as well as onstage. Each day a little more of the ballets were added—the pas de deux, the coda—until finally she possessed the whole and, with it, eventually, some hard-earned recognition, as she recorded:

January 13, 1957—Salem, Ohio. Yesterday we drove for 13 hours. Today we had a matinée at 3 o'clock. We rehearsed from 10:30 to 1 p.m., ate and got ready. I did the Chabrier [Le Bal] *very well for the first time. Pas des Déesses was okay. Now that I know it better, I will have to improve it. My toes were very sore, but at least I danced well. My arms are still bad. Too skinny. Then I had dinner and rehearsed for two and a half hours.*

January 14, 1957—Mount Vernon, Ohio. The theater floor was so uneven, full of holes and each board at a different level. I messed up my fouetté *in Chabrier, when my tiara and glove caught and I couldn't keep turning and had to let go of Glen's [Tetley's] hand. I was on Glen's feet more than my own. Otherwise, I did pretty well. Bob [Joffrey] said that I had danced very well and commented on the clapping after my solo.**

January 17, 1957—Albion, Michigan. We had just oodles of autographs.

February 5, 1957—Cedar Falls, Iowa. We had a reception with hundreds of the university kids. I was cornered on a sofa by a group of about fifteen and, for quite a while, talked like a magpie. I was so relieved that all had gone well.

February 6, 1957—Menomonie, Wisconsin. My feet were so sore and I had very bad old shoes. The Chabrier still eludes me. I don't feel sincere. I feel like an old woman putting rouge on her cheek. Trying, but pathetic. Pas des Déesses is nice.[17]

Martinet stood in for Tompkins for two weeks, and on the fifteenth day Tompkins returned to the stage, but in the middle of her performance, she collapsed. The curtain was prematurely closed, and Jack Harpman went in front of the audience and said, "Is there a doctor in the house?" They were performing at the site of the Mayo Clinic in Rochester, Minnesota, and everyone in the audience laughed. "No, seriously," said Harpman. "One of our dancers is hurt."[18] Five well-meaning

---

*Joffrey was parsimonious with compliments, and for him to say anything to Martinet was highly unusual. John Wilson told the story of going up to him on tour and saying, "Look, Bob, I know you're concerned with every bow on the dress, but don't we ever do anything right? We're never told we danced well. There's never any praise." And Joffrey replied, "If I didn't feel you were worthy, you wouldn't be here in the first place." (Wilson, November 5, 1991.)

heart surgeons raced onto the stage to help with Tompkins's freshly retorn calf muscle.

Incredibly, Tompkins's was the only grave injury sustained during eight national one-night-stand tours. She insisted on remaining with the company, and was one of their most captivating dancers and then ballet mistress until 1960. Joffrey expected complete fidelity. It was the quality he cared about most in his dancers and employees.

The company rarely repeated visits to towns in its early one-night-stand tours. "We never got bad reviews," Harpman said, "but the community-theater people had to put out so much energy toward having a ballet company that, as much as they loved it, many of them said, 'We'll never book a ballet company again.' "[19]

Being a member of the Joffrey bandwagon and evangelizing, however, was not everyone's ambition. At the end of the 1957 tour, Glen Tetley left the company; his reasons provide another kind of insight into what the Robert Joffrey Theatre Dancers was, by describing what it was not:

> Sometimes we arrived in the theater with the audience already sitting in their seats, which was an awful feeling. We would have to warm up quickly. I developed some knee problems. . . . When we played Chicago, it was marvelous. We had a real dance audience and there was an enormous response. But we played other places where they really had not seen live dance. One time we came into this high school and Jerry [Arpino] and I went out onstage to warm up. We were wearing normal warm-up clothes—tights, dance belt, ballet shoes. I was lying on the floor doing stretches and so was Jerry, and the high school principal, who was a big, tall man, stalked in and looked at us and said, "I think I am going to be sick." It was outrageous. That was the kind of uninformed audience we had in some places. . . .
>
> We were on our own. Bob did not come on tour. After a while I resented it very much. I felt deluded. We were working awfully hard and holding this whole thing together, and it is called the Robert Joffrey Ballet, and his presence is not there.[20]

Tetley next joined Martha Graham's company and then Ballet Theatre and later he became an internationally respected choreographer. In the late sixties he also helped Marie Rambert transform her company from classical ballet to contemporary dance by staging four of his works for her.

The troupe's next few years would bring satisfying evidence that people's lives were being changed, and new dancers would enter the troupe who (like both the renegade Tetley and the devoted Martinet) would choose to stay with ballet professionally in some capacity for the rest of their lives. Of the fifty-one dancers represented by the eight national tours until 1964, almost half of them—twenty-four in total—are still choreographers, artistic directors, and teachers today.

To its members the company was bigger than Robert Joffrey, the company aspired toward life at its most impudent, its most present, its most optimistic—its most danced. "We were not an ensemble that was built on repertoire or around a single choreographer," said Arpino, "and this was very difficult for some people to understand. The company is what dreams are made of. It's what real dreams are made of, and in a rational, practical world, few are going to accept that."[21]

CHAPTER 10

Quarrying the Repertoire

In New York, Joffrey had stuck little red pins into a map, charting the company's progress across America. When Robert Joffrey Theatre Ballet returned on May 9, 1957, its members found a transformed American Ballet Center. There were additions to the school's faculty: Lillian Moore was now regularly giving classes in pointe and in variations, and increasing the number of her highly respected pirouette classes. *Dance Magazine* claimed Joffrey's school was perhaps the only one in the nation to focus on specific technical elements for the duration of an entire lesson.[1] Fernand Nault, who was about to become a ballet master at Ballet Theatre, had also been added to the faculty; and Erik Bruhn routinely accepted Joffrey's invitations to guest teach.

In his own classes, Joffrey continued to pay distinct attention to the men, and he often made them execute combinations *before* the women (an unheard-of practice) because he believed this prevented the males from "hanging back" and feeling like second-class citizens.[2] "Girls always have the advantage in classical ballet in America because they have had earlier training at ten or twelve years of age, so that there is a coordination that men often lack," he said.[3] His modus operandi was to build the men's confidence by forcing them do some of the exercises first, thereby subverting the old order.

In a small storage room adjacent to the studio's air shaft, Ann Hutchinson, a former dancer and an expert in dance notation, had opened the first office of the Dance Notation Bureau. It was around this time, she remembered, that Joffrey was given a private donation for the creation of a new ballet. To Hutchinson's astonishment, Joffrey applied the money toward improving the school's facilities. "He used the money to fix up the school and to get in decent furniture, partitions, and lavatories. And I thought, 'How dare he?' " said Hutchinson. " 'That's not what the money was given for.' And somebody said, 'Well, when he fund-raises, he brings the prospective donor to the school to watch class. If the school is nice looking, they are going to be impressed. Wealth breeds wealth. If you look poverty-stricken, then people aren't going to consider you in the same way.' "[4]

Alex Ewing, who continued to drop by the school daily to manage business affairs, understood Joffrey's positive and flexible attitudes toward money. "Bob firmly believed that he was very lucky and that things would come his way. And they did," said Ewing. "He had quite a record for finding out who would step into the breach at a crucial moment, and he always had the capacity to spend up to the limit of whatever money there was. It's a much better kind of person to work with than a born loser."[5]

Joffrey's priorities were always to put the art first—to procure the choreographer who really excited him, hire the most desirable designer, shore up the school—then set about paying for it. He was an incorrigible optimist, a person who flew high over the miasma produced by penny-pinching clerical exactitude and the need to be secure, perfect, righteous, and invincible in one's financial affairs. It helped that he exhibited an uncanny ability for surrounding himself with people who would zero in on administrative matters, people who would do the small work, attend to the details, and recommend substantive plans for how something could be accomplished when there wasn't any wherewithal. Joffrey's apparent grace unblemished by hubris made many feel good about volunteering their assistance to him. Hubbard Miller, a member of his artistic team from the sixties, said it best: "You know the thing about Robert Joffrey? One day you found yourself rolling a peanut down the center of Third Avenue with your nose and you said to yourself, 'Why am I doing this?' And it was because Robert Joffrey had asked you to do it. You would do anything for the man, to the point of making yourself ridiculous."[6]

Columbia Artists wanted the company back for a tour that would not actually begin until January 3, 1958. For the next seven months, therefore, Joffrey had to find work for his dancers to dissuade them from joining other troupes. Then, quite out of the blue, Julius Rudel, the newly installed general director of the New York City Opera, approached him with an offer to choreograph for the fall season at City Center. There would be seven productions from October 9 to 24, and each required a ballet. Rudel envisioned an eclectic repertoire stressing original works and American operas. It was a prospectus similar in many respects to Joffrey's for ballet.

Rudel and Joffrey had never met. Trudy Goth, founder of the Choreographers' Workshop, had recommended Joffrey to Rudel, and Joffrey seized the chance. Joffrey staged ballets for the New York City Opera under Julius Rudel for the spring and fall seasons until 1969, taking two three-year breaks. He more than fulfilled Rudel's aims. "Joffrey and his dancers became an important part of the whole opera," said Rudel. "When we put our faiths together, ballet became integral, instead of a little jewel in a specific setting."[7] Joffrey benefited because he was forced to choreograph quickly for Rudel; his self-confidence returned when the results proved consistently solid, and he used the opera ballets to test new material and stretch his dancers. The Joffrey members were supplied the opportunity to work creatively with him, and they assumed dual status as the official New York City Opera Ballet. This guaranteed them employment, broader training, and the chance to be seen by the discriminating New York audience.

Balanchine and Kirstein's New York City Ballet was the official resident at City Center and had been since 1948. Once Joffrey's company was introduced to City Center's stage via the opera, Joffrey decided that the height of accomplishment would be someday to see his company perform in that theater. He embraced the gloriously impossible goal.

"I kept badgering Morton Baum [who governed City Center of Music and Drama] to let me have performances of my company at City Center," said Joffrey several years after he had been working successfully with Rudel. "Because the opera didn't perform the whole week. Monday, Tuesday, and Wednesday were dark. I suggested he turn Tuesday over to my ballet company. He sort of laughed at me and sent a telegram, 'Sign your opera contract. We have one company, that's enough.' I wasn't going to sign my contract unless he gave me a performance—which was funny and precocious on my part. It was as if I thought Baum really cared whether or not *I* was the opera choreographer."[8]

While counting the days until January 3, Joffrey was invited to substitute-teach for William Dollar at the American Ballet Theatre school in addition to his regular schedule there. At American Ballet Theatre, Joffrey encountered authentic stars and many of the best young dancers. He took advantage of its studios as a scouting ground from which he could lure seasoned performers and unspoken-for neophytes and add them to his company, which on the 1958 tour would expand to eleven members.

Into his first substitute class walked Rochelle Zide, a twenty-year-old who had been a teenage prodigy and was waiting to sign another seasonal contract with Ballet Russe de Monte Carlo. She had not actually intended to take the class, but had been packing her bags in the hallway when she spied Erik Bruhn entering the studio, which led her to think, "Bruhn's the greatest dancer alive. If he's taking class with this stranger, whoever he is—Bob Joffrey? Bob Joffrey!—so am I." The decision produced a startling result, as Zide recalled:

> In that first class were not only Bruhn, but Job Sanders, Sonia Arova, Mary Ellen Moylan, Michael Lland, Jillana, Scott Douglas, half of the New York City Ballet and half of Ballet Theatre, and, I think, Nora Kaye. The energy

was very crowded. There was tremendous excitement. And Joffrey kept moving me closer to the front of the class with each combination we did.

Later, in August, he offered me a position in his company. I had just signed my contract with Denham [Sergei Denham, director of Ballet Russe] that morning. Joffrey tried, and I tried, to get me out of the contract. I was so excited, but Denham wouldn't let me out. He couldn't understand—it just didn't compute. Why would I want to leave the Ballet Russe de Monte Carlo to go with this little company in a van?

When I went back to Ballet Russe, everyone—even Alicia Alonso— asked, "Where have you been? Where have you been studying?" Because in the two or three months of our summer layoff, I had turned from a very talented little girl into a mature dancer, and with great control, which I really hadn't had before. I had always had this flashing talent, but I hadn't had any control. They were all asking me and I kept saying, "Bob Joffrey, Bob Joffrey, Bob Joffrey."[9]

In 1958, there were seven vacant slots in the Robert Joffrey Theatre Ballet, now that John Wilson and Brunilda Ruiz were tending to their newborn daughter, Glen Tetley and Helenka Devon had left, and Joffrey was waiting for Zide. Joffrey never held auditions. He handpicked dancers mostly from his and Fernand Nault's classes at ABT or from the Seattle Aqua Theater casts. Columbia Artists was not covering the troupe's total expenses on tour, and to compensate for the difference and enable Joffrey to increase the number of dancers and change the repertory, Arpino helped by opening the Health Stall, a health-food store in Greenwich Village. Among his regular customers were e. e. cummings and José Ferrer.

Between Arpino's income, Columbia Artists' fee, and his own salaries, Joffrey pooled enough capital to hire dancers Nels Jorgensen, Marie Paquet, Vicente Nebrada, Alfonso Catá, Maria Grandy, and Gayle Young. Jonathan Watts would also come along as a guest artist from the New York City Ballet, and in late January, Wilson and Ruiz would join them in Juárez, Mexico.

Pianists Helio de Soto and Howard Barr were the accompanists. Françoise Martinet's mother, Manet Seguin, was wardrobe mistress. The repertory included Joffrey's *Pas des Déesses* and *Le Bal*, and Balanchine's *Nutcracker* Grand Pas de Deux, for which Watts had secured Balanchine's permission. For the first time, there were also ballets specially commissioned from choreographers that Joffrey had selected: Todd Bolender with *Whirligig* (music by Mozart) and Job Sanders with *Contretemps* (music by Fauré).

The tone of the 1958 repertory was as sweet and chirpy as Joffrey Ballet's repertory was ever to sound. *Whirligig*, a straightforward let's-show-off-the-company piece, with the dancers in Greek tunics or sweatpants playfully jiving to Mozart, replaced Joffrey's departed *Kaleidoscope.* Sanders's *Contretemps,* which told a story about disappointed love between an older woman and a younger man at the seaside, supplanted Joffrey's *Within Four Walls,* and the pas de deux from Balanchine's *Nutcracker* replaced Vilzak's from *Sleeping Beauty.* Much had changed on the menu, but the menu plan had stayed the same: one abstract dancey-dance, one dramatic, one romantic, one ballroom-scene ballet, and one classical pas de deux.

This was to be the basic programming structure, with variations in tone, for decades. As director, Joffrey's confidence never betrayed him. He scripted messages for his audiences, cultivating their trust in his taste and building an identity through a repertory that drew upon his God-given talents as a collage artist. The program wasn't four separate works and a pas de deux, but four-as-one, leading the viewer to know the complex range of feeling and thought it was possible to express in dance.

Joffrey decided, for the first time, to travel with the company. That winter, the mode of transportation was a bus: a sleek, silver-metal commercial vehicle with ROBERT JOFFREY THEATRE BALLET stenciled along its sides. Joffrey commandeered the front left seat and Jack Harpman took over the right, and they set up their offices. Harpman removed every other seat behind them and installed hassocks on which the dancers could rest their feet. Each individual had his or her own space. There was neither any running water nor a commode on board, and so, when they were late to a performance, the men would sometimes catch rain in a cup or scoop up snow to melt for shaving en route.

Sixty-nine concerts were planned, and detours between cities and towns in which the company performed were sometimes unavoidable. For example, during the rainy season in northern California, the company was forced to turn what should have been a relatively easy 170-mile trip from Ukiah to Eureka into a 530-mile, fourteen-hour, grueling inland trek. Escorted by a state patrol car with sirens screaming, the Joffrey bus pulled into the theater's parking lot at 10:30 P.M., to be greeted by the three-quarters of the audience, who had remained despite the fact that it was Tuesday and the next day was a workday. The dancers warmed up onstage in front of the crowd, and Beatrice Tompkins explained arabesques and entrechats. Except for *Whirligig,* a full program, including a Brahms waltz piano duet, was given. The next day the Humboldt County newspapers called the experience their "privilege."[10]

It was episodes such as this that inspired the company members to continue, because at times it was extremely tempting to quit. "After a tour, you think, 'I don't need another one and another one.' I mean, with all the struggling every night and the problems we had," said Jack Harpman. "But then one man from the audience came backstage with his coveralls and his farmer look, and he said, 'You know, my wife drug me here and I didn't want to see no ballette, but, you know, I liked it.' And that would change everything."[11]

The dancers looked forward principally to San Francisco, Seattle, and at the tour's conclusion, the Brooklyn Academy of Music across the East River from Manhattan, in part because Joffrey never missed a major destination. During the tour he had occasionally flown back to New York to supervise the school and to stage *Rigoletto* for NBC-TV Opera,* and the dancers keenly felt his absence. "We rehearsed *Pas des Déesses* like a prayer when he was with us," said Marie Paquet. "He cared intensely about that ballet."[12]

In the course of its national sweep, the Robert Joffrey Theatre Ballet educated dance writers. The sold-out tour was attended at nearly every performance by at least one critic. Many of the reviews in 1958 were up-front about the author's naïveté, and perhaps because they were written without the claptrap of excessive advance publicity, they exposed honest reactions. A typical review would open with this kind of proviso: "I do not know what a real ballet fan would say about the show" (*Record-Searchlight,* Redding, California). The writer then almost unfailingly turned his attention to the costumes—when one doesn't know what one is looking at, one describes what it looks like, surface first: "Outstanding was the marvelous use of color in the costumes, especially the men's and women's matched in a perfect blending which was characteristic of the entire program" (*Tribune-Herald,* Casper, Wyoming). And then, there was always a word about the audience: "A definite hit with the crowd, which called the players back for repeated curtain calls" (*News-Review,* Roseburg, Oregon).

Usually the rest of the column's inches were spent addressing the dancers' individual qualities; critics couldn't help but pick out favorites. Gerald Arpino, Dianne Consoer, and Beatrice Tompkins received top billing from Joffrey. It was his way of indicating who had been with the company from its inception, yet, in private, he continued to tell the dancers they were operating with a no-star, all-star policy. "You're all soloists!" he declared. "No, we're not. We're all corps de ballet," some whispered beneath their breath,[13] knowing full well that he meant they might dance a leading role in one ballet and be part of the background in the next. Still, Françoise Martinet drew numerous accolades with her Taglioni in *Pas des Déesses,* and Nels Jorgensen was also often singled out for his Saint-Léon.

*Prior to *Rigoletto* on February 16, 1958, and aside from *Griffelkin,* Joffrey had choreographed ballets for NBC-TV's opera production of Verdi's *La Traviata,* directed by Kirk Browning, with Eda Lioy and Jonathan Watts as lead dancers. *La Traviata* aired on April 27, 1957.

A critic for the *Argonaut*, writing about the company's debut in San Francisco on February 11, 1958, was the lone negative voice heard, meekly bewailing the lack of dynamic contrast in the repertory: "One suspects that given the proper circumstances they could do much with a serious program"[14]—a prophetic warning about what they could expect in Brooklyn. But otherwise, Joffrey seems to have accurately gauged his audience's capacity for ballet appreciation; Martinet noted in her diary that they received bravos in San Francisco. Then they moved on to Seattle, where the hometown boy was expected to make good.

Joffrey flew from New York to join the company for the Seattle debut. "Bob was anxious for us to do well," observed Martinet. "Fussing around, being onstage until the curtain went up, painting my lips, tucking Brunie's [Ruiz's] hair in, straightening a skirt. I sometimes wished he would disappear."[15] Fancy receptions were given by Ivan Novikoff and Mary Ann Wells. Uncle Marcus, who had paid for Joffrey's first years of ballet lessons and taken him to his first performances, had died a year before. Mary Joffrey, his mother, still chose to speak to his father as little as she could; her dumb stoicism was seen by Joffrey and Arpino both as a protest against Joseph's chauvinism and as a self-serving, unnecessary act that ruined the family atmosphere. Mary, who suffered from arthritis, did not go to see the company perform; Joseph did. The critics reported that Joffrey "has put Seattle (and Mary Ann Wells's teaching) on the map."[16] Four months later, Wells retired.

The company's next hurdle, on March 30, 1958, was the Brooklyn Academy of Music, which, although it was located in a New York City borough, was not considered New York by many.* BAM was the Joffrey Ballet's first union house. The company was nonunion, however, and so the performance ran without stage lights because Joffrey was not allowed stagehands.

"I must confess to a tug of disappointment at the present state of the Robert Joffrey Theatre Ballet," Doris Hering wrote in *Dance Magazine*. "It seems as though his image has tarnished a bit. A few years ago, Mr. Joffrey came out of the West like a balletic Lochinvar. He began creating works, sometimes with daring and sometimes with simple, youthful verve. And through them all there flowed a fresh concept of dancing style—an almost Romantic minuteness of detail quickened with a light, young, American bounce. This was indeed the beginning of a bright new

---

*Joffrey asked John Martin of the *New York Times* to come to the concert. Martin replied, "I am not going to Brooklyn to see dance. When you play Manhattan, I will be happy to see you." ("Conversations on the Dance: Robert Joffrey and Clive Barnes," November 25, 1985.)

ballet image. . . . But if one can judge by this single performance (the first full one in New York in three years), his theatrical approach is now more conventional."[17]

P. W. Manchester in *Dance News* seemed slightly worried: "The overall impression given by this program . . . before an audience which included every unoccupied dancer in New York . . . was that it was beautifully presented in every way, though a little lightweight and possibly a little unsophisticated for New York."[18]

For a multitude of reasons, Joffrey was not to show his company in New York City again until 1964, yet some of these discouraging responses may have contributed to his wariness and procrastination. "As a director, you look at reviews in another way than a dancer or choreographer does," he once said. "We don't have the same eyes. As a director, you usually are very committed to what you are doing and you have a great belief or you wouldn't be doing it. No matter what anyone says."[19]

Soon after the Brooklyn engagement, however, Joffrey took his first steps toward variegating the esthetic tone of his programs and presenting works of higher sophistication. His efforts were rewarded. In the next few years critics in cities on the Joffrey Ballet's national expeditions began to show that they, having seen more, were prepared to report minutely and discriminately about ballet. Some compared Joffrey's staging of *Pas des Déesses* to the one they had seen at American Ballet Theatre. One referred to a Merce Cunningham concert he had seen, which made him look more insightfully at Joffrey's ensemble. The writers discoursed about what dancing means, how it is accomplished, how it made them feel, and they analyzed choreographic design.

For the next Robert Joffrey Theatre Ballet tour, launched on October 5, 1959, Joffrey initiated his crusade to bring Columbia Artists Management up-to-date with what he sensed the public wanted: ballet that was more radical and experimental. He commissioned a work from Dirk Sanders, a Dutch-born dancer and choreographer who had studied with Kurt Jooss and was currently performing with Roland Petit's company in the United States. For Joffrey, Sanders created *Yesterday's Papers,* about a young newspaper boy (Gerald Arpino) who is so lonely that he populates his world with characters made out of yesterday's newspaper. First he invents a girl (Rochelle Zide), and when he realizes that she is forlorn, he fabricates her boyfriend (Nels Jorgensen). His sense of isolation is compounded when girl and boy saunter off, and he hurls himself into making more and more "newspaper" people, none of whom pay any attention to him.

The music was Béla Bartók's Sonata for Two Pianos and Percussion, and when Columbia Artists managers viewed the ballet's premiere in Princeton, New Jersey, they told Joffrey that *Yesterday's Papers* could not possibly be taken on the road because the score was too disturbing, emotionally dark, and complex for their kind of audience. And besides, the production required bales of leftover newspapers, and how was Joffrey planning to organize that for all sixty-two stops on the ten-week tour? Joffrey decided to present *Yesterday's Papers* at his discretion, in a limited number of cities. The ballet favorably impressed many critics, yet the reviews were usually mixed, such as this one by Alfred Frankenstein of the San Francisco *Chronicle:* "[*Yesterday's Papers*] is full of ache, frustration and rather thickly laid-on pathos, but it has some strongly dramatic moments, too, and it was astonishing to see how Gerald Arpino, Rochelle Zide, [Nels] Jorgensen and the others could dance to rhythms so complex and involved."[20]

For the 1959 tour, Dianne Consoer was no longer with the Joffrey Ballet; she and Jonathan Watts had married in February, with Arpino serving as best man and Joffrey giving away the bride at a ceremony attended by Lincoln Kirstein, Felia Doubrovska, Pierre Vladimiroff, Lillian Moore, and P. W. Manchester, among others. "I got married because I was terrified of finishing off my life alone and without the experience of family and children. And, of course, being gay was absolutely unacceptable," said Watts. "Dianne and I were always good friends. We had fun together. She was extremely beautiful, and we shared a passion for dance. I think she might have been warned that I was gay, but she either didn't believe it or she didn't care."[21]

After the wedding, Consoer left the Robert Joffrey Theatre Ballet and joined her husband at the New York City Ballet, and Joffrey hired Richard Beaty, James De Bolt, Suzanne Hammons, Mary Ellen Jackson, Paul Sutherland, and Zide, who together with Arpino, Jorgensen, Martinet, Nebrada, Ruiz, Tompkins, and Wilson comprised the thirteen-member troupe. There were important additions to staff personnel as well: Alex Ewing was officially made company business manager and Barbara Johnson, administrative assistant. Lalan Parrott and Muriel Kilby were the new pianists, providing live music for every work in the repertory, which included Sanders's *Yesterday's Papers,* Francisco Moncion's *Pastorale,* Antony Tudor's *Soirée Musicale,* the Peasant Pas de Deux from *Giselle* (with music by Friedrich Burgmüller), and Joffrey's *A la Gershwin* and *Pas des Déesses.*

Yesterday's Papers was the first work in the Joffrey repertoire to mix classic and modern dance techniques without apology, allowing the seams to show and pointing to them. In Joffrey's programming schemata, Sanders's commissioned work was the progenitor of Twyla Tharp's *Deuce Coupe.* He commissioned *Deuce Coupe* in 1973 from the then little-known modern choreographer, and it paved the way for her mainstream success. *Deuce Coupe* was one of the most important works in contemporary dance history and certainly one of Joffrey's finest achievements. *Yesterday's Papers* opened a slot in the repertoire for original, modern, and audacious works, and Joffrey kept that slot open until he died.

"This kind of ballet is controversial, like some modern art," wrote Alice Amory of *Yesterday's Papers* in Charlottesville, Virginia, adding, "The sound was much like that of a busy street . . . jarring. . . . But the audience enjoyed the unusual patterns and acrobatics."[22]

The other ballet on the program with some metaphoric and compositional grist was *Pastorale,* created originally in 1957 by Francisco Moncion, a principal with the New York City Ballet, for City Ballet's Allegra Kent, Roy Tobias, and himself. *Pastorale* told the story of a blind man who, as a man of nature, is sitting contemplatively in a glade of saplings when he is chanced upon by a blithe, superficial, sassy, and blindfolded young girl, who belongs to a nearby picnic and is playing blindman's buff. They sense each other's presence, the blind pursues the blind, and like the mythical Sylphide and her James, or the ghost-maiden Giselle and her Albrecht, they brush past each other, feel the whir of wind, and turn. The Girl believes the Stranger to be her boyfriend. When she discovers the truth, she is emotionally transformed and cannot return to the arrogant boyfriend—nor remain with the Stranger, with whom she is in love.

Brunilda Ruiz most frequently danced the Girl, and Arpino assumed Moncion's role as the Stranger; there was consistent agreement about Arpino's portrayal. The ballet in which Arpino was "blind" ironically taught him to recognize the value in dancing not as if through the eyes of the audience, but through his own.[23] *Pastorale* transformed him from an effervescent showman into a mature, luminous artist.

Moncion recounted the process by which he shepherded Arpino into the role that was Arpino's signature until 1964:

"In the early rehearsals, Jerry's idea of a blind person moving was not mine. He made stabbing, spasmodic gestures and he squinted his eyes. But I wanted a serenity that conveyed the Stranger's comfort with his affliction. 'Less is more,' I kept saying. I had to scrub him down like a thoroughbred after a race and get him down to the real him and adapt the movement to him, movement that I felt in my body. He couldn't see himself doing it. Then, finally, by holding down his shoulders and pressing down, I made him feel the restraint, and perhaps taught him to see. His performance was very good."[24]

The other new ballets in the repertory were Joffrey's revised *Kaleidoscope* (now called *A la Gershwin* and built around John Wilson as the singer), the *Giselle* Peasant Pas de Deux, and Antony Tudor's *Soirée Musicale* (music by Rossini and Britten). Staged for the company by Peggy van Praagh and rehearsed by Tudor, *Soirée Musicale* had never before been performed in the United States. It was a minor work, often referred to as "high school" Tudor, but incorporating some complex maneuvers that gave the dancers a new technical experience. Zide remembered having to nail a particularly difficult jump that gave the impression she landed on pointe with one foot while the other foot sailed behind her into arabesque.

The true importance of *Soirée Musicale* in Joffrey's repertoire is that he viewed it as the beginning of his revival and reconstruction period as a director. He said *Soirée Musicale* was his first attempt to quarry the world's repertoire. It prepared him for the large-scale revivals and reconstructions that defined his troupe beginning in 1969.[25]

Of all aspects of his life, Joffrey is most respected for preserving twentieth-century masterworks. The revivals won him international acclaim and identified the Joffrey Ballet by the late seventies as one of America's foremost dance companies. Joffrey's contribution was, in part, to refresh works grown stale from overperformance and rescue lost masterpieces. The meticulous attention he paid to detail, and the insistence on being authentic, distinguished Joffrey's revivals and reconstructions. He would accept nothing less than Léon Bakst's original blue in the 1912 decor for *L'Après-midi d'un faune*, for instance. His orientation elevated the standards and gained its first bearings with Tudor's unnoted *Soirée Musicale* in 1959.

Company morale was boosted that year by the arrival of Vera Volkova. The renowned teacher lived in Denmark, was adviser to the Royal Danish Ballet, and had in her student days been privately coached by the celebrated Agrippina Vaganova. A classical perfectionist, Volkova was nonetheless highly imaginative in her teaching. She conducted special classes for about four weeks at Joffrey's school, and her presence stirred New York's dance universe. Zide's diaries provide a picture:

June 7, 1959: Went to the reception. Was in charge of the "Guest Book." MET MME. VOLKOVA, and she's absolutely charming! She's much younger than I thought and seems genuinely interested in people. Met Eddie Villella! We talked for a few minutes, and when he left, he came over to say good-bye! Fedorova, Pereyaslavec, Danilova, Jillana, Pat Wilde, Harry Asmus, and Olga Tavolga, Gemze de Lappe, Royes Fernandez, Grantzeva, Butsova (as sweet as ever), Miss Moore, and many others were there.

June 8, 1959: Well, it's over! The first class (with Volkova) I mean, and she is wonderful, and I did better than I expected. Allegra Kent and Violette Verdy took our class and I spent the whole time between them. Mme. Volkova is utterly charming and forthright. Mr. Joffrey looks at her as if she were a god! He seemed pretty pleased. Then he said if I'd take notes, I could watch the second class, so in I went. Jacques d'Amboise, Dirk Sanders, Michael Lland, Jillana, took. And, a little late, Eddie Villella![26]

By 1960, Joffrey's American Ballet Center had moved and reopened at 434 Sixth Avenue, the building next to its original home. The faculty boasted seven permanent staff members, and the school was no longer for professional dancers and children only. Classes were now being offered for adult beginners. Joffrey's net profit from the school averaged about $150 per month. This, plus approximately $240 per month that he made from teaching jobs and touring, was funneled back into the support of the company. He hoped that accepting nonprofessional adults would enable the school to pay for itself and the company. Joffrey also relied upon gifts from individuals to supplement his personal income; his father was foremost among his private donors.

Perhaps out of tribute to the school, he rechristened the company the American Ballet Center Company and, incredibly, for the next Community Concerts Series tour, which commenced on February 1, 1960, declared the tour the troupe's "debut." He was filling the dates left suddenly vacant by *Dance Jubilee*, starring Bambi Linn and Rod Alexander, which at the last minute had canceled with Columbia Artists[27]—and perhaps changing his company's name was a condition of the unexpected contract. But this would be the only time Joffrey would let his name slip from the title. The company was his, and he was his company.

CHAPTER 11

The Models

The distinctions between American Ballet Center Company and its predecessors were more than cosmetic. By 1960, people were divided over interpretations of Joffrey's esthetic, in particular, his taste in the dancer's body type. Some said that he always went for the oddball, that he was consistent in liking dancers who were different. Others said that despite his natural inclination and sympathy toward the oddball, he was really uncomfortable with it. Around 1960 he began to show concrete signs of wanting a more classically proportioned dancer. Suddenly irritable and testy, he demanded radical physical changes in dancers who were not perfect and never would be. While the spirit of Joffrey's word had not wavered, the letter seemed suddenly ambiguous.

Do I want to be Balanchine or do I want to be Diaghilev or do I want to be Rambert or Petit or Massine? These names glimmered close to the surface of his conversations during the next few years, and many of the dancers felt the consequences. Uncharacteristically edgy, he drove them harder. Most of the company's original members—Arpino, Ruiz, Tompkins, Martinet, Jorgensen, Wilson—were sacrosanct and could say just about anything to him in any tone of voice, but others were victims of his frustration. Zide, for example, who had heard through Arpino that she so inspired Joffrey that he had briefly contemplated returning to the stage as her partner, bore the brunt of his new emotional weather. She was five feet two inches, dark-haired, pale-skinned, and her wide, almond-shaped eyes summoned an *Arabian Nights* atmosphere. Fastidious, complex, scintillating, and energetic, Zide's dancing announced to many, "Here is a ballerina." She and Joffrey would have made a blissful pair, and he rejoiced in her intelligent understanding of placement and technique. But couldn't she do something to change her body? He told her to lose ten pounds and bind her ample bosom. He wanted a longer, leaner elegance—a fluid maiden with a small, sleek head who moved with jet speed. He wanted a more Balanchine look, he said.

"Then why don't you pursue that kind of dancer?" she asked.

"Because all the best tall people go to Balanchine," he answered.[1]

Zide tucked pads into her toe shoes to give her feet the illusion of higher arches. She reconfigured her hairstyle, remembering that one day he had said he liked the way it looked when she had worn the bun higher. She considered surgery to reduce her breasts, wrestled with the option of wrapping her chest flat with Ace bandages, and then decided against taking unnatural measures. She was who she was: an accomplished dancer with a magnetic personality and flair for dramatic interpretation. She trusted that Joffrey still appreciated these qualities.

Zide's efforts to placate him, however, were indications of the seriousness and depth of her response to his esthetic reorientation. Joffrey had asked dancers before to lie about their ages, to fabricate stage names, and to lose weight, but never had he suggested dramatic alterations in their physical form, over which they had little control. (Zide was not the only woman to whom he hinted about breast-reduction surgery.) He was after a "look"; Zide was womanly, and possibly his efforts to defeminize her related to his sexual preference for men. He was experiencing a slight dissatisfaction with his dancers that perhaps accidentally coincided with the arrival of Una Kai as ballet mistress, succeeding Beatrice Tompkins, who left to teach at Joffrey's school. Kai had also danced with Balanchine, she taught a Balanchine-style class, and following her arrival, there would be more Balanchine ballets in the Joffrey repertoire.

His concern for presenting a proper image extended to himself. By 1960, he was telling the public that his true name was Abdullah Jaffa Anver Bey Khan and that he descended from royal Afghan lineage.* Some people used the information to explain away his pompous behavior, because around this same time, Joffrey started insisting that everybody professionally associated with the studio (with the exception of his intimate colleagues) call him Mr. Joffrey. Alexandra Danilova, the former Ballet Russe prima ballerina, who had inspired Balanchine and collaborated with him and taught at his school, and who sometimes taught at Joffrey's, remembered sensing from Joffrey's body language and eye contact that even she was expected to address him as Mr. Joffrey. She attributed his snobbishness to his alleged Afghan nobility.

At age thirty-two, perhaps Joffrey felt he deserved a formal appellation. He cared intensely about propriety, both for himself and his

---

*"A School with a View," by David Leddick, published in the August 1960 issue of *Dance Magazine,* recorded Joffrey's full name as Abdullah Jaffa Anver Bey Khan. In July 1960, Rochelle Zide wrote in her diary (published in *Dance Chronicle* 12, no. 1 [1989]) that she had learned the same information, wording the news with a sense of excitement that suggested this was the first time Joffrey's heritage had been made public. In later years, company biographical information established his name as Anver Bey Abdullah Jaffa Khan, which agrees more closely with his birth certificate and is the accepted form.

dancers. It would be all too easy to say that at this point he wanted to be like Mr. Balanchine, to direct the same caliber of dancers and command the same respect, but he recognized vital distinctions between himself and Balanchine that rendered most comparisons meaningless. The American classicism that Balanchine was steadily developing was more unique (and more creative) than his. Joffrey, on the other hand, wanted everything: he wanted to be *demi-caractère* in the manner of Ballet Russe, neoclassical as Balanchine, pop and old-fashioned, fun and serious—everything that had more to do with the atmosphere around dance than with dance.

Joffrey's repertoire had, so far, been designed to suit *demi-caractère* dancers and dancers whose proficiency as actors outshone their technical abilities. But over the past four tours, his dancers had improved, and this factor compounded Joffrey's urgent need to banish every vestige of musical theater. Out went his song-and-dance *A la Gershwin** and in came Balanchine's *Pas de Dix,* a neoclassical ballet with tiaras and short black tutus, to music by Alexander Glazunov.†

Pas de Dix capitalized on the score's amiable Hungarian mood with the dancers clicking their heels, tossing their heads, dipping far backward, and flashing broad smiles. The solos, duets, and quartets hinted of mazurka and czardas. Joffrey had grown up seeing the Ballet Russe production of *Raymonda,* of which the music for *Pas de Dix* was from the last act. *Pas de Dix* was an audience pleaser that showcased the dancers and complemented the Joffrey's dominantly sunny tone.

Jonathan Watts had been in the first New York City Ballet cast of *Pas de Dix* in 1955. He had danced in the extremely difficult male pas de quatre. Watts had returned as a guest artist with the Joffrey Ballet, and Joffrey requested *Pas de Dix* particularly for him. Balanchine obliged and sent Vida Brown to stage the ballet and Kai to polish the final product.

Pas de Dix required the cast of ten sometimes to move, work, and breathe as one. By taking on *Pas de Dix,* Joffrey exercised a stronger mandate to transform his chamber ballet ensemble into a small symphony. There would be more people onstage, fine-tuned and trained for unity and precision, with a requisite emphasis on conformity. Conformity in ballet is not an evil, implying lack of original thought or forfeiture of individual char-

---

*Charter Joffrey member John Wilson did not come along on the 1960 tour, and because *A la Gershwin* had been made for him, his absence is another reason the ballet was dropped. Joffrey brought *A la Gershwin* back for several performances in 1961, when Wilson returned midseason to the troupe.

†Joffrey listed *Pas de Dix* as *Raymonda Variations* in his company's *Playbills* to avoid confusion among audience members with his *Pas des Déesses.* But to his dancers, Balanchine's work was always known as *Pas de Dix.*

acter. When multiple bodies onstage agree with one another, the differences between their inner natures and musical sensibilities stand out in bolder relief. *Pas de Dix* would push them to places they never thought they could go; by working as one, they would actually gain individuality. They would sharpen.

The tour ahead was short, running from February 1 to March 20, 1960, and close on the heels of the previous tour. Joffrey quickly hired Gage Bush, Jeremy Blanton, Sara Leland, and Richard Zelens. It did not matter whether they could act. They were technicians with solid instincts for dance spirit and gesture, and their clean-cut physiques harmonized with those of most of the company members.

Dianne Consoer had also returned as a guest artist with Watts, bringing the total number of dancers to seventeen. The orchestra, production, and managerial staffs had twenty-two members among them. Although still considered small, the American Ballet Center Company was as large, specialized, and expensive as it had ever been. The Columbia Artists managers tried to discourage the expansion as being beyond their means. Joffrey ignored the protest.

One of the most important formal additions to the full-time company roster was lighting designer Thomas Skelton. For each of the ballets, he manufactured sophisticated but simple lighting plots. Skelton—who would later design *Peter Pan, Guys and Dolls,* and *The King and I* on Broadway and become the associate director of the Ohio Ballet—interpreted dance as movement in space, the space as light, and the designer as an invisible partner with the power to reveal more of the dance. "It is my job to comment on the dancer," he said. "It is my responsibility to create the space in which the dance happens. . . . As to color, I control the palette, using a color-mixing process quite different from painting. Since white does not exist in lighting, I can decide what white is for each ballet." His philosophy was in accord with Joffrey's "Lights carry the dancer's movement into another dimension,"[2] and the two men formed a collaboration that lasted really until Skelton's death in 1994.

In 1960, the company further diversified when Joffrey employed a musical director, Ted Dale; an orchestra manager, Maxim Gershunoff; a concertmaster, David Pokotilow; and a staff pianist, Mary Roark. A new stage manager, Dan Butt; a costume supervisor, Zena Romett; and a design consultant, William Pitkin, also came on board. Joffrey's father had advised him to surround himself with the best; he had produced a highly evolved team that was a testament to his talent for detecting theatrical potential in young unknowns.

For the first time, the dancers would perform a rotating repertory, which included Joffrey's *Pas des Déesses* and Moncion's *Pastorale,* and they would not have to dance in every work. *Pas de Dix*—which was led by a principal cast of either Ruiz, Martinet, or Zide, partnered by Watts or Arpino—alternated with Fernand Nault's staging of *La Fille mal gardée*. *Fille* was a wonderful, rollicking story ballet that had been around in various forms since 1786; Nault based his version on Bronislava Nijinska's production, which had been staged in 1940 for Ballet Theatre. As a one-act piece that lasted for an hour and a half, *Fille* gave audiences the sense of having seen a sumptuous, traditional ballet. *Fille*'s pantomimic action and buffoonish characters also appealed to children and ballet novices. For the cosmopolites, Joffrey reserved *Pas de Dix*, but *Fille* was danced almost every night, and unlike on the previous tours, Joffrey was often there to see it.

The company was still performing in out-of-the-way places. In Greenville, North Carolina, a critic remarked that the townspeople had not been host to ballet since 1947. Even though much had changed since Joffrey had linked with Columbia Artists Management, the public's education was ongoing. He shouldered the responsibility as if he were an ambassador of American dance.

Zide, having recently left Sergei Denham's Ballet Russe, was acutely aware of Joffrey's perspective. To illustrate the way he operated, she compared the differences between the Ballet Russe's arrival at a performance destination and the Joffrey troupe's welcome. Whenever the Ballet Russe bus pulled into a city, Zide noted, the dancers were often greeted by flashing cameras, reporters, and autograph hounds. Interviews had been prearranged for some dancers; the occasion was cause for municipal celebration. The arrival of the Joffrey bus, however, disrupted nothing. Still, the Joffrey troupe was invited to receptions and introduced to their public, and Joffrey carefully applied himself to these interactions so that they left enduring and favorable impressions.

Whereas Denham had insisted his ballerinas wear dresses and look glamorous even when traveling, Joffrey aimed for a more accessible human identity. He understood that ballet is implicitly not for everybody. It beckons an elite of an elite. But he was not interested in excluding anyone in his audience. He allowed his dancers to appear in public in clothes that were like the public's. The women could wear pants on the bus. At receptions, simple cotton shifts, instead of silks and furs and elbow-length black gloves characteristic of some Ballet Russe *étoiles,* were the order. The men wore suits and ties.

The image, whatever it was, was noticed by the press. Beth Cook, in her column, "Coffee Time Talk," in the *Modesto Bee,* observed that "when the [Joffrey] troupe members arrived [at the reception], they looked like youngsters, too, a bit astonishing considering their ability onstage. The ballerinas had changed into skirts and blouses or simple dresses; most of them wore flat shoes and their long tresses were swept

back above their ears into severe chignons—the Russian Influence perhaps? The result was refreshing."³

Incredibly, the fashion consciousness helped breed the reputation Joffrey intended, and Zide spelled it out:

"They used to call us the Palmolive company. We all looked like we
smelled of Palmolive. We were clean. We were neat. We were American.
We dressed American. Our contribution was the enthusiasm we brought.
We allowed people to think that dance was accessible. It was something
that, if they couldn't do it themselves, maybe their children could."⁴

By the tour's conclusion, Zide had prominently risen and established herself as a prototypical Joffrey dancer. Try as he might over the next few years
to flush the too-short-yet-intoxicating dancer from his system (by denying
her roles or making her third cast), Joffrey continually found himself drawn
back to her. There had been a Zide-esque member in the company
through to Tina LeBlanc, a sublime classical minx who was a Joffrey Ballet emblem in the late eighties until she left in 1991. Although he never
seemed to realize that in Zide or LeBlanc he had ballerinas, mitigating circumstances usually prevented Joffrey from quashing such dancers' progress.
Favorites with the audience, they embodied his credo that spirit in dance
means everything, and as a rule, he never fired anybody.

In Zide's case, she was also Arpino's partner. They argued bitterly in
rehearsals, yet onstage they shot sweet adrenaline through the souls of
those who watched. The chemistry worked. Moreover, Zide's uncanny
ability to remember almost every step performed by almost every dancer
in almost every ballet meant that when someone was injured or sick, she
stepped in. Her memory often spared the company embarrassment, and
Joffrey grew accustomed to her feisty challenges to his authority.

While he was more comfortable with artists who did not question
him, he would not hold it against them if they did. His office door at the
American Ballet Center was always open in 1960. A good listener, he
heard few complaints. Although he had assumed some airs and cherished
the small bronze bust of Napoleon that sat on his desk, his living habits
were still relatively simple. He and Arpino shared a small brick-walled
storage room in the back of the school. This room where they slept had
two windows and the ceiling was high, but it was almost possible to stand
at the center and touch opposite walls with one's hands. Their bathroom
was the boys' dressing room down the hall. There was no kitchen, no
heat at all on Saturday and Sunday, and no heat or hot water after 6 P.M.
the rest of the week. They lived there for five years. Almost everything
they owned had gone into storage.

When Joffrey and Arpino moved out of the school and into a house in
the Village, every inch of wall space was crammed with framed photographs, lithographs, paintings, sculpture, animal heads, and tapestries,

and table surfaces were filled with collections of ivory, tortoiseshell objects, and handmade wooden artifacts. Joffrey said he thought he became a collector because he had endured so long a time without things. "I find that they are very calming."[5]

On July 12, 1960, the company returned for a weeklong engagement at Jacob's Pillow Dance Festival. Ted Shawn, the Pillow's director, insisted that Joffrey present *Pas de Dix* with Maria Tallchief and Michael Maule as guest stars. Tallchief had originated the role for Balanchine; she and Maule would certainly draw a crowd. Joffrey accepted Shawn's terms and invited Roy Tobias from the New York City Ballet to perform with the company as well. The program was completed by *Pastorale* and the world premiere of *Clarissa,* choreographed by Thomas Andrew.

When Joffrey had procured Tallchief and Maule as guests for *Pas de Dix,* Walter Terry thought it would also be wise for Joffrey to present a new ballet featuring them. At the time, Andrew was Walter Terry's companion, and it is possible Joffrey selected him as choreographer with the assurance of a positive review in the *New York Herald Tribune.* "An enormously successful world premiere . . . Intensely theatrical and visually stirring," wrote Terry of *Clarissa* in the *Tribune.*[6] Because of scheduling conflicts, however, Tallchief was unable to learn *Clarissa* for the premiere, and so Zide stepped into the title role, dancing opposite Maule as her lover and Arpino as her father.

Along with Terry, P. W. Manchester and Edwin Denby were also among those who were aware of how the Joffrey troupe functioned internally. These critics saw practically every Joffrey program in rehearsal before it went out on the road. Denby usually sat quietly in a studio corner. Whenever Joffrey asked him what he thought of the work, the dancers gathered. Joffrey shared the esteem that both dance and literary aficionados had for Denby as the most perceptive and engaging American dance writer of the twentieth century. Interestingly, though, Denby never reviewed Joffrey's company for any of the numerous magazines that he contributed to over the years *(Dance Magazine, Dance News, Saturday Review, Hudson Review,* and the *Nation.)*

Although Denby did not write about Joffrey, he also did not completely ignore him. Instead, he offered valuable suggestions about casting, and referred theater professionals to his school and troupe. "Edwin Denby was a devotee of the New York City Ballet, but he was an adviser to Bob," said Arpino. "He was concerned with the company's structure and what the company was about. He believed in Bob and this young company, and he sent many, many people to the school."[7]

Lincoln Kirstein recognized that in Denby he had a voice for his cause. Denby's interest in Balanchine's work was at the core of his artistic philosophy. For him, momentum and its relationship to music were paramount. He was not interested in dramatic gesture. He was just as enthusiastic about Merce Cunningham as he was about Balanchine. In the dance critics' code there developed, around 1966, an unwritten rule that if you were pro-Balanchine, you could not possibly be pro–anybody else. Critics made choices and broke the rule constantly. Yet the rule persisted and clouded the air for the next three decades, though it cannot be attributed to any single figure or factor. But since Denby was the acknowledged leader of the pro-Balanchinean coterie for the press, one must stop to think, What if he had written something about Joffrey? What if his encouragement of the Joffrey Ballet had been better known?

Denby was certainly interested in one dancer on whom Joffrey was also fixated beginning in the summer of 1960.[8] Her name was Rita Bradley, but Joffrey soon rechristened her Lisa Bradley. She eventually became his greatest muse. He did not choreograph more than one ballet for her; instead he solidified his company around her.

Joffrey and Beatrice Tompkins had discovered Lisa Bradley a year earlier, when they had attended a performance by the Garden State Ballet of New Jersey. Her dancing worked Joffrey into such a euphoric state that he went backstage, introduced himself, and invited her to take his classes. When Bradley showed up at the American Ballet Center, Françoise Martinet declared that she was "the first perfect body we had ever had," and it wasn't long before the company members understood that "Bob had realized his dream."[9]

Martinet explained that the Joffrey Ballet's evolution could be delineated by pre-Bradley and post-Bradley eras: "There were many dancers during the company's first generation that he didn't take. He kept a group that would work very well together. We could really move. We had a little sickled foot here and there, but we were highly disciplined. We were all high achievers. But looking back, I know that Bob thought of us a little bit like lovable klutzes. We were artists, but we did not have good enough bodies."[10]

Joffrey obsessed over Bradley's training at his school. Seventeen years old, she had been a student of Marie Jeanne's for the past two years at Fred Danieli's studio in her native New Jersey. She had come to ballet late, starting when she was thirteen, but not studying seriously until she arrived at Joffrey's. Even then she was reluctant. She did not have many financial resources, and therefore, Alex Ewing sponsored her at the school. When Joffrey learned that she had never seen a ballet performed by a major company, he invited her regularly to accompany him to American Ballet Theatre performances. He taught her how to look at dance, and how to freeze-frame mental images as visual aids in performances later on. When her ignorance of advanced ballet terminology clearly impeded her progress, he lent her books from his library. If he said, *"Grand rond de jambe jeté en dedans,"* she should be able to do it. He tailored company classes to her specifications and gave her private lessons. She took as many as five classes a day, an almost physically impossible schedule that represented an irresponsibility on Joffrey's part.

Reed-thin, almost emaciated, the skin pulled taut between her two hips, Bradley seemed erased. Yet somehow she was beautiful. Bradley had been ordered by her pediatrician to dance as a means of putting on muscle. Her frailty notwithstanding, she was like a musician with perfect pitch; her corporeal instincts were clean, precise, and eloquent. Zide said, "There wasn't anything she could do without taste."[11]

Joffrey had learned from Mary Ann Wells and from his own experience that nothing is more powerful on earth than the human will. Bradley tested his patience: she was headstrong, often belligerent, sometimes deceitful, and unquestionably complex. Refusing to wear a black leotard and pink tights to class, she straightaway broke one of Joffrey's most valued requirements. He ordered her out of the school and told her not to return until she was properly attired. The next day she knocked tentatively on his door.

"Why is it that you only like black and pink? It drives me crazy. I want to wear some color," she said.

"It's very simple," he replied. "I have a lot of dancers that I see all day long. Try it yourself. Just stand in the back of the studio and look at a classful of bodies. See how much better you see a single body when each student wears the same-colored leotard and tights."[12]

Bradley obliged him, agreed with his sensible viewpoint, and adopted the black-and-pink uniform. But there were other tempests. She appeared to want to run her own classes, stopping herself in the middle of a combination to give herself corrections. Joffrey told her to keep moving. Not to think, but to dance. She argued. He was impossible to ruffle. "He was always so calm and gentle and always, always kind," she said.[13] She had thought that he wanted to destroy her or make her his. Then she realized that perhaps she was perceiving him incorrectly. Mentally she revolved 180 degrees, to another vantage point:

"The rules he was giving me were a way of centering my attention on dance, which was centering my attention on life, lifting myself above myself. I was rebellious. I had a lot of garbage. But Mr. Joffrey didn't want me to bring that garbage to class. He was inviting me to do better, not better than the dancer next to me. I was surrounded by people who could dance reels around me. But better by stopping the fight against myself. . . . To become an instrument. To realize that art is born without the ego."[14]

Lisa Bradley made her debut with the company on August 12, 1960, as one of Lisette's friends in *La Fille mal gardée* at the Chautauqua Amphitheater, located in a heavily wooded hillside region in New York's westernmost county. The community's stronghold, the Chautauqua institution offered an impressive array of courses in music and drama. A year earlier Joffrey had been brought in by Julius Rudel to choreograph two productions for the Chautauqua Opera Association's summer season: Bedřich Smetana's *The Bartered Bride* and Lerner and Loewe's *Brigadoon*. In 1960, Joffrey had been invited back to choreograph Rodgers and Hammerstein's *Carousel* for the week of August 19. To Bradley's astonishment, Joffrey cast her in the musical's plum leading role of Louise, thereby sending a jealous shiver through some of his tried-and-true women dancers. They admired Bradley's dancing, but often found her too unpredictable and flirtatious to earn their trust.

On November 16, the stakes were higher. The Dallas Civic Opera Company presented the American debut of coloratura Joan Sutherland and the first American staging of Handel's *Alcina*. Franco Zeffirelli directed the production, and the "stunning corps of dancers" (Robert Joffrey's troupe, so described by the *New York Herald Tribune* music critic) performed no less than twelve baroque ballet sequences choreographed by Ani Radosevic.

Joffrey used *Alcina* as an excuse to restock the troupe, and while opera aficionados celebrated Sutherland's premiere, he rejoiced in the first performances under his auspices by Eleanor D'Antuono, Diana Cartier, and Lawrence Rhodes. D'Antuono had come from Ballet Russe and was a regular in Joffrey's classes. Once in his company, she remained for half a year before moving to American Ballet Theatre, where she rose to principal rank in 1963. Cartier and Rhodes stayed with Joffrey considerably longer and, for independent and memorable reasons, refined the company's identity. Everything about Cartier's dancing seemed angled, from her long, sharp bone structure to her wonderful, pointed wit.* Rhodes was Mercury incarnate: graceful, evanescent, fleet, and classically honed.

Why were experienced dancers now lining up to join? A former Ballet Russe member, Rhodes matriculated in Joffrey's company, in part, because American ballet training was clearly coming of age and Robert Joffrey was partly responsible. His teaching methods were nothing short of revolutionary, said Rhodes, adding, "Bob was talking about ideas in class that were concrete and scientific. I responded to an intellectual idea about dance. The old Russians were not very instructive. Their method was survival of the fittest. Whereas Bob was talking about 'squaring off the hips'—scientific, anatomical ideas.

*Cartier stayed with Joffrey briefly at this juncture, but returned in 1965 and remained until 1979, ending as one of Joffrey's ballet mistresses.

"He loved the material that men did, too. Setting up a longer period of time to do a pirouette. He loved that vocabulary. He had an energy that was very infectious and very male.

"We worked much, much harder with Bob than with Ballet Russe. Ballet Russe was in a situation where there wasn't even a company class offered. There were many dancers who never did class. When you think about it, it was really quite bizarre. In rehearsal, Freddie Franklin offered a class, but on tour there was no Freddie."[15]

On January 22, 1961, the troupe headed for the road again. It had a new name: the Robert Joffrey Ballet. The forty-seven-city tour began in Hempstead, Long Island, snaked through Florida townships, and concluded by way of Chicago. There were seventeen dancers in all, including Carolyn Borys, Robert Davis, Richard Gibson, and Jacquelyn Gregory. Gershon Kingsley, a young German brought to New York to direct a Broadway musical, supervised the orchestra as the new music director. The ballet mistress was still Una Kai. Joffrey accompanied them, often taking the final bow with the troupe and granting interviews to reporters.

On this tour, his habit of writing notes to the dancers and crew, correcting faults observed during performance, reached maturity. "He has the eye of a hawk when it comes to noticing a hesitant step, a faulty light, a careless hairdo, a spot on a costume," remarked Alex Ewing, the business manager.[16] The notes were intended to achieve perfection, and Joffrey rarely missed a performance. If he was forced to be absent, then a ballet mistress wrote and delivered the postperformance critique in his stead.

The repertory for the 1961 tour was larger than ever, including Balanchine's masterpiece *Allegro Brillante* and Lew Christensen's humorous *Con Amore,* both staged by Kai. Thomas Andrew's *Invitations* was also new, while Nault's *La Fille mal gardée,* Moncion's *Pastorale,* Balanchine's *Pas de Dix,* and Joffrey's *Pas des Déesses* completed the bill.

Because the company was playing in some of the same cities it had visited five years earlier, returning critics jumped at the opportunity to note change. "Ballet Company Improved," read the headline of one newspaper review in Raleigh, North Carolina. "New Maturity Shown by Joffrey Ballet," announced the *Courier-Express* in Buffalo, New York. The rise in technical caliber struck them head-on, and Ruiz epitomized the new beauty and power. "[The company] has its share of budding talent and at least one outstanding dancer . . . Brunilda Ruiz," wrote Claudia Cassidy in the *Chicago Tribune.* "Her sense of fun can skim a ripple of laughter to the back row."[17] Paquet, Martinet, Zide, Jorgensen, Sutherland, and Arpino routinely prompted sincere hyperbole, and Bradley's reputation ascended with her debut as Eros in *Con Amore* ("an eye-opening creature in a pink costume that fitted like her skin"—*Virginian-Pilot,* Norfolk, Virginia).

Making dance look like fun was still perceived to be Joffrey's priority. "The company has a definite point of view," wrote Ann Barzel in the *Chicago American*. "It is that the most important part of ballet is dancing, and good dancing includes a human quality as well as technical skill."[18] Others, such as Betty Kovach from the Raleigh *Times,* were more circumspect: "The lack of subtlety in interpretation is more than compensated for by the amazing energies of the entire group. If one remembers that this is, in no sense of the word, a classical company and does not expect traditionally ethereal performance, then pure enjoyment is the result."[19]

Arpino often sequestered himself during the tour to choreograph. At the time, he had no intention of becoming a choreographer; his private exercises in vacant studios were solely for the purpose of playing with movement to amuse himself, and sometimes Zide. But John Wilson, his old friend and a charter Joffrey member who had reunited with the troupe midseason, cornered Arpino on the Joffrey bus and informed him that Wilson and choreographer Joyce Trisler were planning a one-night program in the spring at the 92nd Street YM–YWHA's Kaufmann Auditorium. There were a couple of problems, however. They needed a third party to help with the down payment for the space. And they had to fill out their program. Would Arpino consider joining them?

On May 16, 1961, Gerald Arpino and Company appeared, sharing a bill with Trisler and Wilson's separate ensembles, presenting Arpino's first ballets, *Partita for 4* and *Ropes*. The reviews heralded that a choreographer, the genuine article, had been born that night. The pair of works that ignited Arpino's career could not have been more different. *Partita for 4,* with music by Vittorio Rieti, consisted of formal patterns and geometric designs executed by Lisa Bradley, Paul Sutherland, Lawrence Rhodes, and James De Bolt. Lisa Bradley wore a short pink skirt and the men were in navy blue, sleeveless unitards with white socks and shoes. Lillian Moore suggested in her article in *Dancing Times* that, on a small scale, *Partita* was Balanchine's *Apollo* reimagined with the sexes reversed.[20]

Walter Terry could not help noticing that something was off with Arpino's musical sense. "I was somewhat troubled by the relationship between action and sound," he wrote in the *Herald Tribune*. "Obvious musical climaxes were clearly exploited in the dance but other visual patterns were associated with the music in a rather tenuous fashion."[21] Arpino's recurring problem with music—keeping the counts—would seem to have reared its embattled head. He had a solution: for this concert and for rest of his lengthy tenure as a choreographer, Arpino would engage an assistant. The first one was James Howell.

Strapping, blond Howell had wandered into the American Ballet Center in late 1960, professing that he wanted to dance with Joffrey. He had grown up in Zillah, Washington, where his parents ran an orchard. His mother had started him out on the piano, but Howell had contracted polio and, by twenty, was taking modern dance as therapy with Martha Nishitani in Seattle. Obsessed with movement, he attended Connecticut College School of the Dance in New London one summer on scholarship with Martha Graham. Committed to remaining in the East and making a career in dance, he had ended up on the American Ballet Center doorstep.

Arpino, age thirty-eight, and Howell, age twenty-five, inspired and warmed to each other from the moment they met. When Arpino returned from the 1961 tour, he unhesitatingly tapped Howell to help with the music for his upcoming choreographic debut. They worked together on *Partita for 4,* with Howell calling out the counts for the dancers. *Ropes,* however, was far more challenging. Arpino had selected a Charles Ives score, Set for Theatre or Chamber Orchestra. Howell had never heard of Ives. "What the hell kind of musician are you?" exclaimed Arpino, but he kept him in the studio.[22] "The great thing about Jim was he was a tremendous censor and disciplinarian," said Arpino. "If I wanted to cop out and just repeat something that had been done before, he never allowed it. 'You can do better than that,' he'd say."[23]

For the classical ballet genre and for its time, *Ropes* was an innovation. Arpino suspended six thick ropes from the ceiling, a semicircle of five from which hung five men (Charles Leslie, Jack Weber, Howell, Rhodes, and Sutherland), and one in the center for the woman (Brunilda Ruiz). He conceived of the men as predatory creatures; their shapes as they clambered up and down the ropes were distorted, their gestures reminiscent of a troop of anxious primates. "The music was difficult because you couldn't really count it, and the men had to breathe together in order to stay together," said Rhodes. "We each held a rope and started in a fifth-position deep plié, then ran up the rope and threw our heads back at the same time. It was animal."[24]

The woman was their antithesis, delicate and tranquil, and on pointe with her hair loose. The ballet revealed their paths toward violent conflict, described by Moore in the following extract from *Dancing Times:*

The rope seemed to symbolize the dancers' personal identity. At one point the girl, after a frantic and confusing passage in which she danced with all of the men and seemed almost crushed by them, fled back to her rope as though it were a refuge and a protection, and danced with it a strange and touching pas de deux. In the ballet's stunning climax, the girl was suspended high above the stage, caught in a tangled mesh of ropes like a fly in a spider's web.[25]

On opening night, Ruiz accidentally ensnared her long brown locks in the ropes. "Scissors," she whispered to the men while being lowered to the ground during a blackout. "Someone get the scissors." The men tugged at her hair. In the orchestra pit, the conductor, Maurice Peress, held silent for a minute and a half, uncertain what to do. "I'm hanging there like Jesus Christ crucified," said Ruiz. "We had rehearsed the ballet to death. Nothing like this had ever happened. I'm thinking, 'I've ruined the ballet.' "[26] She yanked herself free and finished the dance. Nobody in the audience ever knew of the torture.

As a spontaneous and instinctual choreographer, Arpino relied on a degree of improvisation in rehearsal. He picked dancers who were uninhibited about elaborating upon the choreographic material, presenting him with their own ideas and showing off their natural strengths. His methods, as described by Paul Sutherland, changed little over time:

"Jerry isn't the sort of person who sits down and saturates himself with the music or comes into the studio with the steps all laid out. It's a struggle for him. He has to drag the ballet out of his guts, and your guts. I might give him a step and someone else might do a set and give him lighting, but it's his guts. His struggle is not to think of steps, or to figure out a pretty story. His is a struggle toward wholeness."[27]

In the summer of 1961, Arpino was commissioned to choreograph another ballet both by Alex Ewing individually and by Nancy Lassalle through Ballet Society, a corporation that had been formed fifteen years earlier by Balanchine and Kirstein as a funding arm of the New York City Ballet to encourage new works. Selecting Bradley and Sutherland, Arpino choreographed *Sea Shadow** to the adagio movement of Ravel's Piano Concerto in G.

In the ballet, a restless boy languishes near a large conch shell on a dark-lit beach. The filtered light suggests the possibility that he is underwater, an inhabitant of the ocean floor. The whole ballet could be his dream. As he presses himself into a chest stand, his torso and legs ascend so easily into the air that the impression of unreality, buoyant weightlessness, and the supernatural is compounded. When he holds up the shell, a female apparition enters. She travels on pointe toward him with fluttering feet. Wearing a simple unitard with her hair flowing loose, she suggests a sea nymph, a phantasm, and she is clearly the answer to the man's romantic distress, although she gives not the slightest impression of wishing to be so. She seems remote. Their athletic pas de deux occurs mostly on the floor. On his back, he lifts her with both hands around her rib cage to face him, and she sways with a beautifully arched spine and seemingly endless limbs in the water's currents. If he lets go, she might drift

---

*The working title for *Sea Shadow* was alternately *Fantasy for Two* and *Undine*. Arpino was inspired to create the pas de deux in part by Paul Sutherland, who was trying to build his upper body by executing repeated chest stands. Arpino watched him work out in the studio—the scene was similar to the beginning of Jerome Robbins's *Afternoon of a Faun*.

away. *Sea Shadow* had atmosphere, and as physical poetry, Arpino rarely matched it. The ballet was lovely and sensual, and convinced people that chief among Arpino's attributes was his lack of fear about "baring his soul to an audience of strangers."[28]

That same summer of 1961, Joffrey had also been given a $5,000 grant from an anonymous donor to use for a workshop. For four consecutive weeks, he turned the American Ballet Center into a hothouse, paying choreographers Lee Becker, Gloria Contreras, and Arpino to experiment with his dancers. Joffrey did not care whether or not they generated work that qualified for the repertoire. His objective was to give his dancers a chance to participate in the creative process, and for the first time to be paid to rehearse. The three choreographers were, by intention, practitioners of three distinct idioms. "If a dancer is intelligent, he takes something away from each choreographer he has worked with," Joffrey said. "He enriches himself. It's like another layer has come off."[29]

Lee Becker was a former Joffrey student from the High School of Performing Arts and an original cast member on Broadway in *West Side Story*, choreographed by Jerome Robbins. Her style was somewhat reminiscent of Robbins's work in that musical. After giving the company members daily classes in jazz dance to loosen and prepare them for improvisation and unfamiliar muscular isolations, she tackled a Dave Brubeck score.

Gloria Contreras, a choreographer from Mexico who had once been a student in Balanchine's school, wanted to try her hand with an Anton Webern score, and using her charged, dynamic, and tight vocabulary, considered at the time to be avant-garde, she made *Bagatelles*.

Arpino used the grant and workshop to produce *Sea Shadow*.

The workshop allowed Joffrey to retrench and to solve a problem that he believed was endemic to American dancers, namely that their training is compartmentalized. He wanted his company members whole, alert as creative instruments and stimulated by the diversity of movement. He encouraged them to know music and to analyze scores, educational exercises for which there was not time under normal rehearsal conditions. In many foreign countries where the ballet institutions are state supported, these activities are a given, and in his opinion, they produced better, more well-rounded dancers.

"America has produced very good dancers under difficult conditions, not ideal conditions," he said.[30] For the Robert Joffrey Ballet and for Gerald Arpino's career, the workshop was a milestone.

CHAPTER 12

Rebekah Harkness Kean

At the conclusion of the workshop, Joffrey absorbed Arpino's *Partita for 4* and *Ropes* into the repertory for the 1962–63 season. Later, looking back on his decision, he said that he had long suspected Arpino was a born choreographer.[1] People other than Arpino heard Joffrey's opinion of Arpino's early work and potential. "Bob was very excited," said Una Kai. "He realized Jerry was good, and from that point forward, he made sure Jerry's career flourished."[2]

Joffrey also wanted *Sea Shadow* in the repertory, but Kai cautioned that John Cranko had choreographed *The Witch* to the same Ravel score for the New York City Ballet when she had been a member and that the Ravel estate had protested that the music was not written for dance and, therefore, could not be used by Cranko. After City Ballet gave the premiere on August 18, 1950, and had completed its Covent Garden engagement, customs officials destroyed the expensive sets and costumes. *The Witch* had the distinction of being the only City Ballet premiere presented overseas and never seen by its New York audience.

Arpino, likewise, did not have permission from Ravel's executors, Elkan-Vogel, a Philadelphia music publishing house, to play the adagio section he had used for *Sea Shadow*, so Joffrey decided against presenting the ballet in the 1962–63 season. The ballet was also not yet finished.

At the time, Arpino understood that the ballet's incompleteness was Joffrey's reason for not wanting to present *Sea Shadow*. He later discovered, however, that he was often the last to know Joffrey's true motives or reservations. Joffrey seemed to like to keep Arpino off-balance by withholding praise. "*Sea Shadow* had been discarded after the workshop. Bob liked the Lee Becker piece and the Contreras, and I was there," Arpino said in 1994. "He dismissed *Sea Shadow*, he just dismissed it. Bob never indulged or overpraised me. He was my biggest critic. He was my adversary in the sense that we would argue about something in my work, and almost every time he would win because he was esthetically right. In his heart he loved what I did, but in truth he looked to the other choreographers."[3]

Two fundamental advantages of Arpino as house choreographer were his loyalty and his price. Joffrey was sure Arpino would never leave him. As dedicated as Joffrey was to the troupe, so Arpino was to him. Their dynamic seemed in this regard to be uneven, but through their relationship Arpino had access to fine dancers; most of the time he had a rehearsal studio at his disposal; he could even fail and not find his job in jeopardy. In addition, he did not have the responsibility of running a company. He was in these respects a most fortunate choreographer. To Joffrey's benefit, Arpino welcomed being told what to do. He worked fast, and he did not expect to be paid one red cent.[4]

This final point mattered because the company was teetering on the brink of dissolution. "It entered a rough phase around 1962 and had outgrown Columbia Artists," said Ewing, explaining that the company stayed with Columbia Artists even though it kept growing and diversifying, and the income from tours, the school, and the New York City Opera could not compensate for the rising costs.[5] It was uncommon in those days for a school to support the company. Usually the two were kept scrupulously separate, and the school was where the artistic director drew his or her salary. In February 1961, Ewing had sent a memo to Joffrey and others within the administration reporting that American Ballet Center's anticipated budget of $5,375.30 for that month would furnish the payroll and pay some bills, but that "little or no funds [would] be available for company use."[6] Ewing also told Joffrey that it would be necessary to take $1,000 from the company to pay the school's taxes.

Jack Harpman, the company manager, said that he never knew if there would be enough in the bank to cover the dancers' weekly paychecks.[7] He felt certain that, short of a miracle, the company would have to close. His fear proved justified, because prior to setting out on January 28, 1962, for the fifty-five-city tour, Joffrey appealed to Gloria Gustafson for help. Her mother had assisted the company on its inaugural tour with a $5,000 donation and had donated her daughter's station wagon. He told Gustafson the troupe would have to shut down.[8] He also reached out to William J. Blanken Jr., a consistent Joffrey Ballet supporter, who was a friend of Lincoln Kirstein's and of dancer Nels Jorgensen's. Finally, he called upon his father for advice. Joseph Joffrey had been aiding his son financially since the early 92nd Street Y performances. Having lived through the Depression, Joffrey senior recommended he hang on. "There are many roads to Mecca," he told his son. And Robert Joffrey believed it.[9]

When Joffrey surveyed the national landscape, he saw several reasons to be encouraged, not the least of which was that the "One and Only" Ballet Russe de Monte Carlo had canceled its 1961 national tour, then calmly shut down for good. The loss saddened Joffrey, but it was ultimately his gain, because some of their tour bookings were siphoned off to the Joffrey Ballet.

By 1962, the national mood had also dramatically shifted since Joffrey's company had first set out six years earlier. Since then, the Russians had launched *Sputnik* and successfully landed spacecraft on the moon, beating the Americans in the race to conquer outer space. Because of these defeats, wrote historian Eric F. Goldman in *The Crucial Decade— and After*, doubt about the American way of life seemed to be the underlying American crisis in 1962.

In the home, in the office, everywhere, people questioned their values. College-educated women (who were thought to be ballet's principal audience) entered the job market, not only because they needed money, but because they had newly made the conscious decision to have careers before having babies. The ubiquitous TV dinner was one sign that priorities were being placed on convenience, economy, and time-saving—and that the rhythm of American life had accelerated.

An upside to the doubt was that people sought ways to improve themselves. Schools, hospitals, libraries, civic centers, and the arts benefited from new private donations because simple consumerism would not change the past and land Americans on the moon any faster. "What was needed was not the better-equipped American, but the American who was a better human being," wrote Goldman, "his life enriched by an altered community atmosphere and by greatly improved facilities for education, medical care, and recreation."[10] Campaigning on hard-line anticommunism, John F. Kennedy was elected to the presidency in 1960, and with him came a new attitude and passion for the arts. "I see little of more importance to the future of our country and our civilization than full recognition of the place of the artist," Kennedy would say three years later. "If art is to nourish the roots of our culture, society must set the artist free to follow his vision wherever it takes him. . . . Art established the basic human truths which must serve as the touchstones of our judgment."[11]

One night in 1962 at a New York social gathering, the composer Gian Carlo Menotti introduced Joffrey to Rebekah Harkness Kean. She was the widow of William Hale Harkness, a Standard Oil Corporation heir. Her blond hair in a neatly coiffed wave, her small eyes, her sleek figure, and the occasional bursts of delightful naughty laughter gave Joffrey the impression that she was vivacious and fun-loving.[12] When her husband, who was much older than she, had died in 1954, Rebekah, who had grown up affluent in St. Louis, was reported to have inherited $60 million from him. Her third marriage, in 1961, was to Dr. Benjamin H. Kean, a New York parasitologist of considerable reputation.

Mrs. Harkness, as she was known professionally in dance circles, had trained as a composer; the International Ballet of the Marquis de Cuevas had used her score *Journey to Love* for a ballet of the same name at the

1958 Brussels World's Fair; Renzo Raiss of the American Festival Ballet had choreographed to Harkness's *Letters from Japan;* and her work had also been presented at Carnegie Hall. Since childhood, she had been intrigued by ballet, and she now applied herself almost daily to private lessons. As an arts patron, she had established the Rebekah W. Harkness Foundation for the sole purpose of fostering dance in America, particularly a new generation of choreographers. She had placed her resources behind Pearl Primus, sponsoring her African tour in 1961, and behind Jerome Robbins's Ballets: U.S.A., an esteemed ensemble that had had its debut at the first Festival of Two Worlds in Spoleto, Italy, and had also performed at the Brussels World's Fair. The Spoleto Festival was directed by Menotti, who was Rebekah Harkness's frequent house guest. In 1962, Harkness withdrew from Jerome Robbins when he demonstrated resolutely that he would not let her participate in Ballets: U.S.A.'s artistic direction. She, with Menotti's guidance, then reached out for another dance company to sponsor.

Robert Joffrey, age thirty-four, was vulnerable. Vulnerable but also "very diplomatic and very ingenious and very devious," said Ewing, adding that the Robert Joffrey Ballet was not eligible for conventional patronage at the time because the company did not have a not-for-profit status, which meant that it could not receive tax-deductible individual contributions.[13] On the other hand, the company could accept money from a foundation. Harkness, therefore, seemed an ideal prospect.

She made a phone call to Joffrey and requested he arrange an exclusive performance for her at the Phoenix Theater in the East Village (Second Avenue and Twelfth Street).[14] At the same time, Menotti had invited Joffrey to audition for the next Festival of Two Worlds in Spoleto. Delighted, Joffrey agreed to accommodate both requests, and the space was rented. Gathering his dancers onstage before the performance, he announced, "This is an important showing. I can't tell you whom you're dancing for, but if the audition is a success, our futures are assured."[15]

He asked the dancers to remain in their practice clothes and ordered his stage manager to raise the backdrop and legs to reveal the theater's walls and internal machinery. The simplified setup struck some of them as atypical of Joffrey, who usually prided himself on ballet's contrived illusion. It reminded others of the well-attended preview Robbins's Ballets: U.S.A. had given in New York.[16] Robbins had also worked on a bare, unlit stage with the rigging and brick wall exposed. So the Joffrey dancers interpreted Joffrey's radical esthetic transformation to mean that they, like Ballets: U.S.A., would be dancing before a throng of potential investors. When the program began and they performed an excerpt from every ballet in the repertory, they could make out the silhouettes of only five people in the theater.

"It was spooky because we started dancing and the whole place was deadly silent," said Lawrence Rhodes. "There was no response. We thought there would be a thousand people. There were five. And at the end, Bob said nothing. He was not a great communicator. We didn't know what had happened."[17] The dancers imagined they had failed and modestly slipped back into the routine of preparing for the next ten-week tour, which would commence on January 28, 1962, covering twenty-six states.

It seemed like business as usual, but there was a significant difference: someone new was running Joffrey's life. Edith D'Addario had come to work at the school, answering the phone, taking roll call for the classes, and keeping the books. Her desk was immediately outside Joffrey's office door. She sat scheduling his appointments and protecting him from interruptions. As Joffrey's fierce but benevolent watchdog, she also sometimes made donations to rescue him and the school from financial trouble. Her generosity extended to Joffrey's students; she contributed toward the electricity bills of many teenage scholarship students and often steered them patiently through the terrors of living in New York. Loved and feared (because her adamantine eyes could be most disapproving), she single-handedly organized the American Ballet Center and is probably the reason the school exists today. In late 1961, D'Addario assumed a minor role with the force of a major player, but with her out front, Joffrey's accessibility decreased. New dancers, in particular, now had to satisfy D'Addario's requirements in order to reach him.

For the sold-out tour, Joffrey expanded the company to a ten-member orchestra and twenty dancers. New to the company were Helgi Tomasson and Lone Isaksen, dancers in Denmark and recommended by Erik Bruhn. Tomasson had studied with Vera Volkova and at the School of American Ballet; Isaksen had danced with the Scandinavian Ballet. After Tomasson auditioned, Joffrey played hard to get. He would not give Tomasson the satisfaction of knowing whether or not he had made it into the company until Tomasson's money ran out. At that point, Joffrey offered him a loan, told him he would not be paid for rehearsals, and said he could join the troupe only if he changed his name to Harold. Tomasson reluctantly accepted the conditions.*

---

*On tour in Seattle, where there was a large population of Swedes, Norwegians, and Finns, "Harold" Tomasson opened a telephone book to a standard Scandinavian name, such as Andersen, and showed Joffrey the extensive number of men with the first name of Helgi. Joffrey capitulated. When the next programs were printed, they read "Helgi Tomasson."

After two more years with the Joffrey Ballet and a stint in the Harkness Ballet, Helgi Tomasson would go on to become one of the most elegiac of the New York City Ballet principals and, in 1983, artistic director of the San Francisco Ballet.

In contrast to his dealings with Tomasson, Joffrey pursued Isaksen, calling her on the phone to make certain she auditioned for the company. Isaksen was a dark, ethereal beauty, similar—in many ways that did not go unnoticed by her—to Lisa Bradley.* Both were small-boned, delicate, limber, and seen to their best advantage when being partnered in adagio. From Isaksen there emanated a tenderness that touched her audiences. While Bradley was a mystery, Isaksen had mystery. There was room for both women in the company.

In their first season, Tomasson and Isaksen were offered mostly corps de ballet roles. They were also provided with salaries that, at $65 to $75 a week, were substantially lower than what the Joffrey veterans were earning, and as much as $45 less than what the charter members had received in 1956. Joffrey was continuing to use his familiar cost-cutting measures so that he could amplify the company roster (adding Anna Marie Longtin, Joseph Nelson, and Sandra Ray, and bringing back Vicente Nebrada to the 1962–63 lineup) without escalating expenses.

The most frequently performed ballets on the tour were by Balanchine. "We were bringing *Square Dance* and *Pas de Dix* and *Allegro Brillante* to a lot of places that were seeing Balanchine for the first time," said Joffrey.[18] Jonathan Watts and Brunilda Ruiz led the cast in *Pas de Dix*. Arpino and Rochelle Zide were the principals in *Square Dance,* a ballet new to the repertory that incorporated a live caller (John Wilson) onstage, announcing the patterns as in a real square dance, only here the music was by Vivaldi and Corelli and the steps were balletic.

Another novelty in the season was the pas de deux from August Bournonville's *Flower Festival in Genzano*. Fredbjørn Bjørnsson, a renowned Royal Danish Ballet dancer, had offered a course in the nineteenth-century choreographer's technique at Joffrey's school in the spring and had taught Eleanor D'Antuono and Lawrence Rhodes the pas de deux. In 1962, the Robert Joffrey Ballet was the first American company ever to perform Bournonville, with Rhodes partnering Ruiz.

The formal Joffrey Ballet premieres of Arpino's *Ropes* and *Partita for 4* added more novelty. "By all odds [*Ropes*] was the most exciting new ballet shown here this season," wrote Ann Barzel in the *Chicago American*.[19] The critics in Seattle, however, determined that the "half-theater, half-ballet" piece was dispensable. Arpino experienced his first taste of

---

*On the 1962 tour, Rita Bradley for the first time appeared on the program as Lisa Bradley. She said Joffrey had thought her given name was "too Spanish-sounding," and he wanted something more American. He was still in the mind-set of wanting his audience to identify with the dancers as the kids next door and to take national pride in them. By the late sixties, with the student uprisings, Vietnam protests, and civil rights activism, he changed his attitude and no longer tinkered with names because they were "too ethnic."

being at the center of a small controversy, but at this point he did not yet identify himself as a choreographer.[20] He was still a dancer, although, at thirty-nine, he was pondering retirement from the stage.

On its way back to New York from the West Coast, the company performed on March 30 in Detroit, Michigan, a date and place most of them will always remember. They knew by this time that the five people in the audience for the bizarre audition at the Phoenix Theater had been Harkness, Léon Fokine, Gloria Fokine, Jeannot Cerrone,* and Joffrey. Cerrone was now waiting backstage to speak to the dancers. Joffrey and Arpino had known "Papa" Cerrone since his Ballet Russe days in Seattle, when Cerrone had been the company's assistant director. Cerrone had later joined American Ballet Theatre as its company manager, and at present he was employed by Harkness. The dancers put two and two together and presumed Cerrone was about to give them the glad tidings that they had "won" the audition and were on their way to Spoleto. But to their chagrin, Cerrone announced instead that they were being invited by Harkness to visit her Watch Hill estate that summer for a twelve-week rehearsal period. "Watch Hill? What is Watch Hill?" they asked. "I remember Brunie [Ruiz] and I thinking that we'd be old ladies clicking our false teeth before we ever got to Spoleto," said Françoise Martinet.[21]

Menotti had encouraged the Joffrey troupe to perform in Spoleto, and Harkness agreed to foot the $100,000 bill for transportation and set and costume refurbishment. Menotti and his colleague, the composer Samuel Barber, had seen the Joffrey Ballet on tour. Arpino's *Ropes* had enthralled them, and they persuaded Harkness to back Joffrey and Arpino. Complimented though Joffrey and Arpino were, they asked Harkness to sponsor a choreographers' workshop and paid rehearsal period instead of the Spoleto engagement. She completely understood Joffrey's need to work unencumbered by financial pressure, and she agreed to his proposal, but there was a catch: the workshop could not be in New York. She wanted the choreographers, dancers, composers, and teachers on her sprawling Watch Hill estate facing Rhode Island's Little Narragansett Bay.

Joffrey, Harkness, and members of her foundation board commissioned Arpino, modern dance choreographer Alvin Ailey, Broadway choreographer Donald Saddler, and Canadian ballet choreographers Brian Macdonald and Fernand Nault for the Watch Hill summer. Vera Volkova agreed to teach a course, joining Joffrey and Kai, who taught company class. Mayne Miller and Rachel Chapman were the troupe's pianists.

---

*Jean B. Cerrone's nickname is Jeannot, by which he is widely recognized. Gian Carlo Menotti was not in attendance.

Joffrey would be doing triple duty; he planned for the first time in six years to make a new ballet. He had in the interim produced many opera ballets. One of these was for Verdi's *Aïda* in the fall of 1961. And on June 7, 1962, he would reprise *Aïda* for the Seattle World's Fair, to inaugurate the city's Opera House.

Joffrey cast Françoise Martinet and Arpino as the *Aïda* leads and brought to Seattle for supporting roles James Howell, Suzanne Hammons, Nels Jorgensen, Ruiz, Bradley, Nebrada, and Tomasson. He also employed three dancers with whom he had never before worked: Finis Jhung, Noël Mason, and a nine-year-old prodigy, Francesca Corkle. Corkle had grown up in Joffrey's home city and had been trained by her mother. She was able to do six pirouettes on a dime. Joffrey had watched her progress since she was three and decided she was now ready to leap out of a lotus blossom and astonish the *Aïda* audience with her virtuosity.

Joffrey had also choreographed a difficult lift for Arpino: he was to be carried on a human throne formed by Tomasson and Jhung, who stood at either side of Arpino and hoisted him above their heads by placing one hand under his buttocks. With their other hand, they each clasped one of his. The lift was precarious under any circumstances, but for the Triumphal March, Joffrey wanted Tomasson and Jhung to bear Arpino across the stage and up a precipitous staircase. They were trying out the maneuver in rehearsal and had almost succeeded in climbing the stairs when suddenly Tomasson's shoulder contracted in a spasm. "Come down!" he cried to Arpino.[22] But it was too late. Arpino toppled twenty-five feet down the steps. When he landed on the floor, he couldn't walk.

Both Arpino and Tomasson were rushed to the hospital. Arpino was put in a body brace; he had broken four transverse processes off his lower spine. The fracture missed his spinal column by an eighth of an inch; he had narrowly escaped becoming a paraplegic. As for Tomasson, he had badly strained his shoulder muscles, and his arm required a sling.

Arpino did not return to New York with Joffrey after *Aïda*. Howell stayed behind with him in Seattle to nurse and rehabilitate him. "Bob kept calling and telling me I had to come to Watch Hill," said Arpino. "I kept telling him I was in horrible pain. That's when, in bed, I started to choreograph *Incubus*. The thing that saved my sanity was listening to the [Anton] Webern pieces. I was in love with them, and against doctor's orders, I started to move my head and my arms and tell Jim [Howell] what I saw and how I felt."[23]

By the time Arpino arrived in Watch Hill five weeks later, he had mentally prepared his ballet, *Incubus*. Incredibly, he also started to take class again, and Joffrey cast him in the master-of-ceremonies role for his new ballet, *Gamelan*. Arpino has often said, "That fall became my rise,"[24] marking the accident as the start of his conscious decision to earn the appellation *choreographer*. He approached Lone Isaksen to work with him on *Incubus*, his ballet about a young girl driven mad by internal demons and rejection from her family and lover. With the benefit of hindsight, Arpino said that *Incubus* sprang from his pain, but at the time Isaksen knew nothing about his broken back and did not notice the corset with metal stays that was concealed beneath his sweater. Isaksen was not alone in her unawareness. Arpino, the stoic, told few about the mishap.

For him and Joffrey, an entire summer stretched ahead to concoct ballets. "How often can we dancers and choreographers have the luxury of time, as paradoxical as this may sound, to work hard, really hard? We have time here in Watch Hill . . . to create, time to edit, time to rehearse, and that extra miraculous time that every choreographer and director dreams about, time to do what we call 'clean,' to polish and perfect," proclaimed Joffrey.[25]

On July 6, 1962, Ailey, Macdonald, Saddler, and Nault began arriving in weekly shifts. Joffrey had emphasized to them all that the purpose of Watch Hill was experimentation. Moreover, practically anything they desired (pianos, rosin, tape decks) would be provided on demand by Harkness, who had opened her mansion, called Holiday House (with its seventeen separate apartments, over forty rooms, twenty baths, and eight kitchenettes, and one small studio), to the choreographers and Joffrey for their living quarters. Most of the dancers were housed within walking distance in the resort's town center at the Bay View Guest Apartments; Harkness paid them full union scale, working on an Equity schedule of six hours per day and weekends off. They rehearsed mainly in Watch Hill's old firehouse, which Harkness had appropriated and renovated, raising the roof and transforming the interior into two studios. The local high school auditorium was also on reserve for run-throughs with lights.

Commandeering one studio, Joffrey said he envisioned a Japanese ballet inspired by haiku. He chose a score by Lou Harrison, a polyglot composer, the dean of West Coast composers from California, who was known to put Elizabethan music with Indonesian music with 12-tone music. Harrison's Suite for Violin/Piano and Small Orchestra was strongly influenced by, among other things, the Indonesian Gamelan orchestra. Joffrey chose this piece and titled his ballet *Gamelan*. He asked Isaksen, Bradley, Jorgensen, Sutherland, Watts, and Arpino to be his principal dancers, and when Watts dropped out, he cast Rhodes.

Although some of the dancers were eventually given specific roles (for example, Wind, Bird, and Hunter), *Gamelan* was not a story ballet. It was a kinetic landscape painted against Harrison's formal score that summoned an abstract courtly atmosphere. "I felt that my curiosity about weight and weightlessness, about movement and the physics of movement, was being immensely satisfied," Isaksen recalled of *Gamelan*. "I remember very strongly being more aware than I usually am of the floor beneath me; and more aware than I usually am that the air around me was tangible and I cut through it; and more aware when someone was lifting me that I was floating."[26]

When Alvin Ailey arrived, he launched into preparations for *Feast of Ashes* with principal dancers Martinet, Bradley, and Sutherland. Ailey had never worked with classical dancers, and many of the newer Joffrey members had never learned the modern idiom. *Feast of Ashes* was based on Federico García Lorca's *House of Bernarda Alba* and was accompanied by an arrangement of music by Carlos Surinach, who had written some original pieces specifically for the ballet. Dramatic and fierce, the choreography compelled the players to hide nothing of themselves, and they devoured the experience.

Brian Macdonald had written his own scenario for *Time Out of Mind*. Outlining the idea to Joffrey in a letter, he said, "The work would in no way be vulgar, or even overtly erotic, but would deal with sex, and explore the need of man for woman . . . not simply displaying her, but playing with her, obeying the mating instinct. I hope this description doesn't alarm you. As I said it wouldn't be at all vulgar, the gray-haired grannies at the matinée would love it."[27] More than three decades later, *Time Out of Mind* was still being performed by companies all over the globe. In Watch Hill, Elisabeth Carroll and Rhodes led a large cast to the hard-driving score from Paul Creston. Most of the dancers responded favorably to Macdonald's perceiving them as sexual creatures and quickly came to understand the advantage of working with so many choreographers: each choreographer read them differently.

On the weekends, Harkness invited the company members* to swim in her pool; she threw parties for them and once tucked ten-dollar bills sheathed in tinfoil packets inside a cake to surprise them.[28] She furnished them with a masseur. She rented a bus to transport them to an Alvin Ailey company performance in New London, Connecticut. "We were in heaven," said Isaksen, adding that what was important about the summer was that they were respected as artists. "Not dancers—dancers are workers," she said. "Dancers as artists bring something to the work that the work cannot live without."[29]

They felt irreplaceable. romantic relationships abounded, one of which (Helgi Tomasson and Marlene Rizzo) resulted in marriage. "All

---

*Company members included several new dancers: Lawrence Adams, Elisabeth Carroll, Janet Mitchell, Joseph Nelson, Marlene Rizzo, Felix Smith, and Richard Wagner. Dianne Consoer and Jonathan Watts were also back.

those new ballets that had never been seen before—sometimes dancers involved in that kind of atmosphere are not the best judges of how good the work is itself," Tomasson commented. "But we were not thinking of that so much. We were having our minds opened by the excitement, the enjoyment one gets from being part of the creative process."[30]

Harkness also wanted to partake of the process. Before anyone arrived in Watch Hill, Cerrone had sent a score to Arpino with the request that he consider using it for his next ballet. Arpino rejected the score, not knowing that it had been written by Rebekah Harkness. Joffrey respected his decision and, after discovering the true identity of who had written the music, he sent the score by "R. West" to choreographer Donald Saddler. Saddler was a good friend of Walter Terry's, who was also an integral member of Harkness's entourage. Saddler proposed a story ballet about American children visiting a museum. Inspired by portraits of the nation's leaders, one boy dreams that he is President John Fitzgerald Kennedy. Saddler called it *Dreams of Glory,* and Rhodes was given the JFK role. "It was one of the few times I was really embarrassed to be in a ballet," Rhodes commented. "But we knew it was Harkness's music and thought, 'Okay. This is it. This is the compromise for having this location and the studios.'"[31]

From all appearances, Joffrey did not seem to mind accommodating Harkness. "Bob was happy somebody was doing something for her," said Saddler. "We all got along very well. Harkness was amenable. I had carte blanche to do whatever I wanted."[32]

Aside from *Dreams of Glory,* Harkness was preoccupied with an Arpino ballet. It seemed that Lisa Bradley and Paul Sutherland had not been able to forget about *Sea Shadow* and were rehearsing the pas de deux in their spare time. Harkness had chanced upon them and declared, "That's the most beautiful pas de deux I've ever seen."[33] She insisted that Joffrey allow Arpino to finish the ballet and add it to the repertoire, despite the fact that Arpino lacked proper permission for the Ravel music.

As the cool fall winds blew across Little Narragansett Bay and the leaves turned, all of the choreographers returned to make last-minute changes, and rehearsals ended. Aside from a few trial runs on the Stonington High School stage, the ballets had not been tested in performance. Joffrey and Harkness decided that when the company returned to New York, they would present an informal showing at the Fashion Institute of Technology.

On September 28 and 30, the works-in-progress from the Watch Hill summer were previewed without scenery and costumes. Also included were Arpino's *Sea Shadow* and *Ropes,* and *Roundabout,* the piece Fernand Nault had done at Watch Hill. The audience attended the two programs by special invitation, and the critics, following standard procedure for workshop performances, refrained from writing reviews. (A brief, unsigned rave did appear on the front page of *Dance News,* where P. W. Manchester was managing editor.)

In the next few months, however, *Dance Magazine* paraded the Robert Joffrey Ballet across its cover. The American National Theater and Academy (ANTA) had selected the company to perform a fifteen-week tour of Europe, the Middle East, Southeast and Central Asia, sponsored by the U.S. Department of State and the Rebekah Harkness Foundation. In advance of the Joffrey's departure on December 1, 1962, Adlai E. Stevenson, U.S. ambassador to the United Nations, hosted an extravagant send-off party for the troupe, during which excerpts from the repertory were danced for the U.N. General Assembly delegates.

Interviewed by Walter Terry in the *New York Herald Tribune,* Joffrey told his rags-to-riches story and reminisced about the original vision he had had as a nine-year-old boy of "choreographing a snowflake ballet down a ramp."[34] The hardships of pursuing his childhood dream to have his own company were laid out in melodramatic detail:

> *I was desperate. I had begged and borrowed all I could. The kids [dancers], too, invested in the company. We've all skirted union rules—who hasn't?—because without selfless dedication there would be no dance company in America today.*
>
> *Even our big-business managers helped. They took on responsibilities they didn't have to in order to keep us going. Now, with this support of the Rebekah Harkness Foundation, we'll make the grade. We can even abide by the union rules. . . . This trip is a dream come true.*[35]

Joffrey and Harkness hastily arranged for costumes and scenery for their productions, sparing no expense to hire, among other designers, Karinska, Willa Kim, Jac Venza, and Rouben Ter-Arutunian. For lighting, they enlisted Jean Rosenthal of the New York City Ballet and the Martha Graham Company. Time permitted few rehearsals before the company departed for Lisbon, Portugal, the "gateway" to destinations farther east that included Jordan, Syria, Lebanon, Iran, India, and Joffrey's ancestral home, Afghanistan. But there was time enough for Harkness to dispatch the dancers to Saks Fifth Avenue with strict instructions to "get what they wanted."[36]

Françoise Martinet recalled that when they returned with their purchases, Harkness was disappointed. "We had been careful to buy clothes that were not too expensive, and she had wanted us to buy much better things. I got the feeling she might have traded half of the sixty million dollars to be one of us!"[37]

CHAPTER 13

Ambassadors

From the New York City Ballet's ongoing triumphs in Western Europe and the USSR in the fall and winter of 1962, U.S. government officials had concluded that dance was the most easily grasped and understood American art form in countries whose citizens did not speak English. The Robert Joffrey Ballet had received favorable notices since its inception and had the advantage of Rebekah Harkness's funding, which the State Department felt meant the company would look good because it would have well-made costumes, substantial rehearsal time, and other expenses paid that "enhanced their chances of success abroad."[1]

State Department members expressed to Joffrey that his 1962 winter tour was intended as a peace gesture to convey the idea that "the human body [is] common to all human beings all over the world."[2] Joffrey recognized such a premise as an extraordinary high thought for the government to express about dance. He asked his company members to think of themselves as "ambassadors."[3]

While the Robert Joffrey Ballet's first trip abroad had an external political purpose, it turned out to be, as well, a trip about internal company politics. The tour signaled the end of the Joffrey's troupe as it had been known. The members would grow up, shed naïveté, and come to terms with what it meant to have a Rebekah Harkness. Joffrey faced his motives and economic reality and asked the hard question, "Who owns the artist and whom does the artist owe—and what?"

Harkness was a homebody in many senses, and long-distance travel made her nervous; she often consulted a guru or spiritualist to plan trips. On November 30, she accompanied the company to the airport. In her diary she wrote that night: "See dancers off. [I] come to life when I am with them and wish I were going along. It's [a] life I should have had when young."[4]

With Christmas ahead, Harkness, with her mother, her husband, and her daughter, Edith, flew to their house in Nassau (Bahamas) for an extended vacation. The company had performed three excerpts from her ballet *Dreams of Glory*, choreographed by Saddler, before Adlai Stevenson and the U.N. General Assembly. She had thought they looked "lovely." She said for the first time she felt "right"[5] about her work and was confident about letting the troupe go off without her and her husband. They would rendezvous with Joffrey and company in Teheran, Iran.

Eight dancers, new since the last tour, but most of whom had been in Watch Hill, now bolstered the Joffrey ensemble—Lawrence Adams, Finis Jhung, Karina Rieger, Rosana Seravalli, Felix Smith, June Wilson, Carroll, and Rizzo*—forming his largest troupe so far at forty-five members, including orchestra and stage technicians. Jonathan Watts and Dianne Consoer, who were with the New York City Ballet in Russia, would connect with the troupe by the middle of December. Ted Dale was enlisted as the new musical director, George Bardyguine as technical director, and Rupert Heitzig as stage manager. Manet Seguin returned as wardrobe mistress, and Jack Harpman held his position as the valiant production stage manager.

At Lisbon's Cine-Teatro Tivoli, Saddler's *Dreams of Glory* was consuming most of the rehearsal time. Only a one-act ballet, the production involved fifty costumes and so many set pieces that when the company passed through customs in Portugal, the scale used for weighing theatrical cargo shot twenty thousand pounds past the State Department's limit. *Dreams of Glory* was labeled the culprit by company members, partly in jest and partly in truth. "The more Mrs. Harkness spent on the sets and costumes—we heard some material was forty dollars per yard—the more we lost respect for the ballet," said Françoise Martinet.[6]

Without Saddler present in Lisbon, Joffrey conducted rehearsals for *Dreams of Glory*. At the final dress rehearsal, he ran the ballet from the beginning, starting with Martinet as a White House guide leading a group of tourists across the downstage area and tapping her pointer at portraits of American heroes depicted on the front drop. When the drop rose, a schoolboy (Lawrence Rhodes) and a girl (Lisa Bradley) were asleep in front of a television. The TV announcer said, "And someday you, too, shall be president," prompting the boy to dream of himself as President Kennedy. Delegates from many lands congregated in the Oval Office, tossing a basketball that resembled a globe.

At the rehearsal everything went wrong. Lyndon Johnson's lariat tangled in Lady Bird's feathers; the Statue of Liberty's crown fell off; the jacket buttons of the Spirit of '76 (Paul Sutherland) popped off on the first grand jeté; the ball hit an admiral (John Wilson) hard enough in the stomach to cause the general (Helgi Tomasson) riding on his shoulders to fall facedown on top of the ball on the stage floor—and then the ball bounced into the orchestra pit.

---

*Rochelle Zide sustained an eye injury on the first day of rehearsal in Watch Hill and had to leave the company.

"Stop the ballet!" Sutherland remembered Joffrey shouting, drumming the fingers of one hand on his stomach and twidding a pencil in the fingers of his other. "This ballet is canceled and if anyone asks why, just say that the costumes weren't ready."[7] Joffrey's excuse was partly true, because every seamstress from the San Carlos Opera was working overtime to finish them. But Joffrey had been known to put a show on without costumes before. Said Arpino, "The work was not up to our standard."[8]

Twenty-two days later, Joffrey contacted Harkness through her husband to tell her the ballet had not been danced. In her diary, Harkness recorded the following response:

> Dec. 27, 1962—B. [her husband, Ben] gives me bad news that Dreams of Glory hasn't been done yet—can't decide about trip to Persia—don't get too upset but am irritated with Bob [Joffrey]. . . . Am learning, I hope, not to let things upset me so much. Must learn to be happy even when everything goes wrong.

In 1993, eleven years after her death, Rebekah Harkness's diaries were given to the Dance Collection of the New York Public Library for the Performing Arts by the painter Jasper Johns. Craig Unger did not have access to the diaries before his Harkness biography, called *Blue Blood*, was published in 1988—the year that Joffrey died.

Harkness kept diaries. Joffrey did not. Her irritation with Joffrey, described on December 27, 1962, marked the beginning of the breakdown in their partnership. By March 1964, Harkness and Joffrey would sever all ties in an acrimonious feud that raged mainly in the most visible possible forum—the press. The diaries reveal Joffrey through the prism of Harkness and, most important, show Harkness in her own words. The story they tell is of power-playing at the highest level in New York's cultural milieu. Joffrey was not beyond reproach in his dealings with her and would admit, "I was stubborn."[9] But it has most commonly been presumed that his fall from Harkness's grace happened overnight in one explosion reported by the press. The diaries demonstrate a long buildup. Joffrey was not caught by surprise. The war between patroness and artist ignited with his decision to drop *Dreams of Glory* from the program in Lisbon. With that stroke, Joffrey, who avoided conflict whenever possible, set into motion the process that would eventually undo his first company.

Until the foreign tour, he had yielded to Harkness: he had let her act upon Walter Terry's recommendation of Donald Saddler to choreograph *Dreams of Glory;* he had agreed to her choices of ballets for the Adlai Stevenson dinner; he had supported her request to let Arpino complete *Sea Shadow* and incorporate the finished ballet into the repertoire. "When

Harkness entered our lives, we were very poor," he said. "The dancers were never paid for rehearsals. They took outside jobs. Françoise [Martinet] worked at Schrafft's. Jerry taught. They all did other things."[10] He surrendered to Harkness partly because he could not bear to see his dancers still, after six years, performing work unrelated to dance. But, mostly, he believed that he could outsmart her: provide for his dancers, build up the repertoire, minimize her trespasses, and still hang on to her patronage.

The Lisbon critics were disappointed not to see *Dreams of Glory,* but Joffrey's *Gamelan* had deeply moved its audience on December 6, 1962, and even though the ballet was incomplete (presented without the fifth movement), virtually all three of the city's critics felt certain they had viewed a masterpiece. *Gamelan* inspired lyrical effusion, but Ailey's *Feast of Ashes* and Arpino's *Incubus* sparked standing ovations. Ailey's handling of the Lorca story without "losing the resonance and breaking its dignity," as one critic wrote,[11] was admired because it was felt that the choreographer had found the dance language to match Lorca. The Portuguese had seen little or no modern technique until *Feast* and *Incubus,** and they picked up on the idea that the Robert Joffrey Ballet was a synthesis of ballet and modern. *Incubus* was so popular that Joffrey had it repeated on the final evening in place of *Dreams of Glory.* "Even more violent and dramatic than at the premiere," raved the critic for *Diario Ilustrado,* predicting the company's visit would leave an enduring mark on Portuguese choreographers and dancers.[12]

By December 14, the company had performed three times in Amman, Jordan, where ballet had never before been seen. King Hussein had invited the dancers to a reception at his palace and personally opened the door. Soon thereafter, in the West Bank cities of Ramallah and East Jerusalem, the company had offered a lecture-demonstration and performances. The Joffrey ensemble then toured the Garden of Gethsemane and the Old City. The U.S. State Department wrote in its evaluation that the so-called dean of the Jordanian press "in midst of taking broad editorial swipes at American policy in the Middle East . . . felt himself constrained to say that . . . [the Joffrey Ballet] was able to win the sympathy of the Arab audience." The report added, "We have heard literally nothing but praise for the entire company as artists and people. . . . If the Department on occasion has doubted the wisdom of its presentations program, the Joffrey Ballet should reassure it that the program has a significant role and purpose."[13]

In Damascus, Syria, the company gave three performances, then trav-

---

*In 1962, Alvin Ailey's own company was touring Southeast Asia under the auspices of the State Department.

eled to Beirut, Lebanon, where it resided and performed in a casino resort that within a matter of years would be leveled by war. "Lebanon has seen some of the finest ballet from France, England and even Russia, but no audience ever thrilled to a ballet troupe as at the opening of the Robert Joffrey Ballet," remarked a local critic.[14]

By the time Harkness and her husband united with the company in Teheran, Joffrey and his dancers were brimming with a sense of accomplishment. Harkness noted in her diary that the dancers "seemed really glad to see me." But Joffrey? She wrote: "Bob avoiding me because of 'Dreams' not being done in Lisbon."[15]

Harkness's diaries disclose that although she was crestfallen about *Dreams of Glory*, she minded more that her name was left out of the Teheran newspapers, and she blamed Joffrey for the oversight. The game she played with him concerned whose name appeared where, and how big. Who got the most credit for the company, she who had refurbished it and cosponsored the tour, or he whose name was in the company title?

He matched her tactic for tactic, blow for blow, but his methods were entirely passive. In Teheran, he steered clear of her by going shopping; his consumerism knew few bounds. He bought rugs, tapestries, masks, and artifacts and stashed them in the costume trunks. (The dancers learned to unpack their tutus at peril of dropping a hidden Joffrey treasure.) He rationalized that the full production of *Dreams of Glory* would soon have its tour debut in Kabul, Afghanistan, and the ballet would speak for itself. He thought Harkness would understand his Lisbon decision when she saw the full ballet.

On January 11, the company's sets and costumes were transported to the Teheran airport in preparation for the next day's journey to Kabul. But that afternoon, Shah Mohammad Reza Pahlavi of Iran requested that the company stay an extra day to give him and the Empress Farah Diba a command performance. Joffrey naturally accepted the Shah's invitation and retrieved from the airport *Pas des Déesses, Sea Shadow,* and *La Fille mal gardée;* the theater's front-row seats were removed and in their place Persian carpets laid down and ornate armchairs installed for the royal members and their new friends, Dr. and Mrs. Benjamin Kean.

The next week on a free day in Afghanistan, an event occurred that symbolized the end of the original Robert Joffrey Ballet. The company was invited to attend a children's dance-school recital held in their honor in Kabul. Joffrey and most of his dancers went. The program inspired him to promise to return later that evening with ten dancers and a program of ballet basics; the children were clearly struggling to find out everything they could about ballet. When Joffrey's members returned, they flung open the doors to the 250-seat assembly hall, expecting to find the same few children who had barely occupied the space earlier, and discovered an audience of five hundred people, young and old, women and men, who had been waiting for one hour.

Rupert Heitzig recorded the event that followed, bearing in mind that until 1959 Afghan women in Kabul were pressured to conceal themselves from everybody except close relatives in the traditional *chador* (a full-length, heel-to-head garment).

> *The entire crowd of people rose and applauded the dancers as they filed through the audience and self-consciously threaded their way to the front of the room, where a small platform had been sectioned off. A piece of flimsy black cloth was drawn across it, cutting it off from the rest of the area. The dancers shyly shed their outer clothing. When they were ready, the black cloth was pulled back, and ten dancers in practice clothes were revealed to the anxious crowd.*
>
> *There was a gasp, complete silence, a suppressed giggle or two and then—thunderous applause.*[16]

Joffrey led the dancers through their paces at the barre, explaining ballet's academic positions through an interpreter. Then, because the situation warranted a greater performance, the youthful idealists who had cut their teeth pioneering ballet in small American towns started dancing as the spirit moved. Brunilda Ruiz improvised a mambo with her husband, John Wilson, playing on an Afghan skin drum. Wilson, once the company's resident court jester, concocted two pantomime numbers for the kids. Nels Jorgensen, shy, noble, and the quintessential Joffrey male partner, danced his variation from *Pas des Déesses,* while backstage Joffrey readied the girls for a waltz from *La Fille mal gardée.* Then, with only Heitzig on a violin, the entire company brought the evening to a climactic finish with Balanchine's *Square Dance*—a ballet that was not in the repertoire at the time, but which spontaneously emerged in the rightness of the moment.

Nobody said a word afterward. Joffrey and the dancers left the hall, where there had been no reporters, no government officials, no publicists, no managers, and no photographers. "All of us felt that if nothing else happened on tour, our company, the Harkness Foundation, the State Department, or whoever was responsible for that single hour," wrote Heitzig, "had given us each something unforgettable, thrilling and more meaningful than anything we could have imagined."[17] It would not be until several years later that the Kabul experience would be seen as the last gasp of innocence for the company as a body. "Bob would never again connect with us as a group in this way," said Paul Sutherland.[18]

From Kabul, where *Dreams of Glory* was performed without remark from Harkness, the company toured India for almost eight weeks. It danced on a stage specially built over a pool, on the surface of which flowers and candles floated to honor the inauguration of the American embassy in New Delhi for Ambassador John Kenneth Galbraith and his wife, Catherine. During the Galbraiths' reception, Joffrey and the dancers met Prime Minister Nehru and Indira Gandhi, his daughter. Joffrey was approached by the Soviet ambassador, who said he enjoyed the company so much, he wanted to bring it to the USSR. "I said, 'Oh, how nice,' " remembered Joffrey. " 'We would love to go to Russia'—and all of a sudden, he called, and we *were* invited to Russia."[19] The Robert Joffrey Ballet was the first troupe whose presence was requested in such an informal manner by the Soviets; in the past, American companies had only been sent by special arrangement with the U.S. State Department. If the Joffrey's engagement came through, the occasion would be historic.

In New Delhi, *Dreams of Glory* was performed for the second time since its premiere in Kabul. "Music sounds horrible," wrote Harkness in her diary on January 26, 1963. "Am depressed and confused by it all." Four days later, the composer noted that she met with Joffrey and Arpino to "discuss ideas to re-do *Dreams.*" She wanted Arpino to jump in as a choreographer and save the ballet, even though Donald Saddler was the ballet's original choreographer. Arpino remembered trying to explain the ethics of the situation to Harkness and her husband simply:

"I took them one day and I said, 'Look, Dr. Kean, you have a patient and you are treating him, and the patient brings in another doctor who wants to counteract all your treatments. You know that will injure the patient. You will not permit it. Or, it would be like if Picasso painted a painting, and you bought it and you didn't like some of the colors, and you asked another painter to alter the work. You just don't do it. So, too, a choreographer does not go into another choreographer's work. I can't possibly change Saddler's ballet."[20]

Harkness persisted and as a compromise Arpino agreed to consider her suggestion for a new ballet. The piece would be based on vaudeville and would be called *The Palace,* with music by Harkness. Arpino convinced her to structure the piece as a work that could be choreographed to easily by committee. Then she would have more than one person to blame or praise.

By the time Harkness had accepted *Dreams of Glory* as a failure, Arpino and Joffrey had perfected their routine of dividing their duties with her, according to their strengths and inclinations. They were perceived by her to be a team, because they acted, worked, and lived in New York as a team. Arpino, as Harkness once wrote, "fixes everything."[21] He was more apt to take her complaints seriously and bend over backward to accommodate her, whether it was getting her hotel room changed or explaining the artists' ethical code. Joffrey was the director, and, for the moment, Harkness acted as though she respected his opinion. She eagerly sought his affirmation; she cared what he thought. But Joffrey had grown to believe that it was in his best interests to keep her at arm's length, both fearful of him and conciliatory toward him. "He did not want her intruding in his affairs," remarked Arpino.[22]

On March 7, the company concluded the tour with a performance in Calcutta. When Joffrey returned to New York, he did not call, write, or acknowledge to Donald Saddler anything about *Dreams of Glory*. Months later, when Saddler showed up unexpectedly in Watch Hill with Walter Terry, Harkness noted in her diary that "having Don appear is like having a cast-off lover showing up. More moral, but no less embarrassing."[23] But while Harkness confided to Saddler that she had originally been furious with Joffrey for not giving the ballet its premiere in Lisbon, Joffrey never told Saddler anything. "Not a word of thanks," said Saddler later.[24]

Immediately after the tour, in fact, Joffrey and Harkness were probably the most unified they would ever be. He arranged private ballet lessons for her (something he did only for people in whom he had faith). On April 10, she wrote about his classes: "I learn more than ever did before. Am always ahead of the music and not in the 'now.' Off rhythmically—also in life." The next day: "Bob notices how different I am—can talk to him quite freely."

After Joffrey returned from the tour, he started meditating again. He had initially learned to meditate not only through the Seattle public school system, which had mandated a three-minute period of meditation at the beginning of each day at Summit Elementary, but from Mary Ann Wells and the I AM, and from his father. His spiritual background was a mishmash of faiths—Christian from his mother, Muslim from his father, New Age from Wells—and the ideologies he actually applied to himself were unclear. Sometimes he seemed to be more of one faith than another; when he was in the New York University Hospital on his deathbed, he was asked his religion and replied, "Catholic." "But when a Catholic priest came, Bob did not want to have his last rites," said Joffrey's colleague Rima Corben. "I don't know whether that is because he was troubled by the Catholic part or because he did not want to think he was going to die. He didn't talk about it. His spirituality was very complicated."[25]

Most of Joffrey's friends were certain that throughout his life he believed in reincarnation, and they observed that he repeatedly returned to the discipline of meditation. "Joffrey loved India. He was absolutely enamored of India. The weeks there deeply affected him," observed Alex Ewing.[26] Ravi Shankar had invited the company to his house and played sitar for them until four in the morning; Joffrey was transported. In 1963, he was immersed in an Eastern-religion phase (which culminated in his 1967 ballet, *Astarte*), and so was Rebekah Harkness.

Harkness had been practicing yoga almost every day for over a year; her husband nicknamed her Karma. "It means that you are the sum total of your past," she had said proudly.[27] She also performed trance meditations and dabbled in psychic activities, such as palm reading, séances, and the Ouija board. In New Delhi she had made it a point to contact masters and be taught yoga by them. Curiously, she wrote more in her diaries about yoga than she did about ballet, she read more about yoga than she did about ballet. She gossiped less about yoga and her gurus, however, than she did about ballet and the New York scene.

It is possible Joffrey picked up on Harkness's sincerity for yoga and, as a teacher, saw an opportunity to connect and bring Harkness into the fold, so to speak, making her understand that the relationship between the body, the mind, and life is as comprehensible and meaningful in ballet as it is in yoga. "He thought she could be taught," said Arpino. "And he tried."[28] Teaching was Joffrey's purest activity. To him ballet's discipline was the great leveler; he knew he could situate Harkness on the same plane as himself in his classroom, where they would be able to be partners—on his terms.

CHAPTER 14

Treachery at Watch Hill

Joffrey escorted Harkness to the important dance events in town. They attended the Dance Magazine Awards, London's Royal Ballet at the Metropolitan Opera House, and Juilliard's spring program (specifically for the work of Anna Sokolow, a choreographer Joffrey admired and whom he was contemplating asking to make a piece for his troupe). "A little disappointed in Sokolow," wrote Harkness that night,[1] although she seems to have said nothing to dampen Joffrey's enthusiasm. Their rapport was formal, polite, cheerful, mechanical. In many senses, they were still getting to know each other, perhaps more hesitantly than at first; they had already tried each other's mettle.

On May 13, 1963, Harkness and her husband presided over an extravagant welcome-home party at their Westbury Hotel penthouse in Manhattan to honor the Robert Joffrey Ballet's return from the U.S. State Department tour and the Royal Ballet's return to the Met. The guest list included almost every choreographer, composer, and dancer of note from the fields of modern dance and ballet. Many New York critics, teachers, and arts administrators were also invited, in addition to the whole Royal Ballet and Robert Joffrey Ballet. Harkness spent days preparing for the event, and her diaries reveal that she wondered, as she expended herself on Joffrey's behalf, if he was an opportunist. Her husband, Ben, had planted the first potent seed of doubt. Wrote Harkness: "Bob pushing too much Ben says"[2] and "Ben picks on Bob—not too much tho."[3]

Harkness soon concluded that her husband was jealous of the attention she was lavishing on Joffrey, and then she instantly worried that she was losing her husband. By the night of her gala affair, Harkness was convinced that the whole ballet world was duping her. She acknowledged that it had been a grave mistake to strive for fame as a composer instead of settling for wife and mother.

This was the great divide in her life. She loved ballet mostly because there was no place for motherhood in it, she said. The women were not supposed to have bosoms, they were not to suggest maternity on any level. Harkness had three children, one of whom at the age of twelve had thrown herself from the fifteenth floor of the Westbury Hotel and been spared from death by an awning that caught her. Harkness struggled during this period to detach herself from anything or anybody, including her children, that robbed attention from her work as a composer and ballet patroness. She cast herself as a professional artist, and as such, she abided by the rule that work and the discipline of daily practice at the piano, writing scores for Joffrey and Arpino, took precedence over her children and husband. She acted on these choices with tremendous feelings of doubt and guilt. She suffered from moral conflict, turning with increasing frequency over the years to antidepressants and cult leaders, anything that promised to provide her with a sense of wholeness.

There was in the party's atmosphere an intoxicating tang of romantic sophistication that emanated from Margot Fonteyn and Rudolf Nureyev. Their partnership was new, and in their presence everybody was filled with an unembarrassed sense of awe. The joy and comradery that stole over most of Harkness's esteemed guests was also derived, in part, from the sudden awareness that their art had been discovered by people beyond the small band of the world's balletomanes. Dance was booming—and everybody was giddy.

Harkness focused her attention upon George Balanchine and Frederick Ashton—Balanchine because his absence was a glaring insult to her, and Ashton because he made an innocent statement to the wrong person.

Ashton, now the artistic director and choreographer of the Royal Ballet, had a conversation during the evening with someone named Sam in Harkness's diaries—possibly Samuel Barber, the composer and a member of Harkness's entourage. According to Harkness, Sam said that Ashton told him:

> He hears Bob [Joffrey] has to use my music. Sam straightens Ashton out. I am tired and upset over this but decided to hell w/ them—they're god damn lucky to get the music—Fed up with people, but a few are coming on my side. . . . Brings up doubts in my mind and guilts about work in regards to children.[4]

Harkness ultimately blamed Joffrey that Ashton had misunderstood; she was certain that he had fed Ashton the line. Ashton had, of course, told the truth, which was self-evident to most people. The limitations of Harkness's talent were abundantly clear, as were her methods of strong-arming choreographers into using her scores. In the past she had tried with Jerome Robbins, and she had also offered Balanchine a handsome sum of money to choreograph to her compositions. Both men had turned her down. She had a similar history within the music industry: Ella Fitzgerald had been asked by Harkness if she would record some of Harkness's pop songs for pay, and Fitzgerald had rejected the proposition.

A preoccupation with forcing people to choose sides influenced Harkness from May 13 forward; she saw the dance world as cleaved neatly and uncompromisingly between those who were for her and those who were against her. In the spirit of such simplistic thinking, Joffrey was cast into the camp with Balanchine. Balanchine had snubbed the party, and Harkness scribbled in her diary that same night, on May 13: "Dying to revenge Balanchine but feel it's wrong approach." Balanchine and Joffrey were her simultaneous targets, yet the two could not have been further apart: Joffrey depended on Harkness, Balanchine had nothing to do with her.

In the early sixties, when government was chugging toward formal support of the artist but the National Endowment for the Arts had not yet been established and private foundations were gleaning evidence that American dance was worth their attention, the Harkness diaries above all show us how vulnerable was the artist who had no money. An artist without funding, sponsorship, or grants had limited exposure. To be seen, to be appreciated directly, resulted from the personalities and cash behind you. If the measure of art in America was money, then a dilettante such as Harkness could buy herself in. She could play against Balanchine and Kirstein; she could pay off Joffrey.

As for Joffrey, he was almost childlike and insensitive to the growing role of money in the American performing arts; his value system collided with Harkness, and he failed to judge her character properly and to comprehend the game. He did not understand that his company, just because he had dreamed it up and created it, was not beyond anyone's reach to purchase. He used Harkness's music, he let her pay for his dancers' clothing, he accepted her limousine driver to ferry him around the city, he listened to her ideas about repertoire, and he was completely unprepared to compensate her. On some fundamental level, he felt Harkness's patronage was his inalienable right and that she was to him as Chase was to American Ballet Theatre and Kirstein was to the New York City Ballet.

On May 29, Harkness accomplished her first aggressive move to dominate Joffrey's enterprise. She held a meeting with Anthony A. Bliss, general director of the Metropolitan Opera Company, to discuss merging Joffrey's school with the Met's school, then directed by Alicia Markova. Joffrey was not in attendance and would not have been, because his school, as far as he was concerned, was strictly off-limits to Harkness. He did not know that she had ever given his school any thought. Wrote Harkness:

May 29, 1963: Lee [Hoiby, the composer and Harkness's teacher] says people don't believe I write music myself—decide not to brood over anything, let them think what they will.

> *Meeting Bliss—discuss merger of schools—Bob and Marcova* [sic]*—say what I think about Balanchine. Budget with Bob—Ben difficult with them but they must realize what they spend.*

The future imperative for the Robert Joffrey Ballet was to produce more ballets on a grander scale for a wider audience. Several important people had high expectations for the company; Joffrey knew it. The members of the Soviet Ministry of Culture were still interested in having the company tour the USSR in the late fall, but there was a hitch—as yet, Joffrey's company had not publicly performed in New York City. The Soviet cultural attachés wanted to see the troupe for themselves. So did Sol Hurok, the impresario, who had cosponsored the New York City Ballet's USSR tour in 1962 and was thinking of similarly supporting the Joffrey in 1963 if the troupe went to the USSR. Then there was W. McNeil Lowry, director of the Ford Foundation's Humanities and Arts Program. He was spearheading a project to finance dance. He wanted to meet with Joffrey and Harkness. And William Schuman, president of Lincoln Center, had told Harkness that he was interested in presenting Joffrey's company at Lincoln Center and had suggested to Harkness the possibility of housing the troupe there in the small concert hall.

Still unaware that Harkness bore him any ill will, yet sensitive to these new expectations, Joffrey proposed to her that they tackle the production of no less than seven new ballets at Watch Hill the following summer. He wanted some big names, and she agreed. He contacted Kenneth MacMillan at the Royal Ballet, who met with Harkness and told her he was "very interested."[5] Joffrey wrote to Erik Bruhn, sending along recordings of Vittorio Rieti's *Chess Serenade* and *New Waltzes,* advising that Rieti was willing to orchestrate the scores. It was an invitation that Bruhn could not refuse, and he agreed to spend the summer at Watch Hill. Anna Sokolow, Brian Macdonald, and E. Virginia Williams were also engaged by Joffrey, with Harkness's consent, to choreograph. Arpino had already started work on *The Palace,* and Joffrey planned for a new ballet called *The Zodiac,* commissioning Carlos Surinach to compose an original score.

Seven new company members came to Watch Hill: Nancy Fenster, James Howell,* Noël Mason, Margaret Mercier, Christine Sarry, Burton Taylor, and Robert Vickrey. Stanley Williams, who had taught at Balanchine's School of American Ballet, presided over Joffrey's faculty, and the dancers profited from his exceptional abilities as an instructor, particularly of men. Joffrey had summoned Williams from his native Denmark that summer with plans to ask him to serve as the company's next ballet master. The lineup of dancers, choreographers, and instructors was impressive.

---

*Howell had been Arpino's assistant and danced in Arpino's concert, but this was the first time he was a member of the Joffrey Ballet.

In the meantime, Harkness allied herself with William Schuman of Lincoln Center. She was under the impression that she was hatching with him a mutually agreed upon plot to oust Balanchine from Lincoln Center and fill the vacancy with her company, which, if it was to be the Robert Joffrey Ballet, was perhaps "too small and maybe too modern" for Lincoln Center.[6] She wrote:

June 4, 1963: Meeting Wm. Schulman [sic]. Fantastic wants us to run dance co. at Lincoln Center starting in 1966 after he gets rid of Balanchine whom he really dislikes. Says I'm not chairman type & would Ben do that part for me—Expressed most of my ideas for a dance co. . . . He seems an organized happy man & good administrator which I told him I am not.

Several days later, W. McNeil Lowry of the Ford Foundation presented Harkness with an offer to help support Joffrey's school.

June 13, 1963: Meeting Lowry of Ford Foundation—big disagreement over Balanchine—Bob would only get $30,000 a year from them [Ford Foundation] for 10 years for his school.

B [Ben] tells me trick Bob pulled about budget & contract. They really are trying to put one over on us, but I don't care that much & unless they behave there will be no opening [possibly a reference to the Joffrey Ballet's New York City debut, which was being planned for the fall of '63 in Central Park, cosponsored by Harkness and the New York Shakespeare Festival].

Harkness rejected Lowry's offer on the grounds that she was supporting Joffrey and "one foundation was enough."[7] Her remarks about Balanchine, if they were spoken in Joffrey's presence, probably chilled his blood. Joffrey esteemed Balanchine utterly, as did Lowry, who would throw the Ford Foundation's considerable weight behind Balanchine later that year.

After Harkness spurned Lowry, the thought dawned on Joffrey and Arpino that she might not have their best interests in mind. If she had enough money to tell Lowry to withdraw, then why didn't she have enough to stop pestering Joffrey about what the company was costing? They came to realize that her disagreements with them were personal and political rather than financial.

In the June 13 diary entry, Harkness accused Joffrey and his business manager, Alex Ewing, of attempting to "trick" her and Kean. When asked three decades later if such was the case, Ewing explained that Harkness often misconstrued their actions, or rather their lack of action, as deliberate attempts to oppose her, when, in fact, the problem for Joffrey, Arpino, and Ewing was that they were simply unsophisticated about the company's business practices. The accounts were still being kept in the proverbial shoe box; Harkness was frustrated by Joffrey's and Ewing's inability to measure up to Wall Street and Madison Avenue. "Bob wasn't used to accounting formally, which is what Harkness's accountants and lawyers wanted. I had been hired as Bob's business manager, and even I wasn't prepared," said Ewing. "And so, there was not much of the easier Greenwich Village bohemian life anymore. Suddenly it was a bigger company and we were getting involved with designers and composers. There was no relaxing; if anything there was intensification."[8]

Harkness's suspicions increased that Joffrey and Arpino were vengeful. She seems to have thought more seriously about starting a company of her own from scratch. She wrote in Watch Hill, where most of the company had assembled to rehearse:

June 14, 1963: Am just as much of an artist as Bob. Suddenly feel surer of myself.

June 16, 1963: Decide I want ballet co. with school, company and theatre of about 25–30 people.

The summer had so far been disappointing to Joffrey: both MacMillan and Bruhn had been unable to participate. "It's a good feeling to feel wanted," Bruhn had written to Joffrey three days before he was supposed to show up in Watch Hill, saying he had opted for a restful vacation in Denmark instead. He added, "One day I feel we will get together. . . . I am sure you understand, though as a director you must keep things going, and even as a friend."[9]

The dancers were disillusioned because Joffrey was nowhere to be found on the premises. Stanley Williams had replaced him, teaching company class. Paul Sutherland recalled seeing Joffrey once lying on a chaise longue by the pool with the Surinach score on his lap and eyes shut. Otherwise he seemed to spend more time in New York than in Watch Hill. "We thought he had given up," commented Lawrence Rhodes.[10]

The dancers were also, in Sutherland's words, not as "handpicked" by Joffrey as they had once been.[11] Harkness had weighed in with her opinions at the company auditions. Company morale ebbed. Dianne Consoer was pregnant and out. Françoise Martinet planned to leave. The old guard, including Jonathan Watts, did not see the point of dancing for Joffrey when he withdrew from them for days on end. Other peculiar events had occurred that exacerbated their disaffection. Howell, Arpino's unofficial musical assistant, had been hired as a dancer. " 'You say that we're all equal,' " Sutherland exclaimed to Joffrey, " 'but some of us are more equal than others. James Howell can't dance. He's about how to succeed in ballet without really trying. You know, he's improved—when he does a sauté in first position his toes are almost a foot off the ground; of course his heels are, too. How can you hire him along with the rest of us?'

"In a sense Mrs. Harkness corrupted Bob," continued Sutherland, "in the sense that Bob was seduced by the trappings of power. He had always had a houseboy. He never learned to drive a car. We, the dancers, had done a lot of things for him. There was always somebody to get his shirts from the laundry, to drive him around."[12] But when Harkness entered the company, the dancers felt Joffrey's self-aggrandizement to be more acutely at their expense. He rode in limousines, they in subways; he stocked up on fashions from Bloomingdale's, they dressed in the same clothes they'd had for years. Some thought he had forgotten who he was, forgotten where he had come from.

With the exception of Howell, the caliber of dancer that Joffrey now attracted was extraordinary, and those who had been with him for a while were, as they say in dance parlance, ready to go beyond technique. They could transcend the skin; enhance, explore, and change perceptions of the commonplace through movement. They had matured into a special breed of artist. Why did Joffrey seem so uninterested in them?

For answers, they collected evidence from the trail Joffrey left as he prepared for Watch Hill. He had, for example, kept Helgi Tomasson waiting outside his office for two hours while he went through photographs inside, before telling Tomasson at their scheduled meeting that he would indeed renew his contract. He treated Lawrence Rhodes with similar condescension. Yet, when sixteen-year old Noël Mason came on board from Tacoma, Washington, Joffrey met her at the airport at five-thirty in the morning in a limousine, then gave his youngest company member a personal tour of the Village, and later continually verified that she was happily settled into her new apartment. Was his problem that he felt threatened by mature, responsible classical dancers? He panicked, procrastinated, and was often discourteous to dancers who had graduated beyond the student stage.

"Bob had great difficulty dealing with dancers as individual artists," said Sutherland. "He could deal with you if you were a student, but Bob could not have had a company that was a bunch of dancers with mature minds. He wanted you to be very obedient. By keeping Helgi waiting, he was controlling him. That behavior was always there, it just didn't manifest itself until Bob got into a situation where the company was getting bigger."[13]

By late June, Harkness, delighted with the choreographic direction Arpino was supplying her music for *The Palace*, decided that she wanted Arpino to direct the mythical company she was arranging for William Schuman at Lincoln Center. Then, she received a threat from her husband that caused her to lose her equilibrium. She wrote:

June 23, 1963: B. [Ben] says he'll have no more to do with the ballet [company] if I put it on without Palace a success. I wish I knew who was right and then I could act on what I believe. As it is there is always conflict and I go from side to side depending on person I'm with.

Understanding that her future in ballet depended on *The Palace,* Harkness in the next weeks intensified her friendship with Arpino and Howell, inviting them to her Holiday House for dinner.

By early July, Joffrey was spending most of his time with Anna Sokolow, while she worked on *Perspectives,*[14] her first piece ever for classically trained dancers, to a score commissioned from Teo Macero, a jazz composer and frequent Sokolow collaborator. Joffrey revered Sokolow, and as his respect for her became increasingly apparent, Harkness asserted herself as Sokolow's adversary.

Sokolow did not flinch. She did not compromise, nor did her strong, socially aware choreography.

Harkness eyed Sokolow coldly, simultaneously despising and envying her.

July 15, 1963: . . . Anna Sokolow old and ugly as she is has a 28 year old lover who has been in her room for 2 days . . . worry that her ballet isn't technical enough.

July 20, 1963: . . . Anna's ballet irritates me—decide not to do it—should have realized after Juilliard performance what it would be like.

Harkness paraded her sentiments before Joffrey. "Anna had done a wonderful ballet for us . . . and Rebekah saw it and didn't like it at all," he remembered. "She said, 'You can't do that ballet. It's morbid. Dark. You must ask her to leave.'

"I said, 'I can't ask her to leave.'

" 'The ballet's finished—pay her off and get rid of her.' "[15]

Instead, Joffrey himself left Watch Hill on an expedition to corral some of the nation's critics to see Sokolow's work in rehearsal. He hoped the acclaim of these critics would convince Harkness that *Perspectives* was the masterpiece he believed.* Ann Barzel flew in from Chicago. Walter Terry dashed up from New York with Walter Sorell, Sokolow's friend and a dance writer. Harkness noted their arrivals, and she also took advantage of Joffrey's disappearance:

---

*His father, Joseph Joffrey, also paid a visit to Watch Hill. He had retired in 1959 and sold his Joe's Tavern & Restaurant on Pine Street in Seattle. Needing some surgery on his left eye, he had come on his son's advisement to New York City to have the operation. He recuperated at Watch Hill, where his son was pleased to show off his improved circumstances.

July 28, 1963: Bob returns [to Watch Hill] Redhaired critic [Ann Barzel] from Chicago arrives.

August 1, 1963: Bob calls from Miami having never told me he was going.

August 2, 1963: Tell Cerrone no more rehearsals of Sokolow's ballet. It's about time I gave a few orders.

August 8, 1963: Bob comes [to Watch Hill]. . . . Walter Sorrell [sic], critic, interviews me. . . . He wants to see Sokolow ballet.

August 10, 1963: Walter Terry & Don Saddler arrive.

August 11, 1963: Run through [sic] at firehouse—Sokolow's impossible.

No one was more sacrosanct in Joffrey's view than the choreographer. He did not let Sokolow know that Harkness objected to her work; he gave her every reason to believe that her presence at Watch Hill was his honor. Years later, when asked, Sokolow said, "Rebekah never talked to me about *Perspectives*. She was a strange woman. . . . Bob Joffrey treated me beautifully, and Gerald Arpino and I had a nice rapport, too."[16]

Recalling the experience, Arpino said, "Anna Sokolow—that was the first violation that Rebekah did. That bothered Bob tremendously. That was the beginning of it. Bob could never forgive you if you violated his artistic standards. That was one thing about Bob. He would harbor it. Keep it. Never forgive that."[17]

Shortly after the critics had visited, Harkness entertained William Schuman and his wife, and she wrote:

August 16, 1963: Schulmans [sic] arrive. We get along fine—he's very complimentary & says [I] work like a professional. Likes company & asks us to perform at Lincoln Center.

By summer's end, only three of the originally proposed seven ballets had been made: Arpino's *The Palace*, E. Virginia Williams's *Patterns*, and Brian Macdonald's *Caprices*. Harkness apparently did not share with either Joffrey or Arpino her news that the company was going to perform at Lincoln Center. Her negotiations with Schuman undisclosed to them, she plotted for the launching of a new company, one only tenuously related to the Robert Joffrey Ballet. In her mind, therefore, perhaps she had already dismissed Joffrey; Arpino's worth to her would depend on *The Palace*.

On September 5 and 6, the Robert Joffrey Ballet was presented for the first time to the Manhattan public. The long-awaited debut was held on a Ballet Gala program that was part of a weeklong dance festival cosponsored and produced by the Rebekah Harkness Foundation and Joseph Papp's New York Shakespeare Festival, with cooperation and financial support from the city. The dance festival had been conceived the year before as a way to fill Central Park's Delacorte Theatre on "dark" nights by offering free admission. People had only to stand in line in the afternoon to obtain tickets, then return in the evening to see some of the most distinguished dance artists in America. On the Joffrey's first night, the company shared the bill with Edward Villella, Violette Verdy, Oleg Briansky, Patricia Wilde, and American Ballet Theatre. The box office queue trailed off the asphalt path and across the meadow. This was the dawning of the arts-are-for-everyone period, as the government collaborated with private citizens and foundations to make the arts accessible. *Life* and *Time* magazines carried full stories and photo spreads.

Arpino's *Partita for 4* and *Sea Shadow,* and the world premiere of Brian Macdonald's *Time Out of Mind,* introduced the troupe to New York. The last named was presented in practice clothes because the Rouben Ter-Arutunian costumes weren't ready. Joffrey clearly lacked confidence in the new ballets produced at Watch Hill since not one was featured on this auspicious occasion. "Judged on the basis of its performances in the 'Gala,' the Joffrey company must be accounted a major addition to the American ballet world," reported Allen Hughes (John Martin's successor) in the *New York Times.*[18]

But it was *Time Out of Mind* with Margaret Mercier and Lawrence Rhodes in the leading roles that brought down the house, and Jacqueline Maskey, writing for *Dance Magazine,* broached the possibility that the ballet represented a dramatic shift in the Joffrey Ballet's esthetic. *Time Out of Mind,* in fact, was the first in a long line of overtly sexual ballets of questionable taste. Maskey described it:

> *An orgy of predatory sex, mercilessly animated by animal appetite, it drew a sharp performance from the Joffrey troupe, usually more noted for its genteel classicism than its grasp of earthier dance styles. . . . Mr. Macdonald showed a truly remarkable ability to sustain without faltering an intense action level.*[19]

Having announced before the Central Park debut that the company would tour the Soviet Union for nine weeks, Joffrey and Harkness stood as open targets for those concerned about American image. "Since this is definitely a junior scale company, with neither great stars nor great choreographic works, with the exception of *Time Out of Mind,* many of us in the American dance field," wrote Arthur Todd in *Dance and Dancers,* "are concerned over its effect on Russian audiences so recently exposed to the historic triumphs made in the USSR by the New York City Ballet."[20]

In addition to the Russian tour, the company had also been asked by President and Mrs. Kennedy to perform at the White House in October for their guest Haile Selassie, the Ethiopian emperor. Both of these invitations subjected the company's repertoire to acute scrutiny. Hardly a day passed without either Sergei Shashkine, head of Goskoncert, the USSR's official booking agency in New York, or someone named Mr. Wolf from the White House, auditioning the troupe. Their purpose was to choose the repertoire for their respective occasions.

Both Shashkine and Wolf instantly eliminated Arpino's *Incubus* from their programs because they thought Webern's twelve-tone score was too difficult for their audiences to listen to with pleasure. Shashkine also objected to the religious symbolism in the ballet, an excuse he likewise applied to Alvin Ailey's *Feast of Ashes,* rejecting that ballet as well. Upon hearing the objections, however, Ailey agreed to eliminate the crucifixes and other Christian symbols. On the other hand, Arpino refused to alter *Incubus.* Joffrey supported Arpino, whereupon Harkness informed them that she had never been fond of *Incubus.* Joffrey interpreted this comment to mean that she was now turning against Arpino, and he threatened Harkness with the possibility that Arpino would quit.

Harkness recorded Joffrey's reactions:

September 6, 1963: . . . Wolf hates Incubus *which I can understand & music is unplayable. . . . Joffrey acts like a stubborn ass over* Incubus—*have some bad words in the park. . . . Bob says Jerry [Arpino] might walk out if we didn't take* Incubus.

The next day Harkness invited Arpino to lunch and told him she had obtained permission from Shashkine to have another *Incubus* audition. Shashkine saw the ballet a second time, but remained in the end unimpressed. *Incubus* would not go to Russia. Yet, by her willingness to show Arpino compassion, Harkness had proven to him that she was still his loyal friend. Their bond strengthened.

"I never kept anything from Bob. I was the catalyst between Bob and Rebekah and he wanted me to keep on her good side, so that he would know what she was thinking. And I liked her. I did not have a problem being her friend."[21]

The closer Joffrey's original vision of the company edged toward reality, the less control he seemed to have. The troupe was bigger, the repertoire reflected his eclectic taste, and the one-night stands were a thing of the past. But he was at the artistic mercy of Harkness, who opposed him on every issue. The waste at the end of the summer was, to him, unconscionable. He tallied it up: Harkness had successfully squelched Sokolow's *Perspectives;* she had dismissed Stanley Williams as company teacher and, thereby, left Joffrey without a ballet master for the Russian tour; she had rejected his proposal to produce *The Sleeping Beauty;* she had distracted him to such an extreme that he had not been able to choreograph, and Surinach's score for *The Zodiac* was not put to use; and Arpino's *Incubus,* which had been a hit in Lisbon the year before, was out of the repertoire.

From Harkness's point of view, Joffrey had spent the summer sabotaging her. His worst transgression was that she had recommended music for E. Virginia Williams's ballet and been notified by him that Williams was not interested. In fact, Joffrey never gave Williams the recording that Harkness wanted her to hear. He had fibbed to Harkness. Moreover, he had demonstrated that when anything went wrong between them, his response was to rush to the press and communicate to her through the critics. He avoided direct confrontation, failing to return phone calls or to attend meetings. Describing him as getting "mentally queerer," Harkness, by the end of 1963, was convinced that Joffrey had lost his grip.[22] Several of his oldest friends and colleagues, ones as close and dear to him as John Wilson and Walter Terry, came to Harkness privately and told her they also thought he had gone insane. They sided with her. She recorded such actions.

Joffrey felt "very, very alone," observed Arpino. "He was a believer. He knew how great his product was, how great his company was, and he expected that recognition would come, that we'd be accepted by Rebekah. But he didn't realize the power of evil. It's as powerful as faith. It's the opposite of faith."[23]

CHAPTER 15

President Kennedy
and the USSR

On the afternoon of the White House performance, Joffrey rehearsed the dancers in the East Room, having made a pact with himself to forget his daunting surroundings. He distrusted celebrity, not for what it was, but for how he behaved before those who were famous and powerful.

Jacqueline Kennedy attended the rehearsal of October 1, 1963, bringing along Caroline and John, her daughter and son, to see the run-through of Arpino's *Partita for 4* and excerpts from *The Palace,* which were the only pieces on the program. *The Palace* was not a ballet in the strictest sense, but closer to a Broadway or Paris or even a tame Las Vegas revue. Although Arpino received full credit for the choreography, no fewer than three others had contributed bits. Joffrey, Harkness, and Sokolow (who later was the first choreographer to work on the James Rado and Gerome Ragni musical, *Hair*) were his collaborators. *The Palace* was a ballet by committee, just as Arpino had originally envisioned it in India, where he had initially suggested a vaudeville ballet to accompany a Harkness score. Even Harkness's husband had offered suggestions, one of which—a dog act—was not used, and Walter Terry, without public acknowledgment, wrote the libretto.

Terry had arranged the ballet in a series of scenes in nostalgic tribute to the 1920s and early 1930s in America, when musical entertainment acts enjoyed the height of popularity and "every vaudevillian's dream" was to perform at the Palace Theatre in New York. Each scene vivified a dance hall number that might have been seen at the Palace. They included one of ladies rhythmically wafting body-covering, ostrich-feathered fans; top-hatted male tap dancers serenading a leggy femme fatale; a Loie Fuller fantasy of swirling silk drapes and dramatic lighting effects; and a Charleston finale reminiscent of Busby Berkeley movie routines. *The Palace* was meant to be amusing as opposed to "naughty," insisted Terry.[1]

At the White House rehearsal, John junior cavorted with Arpino and offered him an ivory soldier with a spear that had been given to him earlier by the visiting Ethiopian emperor, Haile Selassie. Caroline played with a Raggedy Ann doll and Arpino told her about *Incubus,* his rag-doll ballet. While Arpino amused the children, Mrs. Kennedy and her social secretary, Nancy Tuckerman, pulled aside Joffrey and Harkness and informed them that some of the choreography for *The Palace*'s Riviera scene was too risqué. The women's short, beaded dresses in the Charleston revealed too much cleavage and the tap-dancing men could not wear tights. Changes would have to be made, they said, before the Ethiopian emperor attended the formal program. Mrs. Kennedy explained that she knew what she was asking was not easy, nor should it have been a necessity, because the company's repertoire had been carefully screened in advance. However, when she had greeted Selassie at the airport, he had given her children crosses. Unexpectedly, the emperor had become a religious ascetic since Tuckerman last communicated with his officials. Mrs. Kennedy was now anticipating that because of his orthodoxy, he would be affronted by the sexiness of *The Palace.*

Harkness huffed to Mrs. Kennedy that she would not change *her* ballet, and that she was leaving.

"You can't leave," said Mrs. Kennedy.

"Just remember who put you in the White House," replied Harkness.[2]

Joffrey calmly told Mrs. Kennedy that he understood the dilemma and would alter the choreography and the costumes, authorizing the Charleston girls to wear flesh-toned leotards beneath their regular outfits and the boys to don tuxedo pants instead of black tights. There were, however, neither flesh-toned leotards nor tuxedos available to him. Mrs. Kennedy responded by arranging for stores in Washington to measure and properly outfit the dancers to her specifications.

Minutes prior to the performance the company was still learning completely new steps in the hallway adjacent to the East Room. This kind of impromptu ballet production compromised Joffrey and Arpino's integrity, but it seemed impossible to avoid under the circumstances. Switching the costumes and basically censoring the ballet was artistically a "very illegal move," said Alex Ewing,[3] and Joffrey was not too happy. Yet, it seemed the unfortunate price of moving out of obscurity.

Jacqueline Kennedy's presence at the rehearsal was not an accident. She was instrumental in raising the president's awareness of the arts, coaxing him to speak out on behalf of artists. His words inspired those within the Senate, such as Hubert H. Humphrey, Jacob K. Javits, Joseph S. Clark, and especially Claiborne Pell and Pell's staff writer, Livingston Biddle, who were trying to legislate a government arts program that would evolve into the National Council on the Arts. The United States was the only country in the Western world that did not subsidize the arts, the only one. So far, the American artist relied upon philanthropy and the public who bought tickets, recordings, books, paintings, and sculpture. These senators were attempting to ask for a mere five cents per citizen per year to support artists and arts institutions,[4] and they had allies in President and Mrs. Kennedy.

That evening the president's official hostess was his mother, Rose Kennedy. Before the dinner and the Joffrey Ballet's performance, Jacqueline Kennedy had left the country with her sister, Lee Radziwill, for a holiday in Greece on Aristotle Onassis's yacht. Mrs. Kennedy had given birth the past summer to a son christened Patrick, and the child had died. She was convalescing and made her excuses to Joffrey, Arpino, and Harkness.

The White House performance for 120 guests went well, although some observers felt *The Palace* was too much cheesecake and razzle-dazzle for an occasion "honoring the dignified Lion of Judah."[5] A columnist reported that a State Department official on hand joked, "We've just lost Ethiopia!"[6]

In the reception line afterward, Arpino was thanked by Rose Kennedy. He responded, "Oh, I'm pleased that you liked the ballet."

"I'm not thanking you for that," she said. "But this is the first time I have ever seen my son Jack stay awake for a performance. That's what I'm thanking you for."[7]

Later, as Arpino and the senior Mrs. Kennedy were continuing their conversation over champagne, the president entered the room and spied Noël Mason, Joffrey's youngest and perhaps most attractive dancer. The president asked Arpino if he would be so kind as to introduce her to him. Only sixteen years old, Mason had a genuinely guileless elegance. Joffrey intervened and did not let Mason meet the president; years later he would disclose to Mason that the president had sought her introduction beyond the formal reception line.

Joffrey had brought her into the troupe against his colleague Lillian Moore's wishes. Moore thought the company had outgrown the student stage and that it would be too much effort to train Mason,[8] but Joffrey saw too much talent in her to let her go. Lisa Bradley had been Joffrey's last young trainee. Mason was the next.

Two days after the White House event, Harkness met with her lawyer Aaron Frosch and recorded in her diary on October 4 that she must decide soon if "I want ballet co. in my name." This was the first time the issue of her name being substituted for Joffrey's arose in the journal. By the next year, Harkness would go public with her ambition and inform Joffrey that he had to accept the change to the Harkness Ballet, possibly because the law was behind her. Jeannot Cerrone, who acted as the liaison between Harkness and Joffrey in their negotiations, understood from Harkness that the Internal Revenue Service had notified the Rebekah Harkness Foundation in 1963 that it would lose its nonprofit status if it continued providing the Robert Joffrey Ballet with 90 percent of its funding and did not incorporate the foundation's name in the title.[9]

Interestingly, however, there was no mention of an IRS deadline or mandate in Harkness's journal on October 4 or in the days and weeks leading up to the final split between the Rebekah Harkness Foundation and Joffrey. From the journal it would appear that the impetus for the formation of the Harkness Ballet originated strictly from Harkness. On October 4, 1963, she was full of her own self-importance, adding, "No one has ever mounted five [sic] new ballets so fast or gone with nothing but premieres on tour [to the USSR]."

At this point, Joffrey seemed to be thinking defensively because, before departing for the USSR, he and Alex Ewing arranged to send the company out on yet another one-night-stand, transcontinental American tour with Columbia Artists Management, which would begin immediately after the company returned from the USSR.* Ewing said they told Harkness and Frosch about the plan, but later, Harkness and Frosch would say they had never heard about it.[10] By renegotiating with Columbia Artists, it would seem Joffrey was protecting himself from a Harkness takeover and salvaging whatever remnant of so-called independence he had left.

To prepare them for Leningrad, Kharkov, Donetsk, Kiev, and Moscow, officials from the U.S. State Department and the Soviet Ministry of Culture assembled the Robert Joffrey Ballet members and briefed them in New York's Steinway Hall, where the Ballet Foundation retained a small office. Incredibly, they were told up front that their Russian hotel rooms would be bugged. Interpreters would follow them everywhere. Tipping was welcomed. But they were "severely warned"[11] that any exchange of clothes or selling of an item was considered black-market activity and the wrongdoer would immediately be transported back to the United States. "The main thing is we were to be diplomats," continued Arpino. "We could not fraternize in any way with the Russians. We were told what to say. What not to read. No psychology or religion books. Well, we violated everything."[12]

The first stop was Leningrad, where on opening night the Joffrey would perform on the Kirov stage (before the revolution, and now again, after glasnost called the Maryinsky), which had engendered

---

*Once Harkness lent her financial support to the company, Joffrey and Ewing discontinued their association with Columbia Artists. The post-USSR tour was a new negotiation.

almost every legend of nineteenth- and twentieth-century ballet: Nijinsky, Pavlova, Karsavina, Bolm, Vaganova, Fokine, Balanchine, Danilova, and Nureyev. At the Maryinsky Theatre, Tchaikovsky's *Nutcracker, Swan Lake,* and *Sleeping Beauty* had been introduced to the world. The Russians had been bred for decades and decades on huge three-act productions, ballets that told fantastic stories, defined pure classical form, and were drenched in luxurious costumes and décor. They were further articulated through an alphabet of symbolic, gestural mime. The Joffrey Ballet did not have a single such ballet, nor was it definitively connected to the classical heritage. The repertory was entirely new to the Russians and almost entirely new to the Joffrey. Compared to the Kirov and Bolshoi Ballets' two hundred plus years of existence, the Robert Joffrey Ballet was a seedling. What could the Russians possibly expect of classical orientation, technique, and skill from a company that had existed for only seven years?

The tour was cosponsored by the Rebekah Harkness Foundation and U.S. State Department under the auspices of the State Department's Cultural Presentations Program. Sol Hurok also contributed $21,000 toward transportation costs, a meaningful statement of support for the Joffrey Ballet because Hurok generally did not concern himself with small companies. By comparison to the New York City Ballet with sixty-three dancers and American Ballet Theatre with forty-five members in 1963, both of which had previously toured Russia with Hurok's help, the Joffrey Ballet was small. There were twenty-six dancers in total, plus a thirteen-member orchestra and a minimal staff that included Yuri Krasnopolsky, the Russian-speaking conductor, who had accompanied American Ballet Theatre on its USSR tour (and to whom Harkness paid a higher salary than she did to Joffrey); technical director George Bardyguine, who also spoke Russian; general manager Jeannot Cerrone; business manager Alex Ewing; production stage manager Jack Harpman; lighting supervisor Tom Skelton; and ballet master Richard Thomas. The new dancers were Salvatore Aiello, Virginia Stuart, and William Tarpy.

The five ballets that Joffrey and Harkness called world premieres were Arpino's *The Palace,* Joffrey's completed *Gamelan,* E. Virginia Williams's *Patterns,* Brian Macdonald's *Caprices,* and, seen for the first time with costumes and scenery, his *Time Out of Mind* (in the USSR called *At the Dawn of Humanity*). The repertory also included Francisco Moncion's *Pastorale,* August Bournonville's *Flower Festival in Genzano* pas de deux, Ailey's *Feast of Ashes,* and Arpino's *Sea Shadow* and *Ropes.*

The programs were loaded to give the Soviets their first experience with modern dance through Ailey's piece (restaged by him in a secular version without reference to Christianity and called in Russia *House of Sorrows*); their first exposure to the composer Charles Ives, who had never been heard behind the Iron Curtain and whose score accompanied *Ropes;* and their first taste of Bournonville with the *Flower Festival* pas de deux. Aside from *Flower Festival,* every choreographer and score presented was North American.

The opening night at the Kirov Theatre was October 15. But on the fourteenth, the costumes and sets for three of the four ballets on that program, plus all the women's pointe shoes, the piano rehearsal scores, and the dancers' practice clothes, were still stranded in Frankfurt, Germany. Paul Sutherland and Marie Paquet were also missing; the married couple had lost their passports in London and had to secure their own transportation to Leningrad. Worse, the Kirov management had backed out of its agreement to let the company rehearse on the stage, which was raked (inclined from front to back, as most traditional stages were until the twentieth century), and the company had never before danced on that kind of surface. Sergei Shashkine from Goskoncert was running around demanding "fewer screams and less spanking" in *The Palace,*[13] as the troupe rehearsed instead in a raked Kirov studio. And when the costume and scenery trunks finally appeared, a member of the Joffrey's technical crew was reprimanded for challenging a Kirov stagehand with the remark, "We'll get to the moon quicker than you unload those boxes."[14]

The company was staying at the Hotel Astoria in Nicholas Place and had spent lots of time there because of the problems and glitches. Arpino, who shared a room with Howell, said, "I discovered we had barely any soap. We had very few blankets. The light in our bedroom was so dark. There was an orange velvet shade covering a single twenty-five-watt bulb in the center of the ceiling."

Turning to Howell, Arpino announced, "I've got to do something about this. They said our room is bugged. I'm going to talk to Mr. Khrushchev."

"Just cool it," said Howell.

Arpino climbed on top of a bureau and addressed the light fixture. "Mr. Khrushchev, I am a member of the Joffrey Ballet, and in America we are not treated like this"—he was absolutely kidding. "This room is dismal. In my bedroom, the light is so dim. In America we'd have a pink shade and bright lights. We need more soap in our bathroom. You know, you have one small piddle of a scraping of soap. In America we have lots of soap."[15]

The next day, Arpino and Howell returned to the hotel after rehearsal, and to their amazement, on their bedroom ceiling was a pink shade covering a bright bulb. So much soap was stacked in the bathroom that Arpino said he could have supplied the whole company for weeks. "Mr. Khrushchev, thank you for the soap," he said to the light fixture, and immediately informed the rest of the dancers that if they wanted anything, they had only to ask Mr. Khrushchev. For several days the dancers requested fresh coffee, scrambled eggs, fresh vegetables, soap, extra towels, and blankets. Then the hotel management summoned Joffrey.

"Mr. Joffrey, these demands on us must stop," said the hotel's director, who could not admit the rooms were bugged.

"I don't understand what you are saying. I've made no demands on this hotel. I've asked for nothing," Joffrey responded.

"Oh, yes. They must stop."

"I don't know what you are talking about."

Another day passed and Joffrey was again brought into the office with the same complaint lodged. He called a company meeting, and one dancer piped up, "Oh, there is something Jerry did tell us . . ."[16] Then the dancers confessed their exploitation of the Soviet communications system. They agreed to cease taking advantage of it, but the story survived, and any American company in Leningrad for years afterward heard about the Joffrey Ballet members' ingenuity.

Meanwhile, on October 19, President Kennedy received an honorary degree from the University of Maine, where he delivered a speech about a rapprochement with the Soviets, warning that there might be nuclear war unless every avenue of peace was pursued. Joffrey picked up a copy of the speech from the American embassy, and the transcript was passed around the company. In it, Kennedy described in vivid detail the ravages of nuclear holocaust and told his audience that he did not want one American, Soviet, or European survivor of that potential devastation to ask another, "How did it all happen?"[17]

Joffrey and his company were reminded that this was a strained time to be in the Soviet Union. They could not take lightly their obligation to perform as diplomats. Despite the hilarious means of procuring room service, each knew that the most crucial job would happen on stage.

On October 15, 1963, the Robert Joffrey Ballet made its Russian debut at the Kirov Theatre with *Feast of Ashes, Gamelan, Time Out of Mind,* and *The Palace. The Palace* was an instant winner, although John Wilson reported some boos when company member Virginia Stuart held up the "Americana" sign as part of the ballet. Ten curtain calls and a twenty-minute standing ovation gave choreographers Joffrey, Arpino, and Macdonald enough time to rush onto the stage themselves, leaving Harkness behind with her husband in the theater's royal box. She was ecstatic that *The Palace,* performed to her music, had warranted an encore, but in her diary her vitriol reached new peaks when describing Joffrey onstage garnering all the accolades without her. *The Palace* would become the most popular ballet of her life as a composer, and with that stroke Arpino presumably provided her with the evidence she needed to show Ben Kean, her spouse, that she was more than a dilettante.

Onstage, Konstantin Sergeyev, director of the Kirov Ballet, stood beside Joffrey and proclaimed to the audience that it had been "one of the most thrilling performances" he had seen.[18] Joffrey remembered thinking, "We opened on the Kirov stage! This theater is so beautiful with the blue and gold. On the same stage that Nijinsky danced upon. I can't believe it, it was just history. Four contemporary choreographers all using American music."[19]

The next day the company relocated as planned to the larger Len-Soviet Theater for three weeks of sold-out performances, giving eight performances a week, which for some dancers meant performing as many as fourteen ballets on the weekends. *The Palace* continued to win public favor. In gratitude, Harkness offered Arpino a Rolls-Royce.

"A Rolls-Royce? What do I want with a Rolls-Royce, Rebekah?" he asked. "I don't even drive."

"I'll get you a driver," she said.

"But I can't go around New York like that."

"Well, how about a fur? What's your favorite fur?"

"Chinchilla's nice. I like chinchilla. But if you really want to do something—I mean, you've already done enough—but if you really want to help, you know that building you showed Bob and me on Seventy-fifth Street? Now if you really want to do something, you should convert that building into a Harkness school."[20]

Harkness put her mental gears into action and decided that not only would she like to have her own company, but also a school *and* theater (eventually founding the Harkness School of Ballet at 4 East Seventy-fifth Street in 1965 and the Harkness Theater at Sixty-second Street and Broadway in 1974). She wrote:

> *Decide on life course. Dance Center—build theater like Kirov for dance only. Develop company under national name, and my name. Not Joffrey— he can be director—is also too jealous of me and not big enough person in any sense of the word for such a position.*[21]

Harkness left the Soviet Union within the week and immediately acquainted William Schuman and her lawyer Aaron Frosch with her refined scheme. She recorded the developments:

> *Oct. 30, 1963: Aaron comes—discuss ballet. . . . Ballet name we have American National—it's very good I think.*
>
> *Nov. 4, 1963: See Schuman and Lincoln Center and Mr. Young—Phil[har-monic] Hall terrible acoustical problem. State Theatre ugly color, all glass boxes and modern inside.*
>
> *Discuss possibility of my taking over new chamber music hall and mak-ing it big enough for dance—have layman board of directors, he suggests, then you can rule. Wants us if Balanchine stays or goes as permanent co.*

Am anxious to build my own beautiful thing, but not have it part of Juilliard. Loathe institutions.

Nov. 8, 1963: Walter Terry, Don [Saddler] and Tom [Andrew] came for dinner, also [Léon] Fokine.

Nov. 13, 1963: Schuman calls and I become very elated—I wonder why. B. [Ben Kean] says be prepared for a difficult time with Bob.

Nov. 15, 1963: Eric [sic] Bruhn comes to lunch, says ours is the only company he wants to dance with and is trying to cook up a tour of Europe to come with us and add pas de deux—says Balanchine is destructive to dancers.

Schuman and Young—theater a problem, no place easily available. Recital hall not adequate. Am getting cold feet about being in an institution. State Theatre is too large and other [chamber music hall] is not adequate, nor can I put my name on it. Schuman is nervous out of an institution.

Nov. 19, 1963: Walter Terry for dinner. [He was her frequent dinner companion.]

Meanwhile, back in the Soviet Union, Joffrey remained blissfully ignorant, presenting the occasional lecture-demonstration and observing class at the Kirov School. Some of his dancers continued to gripe about his lack of attention toward them. Richard Thomas had assumed the position of ballet master and supervised their classes.* With no previous experience with the Joffrey repertoire, Thomas seemed to many of the dancers to have been a curious choice. When some refused to take Thomas's class, Joffrey was heard to say, "I wish I was still only six dancers."[22]

Lawrence Rhodes said that in Russia he suddenly comprehended that Joffrey was actually more akin to a producer than a director. His fetishes for perfection and the way the ballets *looked* interested him more than the process. "I decided in Russia to leave the company. Bob never talked with us about the value of a dance: What is this dance about? How do we need to think about it?" continued Rhodes. "He had turned the company over to Dickie Thomas. Bob left our lives, and we had no real explanation for it. In Russia, he was always off in the antique stores. He never taught or rehearsed the company, except maybe *Gamelan*. We did a couple of lecture-demonstrations and it was like the old Bob, but they were isolated [events]."[23]

By October 22, the entire repertory had been danced in Russia. Lisa Bradley and Paul Sutherland inspired rhythmic clapping—the height of

*Richard Thomas had danced with the New York City Ballet, American Ballet Theatre, Ballet Russe, and Ballets Alicia Alonso. He was married to Barbara Fallis and had been teaching since 1960.

Soviet approbation—at every performance of Arpino's *Sea Shadow.* Sutherland said that Arpino intended *Sea Shadow* as an echo to the Bolshoi's acrobatic, over-the-top, thrilling pas de deux *Spring Waters.* In the ballet, Bradley as the ineffable sea nymph ran up a ramp and dove off into the darkness to be caught by Sutherland. It was a climactic moment. But then, during one Leningrad performance, Bradley had slipped and fallen while running up the ramp. Disoriented and terrified, she tumbled into the arms of Sutherland, who had fortunately seen her accident and adjusted the stunt. Bradley refused to dance *Sea Shadow* again unless the ramp was removed. Arpino made sure it was.

Ming Cho Lee had designed sets for the ballet, decorating the stage with poles that resembled abstract kelp beds; utilizing the poles, Arpino choreographed a new section for Bradley and Sutherland. Ticket scalpers surrounded the theater because word of mouth had spread through Leningrad of Bradley's fragile beauty. On the Russian tour, various Joffrey members had their first taste of stardom; Bradley dominated Leningrad artistic conversation. "A treasure of a dancer," exclaimed Natalia Roslavleva, the esteemed Soviet critic.[24]

Aside from his own triumph as choreographer of the hour, Arpino found himself, too, in the unfamiliar position of celebrity, being hailed as an exceptional dramatic dancer for his performance as the blind man in Moncion's *Pastorale.* Jorgensen, Rhodes, and Sutherland were also singled out as leading classical men; Isaksen, Ruiz, Paquet, Mercier, Hammons, and Bradley as the women. Measured by their "truly fanatical love for their work . . . to be a company of most interesting personalities," wrote Roslavleva in her summary report for London's *Dancing Times,* "[the company is] the most American of all the American companies that have been seen by us, and its very vigor, variety of style, subject and technique make it the more interesting."[25]

On the whole, the Russian critics fretted over the Americans' penchant for modern dance and worried that ballet was transforming into cool abstraction. Arpino's *Ropes* was cited, along with Macdonald's *Time,* as examples of this grievous direction. By contrast, most critics championed Joffrey's and Ailey's pieces because they engaged "deep emotion," and *Flower Festival* because it showed that Joffrey "rightly"[26] understood the classical legacy's importance to the dancers' development.

Tass, the official Soviet news agency, reported that the Robert Joffrey Ballet was having "the greatest success of all the American companies that had danced in Leningrad."[27] It is possible that some of the overwhelmingly positive reaction to the Joffrey was a backlash from the visit by Balanchine and the New York City Ballet the year before. Many of the Soviets may have linked cool neoclassicism and abstraction with American ballet because of their prior experience with the New York City Ballet. Balanchine did not want his dancers emoting onstage, he wanted them just to dance. Joffrey pushed for spirit, enthusiasm, and hot energy. "I believe that ballet is about the life of the human spirit," Roslavleva would write in a letter printed under the heading "Nyet to Balanchine."[28] Many of the critics focused in their reviews on the upper-body work—the arms, hands, and *épaulement,* the emotionally expressive parts of the body. Balanchine cared less about the arms than Joffrey, and the Soviets loved arms.

The troupe concluded the Leningrad engagement with twenty-eight curtain calls, then moved on to Donetsk for a week, Kharkov for a week, and Kiev for a week—a week in which the world was rocked.

On November 22, President John F. Kennedy was assassinated. The dancers had just given their first Kiev performance. They were eating dinner at the hotel when a member of the American embassy entered. His face was sheet white; the company thought war had been declared. On television they later saw Kennedy's body lying in the White House East Room, where only a month before they had danced for him.[29] The American embassy ordered Joffrey's performances canceled for three days.

"The theater plunged into mourning," wrote John Wilson in his journal. "The musicians were drunk the entire time, and people were weeping openly in the streets. As they approached us (this happened several times) they would mime, as in an old ballet: 'you,' 'me,' 'heart,' 'eye,' 'tears.' Never, never . . . have I felt such a deep and unspoken bond with a people so remote."[30]

Before Kennedy's assassination the dancers had been scolded and warned to be even more careful because of the recent arrest of Frederick Charles Barghoorn, a Yale political science scholar, who was jailed in Moscow on espionage charges.[31] They were told to stop teaching the Soviets the twist, which had been banned in the discothèques, and to desist from consorting with the stagehands and buying the anti-American posters they found in the bookstores. But after Kennedy's death, all rules seemed suspended. When Joffrey requested permission to hold a memorial service, St. Vladimir's Russian Orthodox Church was opened and a choir provided that included soloists from the Kiev Opera. The church bells silenced for so many years rang out. More than a thousand Soviet citizens, who had grown accustomed to their churches being closed in compliance with the Communist ban against organized religion, joined the Americans.[32]

At the tour's final destination in Moscow, Joffrey dedicated the opening-night performance to Kennedy and gave a speech before the curtain. "He expressed confidence that President Johnson would continue the Kennedy policy of promoting understanding between the two countries through cultural and informational exchanges," reported the *New York*

Times Moscow correspondent.[33] The company gave thirteen sold-out performances in ten days and on closing night took thirty-four curtain calls.

While in Moscow, Lisa Bradley captured the interest of Galina Ulanova, the former Bolshoi prima ballerina *assoluta*. Ulanova (whom Joffrey had seen perform *Romeo and Juliet* when the Bolshoi visited New York in 1959) spoke to Joffrey about coaching Bradley herself; she had Juliet and other classical roles in mind.

Joffrey was filled with trepidation. "I can't let Lisa take her class. I can't let Ulanova see her," he said to Sutherland,[34] because he knew that Bradley was technically too weak to survive Ulanova's close inspection. The Arpino ballets that Bradley mostly danced hid her liabilities; she looked strong, in part, because Arpino and her partners had made her look strong. So Bradley was not allowed private tutoring with Ulanova, and far from being brokenhearted about the missed opportunity, Bradley thanked Joffrey for his protection. She said, "People would watch me in class and be like, 'You've got to be kidding. I saw her last night and this is the same dancer?' It was on the table with Joffrey."[35]

Ulanova then personally invited Bradley to return to Moscow to study privately with her (an invitation that was also extended to Joffrey and Arpino as choreographers in 1965, but which could not be accepted).* Ulanova told Anna Llupina, Soviet reporter for *Dance News*, "I saw two of [the Joffrey Ballet's] performances and found them a very interesting company. I liked Lisa Bradley most. She has a splendid body and features for dancing, and an excellent technique."[36]

The company left the Soviet Union on December 9, returning to an America that was to become irrevocably altered. Illusion, idealism, youth, innocence—some of the stuff of ballet, and the very stuff of the Robert Joffrey Ballet—sank like damaged goods beneath a crush of cynicism. In the post-Kennedy era, almost everything emerging from the arts had to be new art, progressive art, attached to the present as ahead of its time, and therefore capable of being marketed, of spawning cottage industries. What would happen to ballet in the political arena, to artistic standards, grace, and discipline?

---

*Bradley could not take up Ulanova's offer to return to Moscow, but when the Bolshoi Ballet visited New York in August 1979, Ulanova taught Bradley *The Dying Swan;* it was the first time she had taught Fokine's famous solo to anyone. They worked together for two and a half weeks daily; it was a difficult period between the Soviets and the Americans because Alexander Godunov, the Bolshoi's leading male, had recently defected in New York. Incredibly, no restrictions were placed on Ulanova and Bradley. "Every moment with her was a kind of secret," said Bradley. "Few dancers in Russia are chosen to work with Ulanova." (*Dance Magazine*, "Presstime News," December 1979.)

CHAPTER 16

The Split

On December 16, 1963, the Ford Foundation announced its first multi-million-dollar grant to ballet. The $7,756,000 program would strengthen professional companies and schools over ten years in the United States. The principal beneficiaries were Balanchine's New York City Ballet (receiving $2 million) and his School of American Ballet ($3,925,000), while six other regional ballet companies (all with schools and more or less direct ties to Balanchine) received lesser amounts. The objective was to upgrade standards of instruction and to provide young ballet dancers with stable companies to join.

Joffrey's company was not one of the Ford Foundation's recipients, and he had not expected it to be. W. McNeil Lowry, the foundation's Humanities and Arts Program director, had for several years been surveying America's ballet scene. Lowry had earlier offered to help support Joffrey's school, and Harkness had turned him down. Lowry did not hide what he was doing; Balanchine and Lew Christensen from San Francisco Ballet had already tested certain elements of the foundation's ballet program. Yet the outcry following the foundation's announcement was strong and indignant. Not one modern dance company—not Martha Graham, José Limón, Erick Hawkins, Merce Cunningham, Alvin Ailey, or Paul Taylor—had been recognized for his or her contribution to the most American of concert dance forms. The modern dance community felt rebuked and abandoned.

American Ballet Theatre, which had for twenty-four years generated American choreographers and dancers and toured across the country, was likewise completely overlooked by the foundation. "There are minor grants possible in the future," said Lowry. Lucia Chase told *Newsweek,* "We are astounded."[1] The majority argued that the Ford Foundation's actions were undemocratic, un-American, and immoral, because by concentrating the grant on Balanchine, the foundation was setting one national esthetic, one academic standard.

Lydia Joel, *Dance Magazine*'s editor in chief, while not wanting to begrudge Balanchine his good fortune, explained why so many in the dance world were irked:

The Ford Foundation in recent years has given over $700,000 to the City Center Opera. But was that to produce only the works of Gian Carlo Menotti? No. . . . Did the [Ford Foundation] Board feel it could dispense funds to scientific research in the area of behavioral psychology to, let us say, only the followers of one great scientist? No, it did not. Over a period of 20 years it has given millions of dollars to many hundreds of qualified researchers.

Yet in dance it has, for instance, refused assistance to the 24 year old American Ballet Theatre and to the younger, but proven Robert Joffrey Ballet—both of which now operate on an all-too-familiar improvisational pattern. And the program has made no provisions for other eventualities in the next decade.

Mr. Balanchine, saluted as the #1 choreographer, is now also our leading educational force . . .[2]

Sol Hurok also said that he couldn't believe American Ballet Theatre and Joffrey's company had been "neglected."[3] Each time Joffrey's name was invoked in this context it jacked his company into a higher league until it was as if, of course, New York had three important ballet companies, and Joffrey was one of them.

On December 18, two days after the Ford Foundation announcement, Harkness invited Joffrey and Arpino to dinner and disclosed her plan to move the company into Lincoln Center. She had met earlier with Arpino privately and told him the same information she would now repeat to them both. But to Arpino alone she had offered the directorship of the company provided he would leave Joffrey. Appalled, Arpino dismissed the proposition, then informed Joffrey of her plot.

"Bob knew I was going to the meeting. I never kept anything from him. She made me an offer I would never again receive for the rest of my life. She was going to have a company with all these stars—like Erik Bruhn and Maria Tallchief—and she wanted me to become director, if I were willing to leave Robert Joffrey. Bob never had to question [my allegiance]," Arpino said. "I went to hear out Rebekah and Aaron [Frosch], just to see where they were going, what they were doing, and to wish them well. And that's what I did."[4]

At the time, Joffrey was pushing for a New York season on Broadway, but Harkness told him the expense was too great. She had heard through Jeannot Cerrone that Joffrey was "losing contact with the company and that lots of the dancers [didn't] like him anymore."[5]

"I was promised a season in New York, and it didn't materialize," Joffrey later lamented, adding, "It was a homogeneous company . . . in wonderful spirits. . . . I was stubborn, and I wanted the season very badly."[6] Eight months before his death in 1988, he told Richard N. Philp of

Dance Magazine that if anyone asked him the "one disappointment" in his life, he would say, "That this company never danced in New York."[7]

Although Harkness wrote in her diary that she envisioned Joffrey as artistic director, Arpino said that at this particular juncture, she offered the position only to him. As far as Joffrey was concerned, that meant he had been eliminated from her plans, and so, when he was later formally asked by Harkness to remain as director, he doubted her sincerity.

He did not attend Harkness's next scheduled meeting at the Westbury Hotel on December 24, 1963—his thirty-fifth birthday. Harkness fumed, reiterating, "Bob is not big enough to put all this money and prestige behind."[8] Ewing guessed that at this point Harkness was spending $40,000 to $50,000 a week on the company.

On January 6, 1964, the Robert Joffrey Ballet went out on its eighth and final cross-country tour with Columbia Artists Management, Inc. The itinerary included many of the major cities—Los Angeles, San Francisco, Seattle, and Chicago—as well as fifty-six nooks and suburban crannies such as Whittier, California. A former Martha Graham dancer, Richard Gain, was the only new dancer in the troupe since the Soviet Union. Arpino, at almost forty-one, was still dancing, but only in Joffrey's *Gamelan,* and he had a new position in the company as assistant director. Robert Mackay was on wardrobe, Leon Hyman was the new conductor of a fifteen-member orchestra, and Richard Thomas maintained his position as ballet master. His wife, Barbara Fallis, who was a fine teacher, also traveled with the company.

The tour was difficult. On February 3, Cerrone paid the company an unexpected visit in Los Angeles after a performance at UCLA's Royce Hall. Joffrey was not with them. Cerrone announced that Harkness was forming a new company, stipulating that the dancers would be absorbed into the new troupe if they wanted to remain. Harkness would release them from their contracts if they wanted to leave. Joffrey had been asked to head the newly named Harkness Ballet, Cerrone said, but had as yet not responded.

Arpino flew to New York immediately to join Joffrey. The company continued on the tour, which was only half-finished at the time of Cerrone's announcement. Joffrey sent no word to the dancers. The dancers frantically telephoned the American Ballet Center. When they couldn't reach Joffrey, they spoke to anyone who they thought knew his answer. Françoise Martinet, for example, relayed some of their concerns to Joffrey, pleading with him to speak with his dancers, even if he did not know whether he was going to direct the Harkness Ballet or strike out on his own.

Joffrey spoke to a few of them, but could not face many of the company members, perhaps because he feared that they were not unified behind him. From their numerous phone calls, however, he must also have known that they cared about how he would want them to react to Harkness's suspicious and unanticipated maneuver. Around this time, he wrote the following notes to himself in an effort to clarify his thinking (the ellipses were his):

> I have to discuss this with my father. He will want to know everything. He isn't like me . . . always wants facts. And he deserves them: put money into the company, has put up with my being away from home all these years. He is proud of my company . . . seeing his son's name . . . has been my silent partner and rooter all these years. Not something to discuss over the phone. Have to sit down in our house.
>
> Also with Jerry: he is devoting his life as much as I am . . . has made the same sacrifices . . . will be associated with the new company, but on what basis? Cannot commit him without discussing it.
>
> Lincoln Center is a long way off . . . at least several years. Furthermore, their buildings to date have not been outstanding . . . N.Y. City Ballet on bad floor, Philharmonic has bad acoustics. Don't want the company to be cemented into a theatre that's the wrong size, has wrong stage. Hurok won't even book Lincoln Center: does better elsewhere.
>
> Dr. Kean [Harkness's husband]: is so impulsive, could turn against me tomorrow. How would I know I wouldn't be fired as artistic director the first time he really disapproved of something I wanted.
>
> What about my salary now? Should be getting $500 . . . was understood, I am artistic director, conductor gets over $400 . . . I am paid less than him . . . and nothing for rehearsal?[9]

On February 9, Harkness granted Joffrey exactly twenty-four hours to decide. She felt she had to supply a deadline because he had not contacted her despite her many attempts to reach him. The deadline passed. On February 10, George Skibine, former ballet master of the Paris Opéra Ballet and husband of Marjorie Tallchief, was named the director of the newly formed Harkness Ballet. According to Harkness, Joffrey was not out of a job, although his position had changed by default. She still expected to hear from him regarding his future role in the Harkness Ballet.

Joffrey had not been idle while hiding from Harkness and most of his dancers. On February 6, three days after Harkness's ax fell, he and Alex Ewing sought the advice of Lincoln Kirstein. Notes from the conversation lend astonishing insight into the proximity of relations not just between Joffrey, Ewing, and Kirstein, but between the institutions they represented.

Ewing's mother was Lucia Chase, codirector and chief patron of American Ballet Theatre. Kirstein was general director of the New York City Ballet, a company that from his point of view had dissolved twice before reaching its present healthy state. In times of distress, when one of their own was under attack, it seemed that ballet's upper echelon—august, educated, and philanthropic—banded together. Kirstein's advice to Ewing (who refers to himself in the third person in this memo) was as follows:

> *Conversation with Lincoln: Should assume that we will be losing everything . . . and plan from scratch. Will be some pleasant surprises along the way. We should write letter, signed by Bob, to Frosch . . . asking him to detail exactly what are the terms under which he would work. What are his rights, his control over personnel and repertory, salary, length of contract, title, designers and technicians, etc. Just what do they intend?*
>
> *Then return to company cheerful and unconcerned. Alex join them in Seattle . . . just there to see the company. Can advise dancers not to be hasty . . . to wait until choice is more clear.*[10]

Jolted out of their confusion and indecision by Kirstein, Joffrey and Ewing played on each other's sensibilities and conceived the blueprint for the new Robert Joffrey Ballet America. They were hoping to outwit Harkness. When she surprised them by hiring Skibine, Joffrey and Ewing had thought they had more time. They had imagined the dancers returning home, whereupon Joffrey would offer them the opportunity to form Ballet America. But Harkness extended her offer to Skibine first, after which Joffrey and Ewing kept hammering out plans for a new troupe anyway, agreeing in principle on the structure to which it should adhere. In this sense, they were prepared.

Ewing envisioned setting up weeklong residencies for Joffrey's Ballet America in universities across the country through Columbia Artists Management. The possibility existed through Kirstein to tie in with the New York City Ballet's season "either one night a week or one week during the season," according to a Ewing memo.[11] Sympathetic, Balanchine had again offered them the use of his ballets without royalty payments. They would apply for nonprofit status and thereby be eligible for Ford Foundation sponsorship. "Make appointment with Lowry as soon as possible," read the memo. New ballets by Joffrey, Arpino, and Eugene Loring were planned for the summer. The company would be based at Joffrey's American Ballet Center. There would be twenty-four dancers, and a South American tour by 1965. Joffrey had prepared a list of eight dancers who, as far as he knew, were contractually free to stay with him.* But he did not have

---

*They were Arpino, Bradley, Gain, Isaksen, Rhodes, Ruiz, Sarry, and Tomasson. Ewing understood years later that for the tour to the USSR it was necessary for Harkness to sign fairly long-term union contracts with the dancers that extended well into 1964. The position of the union (AGMA) in this dispute, regarding to whom the dancers "belonged," was never entirely clear to Joffrey, the dancers, or the public.

the means to pay salaries, and therefore he could not insist with Harkness that he maintain control of the dancers. Harkness was offering the dancers financial security under union contracts. Joffrey did not want to make them feel embarrassed about choosing money over artistic integrity. Furthermore, he misjudged how much the company members already knew, and he vastly overestimated their general satisfaction with him.

In northern California, the dancers held on to thin air and hearsay. No one in an official capacity had informed them about George Skibine. The more that time passed without word from Joffrey, the more the dancers decided to align themselves with Harkness. "We began hearing rumors. We didn't know what was going on," recalled Brunilda Ruiz, who was the only charter member left aside from Arpino. "I know I needed a job. The only thing I could do was my dancing. I think we felt that maybe Joffrey had almost given up. He had struggled, he had tried, he had done everything, and maybe we felt that he was tired, he *wanted* to have a break. So we kept asking him, 'Do you have any job offers for us?' But nothing came out of him. It was so painful. I called him every day and said, 'What's going on?' He'd answer, 'I don't know what's going on. I'm very upset. I don't know what to do!' "[12]

On March 17, Allen Hughes in the *New York Times* printed the contents of a brief press release from the William Hale Harkness Foundation* announcing that $1 million over a ten-year period would be given toward the "creation and operation of a new ballet company to be headed by George Skibine."[13] This was the first time that the William Hale Harkness Foundation had helped any organization in the arts. Hughes, too, implied that the new company would likely be built on the assets of the Robert Joffrey Ballet, which was currently receiving the support of the Rebekah Harkness Foundation. Hughes correctly anticipated that the sets, costumes, and rights to the Joffrey Ballet repertoire that had been created under Harkness's patronage would be rolled over to the new company, thereby depriving Joffrey's troupe of a major body of work and property.

Joffrey decided to compose his own press statement. He still had not spoken directly to Harkness. In private, he wrote in longhand the following draft, in which his outrage and sense of violation are more vivid than anything the public or his dancers ever saw. He wrote: "The foundation has proved itself careless and contemptuous of the values and

*The foundation was established in 1936 by Rebekah Harkness's former husband to assist in the fields of education, health, religion, and social welfare. In 1964, Rebekah Harkness Kean was vice president of the William Hale Harkness Foundation, in addition to being founder of the foundation that bore her name and that had sponsored activities in the performing arts since 1959.

standards of American dance, its artists and traditions. . . . The fact that the foundation will drop the company after major artistic successes is incrimination enough . . . piracy, hijacking . . . The company was not for sale. . . . This is a statement I had hoped I would not have to make."[14]

The next day Joffrey submitted his prepared statement, the full text of which was included in another piece by Hughes in the *New York Times*. He was severing his ties with Harkness, providing as his principal reason the "ultimatum" given him to change the name of his company to Harkness Ballet. He asked, "Should a foundation that has supported a ballet company and its policies suddenly require that the company change these policies and be named for the foundation? Should the foundation's officers have the right to decide matters that are strictly artistic, including the choice of choreographers, composers and designers?"[15] Joffrey answered his own rhetoric with action. Refusing to address Harkness directly, he had first gone to the press. Harkness had her millions; Joffrey had his contacts in the press, and he counted on the sympathy of a majority of the New York dance world. He fought Harkness by painting her the villain.

"Although my decision may temporarily cripple the Joffrey company, I feel the dance world and other foundations will come to its rescue—and I must take the risk."[16] These were the concluding words of his statement, and they suggest the possibility that Joffrey had intentionally engineered the break-up in such a way that he could amass broad support through sympathy and then start the company afresh without depending on a patroness. This may have been his most Machiavellian hour. Or perhaps it was an act of *badal,* in accordance with the centuries-old Pakhtun code of revenge. If he had negotiated with Harkness one-on-one and they had scripted a genteel statement for publication, he would have aroused far less furor and controversy. He would have been put at a disadvantage. As Joffrey anticipated it, the movers and shakers in the performing arts rushed to his defense after Hughes's piece appeared, in which Harkness's lawyer "declined to comment," thus surrendering the control of popular perception to Joffrey. Ted Shawn, Joseph Papp, Balanchine, Isadora Bennett, Jean Gordon (*Dance Magazine*'s associate publisher), and even the Soviet Union news agency Tass stood by Joffrey at this moment, united against Harkness's takeover plot. From such fervor he had a chance to reconstruct his troupe.

In his Sunday piece of March 22, "Dance Philanthropy and a Moral Issue," Hughes wrote:

It was assumed by the innocent (which included most of us) that the Rebekah Harkness Foundation was simply doing good for ballet in general by giving the Joffrey Ballet the new works, sets, costumes and musical scores it needed. . . .

What we did not know was that the foundation was acquiring the very ballet assets it appeared to be giving away. Everything created and bought for the Joffrey Ballet while it was being supported by the foundation is the property of the foundation. . . .

The Rebekah Harkness Foundation has paralyzed the Joffrey Ballet for the present and imperiled the company's future. The situation is legal, of course; and it may be the result, in part, of Mr. Joffrey's lack of wisdom in the past. But legality and wisdom are not everything. A moral issue is involved here.[17]

A week after the Allen Hughes article appeared, Harkness's husband, Ben Kean, stormed the offices of the *New York Times* and demanded one presenting their side of the story be written and published. According to Harkness in her diary, she wrote a letter to other members of the press, all of whom seemed to have refused to print it. She expressed her wrath further in the diary, writing:

March 17, 1964: Article by Hughes saying we practically left Joffrey in the street. All upset, so mad.

March 18: Jeannot [Cerrone] really upset, ready to sue everyone for first time in his life.

March 24: Ben goes to NY Times and changes their minds about Allen Hughes. Accuses him of personal journalism . . . Skibine arrives.

March 25: Reception for dancers to meet Skibine goes quite well. Kids feel as I do about Bob. He was the great hope of the dance world and then suddenly swelled up and couldn't function anymore.

March 30: No action on part of Times *except a call to Aaron [Frosch] from some reporter. We are getting the slow run around.*

April 1: NY Times *to see Mr. [Clifton] Daniel. Apparently I impress him with my sense of humor which smooths things over some.*

April 2: NY Times *takes our picture. I am showing off . . . worry sick after over picture in tights.*

April 11: Aaron and Walter [Terry] who still think I should publish letter about Bob.

On April 14, Joffrey's lawyer notified Harkness that Joffrey and Arpino would like to have the scenery and costumes that belonged to their ballets. Harkness had also kept Joffrey's personal trunk of clothes, and he expected it returned as well. A lawsuit against Harkness was intimated unless she removed their property from her warehouse immediately. Lawyers on both sides were uncertain who legally owned the costumes, scenery, and choreography. Harkness wrote:

April 16: Must plan either to destroy Bob or forget him—in any event he must be frightened into some sort of behavior or we'll have trouble the rest of our lives.

Siding with Harkness, Walter Terry paid her many visits during these eventful weeks; she recorded that Terry comforted her by calling Joffrey a "liar."[18] Terry wrote an article in the *Herald Tribune*, "$1 Million Grant to Ballet Stirs the World of Dance" (referring to the William Hale Harkness Foundation's support of the new troupe directed by Skibine), that provided a platform for both Joffrey and Harkness to vent their arguments. Harkness said that if only Joffrey had told her that he did not want the new post and that he would prefer to continue with a company under his own name, she "was prepared to assure him that [her] Foundation would continue to assist in whatever ways possible the Joffrey Ballet enterprise, including his company and his school."[19] Harkness conveyed that she was deeply wounded that Joffrey had gone to the press with his formal answer, instead of coming to her first. Joffrey's methods of communication ruined his chances for her support on any endeavor in the future, she implied.*

One by one most of the dancers informed Joffrey that they were leaving him. Some would go with Harkness, some would decamp to American Ballet Theatre, some would drop out of ballet altogether. Nine pledged to remain with Joffrey: Arpino, Lisa Bradley, Alfonso Catá, Nancy Fenster, Richard Gain, James Howell, Nels Jorgensen, Noël Mason, and Christine Sarry. Ewing, Jack Harpman, Richard Thomas, and Tom Skelton would also stay. Françoise Martinet and Jonathan Watts were teaching at the school. The plan for Robert Joffrey Ballet America had not yet been mentioned to anyone beyond the chief architects: Joffrey and Ewing.

The eleven dancers who moved to the Harkness Ballet were Brunilda Ruiz, Lawrence Rhodes, Helgi Tomasson, Lone Isaksen, Margaret Mercier, Marlene Rizzo, Finis Jhung, Felix Smith, Suzanne Hammons, Karina Rieger, and Elisabeth Carroll. Joffrey did not speak to Brunilda Ruiz for years afterward. Lone Isaksen and Lawrence Rhodes were made to feel unwelcome at the American Ballet Center.

The division of repertoire, costumes, and scenery was more complex than the division of dancers. Initially, Harkness hoarded everything, including Joffrey's personal belongings in his touring trunk and Noël Mason's in hers. "To accuse them of stealing Joffrey's clothes [which we did] was just so rep-

---

*Before Harkness died in 1982, she gave Joffrey her word that his company would receive $125,000 from her foundation. After her estate was settled in 1985, the Harkness Ballet Foundation, presided over by executive director Theodore S. Bartwink, honored Harkness's promise. Between then and 1994, the foundation gave $664,250 to the Joffrey Ballet.

rehensible," admitted Ewing in 1993. "It was more reprehensible than they were, actually. They were so anxious to get those clothes out of the warehouse, and I was delighted to have them in, because it was like a bomb. In the midst of all the high principles, at the same time we were scrambling around attempting to win a rather dirty war."[20] Harkness eventually returned to Joffrey and Arpino the rights to their ballets, but the works by the other Watch Hill choreographers belonged to her.

The crisis raised important questions about the rights and duties of arts patrons. In the years before the National Endowment for the Arts, there was no form of government subsidy. Joffrey's encounter with Harkness had clearly demonstrated that the means by which an artist supported himself or his company affected his art form. "If he who pays the piper calls the tune, then perhaps we ought to look at the person who is paying," suggested James Lincoln Collier in an insightful article for *Holiday* magazine.

Collier visited Harkness at Watch Hill and concluded:

As it happens, the [Harkness-Joffrey] uproar is symptomatic of a condition which, without anyone really noticing it, has been creeping over art in the United States since the end of World War II—a condition which, for good or ill, threatens to have a serious effect on American art.

. . . Mrs. Harkness must be given credit for spirit and energy. She must be especially credited for putting her money into something other than fast yachts and slow horses. There is no doubt that she knows a great deal about the dance. The trouble is she does not know enough to offer advice to Joffrey or Skibine or Ailey.

If it were merely a matter of a very wealthy woman being foolish with her money, it would be of little moment. Unfortunately patronage can do vast damage. . . . The notion that art should delight or instruct or inspire has been buried in a frantic game of trend-spotting in which dealers, crude naïfs, butterflies and a host of the talentless unwashed scramble in the gutter for a piece of those capital-gain dollars. It will be some time before painting manages to shake out the rubbish elevated to the status of art by people bent on acquiring enough cachet to be spoken to by Ringo Starr. The lesson is plain. It suggests that the new patrons must possess some virtues other than money. Restraint, knowledge and sensitivity are three that come to mind.[21]

In 1964, after the split, Joffrey received the annual *Dance Magazine* Award, one of the field's most prestigious honors. And Ted Shawn of Jacob's Pillow and Joseph Papp of the New York Shakespeare Festival offered to help him reestablish a troupe by lending him their stages on which to perform.

PART THREE

Threshold

CHAPTER 17

The Nation's Closet

His entire enterprise wrenched from him, Joffrey felt that it was time to take stock. The first company had been a cohesive, maybe somewhat disgruntled one confused by the administration, but it was everything a director would want an ensemble to be. The members had known each other intimately, they could "read moods without speaking," as Lisa Bradley put it.[1] They had helped each other in rehearsal and onstage as partners, caught each other, gauged each other's power for that performance at that moment in that step. They had made each other look assured and glorious. Joffrey knew he had had something that only nine years of dancing and working together could produce. To fail to keep control of it was brutally painful. He was "absolutely devastated," said P. W. Manchester, "but not to the point of self-pity."[2]

Joffrey could not imagine himself the vanquished one, the loser, the defeated victim. His ego was huge and healthy. But the Harkness break was the single defining event in the Joffrey Ballet's history. Joffrey's behavior and decision-making from this moment forward would reflect the memory that he had been bamboozled. Harkness transformed him into someone who feared disappointing other people's expectations, so he further distanced himself from people. The Harkness debacle haunted Arpino and Joffrey. Having been dependent on someone they did not respect, they also lost some respect for themselves.

Arpino actually differed from Joffrey in his interpretation of Harkness's action. He remained fond of her because she had once rescued the company, was infatuated with his ballets, and had saved *Sea Shadow* from oblivion. She had paid him more compliments than Joffrey had. Arpino felt she had been turned against Joffrey by "too many Iagos whispering in her ear" and thought she was irresolute, not evil.[3]

"Rebekah was the catalyst that turned the Joffrey around," Arpino said. "She took us out of the bus and truck and gave us our first esteem."[4] Both he and Joffrey firmly believed in reconciling discordant elements. Having privately declared Harkness's behavior a "crime against American dance,"[5] Joffrey threw himself into bolstering Americans who danced. In April 1964, he recommitted himself to teaching, not only at his own school but at the regional ballet festivals and teachers' conventions. Within five months, he would participate in one regional festival and three conventions (lasting about four days apiece). The festivals paid handsomely by performing artists' standards, and Joffrey was also motivated by the money. One of the most popular teachers (particularly in the Southwest), he charged the hosting companies more than any other guest instructor, and he required first-class travel.

From a New Yorker's point of view, he disappeared into America's hinterlands. He retreated. Since he could not fix Harkness, it seemed he was trying to fix the nation—to become, in the British critic Clive Barnes's words, "Mr. American Dance." Joffrey told Barnes, "Dancers must be made aware, from the very beginning, of their traditions, where they came from as performers. They must know about ballet history, and they must go and see a great deal of ballet. . . . I insist on the dancers learning the great classical variations from ballets like *Swan Lake* and *The Sleeping Beauty,* because this is their heritage, as much as Brahms or Chopin is a pianist's heritage."⁶ If he could not institutionalize his company, then he would institutionalize himself at the regional ballet festivals and every dance convention. He would make American ballet dancers know who they were.

What he was doing was nothing new to him. From the company's beginning in 1956, Joffrey had positioned himself as a Johnny Appleseed of ballet by teaching outside of New York, across the land, hoping to inspire students as he had been inspired by Ivan Novikoff and Mary Ann Wells in Seattle. At one national gathering, his pianist played excerpts from *Giselle,* and not a student among fifty recognized the music. Joffrey felt compelled to shape the next generation and to nurture its responsibility to a tradition. In 1956, more than twenty-five ballet companies (of varying sizes) dotted the nation. By 1964, according to the Rockefeller panel report, the number had almost quadrupled. None were close to giving year-round performances, not even the New York City Ballet or American Ballet Theatre. "Next to this glowing picture must be placed another, more sobering one: *Almost all this expansion is amateur,*"⁷ continued the Rockefeller report.

Yet, slight as it might seem, this advancement signified a veritable revolution in the performing arts. After a long, hard haul it seemed Americans were buying into ballet—possibly because companies such as Joffrey's had infiltrated small cities and towns. Joffrey liked to think that he had played a part in showing ballet at the top of its form. By 1966, three male dancers who had seen Joffrey's troupe as children and had decided on ballet partly because of the experience would join his company.

More than any other act, teaching subordinated his ego to goodwill. He told friends that it caused him to remember why he was in ballet in the first place. He liked to work with young talent. While in the classroom, he was actually ferreting out new dancers. The festivals and conventions evolved into one of his primary resources for scholarship students who could eventually be trained for his school's apprenticeship program and then groomed for the main company.

During the regional festival panels and discussion sessions, Joffrey often found himself on the same platform with Dorothy Alexander, Robert Barnett, Ann Barzel, Alice Bingham, Anatole Chujoy, Karen Conrad, Richard Englund, Doris Hering, David Howard, Mosceleyne Larkin, P. W. Manchester, Josephine Schwarz, Ted Shawn, Ben Sommers, or E. Virginia Williams—the whole world of teachers, dance advocates, company directors, and writers committed to national expansion—authentic pioneers of American ballet. This was his chosen milieu, where he felt comfortable and spoke a common language of dedication to dance and to quality performance.

While Joffrey was heading in one direction, Arpino and Ewing were heading in another. They thought the agreement between themselves had been to reorganize the company. To this end, Arpino and his assistant Jim Howell tinkered with movement for a new, sports-theme ballet, *Olympics*. Arpino acted as though nothing had changed; he specialized in denial and optimism, attributes that sustained Joffrey in times of crisis.

In the eight months after the Harkness split, Alex Ewing assumed principal control of the Robert Joffrey Ballet's reconstruction. He organized. He salvaged from the rubble the repertoire and Joffrey's vision of presenting American dancers in ballets by American choreographers to music by American composers. The years 1965–70 were known in some Joffrey circles as the Ewing years. "When the [Harkness] break came, it was Alex who gave us the confidence to form a new company down at the school,"[8] said Arpino.

For Ewing, the key to the Joffrey Ballet's future boiled down to not repeating his mother's mistakes at American Ballet Theatre. "I wanted to establish an existence that was supportable," he said. "The company I knew best—which was Ballet Theatre—that was the model."[9] But the model became a springboard and in some ways the opposite of ABT. Ewing was determined that the Joffrey company would spend a week at each place where it stopped on tour. There would be no more one-night stands. His optimism made Joffrey rest a little easier.

Ewing turned immediately to W. McNeil Lowry of the Ford Foundation and asked for a Ford Foundation grant. "I can't help you," Lowry told him. "You're not nonprofit. You don't have a board of directors. You don't have any kind of plan."[10] (Lowry had previously been able to offer Ford Foundation assistance to Joffrey's school, when Joffrey was affiliated with Harkness, because Joffrey's sponsor, the Rebekah Harkness Foundation, was nonprofit.)

The challenge facing the thirty-two-year-old Ewing was to establish the company's existence formally on paper as a nonprofit, tax-exempt dance foundation. Such a process would likely consume the better part of a year. The legalities were intricate, the cost prohibitive. (Whereas Ewing's mother poured her personal assets into American Ballet Theatre, Ewing dedicated his time to the Joffrey, not his income.) If the Robert Joffrey Ballet took a year to reconstitute, then Joffrey and Arpino risked losing momentum. The public might forget about them. Dancers might not think of the troupe as viable. Repertoire would be forgotten.

Two hours after meeting with Lowry, Ewing visited the law offices of Paul, Weiss, Rifkind, Wharton & Garrison, the attorneys for American Ballet Theatre. Possible conflicts of interest having been cited, the lawyers there recommended that Ewing try Howard M. Squadron. "And the coincidence—this is what happened and this is why Bob Joffrey does have a lucky star," Ewing said, recapturing the scene that followed within a half hour of leaving ABT's lawyers—"Howard Squadron. I'd never even heard the name before. He was on the phone talking to his wife, and I just sat there while he kidded his wife about her freckles, or something, for about five minutes and I liked him. When he hung up and asked, 'What can I do for you?' I told him. And he said, 'How would you like the Foundation for American Dance?'"[11]

From his file cabinet Squadron retrieved a folder with the completed paperwork for some clients in Boston who had decided to drop their project. He handed Ewing a pen and showed him where to sign. The rest of the day Ewing called his former classmates from Yale, asking them to serve on the board of the Foundation for American Dance. They were thirty-two-year-olds who had not yet been tapped by other performing arts boards but were seated in positions of considerable power within their respective firms and Wall Street companies. The next day Ewing went back to Lowry and said, "We have to have a grant."

"Well, I told you that I can't—"

"No, I've got it. Here's the foundation and here's the board."[12]

Lowry was stupefied. Ewing had pulled off the impossible. The Foundation for American Dance board included William H. Donaldson, Ewing's Yale roommate and president of the securities firm of Donaldson, Lufkin & Jenrette; Louis Marx Jr., the president of Deerfield Oil Corporation; John F. Ball, director of programs at a prominent advertising firm; Harold E. Woodsum Jr., a law associate at White & Case and an all-American football player; and Howard M. Squadron. Only one member had queried in advance, "But do I have to *see* the ballet?" To which Ewing had replied, "No, you just have to give your money."[13]

Ewing did not anticipate that most would appear at the meetings either. Surprised in the future by their almost religious attendance, he said he guessed they came because in addition to making a civic difference with their money, they had started to cut deals and engage in business transactions among themselves. "This board was particularly effective because during the early sixties very few men were involved in ballet in any way, even to the extent of being regular patrons or members of the audience, and certainly not on ballet boards," said Ewing. "And here were five."[14]

The complex partnership between the arts and business would become integral to the new Joffrey Ballet, as it was to every company born of this era. Ewing was in step with the times, suggested this report on 1964 dance economics in *Dance Magazine*:

> *The single most important source of support for the dance . . . has been, and will always be, the individual. . . . In fact, individual giving accounted for more than three-quarters of all giving in 1964, surpassing, by far, foundations, corporations and other sources.*

> *Put a businessman and an artist together and the results are unpredictable, but not necessarily disastrous, as they might have been a decade ago. . . . Even the businessman who thinks and admits that all dance is just so much "fol de rol" (and he's probably in the minority today) still may recognize that his company's participation in the arts can be an important asset to his employee relations program and to his personal or corporate image.*[15]

Joffrey on his own without Ewing could probably not have reorganized a major ballet company. In the world of ballet, Joffrey needed to have upper-class connections, and Ewing provided them. Ewing's Yale companions teamed up on the board because they respected him. Ewing gave Joffrey clout.

During the summer of 1964, Joffrey prepared to teach at his own school for the first time in three years. Among those who flocked there were Edward Villella, John Prinz, Dan Wagoner, Joyce Trisler, Matt Turney, and Janet Mitchell—some of the better-known and more highly accomplished American dancers in modern and ballet. Joffrey had apparently lost none of his pedagogical allure. But these students were working professionals, and Joffrey recognized that the school would have to change orientation if he was to mobilize a new company as fast as Ewing seemed to be demanding it.

Among the first group he organized into a company were Robert

Blankshine, Wilhelm Burmann, Zelma Bustillo, Diana Cartier, Alfonso Catá, Joanne Danto, Edwina Dingman, Luis Fuente, Sharon Herr, Susan Magno, Hilda Morales, Ramon Segarra, and Trinette Singleton. But many of these mature and classically trained dancers "rebelled against Joffrey's rules and regulations [the black-leotard-and-pink-tights uniform, for example] and left," said Richard Gain,[16] because Joffrey expected his dancers to act as if they were his children, subordinate themselves to his will, and not question him on any matter, artistic or bureaucratic.

Joffrey quickly realized that the only people who would fully accommodate him were kids. He then focused on his scholarship students and other novices: Charthel Arthur, Frank Bays, Ronald Bostwick, Robert Brassell, Raymond Bussey, Ivy Clear, Esther Jaenn, Ian Horvath, John Jones, Yvonne McDowell, Dennis Nahat, George Ramos, Arlene Shuler, Donna Silva, and Carol Todd. He assumed that they would listen to him because his was the only professional voice most of them had ever heard. The shift in his attitude was subtle, but far-reaching.

The good that emerged from the Harkness debacle was that Joffrey had failed. "It made me work much harder, made me realize how necessary [the company] was," he said.[17] His bronze bust of Napoleon still prominently displayed on his tiny desk, he delivered a credo for the school that he later used as a template for the company, and that was published in 1965 under the guise of company publicity. It read, in part:

> Hardly a week goes by at the American Ballet Center that a very promising student who has just begun to blossom is not lured away by the offer of a job . . . before she is ready, artistically or psychologically, for her professional career.
>
> . . . This is the person who might have gone farther than all the others if only she could have found the really intense, custom-fitted type of training that she needed. . . . The American Ballet Center is the closest approximation to [a graduate school–type education], and this accounts for the school's small hard core of exceptionally talented students who persist in studying there despite the increasing pressure of outside job offers.
>
> The American Ballet Center proposes . . . to take the first step towards liberating itself from having to serve the ballet-student-world-at-large in order to function as an intensive training ground for a very demanding and experimental company.[18]

Joffrey raises the issue three times in his "credo" that the dancers he trains are constantly lured away from him. His immediate solution to the problem was to have Arpino help him pick the right candidates: "exceptional dancers" who "did not fit in."[19] Joffrey rationalized that such students would be loyal because, amazingly, somebody appreciated them despite flawed physiques.

*   *   *

On November 20, 1964, the Ford Foundation's letter of acknowledgment arrived in the morning mail, informing Ewing that the Robert Joffrey Ballet and the American Ballet Center had been granted $35,000 immediately and $120,000 to be matched one-for-one in not more than three installments beginning January 1, 1965, and paid over the course of the year. "What ho! A lot of $$$$$!" wrote Ewing to Joffrey and Arpino that day. "We're ready to act."[20]

Instantly, Ewing hired press agent Isadora Bennett, proclaiming her to be "the best in the field."[21] Although he was preaching to the converted—because Joffrey had long been familiar with Bennett, who had sneaked him into Martha Graham concerts when Joffrey was a newcomer in New York—Ewing wrote Joffrey and Arpino to explain why they must have Bennett, saying:

> Isadora Bennett, a spirited little redhead of about 60 who's the acknowledged pro, who was told by the Harkness Foundation that she could name her price with them and she turned them down cold, saying she thought the best thing they could do was to give Joffrey back all his things and she believed the Times' version of the dispute! She not only agreed to help us, but said she'd do the first release free of charge and would speak to Ford in the morning to clear the logjam . . . also to refer all the press to her.[22]

In December, Joffrey and Arpino began auditioning dancers again for the company, and over the next three months the school faculty at 434 Sixth Avenue in Greenwich Village grew from Françoise Martinet, Beatrice Tompkins, Lillian Moore, and Joffrey to include Hector Zaraspe, Violette Verdy, Scott Douglas, Mary Hinkson, Edna McRae, and Edward Caton. Joffrey authorized Moore to establish an apprentice program designed to prepare students ages fifteen to eighteen for the company. He himself taught pointe classes. Glen Tetley, Lotte Goslar, and Norman Walker were soon also giving classes, exposing the dancers to modern technique and to Goslar's combination of modern drawn from her German background and what might be called mime improvisation.

Interestingly, Joffrey, who traversed the country preaching the gospel of *Swan Lake* and *The Sleeping Beauty*, told his own dancers differently. Noël Mason wrote in a letter to her parents on March 20, 1965:

> Mr. Joffrey feels the time when a dancer specializes in one type of movement is gone, particularly in America. Hence when someone argues that they only want to do classical roles, he really hits the ceiling. . . . "Why should we ever attempt Swan Lake *when the Russians can do it so much better, yet lack the flexibility that we will ultimately have?"* . . . I must say Glen Tetley's modern classes have really made me appreciate modern dance.[23]

Joffrey was far from unique in his synthesizing of ballet and modern approaches. Josephine and Hermene Schwarz in Dayton taught ballet from a modern viewpoint and modern from a ballet viewpoint; their students, such as Rebecca Wright, Stuart Sebastian, Donna Wood, Jeffrey Gribler, and Joseph and Daniel Duell, were manifestations of that claim. Dorothy Alexander of the Atlanta Ballet practiced and taught what she described as American classicism, which was pretty much the same thing as a fusion of idioms. These people, including Mary Ann Wells, were teaching and talking this way back in the thirties. Joffrey represented the second generation.

To accommodate the sudden burst of activity at his school—including Arpino, who was busy working on another new ballet, *Viva Vivaldi!*—Joffrey appropriated the building's fifth floor and added two new studios. His chocolate-brown-painted, cell-like office remained on the third floor, where the school had been situated for six years.

On January 12, 1965, Joffrey's dancers gave their first so-called performance, demonstrating the properties of Celanese fabric for a Burlington Mills live industrial show choreographed by Arpino, assisted by Margo Sappington. The company was paid $10,000, and Arpino turned some of the Celanese fabric they were advertising into costumes for *Viva Vivaldi!* That same month, *Sea Shadow* aired on a WCBS-TV arts special directed and produced by Merrill Brockway.

Then, on June 14, President Lyndon B. Johnson held a daylong White House Festival of the Arts, presenting ninety-six individual artists, four theatrical troupes, one jazz band, and one ballet company. The Robert Joffrey Ballet performed outdoors on the South Lawn, its members oblivious to the controversy brewing inside the White House, where signatures were being sought from the visiting artists to protest the Vietnam War and endorse poet Robert Lowell's position. Lowell had refused to attend the festival, publicly denouncing Johnson's stance on the war as morally wrong. Although only two signatures were gathered, Johnson refused to deliver his prepared speech at the event's dinner, and with that, the partnership between government and the arts temporarily slipped into a downward spiral.

President Johnson had entered his first full year in office positively disposed toward government subsidy of the arts. He had already established the National Council on the Arts, and by March 1965 the National Foundation on the Arts and the Humanities was created by law, events leading to the establishment in mid-September of the National Endowment for the Arts, chaired by Roger Stevens. In late December, the NEA's first grant went to American Ballet Theatre. It was an emergency matching grant of $100,000 to enable the troupe to continue operations, and an additional matching grant of $250,000 to support a nationwide tour. Although nobody within the NEA doubted the wisdom of allocating 14 percent of its entire initial budget for all the performing and visual arts to ABT—because the grant virtually rescued the company from collapse on its twenty-fifth anniversary—some homophobic congressmen protested.

During a public session, a congressman from a rural district in Virginia addressed himself off the record to Roger Stevens, but his remarks were recorded by Livingston Biddle, deputy chairman of the NEA, in his book *Our Government and the Arts*, and they bear repeating because homophobia was probably an operative factor in the way dance was handled and government-subsidized in the future.

> *"Mr. Stevens," said the Congressman when the court stenographer's fingers ceased to move over the keys of his transcribing machine, "isn't it true that most of the so-called male dancers in these companies you're talking about—isn't it true that most of them are—well—homosexuals?" There was a hint of laughter in the voice, to soften the element of probing derision. "Just for my own information, isn't that true?"*
>
> *"It may be true in a few instances," Stevens said without raising his voice, "but I guarantee you this, Mr. Congressman: If any male dancer happened by right now, he'd be strong enough to pick you up by the waist and put you over his head and throw you straight out the window."*[24]

Biddle also recalled that during the NEA's first days, George Mahon, chairman of the House Committee on Appropriations, told Roger Stevens that funding was promised to him as long as the NEA gave "no funding to dance." Stevens and Biddle responded to the threat by placing the American Ballet Theatre grant under the NEA's *theater* category and, in Biddle's words, relocating "the help for the other dance companies . . . conveniently under 'technical assistance,' a marvelously enigmatic and ubiquitous phrase in government, which here could apply to all the arts, not just one."[25] Dance was synonymous with homosexuality in the minds of many, and into the government's closet it went, often unable to procure funds unless in the guise of some other performing art.

Joffrey had helped revolutionize the teaching of ballet, particularly to men, in America. "This country takes more care of football teams than its dancers, even though I've never heard that any of these football teams bring back anything in terms of national prestige," he once said.[26] But, paradoxically, the ballet world was almost as much in the closet as the government. Homosexuality was still the unspoken issue. Within the safe confines of the dance world, homosexuals did not have to hide from each other. Yet those confines were exactly that: confining.

By 1965, Betty Friedan had published *The Feminine Mystique;* within the next six years, the sexual revolution gathered force. On a June 1969 evening in Greenwich Village, police raided a gay bar called the Stonewall and the clients fought back, pelting their uniformed assailants with bricks, bottles, and glass shards. The riot sparked gay activism nationwide. Joffrey, who was apolitical, would see the Joffrey Ballet reap some of the rewards of the 1960s liberation movements.

CHAPTER 18

City Center Joffrey Ballet

On August 9, 1965, the new Robert Joffrey Ballet made its official debut at Jacob's Pillow Dance Festival. Ted Shawn had been the first to approach Joffrey and kindly offer him a theater for his comeback. The troupe's weeklong engagement was billed as a "re-debut," honoring Shawn's presentation in 1952 of Joffrey's first ballet, *Persephone*. Shawn claimed partial credit for having "discovered" Joffrey, writing in one of his newsletters, "Joffrey, as you know, has been one of my protégés since his very beginning, and I think the boy has absolute genius."[1]

Shawn was often called the father of American dance; he had taught Jack Cole, Martha Graham, Doris Humphrey, Barton Mumaw, Gertrude Shurr, and Charles Weidman. He had been married to Ruth St. Denis. In 1929 they split up and dissolved their Denishawn Company, and Shawn later formed his Men Dancers. As half of Denishawn, he had persuaded the public that modern dance was respectable, in part because he was married and the works he and his wife made were charming, atmospheric, and wide-ranging pieces frequently inspired by indigenous dances of foreign lands. With the Men Dancers, Shawn wanted to emphasize that dancing was a respectable masculine activity. "I believe that dancing is a man's art form as much, or more, than it is a woman's," he wrote. "We will not reach the pinnacle of greatness that dance is capable of until we have as many men, and men of the highest calibre as to character, in dance companies as soloists, as we have women."[2]

At the Pillow, Joffrey presented eleven men and ten women, and the company slipped quietly into contemporary ballet history as the first to have more men than women. Joffrey never formalized a policy about the company's male-to-female ratio, which two years later still favored men by two, but he did not feel the need. Men dancers were elemental to his esthetic, and even though he did not spell that fact out, his and Arpino's actions spoke eloquently for them. In 1965, women vastly outnumbered men in the corps de ballets of the New York City Ballet and American Ballet Theatre, rendering the Joffrey Ballet's male majority of one or two significant.* The Joffrey troupe consisted of Charthel Arthur, Robert Blankshine, Lisa Bradley, Robert Brassel, Zelma Bustillo, Diana Cartier, Ivy Clear, Jon Cristofori, Edwina Dingman, Richard Gain, Ian Horvath, James Howell, John Jones, Nels Jorgensen, Susan Magno, Noël Mason, Marjorie Mussman, Dennis Nahat, George Ramos, Trinette Singleton, and Michael Uthoff. Some had come through the apprentice program, and some through scholarships to the school. They performed the world premiere of Norman Walker's exuberant ballet-modern hybrid *Contrasts* (with costumes by Joffrey and Warren Ruud) to a commissioned score by Paul Fetler; the U.S. premieres of Glen Tetley's sweet, playful *The Game of Noah* and Arpino's *Incubus;* plus Arpino's *Sea Shadow* and Joffrey's *Pas des Déesses.*

Joffrey was still interested in entertaining a large audience and presenting dances that were legible, that relied on a classical heritage, but in a modern context. He was not consciously a rebel. He chose to follow a tradition and did not want to alienate his audience by outrageous provocation. He maintained a strong commitment to American choreographers and twentieth-century composers and to the creation of original works. "It isn't an American emphasis. It's an emphasis on dance in America," explained Arpino.[3]

Although Arpino did not present either of his works-in-progress, *Viva Vivaldi!* or *Olympics,* his repertoire formed the company's backbone by 1965. His handpicked dancers were equal parts modern-dance trained and ballet trained, and more charismatic than they were classical. He loved a languid, flexible physique that could both move fast and be manipulated into hyperextended configurations. His dancers possessed personalities that were harder to control than those in the original troupe. "Arpino picks people, rather than shapes. But then he uses them as shapes—a contradiction," observed critic Doris Hering.[4]

The dancers were still listed alphabetically without regard for principal, soloist, or corps de ballet status. Even though Lisa Bradley could have been declared a Joffrey star, even though Nels Jorgensen had been with him since 1957 and was the troupe's superior partner, even though Noël Mason and Richard Gain had also stuck with him after Harkness—the company was still a no-star, all-star democracy with Joffrey's name above it.

More than anything, the dancers were young; although their style was brilliant, loaded with attack and energy, they lacked refinement. "If one could proffer a genuine quibble here and there about a piece of choreography or an aspect of immature performance," wrote Walter Terry in the *New York Herald Tribune,* "there could be nothing but gratitude that another American ballet company was back in business."[5] Curiously,

---

*Simultaneously, the regional ballet companies struggled to find male dancers.

whereas in 1956 Joffrey had gathered the dancers in his first company and said to them, "I want you to be as teenagers," now he really had teenagers. He had culled a fair number of them from the regional companies, and the age range in most of the regional companies at the time was thirteen to eighteen. His company did not have to pretend.

At the Pillow, the dancers were still learning; several had never danced professionally. In six months, an astonishingly short time, Joffrey had put his imprimatur on them. The Pillow performances were standing room only and made a spectacular hit with the audience. "The Robert Joffrey Ballet appears to have a rosy future," wrote Allen Hughes in the *New York Times*.[6] "An auspicious beginning for the young company," concluded Anatole Chujoy in *Dance News*.[7] Although Joffrey and Arpino would continue to view Walter Terry with suspicion and unequivocally state that he had "turned against" them, proof of such actions could not easily be found. Terry's review of the Joffrey's Pillow "re-debut" concentrated on praising Arpino: "Mr. Arpino, one of the genuine choreographic talents of our day—imaginative, searching, rebellious—has given us in [*Incubus*] a macabre and poignant exploration of the soul of an innocent girl [Lisa Bradley]."[8]

On September 8, 1965, the company opened with a benefit preview for a weeklong engagement at the open-air Delacorte Theatre in Central Park, presented by Joseph Papp and the New York Shakespeare Festival (no longer associated with Harkness). Joffrey treated the date as the first time the company had ever danced in New York. He discounted the Bellevue Fine Arts series in 1956 because the performances were auditions. He discounted the Brooklyn Academy of Music in 1958 because it was across the East River and not in Manhattan. He discounted the 1963 Delacorte performance at the Harkness Festival Ballet Gala because he had shared the program with American Ballet Theatre and other artists. And he never regarded any performance by his company prior to 1956 as a performance by *the* Joffrey Ballet.

Arpino's *Viva Vivaldi!* introduced the company's reigning young male classicists, Robert Blankshine and Luis Fuente. In this ballet Arpino, for the first time, used his signature leap-into-the-air-and-kick-the-back-of-your-head* for Blankshine. Blankshine had an almost female hip structure—open, lithe, and comfortable in splits with backbends. His dancing soared on the border of real and unreal; his feet never seemed to touch ground, indicating an eternal truth about human nature: we know not what we are.

---

*Although this became Arpino's choreographic insignia, the jump that was typical of the Bolshoi Ballet had actually first been executed in the Joffrey Ballet by Lawrence Rhodes in Joffrey's *Gamelan* (1962).

Where Blankshine emphasized the aerial, Fuente was solid, square-jawed, exuding peasant fervor, dominating the music, and thoroughly male. Born in Madrid, Fuente had been superbly trained in classic dance by Hector Zaraspe and was conversant as well with flamenco dance.

Viva Vivaldi!—to Rodrigo Riera's arrangement of Vivaldi's Concerto in D Major for Guitar and Orchestra—demonstrated that the company could do classical work, but the ballet was not of typical classical structure or style.* Blankshine and Fuente competed, each trying to outspin and outjump the other. In pure classical work, men did not usually reveal gladiatorial natures. In the third movement, Margo Sappington, only sixteen years old, set a rare sexy tone. Her short hair finished in spit curls plastered against her cheeks almost placed her outside *Vivaldi!* in a French cabaret smoking cigarettes and wearing stiletto heels. For many in the audience, she magnified the feeling that dancing was physical and, therefore, related to sex. Ballet could be human. A woman first, a ballet dancer second, Sappington was a revelation for many. Critic Deborah Jowitt recalled *Viva Vivaldi!* as a "great turn-on for the audience."[9]

Interestingly, Arpino did not see his work as sexually vivid, but as sexually ambiguous. "I use men and women as almost asexual at times. I see no difference. An arabesque is not masculine or feminine to me," said Arpino.[10] In the future, women would assume the Blankshine and the Fuente roles in *Vivaldi!* and prove his point. "The emergence of Gerald Arpino as a choreographer of genuine stature [is now clear]," wrote P. W. Manchester. "*Viva Vivaldi!* takes him a long step forward into the realm of positive achievement."[11]

Still, as different as *Viva Vivaldi!* might have seemed, it was nothing compared to Anna Sokolow's *Opus '65* on the third night. Sappington, wearing a blond fright wig, galvanized the work when, carried aloft by four men, she then slithered like a cat down their bodies toward the floor. Hands groped at her contours. The character appeared to like

---

*Trinette Singleton, who led *Vivaldi!*'s first movement (and caught the attention of Lucia Chase, who wanted her instantly for American Ballet Theatre), told the following story about the making of *Vivaldi!* to Pegeen H. Albig in 1977. Singleton said that the girls had gone to Arpino and moaned that they wanted "something dancey and pretty and on pointe," because the other works, by Norman Walker, Glen Tetley, and Lotte Goslar, were not classical. It was then that Arpino gathered the girls and choreographed the second movement of *Vivaldi!* with lots of jumps and intricate footwork. Arpino also took recommendations, hints, and orders from Joffrey, who had told Glen Tetley to insert *doubles tours* into *The Game of Noah* because "the men needed to work on their *doubles tours.*" Outraged, Tetley refused. Curiously, Arpino's next ballet, *Olympics,* incorporated many *doubles tours.* It became a given that Arpino's ballets would be the ones that Joffrey would use to strengthen the company's weaknesses as he saw them, because Arpino understood the needs behind Joffrey's requests.

being touched. The music by Teo Macero suggested a hungover state of mind, when there is so much static in the brain one cannot hear one's thoughts.

At the work's conclusion, each of the dancers (many of whom were Joffrey apprentices and students, not official company members) removed an article of clothing and hurled it fiercely onto a pile. Then, one by one, they sat at the edge of the stage with their feet dangling. "They take off their clothes because it's like, 'What the hell have I got this on for?' It's what they felt inside that I exposed," remarked Sokolow.[12] The dancers stared at the audience, cried out in anger, and jumped into the orchestra pit. "[*Opus '65*] puts jeans, sweatshirts and twist-based movements on barefoot dancers and ends up being a brilliantly terse direct expression of the feelings of alienation and sullenness that are common to so many young people today," Hughes wrote in the *New York Times*.[13]

All of the ballets seen at the Delacorte were simply produced, with little scenery. Most of the works were enhanced by Tom Skelton's lighting and the costumes. The full orchestra was led by Maurice Peress, with Rodrigo Riera playing guitar for *Viva Vivaldi!* Ted Shawn emceed the benefit performance, introducing the prologue from Arpino's *Olympics*—an all-male ballet that closely resembled Shawn's own *Olympiad*. Arpino's ballet was set to a score by Toshiro Mayuzumi, who had written the music for Balanchine's *Bugaku*. Nancy Lassalle, secretary of Ballet Society and active at the New York City Ballet, had commissioned the Mayuzumi piece. The repertory was completed by Lotte Goslar's clown ballet, *Charivari!*, Norman Walker's *Contrasts*, Joffrey's *Pas des Déesses* and excerpts from *Gamelan*, and Arpino's *Sea Shadow* and *Incubus*. Tetley's *The Game of Noah* and an original work, *Moods IV* by Louis Johnson, were canceled because of injuries.

"The crowds were bigger than they have been for any other event. The theater holds 3,500 and every night between one and three thousand were turned away," Noël Mason wrote, adding that Morton Baum, George Balanchine, Gower Champion, John Gielgud, and Sol Hurok were in the audience. "Even the kids from Harkness came and are dying to get back in; their company is such a mess," continued Mason. "In my variation in *Pas des Déesses*, I did a slow triple pirouette and the whole audience gasped. After that I hit every balance, too. Mr. Joffrey came back ecstatic and was asking everyone in sight if they'd seen me."[14]

Morton Baum, the formidable president and founder of the New York City Center of Music and Drama (the umbrella organization for both the New York State Theater, which housed the New York City Ballet and the New York City Opera, and the 55th Street Theatre, known as City Center), attended the Joffrey's Delacorte performances. Years earlier, he had seen and been amazed by Arpino's *Ropes*. Now he contacted Alex Ewing to invite the troupe to perform for a week at City Center. As with so many of the theatrical luminaries who witnessed the Joffrey Ballet's resurrection, Baum, an unapologetic Joffrey sympathizer, wanted to be counted as a supporter in the moral crusade against Rebekah Harkness.

Demonstrating the wily, imaginative survival tactics that would define the Joffrey, Ewing proposed a deal with Baum and remembered the scene with the kind of fantastic, subdued pleasure of a man who thought he had seen it all:

> *Morton Baum was narcissistic, grand—a one-man impresario of City Center, and he ran it out of his law office. His was a very old-fashioned little office. Dark. He said, "I have a week free in March [1966]." And I said no, that I didn't want a week from him, I wanted a different arrangement. I wanted a partnership. That he would get twenty percent of the box office—this was really very crazy—we didn't have any box office. I said, "You'll get twenty percent, and if we do well, you'll give me three weeks in the fall."*
>
> *And so he said, "Okay." I don't think he thought we could do it. But he had a week that he had to fill, and because he didn't like this Harkness thing—Morton Baum was another of these like Papp and Ted Shawn—he was going to do his bit, which was to give us the theater free. He was going to make a grand gesture. And I was going to make him a partner. That was my concession to him. This was our chance—possibly four weeks at City Center in 1966.*[15]

On September 20, 1965, an ecstatic Joffrey announced to his dancers that they were chosen to play City Center for a week in March, and there was also the possibility of a European tour in the spring. Baum majestically consecrated Joffrey as the company's artistic director, Arpino as Joffrey's assistant director, and then he anointed Ewing with the new title of general director. "Boys, the only thing I insist is you must do *Ropes* in your first season," Baum told them.[16] "You don't get the engagement unless that's involved in the repertory."[17] He had reacted in much the same enthusiastic way that composers Samuel Barber and Gian Carlo Menotti had in 1961. *Ropes*, it seemed, was the troupe's proven breadwinner.

On November 9, 1965, the Robert Joffrey Ballet began a week of performances for the Harper Theater Dance Festival produced by Bruce and Judith Sagan in Chicago. Clive Barnes, newly installed as the dance critic for the *New York Times*, found his seat in the audience. He had not seen Joffrey since 1955, when Joffrey had staged *Persephone* and *Pas des Déesses* for Ballet Rambert in London, where Barnes had been living. The next day, the critic reported:

The Joffrey Ballet ended its season last night with two programs showing the strength and versatility of a company that could and should become a real power in American dance. Just 20 dancers strong, for its size there is not a ballet company in the world to match it.

. . . If only New York had a theater as suitable for this kind of attraction as Chicago's Harper, and a management as adventurous as Mr. and Mrs. Sagan, we could look forward to a New York season for the Joffrey dancers. Has no one any ideas?[18]

The review was bold and not restrained, which said more about Barnes than it did about the Joffrey, especially if one knew the background to Barnes's appointment at the *Times*. When it had become evident to the *Times*'s editors that Allen Hughes, the paper's dance critic, whom they had appropriated from their own music staff and subsidized to educate himself in dance, was overwhelmed by the dance boom's demands, they began searching for someone to replace him. Clifton Daniel at the *Times* turned to Lincoln Kirstein for advice, and to Sol Hurok. He also consulted Frederick Ashton. Barnes was their universal recommendation.

Kirstein, who violently opposed Hughes, felt just as strongly in support of Barnes. In 1963, Kirstein initiated the luring of Barnes across the Atlantic. Recounted Barnes, "Kirstein had brought me over in '63. He paid for me to come and observe New York City Ballet. . . . The first indication I had that I was to be invited to join the *New York Times*—which I intended to refuse—was a letter from the Imperial Hotel in Tokyo from Lincoln Kirstein, and it just said, 'Dear Clive, Why the hell don't you take the *New York Times* job?' And I wrote back, 'Because I haven't the hell been asked.'

"Later I discovered that an unholy partnership [was part of the deal]. . . . In 1965, I decided to accept the job. . . . Balanchine read every word I wrote because I was brought over as a house critic. I didn't realize that not only was Lincoln and everyone instructing me to admire City Ballet almost past the point of adoration, which wasn't bad because I did, so that was easy enough, but they expected me to put down every other company."[19]

Soon after having seen the Joffrey Ballet in Chicago, Barnes authored a *New York Times* Sunday think piece ostensibly about touring companies, in which he found a reason to compare the Robert Joffrey Ballet to the Harkness Ballet, culminating in these words that would seal Joffrey and Arpino's fate.* These words were the tattoo on their skins, the challenge:

*Critical response to the Harkness Ballet (1964 to 1975) was remarkably unanimous, with the exception of Walter Terry, who loved most everything. One theme that appeared quite often was how impressive the men were. The men most often singled out were former Joffrey dancers: Finis Jhung, Helgi Tomasson, and Lawrence Rhodes. The general thrust was that the dancers far exceeded the limited repertoire that was often of questionable taste. Some typical comments were: "The Harkness Ballet, so superbly endowed with

The key to the Joffrey superiority over its rich sibling [Harkness Ballet] is quite simply that it has more entertaining, or if you prefer, more artistic, ballets. It has in Gerald Arpino a choreographer of unusual talent; indeed apart from the trio of Balanchine, Tudor and Robbins, it is difficult to think of a better classic choreographer in America. Indeed again, it is more than difficult, it is downright impossible. This, and presumably Joffrey's own forceful direction, gives the company artistic focus and an individual spirit.

. . . All great companies created in this century, from the Diaghilev Ballet onwards, have originated from the interplay of a first-rate director with a first-rate choreographer. The Joffrey Ballet, like New York City Ballet, like Britain's Royal Ballet, like perhaps Germany's Stuttgart Ballet, complies with these conditions.[20]

There it was in plain print: Joffrey was a first-rate director and Arpino a first-rate classic choreographer. The subtextual comparison of Arpino to Balanchine and the Royal Ballet's Frederick Ashton provoked a political uproar among some leading critics. Arpino had scarcely been tested. How could Barnes be so sure?

The immediate effect of his remarks was that Joffrey and Ewing consolidated Arpino as an integral member of their architectural team. Until the company's reformation in 1965, Arpino had popularly been thought of as a dancer—a leading dancer who was beginning to choreograph. It was invariably understood that Arpino and Joffrey were not coequals in the company's original foundation. By 1964, however, more of Arpino's works were in the repertoire than Joffrey's. (Joffrey had planned for the Pillow re-debut to present two new ballets choreographed by himself, but although he worked with dancer Richard Gain and composer David Amram on them, neither was completed.)

In 1966, the Joffrey Ballet could not have crossed the threshold into City Center without Arpino. The power balance between Joffrey and Arpino had shifted toward equality. Arpino's ballets drew the crowd, the praise, the news. Joffrey no longer dominated; now the company was a solid triumvirate: Joffrey as a gifted and effective teacher with a functioning school; Arpino a fast, enthusiastic, and talented choreographer; and Ewing with his valuable connections and administrative savvy. Arpino and Ewing had been essential to their landing City Center and convincing many that the company deserved to go big, move uptown, and be counted among the majors.

On March 30, 1966, the Robert Joffrey Ballet opened at the City Cen-

---

talent and money, performs like a whirlwind, but without significance" (Daniel Webster, *Philadelphia Inquirer*, November 12, 1967); "What a feeble assortment of works these excellent young dancers were asked to fan into life" (Donal Henahan, Chicago *Daily News*, March 13, 1967).

ter Theatre on West Fifty-fifth Street. Ewing had promised Baum 20 percent of the Robert Joffrey Ballet's box office, a meaningless promise
unless tickets were sold. With no budget for advertising, Ewing relied on
acumen. Each day, he took the box-office money from sold tickets down
to Edith D'Addario, executive secretary at Joffrey's school. There, students were guaranteed one free ticket provided they sold a ticket. When
a student had sold a ticket, Ewing would pay for the student's "free"
ticket out of cash from the box-office till. In 1966, a top-priced ticket
was $4.65. The ruse was illegal, but harmless, and as Ewing recalled, it
achieved the desired result:

"We used the money over and over again. So that way we had a good
attendance. And Baum was absolutely astonished. He walks into the
orchestra on opening night and the orchestra was just about full. And
he's thinking, 'Where the hell do all these people come from?' because it
wasn't the New York City Ballet crowd. It was a totally different crowd.
It was all kids and their roommates and their aunts.

"And that was one of my contributions to the company. I liked it less,
because it was highly illegal—because you can't take the box-office money
until the engagement is over. It's supposed to be held in escrow, or something. But Baum gave us a lot of leeway, and that's the way it worked."[21]

By every measure the Joffrey's debut season was a success. Arpino presented the engagement's only world premiere: *Olympics,* his all-male
ballet based on ancient Greek competitive sporting events. *Olympics*
seemed a direct (though less spiritually dimensioned) descendant of Ted
Shawn's *Olympiad* (1936), and more than one critic wondered if it was
any coincidence that for the premiere Shawn sat on the right of Isadora
Bennett, Joffrey's press agent. Norton Owen, a Shawn historian and
since 1990 director of preservation at Jacob's Pillow, said Shawn was
proud to have influenced Arpino and the Joffrey. They had brought
about a rebirth of male dancing. Owen further elaborated:

"Here, with *Olympics,* was a ballet set in a sports milieu that had very
definite homoerotic undertones that could be presented forthrightly and
in a way that was very respectable. The homoerotic has got to be an element that Shawn was picking up on, because he had an analogous situation. He had a company of men dancers in the 1930s and he was trying
to make a point about 'this is a manly thing for men to do.' But Shawn
meanwhile was gay and he was not up-front about that. . . .

"He had this company of hunks, and there have to have been times
when he would do something about the composition of the choreography that would please that sensibility in him. . . .

"I think Shawn then probably was very taken with the Joffrey Ballet
because it was, in essence, a later generation of this same kind of situa-

tion brought forward to an even bigger public and probably to an even greater acclaim."[22]

The critics from *Ballet Review* and *Dance Magazine* saw what is plainly visible on the 1967 *Olympics* film, stored at the Dance Collection in the New York Public Library for the Performing Arts at Lincoln Center: John Jones and Jon Cristofori as the wrestlers contested each other groin to groin. The wrestling was wrestling in quotes. While one man stood in wide-legged plié, the other straddled him. They pushed and pulled up and down in slow motion until the straddling man swiveled his pelvis in direct alignment with the standing man's pelvis. The standing man then sank to the floor and rolled away, conquered and exhausted.

In any interview in which Arpino was asked to discuss the homoerotic content of his ballets (and he made many in the future that would also warrant the question), he claimed he did not see what the critics and others saw. It is probably testimony to Arpino's choreographic control in *Olympics* that the ballet was not generally confused with a sexual statement. There was far more to *Olympics* than the wrestling pas de deux, and this is what established the dominant tone: Luis Fuente in a brief, white tank-top leotard was the high-leaping, muscular Torch Bearer. Spinning in second position, flying through grands jetés, biting into grandes pirouettes, and lighting the Olympic brazier, Fuente brought down the house. The ballet borrowed from Martha Graham's floor exercises and other modern vocabulary that Arpino had learned from Mary Ann Wells, May O'Donnell, and Gertrude Shurr. Arpino was assisted in its choreographic composition by Richard Gain, Ian Horvath, and Michael Uthoff, who were also familiar with modern technique. The curtain calls lasted "nearly as long as the ballet itself," exclaimed *Time* magazine.[23]

"As a manifesto of the importance of the male dancer it [*Olympics*] might be justified, and certainly it shows the vigor and power of the Joffrey men," Barnes commented in the *New York Times*. "But in their quieter moments, posing around the stage, they do look rather like overpretty advertisements for the body beautiful. In ballet, as in life, there is nothing quite like men and women together."[24] When asked in 1992 about his recommendation that Arpino add women to the *Olympics* cast, Barnes said:

"I may have been slightly worried at what could have been taken as a homoerotic element, which might have been damaging to the company's image. . . . I was concerned in that I perceived there was a dance revolution about to happen, or perhaps was happening. And I perceived the *New York Times* taking a key role in that. . . . It was so widely said in America, more widely in America than Europe, that dance was the fairies' ball game. And I know I was conscious that this was something that had to be corrected if dance were ever to take its place among the ordinarily accepted."[25]

Olympics was not the only newsworthy story that animated City Center that week. Former apprentices Frank Bays, Rex Bickmore, Dermot Burke, Margo Sappington, Donna Silva, and Don Richard gave their first performances as company members. Joffrey stole away Christine Hennessy from American Ballet Theatre, adding her to the ensemble specifically for the leading role as Lisette in Nault's *Fille mal gardée.* ("He needed her because she was classical," said Dennis Nahat. "Everyone else was too weird, too young, too modern.")[26] The dancers totaled twenty-eight (with men outnumbering the women by two). The brilliant casting of Lisa Bradley, Ivy Clear, Noël Mason, and Nels Jorgensen in Joffrey's *Pas des Déesses* would long be remembered after the season. And then, finally, the Maurice Ravel estate caught up with Arpino's *Sea Shadow.* Two lawyers representing Elkan-Vogel Publishing, which controlled the Ravel copyright, stormed into a Joffrey rehearsal and grabbed the scores for the Concerto in G-minor from the orchestra stands because Joffrey had stalled for too long.

Sea Shadow was scheduled to be performed the next day at a matinée. Rather than cancel, Arpino accepted the offer of Michael Colgrass, a young composer and percussionist who had played in the Joffrey orchestra and seen *Sea Shadow* several times. Colgrass thought he could write a new score for the twelve-minute ballet overnight. Arpino accompanied Colgrass to the offices of Merrill Brockway, executive producer of CBS-TV's *Camera Three,* where they watched a film of *Sea Shadow* until Colgrass had a precise idea of counts. Colgrass went to work, and in the morning, racing by taxicab and clutching copies of the score (in those days one had to make formal appointments at photocopiers, which Colgrass had done en route), he arrived at City Center with a completed work.

Lisa Bradley and Richard Gain, the dancers; Maurice Peress, the conductor; and the orchestra (with Colgrass in the pit on vibraphone) performed the matinée, having run through the new score only once. Isadora Bennett successfully quashed news items that were written and prepared to run in *Time, Newsweek,* the *Herald Tribune,* and the *New York Times* about the emergency rescue by Colgrass. The change of music was announced before the curtain lifted; only one critic made note (perhaps because the program failed to credit Ravel in the first place). Joffrey and Bennett did not want the public knowing that Joffrey had been evading the law, that he had been observed running to hide behind his file cabinet whenever Elkan-Vogel people called him, as if they could see him through the phone. For his services with *Sea Shadow* and for sparing Joffrey from having to drop the popular ballet, Colgrass received $500; he waived royalty fees. In April 1989, the Ravel score was made available and *Sea Shadow* was revived, accompanied by it. Critics felt the Ravel worked better than the Colgrass but the latter was more than serviceable.

*   *   *

On June 3, 1966, Baum announced that, "strongly encouraged"[27] by George Balanchine and Lincoln Kirstein, he was appointing the Robert Joffrey Ballet the resident ballet company of City Center.* The troupe would now be called City Center Joffrey Ballet. It would have a three-week season, commencing in the fall. "We believe they ought to have a chance," Baum informed *Newsweek*. "We give them the house, pay all the expenses, a total of some $17,500 a week. All they have to worry about now is themselves." Baum had offered City Center to Lucia Chase at American Ballet Theatre, but, added *Newsweek*, "[She] spurned the prosaic precincts of City Center" because she was used to the Metropolitan Opera House.[28] Alex Ewing responded differently: "The son of Lucia Chase, who had watched Ballet Theatre be an orphan for twenty-five years, knew the value of having a home base!"[29]

For the three-week season, Balanchine offered Joffrey his *Donizetti Variations* plus the costumes, and Ruthanna Boris's *Cakewalk*. Baum was impressed by such generosity toward the Joffrey, and confident that he had a fine new resident ballet troupe, he named Arpino the chief choreographer.

Joffrey rarely acknowledged Arpino's contribution publicly. What was that strange insecurity within him that pushed Arpino down? Why, furthermore, would Arpino want it to seem that he had nothing to do with the company's direction when, in fact, he did by choosing dancers, choreographing, and designing costumes? Incredibly, the answer seemed to have something to do with love and obedience. Arpino was just passive enough to persist in loving Joffrey because he had obligated himself to that ideal. He believed that death was preferable to betrayal or boastful pride. "I would have died for Bob. I would have taken a shot for him. Bob was my family," Arpino said.[30]

To outsiders the partnership appeared uneven. Rochelle Zide, who had returned to the company in 1965 as Joffrey's ballet mistress, said that Arpino for the next two years was never "in the loop."[31] Joffrey excluded Arpino from company meetings involving artistic decisions. "It was not to Jerry that any of us ever went with artistic questions. We went to Bob," she said. "Bob had the office."[32] She further recalled that Joffrey would sometimes take her to a studio to see an Arpino ballet that was almost finished, and that it was clear Joffrey had never seen the ballet before or previously discussed the work with Arpino. It appeared to Zide that Joffrey and Arpino were oblivious of each other.

---

*The New York City Ballet had been the resident at City Center from 1948 to 1964. Balanchine and Kirstein had moved the company in 1964, opening on April 24, to the Lincoln Center complex. The company still resides there in the New York State Theater.

Yet Joffrey's young cousin Naim Shah lived with them for a short while in Greenwich Village, and he observed a completely different picture. Joffrey and Arpino routinely winnowed out bad ideas and improved on the company's desirable characteristics by refining them through lengthy conversations at the kitchen table. There they exchanged detailed observations about dancers, choreographers, and composers. Joffrey respected Arpino's input and vision; the feelings between them were mutual. But Shah was under strict orders not to tell anything he heard or saw. The arguments between his cousin and Arpino sometimes flared and ended with doors slamming. The intimate nature of their friendship and artistic collaboration was their best-kept secret, and weapon.

Marie Gallette Joffrey c. 1930. Having toured her native Italy as an amateur concert violinist in her youth, she had compassion for her son's overwhelming desire to be in the arts. (Credit: Courtesy of Diane Lembo Talley)

After Dollha Anver Bey Jaffa Kahn emigrated in 1916 from Afghanistan to Seattle, Washington, he anglicized his name to Joseph Joffrey and opened the Rainbow Chili Parlor. By the late 1930s, when this portrait of him was made, he was a successful restaurateur who still adhered to many Muslim precepts and traditions of the old country. (Credit: Courtesy of Diane Lembo Talley)

Joffrey's Uncle Marcus frequently convinced him to play hooky from elementary school and catch movie matinées featuring Greta Garbo, Fred Astaire, or Ginger Rogers. Marcus was responsible for introducing his American nephew to the ballet and for paying for his lessons at Ivan Novikoff's School of Russian American Ballet. (Photo taken on February 27, 1957.) (Credit: Courtesy of Diane Lembo Talley)

Mary Ann Wells taught Joffrey ballet and modern dance for only four years, but he claimed that her instruction, philosophy, and esthetic determined his direction at every juncture of his artistic life. When he told her that he wanted to found a ballet company, she responded, "Learn to dance first, Robert." (Credit: Photograph © Ernst Kassowitz)

Bobby Joffrey as a member of Ivan Novikoff's Festival Ballet. This is the first known picture of him as a ballet dancer, and it is probably the way he appeared to his fellow students at the Edmond S. Meany Junior High talent show, 1942. (Credit: Courtesy of Ivan Novikoff and Beuhal Kirberger)

(Left to right) Anna Santanastasio Arpino, Joffrey, and Gerald Arpino on a beach in Staten Island, New York, 1948. (Credit: Courtesy of Ninette Arpino Bandini)

(Left to right) Jonathan Watts, Joffrey, and Arpino in 1952 rehearsing May O'Donnell's *Dance Sonata* in her 56th Street studio. "Wherever he was on stage, that was the center of the stage," said the critic P. W. Manchester of young Joffrey. (Credit: Photograph by Rachael D. Yocom, courtesy of May O'Donnell)

Cast and crew of Joffrey's "nucleus" company onstage at Jacob's Pillow, July 1952. (Left to right, first row) Read Arnow, Helen Murielle, Jacqueline Cecil, Tania Makarova, Diana Dear. (Left to right, second row) Jonathan Watts, Mrs. San Miguel, Eric Creel, Joffrey, Lillian Davies Wellein, Lillian Wellein, Tom Reddy, Electa Arenal, Arpino, Lolita San Miguel. (Credit: Photograph © John Lindquist, courtesy of Lillian Wellein.)

(Left to right) Marie Paquet as Lucile Grahn, Françoise Martinet as Marie Taglioni, Brunilda Ruiz as Fanny Cerrito, and Nels Jorgensen as Arthur Saint-Léon in Joffrey's bread-and-butter ballet, *Pas des Déesses,* c. 1959. (Credit: Martha Swope © Time, Inc.)

The official charter members of the Joffrey Ballet in 1956 (clockwise from the top): Glen Tetley, Dianne Consoer, Arpino, Brunilda Ruiz, Joffrey, John Wilson, Beatrice Tompkins (center). (Credit: Joffrey Archive Photo)

Lisa Bradley in a pose from Arpino's *Sea Shadow,* under the working title of *Undine.* Joffrey had found his greatest muse—"the first perfect body we ever had"—and he solidified his company around her. (Credit: Photography © Jack Mitchell)

Rochelle Zide and Arpino as the leads in *La Fille mal gardée,* choreographed by Fernand Nault. Sometimes affectionately called Arpinsky the poor man's Nijinsky by the other dancers, Arpino lit up the stage. His partnership with Zide is still talked about by Americans who saw them perform *Fille* on the road. (Credit: Photograph © Jack Mitchell 1960)

Brunilda Ruiz suspended in Arpino's *Ropes* at the Fashion Institute of Technology in New York City. Pulling the ropes (clockwise from the bottom): John Wilson, Joseph Nelson, Paul Sutherland, Lawrence Rhodes, Helgi Tomasson, Vicente Nebrada. (Credit: Photograph © Jack Mitchell 1962)

Joffrey's *Gamelan,* an example of Herbert Migdoll's time-lapse photography. "Migdoll does not simply record a specific moment but captures the essence and spirit of the choreographer's intentions," said Joffrey of his collaborator's work. (Credit: Photograph © Herbert Migdoll)

Joffrey and Rebekah Harkness watch the company rehearse in September 1962, during the untroubled early days of their partnership. (Credit: Photograph © Jack Mitchell 1962)

The Robert Joffrey Ballet at the 1962 summer workshop on Rebekah Harkness's estate in Watch Hill, Rhode Island, where guest choreographers Alvin Ailey, Brian Macdonald, Fernand Nault, and Donald Saddler worked with the dancers. (Left to right on the stairs) Elisabeth Carroll, Suzanne Hammons, Lawrence Rhodes, Richard Wagner, Helgi Tomasson, Lisa Bradley, Ailey, Joffrey, and Saddler. (Left to right on the roof porch) Françoise Martinet, Brunilda Ruiz, Finis Jhung, Anna Marie Longtin, Nels Jorgensen, Vicente Nebrada, Marlene Rizzo, Janet Mitchell, Felix Smith, Marie Paquet, Paul Sutherland, Lone Isaksen, Carolyn Borys, and Mayne Miller, the pianist. Arpino and James Howell are absent because of Arpino's back injury in Seattle. (Credit: Photograph © Jack Mitchell 1962)

Joffrey bowing to Emperor Haile Selassie at the White House reception in the East Room after the company's performance on October 1, 1963. Less than two months later President John F. Kennedy (fifth from right, with Lyndon B. Johnson third from right) was assassinated while the Robert Joffrey Ballet was on the U.S. State Department cosponsored tour of the Soviet Union. (Credit: Photograph © Robert L. Knudsen 1963, courtesy of Dance Collection, New York Public Library for the Performing Arts)

The triumvirate (left to right: Arpino, Alex Ewing, Joffrey) who pulled the Joffrey Ballet back together after the split with Harkness and moved it into City Center's 55th Street Theatre as the resident dance company in 1966. (Credit: Photograph © James Howell, courtesy of Dance Collection, New York Public Library for the Performing Arts)

President Lyndon B. Johnson's beagle, Him, lunges playfully for Robert Blankshine, who is brushing the sky at the White House. The newly organized troupe participated in the controversial White House Festival of the Arts on June 14, 1965. In the background, Joffrey Ballet members walk past Alexander Calder's sculpture, *Whale II.* (Credit: Photograph © Jack Mitchell 1965)

(Left to right) Noël Mason, Rex Bickmore, Trinette Singleton, Frank Bays, and Charthel Arthur in Balanchine's *Donizetti Variations*. Balanchine rehearsed the City Center Joffrey Ballet dancers himself, after Victoria Simon staged it. In this photo are "Joffrey's" ballerinas, so-called because they behaved well, worked hard, and were good friends to each other and to him. (Credit: Photograph © Fred Fehl 1966, courtesy of Dance Collection, New York Public Library for the Performing Arts)

Margo Sappington (far right) in Anna Sokolow's *Opus '65* before the dancers take off most of their clothes and jump into the orchestra pit. The men (left to right): Dermot Burke and Jorge Fatauros. (Credit: Photograph © James Howell 1965, courtesy of M. Sappington)

Noël Mason and Maximiliano Zomosa on the fall day in 1967 when she finally felt comfortable with everyone knowing they were a pair. Photo is taken without their awareness at Alex and Carol Ewing's farm in upstate New York, where Mason later hibernated with her son after Zomosa's suicide. (Credit: Photograph © James Howell 1967, courtesy of Noël Mason)

Luis Fuente as the Torch Bearer in Arpino's all-male ballet, *Olympics.* Joffrey was highly regarded for his teaching of men in the fifties, and Arpino choreographed ballets for them in which they were often given as much as, and sometimes more than, the women to do. (Credit: Photograph © James Howell, courtesy of Dance Collection, New York Public Library for the Performing Arts)

When he taught, Joffrey was fierce about details and his students' work ethics. Here he is at the Southeastern Regional Ballet Festival of 1974. (Credit: Photograph © King Douglas, 1974, courtesy of Dance Collection, New York Public Library for the Performing Arts)

Lisa Bradley as the deadly bird in Arpino's *Nightwings,* a ballet created for her and Michael Uthoff in 1966. *Nightwings* inaugurated the company's first season as the City Center Joffrey Ballet. (Credit: Photograph © James Howell 1967, courtesy of Christian Holder)

Maximiliano Zomosa as Death in Kurt Jooss's *The Green Table*. The ballet and Zomosa's performance permanently marked the Joffrey Ballet. Joffrey had seen *The Green Table* when he was eleven. It was the first ballet he saw as an audience member. He promised himself then that he would someday present the masterpiece with his own company. When Zomosa saw *The Green Table* as a college freshman in Chile, he vowed that he would someday dance the role of Death. (Credit: Photograph © Fred Fehl, courtesy of Noël Mason)

In the final scene, Death triumphs over a parade of his victims (Left to right): Marjorie Mussman as the Old Mother, Suzanne Hammons as the Guerrilla Woman, Zomosa as Death, and Jon Cristofori as the Old Soldier. The metronomic actions of Death's limbs continue to drive the rhythm of the dance. Death is the constant, a lesson that was not lost on the Joffrey's audiences during the Vietnam War. (Credit: Photograph © Fred Fehl 1967, courtesy of Dance Collection, New York Public Library for the Performing Arts)

Herbert Migdoll's montage image (a performance photograph combined with a dressing room portrait) of Joffrey's *Astarte* not only caught the psychedelic effect of the multimedia production but it spoke volumes about the sixties gestalt. On March 15, 1968, *Astarte* was the first ballet ever to grace the cover of *Time* magazine. (Credit: © Time, Inc. 1968)

The moment of seduction when the man (Maximiliano Zomosa) forgets himself and steals the lotus, tattooed on the forehead of the ancient Babylonian fertility goddess, Astarte (Trinette Singleton). (Credit: Photograph © Fred Fehl 1967, courtesy of Dance Collection, New York Public Library for the Performing Arts)

Léonide Massine applies the makeup of the Chinese Conjuror to Gary Chryst for the Joffrey's premiere of Massine's *Parade.* Joffrey, who was fascinated by makeup from the Diaghilev period, observes the process for future reference. Claude Picasso, on the left, snaps a photograph. He is the son of Pablo Picasso, who created the sets and some of the costumes for Diaghilev's Ballets Russes original production in Paris, 1917. (Credit: Photograph © Herbert Migdoll 1973)

Gary Chryst as the Chinese Conjuror. *Parade* helped catapult Picasso into the artistic mainstream and contributed to the launching of modernism, but until Joffrey's revival the ballet had never been seen in America. The production, supervised by Massine, established Joffrey as the "foremost historian and archivist of dance materials among ballet directors." (Credit: Photograph © Herbert Migdoll 1973)

A. Aladar Marberger. "Bob was crazy about Aladar. He'd never been with a person who was so open, flamboyant, brave, mischievous, theatrical, a family man who liked famous men." (Credit: Photograph © Joe Nicastri 1986)

Kevin McKenzie and Francesca Corkle in Arpino's *L'Air D'Esprit*. Joffrey had known Corkle, a ballet prodigy from Seattle, since she was three. Her romantic line and old style elegance informed Joffrey's *Remembrances*. (Credit: Photograph © Herbert Migdoll 1978)

(Left to right) Jennifer Habig, Parrish Maynard, and Dawn Caccamo in Sir Frederick Ashton's *Monotones I*. The Joffrey once possessed the largest collection of Ashton's works outside of England, the pride of Joffrey who revered and emulated Ashton almost as much as he did Serge Diaghilev. (Credit: Photograph © Herbert Migdoll 1986)

Christian Holder, one of the most popular and respected dancers both within and without the company, assumed an appropriate leadership role in Arpino's *Trinity*. The ballet was performed every season for the nine years that Holder danced with the Joffrey after its premiere in 1970. (Credit: Photograph © Herbert Migdoll)

James Canfield and Patricia Miller in *Round of Angels,* an elegy choreographed in 1982 to Mahler's Fifth Symphony *Adagietto* and dedicated by Arpino to his musical adviser and friend of eleven years, James Howell. (Credit: Photograph © Herbert Migdoll)

Known for her spinning dances, Laura Dean brought an atomic energy to the troupe for the third time with *Force Field* (1986). Dean proved that Joffrey's acumen for "undiscovered" talent was as strong as ever. (Credit: Photograph © Herbert Migdoll 1986)

(Left to right) Stanley Holden, reprising his role in Ashton's *La Fille mal gardée* as the Widow Simone, rehearses with Joffrey, David Palmer, Tina LeBlanc, and former Royal Ballet dancer, Alexander Grant. (Credit: Photograph © Herbert Migdoll 1986)

Historian and choreographer Millicent Hodson spent more than a decade preparing to reconstruct Nijinsky's, Stravinsky's, and Roerich's groundbreaking *Le Sacre du printemps* (above, Act I, "the calm of nature before the onslaught of a hurricane"). For Joffrey, *Sacre* represented the culmination of an almost lifelong dream to fathom everything possible about his idol, Nijinsky. (Credit: Photograph © Herbert Migdoll 1987)

Beatriz Rodriguez as *Sacre*'s Chosen Virgin, who must "die to save the earth," dancing "as if possessed" by Nijinsky's stylized primitive Slav ritual. Roerich's costume design reveals his fascination with the Stone Age, the Vikings, and ancient Slavs. (Credit: Photograph © Herbert Migdoll 1987)

Joffrey rehearsing with Diane Orio and the large cast of *Petrouchka* in Los Angeles. Fokine's ballet was the one that was perhaps the most dear to him. He would often surprise his dancers by showing up on the stage disguised in a bear costume or a Russian Cossack uniform, dancing around the crowd. "It was only his small size and high energy that gave him away." (Credit: Photograph © Herbert Migdoll 1983)

The all-male Snow Winds in the *Nut-cracker*'s "Waltz of the Snowflakes" choreographed by Arpino. The production was Joffrey's final one. (Credit: Photograph © Herbert Migdoll 1987)

Diane Lembo Talley pours Joffrey's ashes into Puget Sound, releasing them at a spot where Mary Ann Wells's house can be seen on the shore. Behind Talley are two of Joffrey's loyal friends (left to right): Garth Rogers and Bill Leighton, who was his Joffrey Ballet assistant. Dan Brown wears the sunglasses. (Credit: Photograph © Tommy Edwards, courtesy of Diane Lembo Talley)

Arpino's production of *Billboards* involved four choreographers working with music by the rock star Prince. The sets are by Herbert Migdoll. The big, Broadway-like show fulfilled its commercial promise and brought in the mass public, adding substantially to the company's coffers and allowing Arpino to proceed as the company's new artistic director. (Credit: Photograph © Herbert Migdoll 1993)

1966 season's souvenir program there are black-and-white fugues of dancers pursued by tracers—the ghosts of their arms, legs, feet, and heads. The blurry dance photo, suggesting a rush of action, often with a crisp, isolated head or foot as its focal point, became the City Center Joffrey Ballet's—and Migdoll's—signature.

Migdoll wanted to provide a sense of seeing the ballet; Joffrey responded enthusiastically because he wanted the company's image to be that of a troupe of movers—young, exuberant dancers who never seemed to stop—such as the ones in Arpino's *Viva Vivaldi!* and *Olympics*.

"The subtle does not exist for Jerry," said Rochelle Zide. "It didn't exist for him as a dancer. It doesn't exist for him as a choreographer. With Jerry there was sensationalism and exploitation of the human body. If you could do an arabesque of ninety degrees, he wanted it one hundred twenty. If you did it at one twenty, he'd want it at one sixty. As a dancer he did not tend to be outrageous in terms of campiness, but he also did not hold back anything onstage. This characteristic found its way into his ballets. He choreographed to please."[9]

Arpino's racy, crowd-pleasing side was matched by his brooding, loner self. The soulful, dramatic persona that produced *Ropes* and *Incubus*— and would go on to choreograph *Nightwings* and *The Clowns*—also possibly stemmed from Arpino the early Joffrey dancer. In 1956, he had played the demented son in Joffrey's *Within Four Walls,* and in 1959 he had taken on the role of the lonely newspaper boy in Dirk Sanders's *Yesterday's Papers* and the blind man in Francisco Moncion's *Pastorale.* Arpino's significant roles were disturbed outcasts and misfits. Such psychological material was later absorbed into his choreography. In his ballets *Ropes, Incubus, Nightwings,* and *The Clowns,* the central characters were haunted strangers, romantics bearing the burden of the world on their shoulders.

In 1966, Joffrey stood behind Arpino and Migdoll, hiding and masterminding the company. The thing he seemed to fear most was the possibility that he would be seen as just an ordinary man. Various critics picked up on Joffrey's emphasis on image-creating: "The Joffrey trades in romanticized images of a society, images that stress the way we would like ourselves to be rather than in piercing observations of an artist about the way we actually are," Marcia B. Siegel wrote. "People go to the Joffrey not for subtlety or challenge but for clarity, craft, and for a look into the magic mirror of their illusions."[10]

"To me, dance is everything that's good," Joffrey said. "Everything that's beautiful, everything that's difficult. I couldn't exist without dance. It's my whole life."[11] His company's illusion was an honest one. Every angle, shade, tone, and form had precedent in the original 1956

Robert Joffrey Theatre Dancers. His esthetic did not differ from his ethics; there was a bit of the charlatan and a keeper of secrets—but all subordinated to the service of a theater man.

Morton Baum demanded that Joffrey himself choreograph a new work each season. The company was not called the Arpino Ballet, Baum argued; so far, Joffrey had buffeted Baum's pleas. Then, when fall 1966 approached, he surprised everyone and promised a world premiere—his first since 1962 with *Gamelan,* which he would also be reworking for the season.

Joffrey also announced plans for unveiling six additional ballets new to his repertoire during the three-week engagement, September 6 to 25. Balanchine offered him *Donizetti Variations* (Balanchine would work with them at the final rehearsals) and Boris's *Cakewalk.* Boris herself would stage the minstrel-show parody that she had contributed to the New York City Ballet in 1951. Joffrey solicited more choreography from Gloria Contreras, who had participated in his very first workshop in 1961. She agreed to stage *Moncayo I* and *Vitalitas.* But perhaps the news that gladdened him most was that Eugene Loring had agreed to return to the studio. Known as the American legend who choreographed *Billy the Kid,* Loring had not generated anything in New York for a major company in over a decade. Anticipation in dance circles was that he might produce another classic. Loring had chosen a Los Angeles composer, Gerald Goldsmith, as his collaborator on *These Three,* a ballet based on the true story of the three civil rights workers who had been found murdered in Mississippi in 1964.

Gerald Arpino was also preparing a premiere, *Nightwings,* to a commissioned score by John La Montaine, a Pulitzer Prize–winning American composer. The ballet would be for Lisa Bradley and Michael Uthoff, who had married on March 5, 1965. Arpino engaged Ming Cho Lee to design the sets (as he had for *Sea Shadow* and *Olympics*), and Willa Kim to design the costumes. Lee, famous for his stage and opera designs and, in dance, for working for Martha Graham, explained why he was interested in the Joffrey/Arpino vision:

"There's an excitement. They're not ashamed of doing a little bit of show-off, like *Viva Vivaldi!* They're very human.

"Of course, I began to realize that a good deal of it was Jerry Arpino, because he was fantastic at showing off the dancing. He was easy to work with. . . . He had tremendous energy. And the company was close-knit. Everyone enjoyed working with each other. They were not establishment."[12]

Joffrey paced the bridge between the ages of materialism and Aquarius. He was not exactly a card-carrying member of the counterculture, but he absorbed its impact and discovered a rationale for the esthetics that informed his company. Shaping his company as a director, he followed in the path of such choreographers as Jerome Robbins and substituted blue jeans for swan's feathers and T-shirts for sylph's wings, the democratic American middle class for the king's imperial court. American Ballet Theatre had an eclectic repertoire since its inception, but unlike ABT's directors, Joffrey did not view his troupe as a vast museum full of permanent collections. And unlike ABT's directors, he was not producing the nineteenth-century classics—he looked to the past only as far as the memory of the living original cast members or choreographers permitted.

Starting with *Persephone* in 1952 and with his proto-company dating from the same time, his purpose was to integrate contemporary dance and music makers and position them to work with contemporary designers, stretching their ideas on his dancers like canvas on a frame. Joffrey's vision for a company was to provide opportunities for collaboration. Still using Diaghilev as his directorial model, his intellectual impetus for the City Center Joffrey Ballet was exactly the same one that had in 1959 put Dirk Sanders's cutting-edge *Yesterday's Papers* on the same program as the first American staging of Antony Tudor's *Soirée Musicale,* on the same program as Francisco Moncion's *Pastorale.* This eclecticism defined Joffrey, whether or not he was the choreographer, and stimulated the artists involved.

New ballets were unpredictable. Joffrey could not screen them beforehand. He had to trust the people he asked, and often he tried to hedge his bets by bringing the choreographers in early enough so they could teach. Ruthanna Boris arrived in the summer of 1966 wearing her white, Helanca, V-neck leotard with a black bra underneath and banging her drum to teach the counts to *Cakewalk.* Loring concentrated on *These Three,* assisted by Margo Sappington. Zide and Joffrey rehearsed Joffrey's new staging of *Gamelan* and everything but the Arpino repertory, which landed on Howell.

The spirit of experimentation permeated not only Joffrey's company but his school. Hector Zaraspe was instrumental on Joffrey's teaching faculty, preparing company members from the apprenticeship pool. One day, Zaraspe wanted to show off to some of his friends the number of exciting choreographers who were rehearsing. Noël Mason captured Zaraspe's tour for his guests in a letter:

> *Mr. Zaraspe took them upstairs telling them how versatile the company was and how everyone did everything. They looked into one studio and there was Margo Sappington practicing [the all-male] "Olympics"! Looked into the next studio and there was Bobby Blankshine practicing* fouettés *en pointe (in my shoes, I might add) to the Black Swan music.*[13]

New to the group of apprentices in 1966 was Christian Holder, whom Joffrey had selected from the High School of Performing Arts. Sixteen years old, six feet tall, and raised on dance, Holder was born in Trinidad to Boscoe and Sheila Holder. Shortly after Holder was born, Boscoe and Sheila emigrated to London, leaving Holder with his grandparents. Two and a half years later Holder joined his parents. He performed with Boscoe Holder and His Caribbean Dancers in nightclubs and cabarets. He studied ballet and earned a scholarship to the Martha Graham School. This took him to New York in 1964. Dance, intense and majestic dance, was young Holder's food and air. When Joffrey saw Holder, he instantly offered him an apprenticeship and persuaded him to leave Graham.*

Apprentices fell under the jurisdiction of Lillian Moore and were taught, as well, by several important additions to the staff: Perry Brunson from the New York Ballet Russe school; Maria Grandy, who had performed with Joffrey during the 1957–58 tour; Meredith Baylis (by February 1967); and Zaraspe. Apprentices literally apprenticed roles in the main company. They were not, emphatically not, company members. They danced the small roles and watched the major ones from the wings. Along with Holder in the summer of 1966, the apprentices were Ann Axtmann, Richard Browne, Helyn Douglas, Erika Goodman, Pamela Johnson, George Montalbano, Haynes Owens, Rafael Romero, Robert Talmage, Martha Vaala, Karen Williamson, and Rebecca Wright.

In the summer of 1966, the dancers declared mutiny. It all began during a run-through of *Gamelan*. A disagreement between Richard Gain and Arpino over choreographic accuracy had exploded into a full-scale shouting match. The entire company refused at that point to continue the rehearsal unless Joffrey intervened and proclaimed which person was doing the right step. The dancers gathered in a fifth-floor studio at the school and shut the door, locked the apprentices out, and demanded Joffrey's presence. Joffrey arrived, livid, white-lipped, and "screaming and upset," said Michael Uthoff.[14] The dancers told him that they had gone through *Gamelan* again and again—and it was not an easy ballet, with the men lifting and carrying the women so much that it seemed the women's feet never touched the ground. Not once had Joffrey been present to observe their progress. They threatened to quit en masse if he did not attend his own rehearsals.

"Joffrey was in shock. He wanted us to calm down. He said we were going to be successful," said Dennis Nahat. "We said we couldn't be,

---

*At the same High School of Performing Arts concert, Joffrey had also seen Gary Chryst and offered him a scholarship to the school. Together with Rebecca Wright, Dermot Burke, and Francesca Corkle, Holder and Chryst defined the next Joffrey Ballet generation.

since we weren't getting the training we needed. We needed him in the studio. He was angry that we had the power to confront him."[15]

Nahat suggested that, overwhelmed with bureaucracy, Joffrey was running the company from the office rather than the studio, and the company had diverged from the direction of classical esthetics without his awareness. By challenging him, the dancers had unwittingly forced him to acknowledge the disparity between his vision for the company and the reality. Explained Nahat:

"He was creating a modern company, a great company, with a whole different sensibility than what he thought. He was a classicist. He was not a modernist. When he taught class, everything was fine. He would bring his lithographs and talk to the dancers about what he saw, what he thought was good dancing, and what we should be as people—not as dancers. He was trying to replicate the image of the Kirov Ballet. Maybe his company with Larry Rhodes and Helgi Tomasson before us could have done that, but the company he now had was a company composed of all different freaks of nature. Including myself. We came from different corners of the world. We were trained in ballet, but the repertory Joffrey was staging was not a classical repertory, and he did not have the teachers in place to make us classical."[16]

"Here was this incredible man who could have made all of us into much better dancers, if he had just spent time with the company," said Uthoff. "He took me once for forty-five minutes and worked on *Pas des Déesses*. In forty-five minutes, I completely changed. I gave a performance the next day in Toronto that got a review like no other."[17]

Joffrey responded to the dancers' imminent mutiny by rehearsing them in his ballets *Pas des Déesses* and *Gamelan* for seven hours the next day. He taught more frequently, he addressed his weaknesses, and let others on his staff chastise the dancers for having questioned his authority. Immediately after the incident, Edith D'Addario made many of the apprentices feel that they should not speak to any of the dancers—Dennis Nahat, in particular—who had most vociferously threatened to quit. She "discouraged us from talking to Dennis because he was a 'traitor,' " said Christian Holder, adding, "You felt that your loyalty was questioned [by D'Addario, Howell, and Arpino] if you were seen fraternizing with 'them.' "[18]

Nahat, who had injured himself and was teaching at the school, was dismissed from the company and school by D'Addario. He developed into a memorable American Ballet Theatre character dancer. Perhaps his talent may have been too special for the small Joffrey fiefdom, or at least it was too rebellious, and Joffrey, rather than confronting Nahat, allowed D'Addario to do the dismissing. It seemed an act of sheer cowardice and sent a chill through many of the other dancers, who had thought more highly of Joffrey as their leader.

On this issue they were in agreement, but the troupe's members were in most respects a socially divided lot. An invisible line fell roughly between those who were virgins and those who were not; those who drank and those who did not; those who did drugs and those who did not; and those who embraced D'Addario as a kindly mother figure and those who hoped she would keep her distance. They amused each other in the extreme and were, perhaps, more self-centered than the earlier Joffrey Ballet dancers, but no less desirous of pleasing Joffrey. Their point of agreement: they cared about making Robert Joffrey look good. They respected the way he made them look. He had an eye and a standard that they unconditionally trusted. Even Nahat had left with good words for Joffrey: "He was wonderful to be around."[19]

Yet, the *Gamelan* confrontation had failed to resolve several problems. One was Jim Howell. He was responsible for rehearsing Arpino's ballets, therefore the dancers spent most of their time with him. But his experience as a professional performer was limited. He had danced practically only in Arpino works. He knew less about ballet than they did. He also committed the ballet master's crime of playing favorites, awarding good roles to dancers who were not ready for them, but whom Howell wanted as friends.

Other reasons for the dancers' dissatisfaction concerned the no-star, all-star Joffrey system, which struck many as small-minded and discourteous. The dancers argued that the so-called democratic hierarchy also contributed to physical injuries. If a dancer had to perform a lead in one ballet, then switch to the corps in the next, then perform a modern role, then a classical part, all on the same program (which is what Joffrey would require), then he or she would break down.

But every company has its stages: birth, infancy, adolescence, adulthood, and old age. The Joffrey Ballet was in its adolescence, and like a teenager, on September 6, 1966, it snapped out of the bad mood, acted as though nothing were wrong, and jumped into the City Center Joffrey Ballet's inaugural season as though it were going on a date in a red Corvette.

CHAPTER 20

The Green Table

Despite Joffrey's efforts to the contrary, audience members during the company's first season in 1966 at City Center became enthralled by, and even infatuated with, individual dancers. He had set out to attract the "exceptional" dancer, the person who did not "fit in"[1] (his words), and it is astonishing to think that he imagined they would vanish into a democratic corps. Even their names riveted attention: Ivy Clear, Rex Bickmore, Charthel Arthur, Zelma Bustillo, Maximiliano Zomosa. Said aloud, they conjured vivid lines, kinetic rhythms.

In a company of fewer than thirty dancers, many had to perform in three ballets per night and, on days when there were matinée and evening performances, sometimes as many as seven ballets within a twelve-hour period, plus company class in the morning and maybe even a rehearsal between performances. Those days were exceedingly taxing, but they did give audiences the opportunity to become acquainted with the dancers.

Tickets were affordably priced from $1.95 to $4.95. "Of box office significance was the capacity attendance," reported *Variety* on the Joffrey's three weeks (from September 6 to 25) at the 2,935-seat City Center.[2] The company drew a crowd, and artistically the season could be summarized by Alan M. Kriegsman, when he wrote in the *Reporter,* a New York bi-monthly magazine:

> *This handsome, ambitious troupe of some 30 dancers is keenly conscious that it is an upstart in the tight little world of ballet, and, having come this far, it is clearly determined not to give ground. Lacking the choreographic genius with which George Balanchine has built the New York City Ballet or the traditions of the American Ballet Theatre, the Joffrey troupe does have some crucial attributes that its older, larger competitors appear to have lost—audacity and joy.*[3]

There had clearly not been enough time for the refinements, said Clive Barnes in the *New York Times,* and at first, the repertory had a "dress-rehearsal" look. By the final week, however, Barnes and others were waxing poetic. A Joffrey style was discernible, one that Mary Ann Wells, who had emphasized arms, might have recognized as the fulfillment of her teaching. "The girls have the best arms and feet in American ballet," praised Barnes. "Their style and bearing is a privilege to watch."[4]

Although Walter Terry thought that Joffrey's dancers in Balanchine's *Donizetti Variations* behaved too much like "kids let loose in a palace,"[5] Barnes rejoiced in the staging and compared the Joffrey cast favorably with the New York City Ballet's. He declared, "While it would presumably be heresy, sacrilege, high treason, and bad manners to suggest that the young Joffrey dancers performed this bright, sharp-faceted divertissement better than do Balanchine's own dancers, they came, for a first performance, remarkably close."[6] As Joffrey would learn, Barnes's words did not sit well with either Lincoln Kirstein or Balanchine.

Eugene Loring's *These Three* was a massive disappointment, even though Terry tried to obscure the failure in his piece for the *World Journal Tribune,* titled "A Powerful Loring Ballet." Gloria Contreras's *Moncayo I* and *Vitalitas* were relegated to "nice try, but . . ." status. The only premiere to enter the permanent repertoire was Arpino's *Nightwings.*

Nightwings promoted Bradley and Uthoff's partnership and individual celebrity. The hit ballet depicted an urban malcontent (Uthoff) visited by a seductive predatory bird (Bradley) and her five voyeuristic bird henchmen, whose principal function was to lift her while she simulated castrating him with her pointed foot.*

Joffrey's revised *Gamelan* was pummeled by Barnes in the *Times.* The evanescent quality had been drained from the ballet. Ironically, he found it "perhaps a little overdependent upon its beautiful and beautifully rehearsed dancers."[7]

In Ruthanna Boris's *Cakewalk,* it was Ivy Clear whom critics told their readers not to miss as the Wallflower and as Hortense, Queen of the Swamp Lilies. They also recommended two new dancers: Maximiliano Zomosa and Barbara Remington. Other new company members were Stephania Lee from American Ballet Theatre and Suzanne Hammons, who had originally been with Joffrey, but had defected to Harkness. Seymour Lipkin was the new musical director and conductor. William Pitkin was formally made artistic adviser. Regina Quintana headed the costume department.

Joffrey had also a year before hired Dr. Richard M. Bachrach, an osteopath, as the company physician. Bachrach, who had previously served as company physician for Jerome Robbins's Ballets: U.S.A. in Spo-

---

*In Chile, as late as 1948, classical pointes were equated with the devil. Michael Uthoff was from Chile. Two unrelated facts, except for the geography and the possibility that Arpino was thinking of them as linked.

leto and had also worked with both John Butler's company and American Ballet Theatre, was among the first to focus on the special problems encountered in dance. In case of emergency, he was available to Joffrey's dancers at every performance. He was mostly paid in free tickets to the performances and through workers' compensation. He remained with the company until 1978.

At the City Center Joffrey Ballet, if a dancer could not perform because of an injury, often the whole ballet had to be pulled from the program. There were no second casts for most of the repertory. Joffrey and Arpino were unsympathetic to dancers who complained about aches and pains, and they pressured them to dance regardless of their physical conditions. On numerous occasions, Bachrach received angry phone calls from Joffrey doubting Bachrach's judgment that company members were in no condition to perform. Bachrach devised ways to satisfy both his employer and his patient, and to ameliorate his many conflicts of interest. In the event of minor injury and pain that bordered on the debilitating (which for a dancer might be sore muscles, pulled tendons, back spasms—any kind of muscular-skeletal complaint), Bachrach often injected cortisone, rehabilitating the dancer sufficiently to enable him or her to perform without crippling pain. In 1966, the negative side effects of cortisone were not nearly as well known and understood as now. He also gave the dancers vitamin B_{12} shots to maintain their energy, and in time, he administered muscle relaxants, because they unknotted the dancers' spasms overnight, and the next day they could return to the studio.

Margo Sappington described what went on from the dancers' point of view once Bachrach entered the picture. In 1966, at age eighteen, she injured her Achilles tendon and had firsthand experience with Bachrach:

"[Bachrach] gave everybody quaaludes. . . . The muscle-relaxing qualities of quaaludes were incredible. . . . I took one and about half an hour later I was carrying a plate of food and ended up on the floor, but the next day I was out of spasm. They were fantastic things. For a dancer hurting like dancers do, this was a wonder drug. You took one quaalude a night and you woke up the next day and you went to class and you felt great and you could function.

"The terrible side effect was that you developed a tolerance. Then you took two. Then you took three. Then you started taking them in the daytime. . . .

"But Joffrey absolutely needed us to perform and function."[8]

Badly injured, Sappington suffered valiantly through the first season at City Center, but she did not dance much. Quaaludes taken under ordinary circumstances often made people as loose and sloppy as bean bags. They provided a sensation of bonelessness and sometimes heightened sex. Sappington explained that the dancers learned that if they took quaaludes, the "boneless" effect would be avoided provided they started moving right away. Some of the dancers experimented recreationally with the drugs.

Joffrey and Arpino opposed using drugs for entertainment. Arpino carried his "little black bag"—a leftover property from his days as the first pharmacist's mate in the Coast Guard—in which he kept medicines for his back pain and Joffrey's asthma, and sometimes he had diet pills. The dancers teased that it also contained his "stash," but Arpino and Joffrey were confirmed purists about consumption. Their bodies were their temples, as Mary Ann Wells had defined them. But Joffrey also "didn't see what he didn't want to see," said Michael Uthoff, adding there were some blatant episodes of substance abuse.[9] Joffrey ignored one dancer's drinking problem, even when that dancer was frequently discovered asleep under the studio piano. Joffrey apparently did not believe in interfering with his dancers' personal lives as long as their decorum onstage was professional. His notions of responsibility went only so far.

The vast majority of the Joffrey members had long, sustained careers. "The drugs did not interfere," said one. "I worked hard. I played hard. Maybe it was dangerous, but I am also dangerous onstage. Some people can do it, some people can't."

Glenn White was among those who could not. He arrived as an eighteen-year-old apprentice in 1968 and fell victim to drug use. White's diaries illustrate how far out of touch Joffrey and Arpino could be from their dancers. The generation gap was partly to blame.

The following are excerpts from White's 1971 diary:

January 21: Having some trouble with the damn turns, but again I think it's my shoes being so baggy. Roger [not his real name] is gonna give me a down. Have to call Dr. Bachrach for some before Chicago.

April 16: Got myself in late so I decided that I had to have a Dexamyl for breakfast. . . . I got to class and flew through the day. It was a good thing, too, cause Mr. Arpino changed my hours so that I had seven [hours of dancing] that day. . . . When Jerry wanted to do the coda, I wasn't ready. In fact, I was a crashing disaster. So nothing constructive happened . . . and Jerry got sort of mad. So I got upset when he said, "Go home. You're too tired to do anything." By "anything" he meant choreograph for him.

April 28: I also got to the pharmacy again to have my prescription renewed. More quaaludes and Ritalin. God, I seem to be living on them. I know I'm not but . . . all the same I am renewing my prescription.[10]

There was no reason to believe that Bachrach knew the dancers were misusing the drugs. But asked if he ever worried that when the dancers called upon him for quaaludes, they were using the prescribed drugs not only as muscle relaxants or a balm for real physical woes but to get high, Bachrach said, "I was very innocent. To me, what they were doing was to get relaxed, until later I learned that they weren't. And that is, of course, what happened. But I was a jerk. I wanted to be Mr. Nice Guy. I wanted everybody to love me. I wanted to be one of the gang. And so, at the time [prescribing those drugs] wasn't illegal. But I was a jerk. . . . It's the sixties, you know, and the early seventies, and it's the drug culture."[11]

In 1987, White required a leave of absence from the company as Arpino's assistant to dry out in a clinic for drug and alcohol addiction. He is the only Joffrey dancer who has admitted to having needed such formal intervention.

In the middle of 1966, Michael Uthoff visited Joffrey in his office. During their casual conversation, Uthoff's eye wandered to a box marked Jooss.

"Do you know Papa Jooss?" he asked.

"No," replied Joffrey. "But I want someday to do his ballets. I really want *The Green Table*."

"Let me write my parents, and I'll see what I can do."[12]

Uthoff, who had come to Joffrey from the José Limón company, was a son of Ernst Uthoff and Lola Botka. They had recently retired as directors of the Chilean National Ballet. During the thirties, until they settled in Santiago in 1941, they had been members of the Ballets Jooss in Essen, Germany. In 1932, Ernst Uthoff had created the role of the Standard Bearer in Jooss's *The Green Table*.

This was the first ballet Joffrey had seen as an audience member, two months after his eleventh birthday in Seattle. With his uncle Marcus he had watched Uthoff as the Standard Bearer and Botka as the Old Mother. In November 1964, their Chilean National Ballet was presented at the New York State Theater. *The Green Table*, staged for the Chilean National by Kurt Jooss in 1948, was the program's major offering. Joffrey had not seen the masterpiece since his youth, and this performance confirmed the importance he had attached to it as his "talisman." But Joffrey was keenly affected again for another reason. In the company was a dancer like none he had seen: Maximiliano Zomosa.

An antiwar ballet, *The Green Table* had relevance in 1966 to contemporaries living through the Vietnam War. Don Richard, one of Joffrey's dancers, was leaving the company to serve in Vietnam, and although Joffrey did not know it at the time, Richard would not return alive. *The Green Table* resonated. Erupting like a force of nature from behind the black velvet curtain, Death, portrayed by Zomosa, emerged in his leather harness and dark leather boots. The audience could see him, but clearly the soldiers, as they marched off to battle, leaving their women behind, could not.

One by one by one, Death conquered the characters onstage. Each died as each had lived. Death cradled the Old Mother and carried her off; she, poignantly, had been the only one to welcome him. Death, the stealthy and violent caretaker, hovered over the soldier on his watch. Death kept time with his arms and feet—the horrid slap-slap-slap of the soles' metronomic beat. The ballet opened and closed with diplomats at the green baize conference table, firing their pistols and setting war's inevitable cycle into motion again.

Ernst Uthoff and Lola Botka agreed to experiment with the Joffrey Ballet in the late summer of 1966 with Zomosa, whom they called their spiritual son, as their assistant. For three weeks they tried out *The Green Table*. Zomosa taught Death to Richard Gain. At the session's conclusion, Uthoff informed Jooss overseas that the Joffrey Ballet was perfectly capable of performing the masterpiece. Simultaneously, Arpino convinced Zomosa to gamble on uprooting himself from his native Chile to join the Joffrey as a permanent member. A Fulbright grant from the U.S. Department of State was procured for Zomosa. It enabled him to begin dancing with the company that fall in *Cakewalk* and to reprise Death for *The Green Table*'s Joffrey premiere in spring 1967.

On February 5, 1967, Kurt Jooss arrived at the American Ballet Center to polish the production. The City Center Joffrey Ballet was the first company outside Germany in almost twenty years that Jooss allowed to learn *The Green Table*, and the New York State Council on the Arts granted $25,000 for the production in acknowledgment that a momentous event was about to take place. Jooss worked with the Joffrey members, while Joffrey observed the rehearsals and absorbed information. "There are things you never forget," Joffrey said. "Jooss told the [soldiers] when they were walking off, 'They're walking through mud and you have to pick up your feet. It's mud. It's thick.' And during the refugee scene Jooss said, 'No. It's sorrow within you. It's the economy of it. The complete helplessness. You're drained.' "[13] The choreographer fascinated Joffrey.

Michael Uthoff was cast in his father's original role of the Standard Bearer, the Young Soldier was Robert Blankshine, the Young Girl was Lisa Bradley, the Old Soldier was Jon Cristofori, the Guerilla Woman was Suzanne Hammons, the Old Mother was Marjorie Mussman,* the Profiteer was Luis Fuente, and Zomosa danced Death.

---

*At the last performance of the season Lola Botka reprised her Old Mother role for the Joffrey. Two weeks after the company's opening, Fritz Cohen, who had composed the ballet's two-piano score, died. At the Joffrey's first performance, Mary Roark and Patricia Perrin were the pianists, and Seymour Lipkin the conductor.

Zomosa and Death were two sides of one equation. The dancer was born in Valparaiso, Chile, on February 28, 1937. His father was a bank director and an art dealer. His mother doted on the child, planting candies in her mouth before giving them to him to suck upon when he was a small boy. His mother withdrew from him, however, during a time in his life when he needed her most. When he was a young teenager, Zomosa killed another boy with a gun in a hunting accident. "His mother never forgave him for it," said Noël Mason, who would become his second wife.[14]

His father sent him away to boarding school, and later to university, where he played on the national rugby team and represented Chile in scuba diving competitions. Six feet three inches tall, he was an outstanding athlete; he had never taken a dance class or seen a ballet until his college freshman year, when his father took him to a Chilean National Ballet performance in Santiago. *The Green Table* was on the program. When Zomosa saw it, he thought everything in his life paled by comparison. "I was shocked by the whole work," he said. "And especially the role—I decided I just had to dance Death."[15] Against his father's wishes ("I like ballet," his father said, "but I didn't expect it to be in my family"),[16] Zomosa started studying modern dance in the evenings at the National Conservatory. In 1959, Ernst Uthoff invited him to join the Chilean National Ballet. Three years later he inherited the role of Death. He had by then received a biology degree and entered medical college. He had also married and fathered two children—and his father, an alcoholic, had died.

"I can't live by rules," he said. "They don't mean anything to me. I don't have time."[17] In his first City Center Joffrey Ballet season he originated a corps role in Arpino's *Nightwings* and learned Arpino's *Viva Vivaldi!, Olympics, Ropes,* and *Incubus,* as well as assuming important roles in Boris's *Cakewalk.* By his second season the company's character had significantly altered because so many members had left. The troupe was in short supply of men who had enough classical training to partner. Zomosa did not qualify, but it hardly mattered. His ballet was *The Green Table,* and it was to transform the public's perception of the company.

The Green Table was the first full-scale restaging of a historic ballet under Joffrey's auspices. For a long time he had indicated that he wanted to stage revivals within his repertory. He considered that he had started the process with Peggy van Praagh's staging of Antony Tudor's *Soirée Musicale* in 1959, and he had continued his role as a revivalist by collecting Bournonville's pas de deux from *Flower Festival in Genzano* and *La Ventana* (staged by Lillian Moore in 1965, but never performed).

The Green Table was his most remarkable acquisition to date. From its restaging, he developed the fundamental principles for the future reconstructions: bring the choreographer into the company, if possible. Leave him alone in the studio. Give him space, and then watch. Supply everything that is needed to make the production as true to the original as possible. Be authentic. Do not try to project new ways on the old ones. Trust your intuition, and use the dance notation score.*

It is impossible to overestimate Lillian Moore's importance in helping Joffrey think about the position of artistic director as curator. She encouraged him to continue the study of dance notation. As one of America's leading dance historians, she helped shape his posture as a reconstructionist. It is also credible that Joffrey remembered the lecturing from his first ballet teacher, Ivan Novikoff, who might have inspired the idea of an American Ballet Russe that would define itself through the Diaghilev period pieces. Joffrey modified the Diaghilev model and organized his collection around two principles: the fostering of ballets that were collaborations between contemporary artists, and the curatorship of twentieth-century masterpieces.

The previous summer, Joffrey had approached Jerome Robbins and asked for his pas de deux *Afternoon of a Faun* (1953, music by Debussy). Robbins worked on *Faun* with the company. The ballet was an interesting choice because there was no possibility of ignoring the obvious comparisons between it and Arpino's *Sea Shadow*—and Robbins's ballet had already been embraced as a classic. In the end, Joffrey did not accept *Faun* into the repertoire; he successfully pursued Robbins for *Moves, Interplay,* and *N.Y. Export: Opus Jazz*—the Ballets: U.S.A. works.

For the March 1967 season, Joffrey's hands were still tied by fundraising tasks and bureaucracy; although he had planned differently, he did not contribute a new ballet to the repertoire. He and Alex Ewing arranged to open the Stanford Festival of the Arts in June in California and then to spend the next three summers in Tacoma, Washington, in residence at Pacific Lutheran University. They were plotting to keep the dancers employed year-round and yet still cover expenses, which were averaging $10,000 a week. Ewing's central priority was to secure twelve weeks at City Center, plus equally fixed, unswerving engagements each year always in the same cities—Washington, Chicago, Los Angeles, San Francisco— and additional solid weeks in residence at universities throughout the country (but predominantly in New York State). He partly cast the university residencies like choreography workshops, during which the company was paid for three days to rehearse and take class, and the university

---

*Jooss arrived at the Joffrey Ballet with Ulla Soederbaum, who had danced the Young Girl, and who brought with her two *Green Table* notation scores. Jooss had been a student of Rudolf von Laban's in Mannheim in 1921. Laban authored a system of notating dance that was subsequently called Labanotation. Jooss greatly admired Laban, and because of his association with him, *The Green Table* had been one of the earliest ballets to be notated, a task that had been accomplished by the notator Ann Hutchinson.

students were allowed to watch. Then the final two days were for performances without costumes or scenery. Ewing thought this would educate a ballet audience, a Joffrey audience—which was, in his opinion, exactly what his mother at American Ballet Theatre had failed to do. Such unprecedented schemes solved the problem of grueling one-night-stand tours and anchored him and Joffrey to the phone, negotiating with John Hightower at the New York State Council on the Arts, among other forward-thinking people who bought into the idea.

On March 9, 1967, the three-week season opened at City Center. "The new Joffrey production [of *The Green Table*], supervised by Jooss himself, has not only rekindled the enthusiasm of those who saw it with the Jooss company twenty years ago but also it has generated undiluted enthusiasm among a whole new generation of dancers and dance lovers," Terry raved in the *World Journal Tribune*.[18] "Maximiliano Zomosa had a fully justified triumph as Death—a performance of fantastic power," said Barnes of the opening night. The next week, Barnes wrote, "The company, markedly larger than last season, is in fine fettle. There are few dance groups in the world capable of giving more unalloyed pleasure."[19]

There were thirty-six dancers; new members included many former apprentices: Richard Browne, Raymond Bussey, Joel Dabin, Helyn Douglas, Erika Goodman, Christian Holder, Pamela Johnson, George Montalbano, Haynes Owens, Rafael Romero, Arlene Shuler, Karen Williamson, Richard Wood, and Rebecca Wright. Michael Uthoff was out injured; Dermot Burke's partnering skills were earning him a central role in the troupe, but he was still a teenager. The company would have to wait until the summer, when Paul Sutherland would return from dancing with American Ballet Theatre and rescue the Joffrey from male classical bankruptcy.

When Nels Jorgensen snapped his Achilles tendon in the middle of the season and had to be replaced in *Scotch Symphony* by the New York City Ballet guest Anthony Blum (who then also injured himself and was replaced by Jacques d'Amboise, also from City Ballet), one critic, Arthur Todd, cracked, "Had the season lasted longer we might well eventually have seen [City Ballet's] Edward Villella and John Prinz coming forward in this role."[20] Staged by Francia Russell and Una Kai, *Scotch Symphony* had been introduced into the Joffrey's repertoire during the fall 1966 tour through the Southeast. Since Lisa Bradley was on leave, Noël Mason performed the lead opposite Nels Jorgensen, elevating Mason to principal dancer status. Barbara Remington (formerly with American Ballet Theatre and London's Royal Ballet) alternated in Mason's role as Joffrey built up his ballerina constituency. Trinette Singleton and Dermot Burke left an impression in *Sea Shadow*.

Joffrey and Arpino pinned their hopes on them, this new vanguard, the second wave of dancers since the City Center inaugural season. Many in the first group who had laid the groundwork at Jacob's Pillow and the Delacorte for the troupe's reconstitution, performing for a mere $58 a week, were feeling pushed out. Some had already departed. Noël Mason wrote to her parents:

> Ernie [Ian Horvath] asked to leave the company after the [Southern] tour, which they [Joffrey and Arpino] agreed to, and then called him in and told him to leave before the tour (Mr. Joffrey was upset with the way Ernie was working in Houston). Dick [Gain] leaves for Sweden in January and John Jones is leaving too! As a result of all this (most of the kids leaving are upset because they rehearse so many hours with so little result), RJ [Joffrey] has asked Lone Isaksen and Larry Rhodes to guest in March, but it's doubtful Mrs. Harkness will let them.[21]

Richard Gain joined the Cullberg Ballet in Stockholm. He and Ian Horvath, plus George Ramos and Margo Sappington, who (along with Dennis Nahat) had contributed their creative juices to building the resurrected City Center Joffrey Ballet, were no longer on the roster. Sappington's injury left her unable to continue dancing on pointe. Full of regret, she left the Joffrey in the fall of 1966 and joined Nahat in the Broadway musical, *Sweet Charity*. She later choreographed *Oh, Calcutta!*, famous for daring the first totally nude pas de deux in legitimate theater. She returned to the Joffrey several times over the next twenty years and choreographed three ballets. Her ties with Joffrey remained strong and she was one of few women who experienced an intensely charged embrace and kiss from him in a moment of excitement. His allure to women was said to be great, and Sappington was neither the first nor the last to be similarly won over.

Nahat's and Horvath's careers would eventually parallel each other's. After exciting years of dancing with American Ballet Theatre, they focused their vigorous talents on cofounding and directing the Cleveland/San José Ballet.

To achieve his comeback after Harkness, Joffrey had needed strong and extraordinary personalities onstage. But once the company was established, he could not cope with the complexity of so many distinct individuals. He preferred a more tranquil atmosphere at work. Still, Joffrey admired the first group who had been with him at Jacob's Pillow and Central Park, and he remained in touch with most of them, until it was said of Horvath and, to a lesser degree, of Nahat, that as directors they became "more Joffrey than Joffrey himself."[22]

CHAPTER 21

ASTARTE

Joffrey's paramount aim by 1967 was to build a repertoire on the basis of an esthetic continuum. He wanted to teach his audience to observe—to see the historical pattern, the communication of ideas, energy, and techniques across time. He spent hours planning the company's programs, agonizing over the perfect balance of ballets. "The program was a fine art to him," said Sue Loyd, his assistant and ballet mistress in the late sixties.[1] He thought ahead to future seasons and contrived the program so that seasons across the next decade would amount to a single unified experience.

Joffrey thought Balanchine's *Scotch Symphony,* Sokolow's *Opus '65,* Robbins's *Moves,* and Jooss's *The Green Table* were good works. Basically, Balanchine supplied Joffrey his ballets that had been made for the City Center stage: *Donizetti Variations, Scotch Symphony,* the Minkus *Pas de Trois* for the fall 1967 season, when *Pas de Dix* would simultaneously be revived along with *Square Dance.* Having already strongly implied that the Joffrey dancers were better at *Donizetti Variations* than the New York City Ballet casts, Barnes in the *New York Times* hailed Joffrey's *Scotch Symphony* production and probably further fueled Balanchine and Kirstein's indignation. He definitely infuriated Joffrey, who had felt the harsh repercussions from Balanchine and Kirstein. Joffrey subtly warned Barnes to stop.*

By 1967, dancers, teachers, directors, administrators, and the general public were enthusiastic about choosing which New York company they liked best. Ironically, few understood that Joffrey, Balanchine, and Chase at American Ballet Theatre were mutually cooperative. But these various

---

*"I was foolish enough to say, almost jocularly, that [the Joffrey] danced *Donizetti* better than Balanchine's company," said Barnes on April 3, 1992. "Balanchine immediately took it away from Joffrey. Immediately." Joffrey referred to the episode during a question-and-answer period, following Barnes's public interview with him for a series on American ballet at the Dance Collection of the New York Public Library for the Performing Arts on November 25, 1985. Asked, "Do you feel any of Mr. Barnes's reviews have hurt you and your company?" amid lots of laughter from the audience Joffrey responded, "He once gave us a good review that caused me a lot of trouble. I won't go into it."

parties were also competitive, and they knew that the competition was beneficial. At first it was friendly, benign, and Balanchine was the acknowledged leader (Joffrey would never presume to be his equal). But the fervent debate intensified in 1966 as word about *Ballet Review,* a small quarterly publication with a loyal readership among the New York intelligentsia, spread.

Edited by Arlene Croce until 1973, *Ballet Review* was considered by many to be the unofficial New York City Ballet house organ. Many of its contributors were invited inside Balanchine's inner sanctum; the doors to New York State Theater were flung open—the writers could see Balanchine rehearse. "The New York State Theater is a kind of office for the magazine, which does not have one of its own," wrote a *Ballet Review* founding associate editor, Don McDonagh, in an article chronicling the publication's history on its twenty-fifth anniversary. "In Balanchine's day the stage door desk occasionally functioned as a mail drop when our attendance at performances did not coincide. It's the closest thing we ever had to a real office." On occasion, support was more tangible. Kirstein had once endorsed a check to *Ballet Review* "without explanation."[2]

Although its subscription list was small and its influence was not immediately discernible, *Ballet Review* was devoted entirely to thoughtful writing about dance. The division between aficionados and the general audience was given the clearest voice in its pages. As a tool, a grading system was initiated in which each critic marked the New York season's ballets with anything from an A to an F (*A* stood for masterpiece and *F* for insufferable). As many as eleven dance writers contributed to a single issue of *Ballet Review.* The grades they gave to works of choreography were compiled on a single chart at the back of the journal, where they could be compared at a glance. Hierarchy was central to the contributors' critical mentality, and with a few exceptions (Merce Cunningham, Paul Taylor, and Frederick Ashton) everything other than Balanchine's works was given lower grades.

It galled most *Ballet Review* writers that any acolyte of Balanchine's could also delight in Gerald Arpino. Arpino's works received many Fs. Here is Croce's take on *Viva Vivaldi!:*

> It's widely assumed that the Joffrey company at City Center has inherited a large part of Balanchine's old City Center audience—certainly Joffrey encourages the link by borrowing heavily from the repertory of the New York City Ballet. But if this is really a Balanchine-oriented crowd, how is it they are able to tolerate the phenomenon of Gerald Arpino? The last time I saw Arpino's Viva Vivaldi! here is what took place in the pas de deux from the third movement (boy and girl face to face):

1. She: Steps into arabesque on pointe, arms extending backward (the "swan" position). He: Takes her under the armpits.

2. A slow pull away from one another.

3. She: Falls forward, still fully extended.

4. He: Lowers her to the floor. (She still holds the pose. Picture this, please. It's the Swan Queen flat on her nose.)

5. He: Kneels. Bends. And places his left ear to her buttocks.

I wonder if they are still doing it.

If audiences are wrong to like Arpino, it's possible they are also wrong to like Balanchine. Not for the same reasons of course. I should be glad to forget Gerald Arpino and his awful ballets.[3]

With *Ballet Review,* critical politics came of age in the New York world. Its writers' perceptions emerged from the European cultural system: There's a right way. But in America, there is no one established ballet school (despite the Ford Foundation's grants to Balanchine), no single master who can proclaim supreme artistic authority, no common guidebook shared by every student of *la danse d'école.* There is not an audience that has been educated in precisely the same way and that shares a body of historical, social, and economic information that could lead to the same universal conclusion. In America, the climb to the top of the art heap is primarily through self-education that is self-funded, a lonely, arduous path to excellence, using the best of the materials that one can get one's hands on.

In this polarized atmosphere, perhaps it made sense for Joffrey to start thinking about doing more ballets that, as with *The Green Table,* were important to the history of modern art. Shortly after *The Green Table,* he single-handedly revived the reputation of Léonide Massine. In Joffrey's estimation, Massine, who had been Balanchine's archrival, was a hero whose ballets in the thirties and forties were often wrongly dismissed as minor. In 1969, he engaged Massine to revive *Le Tricorne.* He also cultivated a rapport with Sir Frederick Ashton, another choreographer, who, in time, needed a reliable place for his works to be seen. Joffrey began his Ashton collection with *Façade* in 1969 and thereafter added on *The Dream, Monotones I* and *II,* and *Jazz Calendar,* with more to follow. In 1969, Joffrey also engaged Hans Brenaa to stage Bournonville's *Konservatoriet,* building his repertoire of the nineteenth-century Danish choreographer's ballets.

Joffrey's stock rose in the critical community when he started reviving Massine and Jooss, and staging Ashton and Bournonville. It is reasonable to assume that he wanted his place in dance history, but unreasonable to think that he accomplished the development of his historical repertoire—the revivals, reconstructions, and restagings—solely to placate critics who were disgusted with Arpino. Joffrey pursued what he had wanted all along—a company that was about his passion for ballet, and that included Balanchine and Massine and Ashton and Loring and Robbins and Joffrey and, yes, Arpino.

Although he was beginning to hit his stride as a director, Joffrey was still interested in his own choreography. By summer 1967, he was ready to focus his energies on a new work, about the ancient Babylonian fertility goddess, Astarte. An idea from filmmaker Gardner Compton, *Astarte* was a multimedia ballet that, for about five years, Compton had wanted to make with a choreographer. Compton had been in Martha Graham's company shortly after the period in the late forties when she was choreographing the Greek myths. Known then as James Gardner, he had a minor role in the original cast of *Clytemnestra* (1958). His idea for *Astarte* was to put the "whole [hippie] revolution thing"[4] into a mythical format using strobe lights, black lights, and opaque front montage and multiple image film projections. He had recently employed these techniques as a cameraman for producer Midge Mackenzie at the Avant Garde Film Festival in Central Park and had early on studied filmmaking at the feet of Harold Clurman and Elia Kazan.

To accomplish *Astarte,* Compton went straight to Martha Graham because he thought she would relate to the classic mythological protagonist. He told Graham, "Astarte was the goddess of a temple where she helped young men get rid of their virginity. Her essential function was to promote love's art so that there weren't big hang-ups about sex. It was a very practical solution for the young men in ancient times." He mentioned that he wanted to take the story more into the sixties "kind of idea that knowledge and enlightenment is passed to future generations through the ritual of sex."[5]

Graham was not interested in collaborating, although she attended the final performance of *Astarte*'s first season and said to Compton, "Just remember that a pioneer is never employed. He's only imitated."[6] Her words were prophetic. *Astarte* would give rise to a small cadre of imitators and embellish the covers of *Time, Life,* and *Saturday Review,* as well as provoke an illustrated story in *Playboy.*

After meeting with Graham, Compton approached Robert Joffrey. "I went to Bob because I liked his choreography," he explained.[7] Joffrey committed himself to the project with Alex Ewing offering him the threat from Morton Baum that if there was not a new Robert Joffrey ballet in the repertoire by the next season, the company would be dropped from City Center.

Joffrey then traveled with the troupe for its stint of State Universities of New York residencies in April and May 1967. He accompanied it to

Stanford University in California for the late-June week of performances there—a blissful sojourn during the summer of love, an American time and place of hippies, flower children, rock concerts, marijuana, and free love. Then he led the troupe to Tacoma, where a six-week residency and teaching period had been set up for the company at Pacific Lutheran University, to be followed by performances in Seattle.

For the Joffrey Ballet, PLU had replaced Watch Hill: it was an (almost) all-expenses-paid* situation where new choreography could be workshopped—created without the urban static and office pressure. "When the company was performing, it could almost meet expenses out of box office receipts," said Alex Ewing, asking, "But to make new work, how do they rehearse without box office money to sustain the company? The answer was PLU, where Joffrey had free access to the university's Eastvold Auditorium."[8] The PLU residency, designed as a three-year program (which continued for an additional year), was the first step toward procuring the Joffrey Ballet as a permanent fixture in the Pacific Northwest. The interested parties hoped the company would eventually establish a bicoastal residency in Seattle proper, dividing its time equally between New York and Seattle. PLU was where Joffrey would roll up his sleeves for *Astarte*, after weeks of contemplation and research that had included late nights at the Electric Circus in New York's East Village, soaking up the rock-club ambience with Herbert Migdoll.

But when the actual moment for creation arrived, Joffrey stayed rooted inside his on-campus bungalow, claiming he was suffering from asthma.[†] With two weeks left to the residency and still no action from Joffrey, Compton threatened to take the project to Rebekah Harkness. Time and again Joffrey removed himself at crucial moments, which suggested that he had a deep-seated dread of commitment, or, perhaps, that he was lazy. Many of his dancers said that as a choreographer he feared humiliation; he rejected ideas sometimes too soon, he discriminated too harshly. Said Lone Isaksen, "If you are going to create, it's not a good idea to edit yourself before you begin."[9]

Compton's threat snapped Joffrey to attention. On August 17 Midge Mackenzie arrived in Seattle at Compton's request to coordinate the production. She was an experienced director for the BBC in London and had the reputation of being able to accomplish the impossible. "My job

---

*In 1967, the Pacific Northwest Ballet Association was formed. Earmarked money came from the National Council on the Arts and the Washington State Council. This was a partnership between federal and private institutions, a whole new concept.

†Maybe Joffrey was also depressed, because Lillian Moore had, on July 28, 1967, died of cancer at the age of fifty-five. Joffrey adored her and had relied upon her to train the apprentices. Moore and Joffrey had worked closely together since 1959, and before that at the High School of Performing Arts.

was to integrate the music, film, live performance, and kinetic environment in six weeks," she said. "Joffrey ran a very tight ship. He wasn't interested in *everything* related to *Astarte*. He paid attention to the choreography, and Gar to the films."[10]

"Most film people who get involved with dance come from the football field. Follow the ball. That isn't the story," said Compton who, as a former dancer, brought a sensibility to the filming that had rarely been seen before. "The story is about the dramatic relationship of a person to space. And if you don't write the story, the audience will. For *Astarte*, I shot reflections of the dancers in ferrotype tins—think of a highly polished cookie sheet that you can bend and torque, distorting the reflected image. I was using only flesh as the set, the medium, the space. I was painting with flesh."[11]

"There were certain critical factors in constructing dramatic tension between the live performance onstage and the filmed images," added Mackenzie. "They were two separate realities. The performance was at times synchronous and at times strictly in the cinematic imagination as a counterpoint."[12]

The idea of a fugue of images, real and filmed, was similar to Herbert Migdoll's pursuit with time-lapse photography. It was as if the many parts of Joffrey's directorial life were converging in this one ballet, this penultimate collaboration. For the ballet's score, Compton and Joffrey chose rock songs, mostly by Country Joe and the Fish, Moby Grape, and Iron Butterfly, and Compton spliced together a tape. He then handed his tape over to five "scruffy"[13] local Washington State musicians—kids who had been curious about the ballet and had met Hub Miller, a Joffrey affiliate and composer-pianist. They had about nine electronic instruments among them and they loved to jam together. Compton told them to create an original score based on his tape with this one caveat: It had to match precisely the running length of the one-thousand-foot film reel and incorporate Joffrey's request for a raga. Then, calling themselves Crome Syrcus, the band produced the score and arranged to accompany the Joffrey Ballet later to New York and plug themselves in at City Center.

Initially Lisa Bradley had been considered for Astarte, but Joffrey had changed his mind. He was having trouble with her. When the company had arrived at the Seattle-Tacoma airport, a marching band greeted the troupe on the tarmac and dozens of roses were bestowed upon Bradley. People wanted to see her—just simply *see* her. All of the attention, some of which was orchestrated by Joffrey's personnel, unnerved him. He believed that to be a good ballerina one could not have one's head turned by attention and self-glorification. These values he had inherited from Mary Ann Wells and thought he had instilled in Bradley. He slowly repossessed some of her roles because her behavior disappointed him, and new ballets, such as *Astarte,* were given to others.

Joffrey selected Trinette Singleton as Astarte, and Dermot Burke to be her partner, but the next week Burke had an emergency appendectomy. The role was eventually awarded to Zomosa. Zomosa was known for his preoccupation with women. He was a Don Juan. And it was he, in the ballet, who was supposed to be losing his virginity. Joffrey wasn't sure how the chemistry between Zomosa and Singleton would work—Zomosa might seduce Singleton offstage, and Joffrey, while admiring the audacity of those, such as Zomosa, who lived openly according to their passion, also felt protective about his ballerinas. He did not want to place Singleton in a compromising situation.

"Max [Zomosa] was a wonderful, tender, sensual, and creative human being. Trinette was essentially empty. And I mean that in the best sense," commented Mackenzie. "She was the plasticine with none of the interior. She was a mirage. Zomosa was very real. They were opposites."[14]

The chemistry working between Singleton and Zomosa, they completed the PLU residency and performed for a week in Seattle, then left for New York with Joffrey, Compton, and Mackenzie while the rest of the company toured Idaho. There were exactly four weeks until *Astarte*'s opening on September 20; Compton's film had yet to be made, Tom Skelton's set to be built, Joffrey's choreography to be finished, and Singleton's unitard designed by Hugh Sherrer in Day-Glo black-light colors to be painted.

"No one saw the ballet until dress rehearsal in New York because I wanted the fun of making a ballet without outside comments," Joffrey told *Dance Magazine* managing editor Richard Philp. "You see an attractive person and you are attracted to them," he continued. "And then you want to physically enjoy them, to consummate that look and that energy. And that's, in a way, what happened [in *Astarte*]."[15] For Joffrey—who was usually noncommittal whenever the subject of sex arose, but who was known to lead a promiscuous night life—*Astarte* was perhaps an honest step toward admitting to urges that embarrassed him.

On opening night he commandeered his usual place in the orchestra's back row. Compton stood in the aisle next to him. The films started rolling; two projectors were clamped on the theater's balcony rails and two on either side of the stage. Crome Syrcus twanged and vibrated at high decibels. A pair of spotlights raked the audience and a single strobe flickered—the multimedia ballet pulsed to life.

When the stage curtain closed, there was a huge silence. Compton looked at Joffrey, who had not seen the films or the set or heard the music live in conjunction with the movement until the dress rehearsal the day before. "I thought, okay, here's where Bob says, 'Well, this is the only performance.' And then the roar went up. The applause. And Bob looked at me in absolute shock. Like he didn't know what happened. By the end of what seemed an interminable amount of time, he reached over, grabbed me, and grabbed Tom and Midge and pulled us with him to the stage for a curtain call.

"But I saw Bob go from expecting the worst and getting ready for an asthma attack and disappearing into the woodwork to acceptance that he had just created a ballet."[16]

The program for the world premiere of *Astarte* read as follows: "Choreography by Robert Joffrey . . . Film created and photographed by Gardner Compton." By the fall 1968 season, after *Astarte* was the first ballet to make the cover of *Time* and had become one of the hottest box-office attractions ever in dance, Compton's credits in *Playbill* remained as they had been. But Joffrey's were changed. They now read, "Created and choreographed by Robert Joffrey."

"Bobby!" Jeannie Arpino remembered hollering to him, and waving in delight as she dashed across the theater to congratulate Joffrey and her brother on the fall 1967 season, which, at four weeks, had been the company's longest yet in New York.

Joffrey pulled Arpino's sister aside and said, "I am Robert."

"Bobby." She looked him in the eye with a twinkle and said, "You will always be Bobby."

"Behave yourself. I am Robert. In the theater I am Robert, to you."[17]

Astarte became the cornerstone of the Joffrey Ballet's pop dance repertoire. Post-*Astarte,* no matter what it did, the Joffrey was thought of as that tuned-in, turned-on hip ballet troupe that excited young people. Many *Astarte* performances were standing room only.

In the months leading to *Astarte*'s premiere, Ewing had been certain the troupe would have to shut down. Weekly expenses were averaging $10,000; *Astarte* was budgeted at $60,000 and the company was almost entirely dependent on box-office revenue for income. Since the dancers were not continually performing,* sources other than the box office had to be relied upon. Ewing persuaded six Overseas National Airways stockholders to offer $40,000 in personal holdings for the ballet's completion. For the rest he and Mackenzie approached private sources; Compton made the films with some of his own money. After the premiere of *Astarte,* the box office grosses rose from $33,400 the first week to $56,961 for the fourth and final week.[18] By the end of two weeks, *Astarte* had more or less paid for itself. The ballet that had almost "dissolved" the company, said Ewing, also saved the company.[19] Joffrey's administration could breathe again.

But what had been lost? Respectability? It seemed that from the time

---

*Joffrey started choreographing for the New York City Opera again in 1968, but the Joffrey II company was more involved in the productions than the main company.

that the company started dancing in New York, there was a strong suspicion that the Joffrey's agenda was insincere. The word *gimmick* turned up in the early reviews of the company, mostly for Arpino's ballets, beginning with *Olympics* in 1965; but now, Joffrey's *Astarte* was a target. Clive Barnes disdained the "obviousness" of *Astarte* on first viewing, while also calling the multimedia ballet a "milestone." The work seemed to ask him to surrender his artistic ideals to commercialism, and he cautiously approached the challenge. In the end, the only way he could validate *Astarte* was by calling it a "theaterpiece" instead of a ballet. "Go and see it," he advised,[20] and then he returned for a second viewing and scripted an apology that (by his own confession) was not one:

> I had convinced myself that I had been unfair to Robert Joffrey's new ballet, Astarte, *after I had seen it the first time—until I saw it the second.*
>
> . . . This is a new cliché. What happens in Astarte *is conventional. It is the intelligent distillation of happenings, of psychedelic-style rock discothèques, of the entire groovy-noovy thing.*
>
> . . . I saw just what I had originally missed. . . . I failed to notice that it was turning the audience on like magic. I missed also the symbolic quality of the piece. . . . This is the American dream of sex—clean, mystic and uninvolved.[21]

Astarte forced the realization that there was an audience for dance that was bigger than the dance audience. It was up for grabs and the City Center Joffrey Ballet was grabbing with both hands. The company garnered the *Time* cover not because *Time* editors held a serious meeting and argued about which company "symbolized new directions in modern dance,"[22] but because Herbert Migdoll presented a convincing montage photograph to *Time*. Those at the City Center Joffrey Ballet were thinking on their feet; Migdoll's *Time* cover shot of *Astarte* reached nearly four million readers who flipped to an article inside the magazine on March 15, 1968. It said dance is "today the most inventive and least inhibited of the lively arts." It continued:

> In the regal prime of classical ballet, the dancer's craft was devoted to polishing and perfecting an established series of formalized gestures; choreography was as structured as a French garden. Today, however, a ballerina may have to arch on point in one sequence, boogaloo in another, then writhe on the floor like a snake on the make.
>
> Nor is choreography any longer an artistic handmaiden, subservient to the greater demands of the score. In a reversal of precedence, music is now only one of many elements that contribute to the impact of dance.[23]

The litany of broken conventions would cause a lover of nineteenth- and twentieth-century classical ballet to shudder. Joffrey allowed himself to be swept up in the *Astarte* tide.[24] In the *Time* piece he is quoted as saying, "I look upon ballet as total theater. I want to attack all the senses. I want my dancers to express my thing, the now thing, good or bad."[25]

Was Joffrey forgetting himself? *Astarte* was an esthetic stretch for him; it was not his concept, and "attacking the senses" and "expressing my thing" were not his customary language. He possessed a ferocity for excellence, but was he saying he no longer cared? Or was *Astarte* his first real inkling that he had the capacity to communicate to a large audience that knew nothing about dance?

He had choreographed *Astarte,* his first ballet since the five-year-old *Gamelan,* and he was feeling loved. He did not resist.

The first batch of reviews was reservedly positive. Arlene Croce in *Ballet Review:* "Robert Joffrey is more musical than his principal choreographer, Arpino, and has taste. . . . But . . . *Astarte,* the new mixed-media presentation, is a *Life* magazine recap of the avant garde (and so is the avant garde)."[26] Walter Sorell in the *Providence Sunday Journal:* "It is a sensation, for sure. It is more difficult to say whether it is a good ballet."[27] For most American dance arbiters, a choreographer could experiment, but the work had to have structure to qualify as good. Many said *Astarte* did not qualify as good choreography, though there were exceptions. In 1968 Marcia B. Siegel was one who thought *Astarte* was both good dance and a formula for success. Five years later, she scrutinized Joffrey's formula in her book *At the Vanishing Point:*

> [*Astarte*] *was so successful that the Joffrey, which had become established in the City Center and needed to build a clear identity in the competition for audiences, embarked on a whole career of being mod. New ballets in the following season plucked ideas out of the headlines and the shops and draped them with matching movement.*
>
> *These ballets look so unusual and contemporary that the audience mistakes recognition for enlightenment, name-dropping for profundity. . . .*
>
> *Pop dance, while it is not the most creative or profound of all dance forms, is one of the most vital. Audiences love it. Dancers want to work in it because it challenges their technical skills. Choreographers enjoy its freedom from artistic restraints and pretensions. Maybe only critics find it hard to stomach.*[28]

Siegel had her facts straight about *Astarte,* and the Joffrey Ballet could never escape the shadows cast by them. She epitomized the growing faction who speculated about Joffrey's artistic integrity. In 1968, Doris Hering had written in *Dance Magazine:* "Naturally Joffrey has to keep his eye on the box office. And one suspects that his own *Astarte* was originally conceived with that in mind."[29] *Astarte* had provided the City Center Joffrey Ballet with a prescription for insolvency.

CHAPTER 22

The Dance Spirit

Incredibly, after *Astarte,* Joffrey did not choreograph for another six years, handing over the primary dance responsibilities to Arpino. Keeping in mind that all artists steal, the dancers were Arpino's worker bees, gathering movement phrases from other people's ballets and returning to him with the pollen. "Come on, baby, come on, baby—what were those steps you did in such-and-such ballet?" Often that was Arpino's question when he assembled the dancers for a new work.[1] "*Confetti* [1970] and *Kettentanz* [1971] were made in a period when I was obsessed with the Royal Ballet," said Rebecca Wright, who originated roles in both Arpino works. "And if you look at [Arpino's] *Solarwind* [1970] with my extended leg raised and those pirouettes that the other two were doing under my leg, that was out of Ashton's *Monotones* for the Royal."[2]

On occasion, Arpino's dancers would cross their arms against their chests and refuse to help. "By the time Jerry choreographed *Touch Me,* I knew how to handle him," said Christian Holder, for whom this gospel solo was made in 1977. "I didn't demonstrate steps for him to use anymore. I suggested the entrance and the basic shape of the piece, but I did not choreograph it. All steps are his."[3]

By 1968, Arpino's choreographic methodology was developed. He said he worked like an impressionist painter, seeing a vision in his head and creating it by dabbing movement onto the space. The dancers' physicality was his constant source, his paint—how the individual moved, his line, his energy, his musicality, and his past experience speaking through his bones. Arpino invested in his dancers as collaborators. "I want the dancers to be artists, creators," he said. "If they just want to be in a ballet, they might as well be someplace else."[4]

Arpino was slavishly devoted to his dancers, and his passion carried weight with most, but for a few it did not. Richard Gain left in 1967 because he did not enjoy Arpino's collaborative way of working or Howell's inappropriate assumption of responsibility as a "ballet master." Over the next two decades a steady exodus of dancers left partly for the same reason. Joffrey would excuse them from working with Arpino if they asked and let them stay in the troupe as "non-Arpino" dancers, but otherwise he refrained from interfering in Arpino and Howell's rehearsals. By spring 1968, more apprentices moved into the main company. They had fewer issues about working with Arpino. Ranging in age from seventeen to twenty-three, the Joffrey fledglings—Scott Barnard, Donna Cowen, Gay Wallstrom, and Glenn White—saw Arpino in a different and more positive light.

Arpino's choreography would often be imitated in the future, and many of his pretenders would fall by the wayside. But he endured because he made ballets for people who hate ballet. There is perhaps no choreographer in America more controversial than he. To some, nobody did Arpino better than Arpino. "Arpino is a man who, in the kindest sense of the phrase, choreographs before he thinks," wrote Barry Laine, putting his finger on the Arpino irony in *Ballet News*. "That is, his ballets seem sincerely expressive rather than manipulative. He choreographs not for critics but for a popular audience that he has in fact helped create over the pioneering years."[5]

Once Joffrey found mass appeal with *Astarte,* Arpino continued the trend with *The Clowns* (1968) and *Trinity* (1970), ballets that reveal the intricacies of his collaborative choreographic process. The idea for *The Clowns* may well have entered Arpino's consciousness as early as 1963, when, in preparation for the summer in Watch Hill, Joffrey considered a scenario called *Epitaphs for a Circus*. The ballet's author is unknown, but according to the typewritten pages detailing the plot and found in the Joffrey's archives, Joffrey and Arpino were intending to share the choreographic duties. The work's second episode is called "The Clown and His Balloons," and Arpino's *Clowns* resembles it. Here, excerpted, the scene from "The Clown and His Balloons" libretto:

> *Theme: Better to give than to receive*
>
> *Action: The clown appears with his bouquet of many balloons. He offers his balloons to the crowd and, with persuasion, one by one, gets each member of the crowd to accept a balloon. He charms them with his exuberance. They slowly are won over and become in turn very happy. Soon the clown has no balloons left for himself.*
>
> *The thing he loved is gone. His mission in life is completed. He fades and dies. (Stage direction: As the crowd is about him with their balloons, he slips offstage unseen by the audience and is replaced by his symbolic self.) The crowd lifts this [dummy] up and bears it higher and higher (his soul restored to heaven?).*

Arpino's *Clowns* opened with the sound of three atomic bombs exploding. White sawdust-filled dummies tumbled from the sky. One tearstained boy clown survived. He piled up the dead and performed a dance that restored them to life. (Stage direction: the audience should not notice the replacing of dummies by real clowns.) The boy clown handed out transparent helium balloons. First the other clowns loved him, then they grew envious and hated him. They tried to strangle him with a tubular balloon. They pelted him with their rubber noses, neck ruffles, and flowers. A massive mushroom-cloud "bag" filled up with air behind them. They hurled the boy clown onto it, but the "bag" consumed them alive instead. The boy clown alone survived as a bomb exploded. The cycle was doomed to repeat.[*]

On October 16, 1966, the dancer Noël Mason wrote the following news home to her family in Tacoma: "Jerry is going wild with all sorts of new ideas and made us put clown white all over our faces for one rehearsal." At that time, Arpino had recently overseen the premiere of *Nightwings,* and Joffrey was approximately a year away from working on *Astarte.* When Compton offered *Astarte* to Joffrey, he discussed the possibility of incorporating inflatables. Shortly after *Astarte*'s premiere on September 20, 1967, Arpino approached Compton to see about collaborating with him on a ballet that used plastic, sculptural balloons. Sensing Arpino's one-upmanship with Joffrey, Compton turned him down. Compton was not alone in his perception.

"I just had the feeling, an instinctual feeling, that Jerry was spurred on by what had happened with *Astarte.* There is between people a certain kind of rivalry," said Rima Corben, Isadora Bennett's assistant.[6]

Arpino visited Vernon Lobb and Kip Coburn, New York artist friends who lived in a SoHo loft. On their rooftop they played with large inflatable architectural shapes—tying them to the water tower and chimneys.[†] "Vernon and Kip's inflatable sculptures symbolized to me the idea that if you pollute the environment, you self-pollute," said Arpino. "I wanted to make a small attempt to say that we had better think about the preservation of life on this planet."[7]

Arpino first worked with Scott Barnard as he started to formulate *The Clowns.* Then he involved Robert Blankshine as the central clown. He said about choosing Blankshine, "Bobby was so open, vulnerable, and compassionate. I was so hooked on him, I couldn't see straight."[8] Blankshine seemed a numinous air current, and he easily grasped the

---

[*]*The Clowns* also echoes many of Arpino's early roles, most particularly the newspaper boy in Dirk Sanders's *Yesterday's Papers.* Aside from the similarity between the newspaper boy and the tearstained clown as godlike figures capable of bringing humans to life, in *Yesterday's Papers* the ensemble emerges from a pile of newspapers where they have been disguised, much like the real clowns hidden in a heap of dummies in *The Clowns.*

[†]In 1963, choreographer Steve Paxton launched into a series of works that used gigantic, inflatable tunnels with *Music for Word Words.* Merce Cunningham's *Rainforest,* with Andy Warhol contributing the scenery of Mylar pillows, some of which were inflated with air and some with helium, was first performed on March 9, 1968.

predicament of the tearstained clown because as a teenager he had been ridiculed. The ballet opened old wounds.* "I was always devastated by *The Clowns*," Blankshine said. "By the end I'd just be in tears and everyone thought it was sweat, but Jerry touched home. I knew the ballet was quite real. I had known what it felt like to be taunted."[9]

For the music, Arpino turned to his former colleague Lionel Rudko. Previously the owner of several record shops, Rudko had also served as general manager of Carnegie Hall and, in 1964, had managed the Joffrey Ballet. "If you took Jerry to a piano and said play C, you'd have to put a yellow label on it," Rudko said. "But Jerry has this unique ability of hearing something and being able to relate it to movement."[10] Rudko enlisted Hershy Kay to collaborate with Arpino on *The Clowns*. Kay had previously adapted music for Balanchine, but Arpino was the first choreographer for whom he would write an original piece. After watching many rehearsals, Kay composed a twelve-tone, serial-form score with electronic sound effects.

Arpino and Blankshine devised a costume by sewing Blankshine into a shiny chiffon blouson with a double layer of removable ruffles. Costume designer Edith Lutyens Bel Geddes adapted it for the clown ensemble. Arpino often fashioned the costumes for his ballets—indeed if anybody wanted to know where to find him, he was usually with the wardrobe mistress, sewing headdresses, cutting fabrics on the floor. "Arpino is known to hoard every old costume, reusing bits and pieces of them imaginatively in new productions. Delicate dye jobs (for tights, leotards, etc.) are said to be his forte. Before a performance he can usually be found applying the finishing touches to shoes and headdresses in the murky reaches of backstage," wrote Amelia Fatt in *Dance Magazine*.[11]

For makeup, Blankshine went to the library and studied clown faces, eventually devising white Pan-Cake, teased hair, four or five pairs of eyelashes, and white shoe polish on his hands. The jewels and glitter glued onto his face and eyelids cost him repeatedly scratched corneas and one hour's preparation each time he performed the ballet. He had previously learned something about clowns from choreographer Lotte Goslar, a master clown artist and mime, who had responded to Joffrey's commission in 1965 with *Charivari!* Blankshine was in the cast. Many of the routines, characters, and signature Goslar clownisms from *Charivari!* found their way into Arpino's *Clowns*. In *Charivari!* one girl clown wore a calendar of paper hearts pinned to her costume over her real heart. She tore off the hearts and gave them away. In *The Clowns*, Erika Goodman tore paper hearts off the pad on her chest. The red noses, the long shoes, and

*When Blankshine could not take *The Clowns* any more in rehearsals, Gary Chryst would assume Blankshine's place.

some mannerisms—Arpino did not hide the "borrowed" material. Critics noted the similarities.

The Clowns was first performed on February 28, 1968. New York critics were divided; the audiences, for the most part, were not. Blankshine was besieged after most performances by people crying at the stage door. The role launched him to another level of popularity: He was featured in magazine articles. He gained a following.

When *The Clowns* was taken to Vienna the next year, with Gary Chryst in the leading role, the curtain calls broke records at the Theater an der Wien, and Arpino's name was hailed across Europe. The crush at the door for the Joffrey Ballet tickets at the Vienna Festival was so overwhelming that the city's strict fire laws were broken, and people were herded in without seats for them to sit in.[12] In London, however, the critics looked down their noses at the City Center Joffrey Ballet in 1971 and railed against the "tedious" Gerald Arpino, his *Clowns,* and other ballets. The British impresarios tied the Joffrey administration's hands by preventing it from advertising the Coliseum engagement to the extent that Omar K. Lerman, the Joffrey's innovative general manager, had deemed necessary. The engagement did not sell out as had been anticipated. Still, ignoring the critics, a curious public assembled and cheered.

Looking at the next ballet Arpino created after the London visit, *Kettentanz* (1971), many observers felt that his failure there had taught him to exercise self-control. By that time, too, the Joffrey's training system was completely in place and the troupe's incoming dancers were more alike than not. The dancers entering the company possessed more homogeneous backgrounds because, in late 1968, post-*Clowns,* Joffrey had asked his old friend Jonathan Watts to take charge of the school's apprentice and scholarship program. Almost instantly Watts had upset Joffrey by telling him that he did not think the program, which had been left in limbo for a year after Lillian Moore's death, did the job.* Joffrey believed dancers learned by taking as many classes a day as was humanly possible. Watts disagreed, arguing to let him develop a small-scale version of the parent company that would tour small cities with mostly the same repertoire. He would call it Joffrey II. Recounting the day he and Joffrey faced off, Watts said:

"I reminded Bob that I had never taken a pas de deux class in my life. When I joined the New York City Ballet, I was already a very experienced partner because I worked with people who danced in his ballets for his concerts—people like Beatrice Tompkins and Lillian Wellein and Electa Arenal. That's what prepared me for a professional career. Going

---

*Watts officially started as apprentice and scholarship program director on March 24, 1969. He and Dianne Consoer were divorced.

through different ballets with him at the 92nd Street Y and Jacob's Pillow. Those were very concentrated, focused years. The most honest years. We were small. We weren't involved with a lot of ego-tripping and politics. And the values that Bob—as well as May O'Donnell and Gertrude Shurr—instilled in me gave me the respect for classicism. Those values have carried me throughout my career.

"I spoke to Bob about that when I wanted to create Joffrey II. I said to him, 'The way to teach dancers is to give them wonderful choreography to do—not to do a bunch of exercises. Not just class after class after class.' "[13]

Joffrey bought the argument. The concept of a second company with a shared repertoire and administration, though common to many American companies by the end of the millennium, was radical in 1968,* radical and successful. After starting off as the Joffrey Apprentice Company, the name changed to Joffrey II Dancers in 1971 when the troupe started performing. Within five years, Watts and his associate, Sally Brayley Bliss, would be producing 85 percent of the City Center Joffrey Ballet's members, including Richard Colton, Ann Marie De Angelo, Gregory Huffman, Nancy Ichino, Philip Jerry, Krystyna Jurkowski, Beatriz Rodriguez, Russell Sultzbach, and Christine Uchida.†

But that was to come. As the turbulent sixties were drawing to a close, a love affair between two of the company's important dancers turned into a tragedy that jolted the company to its foundation. While working with Joffrey on *Astarte* in Tacoma, Max Zomosa had also rehearsed in *Elegy,* a new Arpino ballet. Zomosa originated a leading role as the Confederate Soldier opposite Noël Mason as His Wife. Mason was ravishing, and during *Elegy* rehearsals, she was intent on deflecting Zomosa's advances. Zomosa "could convince each woman that she was the most perfect in some

---

*As perhaps a backhanded compliment to Watts's very good idea, Lucia Chase at American Ballet Theatre decided to create ABT II in January 1973. When she asked former ABT dancer Richard Englund to found and direct the program, she informed him that it was important to her not to make it look as though they were copying Joffrey II. Therefore, ABT II began as "American Ballet Theatre presents its Ballet Repertory Company." A couple of years would pass before ABT officials gave up trying to prevent the public from calling the troupe ABT II.

Englund and his wife, Gage Bush, who was both a former Joffrey and ABT dancer, were associated with ABT II until spring 1984, when Mikhail Baryshnikov (then ABT's director) closed the doors on it. In 1985, Englund and Bush were appointed artistic director and ballet mistress, respectively, of Joffrey II.

†Joffrey II was initially financed by Bill Blanken, who had quietly been feeding his personal resources into the main company since before 1956. "The Joffrey's history cannot be written without acknowledgment of Bill Blanken," P. W. Manchester had said.

aspect that made it worth returning to him for more,"[14] said a colleague. Mason was the most naïve, the dancer who, in 1963, had captured the special attention of President Kennedy. Now, in Tacoma, during *Elegy* rehearsals, Joffrey was not around to play chaperon. Mason had to fend for herself, succeeding until Zomosa invited her out to dinner to discuss the ballet. "My weakness," the ballerina confessed. "If you talk about ballet, I am completely won over."[15]

On November 21, 1967, Mason and Zomosa were married. The event took place one month after the City Center season with its premieres of *Astarte* and *Elegy* and several weeks after Mason had recovered from mononucleosis. The virus had destroyed nerves in her shoulder and ended her dancing career. A few days after the wedding, a *Dance Magazine* profile revealed that Zomosa was already married and had two children. He lived with his family in New Jersey.

Zomosa had committed bigamy, and Mason had had no idea. She had believed Zomosa to be divorced. Joffrey advised her to stop seeing him, but Mason stood behind Zomosa. "I was still completely in love with Max," she said. "I was very sympathetic and understanding about how a person like him could get himself into a situation like that. He wanted to do the best for everybody, but he didn't know how, and he got himself in too deep with me. He didn't realize how innocent I was. He was my prince, who was going to save me from having to dance anymore."[16] Zomosa did not realize that Mason believed everything he told her, including that love's mystical experience was happening to him for the first time. Mason had spun a fairy tale out of their love and Zomosa had decided to honor Mason by fitting into her myth. He committed himself to the role of prince and took his vows, swearing true love. She would alleviate the torment he had known since his mother had refused ever again to speak to him when he had accidentally killed his friend.

By March 1968, Zomosa convinced Mason that he had divorced his first wife and that she was now living in South America. Meanwhile, his visa was running out and he was not sure how he would be able to stay in the United States. He had bone spurs and other injuries that irritated him when he danced. He told Joffrey that he was leaving the company, then he changed his mind. He had no money and was borrowing "just to eat," said Mason,[17] who had become pregnant in the summer with Zomosa's child.

By the end of November 1968, Zomosa began teaching Christian Holder his Death role in *The Green Table*. At first, because Joffrey thought Holder was not ready to assume such responsibility, Zomosa and Holder worked together privately. One day, Zomosa gave Holder his personal pair of Death's size-10, handmade leather boots to keep. Holder was honored and not disconcerted by what might have seemed an untimely passing of the torch, because Zomosa was generous, unpredictable, and passionate. When younger dancers were making their debuts, he was known to hover in the wings to cheer them on. Holder thought this was another instance when Zomosa was acknowledging the dancer's rite of passage.

Zomosa also told his best friend, Michael Uthoff, with whom he had been quarreling since his marriage to Mason, that he would not see him again after the Southwestern tour in which they were then involved. "He was an individual who loved hard and lived hard. The future and the past didn't make any sense to him," said Uthoff, who had heard Zomosa's refrain about "leaving" too often to notice anything different this time.[18]

Zomosa's immigration papers were not being renewed; he would have to leave the United States, which meant leaving Mason and their unborn child. Zomosa urged Mason to swear to remain together with him even if it meant killing themselves, but Mason refused because she could not destroy the life of their child. The romantic imagery Zomosa had conjured up was straight out of *Romeo and Juliet* and *Swan Lake* and *Giselle,* but he was neither Romeo nor Prince Siegfried nor Albrecht. He was a seriously troubled man, "leading a double life," said Mason,[19] who soon realized that Zomosa's first wife was still living in New Jersey and that he had not divorced her. Moreover, Zomosa was still involved with his children's lives. He had also told their mother that he had divorced Mason. He had lied to everyone. Faced with the possibility that he might not see his beloved children for a long time because of the visa problems, Zomosa was spending more time with them.

Mason warned him their relationship was over. She was moving out of their Manhattan apartment and filing for divorce. He begged her to reconsider. When she refused, he asked for $50 to buy a gun. She refused to give him the money. "This world is just not for me."[20] Those proved to be his last words to Mason.

On January 9, 1969, Zomosa drove to New Jersey, picked up his children at school and dropped them off at their home in Woodbridge. Then he continued down the road, parked, and stabbed himself in the heart with a knife.

"When Max died, Mr. Joffrey just wept," remembered Mason. "He said, 'There will never be anybody like him.' "[21] Joffrey called a company meeting in an empty studio. His face ashen, he told the dancers about Zomosa's suicide and, leaning against a barre and staring out the window, "seemed to ramble" about Zomosa as an irreplaceable model.[22] When Holder left the meeting, he went to the dressing room to gather the boots given to him by Zomosa, but they were gone. Nobody ever knew what had happened to them.

In April, Noël Mason gave birth to a son named Christian and accepted Alex and Carol Ewing's invitation to live with them at Overlook Farm, their estate in Millbrook, New York, where she and Zomosa had once happily courted.

Company morale plummeted after Zomosa's death,* which closely followed the earlier departures of Robert Blankshine and Michael Uthoff—and before them, Lisa Bradley, who, in the eyes of so many, defined the City Center Joffrey Ballet. Why were so many important dancers leaving the company? Bradley and Uthoff were expecting a baby. Bradley had also been hurt by Joffrey's casting choices (he was putting her into third casts) and she wanted eventually to seek other opportunities. There were other extenuating circumstances as well: Bradley rejoiced in the prospect of motherhood; Joffrey and Arpino were less than pleased. Bradley's health, under normal circumstances, was fragile. Pregnant, she was anemic and too weak to dance in her usual confident manner. She had previously miscarried; she asked to be released from touring to avoid another miscarriage. Joffrey kept pressing her to tour anyway.

Joffrey and Arpino's reactions to pregnancy are not uncommon for artistic directors of ballet companies; the condition often permanently transforms the dancer's physique and stamina. "Mr. Joffrey was calm. He said, 'This will change everything. You know it will. You won't come back this time as you were,'" Bradley recalled. "And Jerry was upset, too. I remember him seeing me about eight months pregnant backstage at State Theater and saying, 'How could you do that to your body?'"[23]

After leaving the Joffrey Ballet, Bradley continued dancing for another five years, returning once to the Joffrey in 1976 for a brief period. She had a baby girl and later divorced Uthoff, who was directing the Hartford Ballet. In 1985, Bradley sent her daughter to live with Uthoff. She joined the Cistercians, a nonspeaking Trappist order where she remained for eight years. "My experience in the monastery was the same system I lived with at Joffrey," she observed. "Weren't we silent in the dance? I had for so long been respectful of silence. Dancers' lives are monastically inclined. The fasting. The schedule of the whole day. The selflessness. A monastic's life is to center your attention on Christ. A dancer's is to center it on dance."[24]

By 1966, the Joffrey dancers had smudged more of the classical clarity that they had possessed before Arpino's ballets were the company's acknowledged staple. The dancing now seemed more subject to personal

---

*On November 18, 1969, the National Endowment for the Arts had given $133,000 to the Joffrey Ballet for its full-length production of a modern adaptation of *Beauty and the Beast,* which was to be choreographed by Joffrey, Arpino, Edna McRae, and Mary Ann Wells. Ewing had played an important role in the ballet's concept. Zomosa was to be the Beast. When Zomosa died, the ballet was scrapped.

whim. Except on rare occasion, Joffrey was no longer teaching every day; Basil Thompson was. Perhaps Joffrey's reduced contact with the dancers had permitted a freer approach to classical line and discipline. Pure classicism was taught at the Joffrey, but the education dancers gain in a studio does not always translate to the stage. The stage belongs to the director's taste. Perry Brunson and Hector Zaraspe were teaching the apprentices. They both cared about classical heritage and the precision of line, musical phrasing, and the dancer's intelligent look behind the eye. Their teaching styles, however, were diametrically opposed—"Perry was strict and concerned with technique. Zaraspe concentrated on dancing. It was a wonderful balance," said Glenn White.[25] They beautifully complemented Basil Thompson, the company's perfectionist ballet master and former Royal Ballet and American Ballet Theatre dancer. But perhaps Arpino's extreme athleticism conflicted with the classical restraint learned from Thompson, Brunson, and Zaraspe. Without Joffrey a clear direction was lost.

The departures of Blankshine, Bradley, Mason, and Uthoff in combination with Zomosa's suicide brought a dark closure to an era. Zomosa had found the dignity of meaning in each performance; no matter how many times he danced *The Green Table* or *Astarte*, he said, "I am still experimenting, it's always deeper, deeper, and deeper."[26] Yet his suicide also unified the dancers and dramatically solidified the company's character. They had lived through a tragic experience, and partly in the spirit of the times, many reached for the ultimate early seventies social goal: one peaceful community—no class barriers, no race barriers, no political barriers. These were the circumstances working in Arpino's favor when he applied himself to *Trinity*, his next major work. He said that from the instant he started concentrating on it at Berkeley in the summer of 1970, the ballet seemed predestined. "It was the most perfect collaboration, ever."[27]

The idea for *Trinity* was born when Arpino and Jim Howell heard two sections of the music composed by Alan Raph and Lee Holdridge, live, at a 92nd Street Y concert, "Music in Our Times." Raph's *Sunday*, a fanfare of trumpets and increasingly louder and shorter drum pulses that expanded into organ music, set off the ballet as if it were the first hymn in church. In the second section, Holdridge's *Summerland*, a boys' choir in the pit singing music reminiscent of Gregorian chant intensified the religious atmosphere. The ballet ended with Raph's *Saturday*, sounding almost as it had begun. But the drums had been replaced by electronic guitar chords, suggesting a progression from the primitive to the civilized—the spiritual evolution of humankind from a Westerner's point of view—and the pulse grew weaker and weaker, until there was dead silence. Peace.

There was something stronger than physical and intellectual typecasting to *Trinity* that Lili Cockerille, who danced with the Joffrey from

1969 to 1972, later articulated when she had become a dance critic and author. "I hated being in *Trinity* because I didn't think it worked. It was not musical," she said. "But *Trinity* was a landmark piece because it introduced a new energy into contemporary ballet. It was people enjoying themselves onstage—looking inward, looking outward, and letting that be all that was onstage."[28]

Trinity was made in Berkeley at a time of ineffable "unity within the company," concurred Sue Loyd, who was still Joffrey's assistant in 1970. "We all totally loved each other. That ballet was about love and the energy we gave each other from the wings, in our lives, and onstage."[29]

The title, *Trinity,* also referred to the three men for whom the ballet was made: Dermot Burke, Gary Chryst, and Christian Holder. They were joined by Rebecca Wright, Donna Cowen, plus Starr Danias, James Dunne, Robert Estner, Denise Jackson, Sue Loyd, Diane Orio, Robert Talmage, Robert Thomas, and Glenn White. Scott Barnard sat on the sidelines and gradually forged an association with Arpino, assisting him and eventually taking over, in most ways, for Jim Howell in 1973, except that Barnard's strength was not as a musician; it was as a ballet master.

Trinity was the making of Chryst and Holder as Joffrey stars. Chryst was a former High School of Performing Arts drama major who had been encouraged by Cora Cahan to enter the dance division. Cahan was the leading woman in Norman Walker's modern dance company and one of the most life-affirming contemporary dancers. When Joffrey offered a scholarship to his school, Chryst was already a member of Walker's troupe. In late 1967, Chryst was promoted to company apprentice; the position of company member was offered to him a year later. But, after having witnessed the trouble Dennis Nahat had encountered with Arpino, D'Addario, and Howell and what he construed as ballet politics, Chryst decided to run from dance.

In fall 1968, Joffrey talked Chryst back to the City Center Joffrey Ballet, and under Joffrey's guidance, he mastered the skills that propelled him to the elite as a major American dance-actor (in the European tradition of the *danseurs de caractère*). Chryst was certainly the definitive contemporary interpreter of Léonide Massine's roles and ballets. He inherited the mantle directly from Massine himself, who taught Chryst the roles of Petrouchka and the Chinese Conjuror. Chryst also came close to being the dancer Joffrey might have been. The genealogy—from Massine to Joffrey to Chryst—was quietly understood and observed. Said Tatiana Massine Weinbaum, Massine's daughter and rehearsal assistant:

"My father recognized himself in his youth in Gary. Gary's technique was more developed. In any case, Gary is really a genius of a dancer, and I know my father recognized that. There's a link between Joffrey and Gary and my father. And there's probably a similarity between my father and Joffrey as dancers, sort of converging in Gary. But having watched Gary rehearse with my father, I think he is one of the very few who could absolutely, exactly replicate a movement the way it is shown. I remember the intensity, the feeling of Gary and my father's focus on getting the movement right. And how successful that was."[30]

Christian Holder also captured Joffrey's interest, because Holder was a pop Renaissance man of sorts; while dancing leading roles in the Joffrey, he also choreographed, wrote, and designed and built costumes for rock star Tina Turner. The dynamic among Joffrey, Chryst, and Holder was unprecedented in the Joffrey Ballet. Joffrey seemed almost dependent on Chryst and Holder to lend him a modish social edge. At forty-two, Joffrey seemed to live vicariously through them. He grew his sideburns long, parted his hair in the middle, he went dancing at Arthur's—the hottest discothèque—and bought records by Blood, Sweat, and Tears following their example. Joffrey related to Chryst and Holder differently than any of the other dancers because of their personalities. Chryst and Holder were in their own way larger than life, and they attracted the attention of many famous people to the Joffrey Ballet. Michael Bennett, Cat Stevens, James Ragni, Gerald Rado, Michael Peters, Jerry Grimes, Lester Wilson, and Holder's family friend Penelope Tree were their visitors. "Bob never got over being impressed by a celebrity. He was childlike in that respect," said Bill Leighton, his assistant. "He never quit being a little kid from Seattle, and he never was into the fact that he himself was a celebrity."[31]

Joffrey closely tracked those among the world's legions of stars who saw the Joffrey Ballet, and his company's press agents were sufficiently aware of his preoccupation that they, in turn, recorded names and were able, even decades later, to report that Barbra Streisand, Joan Crawford, Cher, Bette Midler, Hal Prince, and Jennifer Jones had seen the troupe in these early City Center days. Joffrey collected autographs, mostly of famous dead ballerinas, but he liked to expand his collection. Whenever Chryst and Holder lured dignitaries to the company and they came backstage after a performance, Joffrey seemed overly awed. "I was aware I had power. You could see it in his eyes," said Holder. "Even at the *Dance Magazine* Awards. We would flock in with our entourage and he'd be there with Herb Migdoll. It was cute, in its way, endearing. You could tell he'd be in a conversation, but his eyes were over on us to see what he was missing. To see if we were behaving. We'd catch a twinkle in his eye like he'd like to be with us."[32]

Although impressed and intrigued by Chryst and Holder (and dancer Robert Talmage, who was also part of their group), Joffrey maintained his cool professional reserve. They called him Mr. Joffrey. He was using them to shape his company; his interest in them was not only personal. As for

Arpino, he had been watching Chryst's increasing politicization since the Kent State University shootings on May 4, 1970, in Ohio—and Chryst's identification with the Kent State students fascinated him. Chryst had awakened to his own position as a member of a minority group when, as a thirteen-year-old, he first learned that his father was part black, part American Indian, and part Caucasian. His mother, who was Caucasian, had left his father soon after Chryst was born in La Jolla, California. They had moved to New Jersey in 1957, where Chryst at age seven was adopted by his new stepfather, also Caucasian. "I have been Petrouchka most of my life," he said, referring to the tormented puppet in Fokine's famous ballet. "Growing up with my parents in New Jersey where kids threw things at my head and called me a nigger boy. I was not liked in high school because of being so confused about the white group and the black group."[33]

At thirteen, light-skinned Chryst asked his mother directly what race his father's father and his father were. "I think she thought it was not important for me to know until I asked," he said. "I asked, and she did not lie."[34] The truth elicited some relief and identification. Chryst then styled his hair in an Afro like Angela Davis's; he identified with militancy—"as militant as one can be in a ballet company"[35]

Arpino used Chryst's politicized passion in *Trinity*. In the ballet's opening and final movements, Chryst surged into a high arching jump that changed direction midair. Landing "backward," he then repeated the jump on the other side, altering direction midair. The rest of the company joined him; they called the jump the "tank step," recalling Kent State. "Every time the jetés went forward, we were standing up for our rights," said Chryst. "And when we moved backwards, it was because the tanks were approaching. *Trinity*, my sections anyway, was an extension of how I felt about freedom and individuality."[36]

At the beginning of the ballet's last section, Chryst used his fist—the black power fist—to weld the dancers into solidarity. Finally, in almost total darkness (lighting by Jennifer Tipton), the ensemble members placed lit votive candles on the floor. All left the stage.

The year before *Trinity*'s completion, Holder and Rebecca Wright had led Joffrey members on an organized candlelight vigil after a performance of *The Green Table*. Walking out of City Center and singing "Give Peace a Chance," they marched down Broadway to Times Square with a trail of audience members following them. They were joined by many other theatrical companies as they protested America's presence in Vietnam.

While Joffrey cared more that the dancers expose themselves to as many dance performances as possible, rather than involving themselves in protests, moratoriums, and sexual revolution ideology, he and Arpino appreciated that social change affected the company.

Holder assumed the role of leader in *Trinity* since he held that position informally inside the company. "Onward Christian Holder," some jokingly called him—for he was a spiritual person. He was also a true gentleman, who earned the respect of many in the company because he held to his own course and stepped on no one's toes. In 1970, Holder was seriously practicing transcendental meditation. And although he did not identify with African-American militancy (primarily because his strongest roots were in England), he wore long, flowing robes and bells on his toes everywhere he wandered on the Berkeley campus. Arpino asked him to remain in the African robe he wore backstage for *Trinity* rehearsals—which explains why Holder's role is defined by swirling, centrifugal movement.

Arpino had set his highest standard for mass-public "conversion" ballets with *Trinity*. The title does not refer to Catholic dogma or to the code word for the first atomic explosion ever in July 1945. The title was derived from a small incident: Arpino was dabbling his feet in a fountain in Portland, Oregon, when a little child—"more angel than child," said Arpino—started playing with his toes. Arpino commented on the girl's beauty and asked what her name was. "Her name is Trinity," said the woman who was tending her. "She's my hippie daughter's child, and her name is Trinity."[37] Arpino instantly thought, "That's the name of my ballet!" He ran back to the hotel to tell Howell and Joffrey. They laughed at him. Several days later en route to San Francisco, Howell was gazing out of a plane window at a majestic mountain range. He asked Arpino what it was called. The map said, "The Trinity." They gasped—and the ballet was named.

Arpino and Howell believed in karma and cosmic coincidence. They were both schooled Christians who could quote Bible passages, but they were also nascent New Agers, before the term had been absorbed into the popular culture. By 1968, they were beginning to investigate light's power—healing, metaphysical, and destructive. Arpino eventually choreographed *Suite Saint-Saëns* (1978), a ballet in which he was strongly assisted by Howell and Glenn White, which Agnes de Mille described as similar to what she imagined would be the experience of "standing in a flight of meteors."[38] Arpino also produced a success with *Light Rain* (1981), which had been rehearsed for two months with lasers as the only light source (an experiment that was ultimately considered too expensive to continue). *Light Rain* summarized Arpino's view, cultivated from the sixties and seventies, that "we all become light in the end," he said. Light in all its manifestations—from the votive candles he and Howell burned, to the stars in the galaxy—signified to him "the pure essence of being,"[39] which was the same term precisely that he used to define movement.

With *Trinity*, Howell and he were opening themselves to their intuitions; they talked about the fourth dimension—the psychic, the god within, the divine force that could be known provided they refrained from materialism and egoism. Joffrey went along with them to a degree. He was convinced that past dancers' and choreographers' spirits haunted the ballets that he was reviving; he believed in reincarnation. He meditated. But Arpino and Howell had their own special brand of Berkeley-California spiritualism, which did not appeal to Joffrey. California in general and specific words such as *karma* made him uneasy. In contrast, Arpino and Howell bought a house in San Francisco, and the company's experiences in Berkeley informed four of Arpino's works to such a degree that they became known as his Berkeley ballets.* *Trinity* was the first.

About three weeks prior to the premiere, *Trinity* had still not been costumed. Joffrey saw Holder's robe and the motley attire the others were wearing and decided to render them abstract with plain leotards and tights. He and Arpino flew home to New York, and at their new brownstone walk-up on MacDougal Street in the Village, he asked Estelle Sommers of Capezio Ballet Makers for her advice on costuming *Trinity*. "It just needs the right-colored leotards," she told them.[40]

Many years later, Sommers recalled in detail her *Trinity* meeting with Joffrey and Arpino because it was a momentous one for Capezio. She said, "Bob went into another room and brought back this fabric sample, saying, 'This was just made and it's called Milliskin. I don't know where it comes from, or anything about it.' And I went wild. I told him, 'It's the most exciting fabric I've seen for a leotard since Helanca.' And I turned to Jerry and said, 'Jerry, I'm going to find that fabric and I promise you when I have leotards made up, you'll get the first batch.' "[41]

Sommers persuaded the textile firm where Milliskin was invented to let Capezio work with the material. Capezio was the first into the marketplace with a white Milliskin unitard that could be dyed any color. Milliskin—a lightweight stretchy material with a high sheen that gave that wet, sexy look—revolutionized the dance wear and bathing suit industries. Leotards were no longer dull.

On August 20, 1970, *Trinity* premiered at Zellerbach Hall in Berkeley. The dancers wore Arpino's color choices: verdant green, blazing yellow, hot cerise, and electric blue. He described the memorable opening night to Olga Maynard, a writer for *Dance Magazine:*

> Trinity *closed the program but instead of applauding, the audience stayed still for a few moments. Then, from the balcony, young men began throwing themselves over the edge, their friends holding them by their heels,*

*Arpino's Berkeley ballets were *Trinity, Reflections, Kettentanz,* and *Sacred Grove on Mount Tamalpais.*

shouting, "Peace! Peace!" and making the peace sign. It was quite sponta-
neous. I remember feeling scared about the danger of the kids falling from
the balcony, and then I was overwhelmed by the response, by the audience
shouting, "Peace! Peace!"—instead of the usual bravo.

Berkeley was so turned on by Trinity . . . *that the students went to the*
University's concert manager, Betty Connors, and demanded that the big
Picasso banner [the peace flag that Picasso did for Berkeley] be hung across
the gallery at Zellerbach.[42]

On October 9, 1970, *Trinity* was performed in New York for the first
time. The fall and spring seasons at City Center had been expanded to six
weeks apiece—Ewing had finally reached his goal of securing twelve
weeks annually for the troupe in New York. "Three men stand out, tireless and heroic, Christian Holder, Gary Chryst and Dermot Burke,"
raved Clive Barnes of *Trinity* in the *New York Times*. "But the whole cast
is outstanding, including such newcomers as Starr Danias, James Dunne
and Robert Thomas." He thought *Trinity* was Arpino's "most considerable work to date."[43] Most critics for daily newspapers agreed, most for
weeklies or monthlies did not. "*Trinity* is a very noisy ballet, very big and
punchy and calculated," wrote Marcia B. Siegel two weeks later. "It just
wants the audience to be knocked out. The fifteen dancers perform it
with terrific oomph and sincerity, like the people who sing the jingles
about how you can satisfy your libido by driving a Comanche or whatever it is down the New Jersey Turnpike."[44]

Trinity—the Joffrey Ballet's new signature, replacing *Astarte*—was
performed consistently through 1979. Usually it was the last ballet on
the last night, which meant the last image of each season was fifteen lit
candles flickering on a bare, dark stage. "The only thing man can leave
on this earth is the light of himself," Arpino said.[45] In 1970, at the ballet's
candlelight conclusion, many of the dancers were remembering their colleague Maximiliano Zomosa.

CHAPTER 23

Crossing Over

By the end of 1970, Joffrey had experienced enough of Arpino's work and esthetic to comprehend his influence on the company. He could have reduced Arpino's load. He could have stopped using his choreography, if he had wanted to strive only for higher classical principles.

Joffrey reminded reporter Amelia Fatt in October 1970 that central to his original concept for the company was an "all-star casting of *The Sleeping Beauty,* conducted by Toscanini."[1] With Harkness, he had dancers whose qualities would have served *Sleeping Beauty,* but not in the numbers necessary for this most difficult nineteenth-century classic. By 1970, however, *Sleeping Beauty* was out of the question for his dancers. Had he really always yearned to direct a classical company, but his innate attraction to and sympathy for the odd had compelled him in a contemporary direction? Was he scripting a new plan? In no other article until Fatt's for *Dance Magazine* had Joffrey mentioned the all-star/Toscanini *Sleeping Beauty.* Perhaps he was just reminding himself of who he had once been: a dancer tweaked into consciousness by *The Borzoi Book of Ballets,* the Ballet Russe, and the Royal Ballet, which had regularly visited New York. Joffrey was infatuated with Frederick Ashton's choreography for the Royal. He was also acquainted with Royal Ballet members David Blair, Alexander Grant, and John Hart, who sometimes attended City Center Joffrey Ballet performances. Through Zaraspe, Margot Fonteyn befriended Joffrey (toward the end of her life, she was a guest-teacher at the American Ballet Center). Joffrey knew Ashton personally, too; and Ashton responded to his enthusiasm for his work. Ashton was retiring as the Royal Ballet's director in 1970, which to many people, including Joffrey, seemed grievously premature.

In 1969, the Joffrey had acquired Ashton's *Façade,* the first of what would soon be a repertoire the largest number of Ashton works outside England. Most of the Ashton repertoire, with its purity of line, supreme musicality, good manners, and beneficent humanity, contrasted starkly with the crowd-pleasing Arpino repertoire. How could Joffrey justify that he liked both?

"Bob was a very mixed-up person in many respects, because he was a very dichotomous person," noted Clive Barnes about the conflict he perceived within Joffrey, after over two decades of observing him at relatively close range. "There was the sea green, incorruptible museum meister, who really wanted to be a connoisseur and really wanted to sit back in his beautifully appointed study with his little bust of Napoleon, and who wanted to think beautiful thoughts and to develop a beautiful repertory, rather like an eighteenth-century grand seigneur on his grand tour of Europe would have brought back wonderful paintings and mounted them in lovely galleries and invited friends.

"Then, there was the other aspect of Bob, which was sort of—he had the soul of an Afghan rug seller. He wanted to sell as many rugs as he could. He wanted to go into the marketplace.

"So, there was this very calm grand seigneur on the one hand, and there was this little marketplace urchin on the other, and I found it enchanting."[2]

Joffrey, the "grand seigneur," was in the ascendant by 1970, when a new generation of dancers had entered the company. Massine, his daughter Tatiana, and former Ballet Russe de Monte Carlo character dancer Yurek Lazowski had taught the dancers *Le Tricorne,* Massine's Spanish classic, which had been created for Diaghilev in 1919 with an original score by Manuel de Falla and sets by Picasso. *Le Tricorne* by the City Center was greeted with mixed reviews; the second cast of Alaine Haubert and Edward Verso was considered an improvement, but Joffrey, when asked in later years if he had one ballet he would like to revive again, replied *Le Tricorne.*

The City Center Joffrey Ballet would serve as the American repository for Massine's works, as Joffrey brought Massine back into circulation. It seemed that with this new push to revive and restage ballets, Joffrey was moving chronologically through his own life. Massine gave him at age eleven his first experience as a paid dancer onstage in the Ballet Russe *Petrouchka.* Kurt Jooss and *The Green Table* provided Joffrey, also at eleven, with the first ballet that he knew he wanted to have in his repertoire. Ashton was the choreographer to whom he had been compared at twenty-seven. Dancer, director, and choreographer—the parts of Joffrey's career were laid out and represented by the choreographers with whom he worked that season.

By 1970, Rex Bickmore, Richard Browne, Ivy Clear, Jon Cristofori, Susan Magno, George Montalbano, Marjorie Mussman, and Trinette Singleton had left the Joffrey ranks. The company was refortified by more dancers: Martine van Hamel, a leading principal in the National Ballet of Canada, thinking she would like to try some contemporary choreography, accepted Joffrey's invitation. But, also suited for *Le Corsaire,*

Swan Lake, Nutcracker, and *La Bayadère,* van Hamel exited swiftly for American Ballet Theatre, in 1971. Joffrey hired James Dunne, Dennis Wayne, and Robert Thomas from the Harkness Ballet, too. Simultaneously, from Seattle he captured Francesca Corkle, the former child prodigy he had unveiled in his 1962 *Aïda.* Corkle's dancing leaped the synapses between grace, beauty, and the classical codes. She was on first impression unforgettable. Tiny and strong, Corkle set the company's highest standard for stylistic clarity during this period. Starr Danias, Sue Loyd, Alaine Haubert, Burton Taylor, Edward Verso, and Gay Wallstrom also assumed authority. There were, as well, Scott Barnard, Henry Berg, Donna Cowen, Ann Marie De Angelo, Robert Estner, Denise Jackson, Diane Orio, Nancy Robinson, Beatriz Rodriguez, Robert Talmage, Robert Thomas, Glenn White, and William Whitener.

By spring 1970, the company had grown to thirty-seven dancers on an annual budget of $1.5 million, which the Ford Foundation supplemented with a three-year grant of $1.2 million. Jennifer Tipton, who would emerge as one of America's most sought-after lighting designers, was the production supervisor. Press agent Rima Corben was in her third year as a dedicated Joffrey employee working with Isadora Bennett. Bill Leighton, Joffrey's resourceful assistant, devised a reliable hourly schedule both for Joffrey and for the troupe. The schedule transformed them into profoundly more efficient entities. At the weekly cost of $48,000 for seven performances, with a forty-seven-member orchestra and a technical crew of ten carpenters, ten electricians, and four property staff members, it was, as with all professional ballet companies, an extremely expensive enterprise.

Ewing's plan to sustain the troupe through university residencies had carried Joffrey far. But the fruitful Pacific Lutheran University summer residencies, supported by the National Endowment for the Arts and Humanities through the Pacific Northwest Ballet Association, ended in 1970, after four years. The association wanted a permanent company in Seattle and Joffrey would not consider moving. Influenced by the presence of the City Center Joffrey Ballet in Tacoma and Seattle, and the support system it generated, the Pacific Northwest Ballet was founded in 1977.

The City Center Joffrey Ballet had, under the general directorship of Ewing and helped by general administrator Omar K. Lerman, continued to maintain an ambassadorial presence in the arts: In 1968, President Johnson had invited the company to perform again at the White House, this time for King Olaf of Norway. In late June 1969, the Joffrey had spent its week performing in Vienna to standing-room-only audiences. In 1970, Ewing had picked up a summer residency at the University of California at Berkeley. It lasted for two summers. Because of Ewing, the company had a stable home base. Twelve weeks a year were spent at City

Center. It was sufficient time for the Joffrey to build a loyal audience that was interested in cast changes, and more important, provided time for the dancers to develop range.

Ewing, though, resigned from the company at the end of 1970. His wife, Carol Sonne Ewing, had died tragically of a heart attack during the family's summer pack trip in the Sierra Nevada, on July 25, 1969. Ewing was shattered, and with three children to care for on his own, he did not have the spirit to continue as the Joffrey's general director. Although he remained officially connected to the Joffrey's Foundation for American Dance until 1979, the Ewing years were essentially over. It had been a thriving period defined by invisible links that have no name other than affection and respect.

Anthony A. Bliss was Ewing's choice to be his replacement. Bliss had recently stepped down from his position as president of the Metropolitan Opera. Bliss was the same man who had met with Rebekah Harkness on May 29, 1963, to discuss merging Joffrey's school with the Met's school under Alicia Markova. Thus, Bliss had already been tangentially involved in a takeover plot concerning Joffrey—but neither Joffrey nor Ewing probably had any notion of it.

In 1971, Joffrey welcomed Bliss on his foundation as chairman because he trusted Ewing. Ewing said, "Tony Bliss was very much a fan and supporter of Bob Joffrey. He never skimped when it came to paying for dinners or entertaining potential backers, he always paid his own way, never missed meetings, listened to endless discussions and arguments, and he came to the rescue by taking responsibility when I had to step down. We were all on the same side."[3] Bliss's father, Cornelius N. Bliss, had been a Metropolitan Opera trustee for seventeen years during the 1930s and 1940s. Tony Bliss was a partner at the New York law firm of Milbank, Tweed, Hadley and McCloy. He belonged to upper-crust clubs: the Century, the River, and the Wall Street. Although intimidated by Bliss, Joffrey imagined his credentials would serve the company well and he had courted Bliss by inviting his wife, Sally Brayley, to join the company as a dancer in 1967. Joffrey accepted Tony Bliss even though Bliss had acted with open condescension toward Arpino.

Arpino's controversial reputation as a choreographer was impossible to ignore any longer. *Trinity* divided the audience from the critics, whose opinions seemed to have a stronger impact on each other than on the box office. By 1970, Arpino was one of the intellectual elite's least respected American choreographers—just when the City Center Joffrey Ballet was counted as establishment. The emotional capital that Joffrey and Arpino had gained after the Harkness breakup had been spent. The honeymoon with the press was over. With the advent of an economic recession, competition for the dance audience was greater than at any other time in American history. Moreover, Natalia Makarova had defected from Russia's Kirov Ballet; Cynthia Gregory was dazzling people at American Ballet Theatre; so were Fernando Bujones, Ivan Nagy, and Martine van Hamel; Jerome Robbins emerged with *Dances at a Gathering* for the New York City Ballet. The new choreographer on the block, Eliot Feld, was in most critics' eyes everything that Arpino was not. In addition, Feld had launched his own ballet company.

Yet, after *Trinity*, Joffrey seemed to be abdicating to Arpino and the commercial esthetic even more. The press debated the City Center Joffrey Ballet's virtues with sufficient intensity that the debate itself was reported by John J. O'Connor for the *Wall Street Journal*:

> *Though far from being financially secure—no dance company is—the Joffrey is now very much part of the Establishment. Amiable coexistence, rather than competition, with Balanchine has been the pattern, and more than a few professional observers are sulkingly disappointed. . . . There has been criticism of assistant director Gerald Arpino's tendency to control too much of the choreographic output, with highly uneven quality being almost inevitable. . . . But worst of all, aver the snipers . . . How are the masses ever going to learn to appreciate "true art"?*[4]

As Ewing had said, to some extent the Joffrey was formed by the need to survive, the need to support its existence "in a way that is tenable." Arpino presented the most sensible economic answer. "Joffrey knew which side his bread was buttered on," Ewing had continued. "He could hear applause as well as anyone else. He liked the worst of Arpino's work better than the worst of anyone elses."[5]

For the next five years, as his new batch of promising dancers developed, Joffrey searched outside for young choreographic talent. He also added more Massine and Ashton to the repertoire—and shut Arpino out of the office, busying him in the rehearsal studio.

Massine would stimulate the growth of the company's *demi-caractère* reputation, and Ashton would further test its classical potential. The dichotomy between a company of contemporary dance-actors and classical virtuosos had been there since Joffrey was making ballets in the early fifties in the image of Roland Petit and in the shadow of Ballet Rambert. Both Petit and Rambert had shown him that it was possible to be perceived as established with fewer people than the major troupes. Yet Joffrey's guiding spirit had indulged more in the commercial than he had originally planned.

For Robert Joffrey the years 1971 to 1975 were his most expansive, complex, and dangerous. The standout year that perhaps more than any other summarizes the history of the Joffrey Ballet is 1973, when Twyla Tharp's *Deuce Coupe*, Léonide Massine's *Parade*, Frederick Ashton's *The Dream*, and Joffrey's own *Remembrances* entered the repertoire.

Joffrey would schedule repertoire in the future that was its equal, but he would never surpass it. He had reached his zenith as an artistic director. Yet, strangely, if one were to look exclusively at the reviews and news reports, one would think the New York seasons of 1973 had been crippled by poor artistic judgment and worrisome financial surprises. Joffrey received a crushing blow a month before *Parade*'s premiere, when, on February 23, the City Center of Music and Drama management abruptly notified him that because of its $1.3 million operating deficit, and monthly losses in the area of $100,000, his company's annual subsidy was being reduced by 80 percent. The new arrangement—which called for a drop in support from $380,000 to $75,000—would commence on September 1. After that date, the use of an orchestra would no longer be without fee, and the box office and house personnel would be Joffrey's without charge for only one, instead of both, of the six-week performing seasons.

Joffrey and his general administrator, William Crawford, rebounded from the shock and swiftly conceived an alternative plan. They argued that the company had in recent years succeeded in breaking even and had demonstrated fiscal responsibility. The cutbacks were "unmerited," they said. On March 2, they handed City Center officials their compromise in writing, warning that the City Center's "new arrangement" as it had been proposed "would make it virtually impossible to maintain the Joffrey Ballet as a going concern."[6] City Center still underwrote both the New York City Ballet and the New York City Opera, which were its biggest constituents.

Five days later, City Center rejected Joffrey and Crawford's alternative. On March 22, the cutbacks were officially announced in the press.

Joffrey pared his fall season to four weeks and publicly ruminated over whether or not to cancel the 1974 seasons. He explained his grievances to the company's supporters in the form of an incisive and uncharacteristically emotional letter that was reprinted in *Dance News*:

> What is particularly depressing about the Joffrey Ballet's sudden change of circumstances is the extent to which it has been compelled to bear the overwhelming brunt of City Center's belt-tightening. City Center presently lists seven so-called constituents. The New York City Ballet and New York City Opera are among them, both of which effectively look to City Center to underwrite the entirety of their annual deficits.[7]

Joffrey pondered City Center's injustice, listing the facts and figures to show that the New York City Ballet and the New York City Opera received well over half of City Center's total support budget and, by comparison, the Joffrey Ballet only 15 percent. Then, pointing out that under the "new agreement" the New York City Ballet was losing approximately $100,000 and the Joffrey Ballet $305,000, he commented:

> The withdrawal from the Joffrey would appear to be excessively disproportionate. . . . It is the fiscally responsible Joffrey Company which has been singled out to suffer most.
>
> What can be salvaged I don't know. I do know, however, that we have been demoralized and shaken by the precipitateness and seeming inequity of City Center's action. The truth of the matter is that the relationship we thought existed, simply didn't.[8]

But, in the eyes of Norman Singer, City Center's general administrator, the Joffrey Ballet management had not been entirely blameless in contributing to the deterioration of the City Center partnership with the company. On March 24, 1971, an outraged Singer had reprimanded Alex Ewing in a letter for having made disparaging remarks at a National Endowment dance panel meeting. Singer felt that Ewing had wrongfully implied that City Center's support of the Joffrey Ballet was disingenuous and small, that the Joffrey only received help "because it was an advantage" to the Center. Moreover, said Singer, Ewing had incorrectly stated that the Joffrey was there on the "same basis" as American Ballet Theatre, when, in fact, the Joffrey received many advantages as a City Center constituent that were not offered to outside "visiting" troupes. "It is sometimes discouraging not to have endless praise for our support," concluded Singer. "However, it is excruciatingly painful to have it denied in such a crucial forum as the National Endowment."[9]

"Norman Singer interpreted this as a rather gross disloyalty which is ironic because from the very beginning, I was most enthusiastic, grateful, and committed to the idea of having City Center as the home of the Joffrey Ballet," said Ewing many years later, explaining that he had been making the case to the NEA that the City Center support did not cover the Joffrey's expenses as many people generally assumed. Ewing was trying to shift the NEA's thinking and convince its dance panel members that the Joffrey Ballet genuinely needed NEA support.[10]

In the spring of 1973, Singer warned the Joffrey Ballet management that unless Joffrey authorized a ticket price increase "and the increase went to City Center," the $65,000 that had been offered to the troupe "as an advance against independent fund raising efforts" would not come through. Singer further stipulated that the Joffrey Ballet ask its subscribers to contribute to City Center "an amount equal to twenty percent of their subscription price."[11] These were horrendous demands in Joffrey's opinion. Sharing his point of view with Morton Baum, Joseph Papp at the New York Shakespeare Festival, and Ted Shawn at Jacob's Pillow, Joffrey agreed that the arts were for the people and that prices must be kept low, or even nonexistent, so that anyone who desired to enter the theater could do so without hardship.

Those days were over; the realization that not-for-profit meant exactly what it said was dawning on theater producers, presenters, and owners. Although he could not have known it then, Joffrey and his company were crossing into unstable financial terrain, and they would never again traverse firm ground.

Joffrey's troupe was not alone in facing the problems of economic recession. Just as expansion in the performing arts had come in fits and starts, so would decline. Top union scale for principal dancers in 1973 was $30,000, and company directors' salaries were comparable or less; for example, Joffrey was paid $300 weekly (or $15,600 annually) beginning in 1970 and for several years did not receive a raise.[12] These salaries belonged to the elite in dance, and although respectable within the performing arts, they were meager compared to those in most other professions. For instance, Joffrey was making as much in 1973 as a lawyer who had just graduated from law school and passed the bar examination.

At any given time within the United States there were, at the most, about four hundred men and women who were qualified to be members of a professional or topflight regional ballet troupe. Many thought there should be some recognition for that fact. Some who were union members went on strike, demanding tougher regulations and more pay. "We are no longer prepared to subsidize dance with our own talents, time and bodies," said one to the *New York Times* during the 1973 New York City Ballet strike. "We want normal lives and decent incomes comparable to our achievement."[13]

The dancers' union, AGMA, organized in 1936, began more conscientiously enforcing the rules on performing artists' working conditions—their hours, unemployment insurance, paid sick leave, costume fittings, and the number of dance shoes and tights that were supplied. Although AGMA was not a very effective union and few dancers were members, such policing often placed the artistic director in an adversarial position.*

---

*Joffrey experienced a run-in with his dancers and AGMA in late June 1972, when the company was scheduled to appear for the first time for a week at the outdoor Ravinia Festival in Highland Park, Illinois. Fluke weather brought almost freezing temperatures on opening night. The dancers, led by Dermot Burke, their union representative, demanded that Joffrey change the program so that the women would not have to dance on pointe under such conditions and in skimpy costumes. They threatened not to perform unless he went along with their request, for which they were supported legally by AGMA regulations.

Joffrey informed them that the Ravinia debut was important to the company and they should put the company above their individual considerations, or else, he intimated, they should leave the company. Illuminated by Joffrey's apparent lack of interest in their well-

The artistic director as the "boss" who had to be watched for exploitive practices emerged as a common perception. Trust and a shared philosophy between dancers and the artistic administration eroded, usually without basis in fact.

The problems were not endemic to dance troupes alone. Internally, within many performing arts organizations, boards of directors wrested control from their artistic staffs in the name of trying to reconcile internal differences, form a team, institutionalize, and ultimately make money. One of the many reasons why boards could not understand why the arts did not pay is that they came from the profit-making world where efficient management produced financial gains and where the quality of a product was judged by the amount it brought in. Boards perceived the artists as weak and inefficient and treated them as such. Despite everyone's efforts, misguided or not, audiences for the performing arts reached a plateau by the 1980s and the market was pronounced saturated. By the 1990s, attendance actually showed signs of decreasing.[14]

Was the novelty gone, the artistic experimentation stale? In 1973, Joffrey thought he could still achieve anything he wanted. Accustomed to setbacks, he had no reason to believe that he could not surmount the new, restricted arrangements with City Center. He appealed once again to the Ford Foundation for help and was awarded a four-year grant that would accrue $1 million to a cash reserve fund. W. McNeil Lowry at the Ford Foundation was among the few patrons who by 1973 had changed his mind and understood that the performing arts would never be able to "pay their own way," that although it was a common belief in 1961 that the arts would eventually be profit-making (a persuasive thought that had helped gain support for the establishment of the NEA in 1965), the belief was wrong.[15] Lowry argued, therefore, that adjustments had to be made. Said Ewing, "Mac Lowry expected such companies as the Joffrey Ballet to return at least once for more support. He knew the idea of a ballet company surviving on earned income alone was absurd and impossible to realize."[16]

Bolstered by the Ford grant, Joffrey added more ballets, incorporating into the repertoire works by Arpino, Tharp, Eliot Feld, and José Limón.

---

being, some dancers decided not to renew their contracts the next year, but the Ravinia performance of *Trinity, Kettentanz,* and significantly, *Feast of Ashes,* went on as scheduled. (Burke, who was the company's leading male partner, quit practically on the spot.) The parallel between a subzero evening in Kabul, Afghanistan, in 1962, when the Joffrey's male members had performed *Feast of Ashes* bare-chested without threatening to strike, and the debut Ravinia program was evidence to Joffrey and Arpino that dancers had become much more assertive about their rights. The word *abuse* had yet to be introduced into the dancers' vernacular, although Gelsey Kirkland would change that with her book, *Dancing on My Grave* (Doubleday & Co., 1986).

These forced into stronger relief the importance of his main quartet—*Deuce Coupe, Parade, The Dream,* and *Remembrances.*

Of Arpino's new piece—*Jackpot,* a duet for Erika Goodman and Glenn White (and Arpino's fourth collaboration with electronic-score composer Jacob Druckman)—Arlene Croce wrote: "The subject was orgasm and the décor was a box that lit up every time. . . . *Jackpot* was, I think, Arpino's best ballet . . . unabashed, unsolemnized, porn."[17] In *Jackpot,* Arpino drew more and more choreographic material from White because his assistant Jim Howell was leaving the company in the fall to learn the physical therapist's trade in San Francisco. As a dancer White was exotic enough, off-classical-center enough, and generous enough to suit Arpino's needs. He allowed Arpino to depend on him without the promise of formal credit in the *Playbill.* Above all, White was an excellent partner. Arpino also revived *Secret Places* (1968) for Dennis Wayne and Donna Cowen. Having almost routinely turned out three premieres each year since arriving at City Center, his reduction in output did not rank him a key player in 1973.

For different reasons, neither was Eliot Feld. Feld had risen at American Ballet Theatre and emerged at the end of the sixties as one of the most promising young American choreographers. In his early life, Feld had taken the part of Baby John in *West Side Story* (both onstage and in the film version, choreographed by Jerome Robbins), and one of his better known roles at ABT had been as one of the three reveling sailors in Robbins's *Fancy Free.* A good deal of Robbins had rubbed off on Feld the choreographer, yet, until *Jive* for the City Center Joffrey Ballet, Feld had not seemed derivative.

Comparisons between Feld and Robbins were inevitable at the Joffrey because only four months prior to Feld's premiere of *Jive,* Joffrey had taken Robbins's *Interplay* into the repertoire. The music for *Interplay* (1945) was Morton Gould's *American Concertette*—a score that evoked vintage jazz, to which Robbins had responded with jitterbug and swing, cartwheels and double turns in the air. For *Jive,* Feld chose Gould's *Derivations for Clarinet and Band,* the same kind of early-forties jazz that Robbins had used. And Feld vivified it with the same kind of athletic, dance-floor, swing movement as Robbins: jitterbug and swing, cartwheels and double turns in the air.

Joffrey soon dropped *Jive* from the repertoire, concurring with his associates who were worried by the similarities. The reaction was unusual for Joffrey, who generally defended choreographers, but in this instance, he informed colleagues that unless *Jive* was pulled, Robbins would insist on having his ballets *Interplay* and *Moves* removed from the repertoire. Joffrey also decided to let the license run out on Feld's *Meadowlark,* his acclaimed Haydn piece, which had been commissioned by the Royal Winnipeg Ballet in 1968 and which Feld had newly staged for Joffrey in 1972.* Feld was Joffrey's worthy price for Robbins, whose *Moves* (1959) heaped respect upon the troupe because it was generally agreed that the Joffrey's members performed Robbins's difficult silent ballet to perfection.

If José Limón's *The Moor's Pavane* had a place in the Joffrey's repertoire in 1973, it was because Joffrey admired the work. *The Moor's Pavane,* a modern dance classic that was based on Shakespeare's *Othello* and that belonged to Limón's company, was already in the repertoires of American Ballet Theatre, the Pennsylvania Ballet, the National Ballet of Canada, and the Royal Danish Ballet. Joffrey looked upon *The Moor's Pavane* in some respects as a pedagogical tool that would both extend his current dancers' technical range and supply him with a second opportunity to work with dance notation. He, with Limón dancer Jennifer Scanlon, who staged it,† selected Christian Holder as the Moor, Burton Taylor as Iago, Jan Hanniford as Desdemona, and Beatriz Rodriguez as Emilia.

In part, Joffrey was putting himself at greater risk with *The Moor's Pavane* than he had with previous stagings of classics, such as Jooss's *The Green Table,* because more people were still alive who had seen the original cast. He was also opening himself up to accusations that he was using revivals as bait to hold the dance aficionados' interest. Croce framed the dilemma in the *New Yorker:*

> After seven years in residence at the City Center, the company has grown so unattractive that serious dance lovers stopped attending everything but classic revivals—the choices were always interesting, even if the actual performances were not. What this withdrawal of attention meant was that the structure by which the company made its dancers grow was dead. Generally speaking, you can't feed dancers on imports and revivals. Imports and revivals please audiences; they seldom help the dancer, who can't be at his best in somebody else's old part.[18]

Joffrey vehemently disagreed, and in a 1980 interview with Richard Philp of *Dance Magazine,* he defended his theory that dancers grow

---

*On September 13, 1971, William Crawford assumed Omar K. Lerman's position as the Joffrey Ballet's general administrator. Crawford had held the same position in Eliot Feld's American Ballet Company from 1970 until its dissolution a year later. A Joffrey-Feld link was thus established. Lerman left over a dispute with Tony Bliss about Lerman's innovative advertising campaign; under Lerman, the City Center Joffrey Ballet was the first to advertise its season on television, a practice that Bliss (supported by Barnes in the *Times*) opposed on the grounds that it was vulgar and too commercial. By the 1990s, ballet companies would routinely advertise on TV, provided the funds were available.

†José Limón had died on December 2, 1972.

through the performance of revivals: "My dancers perform *The Moor's Pavane* and they are valid in it, but they are valid in the sense that a repertory company can never be as pure as a company that only specializes in one technique. How can you? I mean it's ridiculous. But you may have other advantages. Both kinds of companies—the repertory and the specific company that is devoted to the energies and creativities of one person—are valid. You have to have both."[19]

For someone who was driven by dualism and attracted to juxtaposition, Joffrey could be matched by only one other person in dance: Twyla Tharp. He invited the thirty-two-year-old, modern-and-ballet-trained dancer and choreographer, who worked in her own idiom and who was inquisitive about classical ballet, to devise a new piece for his troupe. A relative unknown from the avant-garde scene, Tharp would be the supreme test for Joffrey's dancers. To be sure, she had already been legitimized by having appeared at the Billy Rose Theater in the 1969 Dance Repertory Event and toured on the basis of her good work from Central Park to Paris, but she was not internationally respected. Would Joffrey's dancers yield to her, respect her, and try something entirely new?

Arpino had first encouraged Joffrey to see Tharp's work—an important point because, while it is true that Joffrey scarcely ever missed dance performances in New York, Arpino hardly ever saw any. But somehow Arpino saw Tharp first at the Delacorte and told Joffrey about her. Together they knew what their company needed: a contemporary and box-office hit.

In a sense the seed for *Deuce Coupe* had been planted with Joffrey's risk on *The Mingus Dances* in 1971. This collaboration between Alvin Ailey and jazz legend Charlie Mingus had been an expensive venture that failed because Ailey had simultaneously been commissioned to choreograph Leonard Bernstein's *Mass* for the Kennedy Center inauguration and had placed *Mingus Dances* on his back burner. The next year, Joffrey tried again with showbiz choreographer Joe Layton, who conceived a lavish extravaganza, *Double Exposure,* that also fell flat. Next up was Twyla Tharp, who had never even seen the City Center Joffrey Ballet. "As I attended the Joffrey performances, I watched the stage less and the audience more, trying to gauge what got through to them," Tharp wrote in her autobiography, *Push Comes to Shove.* "The ballet to come represented my first commercial work since the Alaskan Pavilion's furry hootchy-kootch. I never lost sight of the fact that Bob Joffrey was hiring me to make successful art."[20]

Tharp's and Joffrey's dancers were to join onstage. For music, Tharp picked Beach Boys tunes. "The ballet's name came from a Beach Boys hit titled after a two-door vehicle," she explained. "This seemed an auspicious metaphor for our two companies."[21] For sets, six graffiti artists, kids who usually decorated the subway system illegally, were hired to spray-paint their tags and designs on three white panels that unrolled upward, becoming a backdrop for the dancers during the performance.

Inner-city life comingling with the ballet society, complex ecological themes framed in a simple structure; pop music and formal movement; idiosyncratic Tharpians sharing the ballet stage—Tharp's taste for cross-pollination confused and riled many Joffrey dancers. As rehearsals progressed, Joffrey held Tharp's hand. His dancers were resisting her.

Rebecca Wright, who was not initially cast in *Deuce Coupe*, recalled that rarely before had she seen Joffrey in the studio as much as when Tharp was there. The critical moment hit when Tharp confronted the dancers' skepticism. Wright described the scene:

> *After two or three weeks of all this work, Twyla just stood up and said, "Look, those of you in this room who do not want to do this work and do not like what I'm doing, I really want you to leave. And I don't want you to ever come back. And I won't hold it against you, because I know that my work is unusual. I'm just telling you now. I'm giving you all your options to get the hell out of here."*
>
> *Three-quarters of the room left.*
>
> *Bob—he, too, was trying to figure Twyla out. She was very stubborn and headstrong and had a command in the studio even though she was introverted and shy. And I think it was really one of the few times that I've seen him dealing with an unknown quantity. She was unknown, and the piece was unknown. And he was actually fascinated and kind of learning with her. He did not step in her way when she asked people to leave the studio, which was very unusual. Usually, he would control that kind of element. He'd let the choreographer alone, but he controlled the dancers.*[22]

After Tharp lost her first contingent, Wright asked Joffrey if she could join *Deuce Coupe*. Surprised, he said that he had never thought of her as "that kind of" dancer—thereby betraying that he typecast his dancers despite his protestations to the contrary. By her own admission, Wright fancied herself one of the best ballet dancers around, and she wanted to prove her mettle to Tharp:

> *I went into the studio and within the first hour I was completely lost. Lost! I did not know how to syncopate and reverse and invert. And her people could do it on the spot. And I stood there, and I was flabbergasted and humiliated and pissed and everything. I mean, everything. Tharp brought up everything. And I thought, "I'm not going to leave this studio. I'm not going to let her or anyone see the real truth." And I stuck it out.*
>
> *Then one day I had an interview with a writer and during the interview I had a Bloody Mary. I came back into the studio a little bit tipsy, which I never did. I never did drugs or drank and danced. And I got the segment of*

Tharp's movement that I had been having so much trouble with. I had sort of let go. Just she and me together, and me loosening up, and basically releasing all my preconceived ideas about what I should look like. It was a fabulous experience. But Twyla was a profound experience for the whole company in the end.[23]

On February 8 in Chicago, *Deuce Coupe* commanded its world premiere. On March 1, New Yorkers saw Tharp's new work for the first time at City Center. "The casting of *Deuce Coupe* is weird," observed *Village Voice* critic Deborah Jowitt. "I got the feeling that whoever showed up for a rehearsal was put in a section."[24] Nancy Goldner of the *Nation* launched into her review with, "The Joffrey Ballet's decision to ask Twyla Tharp for a new ballet for its own repertory was daring and sensible." She further elaborated, "Tharp's ambiguous attitudes toward rock and roll, the fun lovin' and affluent America that the Beach Boys represent and to a certain extent extol, and teen-age dancing and attitudes implicit therein are what make *Deuce Coupe* fascinating and thoughtful."[25]

By the early seventies, it was sometimes hard for a choreographer to get a fair trial, and often impossible to escape without being compared to another choreographer. Wrote Barnes: "*Deuce Coupe* has been a great and deserved success—but a shade too easy. It isn't half the ballet *Jive* is."[26] Then there was Marcia B. Siegel, who said: "Every millennium or so a ballet comes around that shatters all your notions of what ballet is or should be. Twyla Tharp's *Deuce Coupe* is one. I thought I was prepared for this. . . . I wasn't prepared a bit. . . . Because Tharp makes these dancers move! All other ballets you can remember suddenly seem like dull posturings and positionings, futile strainings after insipid effects."[27]

Dale Harris for *Saturday Review* suggested that American dance history had been achieved: "Twyla Tharp's *Deuce Coupe* is the best thing to have happened to the Joffrey Ballet in a long time. It is also one of the best things to have happened to dance in America."[28] And Patricia Barnes in *Dance and Dancers* believed *Deuce Coupe* "is one of those works that totally comes together in all its aspects, choreography, music and décor. . . . Another, if less flamboyant, success was provided by Eliot Feld's *Jive* . . . fortunately Feld's work does not at all resemble Robbins's ballet [*Interplay*]."[29]

Croce's review for the *New Yorker* produced a vibrant picture of Tharp's work: "The ballet steps are like a primitive's-eye view of classical style, fascinating in their plainness and angularity, and the social dances are rich with crazy, campily corny suggestion. Neither type of dancing is what it would be in the hands of any other choreographer, and yet neither is what it ordinarily appears to be in its raw state—in the classroom, or in school gyms, ballrooms, and discothèques. Whatever the Tharp eye sees, it changes."[30]

In Croce's view, *Deuce Coupe* would have been better "if the Joffrey members of the cast were better classical dancers." She blamed the Joffrey troupe's ruined "natural grace of movement" squarely on Arpino, accusing him of a monstrous crime: "All those slick, empty, and violent ballets by Gerald Arpino that slammed the audience with the Dionysian ecstasy of dance or appealed to the audience's political convictions and hunger for 'relevance' certainly did contribute to the shaping of a style, but it was a style that rendered Joffrey dancers unfit for anything better."[31]

Unfavorably comparing one choreographer with another was an acceptable critical practice that Joffrey could do little about. With *Deuce Coupe*, in which she went through the alphabet assigning Erika Goodman to perform a classical movement to each letter, beginning with *Ailes de pigeon*, Tharp entered the mainstream. Joffrey's stock as a discoverer of talent skyrocketed, and he asked Tharp to make another ballet the following season. But for Arpino it would be a year and a half (his longest hiatus thus far) until he choreographed again, offering *The Relativity of Icarus* in August 1974. The work is remembered as much for the sensual pas de deux for Daedalus (Ted Nelson) and Icarus (Russell Sultzbach) as for Arpino's anger about people seeing his ballet as strictly homosexual. Controversial or not, *Icarus* sank, and Arpino's confidence and energy sank along with it. More than another year passed before he presented *Drums, Dreams, and Banjos* to rallying music by Stephen Foster, and then it, too, fizzled. The seventies were hard on Arpino.

In the fall of 1973, Tharp produced a fifteen-minute snapshot for Joffrey called *As Time Goes By,* to the last two movements of Haydn's *Farewell* Symphony, which could be seen as the progenitor for her most famous work, *Push Comes to Shove* (music, Haydn and Joseph Lamb), which was commissioned three years later by Lucia Chase and Oliver Smith at American Ballet Theatre for some of their principal ballerinas and the young Soviet dancer who had come to America in 1974 seeking new ways of moving—Mikhail Baryshnikov. Tharp was using Joffrey's dancers to see what she could do in the classical idiom. Even though *As Time Goes By* turned out to be a novelty, it harnessed the power of certain exceptional dancers (chiefly Ann Marie De Angelo) whom Joffrey had not previously recognized.

With Tharp's advent into ballet's realm, whatever lingering arguments there were about the rightness and wrongness of movement seemed arcane and irrelevant. The vision of openness to movement that Mary Ann Wells had seen so clearly and indoctrinated in her students had been realized not out of Joffrey or Arpino, but out of Tharp through them.

But *Deuce Coupe* was not the only attention-getter in the spring season of 1973. Joffrey also staged a reconstruction of *Parade,* the 1917 ballet conceived for Diaghilev's Ballets Russes by Jean Cocteau, who recruited Léonide Massine, Erik Satie, and Pablo Picasso as his collaborators. Picasso's designs for the décor and some of the costumes established Cubism as the theater's new direction in modernism. *Parade* was also regarded as the first multimedia ballet "because the theme, choreography, music, costumes and décor were created as a collaborative effort of the four artists, all under Diaghilev's watchful eye."[32]

Joffrey's *Deuce Coupe/Parade* pairing may not have been accidental. In 1973, historian Millicent Hodson wrote a story for San Francisco's *City* magazine suggesting that the two ballets bracketed the avant-garde in the twentieth century. Joffrey was so excited to read his idea spelled out in print that he met with Hodson to exchange esthetic theories. *Parade* spoke to Joffrey on many levels—as collaboration, as pop, as multimedia—and Hodson was among the first to comprehend his greater design. She had first met Joffrey when she was a student in 1971 in Berkeley, where she was researching Vaslav Nijinsky and began collecting materials for reconstructing his *Sacre du printemps*. Joffrey had told Hodson then that when she was ready to stage the Nijinsky-Stravinsky work, she should contact him before she went to anyone else. With *Parade* they resumed communication sooner than planned. Her memory of their *Parade/Deuce Coupe* conversation offers a rare insight into Joffrey's mercurial originality. It is not necessarily important to be ahead of the times, Hodson believed Joffrey thought, but to be ahead of yourself, to trust your instincts as a director. If Joffrey was like Diaghilev, it was because he possessed the acumen to join the pieces into one magical whole.

Recalling her 1973 exchange with him, Hodson said:

Let me begin by telling you the difference between Joffrey in 1971 and Joffrey in 1973. In those two years he had gone from being Bob Joffrey in his shirtsleeves without a beard to Robert in full suit and with a beard and a belly. He had become more monumental, more institutional, and absolutely as wonderful. But there was a changeover, which was of course very advantageous to the company. A greatness about him had begun to come out. And he was so into image, he knew the beard would do it. The beard would help.*

In 1971, he had seen a big section of Parade *in a Nijinsky-Diaghilev documentary that I had worked on. And he came to me afterwards and said, "That settles it. My company should do* Parade. *You've convinced me that it's still alive."*

---

*On New Year's Eve, 1971, Joffrey's father, Joseph Joffrey, died in a Seattle nursing home. Joffrey grew a beard immediately after. According to Rima Corben, the beard was his visible sign of becoming a man and inheriting the leadership position within his family. Earlier, in 1966, his uncle Aurang Shah, M.D., had been murdered by one of his patients, a Pakhtun. After his father had died, Robert Joffrey was therefore the eldest male in the extended family.

He had some sense that in the seventies, finally, the great twentieth cen-
tury was lumbering towards its end. There was a sense of recapitulation, of
"What did all this mean?" Robert and I talked about that. He knew what he
was doing. He was taking on the history of ballet into the repertoire and, on
some fantasy level, being Diaghilev.

So, in 1973, the whole notion of Parade *and* Deuce Coupe *bracketing*
the twentieth-century avant-garde—he loved it. He wouldn't stop talking
about it.[33]

Parade had been revived after its premiere in Paris only nine times
between 1917 and 1926. Until Joffrey's production on March 22, 1973,
it had never been performed in America. "Joffrey's reason for staging
Parade is utterly disarming to the balletomane," wrote Anna Kisselgoff in
the *New York Times,* quoting Joffrey, who said: "It's one of those things
everyone talks about but has never seen."[34]

The steps to *Parade*'s revival were steep and drew on Joffrey's
immense reserves of patience. Determined to reproduce an authentic
version of one of the most famous of all lost ballets, he had sought—and
received—the blessings of Massine and Picasso, but not without a fight.
"I kept talking to Massine about *Parade*," said Joffrey. "And he'd say, 'No,
no. It is old hat. I was too young. That was one of my first ballets. I don't
think it would go now. It is too difficult to get Picasso to help.' "[35]

After persuading Massine to try remembering his landmark work, Joffrey assigned a design team of Kermit Love, Willa Kim, and Edward Burbridge to begin reconstructing the costumes and décor almost three years
prior to the City Center Joffrey Ballet's premiere. Joffrey envisioned
Massine working directly with his dancers, teaching them the choreography with the help of assistant Susi della Pietra. Picasso's son, Claude,
came to final rehearsals and photographed them for his father.

From the revivals of *Le Tricorne* in 1969 and *Le Beau Danube* in 1972,
Joffrey's dancers knew Massine well. Most Americans, however, recalled
the choreographer in a starkly different context. In the 1948 landmark
dance film, *The Red Shoes,* Massine had portrayed the obsessed ballet
master and shoemaker who demonically coerces a young dancer to her
demise. The role had made Massine famous within some movie-buff circles as a dashing, enigmatic actor. But for his work as a choreographer,
the American establishment was not in the mood to be kind. It had gradually turned against him following such trivial ballets as *Union Pacific*
(music by Nicolas Nabokov, 1934) and *Mam'zelle Angot* (music by
Charles Lecocq, 1943) for Ballet Theatre. Massine was the pupil of
Diaghilev, and the only dancer-choreographer to be cultivated to full-
fledged maturity entirely by Diaghilev. He was immensely popular and
revered in Europe, his promise universally recognized, and yet Massine

was seen by the American artistic vanguard as the scourge of classical ballet.[36] His innovations and large body of work after 1932 were dismissed.
He who had once been so beloved faded out of the picture as Balanchine's star ascended.

Massine's biographer Vicente García-Márquez explained that Massine was victimized principally by Lincoln Kirstein and Sergei Denham,
his director at Ballet Russe de Monte Carlo. According to Massine, Denham "wanted to change the image of the company and make it American
Ballet Russe by bringing in Balanchine, who did not yet have his own
company." Denham aimed for an American Ballet Russe by making life
so miserable for Massine that he resigned as ballet master and eventually
left America around 1947; more than twenty years later Joffrey aimed
for an American Ballet Russe by contacting Massine. The irony of Joffrey's "defiant sense of historical commitment," remarked García-
Márquez, "pleased, amazed, and impressed Massine."[37]

It would be easy to say that Joffrey began rescuing Massine's pieces in
1969 because he felt indebted to Massine.* Hadn't it been Massine's
early affirmation that inspired Joffrey's confidence to become a professional dancer, choreographer, and director? When Joffrey sent his first
troupe out in the station wagon, weren't they the beneficiaries of the
infrastructure that Massine had helped lay down throughout the country
on all levels? Didn't Massine help to generate a sophisticated audience for
Joffrey?

Sentimental debt might have played a small part, but according to P. W.
Manchester, Joffrey was not motivated by altruism to save an unjustly
neglected choreographer. Massine's ballets (*Parade* in particular) and
Fokine's ballets were central to his vision of an American Ballet Russe. Joffrey was old-fashioned and un-American in this regard: he believed that
creation was not limited to making a new work. He believed that by
accessing the past through one's "teachers," one was actually extending
the dimensions of one's present, and therein lay true individual liberation.

---

*Joffrey was not the only American director thinking about Massine as someone
whose works could be revived and restaged. Shortly before Massine brought back *Le Tricorne* for Joffrey, he revived *Aleko* (with its splendid décor by Marc Chagall) for Lucia
Chase and Oliver Smith at American Ballet Theatre. According to Massine's daughter,
however, her father felt Joffrey was reviving his works for the right reasons and with the
proper respect. "My father admired him tremendously," said Tatiana Massine Weinbaum.
"Joffrey reconstructed his pieces with a religious attention to detail, to trueness, to
authenticity, to how it was originally done. His dancers were open. They were easy to
work with for my father—it was a trickle-down effect from Joffrey's attitude about reconstruction." Before Joffrey staged *Le Tricorne*, Massine had also been busy reviving his
works in Europe; he was not inactive, but, until Joffrey, he felt largely misunderstood by
people who had not grown up on the Ballets Russes.

He believed all honor was due to the teacher, in his case not only Novikoff, Wells, Shurr, and O'Donnell, but Massine and Fokine, on whose ballets he had cut his teeth. He felt there should be no embarrassment for having done well at receiving instruction and no shame in keeping the art alive simply by repeating it. "When I do a revival, it's like my own ballet in a way. I am as close to that as I am to doing my own choreography, and I want to make it as perfect as possible."[38]

In 1973, just as he was standing by Arpino against the tide of critical opinion, he would stand by Massine and defy the elder generation of New York ballet snobs. "Joffrey's excitement when he watched rehearsals was the excitement not of a dance historian, it was of a balletomane. And there is a distinction," observed Tatiana Massine Weinbaum. "He looked like someone hungry sitting down before a big feast. He treated my father like a god."[39]

Joffrey had initially asked Massine for *Parade,* but Massine had agreed to stage it on the condition that *Le Tricorne* and *Le Beau Danube* entered the repertoire first. And so, in 1969, *Le Tricorne,* which Cecil Beaton described as "a mystery thriller in terms of the dance,"[40] was reborn. Massine proclaimed the reproduction his most pleasing experience yet as a comeback choreographer.[41] *Le Tricorne* had not been seen in New York for twenty-five years. For Joffrey the experience represented a giant step toward providing a historical continuity not previously thought possible. From Manhattan's Four Seasons restaurant, where it was hanging, he retrieved part of Picasso's original front curtain and had it copied.[42]

In *Tricorne,* Joffrey uncovered new strengths in his dancers, one of whom, Alaine Haubert, would gain a reputation as a sublime interpreter of Massine's ballerina roles, culminating in the Street Dancer of *Le Beau Danube.* Haubert and Edward Verso were the spirited and memorable second cast in *Le Tricorne.* Luis Fuente in Massine's role of the Miller and Barbara Remington as the Wife held their own as first cast.

Fuente, however, stunned and humiliated Joffrey when, in the middle of one performance, he substituted an authentic Spanish dance called a *farruca* for Massine's stylized version of the same. Prior to the performance, Basil Thompson, the ballet master, entered the men's dressing room and informed them of Fuente's scheme. "We stood in the wings with bated breath to see if Luis really would do it," recalled Christian Holder. "He brought the house down! It was the first time the role got a real ovation. It was as if Luis was saying to us all, 'This is what a *farruca* really is!' "[43]

Joffrey fired Fuente the next day by telegram. Since Fuente was one of the troupe's strongest technicians, his loss was painful, but Joffrey refused to buckle and risk further dishonor to Massine. "It's a matter of artistic integrity to preserve a ballet as it is given to you," he told the *New York Times.*[44]

Many criticized Joffrey for not confronting Fuente personally, but Fuente understood. Earlier in the week, a minor argument between him and Joffrey had rapidly escalated, culminating in Fuente's announcement that he would leave the troupe at the season's end. Fuente, who had a long and admired history for spontaneously improvising his solos in Arpino's ballets, then decided to flirt with *Le Tricorne*. He informed Thompson (who wanted no part of it) and a few others. After the applause rang out for the surprise *farruca*, Joffrey punished Fuente primarily because his own staff had not kept him informed and because he wanted the final word on Fuente's departure. "He did not like the stubborn way I said I was leaving. And then I very naïvely risked myself onstage, because I was used to having so much liberty with the company," said Fuente. "If we hadn't had the fight before, I think he would not have fired me."[45]

Eventually, Fuente restored Joffrey's faith in him. He accepted Joffrey's invitation to rejoin the company in 1979, and he created the leading male role in Joffrey's *Postcards* in 1980. After directing the National Ballet of Spain and his own company in Madrid, he returned again to the Joffrey Ballet in 1995 as a ballet master under the directorship of Arpino and his associate, Ann Marie De Angelo.

As for Massine, he ignored the Fuente incident and volunteered to stage Michel Fokine's *Petrouchka* the following year, 1970, assisted by his daughter and Yurek Lazowski.* Massine's name had been associated with the title role since *Petrouchka*'s New York premiere on January 25, 1916—five years after the ballet's debut for Diaghilev's Ballets Russes with Nijinsky as the tormented puppet, a role now synonymous with Nijinsky's very soul. Lazowski, too, was linked to Petrouchka, having assumed the role when Fokine staged the ballet in 1940 for de Basil's Original Ballet Russe. In 1942, Lazowski assisted Fokine in staging it for American Ballet Theatre. His affiliation with Fokine and direct contact with the choreographer were more comfortable and strong than Massine's, though neither Massine nor Lazowski were regarded as ideal to reconstruct *Petrouchka*.[46]

Although *Petrouchka* had been performed over the years by London's Festival Ballet, the Royal Danish Ballet, and Britain's Royal Ballet, *Petrouchka* had not been seen in New York in more than twelve years. It was not a twentieth-century masterpiece that needed saving, but it was

---

*In the middle of the Joffrey Ballet's premiere season with *Petrouchka* in 1970, American Ballet Theatre announced it was mounting a major new production of *Petrouchka*. The battle for authenticity was on. Dimitri Romanoff and Yurek Lazowski were in charge of the ABT version, which the company claimed had been in preparation for two and a half years and was made possible by an NEA grant given in 1969.

definitely an important addition to Joffrey's Diaghilev-period repertoire. He wanted the Benois sets and costumes, the Stravinsky score, and the Nijinsky role.

"Mr. Joffrey worked well with Massine, and even though Massine changed the steps and staging, it was Massine who gave us our characters in great detail," said Holder, who was the first cast Moor and who was thought by Massine to be exemplary. "Massine counted the fiendish music for us. He gave us the flavor, which was sorely missing in the sterile, though 'authentic,' ABT production. From his seat, Massine *became* the Coachman, the Moor, the Nursemaids. It was a truly rich experience. The ballet also afforded Joffrey the opportunity to go incognito among the extras during the performance. His makeup was so good that it took a while to identify him. It was only his small size and high energy that gave him away."[47]

Joffrey's staging of *Petrouchka* was lambasted from all quarters because, among other reasons, Fokine's choreography was practically unrecognizable and the scale of Benois's décor "diminished and grotesquely altered," declared Lincoln Kirstein.[48] Tatiana Massine immediately sent a telegram to the newspapers disassociating her father and herself from the production. Joffrey tried unofficially with Lazowski and David Blair's help to repair the ballet, but without responding to Massine's missive or even acknowledging that he had read it. "I know that no one today can dance these ballets exactly as they were," Joffrey did remark. "But if we try hard, we can come as close as possible."[49]

"Robert Joffrey is an insatiable fan. Among ballet directors, he is our foremost historian and archivist of dance materials," later wrote Nancy Reynolds, a Balanchine historian.[50] Edwin Denby suggested to Joffrey that he rearrange some of the *Petrouchka* casting, and according to Charthel Arthur, Joffrey responded by moving her from third- to first-cast ballerina. *Petrouchka* evolved into a staple of the Joffrey's repertoire, bringing to the company an international cachet that had previously eluded it, but only after the fourth-cast Petrouchka, Gary Chryst, inherited the role the season after the premiere.

Chryst worked closely on Petrouchka with Massine and Lazowski (who had spent much of their time fighting in Russian over the "right steps").[51] But Joffrey was also instrumental. Chryst recalled the insight Joffrey offered that helped him decode the sawdust-filled puppet and develop a portrayal that was ultimately compared favorably to some of the great Petrouchkas:

Everyone did Petrouchka so sad, and I couldn't place the sorrow in the character. And Mr. Joffrey said, "No, no, no, no. Feeling sorry for yourself is the easiest emotion to play." I had done a lot of homework on Petrouchka and went back for more, taking a lot of my characterization from a photograph of Nijinsky in which he has only white on his face and some shading—the photo with his fist up. And that had anger in it. And I thought, "Ah." Because the whole thing about Petrouchka is that he feels pain. I think the Charlatan gave him feelings so that he could feel pain. But he can also feel love. And he feels love and he feels pain, so, he can also feel hatred.

He is just helplessly in this body that can't function. When he sees the Moor, he thinks, "I would kick him, if I could." He cries not because of the pain, but the frustration. It's not the pain. It's almost like having muscular dystrophy. . . .

Joffrey didn't treat me differently after I had so much success with Petrouchka. He said, "Now you have to work harder." Which is very true.[52]

Chryst's next role in a Massine ballet was in 1972. In *Le Beau Danube* he danced the King of the Dandies and during one rehearsal was graced along with most of the company with the rare opportunity to watch Alexandra Danilova and Massine reprise the Street Dancer and Hussar, probably for the first time since they had left Denham's company, where their performance in *Danube* was the company's signature.

Danilova and Frederic Franklin had come to coach the pas de deux, and Joffrey enticed Danilova onto the stage with Massine for a photograph. Remembered Christian Holder, "Pretty soon Joffrey was saying to them, 'Oh, can you go through the motions?' And they started dancing, and she was telling Massine, 'You're not holding me right!' And he was arguing back. And they were having one last fight with that *Blue Danube* music going. She was in her street clothes and high heels, and he was in his Spanish trousers and his hairnet and his little black shoes. They had the stage and one work light. Joffrey exploded with nostalgia. This was really, really great."[53]

Joffrey admitted that he used opportunities such as this to try to mimic the legends, to feel their choreography, their interpretation, so that he could help his own dancers. "I'd get right behind Massine, because he had such a distinct flair for movement. He took his hand up—I could just see the way he would do it. It was so individual," observed Joffrey. "Frederic Franklin is very different. Where some people are angles and exclamation points, other people are curves and quotations."[54]

The practices that developed during *Danube* rehearsals were integral to Joffrey's future reconstructions. He would not have attempted to revive Massine's or any other choreographer's work without the right dancers in his company. To know which ones were "right," he felt he had to feel the movement himself. This was part of his job as a curator. He explained to Richard Philp of *Dance Magazine*, who interviewed him extensively over eighteen years, "When you are director of a company, you don't own the ballet, you take care of it. If you feel you can't take care of it, then there's no point in doing it. It's better to drop a ballet for a season or two, until you have the right dancers to make that ballet live again."[55]

The year following *Danube*, Joffrey scheduled *Parade*. It would be performed in the United States for the first time. After weighing whether to cast Chryst or Holder as the Chinese Conjuror, in the eleventh hour Massine awarded Chryst the part that would ultimately clinch his reputation as a definitive Massine interpreter and a dance-actor exemplar for contemporary times. Although Chryst had many valuable sessions with Massine, it was Joffrey who provided him with a perspective and a historical context. Chryst recalled one "private lesson" with Joffrey that opened his eyes:

> I went to the theater and was on my way to class when Mr. Joffrey peeked around the corner. "Gary, come here," he said. "It's okay if you don't take class today. It's okay." I thought to myself, "What! This is unheard of." We sat on the floor for an hour with open books of pictures of Massine in his makeup as the Conjuror. And we read the different stories, Cocteau's scenario. Joffrey kept talking. He was like a child when he'd get inspired. "Now, I think in this version that Massine was a European posing as a Chinaman," he said. "But I think with you, you can really be a real Chinaman. 'Cause look at this picture. It is painted, but you already have almond-shaped eyes. So, let's see what we can do."*
>
> We sat and worked on the makeup, and I remember him saying he didn't care if anyone liked Parade. "I like it. I think it's brilliant," he said. "I think it's fascinating."[56]

Joffrey's association with Massine would continue in 1974 with the ebullient, commedia dell'arte–inspired *Pulcinella* (music by Stravinsky, 1920), with Gary Chryst as Pulcinella. And, in 1992, after both Joffrey and Massine had died, there would be Tatiana Leskova's restaging of *Les Présages* (to Tchaikovsky's Fifth Symphony, 1933), Massine's allegory about the evils of war. It was produced under Arpino's supervision. Thus, through the Joffrey Ballet, Massine found the positive reception that had hitherto eluded him in America.

---

*For the first performance, Massine himself applied Chryst's makeup and neither Chryst nor Joffrey was ever again able to duplicate it.

CHAPTER 24

Muses

No sooner had the 1973 spring season ended than Joffrey started choreographing again. His instincts, his taste, ran naturally toward the romantic. All of his ballets, every single one, concerned love—the winged, sacred, ideal, sometimes playful, sometimes exotic (never crassly erotic), and always larger-than-life kind of love. He had been tinkering with *Remembrances* for three years, off and on, and the new ballet would be as romantic as the rest, except that its source of inspiration was personal. Ghosts from his past, an evocation of phantoms, a series of portraits drawn from memory of the people who had loved, transformed, and redeemed him, and whom he had loved in return.

What prompted this newly subjective spirit? A week before Christmas in 1970, Mary Ann Wells had collapsed from a stroke and died shortly thereafter on January 8 in a Seattle hospital. The holiday season held great meaning for Joffrey; the Victorian decorations in his house and upon his tree were so extraordinary that *House and Gardens* would one day publish photographs of them. Christmas Eve was his birthday; he would always put official business aside at this time of year and, just as Wells had done, fling open his home for party after party. Wells's death meant the loss of the grande dame who had given him his gentlemanly demeanor, who had supported him in dance and taught him what it meant to be an American, as well as how to be a dignified and ethical one.

Almost a year later, on New Year's Eve 1971, during a celebration at his house, Joffrey received a phone call from Seattle that his father had died in the nursing home. Joseph Joffrey's proudest moment had come in 1969, when Pacific Lutheran University in Tacoma had given his son an honorary degree. Only when his son stood before the flashing cameras, decked out in cap and gown and holding a diploma, did Joseph concede that ballet as a career had not been a mistake. Joseph's brother, the Harvard graduate Aurang Shah, had tried long before to convince him that *Joffrey* was a name in New York. But having a name attached to a ballet company had not been enough to persuade Joseph that his son had been right in opposing him on the issues of speaking Pakhto in the home, on praying to Allah five times a day, and on wanting to sever his cultural ties to Afghanistan. It had not proved to Joseph that his son's rebellion, which he perceived on some level as a rebellion against him as an Afghan, was worth it.

Despite everything, though, Joseph had stood by his only child. He had advised him on business matters and supplied him with constant, practical guidelines. He had told his son that the way to deal with enemies was to give them enough rope "and they will hang themselves."[1] The principle laid the foundation for Joffrey's nonconfrontational management style. A frequent gift to his male colleagues, of whose allegiances and sentiments he was unsure, would be a necktie from Bonwit Teller; Joffrey's idea was they could hang themselves, but only he and a few chosen friends understood when the pun was intended. It was Joseph, also, who lent money at important crossroads. And Joseph had not cut off his son because he was a homosexual. Joseph and Mary had accepted what they knew about him, spoken and unspoken.

Remembrances was shaped by the death of beloveds. Contained within the work were Joffrey's impressions from childhood of his parents and of his relationship to Wells and her husband, A. Forest King.* For *Remembrances* his inner eye fixed intently on the place of women in his life, both the maternal and the romantic figures. By 1970, his mother, Mary Gallette Joffrey, had been moved into a nursing home with her brother, Joffrey's uncle Jo-Jo, where she was visited for the next fourteen years three times a week by Joffrey's oldest female friend, Diane Lembo Talley. Talley was his surrogate sister. He had known her since 1952. She was one of the few he felt comfortable allowing into the Joffrey household; she was the one who had called him from Seattle with the news that his father had died; and she would visit Joffrey and Arpino at Christmas almost every year for a month and decorate their tree three layers deep with ornaments over the course of four days behind closed doors with Joffrey directing where the decorations should be placed, but not touching them himself. Talley was also Joffrey's professional colleague. She had been his assistant during the late 1950s and early 1960s, and she had recently been responsible for auditioning and hiring seventy-five supernumeraries for Joffrey's touring production of *Petrouchka* in Seattle. She was, therefore, intimately aware of Joffrey's hectic, demanding schedule, and she was able to reassure Joffrey's mother authoritatively that the reason he was not by her side in Seattle was his job, not that he did not love her.

Mary Joffrey often cried for Bobby on Talley's shoulder. Stricken by acute arthritis and diabetes, she had been consigned to a wheelchair

---

*King died on August 27, 1972.

many years prior to moving into the nursing home, and even before, she had—as family legend has it—decided to sit down and never rise again to carry out Joseph's bidding. Indeed, she claimed sole right to an over-stuffed armchair at 1010 East Lynn Street in Seattle. When their time came to live in nursing homes, she and Joseph chose separate ones.

The image of an immobile Mary Joffrey possibly found its way into *Remembrances* as She, Who Remembers, portrayed by dancer Jan Han-niford, whose movement is by design severely limited in the ballet. She sits on a Victorian love seat and mimes her memories throughout the piece, while the dancers re-create the action that is presumably being screened in her head. Another interpretation is that the "remembering lady" was Joffrey. He paralleled his thoughts about the maternal role model in *Remembrances* with a meditation on the virtue of romance. It seemed pos-sible that the deaths of important authority figures gave him a certain free-dom to express passion. By April 1973, when he was setting the ballet for a scheduled fall premiere, he had met the great love of his life.

A. Aladar Marberger, twenty-six, was an art dealer and the director of the Fischbach Gallery in the West Fifty-seventh Street gallery district. A native of Philadelphia and a graduate of Carnegie Mellon University, Marberger had been persuaded to move to New York four years earlier by his teacher, the painter Elaine de Kooning. Living in the Village and specializing in contemporary art, he had cultivated affluent Manhattan connections and sophisticated habits and landed the Fischbach director-ship by the time he was twenty-three. Marberger was openly gay and a moderate militant. His eyes were penetrating, ancient; people said they saw centuries in them. His blond hair was cropped and he was balding. He looked older than his years, and he was suave. He introduced Joffrey to the heady New York circles of the nouveau riche and the gay avant-garde; and he routinely sent the dancers bouquets on openings. Difficult, demanding, he challenged Joffrey to be the great artist he was obviously intended to be.

"Bob was crazy about Aladar. He'd never been with a person who was so open, flamboyant, brave, mischievous, theatrical, a family man who liked famous men," said their friend Barbara Schwartz. "Aladar hated dance and it made Bob happy that Aladar was not involved with ballet. Suddenly they were a very hot item."[2]

Joffrey let Marberger spend the whole night until morning in his bed, the first man awarded such a sanction in a long, long time.[3]

By 1973, six years after *Astarte,* Joffrey was ready to tackle the subject of romantic ardor from a personal stance. He was willing to renew his contact with his muses, to transform himself again from director into choreographer. He brought Francesca Corkle and Scott Barnard into the studio. Both were affectionately admired by him, but, in fact, Sue Loyd had worked first on the piece with him in 1971. Loyd was truly his aide-de-camp. He had leaned on her throughout the period when the troupe was settling into City Center. She helped him program, cast, and rehearse; then with a few minutes left before curtain time, she would pull on her clean, pink tights and costume, do a quick barre, leap out onto the stage, and perform to the hilt. She covered every base while also attending her infant daughter. She was known by some as the Joffrey Ballet's Earth Mother, and in this regard, she was a splendid choice to embody love's opposites, the maternal and the sexual, in *Remembrances*.

But Loyd left the company in January 1973 for health reasons—before Joffrey finished. Standing behind her at some of Loyd's last rehearsals had been Corkle, and in late 1973, Joffrey approached Corkle to ask what steps she remembered Loyd doing two years before. "None," Corkle replied. "Because there wasn't any music and I can't recall anything without music."[4]

Since Loyd's departure, Joffrey had chosen two pieces by Wagner, *Album-Sonata for Frau Mathilde Wesendonck* and the *Porazzi Theme*. His music selection was almost assuredly linked to Wells's husband, whom everybody called Fawther. Even Wells herself called him Fawther, because the name fit: A. Forest King was dependable, secure, and patient, the personification of a paterfamilias. Fawther's obsession was Wagner. Whenever Joffrey visited the Kings (which had been frequently when he was a teenager), he heard recordings of Wagner's operas.

The Wagner-Wesendonck romance had long intrigued Joffrey. He devoured Wagner biographies and knew that Wagner was someone whose creativity was fueled by abstaining from sex. Unfulfilled lust sparked divine creation. Furthermore, it had often been speculated that Fawther and Mary Ann Wells practiced abstention as part of the I AM religion, and that Joffrey's parents had early in his life ceased making love to each other, sleeping in separate bedrooms.

To answer the variety of questions that formed the raw material for *Remembrances*, Joffrey eagerly delved into the poetry of Percy Bysshe Shelley and *The Diaries of Anaïs Nin*, and he researched more about Wagner and Wesendonck. By the time he was in the studio with Corkle, he knew Wagner's Wesendonck songs well. The ballet's theme, he announced, was based on Shelley's lines "Music, when soft voices die / Vibrates in the memory."

Corkle could understand. She had known the Kings most of her life. Although she had grown up in Seattle, Corkle was not a Wells product. She had studied ballet with her mother, Virginia Ryan Corkle, who on occasion also played piano for Wells—just as, on occasion, Joffrey would guest-teach for Virginia Ryan Corkle. The Kings, Corkles, and Robert Joffrey were old family friends, and Francesca had memories of young

Bobby sauntering into their yard, announcing that he was ready for the lamb-shank dinner that Mrs. Corkle had invited him to share with them three evenings before, but that he had apparently forgotten, "because he never had any concept of time."[5] Joffrey was known throughout Seattle's serious ballet community for being the boy with his head in the clouds, thinking of nothing but dance.

In 1969, Corkle joined the City Center Joffrey Ballet, creating many Arpino ballets and bringing down the house in Balanchine's *Square Dance*. Joffrey seemed to be waiting for Corkle to grow up, letting her breathe like a bottle of superior red wine. In 1973, she was apparently ready to put her heart on the line. But who could match her?

After working alone with Corkle for many *Remembrances* rehearsals—"Everything just flowed from him," she said. "He knew exactly what he wanted"[6]—Joffrey brought in Scott Barnard, Corkle's usual partner. He was teaching Barnard to be the artistic eyes behind his head, the custodian of his work and the Diaghilev revivals, his associate and inheritor. He revered Barnard's perfectionism. Unfortunately for Barnard, the bursitis in his shoulder soon eliminated him as the leading male figure in *Remembrances*. He was replaced by Jonathan Watts. Watts—for whom Joffrey had made so many of his early ballets.

In 1973, Watts had not danced for five years, but Joffrey's prodigal son wanted to return to the stage. He hoped to right some ancient wrongs. "Bob was quite hesitant because we had sort of a rocky past," Watts said, recalling that a decade before, when the troupe was preparing for Russia, Joffrey had engaged Watts as guest artist and cast him in Brian Macdonald's *Time Out of Mind* opposite Margaret Mercier for the performance at the Delacorte Theater. Only a few hours before curtain time, Watts had walked out of the theater. He had been unable to face the possibility of dancing poorly before the public that had last seen him with the New York City Ballet, where he had orginated roles in *Agon, Donizetti Variations,* and *Liebeslieder Walzer.* "To leave Bob like that was a terrible thing for me to do," he said.[7] Watts's career with Joffrey had been a series of rash departures and sweet, cautious returns—a pattern that might have broken a more fragile friendship.

The heroic, sweeping, broad, and elongated gestures that Joffrey used for Watts in *Remembrances* prompted critics to label the ballet Byronic. The premiere took place on October 12, 1973, at City Center. Costumed by Willa Kim in delicate, sheer material of pale lavender, green, turquoise, and pink, Francesca Corkle and Jonathan Watts drifted, swooned, and swept each other into a blissful reverie. Joffrey surrounded them with another romantic pair (Denise Jackson and Paul Sutherland) and a dozen minor lovers. Rather than narrating their amorous histories, their gestures evoked an aura of romance. "The ballet is dark and luxurious, a mood, an atmosphere," observed the critic Marcia B. Siegel. ". . . [Donna] Roll sings and acts out the words most expressively, Corkle dances beautifully without any particular indication of character, and [Jan] Hanniford glides back and forth between them to no apparent purpose."[8] Clive Barnes, the only critic who fully warmed to *Remembrances,* called it "a most beautiful piece. . . . Mr. Joffrey should arrange for his muse to visit him on a more regular basis in the future."[9]

Little fuss was made about Watts's comeback, although he and Corkle were praised. *Remembrances* endured as a ballet that dancers loved to perform more than audiences cared to watch.

In spring 1973, while rehearsing *Remembrances,* Joffrey had traveled to Galveston, Texas, where he conducted a six-day workshop with Rebecca Wright at the Galveston Art Center. He was tilling the soil in preparation for what grew over the next four years into a permanent summer workshop in San Antonio, Texas. It was staffed by Joffrey and members of his New York team, including Watts, Bill Leighton, Diane Orio, Glenn White, Françoise Martinet, and Charthel Arthur. Every summer until 1986, he would vacation at the two-week San Antonio workshop on Incarnate Word College campus. These teaching stints relaxed him. He was able to do what he thrilled to most: build young dancers.

"His whole being changed in San Antonio," said Susan Treviño, who ran the program with her husband, Buddy. "He'd answer the phone and say he was the cleaning person. He drove them nuts in New York because he wouldn't let them find him."[10]

"He was very orderly. In his office, he wanted all the windows open at the same height. All the blinds drawn at the same time of day. They were old windows. Some didn't stay open. So, we sawed little sticks the same height to prop them open," noted Buddy Treviño. "I think he was teaching us how to prepare for class, how to focus and be exact, because when he finished class, he would have fifteen minutes to meditate in the dark. They'd close everything up, shoo everyone out, take the phone off the hook, and it would be quiet. He'd have gotten into his kimono. He'd cool down. Meditate.

"Afterwards, he'd prepare for his evening class and consume giant glasses of iced tea. He liked iced tea a certain way. Don't stir it too much. And he'd eat with chopsticks, his own personal pair. Now, he didn't say, 'Go get me something to eat. Go get me a cup of tea.' Somehow everyone got the message that he needed to eat. It wasn't a demanding, ugly kind of thing. These were the rituals that made him work well to his capacity."[11]

San Antonio developed into another feeder institution for his company.* He pulled from its ranks and from its prototypes in Galveston and Chicago some of the company's future best, including Cameron Basden, Michael Bjerknes, Lynne Chervony, DeAnn Duteil, Glenn Edgerton, Julie Janus, Jerry Kokich, Edward Morgan, and Elizabeth Parkinson. San Antonio also served another purpose—as the safety hatch. Joffrey later aggressively investigated the possibility of the company having a six- or eight-month residency in the city. He was looking for an alternative home to City Center. Financial necessity was growling at the door. But ever since Watts, Marberger, and Leighton had put the idea of expansion into his head, Joffrey considered the building of his empire to be a top priority.

The Joffrey empire, beginning with the establishment of Joffrey II in 1968 and then the first Galveston workshop in 1973, was constructed upon the following events: In 1974, Joffrey became a member of the National Endowment for the Arts dance panel; that same year he also accepted the opportunity to choreograph his first Broadway show, *Dancers,* for David Merrick; in 1976, the Public Broadcasting System's new series *Dance in America* aired, and millions of television viewers spent an hour with the City Center Joffrey Ballet, the company chosen to inaugurate the special program. Then, in 1978, Joffrey was named copresident with Yuri Grigorovich, the Bolshoi Ballet's artistic director, of the International Theater Institute (I.T.I.) dance committee; in 1979, he was appointed cochair of the judges' panel for I.T.I.'s first U.S.A. International Ballet Competition in Jackson, Mississippi. The biennial event, patterned after the oldest and most famous competition in Varna, Bulgaria, had spawned similar ones in Moscow and Tokyo. Talent from around the globe entered; and Joffrey, who was supposed to co-chair the fourteen jurists, representing as many countries, took charge when Grigorovich canceled.

Alexander Grant, formerly one of the great character dancers with London's Royal Ballet, but currently representing Canada as the director of the National Ballet of Canada, served on the jury in Jackson. He and Joffrey had known each other since 1949, when the Royal Ballet first performed in New York, but their friendship strenghtened in Mississippi. Grant was part of Joffrey's connection to Sir Frederick Ashton. By 1973, Joffrey had already presented *Façade,* and he was ready for *The Dream,* Ashton's humorous, yet touching, beautiful, and profound rendition of

---

*The San Antonio Performing Arts Association and the city of San Antonio underwrote Arpino's *Jamboree* (1984), making it the first ballet to be commissioned by a city. Arpino's *Suite Saint-Saëns* (1978) and *Epode* (1979) were paid for by Mr. and Mrs. Alonzo W. Gates of San Antonio; this helped to secure the city for the Joffrey Ballet as a base of future support.

Shakespeare's *A Midsummer Night's Dream*. Ashton and Joffrey trusted each other.

The Dream entered the Joffrey repertoire on August 9, 1973, at Wolf Trap Farm in Virginia, two months before the premiere of *Remembrances* at City Center. The ballets were matching bookends, in a sense. Joffrey had his reasons for trying Ashton's work out of town first, because many people had informed him they were skeptical of his company's ability—and even right—to perform an Ashton ballet. Joffrey himself harbored doubts. No American troupe had yet performed *The Dream*. He perceived that every gesture was intentionally placed, and the movement's phrasing to Mendelssohn's music was critical. To accomplish the monumental task, he entrusted Titania to Rebecca Wright and Oberon to Burton Taylor. Ashton was not worried, because he believed (in his own words), "Joffrey is a man of great imaginative enterprise. Whatever he undertakes, he wants to do to the fullest detail, and he's a wonderful, devoted friend."[12] Ashton sent his associates John Hart and Faith Worth, a notator, to stage *The Dream*, confident that the best job would be done. Ashton let few people have his ballets; he was cautious.

The Dream challenged Joffrey as a director to bridge over into pure classical technique, if he could develop the ballerina. With customary eagerness, Wright was determined to find her way into the leading role. Explaining her encounter with *The Dream*, she exposed the ripple that would ultimately hit the company like a wave:

> *Titania was a pivotal role in my career. It was my first opportunity to play an elegant, beautiful, lyrical creature. Nothing butch to it. Nothing all-American. It was a pretty role and I didn't have pretty roles. But it was also a transformation because it was also the first time I worked on motivation, that I worked on developing a character through the foot's approach to the floor. Jack Hart had a profound influence on my approach, and he spoke a lot about the foot. How the ballerina tells the story through the foot. It's the details—the small things in Ashton that define a character.*[13]

The Dream was the first narrative ballet that Joffrey presented in which the dancers were divided between soloists and corps de ballet, and the classicists were distinguished from the character roles. In a no-star, all-star company, it introduced hierarchy and the potential for stars to be born. And as Joffrey had feared, hierarchy had its traps.

Immediately after staging *The Dream*, Joffrey began collecting information toward choreographing his own *Nutcracker*. Joffrey, who had foresworn the other nineteenth-century full-length ballets in which the vocabulary was dependent on the five basic academic positions of the feet, and in which the choreographic structure followed laws as traditional and strict, wanted to try his hand at one.

He knew full well that to stage *The Nutcracker* following *The Dream* might accentuate the reversal in his perceived philosophy. He might also attract an entirely different kind of dancer from the ones he had been employing since losing Isaksen, Jhung, Rhodes, Ruiz, and Tomasson to Rebekah Harkness in 1964. And perhaps that was his intent. It was Joffrey's supreme regret that New Yorkers had never seen the company that he had developed before and during Harkness. In his heart of hearts Joffrey did not want to belong to the pop dance category. During an interview with Anna Kisselgoff for the *New York Times,* he had visibly shuddered when she had linked him to the genre.[14]

After the fall 1973 season, the fun for him as a director was, in many respects, over. His job swamped him in fund-raising and bureaucratic activities. He had no way of knowing how long he would be relegated to the desk, but he attacked the work hoping to find the numbers so compelling and challenging that he would forget himself.[15] He had trimmed his annual twelve weeks at City Center to eight weeks to save costs. Perhaps his incentive to choreograph *Nutcracker* sprang from a compelling financial need to fill his house. *The Nutcracker* was the principal source of income for companies all over the country. It was also a major audience-builder.

Interestingly, over at the New York City Ballet, Balanchine produced a full-length *Coppélia* for Patricia McBride and Helgi Tomasson in 1974. The same year at American Ballet Theatre, Antony Tudor had rejoined as associate director, and the era of Mikhail Baryshnikov, Fernando Bujones, Cynthia Gregory, Gelsey Kirkland, and Natalia Makarova dawned, and with it a classical full-length resurgence: *The Sleeping Beauty, Swan Lake,* and *Coppélia,* to mention a few.

Each company director seemed more interested than before in the full-length classics; Joffrey was just doing it his way. He was advancing toward a three-act *Nutcracker* through Ashton's *The Dream,* a one-act work that contained the emotional weight and majestic beauty of three acts. In 1974, Joffrey spoke to Ashton about staging his *Cinderella* for the company, thereby suggesting that, between *Cinderella* and *Nutcracker,* he was very serious about the company's new interest in traditionally structured ballets.

But *The Dream* presented Joffrey with an instability within the troupe that ultimately hurt his chances for *Cinderella. The Dream* had given Rebecca Wright and Francesca Corkle a taste for the classical ballerina role that they could satisfy only by leaving the Joffrey Ballet. Wright joined American Ballet Theatre in 1975, as did Starr Danias. Others who departed at this time were Burton Taylor, Donna Cowen, Erika Goodman, and Pamela Nearhoof. Wright did not know of Joffrey's future agenda—he had not mentioned *The Nutcracker* or *Cinderella*—but she and others could not afford to wait for him, because a dancer's life is too short. In addition, Wright had discovered that she was being paid considerably less than the men who were her equals with respect to roles and seniority. Joffrey defended himself on the grounds that the men were responsible to families and were "expected" to earn more. Wright could not tolerate his sexist attitude.

The Dream thus contributed toward fragmenting the troupe. By 1975, the techno-wizard athletes provided most of the company's electricity. Those with Princess Aurora or Prince Siegfried intentions had either moved on or were calculating their exits. As one Joffrey dancer, Kevin McKenzie, whose hopes were pinned on ABT, explained, "I learned at the Joffrey that there are workhorses and there are racehorses, and you cannot mix their lines. I was not a workhorse, and ninety-eight percent of the Joffrey Ballet are workhorses. They could dance four ballets a night and switch from one style to another and not feel it. But I could not sustain that type of schedule. And I could not mix the modern and the classical, or perform them too closely together. If I was going to do something severely physical and contemporary, I should not expect to get up and do *The Dream* and *La Vivandière* and *Tchaikovsky Pas de Deux* the next day. I just never could. I just broke."[16] McKenzie went on a leave of absence from the Joffrey in the fall of 1978 and joined ABT the following year. He further developed into one of America's most venerated classical partners; and in 1992, he assumed the position of ABT's artistic director.

McKenzie performed *The Dream* for the Joffrey many times. The ballet, as well as his pairing with Rebecca Wright and Denise Jackson, earned favor with the audience. And *The Dream* was only the beginning of the truly solid attachment between Ashton and Robert Joffrey. In 1974, Ashton's *Monotones I and II* were taught to the company, followed by *Jazz Calendar* and *Les Patineurs* in 1977, *A Wedding Bouquet* in 1978, *Illuminations* in 1980, *Five Waltzes in the Manner of Isadora Duncan* in 1983, and *La Fille mal gardée* in 1986. The Joffrey Ballet at one point contained more Ashton in its active repertoire than the choreographer's home company, the Royal Ballet.

Glad to see *The Dream*, the critics mostly wanted to applaud Joffrey for getting the ballet while spreading word that the Joffrey members fell short of their Royal Ballet counterparts. "They indicate that they are working toward the proper style," commented New York critic Jack Anderson of Joffrey's *Dream* cast. Anderson had already said: "I'm delighted that, amidst its snap-crackle-and-pop, the Joffrey this fall produced two ballets by Frederick Ashton."[17]

Over the years most observers continued to note that the Joffrey dancers were "not good enough yet"[18] to perform the Ashton ballets that entered the repertoire. Yet few were willing to give up hope, and slowly the Joffrey members proved to deserve these peoples' patience. Tobi Tobias of *New York* magazine took note, writing in 1980:

> *The steepest challenge to the Joffrey's ability to mount stylistically authentic revivals is its growing collection of Frederick Ashton's ballets. Currently on display are the pellucid* Monotones II, *the lilting* Les Patineurs, *and the witty* Wedding Bouquet. *The Joffrey's renderings hardly rival the finesse of the Royal Ballet's: The broadness of attack they need to execute and sell Arpino blunts them for the delicacy and precision required in dancing Ashton. Yet it is encouraging that the primary American custodian of Ashton's choreography is improving on its own past performances.*[19]

At the time of *The Dream*'s premiere in 1973, the ballet contributed toward subdividing his troupe and distancing its members from each other and Joffrey, but other factors—undoubtedly even stronger ones—were also at work that made many observers comment that the company had lost its cohesive eccentricity. A survey on the arts in America conducted by pollster Louis Harris in late 1973 found that large numbers of people wanted to attend dance concerts, but the availability of performances was so limited that 91 percent of the 3,005 Americans interviewed had not attended a dance performance in the past twelve months. The public was not receiving the supposed dance boom. Harris emphasized that if the vast majority of Americans were underexposed to and uneducated about culture, then it stood to reason that the future financial state of the arts was at great risk.[20] People had to see dance in order to care about it, but dance was still not being seen by enough people.

Joffrey, who had long advocated democracy in the arts, decided to act. He could reach people. If the audience was there, he would find it. In 1974, he replaced the "lost" four weeks at City Center with a tour to Missouri, Kansas, Iowa,* Nebraska, and Illinois sponsored by the NEA and the Mid-America Arts Alliance. Joffrey II dancers would come along, performing in the small cities, while the parent troupe danced in the metropolises. The engagements were mostly sold out. Joffrey seemed to

---

*Under the direction of Dr. Lewis E. January, members of Hancher Auditorium at the University of Iowa in Iowa City approached Joffrey about instituting a local outreach program. Following the company's successful 1974 engagement, Joffrey arranged for Joffrey II to perform in the surrounding cities. The Joffrey II was in residency during the summers of 1982, 1983, and 1985 through the Iowa Dance Residencies. The main troupe had a residency in the summer of 1987 at the University of Iowa. Artistically enterprising, the Hancher Auditorium/University of Iowa Foundation commissioned and sponsored three new Joffrey Ballet works: James Kudelka's *Heart of the Matter* (1986), Joffrey's production of *The Nutcracker* (1987), and Arpino's production of *Billboards* (1993).

be soaking up the interest of the Harris poll's "untapped masses of cul-
turally receptive people."[21] He said after the tour, "We were going into
cities that had never seen our kind of dance before—and the dancers had
a real sense of pioneering."[22] It sounded a lot like the early U-Haul and
bus days, a depressing comparison that he could not have helped making.

In 1974, he received the prestigious Capezio Dance Foundation award,
which was testament to his contributions to American dance. And in
another repeat of history, the troupe returned to the Soviet Union in
November on a monthlong tour sponsored by the State Department. Joffrey had been concerned that the troupe surpass the impression made by
its 1963 visit. He told the dancers this at a company meeting. The repertoire had been censored by Soviet Union officials. *Astarte,* Margo Sappington's *Weewis,* and John Butler's *After Eden* were not allowed
because they were deemed too risqué.

Although rock music had never been heard in legitimate theaters in
the Soviet Union, the City Center Joffrey Ballet was allowed to bring
Arpino's *Trinity* with the Vegetables, a rock band. When the company
closed the first Leningrad performance with *Trinity,* the audience gave it
a twenty-seven-minute standing ovation. By the next day, the city's
underground rock mavens, rejoicing in the unprecedented chance to
hear their favorite sound live in public, begged for spare tickets. Police
manned the entrances to the sold-out theater, pressing their bodies
against the throng. The Leningrad scenario was repeated in Riga, Vil-
nius, and Moscow. And before the Joffrey left the country, it had already
been invited back for the next year. The company had not let Joffrey
down on a trip that in many other ways also resembled the first tour to
Russia.

But by far the most defining event for the City Center Joffrey Ballet was
when, in May 1975, the City Center of Music and Drama board divested
itself of responsibility for the companies that were based at the 55th
Street Theater. The board had been an umbrella organization that split its
energies between the companies at the New York State Theater (New York
City Ballet and New York City Opera) and those that remained at City Center 55th Street Theater (Joffrey Ballet, Alvin Ailey, Eliot Feld, and American Ballet Theatre). But now it would emphasize running the New York
State Theater and the affairs of the New York City Ballet and the New York
City Opera, for which City Center had functioned as a fund-raising arm.
The Joffrey Ballet and the others at City Center would receive its limited
support. Moreover, the 55th Street Theater's future was up for grabs.

Joffrey considered quitting the house, as did the other 55th Street
Theater dance company constituents. The only alternative offered was
for his and Ailey's company to help support City Center, but the burden

of taking on more than they could responsibly handle threatened to send both the Joffrey and Ailey troupes into bankruptcy.

In the fall of 1975, City Center transferred the management of the 55th Street Theater to a commercial theatrical firm, Theater Now, and delegated its booking functions to yet another firm, which began reducing the theater's emphasis on top-quality artistic performance by renting it out to commercial rock groups. The quality of the theater's management went downhill: for example, the Joffrey endured one season when the heat was shut off prematurely and nobody could be found to turn it back on. There were not enough people at the front of the house to take tickets. Remarked Anthony A. Bliss, "It frightens me to think we might wake up in the morning and find the City Center not functioning at all."[23]

Then, in April 1976, the City Center board adopted an even more drastic measure by ending the subsidy of City Center altogether, because the funds in its central operating bank account had been depleted. After initially proposing to have the theater's management consigned to them, Joffrey's and Ailey's companies soon were part of another plan that was accepted by a majority: Howard Squadron's establishment of the 55th Street Dance Theater Foundation.

Squadron—the lawyer who had "saved" the Joffrey Ballet in 1965 by providing Alex Ewing with tax-exempt papers to create a foundation overnight—came to Joffrey's rescue again. He charged $1 rent per year to Joffrey, Ailey, Merce Cunningham, Dance Theater of Harlem, Paul Taylor, Alwin Nikolais, and Murray Louis. The theater was designated a landmark, and it now seemed possible for operations to resume in a stable environment.

But Robert Joffrey, struggling with the stresses of underfunding, never would recover the company's equilibrium. Although a perennial complaint from his dancers had been that he did not teach them, in actuality, up to this time he was fairly routinely offering them a class taught by him. According to the diaries of some dancers, he taught at least once a week—and he still drew individuals aside to solve their specific problems in certain roles. By 1974, however, he had elevated Scott Barnard to the position of assistant ballet master and Joffrey was slowly replacing himself with Barnard in the studio. Said Barnard, tellingly, of Joffrey's esthetic emphasis at the time when he assumed authority:

"He was looking for more classical dancers. And of course better dancers, because he loved the Royal Ballet and was very moved by Ashton and by the idea of a corps working together. That idea also always excited me. It's the way I was trained. He started turning the training over to me more and more."[24]

By 1975, the teaching of company classes fell entirely to Basil Thompson and Barnard, and Joffrey thereby sacrificed contact on a daily basis with his dancers. Arpino, who had never been a principal directorial force, was, strangely, even less engaged in the company's operations than before. The dancers who looked to him for guidance were discouraged to find that he now often expected them to call their own rehearsals and that he paid more attention to sewing costumes and fussing over head-dresses. He had no visible control; Joffrey had too often ignored him and walked away when he spoke. Joffrey's strongest link to the dancers was the obedient, obliging Barnard, the only person with whom Joffrey worked alone in a studio rehearsing *Pas des Déesses,* so that Barnard could prepare a new production for Joffrey's favorites, the most classical and unrebellious dancers among his brood, who were in Joffrey's opinion Charthel Arthur, Francesca Corkle, Denise Jackson, and Burton Taylor. On the twentieth anniversary of the City Center Joffrey Ballet in 1976, Joffrey scrapped plans for *Postcards*—a piece to Erik Satie's music he wanted to choreograph. The business office was his dominant terrain.

Anthony A. Bliss, his board chairman and now executive director of the Metropolitan Opera as well, insisted he attend all meetings and court potential funders. Patrons wanted to know where their money was going, since Joffrey was seeking to raise $1.5 million in contributions in a yearlong campaign that would end in February 1977, and they preferred a personal contact with the artistic director.

At this time, Joffrey was beginning to believe that Bliss possessed an ulterior motive: he wished to procure the company in some capacity for his wife, Sally Brayley Bliss. Bliss had driven away many of Joffrey's most brilliant, honest, and tireless associates, such as his former general administrator Omar K. Lerman and Rima Corben, the company's press representative from 1967 to 1974.* Bliss suspected that too many Joffrey employees were "listening more closely to Joffrey than to him."[25] Moreover, it appeared that Bliss did not want to hear another anecdote from Joffrey or Arpino about the station wagon days.[26] In his view, the company needed to project authentic glamour rather than glamorizing its past. He was also fed an idea by Clive Barnes on to which he latched like a dog on to a bone, namely that the Joffrey should merge with American Ballet Theatre and become ABT's "American wing." While ABT would stick to the classics, Joffrey would preside over the entire enterprise, and Sally Brayley Bliss would direct the Joffrey. Said Barnes:

"That was my idea. I was flying it in print and also with Tony Bliss and before then. My feeling about the idea was the companies should maintain their identities. It should be one company but there should be two, a large company and a small company. And that Joffrey should have con-

---

*Corben would return to the Joffrey to head its publicity department in 1981. She was still presiding over press and public relations in 1996.

trol of both, because it struck me that Joffrey was the ideal person to be head of it.

"Tony Bliss smiled and agreed. I wasn't really aware that he had taken any particular action."[27]

Joffrey noted that Arpino had somehow been left out of the equation. The merger idea was interpreted by Joffrey as a threat. The thought of a takeover put him on the defensive, as he realized that the company's repertoire and financial security might have peaked in 1973. "He was uneasy," said Bill Leighton, his executive assistant through 1975. "He slept later. He was harder to awaken and get motivated."[28]

Joffrey's pattern of indecisiveness and procrastination was legend. He could continue to hide from reality and banish his anxiety beneath a mound of sales slips from Bloomingdale's shopping sprees. He might deny that he and the troupe were not going to live forever. Or he could change things. But working against him was that by early 1976, Tony Bliss and the board were powerful and the schism between the company's artistic and business staffs was real. "This period of the Joffrey history, if translated into a composite picture, would have less and less consistent points and appear more and more blurred. This was a good deal due to the belief people had that it was too expensive to perform long in New York," said Alex Ewing, who was still vice chairman of the Joffrey Foundation board. "I deliberately removed myself as much as possible because I had seen too many instances when people on the outside thought they knew the one and only way, and there are usually many ways. The trick is to pick a single one and run with it and not be distracted by all the other possibilities. I subscribed to the operating plan that there were huge advantages to performing twelve weeks a year in New York. The problem was the Joffrey Ballet threw out one plan that at least in my opinion could be made to work better and better over the years, and didn't replace it with an equally clear-cut long-range strategy."[29]

There existed a fundamental perceptual confusion about the identity of the Joffrey for the public as well. Without requisite financial resources Joffrey was forced to dilute his concepts, his insights, his sense of the connections between disparate pieces in his repertoire even more. Yet, despite all these distractions and obstacles, incredibly he still took large risks with choreographers.

After 1976, the programming tended to hinge on a single major work. The esthetic centered, to a degree, on grandstanding for one ballet, one choreographer: the new *Romeo and Juliet* by Oscar Araiz, an unknown from South America, who envisioned one Romeo and three Juliets in a single production; Laura Dean, a contemporary choreographer who worked with whirling-dervish spinning, geometry, and loud sound; William Forsythe, once in Joffrey II, now a big gun in Europe with a punk mentality and a seductive attitude toward the toe shoe; there was a wide and impressive John Cranko collection that included *Opus 1* and *Jeu de Cartes;* and Nijinsky's *Sacre du printemps* in 1987, followed by Joffrey's own *Nutcracker* the same year.

Joffrey and Arpino would say that they had always thrived on adversity. But the change in the mid-seventies was different from anything they had known, because the company's operating expenses *far* exceeded the earned income—by over $1 million in each of the last four years. "In the current fiscal year [1975–76], ending August 31, total operating expenses are projected at approximately $3.4 million with only $2.8 million, or 82 percent, of that to be offset by box office receipts, performance fees, and other earned income," reported Dan Dorfman, economic columnist for *New York* magazine, in April. "Without another nearly $1.3 million in grants and contributions—which has already been pledged—The Joffrey would be out of business."[30]

Again, they were not alone. Rebekah Harkness announced plans to disband the Harkness Ballet unless enough money was raised to cover its projected $1.5-million deficit for 1975–76. A Harkness spokesperson told *Dance Magazine,* "[Harkness] is no longer willing to assume financial support of the company because of stock market reverses and the rapidly rising costs involved."[31] And though the NEA had increased its grants substantially to applicants, dance-company ticket receipts across America had dropped from 42 percent of the total budget to 27 percent.[32] In 1975, the City Center Joffrey Ballet management, with William Crawford as general administrator and Jane Hermann assistant administrator, chose a peripatetic existence for the troupe, touring the United States and other countries. And even so, for half the year, it either was not performing or was in rehearsal, during which time no income was earned. "The average Joffrey dancer was paid $11,775 in 1975, and no dancer's wages exceeded $15,000," reported *New York*'s Dorfman.[33]

"Ask yourself, what is good for the organization? What is good for the whole?" Joffrey would so often tell his production supervisor Penelope Curry that she said it sounded almost like a mantra. "And when you can answer that, then you can make your decision."[34] The company's struggle for survival had reached panic level.

PART FOUR

HOME

CHAPTER 25

The Ashes

On January 21, 1976, the City Center Joffrey Ballet was the subject of the first program aired on television for the Public Broadcasting System's new series *Dance in America*. The one-hour special reached between 3 and 4 million television viewers—an astonishing figure when contrasted to the 2,835 people who saw the company in one sold-out night at City Center's 55th Street Theater or to the only 11 million who, in fact, attended a live dance performance in America in 1975. Dance was proclaimed "the fastest growing performance art" by the *New York Times*.[1] The numbers clearly indicated that the quickest way to reach the most people was through the small screen. Joffrey commissioned an audience survey during the company's New York season three months after the TV debut. The startling results were recorded in Robert Coe's book *Dance in America*: "Forty-five percent of the audience had seen the *Dance in America* program, and fifty-nine percent of those attending the Joffrey for the first time were doing so because they had enjoyed the company on television."[2]

Joffrey had realized a significant dream: he had reached the broadest public possible. Television had never been part of his conscious game plan, and yet an inordinate number of opportunities for him to work in TV and the related medium of film had fallen into his lap. He had been part of the NBC-TV opera broadcasts of the 1950s, and his troupe had appeared on the *Ed Sullivan Show* in 1965. While choreographing *Astarte* in 1967, he had learned to think of film as a potential component of dance itself. Throughout the late 1960s, Gardner Compton and his partner, Emile Ardolino, had documented many ballets in the Joffrey's repertoire for the Jerome Robbins Film Archive at Lincoln Center. Many of the company members were, therefore, accustomed to cameras, both in the professional atmosphere created by Compton and Ardolino and in the relaxed environment of the Joffrey studios, where Glenn White sometimes videotaped Arpino's works-in-progress.

By 1976, Joffrey and Arpino were perfectly poised for the *Dance in America* experiment. Said Merrill Brockway, *Dance in America* series producer, who developed the programming with Jac Venza, the executive producer, and Emile Ardolino, coordinating producer: "Most of the dance companies we approached about working with us were suspicious and felt an appearance on television would take away from the box office. Bob Joffrey was the one who was willing to take a chance."[3]

Ardolino wished to focus on choreography that was "uniquely American"[4] and it was agreed that the program would be a company sampler. Joffrey selected Russell Sultzbach in the Torch Bearer solo from Arpino's *Olympics;* Gary Chryst as the Chinese Conjuror in Léonide Massine's *Parade;* Francesca Corkle, Paul Sutherland, and Jan Hanniford in Joffrey's *Remembrances;* Christian Holder as Death in Kurt Jooss's *The Green Table;* a film excerpt from *Astarte;* and Arpino's *Trinity* with the three original men—Dermot Burke, Chryst, and Holder. Massine and Jooss were flown in from Europe to prepare their pieces and to be interviewed on-camera. Joffrey and Arpino were also interviewed.

The presentation of *Parade* and *The Green Table* on television—integrated with the snippets of Massine himself painting Chryst's face with the Conjuror's makeup and of Jooss personally coaching the Gentlemen in Black around the famous green-baize table—did more to solidify Joffrey's reputation in dance than probably any other single event. His place in history after that hour was assured. People could name him as important to dance because he restored twentieth-century masterpieces, landmarks of the modern era; he "rehabilitated" and "adopted" the choreographers who created them. He brought generations together, closed the gaps. The American critics said Joffrey's existence could now be "justified" because he was producing such high level work, both qualitatively and quantitatively.[5]

"Robert Joffrey keeps adding laurels to the crown he wears as uncontested master of revivals," Arlene Croce would write.[6] The tenor of dance writers' attitudes toward him significantly changed; whatever skepticism had existed seemed to be almost completely doused by acceptance and respect, except in one area: many critics still had grave reservations about Joffrey's practice of standing by Gerald Arpino's "pop, disposable ballets of little lasting merit" (*New York Times*, March 7, 1976). "What he does is the life of the company," Joffrey retaliated. "Jerry is what makes us the Joffrey Ballet and gives us our individuality."[7]

The figure Joffrey now cut measured up to the role of experienced statesman. He had thickened, gained weight, and emerged monolithic. His bulk was not the bulk of a sybarite; there was no excess, no sloppiness. His visage too had economized; he was cooler, more restrained, tough, and he sometimes flashed people the dagger eyes. His closely cropped hair and beard were turning gray.*

---

*Marberger and Joffrey's sexual relationship ended when Joffrey put on weight. They both had many partners, but their love for each other continued to strengthen. "There was

* * *

Few visitors to the company delighted Joffrey as much as Papa Jooss, and by 1976 the Joffrey Ballet was the world's main showcase of Jooss ballets. The *Dance in America* program had provided Jooss and Joffrey with time enough together to revive two of the choreographer's lesser works from the early thirties: the sentimental *Pavane on the Death of an Infanta* to the famous Ravel score of the same name, and the amusing frivolity *A Ball in Old Vienna*, music by Joseph Lanner. Together with *The Green Table* and *The Big City* (which had entered the Joffrey's repertoire in 1975), they formed part of an all-Jooss evening presented in Chicago, Seattle, and New York, honoring the choreographer's seventy-fifth birthday.

"Robert Joffrey's decision to show us more Jooss is perfectly natural," mused Nancy Goldner in the *Nation*. "The revival of Jooss reflects a new interest in the past. Now that dancing has proven itself to be an entertainment medium as well as an art form, we want to redignify it by digging up its historical heritage. . . . Delving into the past is noble and good, but what if we've already seen what there is to see?"[8]

Goldner had hit upon an irony, namely that just at the moment when dance seemed to be finding its largest audience—in part because it was being marketed as entertainment—directors were simultaneously looking further into the art form's past and dredging up some of the more obscure works, many of which were not very interesting. Goldner supplied several examples other than Jooss's *Pavane* and *A Ball in Old Vienna*. But there could also be gleaned in her comments a deeper concern: Was there any risk that the broad-based acceptance of ballet as entertainment would over time discredit the art form? Should art be marketed?

In 1976, the Joffrey Ballet* was being held up as a "model of financial management by every major government and private funding agency," including the NEA, the New York State Council on the Arts, and the Ford Foundation.[9] Over the last three seasons the company management—with Tony Bliss as board chairman, Alex Ewing as vice chairman, Peter S. Diggins as general administrator, and James E. Siegel as director of

---

Robert and Aladar and no one between them," observed Marberger's youngest sister, Donna (5 March 1996).

*In April 1976, the company's title officially changed to the Joffrey Ballet because it had ceased to be a constituent of City Center of Music and Drama. This was confusing, because the same year, the troupe moved completely from Joffrey's school in Greenwich Village into the City Center 55th Street Theater, renting three large, expensive rehearsal studios in the same building where the company's administrative offices had been located for some years. With a consortium of four other dance companies, the Joffrey Ballet was operating City Center, which placed an unprecedented financial burden upon the troupe. Advised that the alternative was to leave New York, Joffrey responded that such a move was "unthinkable."

finance and development—had more than doubled the Joffrey's earnings on the road, grossing nearly $2 million at the box office, which represented an impressive 65 percent of its total budget.[10] Internally, however, Joffrey and his administrators worried how long they could endure the hand-to-mouth existence that resulted from living off box office. Would they ever have an endowment or know real security? The final installment of the Ford Foundation's four-year grant would run out in 1978. The company would then lose close to three-quarters of a million dollars, and nobody on Joffrey's staff was attempting to replace the Ford Foundation's contribution with grants and gifts from other foundations, corporations, or private funders.[11] In the middle of a recession, they were counting on Joffrey's luck.

Joffrey invited Agnes de Mille to contribute *Rodeo,* her classic about courtship at a square dance on a Texan ranch. It would be part of the all-American fall '76 season, in recognition of the nation's bicentennial and the Joffrey Ballet's twentieth anniversary. The year before de Mille had survived a stroke that left her with no feeling in the right side of her body, but she was eager to work for Joffrey, partly because she was skirmishing with Lucia Chase at American Ballet Theatre, her home company. But a month or so before rehearsals with Joffrey were to begin, de Mille suffered a heart attack and was sent to the hospital again. Undaunted, she delegated the ballet's staging to Vernon Lusby, her trustworthy régisseur, with instructions about the cast.

Rodeo, with music by Aaron Copland, was a landmark ballet that had originally been created in 1942 for the Ballet Russe de Monte Carlo with de Mille as the tomboy who falls in love with the Champion Roper (Frederic Franklin). *Rodeo* led to de Mille's assignment as the choreographer for *Oklahoma!* on Broadway, and it evolved into a signature work for Ballet Theatre, where it was staged with some changes in 1949. De Mille was notoriously picky about the companies she allowed to dance her works, and tough about casting. She admired Russell Sultzbach at the Joffrey ("One helluva dancer," she said to him. "But can you smile?"[12]) and chose him for the Champion Roper. The Cowgirl was Beatriz Rodriguez.

Joffrey and de Mille agreed to restore the ballet to the original production that had been executed for Ballet Russe. Kermit Love and Oliver Smith, who had designed the costumes and scenery respectively, were brought onto the Joffrey team to reconstruct their work.

Rodeo was a great success for the Joffrey Ballet. "The moment the curtain fell the whole cast, headed by Joffrey, was on the phone," said de Mille. "It was very sweet, and when I got out of the hospital, I came to see them and thought it was excellent. Beatriz Rodriguez was lovely. Bob Joffrey told me he thought I was in love with Russell Sultzbach. Russell was excellent."[13]

Arpino, thinking that to give her more to do would speed her recovery, asked de Mille to present her famous "Conversations on the Dance" lecture at the Joffrey Ballet. In November 1977, the special evening of talk and dance was offered at City Center. Joan Mondale, the vice president's wife (who was involved with the NEA and who de Mille would later suspect was partially responsible for federal funding of the PBS television filming of *Conversations*), arrived with her phalanx of Secret Servicemen. The press corps and camera crews were lined up three deep, and de Mille was surrounded by friends with phials of nitroglycerin ready in their pockets in case of an emergency. Her dressing room had been transformed into a makeshift "operating room," she said.[14]

"Bob Joffrey took my hand and we stood [onstage]," wrote de Mille in her memoir, *Reprieve*. "There was absolute silence and electric emptiness and waiting."[15] Joffrey seated de Mille and left the stage. The curtain rose and she began to speak. The audience was with her, willing her to succeed, and at the end of the program, which included Joffrey's dancers and de Mille's guest artists, de Mille threw both hands out to the audience. "*Both*, the right as well as the left, extended and held open, a perfectly natural and spontaneous gesture."[16] She had not used the right arm since the stroke. Her doctors, her physical therapists, gasped audibly, and some cried. The curtain fell. Joffrey led de Mille to center stage as the curtain flew up again. He placed a small nosegay into her right hand, then backed off, confident about her strength. "I had no cane. I had no arm. I had no support. I had no companions. I was out there, absolutely alone," she said.[17]

De Mille had victoriously returned to the stage, and although she appreciated Joffrey and Arpino's kindness, her legendary sharp tongue had not softened. In time, she voiced concern that *Rodeo* was not being properly kept up. She was especially concerned about Beatriz Rodriguez's portrayal of the Cowgirl. "You have to believe that's a girl that has not been kissed, has not been hugged, has not been flirted with. She's dreamt of it, but she doesn't know it," she told Rodriguez. De Mille disapproved of Rodriguez touching the Champion Roper without any "shyness in her."[18] She demanded that Joffrey remove Rodriguez from the role and replace her with someone else. He would not consent. De Mille threatened legal action. Joffrey canceled the next performance and dropped the ballet from the repertoire.

Rodriguez was for Joffrey himself an acquired taste; he had learned to appreciate her stoic beauty that seemed built on a pile of explosives. She had grit, which was why she had seemed right for the Cowgirl. But she was seductive and disquieting, which might have been antithetical to de Mille's vision. Joffrey in this case stood by his dancer and refused the choreographer—something he had never done.

*   *   *

At the beginning of 1977, the Joffrey Ballet canceled its traditional spring season in New York. It was an unprecedented move in the troupe's history. As Joffrey noted, "There's no point in doing a season if you don't have the money to produce it well."[19] Still, the cancellation was effected with "reluctance" and "regret," wrote James E. Siegel, the Joffrey Ballet Foundation treasurer. In a fund-raising letter to Estée Lauder Inc., a national cosmetics company, Siegel added, "We are at a crossroads. We are beset with very serious problems. . . . Between now and August 31, we shall either make great strides in strengthening our financial underpinning or we shall face the threat of insolvency."[20]

Amazingly, in a bankrupt position, Joffrey gambled with the company's first full-length ballet, *Romeo and Juliet,* by Oscar Araiz. In Araiz's unconventional version of the classic to Prokofiev's score, the dancers wore rehearsal clothes and gradually attired themselves in costumes befitting their characters. As time would prove, Araiz's work would fail, but the company did not fall apart because of it, nor did Joffrey's faith in his own judgment waver. "I take full blame for the repertory, nobody else," he said. "I really don't listen to anybody, be it Jerry Arpino or my board or my dancers."[21]

The troupe's problems reflected the negative economic conditions in America that stemmed from the 1973 recession and the corresponding stock market decline. All foundations had grown cautious, and by 1977, the onus of supporting nonprofit arts organizations had shifted onto the private sector. Government support for the arts had slowly declined. The challenge for most dance companies had been to recognize that the support structure was rapidly changing. The Joffrey Ballet's administration had not anticipated this new climate, nor had it believed the Ford Foundation's four-year grant would not be replenished. In response to its oversight, Tony Bliss intensified his efforts to have Joffrey merge the company with American Ballet Theatre. His concept was "unimaginable" to Joffrey,[22] in large measure because it was motivated by marketing concerns and, he thought, Bliss's personal agenda.

The story that follows of the company's disbandment in 1979, while inextricably linked to financial matters, reveals that Joffrey simultaneously carried out the expansion of both himself and his company as forces in the world of dance. It was as if for him, on some fundamental level, money was no obstacle. He had weathered the Harkness breakup understanding that the consequences of his actions were not irreversible; the company could come back. Now he faced a greater test: Could he outbrave Bliss, who was ambivalent about providing him with the conditions under which to be creative, and still maintain the company?

In 1978, Arlene Croce in the *New Yorker* proposed the same idea that

Clive Barnes had already privately suggested to Joffrey and Bliss. The time had come, said Croce, for Joffrey to split his troupe into two wings, "one to do Joffrey's revivals and the other to do Arpino's ballets. No company can serve two ballet masters."[23] The words lent some artistic validity to Bliss's business scheme to reinvent the Joffrey Ballet as the American wing of ABT, limiting the company to one genre. Bliss, too, wanted to divide Joffrey from Arpino by reducing Arpino's role in administrative decisions. "Jerry is difficult to work with," Bliss commented. Bliss's alleged agenda was to replace Arpino with his wife, Sally Brayley Bliss, who was the current director of Joffrey II, and award her whatever repertoire did not fit in at ABT to direct as a separate company. "I can assure you that that never crossed my mind," Bliss later said.[24]

But others had heard and witnessed differently. "Tony felt that Jerry was a hindrance to Robert's career. He had no interest in Jerry when I was there," said Henry A. Young, an executive director for the Foundation for the Joffrey Ballet. "We [Bliss and Young] had many discussions about what Sally's career would be, and I advised Robert of it. I think that Tony didn't necessarily have the Joffrey as an agenda. I think Tony had Sally's ultimate career as an agenda."[25]

Remarked Sally Bliss, "If Bob had said, 'Why don't you be my assistant?' I would have done that. That would have been nice. . . . I would have loved to have gone in and worked with the company, to be anything they wanted me to be. . . . But Tony and I never talked about it because I felt that with him being chairman of the board, the line was very thin."[26]

Starting in 1977, observers continually assailed Joffrey's concerns for being too disparate, too diverse, and ultimately incompatible. They determined that the Joffrey Ballet was torn between the twentieth-century-revival wing and the Arpino-contemporary wing. But variety still interested Robert Joffrey. He believed the two sides could coexist because they coexisted inside of him. And he loved Arpino. Had anyone the right to sever them?

Together Joffrey and Arpino were finding a new sense of American movement. They were a team, curious enough about the inner workings of each other's mind that they continually laid themselves on the line for each other. But few saw the attachment as a strong one because Joffrey had little to do with Arpino during the workday, and their interactions in public were easily misconstrued.

Among those who caught the subtlety was Henry Young, who described the Joffrey/Arpino partnership of the late seventies:

The truth is that in all the time I worked with Bob and Jerry, Jerry was always very ill-treated by Bob with regard to the budget. The rules of the game for Jerry were that he had to raise his own money for the ballets. He could only rehearse with the youngest company members, because they were cheaper. And, in general, rehearsal time and stage-tech time were always kept to a minimum for him. Jerry always put a work on under duress.

Bob was never mean to him, he was simply fixated on his own issues and wrestling with the conflicts of funding the institution. Jerry accepted the relationship that existed. Bob always had respect for Jerry, but I think it was complicated by their own—it's like a husband and wife working in the same business. I simply recognized that there were currents going on in their relationship that I didn't know.

Bob was really the front man for the organization within the board. Jerry was usually not asked to speak, but he was generally present at [board] meetings. There was a long history of wariness about Bliss and his objectives, which created a formal atmosphere. Bob was always on his guard around Tony. Bob was political. He was cautious.[27]

Joffrey and Arpino could redeem themselves in each other's eyes. Yet many of the dancers who had been through the trenches with the company over the past six years had a more difficult time forgiving the way they were sometimes treated by Joffrey and Arpino. Christian Holder said, "We had our own feelings about Jerry, which had little to do with Joffrey's behavior toward him—they merely happened to correspond because Jerry was who he was and behaved the way he behaved. Most of us felt that Jerry was not Joffrey's equal because it was visibly apparent to us over the years that Jerry was unsuited to direct. When Joffrey was away, we, the dancers, and the ballet masters got the show on. Jerry never took charge in any emergency. We did it. He was basically a nice, caring man, and he was our associate artistic director in name only."[28]

The year 1977 was the final one of the Ford Foundation's challenge grant. Joffrey and his board, therefore, had fair warning. "In 1974, twenty-four percent [$683,000] of the Joffrey Ballet's operating budget came from the Ford Foundation. By 1978, it dropped to $100,000, and in 1979 it was zero," said Henry Young, executive director of the Foundation for the Joffrey Ballet at the end of 1978. "When you go from $683,000 to zero, you have a lot of rebuilding to do to maintain your existing budget." The company's escalating costs were shouldered by the audience. In 1975 the average ticket price was $6.41, and in another five years it had increased to $11.[29] Ballet, which had enjoyed spectacular popularity throughout the 1960s and early 1970s, had been easily affordable. One of the concerns that many in the art form had shared during that time was a vision of ballet as inclusive, egalitarian. Low ticket prices had preserved ballet's image as nonelitist. Now, ticket costs were soaring beyond the reach of many. The division between classes in American society was widening; by 1980, pundits would declare that the dance boom was over.[30]

Rising ticket prices were the result of rising expenses. "The crux of the problem can be summed up in one word: unions," wrote Walter Terry in *Saturday Review*, adding, "There is neither villain nor blameless hero. It's a matter of viewpoint."[31] Dancers do not look at dancing as their job; they usually work out of loyalty to one artistic director and expect to be paid what the company can afford.[32] In contrast, members of the stage crew, the ballet orchestra, and the administrative personnel regard themselves as laborers. They belong to a union to insure fair treatment and to gain benefits. Two-thirds of the total Joffrey Ballet payroll in a week in 1978 went to the orchestra and the crew.

People who could afford the higher ticket prices (at $30 tops) tended to be older, while the Joffrey's audience had traditionally been young. In 1978, 20 percent of its audience were students and another 20 percent were young professionals.[33] The rest were middle-aged or elderly. By 1979, the company had succeeded in attracting a more financially stable audience, but not one that was considered wealthy and, therefore, reliable for philanthropic support beyond the purchase of season tickets.

In 1977, Joffrey was appointed by President Jimmy Carter to the National Council on the Arts, where he consistently impressed people because he defended and advocated subsidies for troubled companies without bringing his own onto the table. "He was selflessly for dance," said one council member, who wished to remain anonymous. "He wasn't there for the Joffrey, he was there for dance."

In 1979, he was the only American on the jury for the U.S. International Ballet Competition in Jackson, Mississippi. To have the competition located in the United States for the first time implicitly acknowledged that American ballet had come of age. Joffrey literally carried the lit torch for the opening day ceremony.

"Joffrey was becoming Mr. American Dance," noted Clive Barnes. "I don't know how conscious he was of that, fairly conscious, I imagine. If anyone wanted to represent dance, it was Bob. And so he was institutionalizing himself."[34]

In 1979, Norman Walker, director of Jacob's Pillow, appointed Joffrey to the dance festival's advisory board.* That same year, the Joffrey returned to the White House for its fourth visit and performed a segment

---

*After Ted Shawn's death in 1972, Jacob's Pillow Dance Festival was directed by John Christian (1972), Walter Terry (1973), Charles Reinhart (1974), Walker (1975–79), Liz Thompson (1975–90), Sam Miller (1990–95), and Sali Ann Kriegsman (1995 to the present).

of de Mille's *Rodeo* for President and Mrs. Carter and their guest, Premier Deng Xiaoping from the People's Republic of China. And at his school, a scholarship student was being groomed for Joffrey II. He was Ronald Prescott Reagan, the youngest son of the governor of California, who would possibly seek the Republican nomination for the presidency.

Joffrey seemed to be playing a strategic game to avoid folding the troupe permanently; both wittingly and unwittingly, he was stockpiling ammunition. But then, fate and nature turned against him: the NEA dramatically curtailed funding for touring, a performance week in New Orleans was canceled because of flooding, and a New York newspaper strike perhaps exacerbated the decline in ticket sales. By February 1979, the troupe was floating over $600,000 in loans, and its projected operating deficit was $1.6 million for 1978–79.

When Rudolf Nureyev approached Robert Joffrey through James Nederlander, America's leading private dance impresario,[35] asking if the Joffrey Ballet might be interested in joining him on Broadway for four weeks, Joffrey could scarcely say no. Nureyev was cash in the bank. During the run at the Mark Hellinger Theater from March 6 to April 1, 1979, Nureyev could rescue the Joffrey Ballet with their joint program entitled "Homage to Diaghilev."

Joffrey, agreeing to the flat fee Nederlander offered him, contributed his productions of *Petrouchka* and *Parade*. Nureyev added a production of Fokine's *Le Spectre de la rose* borrowed from the London Festival Ballet, where he had danced it the year before. Nederlander was paying for a revival of Nijinsky's *L'Après-midi d'un faune*, which had not been seen in New York in over thirty years.

"It is no secret that the Joffrey was more or less obliged to undertake this engagement in association with a commercial management, rather than under its own auspices, to offset a deficit that threatened the company's very existence," wrote David Vaughan in *Dance Magazine*. "At the same time, Robert Joffrey, with his keen sense of ballet history, must have welcomed the opportunity to commemorate the fiftieth anniversary of the death of Serge Diaghilev—and the seventieth anniversary of the Paris debut of his Ballets Russes."[36]

The desperate state of the Joffrey Ballet's affairs was unknown to Nureyev, who claimed he was unaware the company was about to go bankrupt. Nureyev was, however, fairly well-acquainted with Joffrey and the company. In 1970, he had arranged to stage his *Laurencia* with Merle Park for the Joffrey, which, although never performed, introduced him to many of the dancers and their work habits. He also valued Hector Zaraspe and so had once been a frequent visitor to Joffrey's school, where Zaraspe taught. Nureyev was Erik Bruhn's close friend, and through him, too, he had long ago learned about Joffrey's ballet standards and philosophy. His choice of Joffrey was approached, as with most everything Nureyev undertook in dance, with seriousness and integrity. "Joffrey's company was a very highly organized company, and I thought it was very, very good for the Diaghilev program," said Nureyev. "Joffrey was charming. His personality was larger than life."[37]

Both Nureyev and Joffrey had discovered Diaghilev through their inquisitiveness, as student dancers, about Nijinsky. Nureyev had often been compared to Nijinsky, and the public yearned to see him dance the roles for which Nijinsky was famous. *Petrouchka* and *Spectre* and *Faune* were on the program. The first two were familiar to Nureyev, but *Faune* would be a first. Nureyev, at forty, was nearly twenty years older than Nijinsky had been when he had danced the Faun at the ballet's premiere in 1912. Although past his prime, at this age Nureyev's intellectual investigation could presumably combine with experience to shape a deep and meaningful performance. This was the plane on which Nureyev and Joffrey now collaborated.

Joffrey never doubted who was the master, the superstar, the boss in charge of "Homage to Diaghilev," and he found that when Nureyev was approached intellectually, he was down-to-earth. Like Nureyev, Joffrey had wanted someday to dance Nijinsky's signature roles. As the next best thing, he lived vicariously through Nureyev. "The 'Homage to Diaghilev' was the resolution of a strong desire," said Nureyev. "I always felt compassion for Nijinsky. Very early on, I wanted to absorb all his work. I wanted to penetrate the reason he was so extraordinary. It is about the way he moved. The attention to the foot has to be very high and never let go."[38]

Most critics were disappointed by Nureyev's performances, even as they admired the Joffrey Ballet members and the program's sets and costumes. "What no words and pictures had quite prepared me for was the icy perfection of Nijinsky's conception," Nancy Goldner wrote in the *Nation* of *Faune*. "The watery shimmer of Debussy finds a countervoice in Nijinsky's bedrock certainty of geometrical line. Were *L'Après-midi d'un faune* to be studied second by second, my guess is that every gesture and every grouping would be echoed in every other one. . . . Yet Nureyev's devotional submission to *L'Après-midi d'un faune*'s self-effacing spirit and impersonal language precluded any thoughts about what it must have been to see Nijinsky's faun."[39]

In contrast, Anna Kisselgoff, who, since November 1977, was chief dance critic for the *New York Times,* said of Nureyev's Faun, "Nureyev in the title role, and the seven nymphs from the Joffrey Ballet . . . give us a very good idea of what this historic ballet was meant to be. Perhaps we are seeing it only in outline. But on its own cautiously-danced terms, this new production . . . makes for a splendid occasion."[40] Kisselgoff was unimpressed, however, by Nureyev's Petrouchka, saying that he reached for the height of tragedy through a "little boy interpretation" that "opted . . . for charm." She resolutely dismissed his *Spectre* as "wrongheaded."[41] Such views were broadly shared by Joffrey's dancers, who were stunned, in light of Nureyev's words suggesting his high standards, to observe his shoddy professionalism during performances. He seemed more interested in looking at the dancers warming up in the wings than at those who were performing with him onstage. He also talked while dancing.

From *Faune* both Nureyev and Joffrey received something of lasting value. *Faune* was the only ballet Nureyev felt comfortable dancing as he grew older, and indeed it was the last ballet he ever danced. He called it his *Dying Swan*, likening himself to Anna Pavlova, of whom he said, "Each time somebody had a big success, Anna Pavlova would scream to her dresser, 'Bring me my Dying Swan tutu!' She would put it on and march onstage. It kept her famous. So, I put on *Faune* everywhere. In fact, this December I danced it for the last performance I did. One is very grateful that there is a ballet I can do anytime, day or night."[42] Less than six months after having said that, Rudolf Nureyev died, on January 6, 1993.

In *Faune* Joffrey gained for his repertoire a new Diaghilev gem. Most important, "Homage to Diaghilev" set an all-time box-office record at the Mark Hellinger Theater, and Nederlander decided to repeat the program in the summer, from July 17 to 28, at the New York State Theater. Joffrey also toured with it to Chicago and to San Francisco. But night after night of dancing the same roles as a backup to Nureyev wore the Joffrey Ballet members thin. Nobody was allowed to substitute for Nureyev on Broadway; when, for example, he suffered a slight injury, three weekend performances had to be canceled.* When Nureyev did not accompany them to San Francisco, they felt some relief. Gary Chryst commanded the title role in *Petrouchka*. Gregory Huffman performed *Faune*, and Ross Stretton *Spectre*, with Nureyev's chosen Joffrey ballerina, Denise Jackson. "A firm exponent of the repertory concept, Mr. Joffrey has always opposed the use of guest stars," wrote Kisselgoff in the *Times*, after having rhetorically asked the pointed question, "Where does the Joffrey Ballet stand now?"[43]

In the same article of May 1979, Kisselgoff announced Joffrey's good news that his company was scheduled to return to City Center on March 10, 1980. It would appear for three weeks in a new, full-evening production of *Cinderella*, which he would choreograph. "Homage to

---

*The contract that Nederlander and Joffrey agreed to sign stipulated that they purchase an insurance policy to cover every performance provided Nureyev danced. If Nureyev injured himself and could not perform, the company could not have someone substitute for him because it would invalidate the insurance. Joffrey's hands were tied; his dancers had to yield to Nureyev and the situation.

Diaghilev" appeared to have restored the troupe's economic confidence—
or had it? Not completely convinced by Joffrey's optimism, Kisselgoff
signed off her article with what could almost be called a eulogy:

> The company has had its moments of greatness. Unique in its exuberance of
> style, a repository of masterpieces rescued from oblivion, and for many, an
> introduction to ballet, the Joffrey has played a vital role in the development
> of dance in the United States. To say it deserves a second chance will be to
> admit that we allowed the first chance to slip by. To our enduring shame.[44]

As it turned out, Kisselgoff had correctly sensed doom. On August 19,
1979, Robert Joffrey let go of approximately ten of his dancers, put
another ten on probation, and retained about twenty under contract. He
informed the group he retained that it did not have to report back to
duty probably for another six months. They were on layoff. He said he
needed time to retrench. There would be no New York season in the
spring, and no *Cinderella*. The European tour had also been canceled. "It
was like the Saturday-night massacre," said Philip Jerry, a dancer who
survived the cuts. "No one had an inkling. It was devastating. People
were up till six in the morning just crying. There was a lot of alcohol
consumed."[45]

Among the company members whose contracts were not renewed
were Diana Cartier (who had first joined in 1960 and was currently a ballet mistress), Robert Estner, Jan Hanniford, Christian Holder, and Seymour Lipkin, the conductor. Gary Chryst elected to leave for a
Broadway show, and Burton Taylor chose to follow Cartier, his wife. The
shock waves were felt throughout the dance world; the Joffrey without
Holder and Chryst seemed impossible to imagine, and Joffrey endured a
pain that was strongly reminiscent of the one the Harkness defections
had caused.

"I love Christian and Gary dearly," he said, adding, "That was years of
building and then not being able to go on—so it was very traumatic.
Probably more than I let on, because I am not a person to let on very
much. There can never be another Christian or Gary. But the company is
a tapestry with many, many colors and lines going through it, and sometimes you see more rust and sometimes you see more blue and sometimes
you see more gold. It is all that weaving in and out that makes the whole.
And without that weaving in and out, you wouldn't have the texture nor
the depth. All those dancers have made lines in the company, and these
lines are there to lead to other lines."[46]

At the company's final ballet, which was *Trinity,* at the outdoor
Ravinia Festival in Illinois, Joffrey did not take his usual place in the wing
for the last performance of the season. He always bowed at the final curtain call with the dancers, then thanked them at the tour's conclusion.

Arpino was missing, too. "Joffrey's absence under these circumstances on the eve of the troupe's dissolution was like a slap in the face to us," said Holder. "We felt abandoned. The captain was deserting his sinking ship. A note on the backstage bulletin board would have sufficed."[47]

Although "Homage to Diaghilev" had provided a lift, the simple fact was that without an endowment or cash reserve, and particularly without the Ford Foundation or at least one major patron, or without a board chairman who could give his full attention and clout to fund-raising, the company needed to pare back to a skeleton staff and try to recoup. During every week of the layoff, Joffrey, Arpino, and Young met with the board, chaired by Bliss, to discuss the first item on the agenda: bankruptcy. "We had the papers for Chapter 11 drawn up," Bliss said.[48]

Then, in November 1979, under the advisement of Livingston Biddle and Rhoda Grauer, chairman and dance program director respectively of the NEA, the National Endowment awarded the company a special matching grant of $250,000. The Joffrey management was required to report monthly on the company's financial status and had been subjected to two audits by the Endowment before the "highly unusual" action had been implemented.[49] Such bureaucratic inconveniences were worth it: the NEA grant reversed the Joffrey Ballet's destiny. The company could start back up.

Nureyev said of the company, "Often I thought, 'Why do they exist?' "[50] Precisely the same question haunted Joffrey. "Always when you have a difficult time, it makes you value what you do. And sometimes out of something that is traumatic comes something good," he philosophized. "Often people create out of pain, death, or something that has happened to them. Sometimes you go deeper into your work. We're reborn each time—but you can't be reborn unless the ashes are there."[51]

Among the ashes were Joffrey supporters in Chicago. They had been noisily tempting Joffrey to relocate the troupe to their city before the NEA grant came through. But the Chicago offer would not cover the moving expenses or the seasons, and so Joffrey had turned them down. Then a man from Los Angeles, tentatively and informally, offered him another plan. Young recalled the effect it had on Joffrey:

Sometime in the summer of '79, somebody who was in the film business— I'm sorry I can't remember his name—called up and wanted to sit down and talk about the company and L.A. It had, I think, no contextual connection that I know of with anything the Los Angeles Music Center eventually had in mind. We met at Sardi's and we talked for two and a half hours, and Bob was doing ninety percent of the talking. Jerry was playing the role at this juncture of "You're right, Bob."

I would say that walking out of that restaurant, the individual in question had a total opinion that Bob was vastly interested in moving to L.A.

We put [the Los Angeleno] in a cab and we were walking up the street, and Bob said to Jerry and I, "We'd never do that, would we?"

I said, "What conditions would need to exist for us to do it?"

And he said, "Well, I guess if they would provide half the funds needed, we might."

That was the only conversation that existed between him and me on L.A. We had to genuinely contemplate whether or not there were alternative sites in America that made sense. I would say that the three most frequently articulated by Bob and Jerry at the time were Chicago, Seattle, and San Antonio. And this question of L.A. was the fourth.[52]

In 1980, Anthony Bliss contacted Baryshnikov, who was the newly installed artistic director of American Ballet Theatre, and again proposed the by-now-famous plan to merge the Joffrey Ballet with ABT. Upon learning of the meeting, Joffrey turned to his boyhood friend and sounding board Richard Englund and to Gage Bush, certain of their fidelity. Englund had come in and out of Joffrey's life, professionally and personally. Their friendship was fraught with antagonism made none the easier because sometimes they were sexual partners, they were competitive about the dance world, and they had started at more or less the same point in Seattle. Englund and Bush were at ABT II at the time; Bush was the heiress to a handsome fortune, and her affluent New York lifestyle with Englund and their two daughters more than matched the Blisses'. "Bob called up one night to ask if he could come over for dinner. When Bob arrived, he was white as a sheet," remembered Bush. "He said Tony had taken him to lunch that day and told him that Sally was going to be his assistant director and his successor. Bob told Bliss that if that happened he would close down the company."[53]

Joffrey was not the only person concerned about Bliss's persistence. Without Bliss's knowledge, Joffrey executive director Robert Hesse summoned ABT executive director Charles Dillingham for a private meeting. "We met in the lobby of a hotel," said Dillingham. "We both intuitively knew that Bliss's plan to merge the two companies was a terrible idea. We agreed that if it became public, it would do us both a lot of damage."[54]

At the time, Bliss, as general manager of the Metropolitan Opera, controlled the number of weeks that ABT played the Met. According to Dillingham, Bliss often did not cooperate with ABT. "The Met engagement was our lifeblood and we needed every bit of help to make it as successful as possible," said Dillingham. "Bliss blocked ABT from getting the dates it wanted and would not give the company a ninth week." Having been dismissed as Metropolitan Opera president in 1967, Bliss was viewed as possibly having a vendetta against the Met that was carried out on ABT. "Tony could be vindictive. It was as though he was trying to get us out of the Met and Joffrey in," concluded Dillingham.[55]

The irony of the political mayhem Bliss caused is that Joffrey and Arpino always thought that Tony and Sally Bliss were pitted against *them*. They had perhaps misinterpreted Tony Bliss's jealousy of ABT's size and stature as disapproval of the Joffrey Ballet. While the rest of the Joffrey Ballet's history might indicate that Bliss was pro–Joffrey Ballet and anti-ABT, Robert Joffrey thought it was the reverse.

CHAPTER 26

Los Angeles

In 1980, Joffrey made a list of ballets for a five-year plan that included John Cranko's *Taming of the Shrew* and *Romeo and Juliet,* Ashton's *Fille mal gardée* and *Cinderella,* and his own *Nutcracker.* They were all full-evening works that had been created in the twentieth century and that could not be produced without a well-matched ensemble led by a ballerina and her premier danseur. Paired couples—Patricia Miller and James Canfield, Dawn Caccamo and Glenn Edgerton, Beatriz Rodriguez and Jerel Hilding, Leslie Carothers and Philip Jerry, Deborah Dawn and Tom Mossbrucker, Tina LeBlanc and Edward Stierle, Denise Jackson and Luis Fuente—were the cornerstone of the company's new repertoire.

The difference between the Joffrey before and after the troupe's 1979 dissolution was so great that audiences reeled. "For a year after we started again it seemed like every review was about 'Where are Gary Chryst and Christian Holder?' " said James Canfield. "And that was really hard for us. But it stopped when we did *Taming of the Shrew.*"[1]

In order to replenish his supply of dancers in 1980, Joffrey drew largely from Joffrey II. Among those he chose were Madelyn Berdes, James Canfield, Leslie Carothers, Lynne Chervony, Erik Dirk, DeAnn Duteil, Glenn Edgerton, Celeste Jabczenski, Tom Mossbrucker, and Luis Perez. They had partially been trained by Sally Brayley Bliss and Maria Grandy, associate director of Joffrey II and a former Joffrey dancer herself. "So does that mean that Sally is really setting the company's standard and tone?" asked writer Lois Draegin of Joffrey, to which Joffrey replied, "We do it together."[2] No matter how suspicious Joffrey was of Bliss's motives, he did not quarrel during this transition period with how she and Grandy were educating dancers; he felt his new members had acquired the Joffrey style and could learn new ballets quickly.

In the first 1980 season, Joffrey risked everything by presenting eleven new productions, more than the troupe had ever before attempted. "What we saw came as something of a shock," said Anna Kisselgoff in the *Times.* "There were so many new dancers on stage and the troupe danced so differently that it looked like a new company."[3] Joffrey was clearly exercising his right to fail. He flopped with Moses Pendleton's version of *Relâche,* but by giving choreographer Laura Dean her first opportunity to work with classical ballet dancers, he empowered an artist whose mathematical, mosaic vision of dance claimed a major share in stimulating the contemporary dance and music scene.

"The idea of Dean doing a piece for the Joffrey is as intriguing as the prospect back in 1975 of Twyla Tharp's making something (*Deuce Coupe,* as it happened) for the company," explained Deborah Jowitt in a *Village Voice* feature about Dean's *Night* for the Joffrey. "Dean's dances are always clearly structured, elegantly patterned; so, often, are ballets. But Dean's movement style is understated, full of little stamps and kicks and hops; no matter how difficult it is to perform, her dancers attack it with the unspoiled verve of people dancing for pleasure."[4]

Joffrey had been eyeing Dean for some time, and when he invited her to choreograph for him, as a measure of his confidence he suggested she think about making three pieces (*Night* was followed by *Fire* [1982] and *Force Field* [1986]). "That was his way of assuring me that I wasn't just some anomaly coming in," said the postmodernist.[5] For *Night,* she wrote her own score to accompany the dance. The basic movement principle was spinning.

Dean proved that Joffrey's instincts for elevating choreographers were still keen. In fact, he had gotten better at it. The 1980 seasons launched a series of choreographers whose works were not familiar to Americans: Jiří Kylián, who was working in the Netherlands; William Forsythe, a former Joffrey II dancer, from Germany; and James Kudelka from Canada. But Dean would become a veritable fixture, generating six ballets for the company, the last of which was a section of *Billboards* (1993).

Arpino was also stimulated by the influx of new dancers. He entered into a prolific creative phase such as he hadn't really experienced since *Kettentanz* in 1971. *Suite Saint-Saëns* ignited it in 1978, after which he choreographed *Light Rain* with the help of James Howell, Glenn White, and Cameron Basden. *Light Rain* had been postponed in late 1979 with the advent of the American hostage crisis in Iran, and Arpino was advised that the Douglas Adams–Russ Gauthier score for the ballet might offend people because it incorporated Middle Eastern rhythms. He shelved the ballet for two years, but in 1981, *Light Rain,* with Celeste Jabczenski and James Canfield in the leads, was given a premiere. It subsequently gained an almost cult status in Los Angeles, and Leslie Carothers, who replaced Jabczenski, was idolized by many.

Light Rain, a showpiece of hyperextensions, swiveling hips, and acrobatics to an exotic combination of banjo, violin, clay drum, and wood sticks, was followed in 1983 by the elegiac *Round of Angels.* At that ballet's beginning, Arpino returned to his most intimate use of male part-nering. For the score, he used the romantic Adagietto in C Minor from Mahler's Fifth Symphony, a work that many protested could not be danced to. The ballet was dedicated to the memory of James Howell, who had died on October 21, 1982, of causes related to AIDS.

Howell was one of the earliest known AIDS cases in America. He had moved to San Francisco in 1973 to practice dance therapy. Arpino had bought with him a two-story house in the Castro district, transforming the bottom floor into a dance studio. Howell lived and taught there, and Arpino visited him as often as he could. He and Howell both went to the same physician, Dr. Roy Leeper, who was part of the vanguard of physi-cians committed to diagnosing and combatting AIDS. Leeper had long been an admirer of the Joffrey Ballet, and he knew Joffrey personally as well. When Howell's condition caused him to be bedridden, Arpino, Leeper, and Sue Loyd cared for him.

With AIDS came a new picture of life shaped by death, despair, shame, and fear of sex. Toward the end of the millennium, the worlds of the per-forming and visual arts and entertainment would be painfully impacted. By 1996, nineteen men who had at one time been associated with the Joffrey Ballet had died of AIDS-related causes. Among their number were Ian Hor-vath, Gregory Huffman, Robert Joffrey, Edward Stierle, Burton Taylor, Glenn White, and John Wilson.

The Music Center of Los Angeles task force first approached Joffrey in October of 1981. At the same time, the company was in rehearsal for John Cranko's *Taming of the Shrew,* a full-length production that was budgeted at $376,000. Joffrey had been unable to raise the full amount, and *Shrew,* while ultimately well-received, threatened to sink the company once again on the eve of its twenty-fifth anniversary season. Joffrey looked closely at the Los Angeles offer. "One finds out after twenty-seven years that, no matter how wonderful the reviews are or how well the new ballet is going, if you don't have the funds for new costumes or to pay the royalties or the composer, then you will not have what you envision," he told Irene Borger of the *Wall Street Journal.* "You can't do it alone. You have to get peo-ple to help you."[6] Recognizing that if he was to be the first ballet director to try a bicoastal arrangement, his fund-raising resources and board would double, he felt compelled to consider the Los Angeles proposition seriously.

The Music Center existed for seventeen years without a ballet com-pany. John Clifford's ten-year-old Los Angeles Ballet (along with the San Francisco Ballet, Pennsylvania Ballet, Houston Ballet, Eliot Feld Ballet, Lewitzky Dance Company, and Alvin Ailey American Dance Theater) had briefly been discussed for the Music Center residency, but Clifford's troupe was ultimately deemed to "fall short of the standards that the

Music Center represents."[7] Joffrey could have Los Angelenos' ballet dollars practically to himself. He was enticed by the Dorothy Chandler Pavilion, which was the perfect scale for ballet and set a glamorous, opulent tone. The possibility of increasing the company's season was also held out by the Music Center officers, on the basis of which Joffrey aimed to expand the troupe to sixty dancers.

Los Angeles allowed him to think big. He trusted his dancers. The company that would reside in the Music Center was almost as conservative as the people who were interested in bringing it west. Under Joffrey's ballet master, Scott Barnard, and assistant ballet mistress, Trinette Singleton, the dancers were more uniform, more classically attuned than in the late 1970s. They posed no threats; they were safe. Outstanding, unusual personalities had been sacrificed for the elegance of a coherent stylistic ensemble. Their kind of dancing could be admired tremendously, but often from an emotional distance.

On April 30, 1983, the Joffrey Ballet gave its inaugural performance at the Chandler Pavilion.* Nancy Reagan, the president's wife and the mother of Ron Reagan, now an ex–Joffrey dancer, was the honored guest. Conservative Californian Republicanism had swept into the White House. A former movie actor and his former movie actress wife were at the country's helm, and they had taught their son that it was acceptable to be a ballet dancer.

Ron Reagan had submitted his resignation to Joffrey three and a half months before the company's Music Center debut. He then wrote an editorial for *Newsweek,* explaining his precise reasons for quitting the career to which he had dedicated six of his twenty-four years. He railed against the treatment of dancers by the Joffrey Ballet staff. "Deprivation of education is unfortunate but dehumanization is inexcusable. I have heard ballet masters and choreographers berate dancers in a way which, on the street or in a boardroom, would provoke a fistfight," he wrote. "The belief seems to be that humiliation is necessary to keep ballets and dancers looking crisp. The truth is that ballets are danced best by artists who are confident and relaxed. How can one be larger than life onstage if one is belittled each day in rehearsal?"[8]

Ronald Prescott Reagan, the youngest son of President Ronald Wilson Reagan, had come to ballet late. When Baryshnikov and Leslie Browne (with Joffrey dancer Starr Danias in the supporting cast) blazed across the silver screen in 1977 in Herbert Ross's *The Turning Point,* boys everywhere who liked to dance, move, and be physical saw ballet presented as an exciting career. Reagan, eighteen, studied ballet with Stanley Holden in Los Angeles. When he began, he had never seen a live ballet perfor-

---

*The same day that George Balanchine died.

mance, but he admired *The Turning Point*. He also studied ballet during his brief time at Yale University.

Young Reagan's *Newsweek* piece indicated that he was unaccustomed to the art form's discipline. On the other hand, as the president's son, he had endured his fair share of criticism in the press. Reporters had followed Reagan to the unemployment line, for example, when he was picking up his check during a monthlong layoff from the Joffrey Ballet in 1982. They had frequently speculated that he was gay because he was a ballet dancer.

"There was the predictable right-wing conservative rumbling about guys in tights. You know, the redneck perspective on dance," said Reagan. "But what surprised me, actually, was the *gay community's* immediate assumption that I must be homosexual because I was a dancer. It seemed to be so homophobic in its own way."[9]

Reagan ended the *Newsweek* piece exhorting dancers to "take the first step" toward abolishing "financial exploitation and degradation"[10] within the ballet company system. He did not volunteer to be their leader. He vanished from the scene and has attended few dance performances since.

Almost everyone connected with the Joffrey Ballet and the Music Center thought that it was particularly considerate under the circumstances that the First Lady still came to the Los Angeles opening. But then, although few realized it, Nancy Reagan had initiated the Joffrey Ballet's move to L.A. The chain of command was described as follows by Dr. Robert Hesse, who became the Joffrey Ballet's executive director after the move. Among the key players was Armand Deutsch, an investor and a Reagan confidante, who, in 1924, was the intended kidnapmurder victim of Nathan Leopold and Richard Loeb; Michael Newton, an Englishman and the popular former president of the American Council for the Arts in New York, who was now president of the Music Center's Performing Arts Council; David H. Murdock, who was a billionaire developer friend of President Reagan's, and the chairman and chief executive of Pacific Holding Corporation; Gabriele Murdock, David's wife, who was genuinely keen on the ballet; and Harry Wetzel, who was chairman of the Garrett Corporation, a major producer of aerospace components and systems, and the owner of Alexander Valley Vineyards in Sonoma County, California.

Hesse explained, "When Ron was with the company, Nancy asked Artie [Armand] Deutsch to bring the company to L.A., and he did it. Deutsch and Michael Newton recruited David Murdock to make it happen. Murdock had become a member of the Performing Arts Council [of the Music Center]. He wanted something big to do. Harry Wetzel said, 'Do it!' "[11]

The Joffrey Ballet had entered the Music Center's consciousness through Nancy Reagan and her husband. "I think my mother's agenda was probably a personal one of, 'When we move back to L.A., my son will be in the same city I am,' " said Ron Reagan. "There are always plenty of people who are looking to suck up to people who are in power. They saw the Joffrey's move to L.A. as a way to make Nancy happy."[12]

The Reagan association with the Joffrey Ballet had been initiated in July 1979, when Meredith Baylis of the Joffrey school chose Ron to be a scholarship student. Baylis had no idea who he was. Nor did Edith D'Addario, the school's executive director, who said to him when he registered, "Well, I'm glad you're not *that* Reagan!"[13] He had been accepted on his own merits. By 1981, a year after Ron joined Joffrey II, Nancy Reagan's friends were donating large amounts of cash to Joffrey II (for example, Marjorie L. Everett, part owner of Hollywood Park, gave $10,000, and there were other anonymous donors), and Mrs. Reagan had agreed to be the honorary chairwoman of the national committee for the Joffrey Ballet's twenty-fifth anniversary. As a member of Joffrey II, young Reagan rose quickly through the ranks, coaxed, groomed, and attended at many photo opportunities by Sally Bliss, the troupe's director. Bliss recalled their first encounter:

> I heard a rumor from my masseur. He said, "Ronald Reagan's son is in the ballet school." And I said, "Oh, you have got to be kidding!" About two or three months later I went to the school because we needed dancers. I saw this—he was like an antelope, thin, beautiful feet, no turnout, and he jumped like an angel. He was just beautiful. I said, "He's green, but I really want this boy. What's his name?"
> "Ron Reagan."
> "Oh, no!" I said.
> . . . Bob liked Ron, but you have no idea what we lived with. We lived through the presidential campaign and through Ron's coming to me and telling me he was going to get married the next day. I was on the phone with Nancy that night, saying, "I want you to know that Ron is eloping and getting married at nine a.m. tomorrow morning." She said, "You have my promise [I will not tell Ron that you called]."[14]

Joffrey had wanted Reagan to join the main company a year before he actually did in August 1982, but Sally Bliss dissuaded him, Reagan claimed, because she had booked a national tour for Joffrey II based partially on the lure of Reagan's name. Although Sally Bliss denied that her cultivation of Ron Reagan was calculated, she knew that what she was doing could not hurt her cause of strengthening Joffrey II and proving herself indispensable to the Joffrey enterprise. By the same token, a battle line between Joffrey and Sally Bliss had been drawn over Reagan because he was attracting so much money to Joffrey II, and Joffrey felt that the main company's survival should come first. To Joffrey and Arpino, Sally Bliss's reluctance to release Reagan was an additional sign of her growing power. In the middle of this infighting, Reagan was promoted into the Joffrey Ballet, where disenchantment beset him. He said that he was aware in 1981 that a move to Los Angeles was being planned, but Joffrey was not telling the dancers about it. At company meetings, when asked about the rumors, Joffrey and Arpino denied that they were pursuing a permanent residence in L.A. "The dancers were being lied to, basically," said Reagan, adding that whenever he spoke up at the meetings and informed the dancers about what he knew through his mother about the Los Angeles plans, there would be a "shocked silence" while Joffrey and Arpino regrouped.[15] Reagan thought they were treating the dancers like children. Incensed, he saw the same kind of attitude prevail in the rehearsal studio: dancers were severely reprimanded for making minor mistakes. He also realized his limitations, and so he quit on January 18, 1983.

Although Ron Reagan had lasted only five months with the Joffrey Ballet, his presence had provided spice and encouraged many at the Music Center to acknowledge Joffrey's good sense for having made the most out of Reagan while he was there. The association linked the company to the Republicans and changed the perceived context of Joffrey's vision. "Lest it be assumed that its Presidential ties have been nothing but nuisances to the Joffrey, it should be noted that the Los Angeles Music Center, the company's future home, recently raised $1.8 million to support the troupe's upcoming move west, which may have been in some financial jeopardy. Much of the money is said to have been donated by members of the state's Republican Party. Enough said?" wrote Eric Taub in *Ballet News*.[16] Taub reminded people that the NEA, which had as recently as 1980 rescued the company from certain bankruptcy, was now being largely supported by people who had applauded Reagan's slashing of the NEA budget. Furthermore, the NEA was drawing nearer and nearer to a strange-bedfellow relationship with corporate funding.

In 1983, Frank Hodsoll, Reagan's NEA chairman, created the first National Medal of the Arts awards. Among the twelve recipients at the White House ceremony were Philip Morris and Texaco. "The inclusion of two corporations underlined the striking role that business corporations were playing in supporting the arts," observed Alice Goldfarb Marquis in her *Art Lessons: Learning from the Rise and Fall of Public Arts Funding*. In Marquis's view, the NEA had a long history of trying to involve American business in government subsidy of the arts, but business leaders wanted some control over who received their money and also wanted recognition. By 1983, corporations, "encouraged by a tax law that allowed deductions for charitable contributions of up to 5 percent of net profits," were contributing more to the arts than the NEA.[17]

Many struggling arts institutions, such as the Joffrey Ballet, could not turn away corporate sponsors. Starting with the 1981–82 season, a major Joffrey Ballet sponsor was Philip Morris Companies Inc. Joffrey patrons would grow accustomed to thinking of the company as the "Johnny Appleseeds of the dance" because that was what the Philip Morris ad campaign claimed.

But Joffrey had learned from the Harkness debacle that nobody gives something without wanting something in return. The Republican patronage and corporate philanthropists' contributions carried with them the implicit understanding that experimental work was less valued than the tried-and-true. It is possible that Joffrey and Arpino distanced themselves from each other at work because they were concerned about homophobia. They felt that David H. Murdock, the new chairman of the Joffrey Ballet board and now the chief executive officer of Castle and Cooke, was on the watch for homoerotic content in the Joffrey's repertoire. To them, Murdock appeared to expect some artistic influence in return for his patronage. Murdock had raised the $2 million the Joffrey Ballet needed to underwrite the company's first two L.A. seasons. "It takes a great deal more money to put on ballet than I had initially realized,"[18] Murdock told the *Wall Street Journal* in 1984.

There was, of course, much more to the company's Los Angeles move than Nancy Reagan's concerns. Without Tony Bliss's efforts, the Joffrey Ballet would likely have folded. He had played a large and invaluable role in establishing the company at the Music Center, during a time when the company's accumulated deficit totaled $700,000 and a condition of the contractual agreement with the Music Center task force was the elimination of this deficit. After Bliss resolved the problem of the deficit, the Joffrey Ballet qualified for support from the Music Center Unified Fund, which raised an additional $2 million to underwrite the first two seasons.

Bliss had not worked alone. Although Murdock was instrumental in the Los Angeles move, the Music Center residency would also never have happened without Michael Newton of the Music Center's Performing Arts Council. Newton had first seen the company in 1966. It hooked him, and unlike anyone else within the Music Center, he knew firsthand whereof he spoke. "I feel we gave the company a whole new shot in the arm," he told Draegin in 1985. "The company's invigoration, I think, dates to the L.A. arrangement. It would have to. You wander around the wilderness and you're on the edge of calamity after calamity, and then you find, to a degree, a place of refuge. Robert said on the first night of the season in '83 that he felt he'd come home when he played in this house. It's probably true. Stability doesn't buy the esthetics. But also, you can have the greatest vision in the world, but if you don't have money, you're not going to work for very long."[19]

But Newton would die of an AIDS-related illness in October 1986 and the Los Angeles residency, a daily gamble, would never recover from the loss. Indeed, the Music Center had been woefully unprepared. By 1985, the residency was teetering on the brink of collapse mostly because the Music Center's tight schedule did not allow for the company to expand its seasons and, in any sense of the word, to develop into a true resident. Joffrey had not lived up to his part of the bargain, which was to present other dance events at the Dorothy Chandler Pavilion and to provide the staff capable of performing that function, but he had reasoned that if the Joffrey could not perform as much as it had been promised there, why should other companies be given the weeks?

Unable to weather Newton's and, in 1988, Joffrey's deaths, and Arpino's acrimonious struggle in 1990 with Bliss, Murdock, and Pennie Curry, among others, the Music Center residency formally ended in 1991. But throughout the company's eight-year relationship with the Performing Arts Council of the Music Center, some of the very basics were never supplied to the troupe. The studios, for example, never had mirrors, which dancers need to correct their line. The company was shortchanged on rehearsal space and time, and on offices. The Music Center's unrealistic contract with the Joffrey had called for the company to be ready to move its operations to Los Angeles by August 30, 1984.

"Quite obviously, we put this together on paper, but the implementation of it doesn't always follow the blueprint laid out," said Newton in January 1985. "We didn't know where the company was going to perform. Five weeks was as much as we could find this year. The contract signed by all parties calls for the Joffrey to move its principal administrative offices here, but it can't simply move and then have to rehearse the ballets on the streets. . . . This has been a nightmare, but what gives me hope is the consistency of Robert Joffrey's vision. All the news from the box office has been good, and the press has treated the company well."[20]

In 1985, however great his disappointment with Los Angeles, Joffrey had compelling reasons to hold on to the spectacular Dorothy Chandler Pavilion and sweeten his relations with the Music Center's administrators. He still wanted to realize major ballets on that stage. "My father once told me that I could do anything if I worked enough hours," he told *People* magazine, adding, "You have to dream like a rich man and work like a laborer; the trick is to take the risks."[21]

On October 29, 1985, Aladar Marberger learned that he had Kaposi's sarcoma, a rare form of skin cancer that is associated with the AIDS virus. Programs to test people for infection with the virus had become available. Sometime around then, Leeper learned from a colleague in Manhattan that Joffrey had tested HIV-positive and been put on the drug AZT. Whereas Marberger was outspoken about his illness and discussed his "spirited way of dealing with the disease" in several newspapers and such magazines as *Time* and *Vanity Fair,* as well as in a television documentary,[22] Joffrey elected to be silent.

"Robert did not open up to Aladar about AIDS, but Robert was so proud that Aladar could be what he couldn't be," said Barbara Schwartz. "Robert admired Aladar's courage to speak out in public and draw people's attention to finding a cure."[23]

"AIDS was not a gay issue for Aladar," said Donna Marberger. "It was a disease, and he wanted to break the stigma. He [put] down people who hid from it. But he loved Robert and respected his privacy, even though it made him so sad not to be able to talk about AIDS with him. They were both so scared."[24]

After Ben Sommers, president of Capezio Ballet Makers and Estelle's husband, had died, Joffrey called her every night. "I think Aladar and I were the only two people who knew about his health," said Sommers. "He was ashamed."[25]

"There is no question about it. AZT is not given for the common cold," said Leeper. "It's an unquestionable truth. Robert Joffrey was HIV-positive and developed AIDS. As to his own realization of that fact, I think he can perhaps be forgiven. So many people feel invincible. They couldn't be sick, they couldn't have anything really wrong with them. There are people who are informed that they have HIV-positive blood and refuse to hear it."[26]

Other factors contributed toward Joffrey's heightened sense of life's brevity: on June 22, 1985, Joffrey's mother, who suffered from dementia, died of renal failure at the age of eighty-nine. Joffrey could not bring himself to sell off his boyhood home in Seattle. He was in denial about the news he had received about the terminal nature of his disease. In 1985, though, reporter Lois Draegin spent more than two weeks with him, on and off, including celebrating New Year's Eve, 1984, with him and Arpino in their Greenwich Village home. Joffrey opened up to Draegin as he did to few other interviewers; it seemed to be the time to tell his life story and set the record straight. Although he ignored his prognosis, he spent every minute he had, from then until the end, in the theater, struggling to complete his dream as he had imagined it. The deadline of his health compelled him. The disappointment of the Music Center's failure to live up to its contract was negligible by comparison.

During her interviews with Joffrey, Draegin wrote detailed notes on Joffrey and Arpino's redbrick walk-up on MacDougal Street, which had become famous in the dance world for its museum-like atmosphere, especially at Christmas. It would be the subject of an *Architectural Digest* story, and the rooms were like an inside view of Joffrey's mind, as well as a retrospective of the Joffrey Ballet repertoire:

Floor to ceiling, everywhere, paintings, prints, photos, a combination of dark antique portraits, nineteenth century ballerina lithographs. Where there aren't paintings on the walls there are dark shelves of books and more books, dance, ballet, art. Marble fireplaces, heavy wooden hutches, curved velvet settees.

In the dining room they combine a collection of antlers and dark portraits—no one's ancestors. Ancestors appropriated for effect and esthetics (not unlike company esthetics—appropriate best of old and new, preserve, in an American form for consumption and enjoyment—that might bristle purists, but then, this crowded room works). The central portrait in the living room is one Joffrey bought because it looks like his mother.

The Christmas poinsettias are everywhere. The magnificent tree full of ornaments collected from their travels. The house is decorated with masses of balloons. Decorated with the concept that more is better. Presents upon presents. Even one for me.

Joffrey's room, a space dominated more by books and prints than its narrow bed. He takes me out to the porch they built—a six-foot-long deck that looks out on the Village. He loves to sit out here and drink his morning tea. He can't wait to show me the real prime collectibles—a rare photo of Pavlova, a photo of Nijinsky, an original litho of Pas de Quatre, *a photo of Mary Ann Wells, a book on Spanish dance, photos of the company at the Bolshoi, a costume sketch for the Chinese Conjuror in* Parade, *a framed piece of the graffiti used during the original* Deuce Coupe.

A generous satisfied man, surrounds himself with objects that fascinate, people who are loyal. [Arpino, Diane Lembo Talley, Herb Migdoll, and Jonathan Watts are downstairs.] Loyalty is overall feeling. Nothing random about it. He's the locus of all the activity.[27]

After the New Year's party, Draegin traveled with Joffrey and Arpino to Los Angeles, intending to assess the company's bicoastal residency for the *New York Times Magazine* and to watch Cranko's *Romeo and Juliet* being fitted into the Music Center. By 1985, aside from *Romeo and Juliet*, several major projects were in development: the reconstruction of Nijinsky's *Sacre du printemps*, which was being undertaken by Millicent Hodson and Kenneth Archer, and Joffrey's own production of *The Nutcracker*. Joffrey wanted to produce a nineteenth-century classical ballet to a Tchaikovsky score. He conceived his *Nutcracker* as an American version, set during the Victorian era. Replicas of Victorian American toys that he had started collecting when he was a boy would be placed under the ballet's Christmas tree and subsequently into the hands of the party children. He would build *The Nutcracker* out of his life; the generous atmosphere that Draegin soaked up from her New Year's Eve at MacDougal Street would suffuse the ballet. To prepare the dancers for its classical demands, Joffrey appointed

Richard Englund to be the director of Joffrey II in May 1985 and antici-
pated asking Englund to collaborate with him on choreographing *The
Nutcracker*. They had both been students of Ivan Novikoff and Mary Ann
Wells in Seattle; this would be their first experience working together.
Jeremy Blanton, a former Joffrey member, succeeded Maria Grandy as the
Joffrey II associate director. Englund's wife, Gage Bush, also a former Jof-
frey dancer, was hired to be ballet mistress. (Both Englund and Bush had
recently lost their positions as the founders and directors of American Bal-
let Theatre II; cost-cutting was the stated reason.) Joffrey's mandate to
Englund and Bush was to make the young up-and-comers pure of line and
technically strong enough for *Nutcracker, Les Sylphides, The Sleeping
Beauty*, and more Bournonville, Ashton, and Balanchine.

The selection of Englund and Bush for Joffrey II was, in part, Joffrey's
way of safeguarding himself against Bliss's inevitable takeover. Joffrey
easily awarded those jobs to Englund and Bush because Sally Bliss had
surrendered her position as Joffrey II's director without complaint or
argument in the middle of 1985. She would later say that she had hoped
that Joffrey would interpret her resignation as the cue to offer her a position at his side with the main company. The Blisses believed they always
had the Joffrey Ballet's best interests in mind, and their loyalty to Joffrey
could be substantiated. In 1985, Bliss was sometimes spending as much
as fourteen hours a day on Joffrey-related tasks, while he simultaneously
held his full-time position as general manager of the Met. He had supported Joffrey 100 percent—even Joffrey said so—on the production of
Cranko's *Romeo and Juliet*, which was costing the company close to a
million. Sally Bliss, claiming that she raised $150,000 for Joffrey II over
the fifteen years she was with the second company, said, "I gave my life,
my blood, my soul, and I loved Bob Joffrey."[28]

But Joffrey mistrusted their words and actions, and in his final years,
he intended to surround himself with people to whom he could delegate
responsibility and then confidently turn his back. "Bob was very concerned when he brought me in to direct that I develop a clear, classical
image," said Englund. "He was anxious for the company's future to be
along the lines of any true classical company. It was my position to be as
understanding as possible."[29]

Englund felt he was being "groomed" to eventually, take an artistic
position with the company, and indeed, in Joffrey's final will and testament, he was named the associate director with Arpino as director.
Although Joffrey would posthumously be accused of having been unprepared for the inevitable, he was clear-eyed about the company. He knew
what he wanted for its future, and he prepared for it to run without him,
telling Englund in 1985 that "its continuity would be maintained"
through the classical repertoire.[30]

CHAPTER 27

Sacrifices

In 1985, people beyond Joffrey's most intimate circle began to realize that he did not seem himself. He asked one of his dancers, who had been with him for ten years and been recently trying to break out as a choreographer, to produce a piece for the company. Philip Jerry choreographed *Hexameron* and invited Christian Holder to design the costumes. Meeting with Joffrey for final approval of the designs, Holder noticed something strange. Joffrey was colorless and uninterested in the drawings. After a cursory glance, he waved his approval. Where were his energy and enthusiasm? Ordinarily, Joffrey would bustle around the table, pencil twirling in the fingers of one hand or fingers snapping, eyes beaming, memories tumbling out of him. He would have been glad to see Holder and encouraging to Jerry. Holder wondered if he was sick.

Joffrey's episodes of looking pale and distracted stacked up like cards, but from the top each card looked the same and Joffrey was bluffing. "He should have been a diplomat," his mother had observed years earlier. Joffrey wanted nobody to know the truth, in part because, what good would it do? Telling people about his disease could only jeopardize the company's future. He believed a mainstream American ballet company could not afford to lose the image of propriety, security, and gentility.

"In the greater sense, [denial] by dance company administrators only entrenched what I believe to be the homophobic aspects of the business," commented Leslie E. Schoof, the Joffrey's director of operations at the time. "The reason for not stepping forward was twofold: it was certainly as much homophobic at that point [in 1985–86] as it was against AIDS. The fear for their company, whether they directed it, danced in it, or simply worked in it, was that somehow the exposure of this disease, and therefore homosexuality, was going to eliminate funding and the audience."[1]

As one of the first among leading figures in dance to have AIDS, Joffrey in time commanded the attention of both the dance and gay communities. They watched how he handled the suspicions. Some people were bitterly disappointed, even angry that Joffrey did not come forward; others accepted his right to privacy. Some simply believed he did not have AIDS. After he died, most of those from whom he had been careless about hiding the nature of his condition stated that they felt his reason for not going public was his profound sense that a sexually transmitted disease was not, to his mind, a noble way to go.

He preferred that people believe that that he had died from complications related to his asthma. Gerald Arpino, Rima Corben, Aladar Marberger, Herbert Migdoll, and Diane Lembo Talley, together with Corben's sister Roberta, a physical therapist, were Joffrey's primary caregivers when, by late 1987, he was forced to run the company from his sickbed. Joffrey officially appointed Talley his executive assistant, bestowing upon her the clout to work in his office at City Center and to act as his Joffrey Ballet mouthpiece should the need arise. Marberger lived on West Eleventh Street, which was practically around the corner from him and Arpino, but since Arpino was uncomfortable being in the same room with Marberger, Marberger was not at liberty to extend his concerns for Joffrey's well-being too far.

But in 1985, Joffrey's good days still vastly outnumbered his bad. As a dancer he was accustomed to reading his body's messages. The only difference was that he was now acutely aware that the difference between being alive and being dead was the presence of the body. "I have to be very careful of what I eat, because I want my body to function," he told Draegin in 1985. "I think one should take care of one's body. It's the only thing one has."[2]

As he had found throughout his adult life, he still only needed four to five hours of sleep. He considered his low maintenance the "gift" that had perhaps allowed him to succeed with the Joffrey Ballet. He worked while others slept. At night, he exerted complete control over his world, turning on the classical music and mapping out new repertory. There were no phone calls, no interruptions. Having announced on October 2, 1985, in Los Angeles that Sir Frederick Ashton had consented to let the company mount a production of his *Fille mal gardée* and that a revival of Nijinsky's *Sacre* and a production of *Nutcracker* were also forthcoming, Joffrey had a lot to ponder after midnight. With *Fille,* the dancers would build on Cranko's *Romeo and Juliet,* in which they had proven that they could captivate audiences for a full evening. *Fille,* being comic and by Ashton, was entirely different in style. But it was equally demanding in requiring the dancers to evolve their characters over more than one act. *Fille* would be directed by Alexander Grant, who squared in with Joffrey's other plans. Grant would revive Ashton's *Dream* for Los Angeles in 1987, and as a character dancer of the highest order, he would be asked to assume the role of Drosselmeyer in *Nutcracker.*

Joffrey was indulging in reminiscences. He pointedly admitted to his friend Richard Philp around this time that through the repertory he was restricting himself to "people who I really felt comfortable working with . . . comfortable exchanging ideas with, people I've respected for many years and am happy to bring all together."[3]

With *Fille*, Grant and John David Ridge and John Wilson (as second cast Widow Simone) would return to his fold. Each man was of paramount significance. Grant and Joffrey went back to 1949 and the years during the 1960s dance boom when the Royal Ballet routinely visited New York. In *The Dream* as the original Bottom, and in *Fille* as the clueless, endearing Alain, Grant had given performances that were among Joffrey's most cherished memories. He and Joffrey had been jurors on the International Ballet Competition panels since 1979, which had intensified their bond. As for costume designer John David Ridge, he had first worked with Joffrey manufacturing the masks for the company's premiere production of *The Green Table* in 1967. He had also designed the costumes for Joffrey's last ballet, *Postcards*, in 1980. Joffrey respected his work and counted him as an important personal friend. Then there was John Wilson, a charter Joffrey member who had been Joffrey's first musical adviser, arranging John Field's piano scores for his most enduring ballet, *Pas des Déesses*. On the maiden 1956 station wagon tour through the South, Wilson had jumped into the orchestra pit to play the piano for *Pas des Déesses* after dancing three previous ballets. He had virtually defined the Joffrey Ballet's legendary reputation for versatility. As Widow Simone, he would reprise the role that he had danced in the Fernand Nault version of *Fille* for Joffrey in the 1950s and early 1960s.

With *Sacre*, to the famous Stravinsky score, Joffrey was summoning the ghost of Nijinsky once again to his stage. He had been corresponding with Millicent Hodson since 1980, hoping that she and her husband and collaborator, Kenneth Archer (an art historian who was reconstructing Nicholas Roerich's original costumes for *Le Sacre du printemps*), would remember their spoken agreement to approach him when the moment arrived to resurrect the ballet onstage. He had borne an inestimable fondness for Hodson ever since 1971 and the Berkeley days. They were kindred spirits. He could not wait to collaborate with her and Archer. "I'm sure Diaghilev would have smiled to see us discussing our forthcoming revival of Nijinsky's *Sacre* over high tea at the Savoy; the perfect place and so in keeping with the tradition," he wrote in a letter to Hodson and Archer on October 3, 1985. "I want to tell you both again how excited I am to know at last that this production will indeed be possible. I am most grateful to you both for all your efforts to make this dream a reality."[4]

With *The Nutcracker*, it was he who had been amassing material and planning for almost a decade and a half. This was his baby and he put everything he had into it, but he was also willing to wait until the other two projects—*Fille* in 1986 and *Sacre* in 1987—were launched.

In 1986, Joffrey began saying farewell: he and Richard Englund returned to Jacob's Pillow, where in 1952 both of them had been chosen by Ted Shawn to show their works on a program of Trudy Goth's Choreographers' Workshop. The Pillow was the scene of Joffrey's first legitimate choreographic debut, and the place where the company had first performed after the Harkness debacle. Joffrey and Englund stayed for two days in 1986, perusing the archives, touring the grounds, talking to people who remembered them and who had known Shawn. "I don't think the visit had a stated purpose," noted Norton Owen, the Pillow's archivist. "They were very open to being here, very appreciative and down-to-earth. Both spoke warmly about their beginnings here and were full of detail about it. They spoke about what an important time it had been for them in their careers, remembering it very fondly."⁵

In 1986, Joffrey went to the Joffrey Summer Workshop in San Antonio for the last time and taught the last class of his life. And in 1986, members of the Performing Arts Council of the Music Center reevaluated the Joffrey Ballet residency. That year the Joffrey Ballet was alloted six weeks at the Music Center. According to the original plan, there should have been twelve weeks. The bicoastal deal seemed to be falling apart.

On October 16, 1986, in celebration of the company's thirtieth anniversary, *La Fille mal gardée* premiered at City Center. Of all the Ashton ballets acquired by Joffrey, *Fille* was the most easily received. Critics who had so often in the past grumbled over the company's failure to accomplish Ashton's lyrical style rhapsodized about *Fille*. After eight Ashton ballets, the dancers had absorbed the proper attitude and could reflect his style with comprehension. Alexander Grant and Faith Worth had taught them well. *Fille* called attention to Tina LeBlanc as Lise, David Palmer as Colas, and Edward Stierle as Alain. They were dancers who could deliver to Joffrey something that he always prized—absolute joyousness in dancing, along with conscientious attention to technique. LeBlanc was his new classic ballerina, Stierle his new virtuoso and energetic comedian.

After writing about Stanley Holden's great performance as Widow Simone (reviving the role for which he had been originally cast by Ashton in 1960), Joan Acocella talked about LeBlanc in *Dance Magazine*, saying:

> LeBlanc, to begin with, looks *like a country girl. She is dark-haired, rosy, and well built, and her body, when still, has a genuine repose, like a Degas dancer. More important, she is a natural actress and a robust dancer. Indeed, the two qualities are one. What makes her dancing so red-blooded is*

*that the drama is flowing through its veins, making her plié deep, cutting
her second position big and clear, throwing her arms back wide, wide, in her
huge jetés. And what makes her acting so natural is that it is in the dancing.
. . . But LeBlanc made it seem utterly spontaneous, as if, her cup of love
running over, she were asking us to take some: "Here is my happiness—
share it with me."*[6]

Le Blanc was an unconventional ballerina, a Joffrey ballerina, trained
originally by Marcia Dale Weary and then elevated through Joffrey II by
Sally Bliss. She had joined the company in 1984. As often in the past, Joffrey would fight within himself to accept someone of her short stature
and ample bosom; he would make her second cast Sugar Plum Fairy.
Despite her training, which did not belong entirely to his school, she
embodied Joffrey's esthetic values. Her frequent partner in the years to
come would be Stierle, who would be the first cast Fritz and the Snow
Prince in *The Nutcracker.*

Also in the fall 1986 season, Joffrey opened his repertoire to include
Mark Morris's *Esteemed Guests* (music by C. P. E. Bach). Ever since Lois
Draegin had called his attention to Morris over a year before, Joffrey had
not been able to stop talking about him. He would ask anyone who
entered his office what they thought about the controversial young
choreographer and modern dancer, who was born, raised, and introduced to all kinds of movement in Seattle. This was vintage Joffrey: skirt-
ing the business at hand by directing conversation to a new dance
personage who fascinated him. In *Esteemed Guests,* Morris "used a ballerina, the way ballet says one should, but he gave her no partner, so that
in the slow movement she seemed to wander forlorn in search of the
dance she was supposed to be doing," wrote Joan Acocella in her biography, *Mark Morris.*[7] Only the second piece by Morris for a ballet company,
Esteemed Guests did not linger in Joffrey's repertoire, although Morris
pursued his curiosity about classically trained dancers long after. He
choreographed many original roles for Baryshnikov.

When the 1986 fall season concluded, Joffrey devoted himself to
Nijinsky's *Sacre du printemps,* the 1913 collaboration between Nijinsky,
Stravinsky, and Roerich, whose premiere caused a riot at the Théâtre du
Châtelet in Paris. At that time, the performers could scarcely hear the
music because of the ruckus in the audience. People shoved hatpins into
each other, thwacked their neighbors with their canes, and bellowed in
protest of the score and, to a lesser extent, the choreography.

Sacre unleashed the energy inherent in modernism. A groundbreaker,
the original *Sacre* would, however, be performed only five times in Paris
and three in London, and then Diaghilev retired it from his repertoire.
Nijinsky was his lover, but the young dancer had developed a relation-

ship with Romola de Pulszky, a Polish dancer. The two had left for the South American tour of Diaghilev's Ballets Russes after the Paris season in which *Sacre* premiered (May 29, 1913), and aboard the ship, Nijinsky's proposal of marriage to de Pulszky was accepted. Diaghilev then banished Nijinsky and his ballets. ·

As a young student at the University of California, Berkeley, Millicent Hodson had zeroed in on Nijinsky in her studies. When Joffrey visited with his company in 1971, he met Hodson. She was wearing a T-shirt dress that went straight to the floor and fit her like a tube. When she bent down, she had had to twist and flatten herself in a tight lunge because there wasn't room for her knees to separate wide. It made her look two-dimensional, like an Egyptian frieze figure. Joffrey commented that the move looked just like something out of Nijinsky's *Après-midi d'un faune*. Hodson's ears perked up. She remembered, "That's what led us into the conversation on Nijinsky. I told him how I'd started this documentary project collecting material on *Le Sacre du printemps*, and how I dreamed of seeing it onstage and that I was going to try to find all the missing pieces. He said, 'Well, that's a very good idea.' "[8]

In February 1980, word reached Joffrey that Hodson—by this time a choreographer and a doctoral candidate—was in the throes of reconstructing *Sacre*. Joffrey immediately contacted her. Hodson wrote back:

> *After some consideration, I feel certain it is too early in the process for me to discuss the reconstruction, so I will not be coming to meet you tomorrow. . . .*
>
> *The choreography for* Le Sacre *has truly been lost. It is not among the Diaghilev ballets which had simply been put out of repertory and so now require putting the pieces back together. In the case of* Le Sacre *each single piece—each movement and its relationship to the music—requires an arduous search. . . . In a year or two it is possible that we could have a constructive discussion about the project.*[9]

Curiously, however, a few months later, in June 1980, Hodson published the results of her *Sacre* research in *Dance Magazine*. John Neumeier, director of the Hamburg Ballet, and Bruce Marks of the Boston Ballet immediately attempted to produce the reconstruction. Robert Craft, Stravinsky's biographer, told Hodson that if she went ahead, she would incur the "enmity of the entire Stravinsky establishment."[10] Craft also tried to procure the project for Gillian Lynne, the choreographer of the Andrew Lloyd Webber musical *Cats*.

The *Sacre* revival was a much-desired and very polemical project, in part because Stravinsky had claimed as late as 1967 that he *and* Nijinsky had choreographed the ballet. Stravinsky had earlier appropriated Roerich's credit for the scenario, and he had continued to promote the idea of his dominance in the collaboration. Some still wished to protect Stravinsky after the composer's death, and Hodson encountered resistance.

Two years later, as Hodson had suggested, she, Joffrey, and Kenneth Archer were working together. Hodson had been awarded a $10,000 grant from the L. J. Skaggs and Mary C. Skaggs Foundation, and Joffrey's main purpose at this point was to build funding for *Sacre*. While his enthusiasm was great in person, once Hodson and Archer were out the door, Joffrey strangely did not go after funding even though Hodson had already set the stage. Again, he vanished at the instant his presence was most needed. Since he did not respond to Hodson's letters, she could have gone elsewhere. She had other offers, but she held on to Joffrey.

On September 14, 1985, they signed a tentative agreement. Joffrey, it seemed, had needed to feel that he could defend the project; putting a ballet together step by step, gesture by gesture, note by note, laid him open to claims that he was inventing Nijinsky and had taken reconstructing too far. He maintained that his company was the world's storehouse for Diaghilev ballets. *Sacre* would be the crowning achievement—he had never before achieved a revival so complex, nor one that had been so monumentally expensive. To accomplish this daunting task, Joffrey depended on the constant assistance of Penelope Curry.

In 1986, Pennie Curry was general director of the Joffrey Ballet. For years she had served as Joffrey's strong right arm. She had worked behind the scenes at Joffrey II and moved through the main company as production stage manager (where Joffrey felt she accomplished her best work), lighting designer (trained by Jennifer Tipton), production budget manager, arranger of transportation—there was not any production angle that Curry had not covered.

By 1986, it was observed that Curry could practically read Joffrey's mind. He did not receive her as a friend, however. Rejected by his inner circle, Curry was adopted by Tony Bliss, who had trained her for another promotion, to the lofty position of executive director. Bliss, in fact, had insisted on Curry's appointment as general director, sharing top billing above the dancers' names on the program. Joffrey had not wanted her up there with him and Arpino. Bliss had promised Joffrey that he would not proceed with Curry's accession to general directorship, and then he broke his word. He repeated the transgression when Curry was elevated to executive director in 1987. Bliss thus fixed Curry as a point of conflict between himself and Joffrey.

But she was committed to Joffrey's vision, although Joffrey did not trust that commitment, and this difference would eventually affect the way in which he wrote his will. As for *Sacre*, the reconstruction benefited from Curry's dedication. He accepted her unstinting efforts; without them, *Sacre* might not have been accomplished in time for him to see it.

In June 1987, the company relocated for several weeks to the University of Iowa, where rehearsals for *Sacre* and *Nutcracker* commenced. Joffrey's workshop principle was still an operating, fundamental part of the company's philosophy, because the university had for some years sponsored the company and Joffrey II. Hancher Auditorium/The University of Iowa Foundation was a major backer of *The Nutcracker*. The Iowa patrons connected with the project seemed to possess an inveterate understanding of a ballet company's needs. They gave Joffrey space and support—commodities that were unavailable in Los Angeles and too expensive in New York.

Joffrey did not travel to Iowa City with the company, which confounded many because the two ballets were understood to be so important to him. His excuse was asthma. Scott Barnard assumed principal responsibility for producing *The Nutcracker*, while Arpino choreographed, also with Barnard close by and Diane Lembo Talley present. *Sacre* belonged to Hodson and Archer, who worked with pianist Stanley Babin, and with Beatriz Rodriguez as the first cast Chosen One and Carole Valleskey as the second. The afternoons were reserved for *Sacre*'s complex group sections with forty-six dancers.

On September 30, 1987, the curtain rose on *Le Sacre du printemps* at the Dorothy Chandler Pavilion in Los Angeles. An earthquake strong enough to level buildings occurred later that night. Few who had been in the audience could help wondering about the significance of Mother Nature's seismic response. *Sacre* is from first to last a ritual; a virgin is chosen who will be sacrificed so that the world can be reborn to springtime.

"Instead of the rioting that marked the Paris premiere by Serge Diaghilev's Ballets Russes in 1913, tonight's keyed-up crowd at the Dorothy Chandler Pavilion responded with a standing ovation," wrote Alan M. Kriegsman, chief dance critic of the *Washington Post*. "Hodson, Archer, and principal dancer Beatriz Rodriguez, who portrayed the Chosen One, were pelted with bouquets, and a veritable fusillade of bravos greeted Robert Joffrey whose unwavering persistence of vision made the miracle possible.

"The new production of 'Sacre' grabs one at a deep, gut level, just as the original must have done for the spectators of its day, favorably disposed or not. That's because the ballet, in its very choreographic, musical and visual form, speaks to us of profound, primal and timeless matters."[11]

Stravinsky's music had shocked people at first, and it was not until two years after the ballet's 1913 premiere, when Stravinsky's score continued to be played in concert, that audiences recognized its seminal value. Stravinsky revolutionized rhythm, but it was Nicholas Roerich, the painter, an expert in ancient Slavic ritual, who provided the ballet's scenario and the raw, savage colors and geometric patterns that provided the setting for the avant-garde.

Hodson observed, too, that "every time in this century when there is a new burst of creative activity, there's a return to indigenous culture."[12] Unlike the other Diaghilev Ballets Russes works that had launched major movements in dance, music, and décor, such as Nijinsky's *L'Après-midi d'un faune*, Massine's *Parade*, and Fokine's *Petrouchka*, *Le Sacre du printemps*, based on pre-Christian Russian folklore, echoed real experience. Although hard evidence suggested human sacrifice was not actually practiced in the society depicted by the ballet, the sense that the ballet was anchored to authentic ritual prevailed. "What was going to be performed wasn't just a dance," explained Archer. "Everything was done for a purpose."[13]

Many critics in 1987 anticipated the chance to see a ritualistic ballet; some approached Joffrey's premiere having pored over books about myth and ritual and having weighed the pertinent cultural history issues. Marcia B. Siegel described her first impression in the *Christian Science Monitor:* "For me, the event was overwhelming. The ballet in the flesh exceeds every sensational claim in its dossier. It is tremendous—emotionally powerful, structurally ingenious, and beautiful besides."[14] And, for the *Hudson Review,* she described *Sacre*'s unfolding panoramic scenes: "[The first act begins on] a day in early spring when the sun first appears over the arctic horizon, and the people emerge to dance once more on the earth after the winter's hibernation. In little organized groups, then all together, they celebrate their survival, look for auguries of the future, enact ritual combats and matings, and, after the tribal Sage has kissed the ground, they gaze straight at the sun and fling themselves into spasms of archaic joy."[15]

Extremely ill, Joffrey rose to the occasion and flew across the country to witness the Los Angeles premiere and bow with his company at the end. His participation in *Sacre*'s rehearsals had been greater than anyone had expected. "Mercifully," said Hodson, "when he was so sick, he came to technical rehearsals to put it on the stage."[16] Archer added, "It was very important that he was there. He was the best artistic director because he had the whole thing in his mind with *Sacre*. He could make adjustments. Who else would bother to look in that detail so that he could say with total conviction, 'They [Hodson and Archer] have it'?"[17]

The reviews arrived over the next days, weeks, months, and years from that night in Los Angeles and subsequent performances of *Sacre*. It was accepted, not as *the* authentic Nijinsky choreography, but as a close approximation, and a fine piece of theater on its own terms. "This unprecedented attempt to revive Vaslav Nijinsky's lost choreography succeeds in revealing the full meaning of the ballet," wrote Anna Kissel-goff in the *New York Times*.[18] "From what one can tell, [Hodson's version of *Le Sacre*] was based on evidence too fragmentary to allow it to be counted as one of Nijinsky's works," commented Joan Acocella in the *New Yorker*.[19]

Joffrey returned home to MacDougal Street and his condition worsened. He was admitted to New York University Hospital, where Jonathan Watts spent Thanksgiving with him.

"Bob was in a lot of discomfort," said Watts. "He was going through hell, that's what he was going through. He seemed pleased by the simple pleasures at that point, such as popcorn, which he craved. He wanted nothing complicated in the way of conversation. I heard him talking to Jerry on the phone and he said, 'I should never have gone to Los Angeles for the premiere of *Sacre*. My T-cell count is way down.'

"He never said, 'I have AIDS.' And I asked him, 'Bob, have you made any kind of preparations for what will happen to the Joffrey Ballet?'

"He said, 'I am going to direct the company. I am directing it right now.'

"I said, 'Why don't you just remove the burden from yourself for a while until you're feeling better, and put someone else in charge?'

"Once I got the idea that he wasn't acknowledging that he was going to die, I then just said, 'Well, try to do it as an interim measure anyway,' hoping that he would make intelligent, rational decisions while he still could. But he wasn't prepared to. He wasn't going to let go.

"Four months before his death, he had John David Ridge there in the hospital busy with the designs for *Nutcracker*, and he was going through them all, working on it. . . . He probably thought he could beat AIDS."[20]

CHAPTER 28

The Nutcracker

On December 10, 1987, at the University of Iowa's Hancher Auditorium, the company presented the world premiere of Joffrey's *Nutcracker.* He was unable to attend. Feeble, he rested in New York University Hospital, where the company members later phoned him. "There must have been a line of twenty people waiting to talk to Mr. Joffrey on the night of the premiere," said Francesca Corkle, who was now a teacher at the Joffrey School. "He sounded so weak, and he was teary, too."[1]

The next day, he watched a videotape of the opening with Herb Migdoll and Val Golovitser, his and Arpino's assistant. This is what he saw: The front curtain for Joffrey's last ballet is designed by Oliver Smith, the dean of American designers *(West Side Story, Rodeo, Fancy Free).* Painted at the top is a nutcracker in a handsome military uniform. He is surrounded by toys, including a kite with a face, a lamb, a bear on wheels, and a soldier. Behind this curtain a party at the Stahlbaum's rollicks. (Diane Lembo Talley, a behind-the-scenes collaborator on the production and the person in charge of the children, said that she thinks the stairway leading down to the Stahlbaum living room was based on the Arpino family stairway at 297 Pelton Avenue.)[2]

The Stahlbaum house is drawn from New York City's upper-class society around 1860, before the Age of Innocence. From the high ceiling, an imposing chandelier of many brilliant crystal strands casts a festive, shimmering light; an ornate fireplace opens upon two needlepoint stockings and throws warmth into the formal-looking room that abounds with lively, jubilant guests. Near the front door, an austere grandfather clock, topped by an owl whose wings spread each time the clock strikes, summons the final guest. Dr. Drosselmeyer surges into the room with an air of nervous importance. He flings his black cape lined with purple satin— the color that Joffrey most associates with Mary Ann Wells, the color that he believes protects, heals, and radiates hope—over his arms and around his shoulders.

(When Joffrey spoke about Drosselmeyer to Richard Philp, who later in 1988 would become editor in chief of *Dance Magazine,* he implied that he was talking about himself. Similarly, he seemed to view Clara as the personification of his audience. She is everyone he performed for, created for, worked hard for; she is why he has tried, why he has cared so much. He said: "Through Drosselmeyer [read: me], Clara [read: the audience] is able to see things and to experience things that she would never have the opportunity to experience otherwise, because he is a magician, a mystic, and a strange person. We do it a little bit differently in that Drosselmeyer is not an ancient man. He's intelligent and bright and charming and mischievous and very mysterious. He is the one who has conjured this whole thing up. He has done all these special things for Clara because he, in a way, is this eccentric person who loves Clara as Clara loves him.")[3]

Drosselmeyer has a gift for each child at the party. (Sixty children are in Joffrey's $1-million production, though not all participate in the opening scene.) The children rejoice in their gifts. Abandoning themselves to twirling and leaping gleefully toward the downstage area, they lift the real wooden Indian or the doll-sized rocking horse or the new brass doll bed with lace cover and pillow and show them to us. The qualities of beneficence and spontaneity define the first act.

Drosselmeyer beckons Clara to descend the stairs, which she does as if in a trance. She curls up on the Victorian settee and he scatters a handful of silver glitter-dust over her. ("She is a more interesting person because of the dream," commented Joffrey.)[4] She dreams that the male nutcracker doll Drosselmeyer has given her and with whom she has fallen in love grows to life size. (The Nutcracker doll looks like Joffrey's photographer and friend Herbert Migdoll. He has large, wistful, sad, sweet eyes like Migdoll's. Even Migdoll notices the resemblance.)

After the battleground scene, in which the Nutcracker and Clara reign victorious, Drosselmeyer leads her to the Land of Snow, where the dashing, split-jumping, irrepressible Snow Prince resides. (The Snow Prince is pure Arpino, who is one of the four choreographers on this production. George Verdak, Scott Barnard, and Joffrey are the others. Richard Englund had originally been assigned, but was let go by Joffrey early on. Arpino was "wonderful" about fabricating movement, Joffrey said of him on this project.[5] It is not just the movement he makes, it is that he has been in a good spirit, in the right frame of mind to help Joffrey when Joffrey needed him. He has been a prince. Scott Barnard, too, had helped much more than anyone gave him credit for, but Joffrey knew this. It did not go unnoticed that Barnard was an excellent ballet master when Joffrey was too ill to be at rehearsals every day to pull the production together.)

The third act takes place in the Kingdom of Sweets, a series of divertissements, capped by the pas de deux for the Sugar Plum Fairy and her Cavalier. But it is the Ukrainian dance called Nougat that seems closest to

Joffrey's identity. (The three boys in the *trepak* are wearing pants that assume the shape of mushroom caps when the dancers whirl. These pants are designed after Joffrey's *trepak* pants from his performances with Ivan Novikoff's troupe at the bond rallies in Seattle. He had kept a pair for old times' sake and asked John David Ridge to copy them. They call to mind the boy who went to Novikoff's school, thinking he was going to learn to tap dance, then discovering that Novikoff taught Russian folk dancing and ballet. That boy reveled in the physicality of movement, the heady sensation of jumping, and the challenge of gliding through air, defying his teacher, who had told him he should under no circumstances appear in front of people onstage, that he should bow and leave, that he shouldn't be a dancer.)

Drosselmeyer steps forward with a tambourine, upon which he taps a bouncy rhythm that summons Mother Ginger from the wings. (Joffrey, the tambourine dancer, dazzled customers for small change in his parents' restaurant.)

At the ballet's conclusion, a colorful hot-air balloon descends, and Drosselmeyer and Clara step into its basket. The balloon rises, and they wave good-bye.

On December 23, 1987, Robert Joffrey signed his last will and testament in front of witnesses Diane Lembo Talley, John David Ridge, and Val Golovitser. "During my life, I have sought to make a contribution to the world of dance," it read. "Ever since I formed my first company in 1956, my primary artistic goals have been to commission new ballets from contemporary choreographers and to revive twentieth century classics. . . . As my legacy to the world, it is my express desire that the Joffrey Foundation continue its services and contributions to dance. . . . I request that the Board of Directors appoint my very good friend and close associate, Gerald Arpino, as my successor Artistic Director of the Joffrey Foundation. I further desire and request that my very good friend and close associate, Richard B. Englund, currently the Artistic Director of Joffrey II, be appointed as Associate Director with Gerald Arpino and as General Administrator of the Joffrey Foundation. It is also my express desire and request that the Board of Directors appoint Scott Barnard as Chief Ballet Master of Joffrey Foundation."

These were his wishes. They were not done deals. None of what Joffrey had requested was legal and binding to his board of directors, who would, after he died, have to vote upon the positions that he discussed. Shockingly to many, the will did not mention Pennie Curry, whom they had assumed Joffrey would name to remain as the executive director. Nor was Sally Bliss mentioned; she had lost her place to Richard Englund. The will also specified that Arpino and Edith D'Addario were to divide equally Joffrey's shares in the Joffrey School. His personal effects, jewelry, furniture, and household goods were to be split among Arpino, D'Addario, and Aladar Marberger. Arpino and D'Addario were appointed coexecutors of his will.

His signature looked nothing like its former self; its round, bold shapes had collapsed, the lines were tentative, faint, like the markings of an old person's pen.

A week later to the day, on December 30, *The Nutcracker* opened in New York at City Center, and Joffrey, who had been discharged from the hospital, was determined to attend the performance of a ballet that he had worked on intermittently for fifteen years. He had not seen the dancers in months. They had been told that the AIDS rumors were false. They understood that Joffrey had been hospitalized because of his asthma, that one of his asthma medications had adversely affected his kidneys.

By December 30, he had lost so much weight that Arpino said his "heart could be seen beating beneath his pajamas like a hummingbird's wings."[6] He required a wheelchair to move from room to room. Arpino, Migdoll, Talley, Curry, and Corben tried to dissuade him from donning his tuxedo for the New York debut. He was frail, but he had a mission. He was choreographing his final curtain call in scenes here described by Diane Solway, author of the biography of Edward Stierle, *A Dance Against Time:*

> The houselights were dimming when Golovitser wheeled Robert Joffrey to the enclosed sound booth at the back of the orchestra, where he went unnoticed for almost the entire performance. . . . During the final divertissements of "The Kingdom of the Sweets," Joffrey turned to Pennie Curry, who was next to him in the sound booth. "I want to bow with my company," he said suddenly. "I don't think that's wise, Bob," Curry answered cautiously.* "To go onstage just as the curtain is going up, with the dancers not knowing how ill you are—I'm not sure they can emotionally handle it." Joffrey just grinned back at her. "I want to bow with my company," he repeated.
>
> . . . In the dark, Leslie Carothers almost tripped over Mr. Joffrey. She had danced the Snow Queen in the First Act and had come backstage to watch the end of the ballet. "I was completely stunned. Mr. Joffrey was such a vital man and here he was looking very, very ill. I went to the back of the wings and cried."[7]

---

*Roberta Corben, his physical therapist, told him simultaneously that there was not a problem. "You'll be able to do it," she said. Corben went backstage with him and showed Alexander Grant and the conductor, Allan Lewis, how to hold him. Corben did not expect him to walk, but only to stand.

The curtain came down, and Golovitser wheeled Joffrey to the center between Allan Lewis and Alexander Grant, who were also unprepared for Joffrey's dramatically changed appearance. Joffrey asked Grant to hold him up, while the wheelchair vanished into the wings. "When the curtain went up, his iron will, adrenaline, and love for his company made him let go of my hand, turn around, and raise his arms to salute the dancers," Grant recalled. "He was so weak and yet he stood for a moment on his own. The company burst into tears. The curtain came down. The wheelchair returned and he was taken off. That was the last most of us saw him."[8]

Incredibly, within a few weeks Joffrey was focusing on the next season, planning a reconstruction of Balanchine's so-called lost *Cotillon* (music by Chabrier, book by Boris Kochno, and décor by Christian Bérard), which would be carried out by Millicent Hodson and Kenneth Archer; a revival of Eugene Loring's classic *Billy the Kid;* and a production of James Kudelka's *Concerto Grosso.* There would also be a *Dance in America* television program on Hodson and Archer's reconstruction of *Le Sacre du printemps* for his company. Although Joffrey remained at home, he showed no signs of improvement.

Tony Bliss, without saying the words directly, began insisting that Joffrey accept reality and prepare for death. Who would carry on the artistic directorship? Bliss, who had no knowledge of the contents of Joffrey's will, arranged for a meeting with Richard Englund and Gage Bush Englund at his law office. He presumed that they would coerce Joffrey into acting rationally. "Tony opened the meeting by saying that this would be the first of several, and that when his wife, Sally, got back in town, the four of us were going to have to sit down and decide the future of the Joffrey," recalled Bush. "And Richard and I looked at each other, and Richard said, 'But, Tony, I don't understand. It's not like the leadership of the Joffrey has been suddenly wiped out.' Tony looked Richard straight in the eye and said, 'We all know there is no way that that company is going to be turned over to Arpino.'

"Richard and I gulped. Then I said, 'Well, Tony, I don't really think that we're the proper people for you to be having this kind of conversation with, because if you feel that Jerry is not adequate to be running the company—and I must admit I am very puzzled why you feel that way—then don't you think you should be having this conversation with your board members?' Tony's reply to that was, 'They don't do what I tell them to.' "[9]

The Englunds promptly left Bliss's office and reported Bliss's comments to Arpino. "It was very difficult when we knew the nature of Bob's illness, because we knew what the outcome was going to be," said Gage Bush Englund. "Richard and I made a few attempts with Bob by saying,

'Bob, while you're not around, chances are that Tony is going to go after Jerry. Don't you think you should take some steps when you're not active with the company to protect Jerry?'

"Well, Bob knew what we were talking about, but he just wasn't ready. I mean, he was going to get well. . . . Nobody was even to know that a will existed. . . . Bob was going to get well, and Bob did not have AIDS, so none of this could be discussed. . . . We were all sworn to secrecy about AIDS because Bob felt that the minute it became known, the board would do one of two things: it would resign and walk away, or it would replace him with Sally. It [AIDS] was a totally open secret, but Jerry and Rima and Herb said this must never get out."[10]

Then, one morning in early March, Joffrey summoned the Englunds to his house. When they arrived, Pennie Curry, Rima Corben, Herb Migdoll, Sally Bliss, Val Golovitser, and Jerry Arpino were standing around Joffrey's bedside. Joffrey had a press release that needed approval from the Englunds. On page three of the release, positioned where few but the most scrupulous dance writers and editors would notice it, Joffrey announced that the Englunds *plus* Sally Bliss were members of a newly formed advisory group that would be available for Arpino to call upon should the need arise. That bit of curious news was preceded by the first public statement about Joffrey's illness:

> During Mr. Joffrey's convalescence from his illness (diagnosed by his doctors as myositis, liver disease, and asthma), he will continue to work from his home, and Mr. Arpino will serve as his artistic liaison.

Bliss had long felt that he was having trouble raising funds for the company because people were worried about Joffrey's health. Arpino, Corben, and Migdoll claimed that Bliss had insisted on making a public statement. It was perhaps the hardest moment for Joffrey in his life, they said. He was being forced against his will to let go, to surrender the company, to admit that he was sick. That night his remaining strength dissipated, and the next morning, on March 11, he returned to the hospital. A week later he lapsed into a coma.

Arpino stayed with him instead of touring with the company to Chicago. The last time Joffrey spoke, he said to Arpino, "I love you and that must never be violated. Never." He also made clear to Arpino that the company was his now to direct and to defend. "I know the company is important, I know what it meant to Bob, and his words to me—making sure that I look after the company, take care of the company."[11] No matter what happened, "they" should not get the company, Joffrey told him. By "they," Arpino understood Joffrey to mean the Blisses. Bliss recalled Joffrey's final words to him thus: "Don't lose Pennie."[12]

On March 25, 1988, at six in the morning, Robert Joffrey died of hepatic, renal, and respiratory failure in New York University Hospital. He was fifty-nine years old.

"He never thought about death. Ever. It was a fluke, a dirty trick," Arpino said three weeks later in a conversation in the Village. "We had plans for the next twenty years. We were brought up on adversity. The best teacher we ever had was adversity. We were survivors. The love and the dedication and the commitment of our lives through this whole process is what made—makes—this company happen.

"I'm never going to be without him, because the plans are laid very carefully. He was a wise man. Oh, was he wise. Gentle and kind. Poised. Great poise. So we balanced each other. I've always said that about us. It's a new challenge. It's a new step. It's a change, but not that radical a change. It isn't going to be that severe. It's going to be an extension. The Joffrey was always changing, that's what gives me my strength, that's how I can bear this sorrow."[13]

On March 29, 1988, at Joffrey's funeral service at the Frank E. Campbell Funeral Home, Alex Ewing stood before the gathering, in a room full of white lilacs that Marberger had arranged in accordance with Joffrey's wishes. Concerned that the memorial would turn into a "rather sycophantic exercise, with everyone piling on tributes and adulations and getting further and further away from Bob,"[14] Ewing recalled what fun Joffrey could be late at night at a party: "He claps his hands and leans back laughing. For some reason it's catching, and you start thinking it's funny, although you don't really quite know why yet. Then he adds a bit to the story, and then another, and soon everyone's involved. I like to think of him like that. He could laugh at anyone and about everyone, yet he was never mean or malicious or cruel. He was a little guy, bigger than life."[15]

That day, Joffrey was cremated, and his ashes divided into three parts. One-third was placed at St. John the Divine Cathedral in Manhattan in a vault exactly one space over from that of Robert Blankshine. One-third was given to Arpino. One-third went to Seattle, where Diane Lembo Talley mixed it with his mother's ashes, which she had saved for him. Then she and her daughter, with Bill Leighton, Garth Rogers, and a friend, sailed out on Puget Sound. When their boat was aligned with Mary Ann Wells's home, they scattered the ashes on the water. "Unless the ashes are there," Joffrey had said, nothing can be created. He had spread himself across the United States, he had symbolically covered the spectrum of his experience, he had split himself into parts that he hoped were greater than the whole.

Afterword

In his will, Joffrey requested that the board of the Joffrey Foundation appoint Gerald Arpino to be his successor as the artistic director. A brief chronicle of Arpino's battle to claim his inheritance may well reflect current turmoil in the United States and mirror attitudes many Americans today hold toward the arts and themselves.

Three weeks after Joffrey's memorial, Anthony A. Bliss, cochairman of the board of directors of the Foundation for the Joffrey Ballet, assembled the company's trustees and managing directors in New York to read the contents of Joffrey's last will and testament. At this meeting, Arpino was voted in as artistic director. Scott Barnard was approved as ballet master, and Richard Englund, of his own accord, resigned as Arpino's artistic associate and chose, instead, to continue directing Joffrey II.

Joffrey had expressed no written wishes regarding the future of the management staff. Bliss wanted Penelope Curry to continue in her position as the company's executive director. He asked Arpino to leave the room (for some unfathomable reason Arpino complied), then the board members voted in favor of maintaining Curry. As executive director, Curry was responsible for arranging the troupe's engagements, shaping the company's direction from a marketing standpoint, developing a fund-raising stratagem, directing the administrative staff, and—most critical—working with the bicoastal board of trustees in New York and Los Angeles to pull off Arpino's artistic vision. But, in keeping with Bliss's design for a Joffrey Ballet hierarchy, one that he had slowly developed over more than twenty years, the executive director was now regarded as an equal to the artistic director. They were equal, but opposing, forces. It was the board that tipped the scales, the board that decided, evaluated, and mediated between the two. The troupe lacked a single leader.

"We are no longer trying to think about it as 'Bob's company' or 'Bob's vision.' It's a new time," said Curry. "Bob was a leader. . . . Now, more people, as opposed to one person, are pulling together to make it work."[1] While Joffrey was alive, Bliss had twice advanced Curry to higher ranks within the company without Joffrey's agreement.

In August 1989, Bliss and Curry, working in consort, promoted Scott Barnard to the position of assistant artistic director—against Arpino's will. A couple of months later, Bliss and Curry accused Arpino of spending $150,000 over budget for the revival of his ballet *The Palace* (the vaudeville extravaganza that had been commissioned by Rebekah Harkness in 1963 to her music). David H. Murdock, Bliss's cochairman of the board, had commissioned an Arpino ballet to honor the office of the American presidency. It would be performed at a gala in Washington, D.C., before President George Bush and the First Lady. Assisted by Scott Barnard and choreographer Louis Johnson, Arpino had reconfigured *The Palace* and renamed it *The Pantages and the Palace Present "TWO-A-DAY."* Although the new ballet for Murdock rivaled its progenitor with respect to lavish costumes and presentation, Arpino firmly believed that he had, in fact, gone under budget. His suspicions were aroused.

Meanwhile, Bliss organized an ad hoc committee of former Joffrey Foundation presidents for the express purpose, he said, of "flanking" Arpino.[2] He told them about Arpino's egregious overage and the company's cash shortfall of around $3 million.[3] (The forty-two-member troupe's annual budget was over $12 million.) One of the ex-presidents moved to hire Sally Bliss as official artistic liaison between Arpino and Curry. Sally Bliss's name would appear above Arpino's in the printed programs with the title *president,* and she would receive a salary of $82,200. It was the same as Arpino's, but less than Curry's at $84,000.[4]

Arpino said that nobody had consulted with him to see if he wanted or approved such a partnership. Sally Bliss also claimed to be in the dark. "I knew nothing about it. . . . A group on the board wanted to bring me in because Arpino wasn't understanding things—I don't want to say what. The point is I know the staff and dancers well. . . . [Arpino] has always been a choreographer, not a director, and he needed the help."[5]

Barbara Levy Kipper, a board member and chairman of the Chicago-based Levy Circulating Company, offered to pay for an accounting firm to scrutinize the books and see if Arpino had really spent $150,000 too much on *TWO-A-DAY.* According to Arpino, when he presented Kipper's plan to Bliss and Curry, he was ignored. Arpino then took it upon himself to examine the company's financial records. His audit disclosed that the full $150,000 could be accounted for as bookkeeping errors. He had actually come in $7,000 under budget for *TWO-A-DAY.*[6]

Incensed, Arpino surrounded himself with sympathetic board members, informing them that the Joffrey Ballet was the object of a takeover plot that hinged on Sally Bliss's eventual appointment as president, and on his own dismissal. A few of Arpino's loyal trustees believed him, but others thought that the Blisses and Curry were not intent on getting rid of Arpino so much as on restricting him to the rehearsal studio as a "pet outside choreographer,"[7] leaving the business operations to them. Tony Bliss said to *Dance Magazine,* "Nobody ever dreamed of wanting to kick Jerry out, but I can see how he would have interpreted it that way."[8] The board soon divided into antagonistic factions, pro-Arpino and pro-Curry.

When Arpino refused to meet with Sally Bliss, she wrote him a long letter in which she diagrammed exactly why she was the right person to be his president and why the troupe's future without her would be hopeless. She challenged his credentials as a director and signed off with, "When your plan begins, the reviews will be speaking about something which is your vision and no one else's. For both sides, the critics and you, reality will set in. Prepare yourself for this, Jerry, it could be rough."[9] Sally Bliss resigned from the board and withdrew herself from consideration to hold a top-level staff position.

Two months later, Tony Bliss drafted a contract that attempted to strip Arpino of the authority to "hire or fire personnel or to make any financial commitment for the company unless specifically approved."[10] The proposed contract also gave exclusive rights to the Joffrey Foundation to produce any Arpino ballets created under the contract—effectively denying him ownership of his work. When Arpino refused to fly out to Los Angeles on April 13, 1990, to discuss the draft with David H. Murdock, who over the past seven years had given at least as many millions to the Joffrey Ballet, Murdock announced that he was "not going to put any more money into the company . . . unless Jerry is removed from a position of responsibility."[11]

Murdock had acquired a reputation for "ruthlessness" when, in 1985, he diversified the Dole Food Company on the Hawaiian island of Lanai, building two large hotels and retraining the local pineapple labor force to make beds and carry luggage for tourists instead.[12] At the time, many Islanders protested that Murdock showed no regard for their cultural history or their land's ecology, and the controversy was sufficient to prompt an investigation by the *New York Times,* which eventually published a front-page story, "After a Long Affair, Pineapple Jilts Hawaii for Asian Suitors." Aware of Murdock's record for taking over, Arpino believed that he would likewise be shown no respect for having been a Joffrey Ballet charter member. He believed that the Los Angeles developer would disregard his history with the troupe, and in self-defense, Arpino began broadly disseminating the claim that he was the company's "cofounder."

In April 1990, before he was supposed to visit with Murdock, Arpino discovered that for the previous two years the company had failed to pay $868,000 in payroll withholding taxes to the Internal Revenue Service. Curry was the executive director and, as such, was directly involved with company finances. Arpino thought she had to have known about the taxes; Tony Bliss had to have known—just as surely as they had known enough about the books to accuse him of overspending. But Bliss said that neither he nor Curry "knew about any of it."[13] The "terrible mistake," he said, had been perpetrated by Lillian Piro, the company's chief financial officer, to maintain a $750,000 cash reserve fund so that the Joffrey Ballet would not lose its grant from the National Endowment for the Arts.[14] On April 6, Piro tendered her resignation. The company was declared to be "two to three weeks away from bankruptcy."[15]

Four months earlier, Penelope Curry had told *Dance Magazine:* "We've replaced our challenge grant money of $750,000. . . . We balanced our budget last year, replaced the cash reserve, and cut the deficit down to about $930,000. We did it by everybody working very hard. That's an honest answer."[16] In the wake of the disclosure in April of delayed payments to the IRS, Curry maintained her innocence and kept her job.

Meanwhile, when the Music Center of Los Angeles finance committee learned that Arpino had jeopardized Murdock's offer to cover the Joffrey Ballet's cumulative deficit of $1 million, plus the $868,000 owed the IRS, its associates moved to supplant the Joffrey Ballet's cumbersome fifty-five-member board with an operating committee of fifteen. The Music Center management was not ordinarily involved with the affairs of the Joffrey board, but the Joffrey Foundation members had asked for—and received—$500,000 in emergency funding from the Music Center in March. David H. Murdock had contributed a substantial part of the unusual donation. The Music Center finance committee attached to the gift the expectation that the Joffrey board would unify and conduct its affairs in a businesslike way.[17] When the Joffrey's members failed to comply, Ron Arnault of the Music Center proposed streamlining the Joffrey's management to a fifteen-member committee that would be chaired by David H. Murdock.

On April 30, 1990, that committee was approved by the Joffrey's Los Angeles board in a 31–9 vote. Expecting to attend the parallel New York board meeting the next day, Arpino was not present in Los Angeles. On May 1, in front of the New York board members, Arpino resigned as artistic director of the company. He took his ballets and those of Robert Joffrey with him.

"I have repeatedly called attention to the financial and administrative mismanagement of this company, and I am frustrated by the failure of the board to hold the responsible parties accountable," he said. "I refuse to participate in an organization which I believe has lost its moral and ethical foundation and which I believe will destroy the artistic vision, reputation, and goals of Robert Joffrey, myself, and all the good people who have worked with us for more than thirty-five years."[18]

Arpino's resignation was not accepted. But he did not accompany the troupe to Los Angeles for the May season that began on May 2. Nor, after May 4, were his ballets on the company's programs. Led by dancers Carole Valleskey and Carl Corry, the Joffrey Ballet dancers rallied around Arpino and presented a statement to the Los Angeles board: "Our presence here is a show of support for the ideals [Gerald Arpino] represents in all of us. . . . We would like to ask that . . . no drastic action be taken concerning the company without first informing us." They emphasized that they could not function "without [their] heart."[19] This was Arpino.

Ten board members resigned. The dancers' plea had helped many realize that without Arpino, they had no artists, and without artists, they had no company.

A petition was circulated to the press, signed by fifteen notable members of the New York dance and theater community. Joseph Papp of the Public Theater was among them. He described to the *New York Post* the actions of those people who were antagonistic to Arpino as "dirty pool," adding: "They were trying to reduce Arpino's function, and I don't like that. . . . All my life I've made it very clear to members of my board that artistic control should be in the hands of the artist."[20] Similar statements in Arpino's support were issued by the nearly one thousand members of the Los Angeles and San Francisco Friends of the Joffrey Ballet. When Clive Barnes, now the *New York Post* dance critic, learned that someone had allegedly been invited to take Arpino's place and subsequently turned down the offer, he commented in print: "This is what Bliss and Murdock are up against with almost anyone they approach. The ballet world is a very small one."[21]

On May 7, 1990, David H. Murdock announced his resignation from the Joffrey Ballet board of directors. Several days later, Anthony A. Bliss resigned, saying, "I decided it was better for me to get out of the way. Either the company will come back completely and go in new directions, or it will die a slow death. I really hope it will survive, because potentially it is a very, very great company."[22] On May 15, 1990, Penelope Curry submitted her resignation. Declining to comment on her reasons, she told Jennifer Dunning of the *New York Times,* "I love this company very much. I have spent the last twenty-two years of my life with it. I will do anything I can to insure the company goes forward."[23]

Having routinely raised funds for his own ballets since 1961, Arpino had solicited $1 million from private and public donations within a month of returning to direct his company on May 23. The support Arpino attracted came from multiple sources, including $300,000 from

Diane Disney Miller, $50,000 from Philip Morris Companies, Inc., and $25,000 from the Harkness Foundations for the Dance. Still, Murdock's resignation had set off a chain reaction among Music Center officers, scared that they were losing their major donor: Murdock.

In 1991, the Joffrey Ballet was asked to leave the Music Center. Hardship, debts, and threats of lawsuits trailed the company. Seasons were canceled; and, in two cities, presenters failed to pay a total of $200,000 owed the troupe for having performed, because the presenters had miscalculated expenses. By 1995, the company had danced in Manhattan for only one season in the previous three years. The relationship with City Center had broken down in the face of escalating rent, the Joffrey's $1.6-million deficit, and the lack of an endowment. The Joffrey Ballet could not be said to have a performing home in New York, and again, there was a movement afoot to relocate to Chicago, where the costs of producing a season were more modest. After having briefly explored the possibility of a merger with American Ballet Theatre in September 1992, and with the less-established Ballet Chicago in the winter of 1995, Arpino decided to close the New York headquarters the following July. Renamed the Joffrey Ballet of Chicago, the troupe moved three months later and set up shop in three studios at 185 North Wabash Avenue.

In 1996, the National Endowment for the Arts is hanging by a thread. The Endowment had several times "saved" the company. The thirty-member Joffrey Ballet of Chicago with a $5-million budget still survives mainly on box-office revenue. The pendulum is swinging back to a time when founders of concert groups and theatrical enterprises tied themselves more closely to their communities.

Before his death, Joffrey had laid out a five-year plan with Arpino. It carried the company only through 1989, when such classics appeared as Eugene Loring's *Billy the Kid,* Bronislava Nijinska's *Les Noces,* and George Balanchine's *Cotillon,* which was another reconstruction by the team of Millicent Hodson and Kenneth Archer. Arpino's initial struggle with the board seriously hampered his ability to lead, although his productivity has been staggering. Twenty-three new works have entered the repertoire in the eight years since Joffrey died. Arpino is a proven fund-raiser.

His directorial vision can be defined chiefly by two evening-length productions: *Billboards* (1993), with music by "the Artist Formerly Known As Prince" and choreography by Laura Dean, Charles Moulton, Peter Pucci, and Margo Sappington, and *Legends* (1996), with music by six famous female vocalists, ranging from Edith Piaf to Barbra Streisand, and choreography by five women. Arpino's 1992 revival of *Les Présages,* Léonide Massine's landmark symphonic ballet of 1933 (restaged by Tatiana Leskova and Nelly Laport), is his only historical reconstruction, and it may have been on Joffrey's long-range list.

Arpino prides himself on encouraging new, young talent.* His initial hopes were pinned to Edward Stierle, whose *Lacrymosa* (1990) and *Empyrean Dances* (1991) suggested that Stierle possessed the ideal qualities for a house choreographer. But Stierle died of AIDS at age twenty-three, and Arpino had to rethink his course. Although, in 1990, he sketched a pas de deux called *The Kiss* for Valerie Madonia and Daniel Baudendistel, he has not choreographed since *The Nutcracker* in 1987.

Today, Ann Marie De Angelo is his associate director, Luis Fuente is ballet master, and Cameron Basden his ballet mistress. Mark Goldweber occasionally assumes ballet-master duties as well. Joffrey Ballet alumni, they are Arpino's choices to be his artistic staff. De Angelo has a proven record of forward-thinking creativity as the former director of Ballet D'Angelo in New York and of Ballet de Monterrey in Mexico. She is Joffrey Ballet to the core, a survivor who takes risks and who has received the benediction of many of the world's greatest ballerinas, such as Alicia Alonso, Margot Fonteyn, Cynthia Gregory, and Melissa Hayden. They either worked with her or saw her in action, and early on believed in her promise. De Angelo calls herself an instrument of Arpino's creation, because his ballets realized her potential. Fuente has also directed ballet companies, and his affiliation with Arpino goes back to *Viva Vivaldi!* and *Olympics,* the Joffrey Ballet signatures from 1965.

Arpino's team is supported by many of the Joffrey old guard. Foremost among them is Herbert Migdoll, who has designed the backdrops for Arpino's two large productions, *Billboards* and *Legends*. He has continued to stand with his camera in the Joffrey studios, theater wings, and audience, shooting every dancer and every ballet in every stage of the process. His tradition of providing the troupe with a look thereby continues, although the look has changed. The bodies are held in space, cleanly lined, and examined as sculpture. The look is composed rather than blurry, realistic rather than fantastic, and the dynamic sense of energy pervades as it always has in a Migdoll frame.

Other familiar people at the Joffrey Ballet of Chicago are Stanley Babin, the solo pianist, Rima Corben, the general press representative, and Roberta Bernard Mitchell (Joffrey's first assistant and the person who accompanied him to Ballet Rambert in 1955), the West Coast administrator. Arnold N. Bremen, who gave the Joffrey Ballet its opportunity to perform for a New York City audience in 1958 at the Brooklyn Academy of Music, is now the executive director. Bruce Sagan plays an

---

*Choreography by Ann Marie De Angelo, Sherry Zunker Dow, Randy Duncan, Joanna Haigood, Mehmet Sanders, and Ann Reinking entered the Joffrey repertoire for the first time in May 1996. Alonzo King (*Lila, Prayer*) was also a choreographer whose work was scheduled for a Joffrey Ballet premiere in 1996.

important role on the board as first vice president. Sagan created the National Endowment for the Arts touring program and helped build the Steppenwolf Theater as its former chairman. He brought the Joffrey Ballet to Chicago in 1965 to perform at the dance festival that he co-organized at the Harper Theater. Also instrumental are board president David A. Kipper and his wife, Barbara Levy Kipper, a long-standing Joffrey Ballet benefactor, whose mother underwrote and commissioned several Arpino ballets. The company has also benefitted from the addition of Harriet G. Ross as artistic administrator and outreach coordinator.

Edith D'Addario still directs the Joffrey Ballet School–American Ballet Center in New York. It continues to be a successful enterprise. Among its staff members are former Joffrey dancers Zelma Bustillo, Francesca Corkle, Edward Morgan, Brunilda Ruiz, and Trinette Singleton. Susan and Buddy Treviño direct the Joffrey Ballet Summer Workshop in San Antonio. Jonathan Watts teaches there along with former Joffrey dancers Eleanor D'Antuono, Brunilda Ruiz, and Paul Sutherland. Françoise Martinet and Charthel Arthur also frequently teach.

Joffrey II folded in 1995 when Gage Bush left to work as ballet mistress at American Ballet Theatre's training company. Her husband, Richard Englund, had died four years earlier on February 15, 1991.

Anthony A. Bliss died on August 10, 1991. As attorney for Antony Tudor, Bliss had drawn up the great choreographer's will. After Tudor's death in 1987, Sally Bliss was named trustee of the Tudor Trust. This means that she oversees and sanctions the dissemination of his ballets. At present, she also serves as executive director of Dance St. Louis, a not-for-profit booking organization.

Penelope Curry worked for Twyla Tharp's company after leaving the Joffrey Ballet; her job with Tharp has ended.

Alexander C. Ewing is the chancellor of the North Carolina School of the Arts in Winston-Salem, a position he has held since July 1990.

Rebekah Harkness died at sixty-seven on June 17, 1982. Her ballet company was dissolved in 1975.

After Joffrey's funeral, Aladar Marberger threw an extravagant party at his home for many of Joffrey's friends, company members, and associates. A few days later, he entered New York Hospital. He remained there for seven months, dying on November 1, 1988. His obituary in the *New York Times* said that he "had had AIDS for three years." It also said: "A longtime friend of Robert Joffrey, [Marberger] served from time to time as informal art adviser to the Joffrey Ballet."[24]

An enduring part of Robert Joffrey's legacy is embodied in the many Joffrey artists who direct companies across the world. The numbers and names speak for themselves: Charthel Arthur and Robert Estner of Grand Rapids

Ballet; Dermot Burke of Dayton Ballet; James Canfield of Oregon Ballet Theatre; Jon Cristofori of Ballet Yuma; William Forsythe of Frankfurt Ballet; Kevin McKenzie of American Ballet Theatre; Dennis Nahat of Cleveland/San José Ballet; Vicente Nebrada of Ballet Nacional of Caracas; Lawrence Rhodes of Les Grands Ballets Canadiens; Lolita San Miguel of Ballet Concierto de Puerto Rico; Margo Sappington of the Daring Project; Trinette Singleton of Bravo! Dance in Pennsylvania; Michael Uthoff of Ballet Arizona; and William Whitener of State Ballet of Missouri.*

Some spent only a short time with Joffrey, but still felt his influence. Helgi Tomasson of the San Francisco Ballet perhaps summarized it best when he said that it was Joffrey's choreographers' workshops and the principle of diversity that affected him most. "As an artistic director, I draw upon my experience with Joffrey, because I had a good experience. He exposed us to so many different styles of moving through such a wide variety of choreographers. I think back on the excitement and pleasure we got from being part of that creative process. He took chances, and he gave us a lot of chances."[25]

With Robert Joffrey's death, the company as he ordered it through the complexity of his esthetic, dancer by dancer, choreographer by choreographer, ballet by ballet, ceased to exist. For the Joffrey Ballet of Chicago perhaps its ability to survive is its closest link to the past. On May 22, 1996, Arpino and his company threw a black-tie, gala ball and gave a performance in Chicago to benefit the troupe. The evening grossed $500,000. Alex Ewing attended the event and admitted that he had accepted the invitation imagining that he would find a company that was a shadow of it former self, one that was not up to the same level as its predecessor. "I thought I would see a company that was the Joffrey Ballet in name only," he said. "But I have not seen women dancers jump like that in years. The dancing was wonderful and I really had to take my hat off."[26]

The lesson of Robert Joffrey is that the artistic spirit is indomitable. Gerald Arpino's vision is not Joffrey's vision. In many ways it is antithetical. Yet it is profoundly true that Arpino provided Joffrey with inspiration, encouragement, and support from the beginning, even before they migrated together from Seattle to New York in 1948.

*Daniel Baudendistel, Rex Bickmore, Laurence Blake, Jeremy Blanton, Diana Cartier, Tony Catanzaro, Gary Chryst, Richard Colton, Patrick Corbin, Carl Corry, Glenn Edgerton, Maria Grandy, Alaine Haubert, Jerel Hilding, Christian Holder, Jeffrey Hughes, Philip Jerry, Finis Jhung, Tina LeBlanc, Noël Mason, Parrish Maynard, Margaret Mercier, Marjorie Mussman, David Palmer, Marie Paquet, Brunilda Ruiz, Russell Sultzbach, Paul Sutherland, Glen Tetley, Carole Valleskey, Robert Vickrey, Dennis Wayne, Ashley Wheater, Rebecca Wright, Rochelle Zide-Booth—the list is too extensive to include everybody who at present contributes to and affects the dance world.

Repeatedly, the Joffrey Ballet was quashed, and repeatedly Robert Joffrey resurrected it in a new form, with new dancers and choreographers. Joffrey thought about the same subject in new ways, he approached the troupe from different points of view. Each time, he aimed beyond his reach. At each fateful juncture, he moved instinctively into a new niche. He adapted—and he prevailed.

If a Robert Joffrey happened once in America, he can happen again. That is the promise of the arts. This is the greatness of American dance.

Notes

CHAPTER 1: THE CHILI RECIPE

1. *Doulat Khan* is inscribed on his gravestone in the plot for members of the Azad Pakhtunistan in Sacramento, California, but generally the family used an alternative spelling, *Dollha*. *Daulat* means wealth, estate, or state (as in government) and is a common Pakhtun name. *Doulat* is the transliteration of local dialect resulting from vowel alliteration. *Anver Bey* is not a Pakhtun name. The sound system of Pakhto does not have the phoneme *v*, and the English *v* phoneme is often read as a *w* in Pakhto. *Anwar*, on the other hand, is a common Pakhtun name that fits the rules of Pakhto phonology. The combination of *Anver Bey* is much closer to Turko/Mughal transliteration and perhaps inadvertently is the result of a Turkish interpreter rendering the name as is, i.e., more Turkish sounding than Pakhto. *Jaffa* means betrayal or treason and is never used as a name; however *Jaffar* is a Muslim name and common among Pakhtuns. *Khan* means chief and at the end of a name denotes social status. The more likely transliteration of the name would have been *Daulat Anwar Bay Jaffar Khan*, or *Daulat Khan*. (Zaman S. Stanizai, notes to author, 11 November 1995.)
2. According to Robert Joffrey's birth certificate, his father was born October 11, 1886. According to Joseph's death certificate and his gravestone, he was born October 11, 1888. Traditionally, Muslims do not celebrate birthdays and birth dates. This often leaves the impression that Muslims do not know their true age.
3. Now the Hazara District of modern Pakistan.
4. Eknath Easwaran, *A Man to Match His Mountains* (Berkeley, Calif.: Nilgiri Press, 1984), 50.
5. Pakhtunistan Day is also known, although misleadingly, as Pakhtunistan Independence Day. It commemorates the naming of Pakhtunistan Square in Kabul, Afghanistan. The square was dedicated to the Pakhtuns by the Afghans in honor of Pakhtun support of Afghanistan Independence. Pakhtunistan has never achieved independence and is now part of Pakistan. (Zaman S. Stanizai, notes to author, 11 November 1995.)
6. Dr. Aurang Shah, M.D., speech on the occasion of the Azad Pakhtunistan Association of America's celebration of Pakhtunistan Day, Hotel Senator, Sacramento, Calif., 2 September 1957.
7. Easwaran, *Man to Match His Mountains*, 55.
8. Naim Shah, interview (unless otherwise noted, all interviews were conducted by author), Kelseyville, Calif., 22 September 1992.
9. Ibid.
10. Robert Joffrey, interview by Lois Draegin, New York, N.Y., 8 January 1985.
11. Gerald Arpino, interview, San Francisco, Calif., 10 July 1991.
12. Garth Rogers, interview, Seattle, Wash., 11 October 1991.
13. Arpino, interview, 10 July 1991.

14. Shah, interview. Within the Islamic context, this would imply a monotheisitic belief system, more specifically, Jewish, Christian, or Islamic.
15. Gerald Arpino, interview, Los Angeles, Calif., 26 December 1991.
16. Arpino, interview, 10 July 1991.
17. Joffrey is widely recognized as having the full name Anver Bey Abdullah Jaffa Khan, which is sometimes published as Abdullah Jaffa Anver Bey Khan. Robert Joffrey authorized Anver Bey Abdullah Jaffa Khan on his biographical sheets for the Joffrey Ballet. His official birth certificate states only "Anver Joffery [sic]." It is likely that the full name was cut short due to space limitations on the document. The misspelling of Joffrey is typed over yet another spelling, "Jaffry." It is also interesting to note that Joseph lists his own birthplace as "Texas," possibly to divert attention from U.S. Immigration.

CHAPTER 2: FINDING BALLET

1. Joffrey, Draegin interview, 8 January 1985.
2. Rogers, interview.
3. Naim Shah, interview, Kelseyville, Calif., 11 July 1992.
4. Conversation with Robert Joffrey, Los Angeles, Calif., 19 September 1985.
5. Gerald Arpino, interview, Los Angeles, Calif., 28 December 1994.
6. Sheldon G. Cohen, M.D., scientific adviser, Department of Health and Human Services, National Institutes of Health, phone interview, Bethesda, Md., 15 December 1993.
7. Arpino, interview, 26 December 1991.
8. Naim Shah, phone interview, Kelseyville, Calif., 11 May 1993.
9. Conversation with Joffrey.
10. Robert Joffrey, interview by Richard N. Philp, New York, N.Y., 18 February 1980.
11. P. W. Manchester, phone interview, Cleveland, Ohio, 2 February 1993.
12. Joffrey, Draegin interview, 8 January 1985.
13. Ibid.
14. Clive Barnes, "Joffrey," *Dance and Dancers,* February 1967, 25–52.
15. Joffrey, Draegin interview, 8 January 1985.
16. Joffrey, Philp interview, 18 February 1980.
17. Ivan Novikoff, phone interview, Seattle, Wash., 20 January 1992.
18. Joffrey, Philp interview, 18 February 1980.
19. Joffrey, Draegin interview, 8 January 1985.
20. Walter Terry, "A Grant Puts Ballet on Its Feet," *New York Herald Tribune,* 18 November 1962.
21. Robert Joffrey, "Remembrances of Kurt Jooss," *Ballet News,* September 1979.
22. Novikoff, phone interview.
23. Joffrey, Draegin interview, 8 January 1985.
24. Robert Joffrey, interview by Richard N. Philp, New York, N.Y., 10 March 1987.
25. Ibid.
26. Françoise Martinet, interview, San Antonio, Tex., 13 July 1991.

CHAPTER 3: GERALD ARPINO

1. Robert Joffrey, interview by Pegeen H. Albig, New York, N.Y., 22 September 1977.
2. Joffrey, Philp interview, 18 February 1980.
3. Catherine Spedden, phone interview, Bothell, Wash., 8 March 1994.
4. Ibid.

5. Ibid.
6. Meg Greenfield, "Bobby Joffrey, We Kids Called Him the 'Ballaydancer,' " *Washington Post,* 27 March 1988.
7. Beuhal Kirberger, phone interview, Seattle, Wash., 20 January 1992.
8. Jan Hodenfield, "Robert Joffrey: Dance, Dance, Dance," *New York Post,* 20 October 1973.
9. Frederic Franklin, phone interview, New York, N.Y., 11 April 1994.
10. Jean Arpino, interview, Staten Island, N.Y., 24 February 1993.
11. Ibid.
12. Rob Baker, "Gerald Arpino, the Architect of Dance," *Attenzione,* February 1984.
13. Gerald Arpino, interview, Los Angeles, Calif., 27 December 1994.
14. Arpino, interview, 10 July 1991.
15. Ibid.
16. Ibid.
17. Arpino, interview, 26 December 1991.
18. Rogers, interview, 11 October 1991.
19. Ibid.
20. Arpino, interview, 27 December 1994.
21. Joffrey, Philp interview, 18 February 1980.

CHAPTER 4: COMING-OF-AGE

1. William Weslow, interview, Seattle, Wash., 26 September 1991.
2. Ibid.
3. Joffrey, Philp interview, 18 February 1980.
4. Françoise Martinet, interview, Iowa City, Iowa, 26 January 1993.
5. Mary Ann Wells, "Some Notes About Teaching," *Dance Magazine,* September 1962, 64–65.
6. Joffrey, Philp interview, 18 February 1980.
7. Coby Larsen, interview, Seattle, Wash., 26 September 1991.
8. Louis R. Guzzo, "Mary Ann Wells, Star-Maker, Retires," *Seattle Times,* 22 June 1958.
9. *Miss Aunt Nellie: The Autobiography of Nellie C. Cornish* (Seattle, Wash.: University of Washington Press, 1964), 99.
10. May O'Donnell, interview, New York, N.Y., 6 November 1991.
11. Martinet, interview, 13 July 1991.
12. Arpino, interview, 27 December 1994.
13. Diane Lembo Talley, interview, Seattle, Wash., 26 September 1991.
14. Joffrey, Draegin interview, 8 January 1985.
15. Hodenfield, "Dance, Dance, Dance."
16. Herbert Migdoll, interview, Los Angeles, Calif., 23 July 1993.
17. Wells, "Notes about Teaching," 64–65.
18. Ibid.
19. Martinet, interview, 13 July 1991.
20. Larsen, interview, 26 September 1991.
21. Wells, "Notes About Teaching," 64–65.
22. Weslow, interview.
23. Ibid.
24. Joffrey, Philp interview, 18 February 1980.
25. Robert Joffrey, phone interview, New York, N.Y., 12 March 1986.
26. Alexandra Danilova, phone interview, New York, N.Y., 30 October 1991.
27. "Conversations on the Dance: Robert Joffrey and Clive Barnes," New York, N.Y.,

Bruno Walter Auditorium, New York Public Library for the Performing Arts, 25 November 1985.

28. Joffrey, Draegin interview, 8 January 1985.
29. Barnes, "Joffrey," 25–52
30. Joffrey, Draegin interview, 8 January 1985.
31. Barnes, "Joffrey," 25–52
32. Joffrey, Draegin interview, 8 January 1985.
33. Maxine Cushing Gray, *Dance News,* August 1948, 5.
34. Joffrey, Draegin interview, 8 January 1985.

CHAPTER 5: NEW YORK, NEW YORK

1. Arpino, interview, 26 December 1991.
2. Jean Arpino, interview.
3. Baker, "Architect of Dance."
4. Gerald Arpino, interview, Los Angeles, Calif., 23 July 1993.
5. Doria Reagan, "Dance—The Twenty-Fifth Anniversary of an American Master: Robert Joffrey," *Interview,* March 1982, 32.
6. Joffrey, Draegin interview, 8 January 1985.
7. "Conversations on the Dance: Robert Joffrey and Clive Barnes," 25 November 1985.
8. Lincoln Kirstein, *Thirty Years: Lincoln Kirstein's "The New York City Ballet"* (New York: Alfred A. Knopf, 1978), 108.
9. Edward Villella, phone interview, Miami, Fla., 23 June 1992.
10. Robert Joffrey, "The Rite of Spring at Seventy-Five," lecture at the New York Public Library for the Performing Arts, N.Y., symposium, 6 November 1987.
11. Arpino, interview, 23 July 1993.
12. Gertrude Shurr, phone interview, Tuscon, Ariz., 28 October 1991.
13. O'Donnell, interview.
14. Anatole Chujoy, "Roland Petit's Les Ballets de Paris, American Debut Winter Garden, N.Y.," *Dance News,* November 1949.
15. Robert Joffrey, interview by Lois Draegin, New York, N.Y., 2 January 1985.
16. Shurr, phone interview.
17. Joffrey, Draegin interview, 8 January 1985.
18. Villella, phone interview.
19. Jonathan Watts, interview, San Francisco, Calif., 10 July 1991.
20. Jonathan Watts, phone interview, Seattle, Wash., 18 July 1994.
21. Glen Tetley, interview, New York, N.Y., 24 October 1992.
22. Lillian Wellein, letter to author, Gryon, Switzerland, 7 February 1994.
23. Theodosia Skowronek-Nassar, interview, Los Angeles, Calif., 7 April 1994.
24. Roberta Bernard Mitchell, interview, Los Angeles, Calif., 26 July 1991.
25. Danilova, phone interview.
26. Marvin Schofer, phone interview, New York, N.Y., 3 December 1993.

CHAPTER 6: DANCER TO CHOREOGRAPHER

1. Doris Hering, "The Season in Review," *Dance Magazine,* April 1952, 9.
2. Joffrey, Draegin interview, 8 January 1985.
3. P. W. Manchester, phone interview, Cincinnati, Ohio, 30 September 1993.
4. Walter Terry, "Reflections on the Joffrey by Critics Terry, Barnes and Kisselgoff," interview by the Joffrey Ballet's in-house newspaper, November 1981.

5. Alexander C. Ewing, interview, New York, N.Y., 6 May 1992.
6. Schofer, phone interview.
7. O'Donnell, interview.
8. May O'Donnell, letter to author, New York, N.Y., 20 February 1992.
9. John Martin, "The Dance: Summary—Some Notable Creative Achievements of the Season—Current Events," *New York Times*, 15 June 1952.
10. Manchester, phone interview, 2 February 1993.
11. Robert Joffrey, interview by Lois Draegin, New York, N.Y., 2 January 1985
12. John Wilson, interview, New York, N.Y., 5 November 1991.
13. Jonathan Watts, interview, San Francisco, Calif., 24 September 1992.
14. Judy Schlein Marlowe, phone interview, Los Angeles, Calif., 16 June 1992.
15. Bernard Mitchell, interview.
16. Walter Terry, "Jacob's Pillow Dance Festival," *New York Herald Tribune*, 6 July 1952.
17. Manchester, phone interview, 2 February 1993.
18. Ibid., 30 September 1993.
19. Louis Horst, "Choreographers' Workshop," *Dance Observer*, January 1953.
20. Jonathan Watts, phone interview, Seattle, Wash., 28 September 1994.
21. Ibid., San Francisco, Calif., 15 September 1992.
22. Brunilda Ruiz, interview, New York, N.Y., 6 November 1991.
23. Doris Hering, "Modern Dance a Ritual for Today," *Dance Magazine*, June 1953, 13–15.
24. Watts, phone interview, 28 September 1994.
25. Hodenfield, "Dance, Dance, Dance."
26. Joffrey, Draegin interview, 2 January 1985.

CHAPTER 7: IN GOOD COMPANY

1. Bradley G. Morison and Julie Gordon Dalgleish, eds., *Waiting in the Wings* (New York: American Council for the Arts, 1987; new edition, 1993), 2.
2. Watts, interview, 24 September 1992.
3. Arpino, interview, 23 July 1993.
4. Eugene J. Hayman, "What AGMA Means to Dancers," *Dance Magazine*, June 1953.
5. "The 92nd Street 'Y' Celebrates Its 75th Birthday," *Dance Magazine*, March 1949, 20–35.
6. Shurr, phone interview.
7. Schofer, phone interview.
8. Brunilda Ruiz, speech at Frostburg State University, Frostburg, Md., 23 April 1994.
9. Ray Kennedy, "The Theater: Dance, The Great Leap Forward," *Time*, 15 March 1968, 44–48.
10. Joffrey, Philp interview, 18 February 1980.
11. Wellein, letter to the author.
12. Manchester, phone interview, 2 February 1993.
13. Doris Hering, "Reviews," *Dance Magazine*, July 1954.
14. Walter Terry, "The Dance World: 'Pajama Game'; a Ballet Concert," *New York Herald Tribune*, 6 June 1954.
15. Hering, "Reviews."
16. Terry, "Dance World."
17. Joffrey, Philp interview, 18 February 1980.
18. Lincoln Kirstein, letter to author, 19 November 1993.
19. Doris Hering, "Reviews," *Dance Magazine*, 24 March 1955.
20. Deborah Jowitt, interview, Copenhagen, Denmark, 1 April 1992.
21. P. W. Manchester, *Dance News*, May 1955.

22. Manchester, phone interview, 2 February 1993.
23. David Vaughan, "Transatlantic View, Choreography in America: 1," *Dance and Dancers,* May 1956
24. "Conversations on the Dance: Robert Joffrey and Clive Barnes," 25 November 1985.
25. Ibid.

CHAPTER 8: ADVERSITY

1. "Conversations on the Dance: Robert Joffrey and Clive Barnes," 25 November 1985.
2. Beryl Goldwyn, interview, London, England, 6 March 1992.
3. Peter Williams, "Campden to Kew—and Back," *Dance and Dancers,* June 1954.
4. Joffrey, "The Rite of Spring," lecture at N.Y.P.L. for the Performing Arts, 6 November 1987.
5. Clive Barnes, "That Fantastic Woman Rambert," *New York Times,* 26 June 1966.
6. "Conversations on the Dance: Robert Joffrey and Clive Barnes," 25 November 1985.
7. Joffrey, Philp interview, 18 February 1980.
8. Cyril Beaumont, "Ballet," *Sunday Times,* 2 July 1955.
9. An entry by Mary Clarke, *Ballet Annual Ten* (London: A. C. Black, 1955), ed. Arnold Haskell.
10. Ibid.
11. A. V. Coton, "London Ballet Month," *Ballet Today,* August 1955, 4.
12. Richard Buckle, "Ballet: A Period Piece," *Sunday Observer,* 3 July 1955.
13. Joffrey, Philp interview, 18 February 1980.
14. Joffrey, Draegin interview, 8 January 1985.
15. "Conversations on the Dance: Robert Joffrey and Clive Barnes," 25 November 1985.
16. Manchester, phone interview, 30 September 1993.
17. John Voorhees, "Sara Dillon Explodes as 'Annie,' " *Seattle Post-Intelligencer,* 8 July 1955.
18. Howard Taubman, "Opera: 'Griffelkin' Has Premiere on N.B.C.-TV," *New York Times,* 7 November 1955.
19. John Voorhees, "New Ballet to Include Dancers Who Also Sing," *Seattle Post-Intelligencer,* 19 June 1956.
20. Joffrey, Draegin interview, 8 January 1985.
21. Schofer, phone interview.
22. Joffrey, Draegin interview, 8 January 1985.
23. Joffrey, interview by Richard N. Philp, New York, N.Y., 22 February 1980.
24. Glen Tetley, interview, New York, N.Y., 24 October 1992.
25. Ibid.
26. Ibid.
27. Watts, interview, San Francisco, Calif., 24 September 1992.
28. Arpino, interview, 28 December 1994.
29. Dianne Consoer, letter home to her parents, 1956.
30. Ewing, interview, 6 May 1992.

CHAPTER 9: SIX DANCERS AND A STATION WAGON

1. Tetley, interview.
2. Joffrey, Draegin interview, 8 January 1985.
3. Tetley, interview.
4. Claudia Cassidy, "On the Aisle: Fresh Young Dance Company of Taste, High Spirits, and Budding Skill," *Chicago Tribune,* 6 March 1961.

5. Morison and Dalgleish, *Waiting in the Wings,* 3–12.
6. Clive Barnes, "Barnes On: The Rise and Presumably the Fall of Americana Spirit in American Ballet," *Ballet News,* December 1982, 8.
7. Anatole Chujoy, *The New York City Ballet* (New York: Da Capo Press, 1982), 92.
8. Lincoln Kirstein, "Blast at Ballet," *Ballet: Bias and Belief* (New York: Dance Horizons, 1983), 200–201.
9. Gerald Arpino, interview, 27 December 1994.
10. Rochelle Zide, phone interview, Jamaica Estates, N.Y., 2 September 1992.
11. Joffrey, Draegin interview, 8 January 1985.
12. Tetley, interview.
13. Gerald Arpino, interview, New York, N.Y., 17 April 1988.
14. Glenna Syse, "Robert Joffrey Dancers Fresh and Inventive," *Chicago Sun-Times,* 23 January 1957.
15. Ann Barzel, "Joffrey Dancers Excel in 'Le Bal,' " *Chicago American,* 22 January 1957.
16. Jack Harpman, interview, Glendale, Calif., 25 May 1993.
17. Françoise Martinet, phone interview, Iowa City, Iowa, 2 February 1992.
18. Harpman, interview.
19. Ibid.
20. Tetley, interview.
21. Arpino, interview, 26 December 1991.

CHAPTER 10: QUARRYING THE REPERTOIRE

1. David Leddick, "Robert Joffrey's American Ballet Center: A School with a View," *Dance Magazine,* August 1960, 48–50.
2. Ibid.
3. Joffrey, Philp interview, 22 February 1980.
4. Ann Hutchinson Guest, phone interview, Lee, Massachusetts, 6 August 1993.
5. Ewing, interview, New York, N.Y., 6 May 1992.
6. Noël Mason, quoting the late Hubbard Miller, interview, Seattle, Wash., 28 September 1991.
7. Julius Rudel, interview, New York, N.Y., 17 January 1995.
8. Robert Joffrey, interview by Richard N. Philp, New York, N.Y., 22 July 1987.
9. Zide, phone interview.
10. Unsigned, "Theatre Ballet Performance Given After Late Arrival of Dance Troupe," *Humboldt Times,* 19 February 1958.
11. Harpman, interview.
12. Marie Paquet, interview, Boston, Mass., 29 August 1992.
13. Rochelle Zide, taped monologue from Prague, Czechoslovakia, to author, 31 October 1992.
14. *Argonaut,* San Francisco, Calif., 11 February 1958.
15. Françoise Martinet, interview, Iowa City, Iowa, 26 January 1993.
16. Maxine Cushing Gray, "In Review," *Argus,* 28 February 1958.
17. Doris Hering, "Reviews," *Dance Magazine,* May 1958.
18. P. W. Manchester, "The Season in Review," *Dance News,* May 1958.
19. "Conversations on the Dance: Robert Joffrey and Clive Barnes," 25 November 1985.
20. Alfred Frankenstein, "Joffrey Ballet Makes Smallness a Virtue," San Francisco *Chronicle,* 8 November 1959.
21. Watts, phone interview, 28 September 1994.
22. Alice Amory, "Robert Joffrey Theatre: Near-Capacity Crowd See First Ballet Given Here," Charlottesville, Va., 1 December 1959.

23. Gerald Arpino, interview, 27 December 1994.
24. Francisco Moncion, phone interview, Woodstock, N.Y., 5 August 1994.
25. Joffrey, Philp interview, 18 February 1980.
26. Rochelle Zide, "Dancing for Joffrey," *Dance Chronicle* 12, no. 1 (1989) (New York: Marcel Dekker, Inc.), 69.
27. Pegeen Horth Albig, "A History of the Robert Joffrey Ballet," vol. 1 (Ph.D. diss., Florida State University, 1979) (Ann Arbor, Mich.: University Microfilms International Dissertation Services, 1994).

CHAPTER 11: THE MODELS

1. Zide, phone interview.
2. Thomas Skelton, his biography, City Center Joffrey Ballet souvenir program, 1967.
3. Beth Cook, "Coffee Time Talk: Ballet Troupe Shares Reception at Wingers," *Modesto Bee,* Modesto, Calif., 25 February 1962.
4. Zide, taped monologue.
5. Joffrey, Draegin interview, 2 January 1985.
6. Walter Terry, "Dance: Jacob's Pillow Festival," *New York Herald Tribune,* 14 July 1960.
7. Arpino, interview, 28 December 1994.
8. Ibid.
9. Martinet, interview, 26 January 1993.
10. Ibid.
11. Zide, phone interview.
12. Lisa Bradley, interview, Elizabeth, N.J., 27 February 1993.
13. Ibid.
14. Ibid.
15. Lawrence Rhodes, phone interview, Montréal, Canada, 25 October 1994.
16. Alexander C. Ewing, article in the 1962 Robert Joffrey Ballet souvenir program.
17. Claudia Cassidy, "On the Aisle: Fresh Young Dance Company of Taste, High Spirits, and Budding Skill," *Chicago Tribune,* 6 March 1961.
18. Ann Barzel, "Joffrey Ballet a Delight," *Chicago American,* 6 March 1961.
19. Betty Kovach, "Robert Joffrey Ballet: Light and Well Chosen Program," *Times,* Raleigh, N.C., 2 February 1961.
20. Lillian Moore, "Ropes, Robbins and Russians," *Dancing Times,* July 1961.
21. Walter Terry, "Dance: John Wilson–Gerald Arpino," *New York Herald Tribune,* 19 May 1961.
22. Gerald Arpino, interview, Los Angeles, Calif., 7 February 1986.
23. Gerald Arpino, interview, San Francisco, Calif., 14 March 1992.
24. Rhodes, phone interview.
25. Moore, "Ropes, Robbins and Russians."
26. Ruiz, interview.
27. Paul Sutherland, interview by Renée Renouf, San Francisco, Calif., 6 June 1976.
28. Doris Hering, unpublished notes, 1966.
29. Joffrey, Philp interview, 22 February 1980.
30. Ibid.

CHAPTER 12: REBEKAH HARKNESS KEAN

1. "Conversations on the Dance: Robert Joffrey and Clive Barnes," 25 November 1985.
2. Una Kai, phone interview, Savannah, Ga., 27 October 1994.

3. Arpino, interview, 27 December 1994.
4. Ibid.
5. Ewing, interview, 6 May 1992.
6. Financial report memo from Alexander Ewing to Robert Joffrey from the American Ballet Center archives, 2 February 1961.
7. Harpman, interview.
8. Gloria Gustafson, phone interview, Milwaukee, Wisc., 1 June 1993.
9. Arpino, interview, 26 December 1994.
10. Eric F. Goldmann, *The Crucial Decade—And After: America, 1945–1960* (New York: Vintage Books, 1960), 345.
11. John F. Kennedy at the dedication of a new library at Amherst College in 1963, from the Rockefeller Panel Report on the Future of Theatre, Dance, Music in America, *The Performing Arts: Problems and Prospects* (New York: McGraw-Hill Book Company, 1965), 4.
12. Joffrey, Draegin interview, 8 January 1985.
13. Alexander C. Ewing, phone interview, Winston-Salem, N.C., 2 November 1994.
14. Craig Unger, *Blue Blood* (New York: William Morrow and Company, 1988), 103.
15. Rhodes, phone interview.
16. Ibid.
17. Ibid.
18. Joffrey, Draegin interview, 8 January 1985.
19. Ann Barzel, "Strangely Compelling Work: *Ropes* and Exciting Ballet," *Chicago American,* 29 March 1962.
20. Arpino, interview, 7 February 1986.
21. Françoise Martinet, phone interview, Iowa City, Iowa, 9 November 1994.
22. Helgi Tomasson, interview, San Francisco, Calif., 24 September 1992.
23. Arpino, interview, 26 December 1994.
24. Marilyn Tucker, "A Fall Led to New Heights: A Virtuoso Choreographer," *San Francisco Chronicle,* 30 August 1971.
25. Ibid.
26. Lone Isaksen, phone interview, Montréal, Canada, 11 November 1994.
27. Brian Macdonald to Robert Joffrey, letter from Seattle, Wash., 28 June 1962.
28. Unger, *Blue Blood,* 105.
29. Lone Isaksen, phone interview.
30. Tomasson, interview, 24 September 1992.
31. Rhodes, phone interview.
32. Donald Saddler, phone interview, New York, N.Y., 16 November 1994.
33. Arpino, interview, 26 December 1994.
34. Walter Terry, "A Grant Puts Ballet on Its Feet."
35. Ibid.
36. Françoise Martinet, phone interview, Iowa City, Iowa, 5 December 1994.
37. Ibid.

CHAPTER 13: AMBASSADORS

1. State Department Statistical Recapitulation Report, Joffrey 1962 Dance Clipping File, Dance Collection, N.Y.P.L. for the Performing Arts.
2. Ibid.
3. Wilson, interview.
4. Rebekah Harkness Kean, 1962 diary, Dance Collection, N.Y.P.L. for the Performing Arts.
5. Kean, diary, 27 November 1962.

6. Martinet, phone interview, 5 December 1994.
7. Paul Sutherland, interview, New York, N.Y., 18 January 1995.
8. Arpino, interview, 28 December 1994.
9. Joffrey, Draegin interview, 8 January 1985.
10. Ibid.
11. D.M., "Music: Triumphant Goodbye Yesterday Afternoon to Robert Joffrey Ballet at the Tivoli," *O Seculo*, 7 December 1962.
12. Tomas Ribas, "Tivoli—The Third Spectacle of Robert Joffrey Ballet," *Diario Ilustrado*, 7 December 1962.
13. Statistical Recapitulation Report.
14. "American Ballet Troupe Gets Enthusiastic Reception Here," *L'Orient*, 28 December 1962.
15. Kean, diary, 4 January 1963.
16. Rupert Heitzig, "Culture in Kabul: Report on the Robert Joffrey Co. Abroad from the Troupe's Stage Manager," *Dance Magazine*, April 1963.
17. Ibid.
18. Sutherland, interview.
19. Joffrey, Draegin interview, 8 January 1985.
20. Arpino, interview, 28 December 1994.
21. Kean, diary, 30 September 1963.
22. Arpino, interview, 28 December 1994.
23. Kean, diary, 10 August 1963.
24. Saddler, phone interview.
25. Rima Corben, phone interview, New York, N.Y., 1 July 1993.
26. Ewing, interview, 6 May 1992.
27. Betty Beale, "Letter from Washington," *Stamford Advocate*, 12 October 1963.
28. Arpino, interview, 28 December 1994.

CHAPTER 14: TREACHERY AT WATCH HILL

1. Kean, diary 11 May 1963.
2. Ibid., 25 April 1963.
3. Ibid., 28 April 1963.
4. Ibid., 13 May 1963.
5. Anonymous memo quoting Jean B. Cerrone on what Kenneth MacMillan said to him, Kenneth MacMillan Watch Hill 1963 file, American Ballet Center archives.
6. Kean, diary, 4 June 1963.
7. Arpino, interview, 28 December 1994.
8. Ewing, interview, 6 May 1992.
9. Erik Bruhn, letter to Robert Joffrey, 12 June 1963.
10. Rhodes, phone interview.
11. Sutherland, interview.
12. Ibid.
13. Ibid.
14. Also called *Time Plus Six*.
15. Joffrey, Draegin interview, 8 January 1985.
16. Anna Sokolow, interview, 20 October 1992.
17. Arpino, interview, 28 December 1994.
18. Allen Hughes, "The Dance: A 'Ballet Gala' Opens in Central Park," *New York Times*, 6 September 1963.
19. Jacqueline Maskey, "A Gift to a Grateful New York City," *Dance Magazine*, October 1963.

20. Arthur Todd, "Letter to Witherspoon," *Dance and Dancers,* November 1963.
21. Arpino, interview, 28 December 1994.
22. Kean, diary, 27 February 1964.
23. Arpino, interview, 28 December 1994.

CHAPTER 15: PRESIDENT KENNEDY AND THE USSR

1. Walter Terry, original libretto for *The Palace,* archives of the Joffrey Ballet school, American Ballet Center.
2. Noël Mason, letter to her family in Tacoma, Wash., 19 September 1964. Harkness Kean's diary corroborates her reaction, Kean, diary, 1 October 1963.
3. Ewing, interview, 6 May 1992.
4. Livingston Biddle, *Our Government and the Arts: A Perspective from the Inside* (New York: American Council for the Arts Books, 1988), 31.
5. "Joffrey Co. Scores in Leningrad," *Dance Magazine,* November 1963.
6. Beale, "Letter from Washington."
7. Arpino, interview, 28 December 1994.
8. Mason, interview.
9. Jean B. Cerrone, interview by Lili Cockerille Livingston, Houston, Tex., May 1982. Transcript sent to author in letter from LCL, 9 August 1995.
10. Ewing, interview, 6 May 1992.
11. John W. Wilson, "My Russian Journal," 6 May 1992.
12. Arpino, interview, 28 December 1994.
13. Kean, diary, no date, but between 12 October and 15 October 1963.
14. Wilson, "My Russian Journal."
15. Gerald Arpino, interview, Los Angeles, Calif., 29 December 1994.
16. Ibid.
17. President Kennedy's University of Maine speech, *Information Bulletin,* American Embassy, Moscow, 21 October 1963, 2.
18. Walter Terry, "Joffrey Ballet Leningrad Hit," *New York Herald Tribune,* 19 October 1963.
19. Joffrey, Draegin interview, 8 January 1985.
20. Arpino, interview, 28 December 1994.
21. Kean, diary, 24 October 1963.
22. Sutherland, interview.
23. Rhodes, phone interview.
24. Natalia Roslavleva, "The Most American? Russian Opinions About the Joffrey Ballet," *Dancing Times,* March 1964.
25. Ibid.
26. Ibid.
27. Konstantin Sergeyev, Kirov Ballet director, unsigned news item, *Dance News,* 5 November 1963.
28. Natalia Roslavleva, "Nyet to Balanchine," letters column, *Harper's Magazine,* March 1965.
29. Noël Mason, letter to her family in Tacoma, Wash., 23 November 1963.
30. Wilson, "My Russian Journal," 16.
31. Marie Paquet, letter to her parents in Boston, Mass., 23 November 1963.
32. Unsigned, "Back from Moscow Tour," *New York Herald Tribune,* 31 December 1963.
33. Theodore Shabad, "Robert Joffrey Ballet in Moscow Dedicates Program to Kennedy," *New York Times,* 30 November 1963.
34. Sutherland, interview.

35. Bradley, interview.
36. Anna Llupina, "Ulanova on Joffrey Company," *Dance News*, January 1964.

CHAPTER 16: THE SPLIT

1. "Ford's Miracle," *Newsweek*, 23 December 1963.
2. Lydia Joel, "Ford Foundation Controversy Pros and Cons," *Dance Magazine*, February 1964.
3. Ibid.
4. Arpino interview, 28 December 1994.
5. Kean, diary, 13 December 1963.
6. Joffrey, Draegin interview, 8 January 1985.
7. Robert Joffrey, interviewed by Richard N. Philp, New York, N.Y., 23 September 1987.
8. Kean, diary, 1963 year-end wrap-up.
9. Robert Joffrey private files, archives of the Joffrey Ballet School, American Ballet Center.
10. Alexander C. Ewing, "Conversation with Lincoln" memo, 6 February 1964, American Ballet Center archives.
11. Alexander C. Ewing, memo #2, "Immediate Action in regard to Harkness Foundation," no date, American Ballet Center archives.
12. Ruiz, interview.
13. Allen Hughes, "$1 Million Given for Ballet Group," *New York Times*, 17 March 1964.
14. Robert Joffrey, handwritten notes, no date, American Ballet Center archives.
15. P. W. Manchester, "Two Harkness Foundations Will Sponsor New Company," *Dance News*, April 1964.
16. Ibid.
17. Allen Hughes, "Dance Philanthropy and a Moral Issue," *New York Times*, 22 March 1964.
18. Kean, diary, 27 February 1964.
19. Walter Terry, "$1 Million Grant to Ballet Stirs the World of Dance," *Herald Tribune*, 20 March 1964.
20. Alexander C. Ewing, phone interview, Winston-Salem, N.C., 14 October 1993.
21. James Lincoln Collier, "Who Pays the Piper?" *Holiday*, December 1965.

CHAPTER 17: THE NATION'S CLOSET

1. Bradley, interview.
2. Manchester, phone interview, 2 February 1993.
3. Arpino, interview, 28 December 1994.
4. Ibid.
5. Robert Joffrey, private files.
6. Barnes, "Joffrey," 25–52.
7. Rockefeller panel report on the future of theater, dance, and music in America, *The Performing Arts: Problems and Prospects*, 13–14.
8. Arpino, interview, 29 December 1994.
9. Ewing, phone interview, Winston-Salem, N.C., 14 October 1993.
10. Ewing, interview, 6 May 1992.
11. Ibid.
12. Ibid.
13. Ibid.

14. Alexander C. Ewing, letter to author, Winston-Salem, 29 March 1996.
15. Alvin Reiss, "The Contemporary Look," *Dance Magazine,* December 1965, 96 and 154.
16. Richard Gain, phone interview, Winston-Salem, N.C., 22 June 1995.
17. Hodenfield, "Dance, Dance, Dance."
18. American Ballet Center brochure, 1964–65 school year.
19. Ibid.
20. Alexander C. Ewing, letter to Robert Joffrey and Gerald Arpino, New York, N.Y., 20 November 1964.
21. Ibid.
22. Ibid.
23. Noël Mason, letter to her family in Tacoma, Wash., 20 March 1965.
24. Biddle, *Our Government and the Arts,* 219.
25. Ibid., 220.
26. Barnes, "Joffrey," 27.

CHAPTER 18: CITY CENTER JOFFREY BALLET

1. Ted Shawn, newsletter, 22 February 1969.
2. Ted Shawn, "Credo," privately printed. Also as quoted in *Update Dance/U.S.A.,* January 1989, 9.
3. Gerald Arpino, interview, New York, N.Y., December 1989.
4. Doris Hering, unpublished performance notes, 18 March 1971.
5. Walter Terry, "Joffrey Ballet 'Redebuts' at Jacob's Pillow," *New York Herald Tribune,* 12 August 1965, 11.
6. Allen Hughes, "Ballet: New Robert Joffrey Company," *New York Times,* 12 August 1965.
7. Anatole Chujoy, "Netherlands, Joffrey Co.'s Debut at Jacob's Pillow," *Dance News,* September 1965.
8. Terry, "Joffrey Ballet 'Redebuts.' "
9. Deborah Jowitt, interview by Pegeen H. Albig, 23 September 1977.
10. Gerald Arpino, interview by Pegeen H. Albig, 24 September 1977.
11. P. W. Manchester, "The Season in Review," *Dance News,* October 1965.
12. Anna Sokolow, interview, New York, N.Y., 20 October 1992.
13. Allen Hughes, "Dance: Joffrey Ballet's Students Seen," *New York Times,* 11 September 1965.
14. Noël Mason, letter to her parents, Tacoma, Wash., 20 September 1965.
15. Ewing, interview, 6 May 1992.
16. Arpino, Albig interview.
17. Arpino, interview, 27 December 1994.
18. Clive Barnes, "Dance: Chicago Festival—Robert Joffrey Company Is Impressive As It Finishes Run in New Series," *New York Times,* 16 November 1965, 54.
19. Clive Barnes, interview, Copenhagen, Denmark, 3 April 1992.
20. Clive Barnes, "Dance: Freedom From Want," *New York Times,* 21 November 1965.
21. Ewing, interview, 6 May 1992.
22. Norton Owen, interview, Jacob's Pillow, Becket, Mass., 28 August 1992.
23. "The Dance: Gamesmanship," *Time,* 15 April 1966.
24. Clive Barnes, "The City Center Joffrey Ballet Opens a History-Making Chapter," *New York Times,* 7 September 1966.
25. Barnes, interview.
26. Dennis Nahat, phone interview, Cleveland, Ohio, 23 June 1995.
27. Unsigned, "City Center Adds Joffrey Ballet," *New York Times,* 3 June 1966.

28. "In Balanchine's Footsteps?" *Newsweek,* 3 October 1966.
29. Alexander C. Ewing, letter to author, Winston-Salem, N.C., 31 March 1996.
30. Arpino, interview, 27 December 1994.
31. Zide, taped monologue.
32. Ibid.

CHAPTER 19: IMAGE

1. Barnes, "Joffrey."
2. Herbert Migdoll, interview, New York, N.Y., 12 July 1992.
3. Herbert Migdoll, interview, New York, N.Y., 20 November 1992.
4. Ibid.
5. Ibid.
6. Ibid.
7. Ibid.
8. Herbert Migdoll, *Dancers Dancing* (New York: Harry N. Abrams, Inc., 1978).
9. Zide, taped monologue.
10. Marcia B. Siegel, *The Shapes of Change* (Berkeley and Los Angeles, University of California Press), 243.
11. John Gruen, *The Private World of Ballet* (New York: Viking Press, 1975), 384.
12. Ming Cho Lee, interview by Pegeen H. Albig, 26 July 1976.
13. Noël Mason, letter to her parents, Tacoma, Wash., 30 August 1966.
14. Michael Uthoff, phone interview, Phoenix, Ariz., 5 June 1995.
15. Nahat, phone interview.
16. Ibid.
17. Uthoff, phone interview.
18. Christian Holder, interview, New York, N.Y., 19 November 1992.
19. Nahat, phone interview.

CHAPTER 20: *THE GREEN TABLE*

1. American Ballet Center brochure, 1964–65 school year.
2. "Joffrey Keeps His Name, His Pace; B.O. Response Marks N.Y. Ballet," *Variety,* 14 September 1966.
3. Alan M. Kriegsman, "The Joffrey Ballet: Small Size, Large Vision," *Reporter,* 1 December 1966.
4. Clive Barnes, "A Proper First Season," *New York Times,* 25 September 1966.
5. Walter Terry, "Elegance Eludes Ballet at Center," *World Journal Tribune,* 16 September 1966.
6. Clive Barnes, "Dance: Joffrey Performs Balanchine," *New York Times,* 16 September 1966.
7. Clive Barnes, "Ballet: Revised 'Gamelan,' " *New York Times,* 16 September 1966.
8. Margo Sappington, interview, Iowa City, Iowa, 28 January 1993.
9. Uthoff, phone interview.
10. Glenn White, 1969–71 diary.
11. Dr. Richard M. Bachrach, interview, New York, N.Y., 23 February 1993.
12. Uthoff, phone interview.
13. Joffrey, Draegin interview, 8 January 1985.
14. Mason, interview.
15. Bruce Johnson, " 'Death' a Fascinating Role—Trip to See Ballet Transformed Budding Physician into Dancer," *Tacoma News Tribune,* 17 July 1968.

16. Mason, interview.
17. Ibid.
18. Walter, Terry, "Joffrey Ballet Finale," *World Journal Tribune,* 27 March 1967.
19. Clive Barnes, "Dance: Dangers Defied," *New York Times,* 15 March 1967.
20. Arthur Todd, "Everything from A to Z: The City Center Joffrey Ballet Gives a Lively Season," *Dancing Times,* May 1967, 414–15.
21. Noël Mason, letter to her parents, Tacoma, Wash., 16 October 1966.
22. Sappington, interview.

CHAPTER 21: ASTARTE

1. Sue Loyd, interview, San Francisco, Calif., 13 July 1992.
2. Don McDonagh, "The Birth and Continuing Times of *Ballet Review,*" *Ballet Review* 19, no.4 (winter 1991, 25th anniversary issue), 45–52.
3. Arlene Croce, "Ballets Without Choreography," *Afterimages* [New York: Alfred A. Knopf, 1977], 326. First published in *Ballet Review* 2, no. 1, (1967).
4. Gardner Compton, interview, Pasadena, Calif., 5 April 1994.
5. Ibid.
6. Ibid.
7. Ibid.
8. Ewing, phone interview, 2 November 1994.
9. Lone Isaksen, phone interview, Montréal, Canada, 27 October 1994.
10. Midge Mackenzie, phone interview, London, England, 1 April 1996.
11. Compton, interview.
12. Midge Mackenzie, fax to author, London, England, 12 April 1996.
13. Compton, interview.
14. Mackenzie, phone interview.
15. Joffrey, Philp interview, 18 February 1980.
16. Compton, interview.
17. Jean Arpino, interview, 24 February 1993.
18. "Joffrey Ballet's Socko Finale of $56,900, 4th Week," *Variety,* 4 October 1967.
19. Don McDonagh, "Joffrey Troupe Seeks Angels to Match Its Muses," *New York Times,* 3 October 1967.
20. Clive Barnes, "The Joffrey's Psychedelic Trip," *New York Times,* 21 September 1967, 57.
21. Clive Barnes, "A Ballet Takes a Trip," *New York Times,* 8 October 1967.
22. James R. Shepley, "A Letter from the Publisher," *Time,* 15 March 1968, 9.
23. Kennedy, "The Theater."
24. William Leighton, interview, Seattle, Wash., 10 October 1991.
25. Kennedy, "The Theater."
26. Croce, "Ballets Without Choreography."
27. Walter Sorell, *Providence Sunday Journal,* 24 September 1967.
28. Marcia B. Siegel, *At the Vanishing Point: A Critic Looks at Dance* (New York: Saturday Review Press, 1973, first paperback edition), 107–8.
29. Doris Hering, "Clowns, Mannequins, Amazons, Sylphs, Naiads, Birds . . . and the City Center Joffrey Ballet," *Dance Magazine,* May 1968.

CHAPTER 22: THE DANCE SPIRIT

1. Holder, interview, 19 November 1992.
2. Rebecca Wright, phone interview, Los Angeles, Calif., 16 June 1995.

3. Holder, interview, 19 November 1992.
4. Barry Laine, "Crowd-Pleaser," *Ballet Review* 7, no. 5, November 1985, 11–15.
5. Ibid.
6. Rima Corben, interview, New York, N.Y., 10 July 1991.
7. Gerald Arpino, phone interview, New York, N.Y., 14 April 1987.
8. Arpino, interview, 7 February 1986.
9. Robert Blankshine, phone interview, New York, N.Y., 14 April 1987.
10. Lionel Rudko, interview, New York, N.Y., 5 November 1991.
11. Amelia Fatt, "The Capricorn Combine," *Dance Magazine,* October 1970.
12. Richard Houdek, "Total Theatre City Center Joffrey Ballet," *Performing Arts,* August 1969.
13. Jonathan Watts, interview, San Francisco, Calif., 24 September 1992.
14. Holder, interview, 19 November 1992.
15. Mason, interview.
16. Ibid.
17. Ibid.
18. Uthoff, phone interview.
19. Mason, interview.
20. Ibid.
21. Ibid.
22. Christian Holder, phone interview, New York, N.Y., 31 July 1995.
23. Bradley, interview.
24. Ibid.
25. Glenn White, interview, San Antonio, Tex., 13 July 1991.
26. Johnson, " 'Death' a Fascinating Role."
27. Olga Maynard, "Arpino and the Berkeley Ballets," *Dance Magazine,* September 1973, 48–61.
28. Lili Cockerille Livingston, phone interview, Pasadena, Calif., 31 July 1995.
29. Loyd, interview.
30. Tatiana Massine Weinbaum, interview, New York, N.Y., 18 November 1992.
31. William Leighton, phone interview, Seattle, Wash., 5 September 1995.
32. Christian Holder, interview, Escondido, Calif., 6 October 1995.
33. Gary Chryst, interview, New York, N.Y., 22 October 1992.
34. Ibid.
35. Holder, interview, 19 November 1992.
36. Chryst, interview.
37. Maynard, "Arpino and the Berkeley Ballets."
38. Agnes de Mille, *America Dances* (New York: Macmillan Publishing Co., Inc., 1980), 179.
39. Arpino, interview, 7 February 1986.
40. Estelle Sommers, interview, New York, N.Y., 20 October 1992.
41. Ibid.
42. Maynard, "Arpino and the Berkeley Ballets."
43. Clive Barnes, "The Ballet: Arpino's Topical 'Trinity,' " *New York Times,* 10 October 1970.
44. Siegel, "Trinity," *At the Vanishing Point,* 117–18.
45. Gerald Arpino, speech for the Joffrey Ballet spring benefit, Los Angeles, Calif., 28 May 1992.

CHAPTER 23: CROSSING OVER

1. Amelia Fatt, "The Capricorn Combine," *Dance Magazine,* October 1970, 33–36.
2. Barnes, interview.

3. Ewing, letter to author, 31 March 1996.
4. John J. O'Connor, "The Dance: Question of Cheers," *Wall Street Journal*, 16 October 1970.
5. Ewing, interview, 6 May 1992.
6. Robert Joffrey, Statement Letter to Friends and Company Supporters, *Dance News*, April 1973.
7. Ibid.
8. Ibid.
9. Norman Singer, Letter to Alexander C. Ewing, 24 March 1971, American Ballet Center archives.
10. Ewing, letter to author, 31 March 1996.
11. Joffrey, Statement Letter.
12. The dancers' pay scale comes from Clive Barnes, "One of the Strangest Strikes to Hit the Arts," *New York Times*, 25 November 1973. Joffrey's paychecks, American Ballet Center archives.
13. Barnes, "One of the Strangest Strikes."
14. Morison and Dalgleish, *Waiting in the Wings*, 45.
15. Ibid., 27.
16. Ewing, interview, 6 May 1992.
17. Arlene Croce, "How to Be Very, Very Popular," *Afterimages* [New York: Alfred A. Knopf, 1977], 88. First published in *New Yorker* (11 November 1974).
18. Arlene Croce, "Joffrey Jazz," *Afterimages* [New York: Alfred A. Knopf, 1977], 14. First published in *New Yorker* (29 October 1973).
19. Joffrey, Philp interview, 22 February 1980.
20. Twyla Tharp, *Push Comes to Shove* (New York: Linda Grey Bantam Books, 1992), 177.
21. Ibid.
22. Wright, phone interview.
23. Ibid.
24. Deborah Jowitt, "Dancing to Beat the Band," *Village Voice*, 8 March 1973 (reprinted in Jowitt's *Dance Beat* [New York: Marcel Dekker, 1977], 164).
25. Nancy Goldner, "Dance," *Nation*, 26 March 1973.
26. Clive Barnes, "Legs Snake Out—Dance Explodes," *New York Times*, 18 March 1973.
27. Marcia B. Siegel, *Watching the Dance Go By* (Boston: Houghton Mifflin Company, 1977), 126–127.
28. Dale Harris, "Performing Arts: Twyla Tharp," *Saturday Review*, 7 April 1973.
29. Patricia Barnes, "Tharp's Coupe," *Dance and Dancers*, July 1973.
30. Croce, "Joffrey Jazz" (reprinted in *Afterimages*, 13–19).
31. Ibid.
32. Martha Shmoyer LoMonaco, "The Giant Jigsaw Puzzle: Robert Joffrey Reconstructs *Parade*," *Drama Review* 28, no. 3 (fall 1984).
33. Millicent Hodson, interview, London, England, 5 March 1992.
34. Anna Kisselgoff, "So Talked About—But Never Seen," *New York Times*, 18 March 1973.
35. Joffrey, Draegin interview, 8 January 1985.
36. Arnold L. Haskell, "Léonide Massine: An Appreciation," *Dance Magazine*, November 1969, 40–55.
37. Vicente García-Márquez, phone interview, Los Angeles, Calif., 11 March 1991.
38. Joffrey, Philp interview, 22 February 1980.
39. Weinbaum, interview.
40. Cecil Beaton, *Ballet* (London, New York: Allan Wingate Publishers Ltd., 1951), 22.
41. Byron Belt, "It's Spring for Ballet," *Newhouse Newspapers*, 29 September 1969.
42. In a piece by Margo Miller, she says that "hard pressed for cash, Diaghilev later scis-

sored out the bullfight scene which he then sold as a painting . . . if you stroll crosstown to the Seagram's building at 375 Park Ave. you can see it." "New York Revival 'Three Cornered Hat,' " *Boston Globe,* 21 September 1969.

43. Holder, interview, 6 October 1995.
44. Kisselgoff, "So Talked About."
45. Luis Fuente, phone interview, Chicago, Ill., 21 February 1996.
46. Clive Barnes, "Was It Ever Really Massine's?" *New York Times,* 22 March 1970.
47. Christian Holder, letter to author, New York, N.Y., 6 October 1995.
48. Lincoln Kirstein, letter to the editor, "Dance Mailbag: Kirstein Argues About *Petrouchka,*" *New York Times,* 1 May 1970.
49. P. W. Manchester, "A Promise Kept," *Playbill,* October 1972.
50. Nancy Reynolds, "Robert Joffrey: The Present Past," Dance Notation Bureau Award Commemorative Program, 1985.
51. Holder, interview, 19 November 1992.
52. Chryst, interview.
53. Christian Holder, phone interview, New York, N.Y., 16 September 1995.
54. Joffrey, Draegin interview, 8 January 1985.
55. Joffrey, Philp interview, 22 February 1980.
56. Chryst, interview.

CHAPTER 24: MUSES

1. Arpino, interview, 23 July 1993.
2. Barbara Schwartz, phone interview, New York, N.Y., 22 March 1996.
3. William Leighton, phone interview, Seattle, Wash., 12 June 1995.
4. Francesca Corkle, phone interview, Pasadena, Calif., 21 October 1992.
5. Francesca Corkle, interview, New York, N.Y., 17 April 1988.
6. Ibid.
7. Watts, interview, 24 September 1992.
8. Siegel, *Watching the Dance,* 46.
9. Clive Barnes, "An Old Love, a New Ballet," *New York Times,* 28 October 1973.
10. Susan Treviño, interview, San Antonio, Tex., 14 July 1991.
11. Buddy Treviño, interview, San Antonio, Tex., 14 July 1991.
12. Sir Frederick Ashton, phone interview, England, 25 March 1988.
13. Wright, phone interview.
14. Anna Kisselgoff, "Joffrey Fulfills a Dream: Reviving Cherished Ballets," *New York Times,* 31 October 1972.
15. William Leighton, interview, Seattle, Wash., 10 October 1991.
16. Kevin McKenzie, interview, Costa Mesa, Calif., 21 January 1993.
17. Jack Anderson, "Reviews," *Dance Magazine,* December 1973.
18. Nancy Goldner, "Dance," *Nation,* 11 November 1978, 522.
19. Tobi Tobias, "Too Much for Everyone," *New York,* 24 November 1980, 73.
20. Richard N. Philp, "Hard Facts on Public Opinion: A Historic Survey on Arts in America," *Dance Magazine,* May 1974.
21. Ibid.
22. Max Wyman, "Joffrey on Joffrey," *Vancouver Sun,* 4 June 1974.
23. Anna Kisselgoff, "4 Ballets Seek to Manage City Center," *New York Times,* 1 April 1976.
24. Scott Barnard, interview, Los Angeles, Calif., 10 July 1991.
25. Rima Corben, interview, San Francisco, 11 July 1991.
26. Arpino, interview, 10 July 1991.
27. Barnes, interview.

28. Leighton, interview, 10 October 1991.
29. Ewing, letter to author, 31 March 1996.
30. Dan Dorfman, "The Bottom Line. The Ballet Business—This Is Not an Offering," *New York,* 5 April 1976.
31. "Presstime News," "Harkness Ballet Faces Demise at End of Winter-Spring Tour," *Dance Magazine,* November 1974.
32. Alice Goldfarb Marquis, *Art Lessons: Learning from the Rise and Fall of Public Arts Funding* (New York: Basic Books, 1995), 102.
33. Dorfman, "The Bottom Line."
34. Penelope Curry, interview, Los Angeles, Calif., 16 May 1990.

CHAPTER 25: THE ASHES

1. Wallace White, "Videodance—It May Be a Whole New Art Form," *New York Times,* 18 January 1976.
2. Robert Coe, *Dance in America* (New York: E. P. Dutton, 1985), 8.
3. Merrill Brockway, phone interview, Santa Fe, N.M., 9 April 1996.
4. Coe, *Dance in America.*
5. Clive Barnes, "The Joffrey Rejoices in the Genius of Jooss," *New York Times,* 28 March 1976.
6. Arlene Croce, "The Spoken Word," Going to Dance [New York: Alfred A. Knopf, 1982], 127. First published in *New Yorker* (6 November 1978).
7. Joffrey, Draegin interview, 8 January 1985.
8. Nancy Goldner, "Dance," *Nation,* 24 April 1976.
9. Anna Kisselgoff, "What Happened to the Joffrey?" *New York Times,* 20 May 1979.
10. Roger Downey, "Robert Joffrey's Just Barely Possible Dream," *The Weekly* (Seattle), 19–25, May 1976.
11. Norma Mclain Stoop, "P.S. We're Coming Home; Dancing Their Heritage Through Thick and Thin: The Joffrey Ballet," *Dance Magazine,* November 1980.
12. Tobi Tobias, "The Joffrey Finds a Home," *New York Times,* 10 October 1976.
13. Agnes de Mille, interview, New York, N.Y., 28 August 1991.
14. Agnes de Mille, *Reprieve: A Memoir* (New York: Doubleday & Company, 1981), 283.
15. Ibid., 285.
16. Ibid., 287.
17. Ibid., 288.
18. De Mille, interview.
19. Joffrey, Draegin interview, 8 January 1985.
20. James E. Siegel, letter to Ronald Lauder of Estée Lauder, Inc., seeking to raise funds for the production of Oscar Araiz's *Romeo and Juliet,* 25 February 1977, Joffrey Ballet archives.
21. Joffrey, Draegin interview, 8 January 1985.
22. Henry A. Young, phone interview, Minneapolis, Minn., 10 May 1990.
23. Croce, "The Spoken Word."
24. Anthony A. Bliss, phone interview, New York, N.Y., 10 May 1990.
25. Young, phone interview, 10 May 1990.
26. Sally Brayley Bliss, interview, Long Island, N.Y., 21 November 1992.
27. Young, phone interview, 10 May 1990.
28. Christian Holder, notes to author, New York, N.Y., 22 December 1995.
29. Stoop, "P.S. We're Coming Home."
30. Ken Sandler, "The Power Brokers II: Broadway Showman, James Nederlander," *Ballet News,* August 1980.

31. Walter Terry, "The Menace of Show Biz Unions," *Saturday Review,* 15 April 1978.
32. Ibid. This idea is attributed in the article to Jane Hermann, director of research and special projects at the Metropolitan Opera.
33. Ibid.
34. Barnes, interview.
35. Unsigned, "Footnotes," *Ballet News,* November 1979.
36. David Vaughan, "Review," *Dance Magazine,* June 1979.
37. Rudolf Nureyev, phone interview, San Francisco, Calif., 18 July 1992.
38. Ibid. First published in *Dance View,* vol. 10, no. 3, spring 1993.
39. Nancy Goldner, "Dance," *Nation,* 7 April 1979.
40. Anna Kisselgoff, "Nureyev in Nijinsky's 'Faune,' " *New York Times,* 25 March 1979.
41. Anna Kisselgoff, "Ballet: Nureyev Dances 'Petrouchka,' " *New York Times,* 8 March 1979.
42. Nureyev, phone interview.
43. Kisselgoff, "What Happened to the Joffrey?"
44. Ibid.
45. Philip Jerry, interview by Lois Draegin, New York, N.Y., 10 January 1985.
46. Robert Joffrey, Draegin interview, 2 January 1985.
47. Holder, letter to author.
48. Anthony A. Bliss, interview by Lois Draegin, New York, N.Y., 19 December 1984.
49. Unsigned, "Joffrey Ballet Gets a $250,000 Grant," *New York Times,* 14 November 1979.
50. Nureyev, phone interview.
51. Joffrey, Draegin interview, 2 January 1985.
52. Young, phone interview, 10 May 1990.
53. Gage Bush, interview, New York, N.Y., 10 November 1991.
54. Charles Dillingham, phone interview, Los Angeles, Calif., 12 November 1992.
55. Ibid.

CHAPTER 26: LOS ANGELES

1. James Canfield, interview by Lois Draegin, New York, N.Y., 10 January 1985.
2. Joffrey, Draegin interview, 2 January 1985.
3. Anna Kisselgoff, "The 'Transformation' of the Joffrey Ballet," *New York Times,* 16 November 1980.
4. Deborah Jowitt, "Two Different Whirls," *The Dance in Mind* [David R. Godine, Boston: 1985], 121. First published in *Village Voice,* (22 October 1980).
5. Laura Dean, interview, Santa Monica, Calif., 2 February 1993.
6. Irene Borger, "Firmer Footing: The Joffrey Goes Bicoastal," *Wall Street Journal,* 7 February 1984.
7. Performing Arts Council of the Music Center members (Sidney R. Petersen, John F. Hotchkis, Diane D. Miller, and Charles Schneider), "Report of the Dance Task Force," 15 June 1982.
8. Ron Reagan, "My Turn: Why I Quit Ballet," *Newsweek,* 14 February 1983.
9. Ron Reagan, phone interview, Seattle, Wash., 7 December 1995.
10. Reagan, "My Turn."
11. Dr. Robert Hesse, interview by Lois Draegin, New York, N.Y., 20 November 1984.
12. Reagan, phone interview.
13. Ibid.
14. Sally Bliss, interview.
15. Reagan, phone interview.
16. Eric Taub, "Footnotes," *Ballet News,* January 1983.
17. Marquis, *Art Lessons,* 165–69.

18. Borger, "Firmer Footing."
19. Michael Newton, interview by Lois Draegin, Los Angeles, Calif., 15 January 1985.
20. Ibid.
21. Barbara Rowes, "Russian Hats Aside, Ballet Boss Robert Joffrey Is As American As Ronald Reagan's Son," *People,* 24 November 1980.
22. Grace Glueck, "A. A. Marberger, 41, Art Dealer, Who Directed Fischbach Gallery" (obituary), *New York Times,* 3 November 1988.
23. Barbara Schwartz, phone interview.
24. Donna Marberger, phone interview, Venice, Calif., 5 March 1996.
25 Estelle Sommers, interview, New York, N.Y., 20 October 1992.
26. Dr. Roy Leeper, interview, San Francisco, Calif., 12 July 1992.
27. Lois Draegin, notes, December 1984.
28. Sally Bliss, interview.
29. Richard Englund, phone interview, New York, N.Y., 28 March 1988.
30. Ibid.

CHAPTER 27: SACRIFICES

1. Leslie E. Schoof, interview, Costa Mesa, Calif., 21 January 1993.
2. Joffrey, Draegin interview, 2 January 1985.
3. Joffrey, Philp interview, 22 July 1987.
4. Robert Joffrey, letter to Millicent Hodson and Kenneth Archer, Hodson and Archer archives, London, England, 3 October 1985.
5. Owen, interview.
6. Joan Acocella, "Ashton and Anniversaries," *Dance Magazine,* March 1987.
7. Joan Acocella, *Mark Morris* (New York: Farrar Straus Giroux, 1993), 201.
8. Hodson, interview.
9. Millicent Hodson, letter to Mary Whitney, Joffrey Ballet's marketing manager, London, England, 27 February 1980.
10. Hodson, interview.
11. Alan M. Kriegsman "Joffrey's Stupendous 'Sacre,' in L.A., a Revival That Makes History," *Washington Post,* 2 October 1987.
12. Sasha Anawalt, "Nijinsky Ballet Rises from the Dead," *Los Angeles Herald Examiner,* 5 July 1987.
13. Ibid.
14. Marcia B. Siegel, " 'Sacre' Ballet Reconstructed," *Christian Science Monitor,* 12 November 1987.
15. Marcia B. Siegel, "Myths for Moderns," *Hudson Review,* Spring 1988.
16. Hodson, interview.
17. Ibid.
18. Anna Kisselgoff, "Roerich's 'Sacre' Shines Light," *New York Times,* 22 November 1987.
19. Joan Acocella, "After the Ball Was Over," *New Yorker,* 18 May 1992.
20. Jonathan Watts, interview, San Francisco, Calif., 11 July 1993.

CHAPTER 28: THE NUTCRACKER

1. Corkle, interview, 17 April 1988.
2. Talley, interview.
3. Robert Joffrey, phone interview by Richard N. Philp, New York, N.Y., 23 September 1987.

4. Ibid.
5. Ibid.
6. Gerald Arpino, interview, New York, N.Y., 17 April 1988.
7. Diane Solway, *A Dance Against Time: The Brief, Brilliant Life of a Joffrey Dancer* (New York: Pocket Books, 1994), 185–87.
8. Alexander Grant, letter to author, 2 February 1996.
9. Gage Bush, interview, New York, N.Y., 10 November 1991.
10. Gage Bush, interview, New York, N.Y., 14 March 1993.
11. Arpino, interview, 17 April 1988.
12. Anthony A. Bliss, phone interview, 10 May 1990.
13. Arpino, interview, 17 April 1988.
14. Ewing, letter to author, Winston-Salem, N.C., 29 March 1996.
15. Alexander C. Ewing's eulogy at Robert Joffrey Memorial, New York, N.Y., 29 March 1988.

AFTERWORD

1. Penelope Curry, interview, Dorothy Chandler Pavilion, Los Angeles, Calif., December 1989.
2. Anthony A. Bliss, phone interview, New York, N.Y., December 1989.
3. Rima Corben, phone interview, New York, N.Y., 17 January 1990.
4. Dennis McDougal, "Joffrey Spent Payroll Tax to Stay in Business," *Los Angeles Times,* 10 March 1990.
5. Gerard Garza and Barbara Isenberg, "Reorganizing Was Needed at Company," *Los Angeles Times,* 4 May 1990.
6. McDougal, "Joffrey Spent Payroll Tax."
7. Letter to the managing directors of the Joffrey Ballet from Carl Epstein, a New York board member, 1 May 1990.
8. Sasha Anawalt, "Arpino Returns," *Dance Magazine,* July 1990, 17.
9. Letter to Gerald Arpino from Sally Brayley Bliss, New York, N.Y., 23 January 1990.
10. Anawalt, "Arpino Returns."
11. Ibid.
12. Robert Reinhold, "After a Long Affair, Pineapple Jilts Hawaii for Asian Suitors," *New York Times,* 26 December 1991.
13. Anthony A. Bliss, phone interview, 10 May 1990.
14. Ibid.
15. McDougal, "Joffrey Spent Payroll Tax."
16. Curry, interview.
17. Anawalt, "Arpino Returns."
18. Statement from Jerry Arpino to the New York board of the Foundation for the Joffrey Ballet, New York, N.Y., 1 May 1990.
19. Statement for the dancers to the Los Angeles Joffrey board of members, Los Angeles, Calif., 9 May 1990.
20. Richard Johnson, "Artists Back Arpino in Ballet Battle," *New York Post,* 9 May 1990.
21. Ibid.
22. Bliss, phone interview, 10 May 1990.
23. Jennifer Dunning, "Executive Director Resigns from Joffrey," *New York Times,* 17 May 1990.
24. Grace Glueck, "A.A. Marberger."
25. Tomasson, interview.
26. Alexander C. Ewing, phone interview, Winston-Salem, N.C., 28 May 1996.

Bibliography

Acocella, Joan. *Mark Morris*. New York: Farrar Straus Giroux, 1993.

Acocella, Joan, and Lynn Garafola, eds. *André Levinson on Dance, Writings from Paris in the Twenties*. Hanover, N.H.: Wesleyan University Press, University Press of New England, 1991.

Albig, Pegeen H. *A History of the Robert Joffrey Ballet*. Ann Arbor, Mich.: UMI Dissertation Services, 1979.

Amberg, George. *Ballet in America: The Emergence of an American Art*. New York: Duell, Sloan & Pearce, 1949.

Anderson, Jack. *Ballet and Modern Dance: A Concise History*. 2nd ed. Princeton, N.J.: A Dance Horizons Book, Princeton Book Company, 1992.

———. *The One and Only: The Ballet Russe de Monte Carlo*. London: Dance Books Ltd., 1981.

Auden, W. H. *A Certain World: A Commonplace Book*. New York: Viking, 1970.

Balanchine, George. *Balanchine's New Complete Stories of the Great Ballets*. Edited by Francis Mason. New York: Doubleday, 1954; revised 1968.

Banes, Sally. *Greenwich Village 1963: Avant-Garde Performance and the Effervescent Body*. Durham, N.C.: Duke University Press, 1993.

———. *Terpsichore in Sneakers: Post-Modern Dance*. Boston: Houghton-Mifflin, 1980.

Beaton, Cecil. *Ballet*. London, New York: Allan Wingate Publishers, Ltd., 1951.

Beaumont, Cyril W. *The Complete Book of Ballets*. London: Putnam, 1937; revised 1949, 1951.

Biddle, Livingston. *Our Government and the Arts: A Perspective from the Inside*. New York: ACA Books, American Council for the Arts, 1988.

Bradley, Lionel. *Sixteen Years of Ballet Rambert*. London: Hinrichsen Edition, Ltd., 1946.

Buckle, Richard. *Diaghilev*. New York: Atheneum, 1979.

———. *Nijinsky*. London: Weidenfield, 1971; New York: Avon, 1975; London: Penguin, 1975.

Caroe, Olaf. *The Pathans, 550 B.C.–A.D. 1957*. New York: St. Martin's Press, 1958.

Chazin-Bennahum, Judith. *The Ballets of Antony Tudor: Studies in Psyche and Satire*. New York: Oxford University Press, 1994.

Chujoy, Anatole. *The New York City Ballet: The First Twenty Years*. New York: Alfred A. Knopf, 1953; New York: Da Capo Press, 1982.

Chujoy, Anatole, and P. W. Manchester, eds. *The Dance Encyclopedia*. New York: A. S. Barnes and Company, Inc., 1949. Revised and enlarged, New York: Simon and Schuster, 1967.

Coe, Robert. *Dance in America*. New York: E. P. Dutton, 1985.

Conner, Lynne. *The American Modern Dance and Its Critics: A History of Journalistic Dance Criticism in the United States, 1850–1934*. Pittsburgh: University of Pittsburgh, 1994.

Copeland, Roger, and Marshall Cohen, eds. *What Is Dance? Readings in Theory and Criticism*. New York: Oxford University Press, 1983.

Cornish, Nellie C. *Miss Aunt Nellie Cornish: The Autobiography of Nellie C. Cornish.* Seattle, Wash.: University of Washington Press, 1964.

Crisp, Clement, and Peter Brinson. *Ballet for All.* London: Pan Books Ltd., 1970, Rev. ed. 1971; London: David & Charles (Holdings), Ltd., 1973.

Crisp, Clement, Anya Sainsbury, and Peter Williams, eds. *Ballet Rambert: 50 Years and On.* London: Scolar Press, 1976. Revised and enlarged edition, 1981.

Croce, Arlene. *Afterimages.* New York: Alfred A. Knopf, 1977.

———. *Going to the Dance.* New York: Alfred A. Knopf, 1982.

———. *Sight Lines.* New York: Alfred A. Knopf, 1987.

Dalrymple, Jean. *From the Last Row: A Personal History of the New York City Center of Music and Drama, Inc.* Clifton, N.J.: J. T. White, 1975.

De Mille, Agnes. *America Dances: A Personal Chronicle in Words and Pictures.* New York: Macmillan Publishing Co., Inc., 1980.

———. *Dance to the Piper.* Boston: Little, Brown, 1951. New York: Bantam Pathfinder, 1964.

———. *Reprieve.* Garden City, N.Y.: Doubleday & Company, Inc., 1981.

Denby, Edwin. *Dance Writings.* Edited by Robert Cornfield and William Mackay. New York, Alfred A. Knopf, 1986.

———. *Dancers, Buildings and People in the Streets.* New York: Horizon Press, 1965.

———. *Looking at the Dance.* New York: Pellegrini & Cudahy, 1949.

Dorris, George. *The Choreography of Robert Joffrey: A Preliminary Checklist.* Vol. 12, no. 1, of *Dance Chronicle.* New York: Marcel Dekker, 1989.

———. *The Choreography of Robert Joffrey: A Supplement.* Vol. 12, no. 3, of *Dance Chronicle.* New York: Marcel Dekker, 1989.

Dorris, Pearl. *Step by Step We Climb: Discourses by the Ascended Masters.* Vol. 1. Mount Shasta, Calif.: Pearl Publishing of Mount Shasta, 1977.

Dunning, Jennifer. *"But First a School": The First Fifty Years of the School of American Ballet.* New York: Viking, Elisabeth Sifton Books, 1985.

Easwaran, Eknath. *A Man to Match His Mountains: Badshah Khan, Nonviolent Soldier of Islam.* Berkeley, Calif.: Nilgiri Press, 1984.

Fonteyn, Margot (presented by). *Pavlova: Portrait of a Dancer.* New York: Viking, 1984.

Fox, Nicholas. *Patron Saints.* New York: Alfred A. Knopf, 1992.

Garafola, Lynn. *Diaghilev's Ballets Russes.* New York: Oxford University Press, 1989.

García-Márquez, Vicente. *The Ballets Russes: Colonel de Basil's Ballets Russes de Monte Carlo 1932–1952.* New York: Alfred A. Knopf, 1990.

———. *Massine.* New York: Alfred A. Knopf, 1995.

Gautier, Théophile. *Gautier on Dance.* Translated by Ivor Guest. Princeton, N.J.: Princeton Book Co., 1987.

———. *The Romantic Ballet.* Translated by Cyril W. Beaumont. London: Wyman & Sons, Ltd., 1932. Revised, 1947.

Getz, Leslie. *Dancers and Choreographers: A Selected Bibliography.* Wakefield, R.I. and London: Asphodel Press, 1995.

Goldman, Eric F. *The Crucial Decade—And After: America, 1945–1960.* New York: Random House, Vintage Books, 1960.

Gruen, John. *The Private World of Ballet.* New York: Viking Press, 1975.

Halberstam, David. *The Fifties.* New York: Villard Books, 1993.

Haskell, Arnold. *Balletomania, Then and Now.* New York: Alfred A. Knopf, 1977.

———. *Diaghilev, His Artistic and Private Life.* New York: Simon & Schuster, 1935.

Hering, Doris, ed. *Twenty-Five Years of American Dance.* New York: R. Orthwine, 1951.

Joffrey, Robert. *Past and Present: The Vital Connection.* Edited by Michael Crabb. Toronto: Simon & Pierce, 1978.

Jowitt, Deborah. *Dance Beat.* New York: Marcel Dekker, 1977.

———. *The Dance in Mind: Profiles and Reviews 1976–83.* Boston: David R. Godine, 1985.

King, Godfré Ray. *Unveiled Mysteries (Original)*. Schaumburg, Ill.: Saint Germain Press, Inc., 1982.

Kirstein, Lincoln. *Ballet: Bias and Belief.* New York: Dance Horizons, 1983.

———. *The New York City Ballet.* New York: Alfred A. Knopf, 1973.

———. *Thirty Years: Lincoln Kirstein's "The New York City Ballet."* New York: Alfred A. Knopf, 1978.

Koegler, Horst. *The Concise Oxford Dictionary of Ballet.* New York, London, Toronto: Oxford University Press, 1977.

Kriegsman, Sali Ann. *Modern Dance in America: The Bennington Years.* Boston: G. K. Hall & Co., 1981.

Krokover, Rosalyn. *The New Borzoi Book of Ballets.* New York: Alfred A. Knopf, 1956.

Lloyd, Margaret. *The Borzoi Book of Modern Dance.* New York: Alfred A. Knopf, 1949. A replication, New York: Dance Horizons, 1974.

Magriel, Paul, ed. *Nijinsky, Pavlova, Duncan.* New York: Da Capo Press, 1977.

Marquis, Alice Goldfarb. *Art Lessons: Learning from the Rise and Fall of Public Arts Funding.* New York: Basic Books, 1995.

Massine, Léonide. *My Life in Ballet.* New York: Macmillan/St. Martin's Press, 1968.

McDaniel, Nello, and George Thorn. *Workpapers: The Quiet Crisis in the Arts, a Special Report.* New York: Foundation for the Extension and Development of the American Professional Theater, 1991.

McDonagh, Don. *Martha Graham: A Biography.* New York: Praeger Publishers, 1973; New York: Popular Library, 1975.

Migdoll, Herbert. *Dancers Dancing.* New York: Harry N. Abrams, Inc., 1978.

Moore, Lillian. *Artists of the Dance.* New York: Thomas Y. Crowell Company, 1938. Republished, New York: Dance Horizons, vol. 18 (no year listed).

Morison, Bradley G., and Julie Gordon Dalgleish. *Waiting in the Wings.* New York: ACA Books, American Council for the Arts, 1987.

O'Neill, W. M. *Coming Apart: An Informal History of the 1960s.* Chicago: Quadrangle Press, 1971.

Payne, Charles. *American Ballet Theatre.* New York: Alfred A. Knopf, 1978.

Qaiyum, Abdul. *Gold and Guns on the Pathan Frontier.* Bombay: Balkrishna Gopal Prabhu Kochrekar, 1945.

Rambert, Marie. *Quicksilver.* London: Macmillan London Limited, 1972, 1983; London: Papermac, 1983.

Reynolds, Nancy. *Repertory in Review.* New York: Dial Press, 1977.

Riesman, David. *Individualism Reconsidered.* Glendale, Ill.: The Free Press, 1954.

Robert, Grace. *The Borzoi Book of Ballets.* New York: Alfred A. Knopf, 1946.

Rockefeller Panel Report. *The Performing Arts: Problems and Prospects, a Rockefeller Panel Report on the Future of Theatre, Dance, Music in America.* New York: McGraw-Hill Books, 1965.

Schmid, Calvin F. *Social Trends in Seattle.* Seattle, Wash.: University of Washington Press, 1944.

Shalizi, Prita K. *Here and There in Afghanistan.* Kabul: Education Press, Franklin Books Programs, 1966.

Shawn, Ted. *Credo.* Privately printed circa 1970.

———. *Every Little Movement.* Pittsfield, Mass.: Eagle Printing and Binding Company, 1954.

Sherman, Jane, and Barton Mumaw. *From Denishawn to Jacob's Pillow and Beyond.* New York: Dance Horizons, 1986.

Siegel, Marcia B. *At the Vanishing Point.* New York: Saturday Review Press, 1972.

———. *The Shapes of Change: Images of American Dance.* Boston: Houghton Mifflin Company, 1979. Paperback printing, Berkeley and Los Angeles, Calif., and London: University of California Press, 1985.

————. *The Tail of the Dragon: New Dance, 1976–1982*. Durham, N.C., and London: Duke University Press, 1991.

————. *Watching the Dance Go By*. Boston: Houghton Mifflin Company, 1977.

Smith, Huston. *The Religions of Man*. New York: Harper & Row, 1986.

Solway, Diane. *A Dance Against Time: The Brief, Brilliant Life of a Joffrey Dancer*. New York: Pocket Books, 1994.

Sorley Walker, Kathrine. *De Basil's Ballets Russes*. New York: Atheneum, 1983.

Terry, Walter. *I Was There: Selected Dance Reviews and Articles 1936–1976*. New York and Basel: Marcel Dekker, Inc., 1978.

Tharp, Twyla. *Push Comes to Shove: An Autobiography*. New York: Bantam Books, Linda Grey, 1992.

Unger, Carl. *Blue Blood: The Story of Rebekah Harkness and How One of the Richest Families in the World Descended into Drugs, Madness, Suicide, and Violence*. New York: William Morrow and Company, Inc., 1988.

Vaughan, David. *Frederick Ashton and His Ballets*. New York: Alfred A. Knopf, 1977.

Walther, Suzanne K. *The Dance of Death: Kurt Jooss and the Weimar Years*. New York: Harwood Academic Publishers, 1994.

Warren, Larry. *Anna Sokolow: The Rebellious Spirit*. Princeton, N.J.: A Dance Horizons Book, Princeton Book Company, 1991.

Chronology of Works

COMPILED BY SASHA ANAWALT
AND JACQUELINE MASKEY

ABBREVIATIONS

Robert Joffrey (**RJ**)
Gerald Arpino (**GA**)
Thomas Skelton (**TS**)
Jennifer Tipton (**JT**)
Stanley Babin (**SB**)
City Center Theater (**CCT**)

Choreographer (**CH**)
Music (**M**)
Costumes (**CO**)
Set (**S**)
Lighting (**L**)
Dancers (**D**)

Staged by (**ST**)
Revival (**RV**)
Assistant to the Choreographer (**AC**)
Ballet Mistress (**BM**)
Joffrey Premiere (**JP**)
World Premiere (**WP**)
Preview (**PV**)
Libretto (**LI**)
Text (**T**)
Conductor (**CN**)
Pianist(s) (**PI**)
Vocalist(s) (**V**)

BALLETS BY ROBERT JOFFREY PRE-1956

ROBERT JOFFREY IN A PROGRAM OF ORIGINAL DANCE COMPOSITIONS

CH RJ (*Malagueña* by Mary Ann Wells) **CO** RJ **WP** 23 June 1948, Woman's Century Club Theatre, Seattle, Wash. **D** R. Joffrey, with (uncredited) Gerald Arpino 1. *Vestris Suite (Grétry):* Salutation, Rigaudon, Minuet, Tambourin 2. *Two Studies* (Hindemith): Dedication, Obsession 3. *Punch* (Prokofiev) Judy: G. Arpino (uncredited) 4. *Suite of Waltzes* (Schubert): Allegro con brio, Allegretto, Allegro non troppo, Vivace 5. *Slavonic Folk Dance* (Bartók) 6. *Malagueña* (Lecuona) 7. *24 Hour Liberty* (Bennett): On the Prowl, Cheek to Cheek, Snake Eyes, Ship Ahoy **PI** Ruth Welke

HIDE AND SEEK

CH RJ **M** Betty J. Walberg; Ray Green, Adagio **WP** 6 June 1951, High School of Performing Arts, N.Y.C. **D** Electa Arenal and Edward Villella

391

PERSEPHONE

CH RJ M Robert Silverman CO Read Arnow, executed by Gertrude Handy S R. Arnow WP 13 Jan. 1952, Theresa L. Kaufmann Auditorium, 92nd Street YM–YWHA, N.Y.C., D Persephone (Lillian Wellein); Pluto (G. Arpino); Demeter (Deidre Stone); Companions of Persephone (E. Arenal, Diana Dear, Marie Kolin, Tania Marakoff, Lolita San Miguel): Lost Souls (Jacqueline Cecil, Eric Creel, Jonathan Watts and E. Arenal, D. Dear, M. Kolin, L. San Miguel) PI Marvin Schofer **Flutist:** R. Silverman **Revised:** 29 May 1954, 92nd Street YM–YWHA, N.Y.C., RV 28 June 1955, Sadler's Wells Theatre, London, Ballet Rambert AC R. Bernard M Antonio Vivaldi, *The Four Seasons* CO Harri Wich S H. Wich

SCARAMOUCHE

CH RJ M John Strauss CO Anver Bey Khan [RJ], executed by Mrs. Frishman and Mrs. San Miguel L Jack Ferris **Preview** 23 Apr. 1952, Brooklyn Museum, Brooklyn, N.Y., D Scaramouche (John Leech [J. Watts]); Girls with Fans (E. Arenal and L. San Miguel, Harriet Fuhrman, Violet Ortiz, Glenda Silverman) PI J. Strauss WP 24 May 1952, Theresa L. Kaufmann Auditorium, 92nd Street YM-YMHA, N.Y.C. S R. Arnow D Scaramouche (J. Leech [J. Watts]); A Hero (Anthony Mordente): Admirers (Carol Frishman, Jean Fishman, Toni Geraldi, Ana Ortiz): A Girl with a Book (Marie Rocco); Girls with Fans (E. Arenal and L. San Miguel, H. Fuhrman, V. Ortiz, G. Silverman)

UMPATEEDLE

CH RJ AC R. Bernard M J. Strauss CO R. Arnow S R. Arnow WP 17 Feb. 1953, Brooklyn High School for Homemaking, Brooklyn, N.Y. D Entrance (E. Arenal and A. Mordente, R. Bernard, Judy Chazin, C. Frishman, Barbara Lucchi, V. Ortiz, Judy Schlein, Dana Sosa, Joel Isaacson, Lloyd Katz, John Montenegro); Adagio or Blues Section (J. Chazin, C. Frishman, B. Lucchi, J. Isaacson, J. Montenegro, A. Mordente); Third Movement, Variations and Finale 1. E. Arenal, L. Katz; 2. A. Mordente; 3. J. Chazin; 4. V. Ortiz; 5. B. Lucchi 6. Ensemble RV 29 May 1954, Theresa L. Kaufmann Auditorium, 92nd Street YM-YMHA, N.Y.C., Robert Joffrey Ballet Concert

PAS DES DÉESSES

CH RJ M John Field, selected Nocturnes, Rondos and Waltzes, adapted by John Wilson CO executed by Parthena Karipides L Spofford J. Beadle WP 29 May 1954, Theresa L. Kaufmann Auditorium, 92nd Street YM–YWHA, N.Y.C., Robert Joffrey Ballet Concert D Marie Taglioni (L. Wellein); Lucile Grahn (Barbara Ann Gray); Fanny Cerrito (Jacquetta Kieth); Arthur Saint-Léon (Michael Lland) PI Steve McDermott JP 2 Oct. 1956, Compton Hall Auditorium, State Teachers College, Frostburg, Md. D Marie Taglioni (Beatrice Tompkins); Lucile Grahn (Dianne Consoer); Fanny Cerrito (B. Ruiz); Arthur Saint-Léon (Glen Tetley) PI J. Wilson RV 27 Feb. 1975, CCT, N.Y.C. RV 4 Jan. 1983, CCT, N.Y.C.

LE BAL MASQUÉ

CH RJ AC R. Bernard M Francis Poulenc LI John Wilson and RJ CO James Trittipo, executed by P. Karipides L Paul Trauvetter WP 29 May 1954, Theresa L. Kaufmann Auditorium, 92nd Street YM-YWHA, N.Y.C., Robert Joffrey Ballet Concert D The Children

(Judy Janaro, Marilyn Smith); The Balloon Man (G. Arpino); The Flower Girl (B. Ruiz); The Organ Grinder (Joseph Edwards); The Newsboy (J. Watts); Mme. Dauphine (J. Kieth); Washerwomen (R. Bernard, Nanette Blair, J. Cecil, Mary Linero, Shirley Neger): The Blind Man (John Wilson); Chimney Sweep (Saint Amant); Blind Woman (B. Tompkins); Her Brother-in-Law (J. Watts); Mourners, Chinese Peasants, Chinese Lord, Steamboat and Waves **CN** J. Strauss

PIERROT LUNAIRE

CH RJ AC R. Bernard **M** Arnold Schoenberg **CO** P. Karipides **WP** 24 Mar. 1955, Theresa L. Kaufmann Auditorium, 92nd Street YM–YWHA, N.Y.C., An Evening of Original Ballets by Robert Joffrey **D** J. Watts and B. Tompkins, J. Keith, J. Cecil, B. Ruiz, S. Neger, Sandra Northrop, M. Smith, J. Janaro, Janet Greschler, G. Arpino, Roy Harsh, J. Edwards, Jerry Burr, Michael Sears, William Guske **CN** Arthur Winograd **Sprechstimme** Alice Howland **PI** Russell Sherman

HARPSICHORD CONCERTO IN B MINOR

CH RJ M Manuel de Falla **CO** P. Karipides **S** Eduardo Sola-Franco, executed by Mary Hipp **WP** 24 Mar. 1955, Theresa L. Kaufmann Auditorium, 92nd Street YM–YWHA, N.Y.C., An Evening of Original Ballets by Robert Joffrey **D** G. Arpino, B. Tompkins, Eda Lioy, M. Smith, B. Ruiz, J. Cecil, Françoise Martinet, S. Northrop, S. Neger, J. Janaro, Rosemary Weekley, J. Burr, J. Edwards, R. Harsh, M. Sears, W. Guske, Baird Searles **CN** A. Winograd **Solo Harpsichordist** Stoddard Lincoln

WORKOUT

CH RJ M Robert McBride, "Workout for Small Orchestra" **WP** 7 May 1956, Phoenix Theater, N.Y.C., Ballet Theater Workshop **D** "Go" (A. Mordente and Dot Virden, G. Arpino, F. Martinet, S. Northrop, Richard Beaty, J. Cecil, D. Consoer, B. Ruiz, M. Sears); "Sweet" (D. Consoer and G. Arpino, F. Martinet and M. Sears, S. Northrop and R. Beaty); "Fast" (G. Arpino and Company)

THE COMPANY REPERTOIRE 1956 TO 1996
Robert Joffrey Theater Dancers

THE BALL (LE BAL)

CH RJ M Emmanuel Chabrier, "Marche Joyeuse," "Habañera," "España Rapsodie" **CO** RJ **L TS WP** 2 Oct. 1956, Compton Hall Auditorium, State Teachers College, Frostburg, Md. **D** Guests (D. Consoer, B. Ruiz, B. Tompkins, G. Arpino, G. Tetley, J. Wilson)

WITHIN FOUR WALLS

CH RJ M J. Wilson, based on themes of Stephen Foster **CO** A. Bey Khan [RJ] **L TS WP** 2 Oct. 1956, Compton Hall Auditorium, State Teachers College, Frostburg, Md. **D** A Young Man (G. Arpino); His Mother (B. Tompkins); His Father (J. Wilson); His Fiancée (D. Consoer); The Intruder (G. Tetley); A Lady (B. Ruiz)

KALEIDOSCOPE

CH RJ **M** George Gershwin, including "My One and Only," "I'll Build a Stairway to Paradise," and "Piano Variations on 'I Got Rhythm' " ("Third Rhapsody") **CO** A. Bey Khan [RJ] **L** TS **WP** 2 Oct. 1956, Compton Hall Auditorium, State Teachers College, Frostburg, Md. **D** D. Consoer, B. Ruiz, B. Tompkins, G. Arpino, G. Tetley, J. Wilson **RV** On tour, 5 Oct.–12 Dec. 1959, beginning in Durham, N.H., under "A La Gershwin"

ROBERT JOFFREY THEATER BALLET

THE SLEEPING BEAUTY: GRAND PAS DE DEUX, VISION SCENE

CH Anatole Vilzak, after Marius Petipa **ST** Ludmilla Schollar **M** Peter Ilyitch Tchaikovsky **CO** RJ **L** TS **WP** 8 Jan. 1957, Newburgh Free Academy, Newburgh, N.Y. **D** Helenka Devon and Ivan Allen

WHIRLIGIG

CH Todd Bolender **M** Wolfgang Amadeus Mozart, Sonata in D Major for Piano Duet, K. 381, **Design Consultant** William Pitkin **L** TS **WP** On tour, 3 Jan.–31 Mar. 1958, beginning in Easton, Penn. **D** B. Ruiz, Maria Grandy, F. Martinet, Marie Paquet, B. Tompkins, G. Arpino, Alfonso Catá, Nels Jorgensen, Vicente Nebrada, Gayle Young **PI** Helio De Soto and Howard Barr

CONTRETEMPS

CH Job Sanders **M** Gabriel Fauré, "Dolly Suite" for Piano Four Hands, op. 56; "Barcarolle," no. 1, op. 26 **CO** William Pitkin **L** TS **WP** On tour, 3 Jan.–31 Mar. 1958, beginning in Easton, Penn. **D** The Boy (G. Young); The Girl (M. Grandy); Their Friends (M. Paquet, V. Nebrada); The Lady (B. Tompkins); Her Admirer (N. Jorgensen); Their Friends (F. Martinet and A. Catá) **PI** Helio De Soto and Howard Barr

THE NUTCRACKER: GRAND PAS DE DEUX

CH George Balanchine **M** P. I. Tchaikovsky **L** TS **JP** On tour, 3 Jan.–31 Mar. 1958, beginning in Easton, Penn. **D** D. Consoer and J. Watts **WP** 2 February 1954, CCT, N.Y.C., New York City Ballet

YESTERDAY'S PAPERS

CH Dirk Sanders **M** Béla Bartók, Sonata for Two Pianos and Percussion **CO** Jack Youngerman **L** TS **WP** 20 Aug. 1959, Chautauqua, NY **D** The Newsboy (G. Arpino); The Printed Paper Girl (Rochelle Zide); The Printed Paper Boy (N. Jorgensen); Four Paper Boys (R. Beaty, James De Bolt, Paul Sutherland, J. Wilson); Four Paper Girls (Suzanne Hammons, Mary Ellen Jackson, M. Paquet, B. Ruiz)

SOIRÉE MUSICALE

CH Antony Tudor ST Peggy van Praagh M Benjamin Britten, "Soirées Musicales" [after Gioacchino Rossini] L TS JP On tour, 5 Oct.–12 Dec. 1959, beginning in Durham, N.H. D Marche (Ensemble); Canzonetta (M. Paquet, P. Sutherland); Tirolese (F. Martinet, N. Jorgensen); Bolero (R. Zide, S. Hammons, B. Ruiz); Tarantella (M. E. Jackson, G. Arpino and Ensemble)

PASTORALE

CH Francisco Moncion M Charles Turner CO after Ruth Sobotka S after David Hays L TS JP On tour, 5 Oct.-12 Dec. 1959, beginning in Durham, N.H. D The Stranger (G. Arpino); The Girl (M. E. Jackson) [B. Ruiz, on tour, American Ballet Center Co., 1 Feb.-27 March, 1960]; The Boy (P. Sutherland); Their Friends (S. Hammons, F. Martinet, M. Paquet, R. Beaty, J. De Bolt, N. Jorgensen) WP 14 Feb. 1957, CCT, N.Y.C., New York City Ballet

GISELLE: PEASANT PAS DE DEUX

CH Nicholas Sergeyev, after Marius Petipa, ST Peggy van Praagh M Friedrich Burgmüller L TS JP On tour, 5 Oct.–12 Dec. 1959, beginning in Durham, N.H. D M. Paquet and P. Sutherland or R. Zide and J. De Bolt WP 20 June 1932, Savoy Theater, London, Camargo Ballet

AMERICAN BALLET CENTER COMPANY

LA FILLE MAL GARDÉE

CH Fernand Nault, after Bronislava Nijinska M Peter Ludwig Hertel LI after Jean Dauberval CO W. Pitkin S TS L TS JP 1 Feb. 1960, Stoneham, Mass. D Mother Simone (F. Martinet); Lisette (R. Zide); Colin (G. Arpino); Thomas (N. Jorgensen); Alain (P. Sutherland); Gossips (D Consoer, S. Hammons); Lisette's Friends (Gage Bush, Sara Leland, M. Paquet, B. Ruiz); Village Notary (J. De Bolt); His Secretary (Richard Zelens); Villagers (Jeremy Blanton, J. De Bolt, V. Nebrada, Richard Zelens) RV 2 April 1966, CCT, N.Y.C. WP 19 Jan. 1940, CCT, N.Y.C., Ballet Theatre, in the version by Bronislava Nijinska, after J. Dauberval

PAS DE DIX (RAYMONDA VARIATIONS)

CH G. Balanchine ST Vida Brown (restaged by Una Kai, 1961) M Alexander Glazunov, from "Raymonda," chiefly Act III L TS JP On tour, 1 Feb.–26 Mar. 1960, beginning in Stoneham, Mass. D B. Ruiz and J. Watts with D. Consoer, S. Leland, F. Martinet, M. Paquet, J. De Bolt, N. Jorgensen, V. Nebrada, P. Sutherland or F. Martinet and R. Zide for B. Ruiz; G. Arpino for J. Watts CN Ted Dale RV 8 Sept. 1967, CCT, N.Y.C. WP 9 Nov. 1955, CCT, N.Y.C., New York City Ballet

CLARISSA

CH Thomas Andrew **M** Maurice Ravel, Piano Concerto for the Left Hand Alone **LI** After Samuel Richardson's *Clarissa* **L** TS **WP** 12 July 1960, Ted Shawn Theatre, Jacob's Pillow Dance Festival, Becket, Mass. **D** Clarissa (R. Zide); Her Lover (Michael Maule); Her Father (G. Arpino); Mourners (G. Bush, Carolyn Borys, S. Hammons, S. Leland, J. Blanton, R. Zelens)

ROBERT JOFFREY BALLET

INVITATIONS

CH T. Andrew **M** P. I. Tchaikovsky, from *The Seasons* and an excerpt from *Pique Dame* **L** TS **WP** 28 Jan. 1961, Dover, Del. **D** Section I (B. Ruiz and Robert Davis with company); Section II (R. Zide and G. Arpino); Section III (F. Martinet and N. Jorgensen with C. Borys, Eleanor D'Antuono, S. Hammons); Section IV (G. Arpino and Lawrence Rhodes with R. Davis, J. De Bolt, Richard Gibson); Section V (M. Paquet and P. Sutherland); Section VI (company)

CON AMORE

CH Lew Christensen **ST** U. Kai **M** G. Rossini, Overtures to *La Scala di Seta, Il Signor Bruschino* and *La Gazza Ladra* **LI** James Graham-Luhan **S** TS **L** TS **JP** 31 Jan. 1961, Center Theater, Norfolk, Va. **D** Captain of Amazons (F. Martinet); Thief (P. Sutherland); Lieutenants of Amazons (E. D'Antuono, B. Ruiz); Amazons (C. Borys, Rita [Lisa] Bradley, Diana Cartier, Jacquelyn Gregory, S. Hammons, R. Zide); Master (N. Jorgensen); Mistress (M. Paquet); Rake (R. Gibson); Sailor (J. De Bolt); Student (L. Rhodes); Eros (R. [L.] Bradley) **RV** 26 Apr. 1967, Harpur Theater, State University of New York at Binghamton, Binghamton, N.Y. **WP** 10 Apr. 1953, Veterans Auditorium, San Francisco, Calif., San Francisco Ballet

ALLEGRO BRILLANTE

CH G. Balanchine **ST** U. Kai **M** P. I. Tchaikovsky, Piano Concerto No. 3 in E-flat Major, op. 75 (unfinished) **L** TS **JP** 21 Feb. 1961, Hammond, La. **D** B. Ruiz and G. Arpino with C. Borys, E. D'Antuono, F. Martinet, M. Paquet, J. De Bolt, N. Jorgensen, L. Rhodes, P. Sutherland **WP** 1 Mar. 1956, CCT, N.Y.C., New York City Ballet

PARTITA FOR 4

CH GA M Vittorio Rieti, "Partita" **CO** G. Arpino and Peter Anthony **L** Tom De Gaetani **WP** 18 May 1961, Theresa L. Kaufmann Auditorium, 92nd Street YM-YWHA, N.Y.C. Gerald Arpino and Company **D** R. [Lisa] Bradley, P. Sutherland, L. Rhodes, J. De Bolt **CN** Maurice Peress **JP** 29 Jan. 1962, Uniontown, Pa. **RV** 13 Mar. 1968, CCT, N.Y.C.

ROPES

CH GA M Charles Ives, "Set for Theater or Chamber Orchestra" **CO** GA **S** GA **L** T. De Gaetani **WP** 18 May 1961, Theresa L. Kaufmann Auditorium, 92nd Street YM-YWHA,

N.Y.C., Gerald Arpino and Company **D** B. Ruiz and L. Rhodes, R. Gibson, James Howell, Charles Leslie, and Jack Weber **CN** M. Peress **PI** Lalan Parrott **JP** 1 Mar. 1962, Salem, Ore. **RV** 1 Apr. 1966, CCT, N.Y.C. **RV** 10 Mar. 1967, CCT, N.Y.C.

SQUARE DANCE

CH G. Balanchine **ST** U. Kai **M** A. Vivaldi, Concerto Grosso in B Minor, op. 3, no. 10 and Concerto Grosso in E major, op. 3, no. 12, (first movement); Arcangelo Corelli, "Badinerie" and "Giga" from "Sarabanda, Badinerie, and Giga" **JP** 7 Feb. 1962, Borger, Tex. **D** R. Zide and G. Arpino with C. Borys, L. Bradley, D. Consoer, S. Hammons, M. Paquet, Sandra Ray, N. Jorgensen, V. Nebrada, J. Nelson, L. Rhodes, P. Sutherland, Harold [Helgi] Tomasson **Caller** J. Wilson **L TS RV** 12 Mar. 1971, CCT, N.Y.C. **ST** Rochelle Zide and Victoria Simon **RV** 13 Oct. 1976, CCT, N.Y.C. **ST** R. Zide **WP** 21 Nov. 1957, CCT, N.Y.C., New York City Ballet

FLOWER FESTIVAL IN GENZANO (PAS DE DEUX)

CH August Bournonville, staged by Fredbjørn Bjørnsson **M** Edward Helsted and Holger Simon Paulli **L TS JP** 17 Mar. 1962, Denver, Colo. **D** B. Ruiz and L. Rhodes **WP** 19 Dec. 1858, Royal Theater, Copenhagen, Denmark, Royal Danish Ballet

SEA SHADOW

CH GA M M. Ravel, Piano Concerto in G, 2nd (Adagio) movement; from 2 Apr. 1966, Michael Colgrass score (commissioned); from 1989, Ravel score restored **L TS WP** 28 Sept. 1962, Fashion Institute of Technology, N.Y.C., under the title *Undine* **D** L. Bradley and P. Sutherland **RV** 14 Oct. 1976, CCT, N.Y.C. **CO** Lewis Brown **S** Ming Cho Lee **RV** 19 Apr. 1989, Segerstrom Hall, Orange County Performing Arts Center, Costa Mesa, Calif. **ST** P. Sutherland

INCUBUS

CH GA M Anton Webern, Six Pieces for Orchestra, op. 6 **CO** Lewis Brown **L TS WP** 28 Sept. 1962, Fashion Institute of Technology, N.Y.C. **D** Lone Isaksen and B. Ruiz, P. Sutherland, H. Tomasson, N. Jorgensen, S. Hammons, L. Rhodes and Lawrence Adams, L. Bradley, Finis Jhung, Anna Marie Longtin, Janet Mitchell, V. Nebrada, Marlene Rizzo, Felix Smith, Richard Wagner, J. Wilson

TIME OUT OF MIND

CH Brian Macdonald **M** Paul Creston, "Second Chorio Dances"; "Invocation and Dance" **CO** Rouben Ter-Arutunian **S** R. Ter-Arutunian **L TS WP** 28 Sept. 1962, Fashion Institute of Technology, N.Y.C. **D** Elisabeth Carroll and L. Rhodes with S. Hammons, A. M. Longtin, J. Mitchell, M. Paquet, M. Rizzo, B. Ruiz, F. Jhung, N. Jorgensen, V. Nebrada, F. Smith, H. Tomasson, R. Wagner

ROUNDABOUT

CH F. Nault **M** E. Chabrier **L** TS **WP** 28 Sept. 1962, Fashion Institute of Technology, N.Y.C. **D** Introduction (L. Rhodes, R. Wagner, H. Tomasson, F. Jhung); Diversion (M. Paquet, S. Hammons, J. Mitchell, M. Rizzo): Fascination (E. Carroll, L. Rhodes, R. Wagner, H. Tomasson, F. Jhung); Flirtation (Company) **PI** Eva Wainless and J. Wilson

FEAST OF ASHES

CH Alvin Ailey **M** Carlos Surinach, "Doppia Concertina" and a section of "Ritmo Jondo," with original music composed for the ballet **LI** after Federico García Lorca's "The House of Bernarda Alba" **CO** Jack [Jac] Venza **L** TS **WP** 30 Sept. 1962, Fashion Institute of Technology, N.Y.C. **D** Matriarch (F. Martinet); Youngest daughter (L. Bradley); Oldest Daughter (S. Hammons); Daughters (J. Mitchell, A. M. Longtin, M. Rizzo); Young Man (P. Sutherland); Limonero (F. Smith); Men of the Village (L. Rhodes, F. Jhung, H. Tomasson, R. Wagner, V. Nebrada, L. Adams); Two Loose Women (B. Ruiz, L. Isaksen) **RV** 6 Oct. 1971, CCT, N.Y.C. **ST** Karina Rieger **RV** 13 Oct. 1976, CCT, N.Y.C.

DREAMS OF GLORY

CH Donald Saddler **M** Rebekah Harkness **LI** D. Saddler **CO** Peter Harvey **S** P. Harvey **L** TS **WP** 30 Sept. 1962, Fashion Institute of Technology, N.Y.C. **D** Boy (L. Rhodes): Girl (L. Bradley); Teacher (F. Martinet); Museum Guard (F. Smith); Students (J. Mitchell, F. Jhung, L. Isaksen, R. Wagner, M. Rizzo, V. Nebrada, N. Jorgensen, A. M. Longtin); Press (L. Isaksen, R. Wagner); VIP & Wife (N. Jorgensen, A. M. Longtin); Persians (V. Nebrada, M. Rizzo); Russian (F. Martinet); Koreans (J. Mitchell, F. Jhung); Divertissements: Pas de Trois (B. Ruiz, M. Paquet, P. Sutherland); and Pas de Deux (E. Carroll, H. Tomasson)

GAMELAN

CH RJ **M** Lou Harrison, "Suite for Violin, Piano and Small Orchestra" **CO** Willa Kim **L** TS **WP** 15 Oct. 1963, Kirov Theater, Leningrad, U.S.S.R.*† **D** G. Arpino with L. Bradley, L. Isaksen, B. Ruiz, Margaret Mercier, M. Paquet, Virginia Stuart, N. Jorgensen, L. Rhodes, P. Sutherland, Salvatore Aiello, F. Jhung, H. Tomasson, Robert Vickrey, J. Wilson. *Four of eight sections were performed 30 Sept. 1962, Fashion Institute of Technology, N.Y.C. (without costumes); †five of eight sections were performed 6 Dec. 1962, Lisbon, Portugal (without costumes) **RV** 14 Sept. 1966, CCT, N.Y.C. **RV** 8 Oct. 1968, CCT, N.Y.C.

THE PALACE

CH GA* **M** R. Harkness **LI** Walter Terry **CO** Robert Fletcher **S** R. Fletcher **L** TS **WP** 15 Oct. 1963, Kirov Theater, Leningrad, U.S.S.R. **D** Card Girl (V. Stuart); I. A Little Bit of Fluff: Dragon Fly (M. Mercier); White Peacock (M. Paquet); Feather Girls (Nancy Fenster, S. Hammons, L. Isaksen, Noël Mason, Karina Rieger, M. Rizzo, Christine Sarry, June Wilson); II, Section 1 (L. Bradley, F. Smith, J. Howell); The Toppers (L. Bradley and F. Jhung, N. Jorgensen, L. Rhodes, R. Vickrey); Bathing Beauties (J. Wilson and June Wilson, N. Fenster, S. Hammons, N. Mason, M. Mercier, K. Rieger, M. Rizzo, C. Sarry); IV Miss Sunny and Her Cavaliers (L. Isaksen and J. Howell, F. Jhung, H. Tomasson, V. Nebrada, L. Rhodes, F. Smith, H. Tomasson, R. Vickrey); V. Pas de Deux Orientale (M. Paquet and P.

Sutherland); VI Rhapsodie Espagñol (L. Bradley, S. Hammons, L. Isaksen, K. Rieger, M. Rizzo, F. Jhung, L. Rhodes, F. Smith, H. Tomasson., R. Vickrey, V. Nebrada); VII. Madame Fenster's Dance of Light (N. Fenster); VII. The Whiz Bangs in "Americana" (L. Bradley, B. Ruiz, and S. Hammons, L. Isaksen, N. Mason, K. Rieger, M. Rizzo, C. Sarry, June Wilson, J. Howell, F. Jhung, V. Nebrada, L. Rhodes, F. Smith, H. Tomasson, J. Wilson, R. Vickrey) CN Yuri Krasnopolsky; *With contributions from RJ, R. Harkness, and Anna Sokolow

CAPRICES

CH B. Macdonald M V. Rieti, "Chess Serenade" and "New Waltzes" CO Motley S Peter Wexler L TS WP 18 Oct. 1963, Len-Soviet Palace of Culture, Leningrad, U.S.S.R. D M. Mercier, M. Paquet, B. Ruiz, C. Sarry, N. Fenster, S. Hammons, K. Rieger, M. Rizzo, June Wilson, N. Jorgensen, P. Sutherland, William Tarpy, L. Rhodes, F. Jhung, V. Nebrada, F. Smith, H. Tomasson, R. Vickrey CN Y. Krasnopolsky

PATTERNS

CH E. Virgina Williams M David Diamond CO A. Bey Khan [RJ] L TS WP 29 Oct. 1963, Len-Soviet Palace of Culture, Leningrad, U.S.S.R. D Allegro Vivace (M. Paquet, K. Rieger, M. Rizzo, C. Sarry, F. Jhung, H. Tomasson, R. Vickrey and N. Fenster, S. Hammons, L. Isaksen, J. Wilson, P. Sutherland, F. Smith); Adagio (B. Ruiz and N. Jorgensen; M. Paquet and P. Sutherland); Allegro (B. Ruiz and N. Jorgensen with entire company) CN Y. Krasnopolsky

THE GAME OF NOAH

CH Glen Tetley M Igor Stravinsky, Eight Instrumental Miniatures; three of the Four Etudes; Symphony of Wind Instruments CO W. Kim S W. Kim L TS WP 10 Aug. 1965, Jacob's Pillow Dance Festival, Becket, Mass. D Noah (Richard Gain); Raven (John Jones); Doves (N. Mason, Dennis Nahat); Observer (Trinette Singleton); Occupants of the Ark (Zelma Bustillo, D. Cartier, Ivy Clear, Edwina Dingman, Susan Magno, Robert Blankshine, Jon Cristofori, Ian Horvath)

CONTRASTS

CH Norman Walker M Paul Fetler, "Contrasts for Orchestra" (commissioned) CO Khan [RJ] and [Warren] Ruud L TS WP 10 Aug. 1965, Jacob's Pillow Dance Festival, Becket, Mass. D 1st Movement (Z. Bustillo and R. Blankshine with Carthel Arthur, D. Cartier, I. Clear, S. Magno, Marjorie Mussman, Robert Brassel, J. Cristofori, I. Horvath, D. Nahat, Michael Uthoff); 2nd Movement (T. Singleton, George Ramos, M. Uthoff); 3rd Movement (Z. Bustillo and R. Blankshine with C. Arthur, D. Cartier, I. Clear, S. Magno, M. Mussman, T. Singleton, R. Brassel, J. Cristofori, I. Horvath, D. Nahat, G. Ramos, M. Uthoff) CN M. Peress

CHARIVARI: OF CLOWNS AND OTHER FOOLS, IN SIX ENCOUNTERS

CH Lotte Goslar M M. Colgrass, "Interlude," "Three Brothers"; Jack McKenzie, "Introduction and Allegro," "Nonet"; Edgard Varèse, "Ionisation" CO Raoul Pène du Bois L TS

WP 9 Sept. 1965, Delacorte Theater, Central Park, N.Y.C. **D** Togetherness (R. Blankshine, R. Brassel, R. Gain, I. Horvath, J. Jones, D. Nahat, G. Ramos, M. Uthoff); Great Grief (D. Cartier, R. Blankshine, D. Nahat, M. Uthoff); The Last Clown [A Dream] (Luis Fuente, C. Arthur, I. Clear, S. Magno, N. Mason, T. Singleton, R. Blankshine, R. Brassel, R. Gain, I. Horvath, J. Jones, D. Nahat, G. Ramos, M. Uthoff); Sleight of Mind (J. Jones); Cupid (I. Horvath, C. Arthur, Z. Bustillo, D. Cartier, I. Clear, S. Magno, N. Mason, T. Singleton); Happy Ending (R. Blankshine, R. Brassel, L. Fuente, R. Gain, I. Horvath, J. Jones, D. Nahat, G. Ramos, M. Uthoff) **CN** M. Peress

VIVA VIVALDI!

CH GA M A. Vivaldi, Concerto No. 7 in D Major for Violin, Strings and Cembalo, op. 11, P. 151, arr. for solo violin and guitar by Rodrigo Riera **CO** Regina Quintana and Anthony **L TS WP** 10 Sept. 1965, Delacorte Theater, Central Park, N.Y.C. **D** E. Dingman, Margo Sappington, T. Singleton, R. Blankshine, J. Cristofori, L. Fuente, I. Horvath; Corps (C. Arthur, Z. Bustillo, D. Cartier, I. Clear, S. Magno, N. Mason, Yvonne McDowell, R. Brassel, G. Ramos) **CN** M. Peress **Solo Guitarist** R. Riera **RV** 14 Mar. 1974, CCT, N.Y.C. **RV** 14 May 1981, Auditorium Theatre, Chicago **RV** 28 Oct. 1988, CCT, N.Y.C.

OPUS '65

CH Anna Sokolow **M** Teo Macero **L TS WP** 10 Sept. 1965, Delacorte Theater, Central Park, N.Y.C. (complete) **D** Ann Axtmann, Esther Jaenn, Y. McDowell, Ximena Quintana, M. Sappington, Arlene Shuler, Donna Silva, Martha Vaala, Frank Bays, Rex Bickmore, Dermot Burke, Raymond Bussey, Jorge Fatauros, George Montalbano, D. Nahat, Haynes Owens, Don Richard **RV** 26 Oct. 1976, CCT, N.Y.C.

OLYMPICS

CH GA M Toshiro Mayazumi (commissioned) **S** M. Cho Lee **L TS WP** 31 Mar. 1966, CCT, N.Y.C.; the Prologue only was performed 8 Sept. 1965, Delacorte Theater, Central Park, N.Y.C. **D** Torch Bearer (L. Fuente); Athletes (J. Cristofori, R. Gain, I. Horvath, J. Jones, M. Uthoff); Attendants (F. Bays, R. Bickmore, D. Nahat, G. Ramos, D. Richard) **CN** M. Peress **RV** 14 Oct. 1976, CCT, N.Y.C. **ST** James Howell

CITY CENTER JOFFREY BALLET

NIGHTWINGS

CH GA M John La Montaine, "Birds of Paradise," op. 34 **CO** W. Kim **S** M. Cho Lee **Associate Designer** Holly Haas **L TS WP** 7 Sept. 1966, CCT, N.Y.C. **D** L. Bradley, M. Uthoff, and N. Jorgensen with F. Bays, Richard Browne, G. Ramos, Maximiliano Zomosa **CN** Seymour Lipkin **PI SB RV** 31 Oct. 1973, CCT, N.Y.C.

CAKEWALK

CH Ruthanna Boris **M** Louis Moreau Gottschalk (7 short pieces) and 3 minstrel tunes (as below), adapted and orch. by Hershy Kay **CO** Robert Drew [on loan from New York City

Ballet] S W. Pitkin L TS JP 8 Sept. 1966, CCT, N.Y.C. D In the First Part: Center (I. Clear, Stephania Lee, Barbara Remington, M. Zomosa); Semi-Circle (C. Arthur, D. Silva, T. Singleton, F. Bays, R. Bickmore, I. Horvath, G. Ramos); Auxiliary Ladies and Gentlemen (Erika Goodman, S. Hammons, Pamela Johnson, N. Mason, M. Mussman, A. Shuler, Karen Williamson, Rebecca Wright, Christian Holder, Rafael Romero); Interlocutor (N. Jorgensen); Left End (S. Magno); Right End (D. Cartier). Programme: Grand Introductory Walkaround (B. Remington and M. Zomosa with Entire Cast); "The Wallflower Waltz" (I. Clear); "Sleight of Feet" (N. Jorgensen); "Perpendicular Points" (S. Magno, D. Cartier); "Freebee" (S. Lee, concluding with a brief "Skipaway"). In the Second Part: Louis, the Illusionist (N. Jorgensen); Moreau and Lesseau (S. Magno, D. Cartier); Venus (B. Remington); The Three Graces (C. Arthur, D. Silva, T. Singleton); The Wild Pony (S. Lee); Hortense, Queen of the Swamp Lillies (I. Clear); Harolde, the Dying Poet (M. Zomosa). In the Third Part (Concluding): Gala Cakewalk RV 13 Oct. 1976, CCT, N.Y.C. RV 8 May 1981, Auditorium Theatre, Chicago WP 12 June 1951, CCT, N.Y.C., New York City Ballet

MONCAYO I

CH Gloria Contreras M José Pablo Moncayo, "Huapango" L TS JP 9 Sept. 1966, CCT, N.Y.C. D C. Arthur, I. Clear, D. Silva, R. Gain CN S. Lipkin WP 1959, Palace of Fine Arts, Mexico City, Mexico

THESE THREE

CH Eugene Loring AC Margo Sappington M David Ward-Steinman (commissioned) CO W. Pitkin S W. Pitkin L TS WP 13 Sept. 1966, CCT, N.Y.C. D First Man (R. Gain); His Wife (M. Sappington); Second Man (N. Jorgensen); Third Man (J. Jones); A Mother (Cleo Quitman*); People: C. Arthur, A. Axtmann, D. Cartier, Helyn Douglas, M. Mussman, D. Silva, T. Singleton, M. Vaala, K. Williamson, R. Wright, G. Montalbano, H. Owens, G. Ramos, R. Romero, Robert Talmage, M. Uthoff, M. Zomosa *Guest Artist CN S. Lipkin

DONIZETTI VARIATIONS

CH G. Balanchine ST V. Simon M Gaetano Donizetti, from "Don Sebastian" CO W. Pitkin L TS JP 15 Sept. 1966, CCT, N.Y.C. D S. Lee, L. Fuente, I. Clear, T. Singleton and C. Arthur, P. Johnson, N. Mason, D. Silva, R. Bickmore, F. Bays, M. Uthoff CN S. Lipkin WP 16 Nov. 1960, CCT, N.Y.C., New York City Ballet

VITALITAS

CH G. Contreras M Peter Dickinson JP 21 Sept. 1966, CCT, N.Y.C. D C. Arthur, I. Clear, R. Gain, D. Cartier, P. Johnson, M. Mussman CN Walter Hagen WP 1961, Palace of Fine Arts, Mexico City, Mexico

SCOTCH SYMPHONY

CH G. Balanchine ST U. Kai and Francia Russell M Felix Mendelssohn, Symphony No.3, op. 56, "Scotch," 2nd, 3rd and 4th movements CO W. Pitkin S Horace Armistead JP 29

Oct. 1966, Junior High School, Quincy, Ill. **D** N. Mason, N. Jorgensen, and S. Magno with M. Zomosa, M. Uthoff, S. Hammons, T. Singleton, C. Arthur, D. Cartier, P. Johnson, M. Mussman, D. Silva, F. Bays, R. Bickmore, D. Burke, J. Cristofori, H. Owens, R. Romero **WP** 11 Nov. 1952, CCT, N.Y.C., New York City Ballet

THE GREEN TABLE: DANSE MACABRE IN EIGHT SCENES

CH Kurt Jooss **M** Frederick A. Cohen **CO** After Hein Heckroth, supervised by W. Pitkin **S** after Hein Heckroth, supervised by W. Pitkin; masks after Hein Heckroth and Herman Markard, supervised by W. Pitkin **L TS JP** 22 Feb. 1967, Royal Alexandra Theatre, Toronto, Canada **D** Death (M. Zomosa); Standard Bearer (M. Uthoff); Young Soldier (R. Blankshine); Young Girl (L. Bradley); Old Soldier (J. Cristofori); Guerilla Woman (S. Hammons); Old Mother (M. Mussman); Profiteer (L. Fuente); Women (D. Cartier, A. Shuler, D. Silva, K. Williamson, R. Wright); Soldiers (F. Bays, R. Bickmore, Joel Dabin); The Gentlemen in Black (F. Bays R. Bickmore, R. Browne, D. Burke, R. Bussey, J. Cristofori, J. Dabin, J. Jones, H. Owens, R. Romero) **CN** S. Lipkin **PI** Mary Roark and Patricia Perrin **RV** 13 May 1981, Auditorium Theatre, Chicago **WP** 2 June 1932, International Congress of the Dance, Théâtre des Champs-Elyssees, Paris, Ballets Jooss

ARCS AND ANGELS

CH GA M William Lawes, Fantasia No. 2 and "In Nomine" from Suite No. 3 in B-flat Major **CO GA L TS WP** 15 Mar. 1967, CCT, N.Y.C. **D** I. Cloister (N. Mason, M. Mussman and C. Arthur, H. Douglas, P. Johnson, D. Silva, T. Singleton); II. Garden (L. Bradley, H. Owens, M. Uthoff, M. Zomosa); III. Paths (R. Blankshine with M. Mussman, J. Dabin and 4 women, 4 men); IV. Heavens (B. Remington, R. Blankshine, L. Bradley, M. Uthoff and 6 women, 3 men) **CN** S. Lipkin

ROOMS

CH A. Sokolow **M** Kenyon Hopkins **CO** Donald McKayle **L TS JP** 26 Apr. 1967, Harpur Theater, State University of New York at Binghamton, N.Y. **D** I. Alone (F. Bays, R. Bickmore, R. Browne, J. Jones, N. Mason, M. Mussman, A. Shuler, D. Silva); II. Dream (R. Bickmore); III. Escape (N. Mason); IV. Going (F. Bays); V. Desire (F. Bays, D. Silva, R. Bickmore, A. Shuler, R. Browne, M. Mussman); VI. Panic (J. Jones); VII. Day Dream (A. Shuler, D. Silva*); VIII. The End? (M. Mussman); IX. Alone (Entire Cast) **CN** Kenyon Hopkins (at CCT premiere) **WP** 24 Jan. 1955, Theresa L. Kaufmann Auditorium, 92nd Street YM-YWHA, N.Y.C., An Evening of Dance Works by Anna Sokolow *M. Mussman added at CCT

CELLO CONCERTO

CH GA M A. Vivaldi, Concerto in E Minor for Cello, Strings and Continuo **CO GA WP** 10 Aug. 1967, Eastvold Auditorium, Pacific Lutheran Univ., Tacoma, Wash. **D** 1st Movement (E. Goodman, J. Cristofori with 9 women, 8 men); 2nd Movement (E. Goodman, J. Cristofori, Nora Esteves, Henry Berg, R. Wright with 4 women, 5 men); 3rd Movement (E. Goodman, J. Cristofori, T. Singleton, G. Montalbano); 4th Movement (E. Goodman, J. Cristofori, N. Esteves, H. Berg with 5 women, 5 men) **CN** S. Lipkin **Cellist** Raymond Davis

ELEGY

CH GA M Andrzej Panufnik, "Sinfonia Elegiaca," 1st and 3rd Movements **CO** Edith Lutyens Bel Geddes **S** M. Cho Lee **L TS WP** 17 Aug. 1967, Opera House, Seattle, Wash. **D** Confederate Soldier (M. Zomosa); His Wife (N. Mason); His Daughter (C. Arthur); His Son (Peter Kahrmann); Young Ladies (7 women); Soldiers of the Union Army (7 men) **CN** W. Hagen

MOVES: A BALLET IN SILENCE ABOUT RELATIONSHIPS

CH Jerome Robbins **JP** 19 Sept. 1967, CCT, N.Y.C. **D** 1. Entrance, Pas de Deux (L. Bradley, M. Uthoff, Z. Bustillo, N. Esteves, M. Mussman, B. Remington, F. Bays, R. Browne, C. Holder, G. Montalbano); 2. Dance for Men (F. Bays, H. Berg, R. Browne, C. Holder, G. Montalbano); 3. Dance for Women (4 women); 4. Pas de Deux (L. Bradley, Z. Bustillo, N. Esteves, Sue Loyd, M. Mussman, F. Bays, H. Berg, R. Browne, C. Holder, G. Montalbano, M. Uthoff); 5. Finale **RV** 12 Nov. 1981, CCT, N.Y.C. **WP** 3 July 1959, Festival of Two Worlds, Teatro Nuovo, Spoleto, Italy, Jerome Robbins' Ballets: U.S.A.

ASTARTE

CH RJ M Composed and performed by Crome Syrcus (commissioned) **CO** Hugh Sherrer **S TS Film** Created and photographed by Gardner Compton **L TS Produced by** Midge Mackenzie **WP** 20 Sept. 1967, CCT, N.Y.C. **D** T. Singleton and M. Zomosa **RV** 27 Oct. 1976, CCT, N.Y.C. **M supervised by** Ted Shreffler; **performed by** Helios; **Projected media created, directed and photographed by** G. Compton; **Produced by** Emile Ardolino

PAS DE TROIS

CH G. Balanchine **ST** André Eglevsky **M** Léon Minkus, from "Paquita" **L TS JP** 21 Sept. 1967, CCT, N.Y.C. **D** S. Loyd, L. Fuente, S. Magno **CN** S. Lipkin **WP** 18 Feb. 1951 (first presented as *Pas de Trais Classique* on 9 Aug. 1948 by Grand Ballet du Marquis de Cuevas in somewhat different form), CCT, N.Y.C., New York City Ballet

SECRET PLACES

CH GA M W. A. Mozart, Piano Concerto No. 21 in C Major, K. 467 (2nd movement) **CO GA S** M. Cho Lee **L TS WP** 20 Feb. 1968, CCT, N.Y.C. **D** L. Bradley and D. Burke **CN** W. Hagen **RV** 23 Feb. 1973, CCT, N.Y.C. **RV** 11 Nov. 1981, CCT, N.Y.C. **RV** 10 May 1985, Civic Opera House, Civic Center for the Performing Arts, Chicago

THE MANNEQUINS

CH Marc Wilde **M** Hall Overton, "Sonorities for Orchestra"; Jimmy Giuffre, "Hex"; Teo Macero, "Pressure" **L TS JP** 21 Feb. 1968, CCT, N.Y.C. **D** Thief (M. Uthoff); Leader (S. Hammons); Mannequin (T. Singleton); Mannequins (Z. Bustillo, D. Cartier, P. Johnson, M. Mussman) **CN** W. Hagen

THE CLOWNS

CH GA AC J. Howell M Hershy Kay (commissioned) CO E. L. Bel Geddes L TS **Special Effects** Vernon Lobb and Kip Coburn WP 28 Feb. 1968, CCT, N.Y.C. D R. Blankshine, F. Bays, E. Goodman, M. Zomosa and S. Loyd, M. Mussman, A. Shuler, R. Wright, R. Browne, D. Burke, Robert Estner, C. Holder, G. Montalbano, H. Owens, R. Romero, R. Talmage, Anthony Williams CN H. Kay RV 23 Oct. 1974, CCT, N.Y.C. RV 20 Mar. 1987, Civic Opera House, Chicago

JINX

CH L. Christensen M B. Britten, "Variations on a Theme by Frank Bridge" for String Orchestra LI L. Christensen L TS JP 5 Mar. 1968, CCT, N.Y.C. D Jinx (M. Uthoff); Wire Walker (S. Loyd); Bearded Lady (M. Mussman); Ring Master (M. Zomosa); Strong Lady (D. Silva); Tattooed Lady (S. Hammons); Second Wire Walker (C. Arthur); Little Clown (F. Bays); Equestrian Boy (H. Berg); First Equestrian Girl (P. Johnson); Second Equestrian Girl (Pamara Perry) CN S. Lipkin WP 24 Apr. 1942, National Theatre, N.Y.C.

DISTRACTIONS

CH L. Christensen M Franz Joseph Haydn, Symphony No. 60 in C Major ("Il Distratto") CO David Barnard S D. Barnard WP 6 Mar. 1968, CCT, N.Y.C. D Adagio (S. Loyd, T. Singleton, A. Williams, C. Holder); First Movement, Section I, Group 1 (Peggy Congdon, H. Douglas, S. Hammons, Carolyn Houser); Group 2 (C. Arthur, Z. Bustillo, Michelle Farr, D. Silva); Group 3 (M. Mussman and P. Johnson, P. Perry, A. Shuler); Section II (P. Congdon, H. Douglas, S. Hammons, C. Houser); Section III (C. Arthur, Z. Bustillo, M. Farr, D. Silva); Second Movement (M. Mussman); Section IV (P. Johnson, P. Perry, D. Silva); Section V (S. Loyd, T. Singleton, A. Williams, C. Holder); Third Movement (Entire Cast) CN S. Lipkin

BOXES

CH M. Wilde M M. Ravel, "Mother Goose" Suite ("Ma Mère l'Oye") L TS WP 13 Mar. 1968, CCT, N.Y.C. D Magician (Robert Petersen); Sorceress (M. Farr); Girl (Jan Miller); Boy (Glenn White) and P. Congdon, Chris Erickson, C. Houser, Gay Wallstrom, Marguerite Wesley CN S. Lipkin

QUARTET

CH Michael Uthoff M Antonín Dvořák, Trio in E Minor, op. 90 L TS WP 13 Mar. 1968, CCT, N.Y.C. D L. Bradley and F. Bays, D. Silva and C. Holder CN S. Lipkin

DIFFERENCES

CH Remy Charlip AC Aileen Passloff M P. I. Tchaikovsky, from "The Seasons"; Jules Massenet, "Meditation" L TS WP 13 Mar. 1968, CCT, N.Y.C. D April and December (Nicole Sowinska); Differences, In Silence (Z. Bustillo and D. Burke); Meditation (M. Zomosa) CN S. Lipkin **Violin Soloist** Lamar Alsop

THE GLASS HEART

CH M. Wilde **M** Norman Dello Joio, "Meditations on Ecclesiastes" **L** TS **WP** 13 Mar. 1968, CCT, N.Y.C. **D** L. Bradley, D. Silva, T. Singleton, D. Burke, M. Uthoff, Scott Barnard **CN** W. Hagen

A LIGHT FANTASTIC

CH GA **M** B. Britten, excerpts from "Gloriana," adapted by Rayburn Wright **CO** Bruce Harrow **S** M. Cho Lee **L** TS **WP** 25 Sept. 1968, CCT, N.Y.C. **D** Fanfare (R. Blankshine and C. Arthur, E. Goodman, P. Johnson, M. Mussman, A. Shuler, D. Silva, T. Singleton, R. Wright, S. Barnard, H. Berg, D. Burke, C. Holder, G. Montalbano, H. Owens, R. Romero); Promenade (E. Goodman and R. Romero with 4 men, 4 women); March (R. Blankshine and 4 women, 4 men); Lavolta (C. Holder, C. Arthur, R. Romero); Coranto (P. Johnson, S. Barnard, D. Burke and 4 women, 4 men); Pavane (E. Goodman and C. Holder); Presto (R. Blankshine); Galliard (T. Singleton, D. Burke, H. Berg); Finale (R. Blankshine and M. Mussman, R. Wright, C. Holder, G. Montalbano with 5 women, 5 men) **CN** W. Hagen; **Consort Guitar** (Rolando Valdes-Blain); **Flute and Piccolo** (Andrew Lolya); **Cello** (Nellis DeLay); **Drum** (Kenneth Monmyer)

THE LESSON

CH Fleming Flindt **ST** Hans Brenaa **M** Georges Delerue **LI** F. Flindt, after Eugène Ionesco's "The Private Lesson" **CO** Bernard Daydé **S** B. Daydé **Associate Designer** W. Pitkin **L** TS **JP** 27 Sept. 1968, CCT, N.Y.C. **D** Pupil (C. Arthur); Professor (P. Sutherland); Pianist (D. Cartier) **CN** W. Hagen **RV** 14 Oct. 1977, CCT, N.Y.C. **WP** Danish Television, 16 Sept. 1963; first stage production 6 Apr. 1964, Opéra-Comique, Paris

FANFARITA

CH GA **M** Ruperto Chapi y Lorente, a prelude and excerpts from the *zarzuela* "El Tambor de Granaderos," adapted by R. White **CO** R. Quintana **L** TS **WP** 9 Oct. 1968, CCT, N.Y.C. **D** L. Fuente, E. Goodman, S. Magno **CN** S. Lipkin **RV** 15 Oct. 1976, CCT, N.Y.C. **RV** 14 May 1980, Auditorium Theatre, Chicago

FAÇADE (A BALLET FREELY ADAPTED TO MUSIC ORIGINALLY WRITTEN AS A SETTING TO POEMS OF EDITH SITWELL)

CH Frederick Ashton **ST** John Hart and Richard Ellis **M** William Walton **CO** John Armstrong **S** J. Armstrong **L** TS **JP** 28 Jan. 1969, Auditorium Theatre, Chicago **D** Scottish Rhapsody (A. Shuler, Diane Orio, S. Barnard); Yodelling: Milkmaid (R. Wright); Mountaineers (R. Estner, R. Romero, R. Talmage); Polka (P. Johnson); Fox Trot (S. Loyd, N. Sowinska, J. De Bolt, G. Montalbano); Waltz (D. Cartier, Alaine Haubert, Nancy Robinson, D. Silva,); Popular Song (F. Bays, H. Owens); Tango: Gigolo (L. Fuente), Debutante (B. Remington); Tarantella Finale (Ensemble) **CN** W. Hagen **RV** 11 Oct. 1973, CCT, N.Y.C. **WP** 26 Apr. 1931, Cambridge Theatre, London, The Camargo Society

KONSERVATORIET

CH A. Bournonville ST H. Brenaa M H. S. Paulli S W. Pitkin L TS JP 29 Jan. 1969, Auditorium Theatre, Chicago D Elisa (B. Remington); Victorine (P. Johnson); Ballet Master (P. Sutherland); Twelve Ladies (C. Arthur, Z. Bustillo, S. Magno, R. Wright and D. Cartier, A. Haubert, S. Loyd, P. Perry, N. Robinson, D. Silva, T. Singleton, G. Wallstrom); Four Gentlemen (Bill Martin-Viscount, H. Berg, J. Cristofori, A. Williams); Violin Player (R. Talmage) CN W. Hagen WP 6 May 1849, Royal Opera House, Copenhagen, Royal Danish Ballet

ANIMUS

CH GA M Jacob Druckman, "Animus I for Trombone and Tape" CO GA S M. Cho Lee L TS WP 5 Mar. 1969, CCT, N.Y.C. D C. Holder, N. Robinson, D. Burke, P. Perry, P. Johnson Solo Trombonist André Smith

WILLIAM TELL VARIATIONS

CH A. Bournonville ST H. Brenaa M G. Rossini, Act 3 of "William Tell" L TS JP 12 Mar. 1969, CCT, N.Y.C. D T. Singleton, L. Fuente and C. Arthur, G. White, S. Magno, J. De Bolt CN S. Lipkin RV 15 Oct. 1974, CCT, N.Y.C. CN S. Lipkin WP 4 Sept. 1842, Royal Theatre, Copenhagen, Royal Danish Ballet

LE TRICORNE

CH Léonide Massine AC Tatiana Massine and Yurek Lazowski M M. de Falla LI Gregorio Martinez Sierra, after story by Pedro Antonio de Alarcón CO Pablo Picasso, supervised by W. Pitkin S P. Picasso, supervised by W. Pitkin L TS JP 25 July 1969, Opera House, Seattle, Wash. D Miller (L. Fuente); Miller's Wife (B. Remington); Corregidor (Basil Thompson); Corregidor's Wife (R. Wright); Dandy (F. Bays); Alguacils [Police] (G. Montalbano and 4 men); Neighbors (8 women, 8 men); Jota (Company) CN W. Hagen V Jean Kraft (in N.Y.C.) WP 22 July 1919, Alhambra Theatre, London, Diaghilev's Ballets Russes

THE POPPET

CH GA AC J. Howell M Hans Werner Henze, Symphonies No. 1 and No. 3 LI after Arthur Miller's play, "The Crucible" CO Patricia Zipprodt S M. Cho Lee L JT Films Stanley Livingston and Henry Roth Sound Score Thomas Boutiller, incorporating verses from Michael Wigglesworth's poem, "Day of Doom" WP 9 Oct. 1969, CCT, N.Y.C. D John Proctor (D. Burke); Elizabeth Proctor (T. Singleton); Abigail Williams (P. Johnson); Mary Warren (R. Wright); Betty Parris (Francesca Corkle); Rev. Samuel Parris (R. Talmage); Judge Danforth (F. Bays); Thomas Putnam (Gary Chryst); Children (Donna Cowen, Denise Jackson, D. Orio, P. Perry, N. Sowinska); Townspeople (5 women, 7 men) CN S. Lipkin

CONFETTI

CH GA M G. Rossini, Overture to "Semiramide" CO R. Quintana L JT WP 3 Feb. 1970, Auditorium Theatre, Chicago D F. Corkle, S. Loyd, R. Wright, S. Barnard, G. White, William Whitener CN S. Lipkin RV 26 Jan. 1985, Dorothy Chandler Pavilion, Los Angeles

PINEAPPLE POLL

CH John Cranko **ST** David Blair **M** Arthur Sullivan, arr. by Charles Mackerras **LI** J. Cranko, freely adapted from the Bab Ballad, "The Bumboat Woman's Story" by W. S. Gilbert **CO** Osbert Lancaster **S** O. Lancaster **L** JT **JP** 4 Feb. 1970, Auditorium Theatre, Chicago **D** Captain Belaye of the H.M.S. *Hot Cross Bun* (Burton Taylor); Pineapple Poll, a Bumboat Woman (R. Wright); Jasper, Pot Boy at "The Steam Packet" (G. Chryst); Blanche, Belaye's Fiancée (D. Silva); Mrs. Dimple, Her Aunt (D. Cartier); The Crew of H.M.S. *Hot Cross Bun* (6 men); Sweethearts, Wives, etc. (6 women) **CN** W. Hagen **RV** 7 Jan. 1983, CCT, N.Y.C. **ST** Celia Franca **WP** 13 Mar. 1951, Sadler's Wells Theatre, London, Sadler's Wells Theatre Ballet

SOLARWIND

CH GA M J. Druckman, "Animus III for Tape and Clarinet" **CO GA L** TS **WP** 4 Mar. 1970, CCT, N.Y.C. **D** E. Goodman, R. Wright, G. Chryst, H. Berg, C. Holder, G. White, W. Whitener **Clarinettist** Arthur Bloom

PETROUCHKA: A BURLESQUE BALLET IN ONE ACT AND FOUR SCENES BY IGOR STRAVINSKY AND ALEXANDRE BENOIS

CH Michel Fokine, supervised by L. Massine, assisted by T. Massine and Y. Lazowski **M** I. Stravinsky **LI** I. Stravinsky and A. Benois **CO** after A. Benois, supervised by Jane Greenwood **S** after A. Benois, supervised by E. Burbridge **L** TS **JP** 12 Mar. 1970, CCT, N.Y.C. **D** Ballerina (E. Goodman); Petrouchka (Edward Verso); Blackamoor (C. Holder); The Old Showman (Yurek Lazowski); Two Street-Dancing Girls (Z. Bustillo, R. Wright); Two Gypsy Girls (A. Haubert, P. Johnson); The Young Merchant (H. Owens); The First Nursemaid (N. Robinson); Coachman of the Imperial Court (G. Montalbano); Two Stable Boys (G. Chryst, W. Whitener); The Devil (F. Bays); Nurses (8 women); Coachmen (4 men); Drunkards (4 men); Masks and Masqueraders, Merchants, Hawkers, Officers, Soldiers, Cossacks, Policemen, A Bear-Trainer, Ladies, Gentlemen and Children **CN** S. Lipkin **RV** 21 Dec. 1976, CCT, N.Y.C. **RV** 22 Oct. 1983, CCT, N.Y.C. **RV** 13 May 1988, Dorothy Chandler Pavilion, Los Angeles **WP** 13 June 1911, Théâtre du Châtelet, Paris, Diaghilev's Ballets Russes

THE STILL POINT

CH T. Bolender **AC** John Mandia **M** Claude Debussy, String Quartet, op. 10 (first three movements), transcribed for orchestra by Frank Black **CO** RJ and T. Bolender **L** JT **JP** 24 June 1970, Eastvold Auditorium, Tacoma, Wash. **D** P. Johnson and B. Taylor with D. Silva, F. Bays, A. Haubert, R. Talmage **CN** W. Hagen **WP** 1954 Tour, Dance Drama Company, Emily Frankel and Mark Ryder

TRINITY

CH GA M Alan Raph ("Sunday" and "Saturday") and Lee Holdridge ("Summerland"), performed by Virgin Wool **CO** GA, RJ and Estelle Sommers **L** JT **WP** 20 Aug. 1970, Zellerbach Hall, Univ. of California at Berkeley **D** Sunday (C. Holder, G. Chryst, R. Wright, D. Burke with D. Cowen, Starr Danias, James Dunne and D. Jackson, S. Loyd, D.

Orio, Dana Sapiro, R. Estner, R. Talmage, Robert Thomas, G. White); Summerland (D. Cowen, S. Danias, D. Burke, J. Dunne and D. Jackson, S. Loyd, D. Orio, D. Sapiro, R. Wright, R. Estner, R. Talmage, R. Thomas, G. White); Saturday (Entire Cast) **Organist** Hubbard Miller **Boy's Choir** St. Luke's Chapel **CN** W. Hagen **RV** 28 Oct. 1981, CCT, N.Y.C. **RV** 25 Oct. 1989, CCT, N.Y.C.

TIME CYCLE

CH T. Bolender **AC** J. Mandia **M** Lukas Foss, "Time Cycle" (Cantata for Soprano and Orchestra) and Prologue from "Echoi III" **L** JT **JP** 25 Aug. 1970, Zellerbach Auditorium, Univ. of California at Berkeley **D** Prologue (D. Cartier, Lili Cockerille, S. Danias, A. Haubert, D. Jackson, Victoria More, D. Orio, D. Sapiro, G. Wallstrom, H. Owens, R. Talmage, G. White); "We're Late" [W. H. Auden] (N. Robinson, Martine van Hamel, C. Holder, D. Cartier, L. Cockerille, F. Corkle, S. Danias, D. Cowen, A. Haubert, D. Jackson, V. More, D. Orio, D. Sapiro, D. Silva, G. Wallstrom, Randall Harris, H. Owens, R. Talmage, G. White); Improvisation I (P. Johnson, F. Bays); "When the Bells Justle" [A. E. Housman] (M. van Hamel with 10 women, 4 men); Improvisation II (Janey Kawaguchi, G. Chryst, V. More, Phillip Hoffman, H. Owens, R. Talmage, G. White); "Sechzehnter Januar" [from Franz Kafka's *Diaries*] (N. Robinson with 12 women, 7 men); Improvisation III (C. Holder); "Mensch! Gib Acht!" [from F. Nietzsche's *Thus Spake Zarathustra*] (13 women, 8 men) **CN** S. Lipkin **V** Marian Marsh **WP** Spring, 1967, Stadtische Bühnen, Frankfurt, Germany, Frankfurt Ballet

REFLECTIONS

CH GA M P. I. Tchaikovsky, "Variations on a Rococo Theme for Violoncello and Orchestra" op. 33 **CO GA** L JT **WP** 3 Feb. 1971, Auditorium Theatre, Chicago, under "Seven Variations" **D** Theme (E. Goodman, D. Sapiro, S. Danias, C. Arthur, F. Corkle, D. Jackson, S. Loyd); Variation I (E. Goodman); Variation II (S. Danias); Variation III (E. Goodman, G. White); Variation IV (S. Loyd, C. Arthur, D. Jackson); Variation V (E. Goodman, H. Berg); Variation VI (S. Danias, Dennis Wayne); Variation VII (F. Corkle and Entire Cast) **CN** W. Hagen **Solo Cellist** Roger Malitz **RV** 2 Oct. 1985, Dorothy Chandler Pavilion, Los Angeles

ABYSS

CH Stuart Hodes **AC** Robert Vickrey **M** Marga Richter **LI** after a story by Leonid Andreyev **CO** W. Pitkin **L** JT **JP** 3 Mar. 1971, CCT, N.Y.C. **D** Young Man (D. Wayne); Young Girl (L. Cockerille); Assailants (Tony Catanzaro, G. Chryst, C. Holder) **CN** S. Lipkin **RV** 16 Mar. 1973, CCT, N.Y.C. **WP** 21 Feb. 1965, The Casino, Cannes, France, Harkness Ballet

VALENTINE

CH GA M J. Druckman, "Valentine for Solo Contrabass" **CO** E. Sommers (conception) with **GA** L JT **WP** 10 Mar. 1971, CCT, N.Y.C. **D** R. Wright and C. Holder **Bassist** Alvin Brehm **RV** 19 Sept. 1986, Dorothy Chandler Pavilion, Los Angeles **RV** 6 Apr. 1994, New York State Theater, Lincoln Center for the Performing Arts, N.Y.C.

WEEWIS

CH Margo Sappington M Stanley Walden (commissioned), performed by Virgin Wool CO W. Kim L JT WP 1 Sept. 1971, Zellerbach Auditorium, Univ. of California at Berkeley, D I (G. Chryst, J. Dunne); II (R. Wright, C. Holder); III (S. Magno, T. Catanzaro) CN W. Hagen

KETTENTANZ

CH GA M Johann Strauss, Sr. ("Gitana Galop," op. 108; "Annen Polka," op. 137; "Erste Kettenbrüke Walzer," op. 4; "Eisele und Beisele Sprunge," op. 202; "Chineser Galop," op. 20; "Seufzer Galop," op. 9; "Hofball Tanz," op. 51; "Cachucha Galop," op. 97) and Johann Mayer ("Schnofler Tanz") CO Joe Eula L TS WP 7 Sept. 1971, Zellerbach Auditorium, Univ. of California at Berkeley D Gitana Galop (S. Magno, S. Danias, E. Goodman, S. Loyd, D. Silva, R. Wright, S. Barnard, H. Berg, D. Burke, J. Dunne, R. Thomas, G. White); Annen Polka (S. Danias, S. Loyd, S. Magno, S. Barnard, J. Dunne, G. White); Kettenbrüke Waltz (R. Wright, D. Burke); Eisele und Beisele Sprunge (J. Dunne, S. Danias, R. Thomas); Chinese Galop (S. Loyd, D. Burke, D. Silva); Schnofler Tanz (E. Goodman); Seufzer Galop (S. Barnard, G. White); Hofball Tanz (S. Danias, E. Goodman, S. Loyd, D. Silva, H. Berg, J. Dunne, R. Thomas, G. White); Cachucha Galop (S. Magno, R. Wright); Gitana Galop (Entire Cast) CN S. Lipkin RV 30 Jan. 1985, Dorothy Chandler Pavilion, Los Angeles

THE MINGUS DANCES

CH A. Ailey AC Karina Rieger M Charles Mingus CO A. Christina Giannini S E. Burbridge L TS WP 13 Oct. 1971, CCT, N.Y.C. D Dance #1 Andante Con Moto [Pithecanthropus Erectus] (P. Sutherland, C. Holder, D. Burke, S. Danias, N. Robinson, S. Magno and C. Arthur, D. Cowen, P. Johnson, V. More, D. Orio, D. Sapiro, F. Bays, R. Estner, P. Hoffman, G. Montalbano, H. Owens, R. Talmage); Vaudeville: Prestissimo [O.P.] (D. Jackson, J. Dunne, T. Catanzaro); Dance #2 Adagio Ma Non Troppo [Myself When I Am Real] (S. Danias, S. Magno, R. Wright, P. Sutherland, D. Burke, D. Wayne and 6 women, 6 men); Vaudeville: Pesante [Freedom] (J. Dunne, T. Catanzaro, R. Thomas, H. Berg, W. Whitener with Henry Felder, Jr. [Observer]); Dance #3 Lento Assai [Half-Mast Inhibition] (C. Holder, N. Robinson and 6 women, 6 men); Vaudeville: Vivace [Dizzy's Moods] (R. Harris, R. Thomas, H. Berg, W. Whitener); Dance #4 Andantino [Diane] (S. Danias, F. Bays, H. Owens, G. Montalbano, P. Johnson, D. Cowen, D. Orio); Vaudeville: Scherzo [Ysabel's Table Dance] (D. Jackson, J. Dunne, T. Catanzaro); Dance #5 Allegro Marcato [Haitian Fite Song] (Entire Cast) CN W. Hagen

DOUBLE EXPOSURE

CH Joe Layton AC Harry Naughton M Alexander Scriabin (Prelude in D-flat, op. 11, no. 15; Nocturne in D-flat for Left Hand, op. 9, no. 2; Prelude in C, op. 11, no. 1; Etude in F-sharp, op. 42, no. 3; Prelude in B-flat Minor, op. 11, no. 16; Poème in F-sharp, op. 32, no. 1; Etrangeté, op. 63, no. 2; Etude in C-sharp Minor, op. 42, no. 5; Prelude in B, op. 16, no. 1; Prelude in A Minor, op. 51, no. 2; electronic music by Henri Pousseur, excerpts from "Trois Visages de Liège" LI after Oscar Wilde's *The Picture of Dorian Gray* CO John Conklin S J. Conklin L TS **Photographs** Cris Alexander WP 4 Feb. 1972, Auditorium Theatre, Chicago D Dorian (D. Burke); Photographer (P. Sutherland); Leader (G. Chryst);

Groupies (R. Wright, D. Jackson, S. Loyd); Couple (N. Robinson, R. Talmage); Young Boy (Russell Sultzbach); Dorian II (G. White) **PI** SB

MEADOWLARK

CH Eliot Feld **M** F. J. Haydn, Flute Quartets, op. 5, nos. 1-4; finale from String Quartet, op. 74, no. 1, arr. and orch. by H. Kay **CO** Stanley Simmons **S** Robert Munford **L** JT **JP** 9 Feb. 1972, Auditorium Theatre, Chicago **D** I. R. Wright and P. Sutherland with S. Magno, D. Jackson, D. Orio, N. Robinson, D. Silva, S. Barnard, H. Berg, J. Dunne, Gregory Huffman, R. Talmage II. S. Magno and J. Dunne III. N. Robinson and G. Huffman with S. Magno, D. Jackson, D. Orio, D. Silva, R. Wright, S. Barnard, H. Berg, J. Dunne, P. Sutherland, R. Talmage IV. R. Wright and S. Barnard, H. Berg, P. Sutherland V. J. Dunne VI. N. Robinson, D. Silva, P. Sutherland and H. Berg, G. Huffman, R. Talmage VII. Full Company **CN** Sung Kwak **WP** 3 Oct. 1968, Manitoba Centennial Concert Hall, Winnipeg, Canada, Royal Winnipeg Ballet

CHABRIESQUE

CH GA **M** E. Chabrier, "Trois Valses Romantiques," "Souvenirs de Munich," "Cortège Burlesque" **CO** A. C. Giannini **L** TS **WP** 10 Feb. 1972, Auditorium Theatre, Chicago **D** First Waltz (S. Danias, C. Holder, P. Johnson, F. Corkle, S. Barnard and C. Arthur, G. White, D. Jackson, Eileen Brady, Christine Uchida, G. Wallstrom, R. Harris, G. Huffman, R. Thomas); Second Waltz (P. Johnson, C. Holder and 4 women); Third Waltz (S. Danias, G. White and 3 women, 3 men); 1st Quadrille (F. Corkle, D. Jackson, G. Huffman, R. Thomas); 2nd Quadrille (P. Johnson, C. Holder); 3rd Quadrille (S. Danias, S. Barnard); 4th Quadrille (G. White); 5th Quadrille (D. Jackson, C. Arthur, E. Brady, F. Corkle, G. Wallstrom); Coda (F. Corkle, S. Barnard, S. Danias, G. White, P. Johnson, C. Holder, and 5 women, 3 men) **CN** S. Lipkin **PI** M. Roark and SB

AFTER EDEN

CH John Butler **M** Lee Hoiby **CO** R. Ter-Arutunian **S** R. Ter-Arutunian **L** JT **JP** 21 Mar. 1972, CCT, N.Y.C. **D** S. Danias and D. Wayne **CN** S. Lipkin **RV** 3 Nov. 1978, CCT, N.Y.C. **ST** Lawrence Rhodes **WP** 11 Mar. 1966, Cannes, France, Harkness Ballet

LE BEAU DANUBE

CH L. Massine **AC** Kate Flatt **B** L. Massine **M** Johann Strauss, arr. and orch. by Roger Désormière **CO** Lois Bewley, after Etienne de Beaumont **S** Vladimir and Elizabeth Polunin, after Constantin Guys **L** JT **JP** 4 Oct. 1972, CCT, N.Y.C. **D** Street Dancer (P. Johnson); Eldest Daughter (S. Danias); First Hand (F. Corkle); Hussar (G. Huffman); King of the Dandies (G. Chryst); Athlete (Russell Chambers); Their Manager (T. Catanzaro); Mother (S. Loyd); Father (H. Owens); Their Younger Daughters (Sakina Jaffrey, Laura DeAngelis, Kathy Montgomery); Artist (R. Talmage); Gardener (T. Catanzaro); Modistes (D. Cowen, J. Kawaguchi, Pamela Nearhoof, G. Wallstrom); Needlewomen (A. Haubert, D. Silva); Ladies of the Town (E. Brady, E. Goodman, D. Orio, C. Uchida); Salesmen (R. Estner, P. Hoffman, Ted Nelson, R. Thomas); Dandies (Richard Colton, R. Harris, R. Sultzbach, W. Whitener) **CN** S. Lipkin **RV** 25 Jan. 1985, Dorothy Chandler Pavilion, Los Angeles **WP** 15 Apr. 1933, Théâtre de Monte Carlo, Monaco, Ballet Russe de Monte Carlo

INTERPLAY

CH J. Robbins AC Wilma Curley M Morton Gould, "American Concertette" CO Irene Sharaff L JT JP 6 Oct. 1972, CCT, N.Y.C. D First Movement: Free-Play (C. Holder and R. Wright, C. Arthur, D. Jackson, F. Corkle, G. Chryst, P. Sutherland, G. Huffman); Second Movement: Horse-Play (G. Chryst); Third Movement: By-Play (R. Wright, P. Sutherland); Fourth Movement: Team-Play (Full Cast) CN S. Lipkin PI SB WP 1 June 1945, Ziegfeld Theatre, N.Y.C.

GRAND PAS ESPAGNOL

CH Benjamin Harkarvy M Moritz Moszkowski, "Spanish Dances," op. 12, nos. 1-5 CO Joop Stokvis L JT JP 12 Oct. 1972, CCT, N.Y.C. D F. Corkle, R. Wright, P. Nearhoof, G. White, P. Sutherland, W. Whitener CN S. Lipkin WP 16 Oct. 1963, Royal Theatre, The Hague, Netherlands, Nederlands Dans Theater

SACRED GROVE ON MOUNT TAMALPAIS

CH GA M A. Raph (commissioned); Johann Pachelbel, "Canon in D" Lyrics A. Raph CO David James S Robert Yodice, from a concept by M. Cho Lee L TS WP 2 Nov. 1972, CCT, N.Y.C. D S. Danias, R. Chambers, R. Sultzbach and P. Nearhoff, G. White, J. Kawaguchi, G. Huffman, E. Brady, D. Orio, D. Silva, C. Uchida, R. Estner, R. Harris, R. Talmage, R. Thomas; The Children (Robin Morse, Gene Harrison) CN S. Kwak

JACKPOT

CH GA M J. Druckman, "Synapse" CO GA L JT WP 7 Feb. 1973, Auditorium Theatre, Chicago D E. Goodman and G. White

DEUCE COUPE

CH Twyla Tharp M The Beach Boys ("Little Deuce Coupe," "Honda," "Devoted to You," "How She Boogalooed It," "Alley Oop," "Take a Load Off Your Feet," "Long Tall Texan," "Papa Ooh Mau Mau," "Catch A Wave," "Got to Know the Woman," "Don't Go Near the Water," "Mama Says," "Wouldn't It Be Nice," "Cuddle Up"); tape compiled and variations on "Cuddle Up" by David Horowitz CO Scott Barrie S United Graffiti Artists: Hugo Martinez, Mike 171, Phase 2, Snake 1, Rick II, Stitch I, Coco 144, SJK 171, Jec, Ray-B 954, Stay-Hi 149, Soda I, C.A.T. 87, Rican 619, Riff 170, Charmin 65, Lee 163, Henry 161 L JT WP 8 Feb. 1973, Auditorium Theatre, Chicago D H. Berg, E. Brady, D. Cowen, S. Danias, E. Goodman, Larry Grenier, Beatriz Rodriguez, C. Uchida, G. White, W. Whitener, R. Wright and Isabel García-Lorca,* Kenneth Rinker,* Sara Rudner,* Nina Wiener,* Rose Marie Wright* *Guest Artist, members of Twyla Tharp Dancers

JIVE

CH E. Feld AC Elizabeth Lee M M. Gould, "Derivations for Clarinet and Band" CO W. Kim L JT WP 21 Feb. 1973, CCT, N.Y.C. D Warm-Up (F. Corkle, A. Haubert, D. Jackson, J. Kawaguchi, P. Nearhoof, B. Rodriguez, C. Uchida, R. Wright, T. Catanzaro, R. Chambers, G. Chryst, L. Grenier, C. Holder, G. Huffman, R. Sultzbach, R. Talmage); Blues (P. Nearhoof, C. Holder and 2 women, 2 men); Rag (3 women, 3 men); Ride-Out (Full Company) **CN** S. Lipkin **Solo Clarinettist** David Weber

PARADE: REALISTIC BALLET IN ONE ACT

CH L. Massine **AC** Susi Della Pietra **M** Erik Satie **LI** Jean Cocteau **CO** P. Picasso, realized under supervision of W. Kim (Chinese Conjuror, Acrobats, Little American Girl) and Kermit Love (Managers) **S** P. Picasso, realized under supervision of E. Burbridge **Curtain** P. Picasso, realized under the supervision of E. Burbridge **L** JT **JP** 22 Mar. 1973, CCT, N.Y.C. (American Premiere) **D** Chinese Conjuror (G. Chryst); Acrobats (E. Brady, G. Huffman); Little American Girl (D. Cowen); Manager in Evening Dress (R. Talmage); Manager from New York (T. Nelson); Manager on Horseback (R. Estner, P. Hoffman) **CN** S. Lipkin **RV** 27 Oct. 1983, CCT, N.Y.C. **WP** 18 May 1917, Théâtre du Châtelet, Paris, Diaghilev's Ballets Russes

THE DREAM

CH F. Ashton **ST** J. Hart **M** F. Mendelssohn-Bartholdy, incidental music to "A Midsummer Night's Dream," op. 21 and op. 61, arr. by John Lanchbery **LI** adapted from William Shakespeare's *A Midsummer Night's Dream* **CO** David Walker **S** D. Walker **L** TS **JP** 9 Aug. 1973, Wolf Trap Farm Park for the Performing Arts, Vienna, Vir. **D** Titania (R. Wright); Oberon (B. Taylor); Puck (R. Sultzbach); Bottom (L. Grenier); Rustics (R. Colton, R. Estner, P. Hoffman, Jeffrey Hughes, T. Nelson); Helena (A. Haubert); Hermia (C. Arthur); Demetrius (R. Talmage); Lysander (R. Thomas); Peaseblossom (D. Cowen); Cobweb (D. Jackson); Moth (E. Brady); Mustardseed (D. Orio); Fairies (Conchita Blazquez, Ann Marie De Angelo, Michelle Hamilton, Jan Hanniford, Nancy Ichino, Krystyna Jurkowski, J. Kawaguchi, P. Nearhoof, Sharon Pederson, B. Rodriguez, C. Uchida, Jodi Wintz) **CN** S. Lipkin **V** Valerie Girard and Jeanne Bowers **Chorus** Wolf Trap Company Chorus, directed by John Moriarty **RV** 2 Oct. 1987, Dorothy Chandler Pavilion, Los Angeles **ST** Alexander Grant and Charthel Arthur

REMEMBRANCES

CH RJ **M** Richard Wagner, "Album-Sonata for Frau Mathilde Wesendonck"; "Wesendonck Lieder," "Der Engel," "Stehe Still," "Im Treibhaus," "Schmerzen," "Traüme"); the "Porazzi Theme" **CO** W. Kim **S** R. Ter-Arutunian **L** JT **WP** 12 Oct. 1973, CCT, N.Y.C. **D** She, Who Sings (Donna Roll); She, Who Remembers (J. Hanniford); F. Corkle and J. Watts with D. Jackson, R. Thomas, J. Kawaguchi, P. Sutherland, N. Ichino, R. Sultzbach, E. Brady, Adix Carman, C. Arthur and K. Jurkowski, T. Singleton, Donn Edwards, Tom Fowler, J. Hughes **CN** S. Lipkin **PI** SB **RV** (Pas de Deux) 28 Oct. 1988, CCT, N.Y.C.

THE MOOR'S PAVANE

CH José Limón **ST** Jennifer Scanlon **M** Henry Purcell, from "The Gordian Knot Untied," Suites 1 and 2; "Abdelazar Suite"; Pavane from "Pavane and Chaconne for Strings," arr. by Simon Sadoff **CO** after Pauline Lawrence, supervised by Charles D. Tomlinson **L** TS **JP** 13 Oct. 1973, CCT, N.Y.C. **D** Moor (C. Holder); Moor's Wife (J. Hanniford); His Friend (B.

Taylor); His Friend's Wife (B. Rodriguez) CN S. Lipkin RV 26 Jan. 1985, Dorothy Chandler Pavilion, Los Angeles WP 17 Aug. 1949, Connecticut College American Dance Festival, José Limón Dance Company

AS TIME GOES BY

CH T. Tharp AC Henry Berg M F. J. Haydn, Symphony No. 45 in F-sharp Minor, 3rd and 4th Movements CO Chester Weinberg L JT WP 24 Oct. 1973, CCT, N.Y.C. D After the Fact (B. Rodriguez); Ten Make Six (E. Brady, A. Carman, P. Nearhoof, B. Rodriguez, B. Taylor, W. Whitener); The Four Finales: I (P. Nearhoof, W. Whitener and E. Brady, A. Carman, B. Taylor with A. M. De Angelo, R. Colton, D. Edwards, R. Estner, Tom Fowler, L. Grenier, J. Hanniford, J. Hughes, N. Ichino, K. Jurkowski, B. Rodriguez, C. Uchida); II (E. Brady with 4 women, 5 men); III (P. Nearhoof with 2 women, 3 men); IV (W. Whitener with A. M. De Angelo, D. Edwards, C. Uchida and J. Hanniford with ensemble); Then (L. Grenier and C. Uchida with 4 women, 2 men) CN S. Lipkin RV 6 Nov. 1977, CCT, N. Y. C.

NEW YORK EXPORT: OP. JAZZ

CH J. Robbins, restaged with W. Curley M Robert Prince, "Jazz Concert" CO Ben Shahn and Florence Klotz S B. Shahn L JT JP 21 Mar. 1974, CCT, N.Y.C. D 1. Entrance: Group Dance (Company); 2. Statics (P. Nearhoof, C. Holder and G. Chryst, L. Grenier, P. Sutherland, R. Estner); Improvisations (Company); 4. Passage for Two (B. Rodriguez, E. Verso); 5. Theme, Variations and Fugue (Company; J. Hanniford, N. Ichino, D. Jackson, K. Jurkowski, P. Nearhoof, C. Uchida, R. Wright, G. Chryst, J. Dunne, L. Grenier, C. Holder, P. Sutherland, E. Verso, W. Whitener) CN Robert Rogers WP 8 June 1958, Festival of Two Worlds, Spoleto, Italy, Jerome Robbins Ballets: U. S. A.

PULCINELLA (BALLET WITH SONG IN ONE ACT)

CH L. Massine AC S. Della Pietra M I. Stravinsky, after Giambattista Pergolesi CO P. Picasso, recreated by R. Ter-Arutunian S P. Picasso, recreated by R. Ter-Arutunian L TS JP 15 Aug. 1974, Wolf Trap Farm Park, Vienna, Va. D Pulcinella (G. Chryst), Pimpenella (F. Corkle), Prudenza (C. Arthur), Rosetta (D. Cowen), Fourbo (R. Sultzbach), Caviello (R. Talmage), Florindo (G. Huffman), Il Dottore (P. Hoffman), Tartaglia (R. Estner), Quatre Petits Pulcinella (J. Hughes, T. Fowler, D. Edwards, R. Colton), Babbo (T. Nelson) CN S. Lipkin V Brenda Quilling, mezzo-soprano; Modesto Crisci, tenor; Donnie Ray Albert, bass. Children courtesy of American Ballet Center WP 15 May 1920, Théâtre National de L'Opéra, Paris, Diaghilev's Ballets Russes

EVENING DIALOGUES

CH Jonathan Watts M Robert Schumann, Davidsbündlertänze, op. 6, nos. 1-7, 10, 11, 13-18 CO J. Eula L JT WP 22 Aug. 1974, Ravinia Festival, Highland Park, Ill. D F. Corkle, A. Carman, G. Huffman, J. Hughes, N. Ichino, D. Jackson, B. Rodriguez, R. Sultzbach, B. Taylor PI SB

THE RELATIVITY OF ICARUS

CH GA M Gerhard Samuel T Jack Larson CO R. Ter-Arutunian L TS WP 30 Aug. 1974, Artpark, Lewiston, N.Y. D The Sun (A. M. De Angelo), Icarus (R. Sultzbach), Daedalus (T. Nelson) V Joanne Bell, soprano

MONOTONES I & II

CH F. Ashton ST Faith Worth M E. Satie, "Prélude d'Eginhard" (Overture); *Monotones I*, "Trois Gnossiennes," orch. by J. Lanchbery; *Monotones II*, "Trois Gymnopédies," orch. by C. Debussy (Nos. 1 and 3) and Roland Manuel (No. 2) CO F. Ashton L JT JP 11 Oct. 1974, CCT, N.Y.C. D S. Danias, B. Taylor, R. Wright (*Monotones I*); Kevin McKenzie, P. Nearhoof, R. Thomas (*Monotones II*) CN S. Lipkin RV (*Monotones II*) 16 Oct. 1977, CCT, N.Y.C., and 23 Jan. 1985, Dorothy Chandler Pavilion, Los Angeles RV (*Monotones I*) 16 Sept. 1986, Dorothy Chandler Pavilion, Los Angeles WP 24 Mar. 1965 (*Monotones II*); 25 Apr. 1966 (*Monotones I*), Royal Opera House, Covent Garden, London, Royal Ballet

DEUCE COUPE II

CH T. Tharp AC Rose Marie Wright **Ballet Mistress** Diane Orio M The Beach Boys ("Little Deuce Coupe," "Honda," "The Welfare Song," "Boogaloo," "Feet Pete," "Texan," Popa Mama," "Water," "Alley-Oop," "Wouldn't It Be Nice," "Cuddle Up"); tape compiled by D. Horowitz CO S. Barrie S James Rosenquist L JT WP 1 Feb. 1975, St. Louis, Mo. D D. Cowen, A. M. De Angelo, J. Hanniford, K. Jurkowski, D. Orio, N. Ichino, R. Wright and E. Goodman, D. Burke, A. Carman, G. Chryst, R. Colton, D. Edwards, T. Fowler, L. Grenier, G. Huffman, W. Whitener RV 30 Oct. 1981, CCT, N.Y.C.

JEU DE CARTES (A POKER GAME IN THREE DEALS)

CH J. Cranko ST Georgette Tsinguirides (restaged by Hiller Huhn) M I. Stravinsky CO Dorothee Zippel S D. Zippel L JT JP 8 Feb. 1975, Auditorium Theatre, Chicago D First Deal: Queen of Hearts (D. Jackson), Ten of Clubs (D. Edwards), Ten of Spades (R. Estner), Seven of Diamonds (T. Fowler), Seven of Hearts (T. Nelson), Joker (R. Sultzbach); Second Deal: Two of Hearts (A. Carman), Three of Hearts (W. Whitener), Four of Hearts (G. Chryst), Five of Hearts (K. McKenzie), Six of Hearts (C. Holder), Joker (R. Sultzbach); Third Deal: Two of Diamonds (R. Wright), Ace of Spades (D. Cartier), King of Spades (P. Hoffman), Jack of Spades (R. Thomas), Ten of Spades (A. Haubert), Joker (R. Sultzbach) CN Robert Rogers RV 27 Sept. 1985, Dorothy Chandler Pavilion, Los Angeles WP 22 Jan. 1965, Württemberg State Theater, Stuttgart, Germany, Stuttgart Ballet

THE BIG CITY

CH K. Jooss ST Anna Markard M Alexandre Tansman, "Sonatine Transatlantique" LI K. Jooss CO Hermann Markard, re-created by Ray Diffen L H. Markard, re-created by JT JP 11 Feb. 1975, Auditorium Theatre, Chicago D Young Workman (W. Whitener), Girl (C. Arthur), Libertine (B. Taylor). Scene I: Street Scene; Sisters (J. Hanniford, Miyoko Kato), Gentleman (E. Verso), Newspaper Boy (J. Hughes), Flower Girl (K. Jurkowski), Landlady (T. Singleton), Businessman (T. Fowler), Nurse (P. Nearhoof), Streetwalkers (A. Haubert, D. Cartier). Scene II; Workers' Quarters, Children (J. Hughes, A. Carman, A. M. De

Angelo, K. Jurkowski), Mothers (J. Hanniford, T. Singleton). Scene III: Dance Hall; Charleston (4 women, 3 men), Musette (4 women, 4 men) **CN** S. Kwak **PI** SB and M. Roark **WP** 21 Nov. 1932, Opera House, Cologne, Germany, Ballets Jooss

OFFENBACH IN THE UNDERWORLD

CH A. Tudor **ST** Celia Franca **M** Jacques Offenbach, from "Gaîté Parisienne" and others, arr. and orch. by George Crum **CO** Kay Ambrose, re-created by R. Diffen **S** K. Ambrose, re-created by E. Burbridge **L** JT **JP** 14 Aug. 1975, Artpark, Lewiston, N. Y. **D** Madame La Patronne (D. Cartier), Her Little Daughter (A. M. De Angelo), Painter (B. Taylor), Waiters (R. Estner, R. Colton), Local Ladies (A. Haubert, M. Kato, Jean McCabe, K. Jurkowski, J. Hanniford, T. Singleton, Ingrid Fraley, P. Nearhoof), Young Men (A. Carman, T. Fowler, Phillip Jerry, D. Edwards), Debutante (S. Danias), Her Friends (Carol Messmer, J. Wintz, D. Orio), His Imperial Excellency (P. Sutherland), Operetta Star (F. Corkle), Young Officer (R. Sultzbach), Queen of the Carriage Trade (D. Jackson) **CN** S. Lipkin **RV** 5 Jan. 1983, CCT, N.Y.C. **WP** 17 Jan. 1955, Palace Theater, St. Catherine's, Ontario, Canada, National Ballet of Canada

OPUS I

CH J. Cranko **ST** G. Tsinguirides **M** A. Webern, "Passacaglia, Opus I" **L** JT **JP** 2 Oct. 1975, CCT, N.Y.C. **D** I. Fraley, B. Taylor and D. Cowen, J. Hanniford, A. Haubert, K. Jurkowski, M. Kato, J. McCabe, D. Burke, D. Edwards, Chris Jensen, P. Jerry, K. McKenzie, R. Thomas **CN** S. Lipkin **WP** 7 Nov. 1965, Württemberg State Theater, Stuttgart, Germany, Stuttgart Ballet

DRUMS, DREAMS AND BANJOS

CH GA **M** S. Foster, variations and orch. by Peter Link **CO** Stanley Simmons **S** R. Ter-Arutunian **L** TS **WP** 9 Oct. 1975, CCT, N.Y.C. **D** C. Arthur, S. Danias, A. M. De Angelo, I. Fraley, E. Goodman, D. Jackson, P. Nearhoof, D. Burke, R. Estner, C. Jensen, K. McKenzie, R. Sultzbach, P. Sutherland, R. Thomas and D. Cowen, J. Hanniford, K. Jurkowski, M. Kato, J. McCabe, C. Messmer, T. Singleton, J. Wintz, A. Carman, R. Colton, D. Edwards, T. Fowler, Jerel Hilding, J. Hughes, P. Jerry **CN** S. Lipkin **V** Charles Leighton **RV** 6 Mar. 1992, Northrop Auditorium, Univ. of Minnesota, Minneapolis **ST** Scott Barnard

FIVE DANCES

CH Christian Holder **M** Sergei Rachmaninoff, "Elégie" and "Mélodie," op. 3, nos. 1 and 3; Prelude No. 9 in E-flat Minor, op 23; Prelude No. 6 in F Minor, op. 32; Prelude No. 1 in F-sharp Minor, op. 23 **CO** C. Holder **L** JT **WP** 16 Oct. 1975, CCT, N.Y.C. **D** D. Jackson and R. Sultzbach **PI** SB

A BALL IN OLD VIENNA

CH K. Jooss **ST** A. Markard, assisted by H. Markard **M** Joseph Lanner, arr. by F. A. Cohen **CO** R. Diffen, after Aino Siimola **L** JT **JP** 28 Jan. 1976, Hancher Auditorium, Univ. of Iowa, Iowa City **D** Debutante (D. Jackson), Her Admirer (K. McKenzie), Her Aunts (D.

Cartier, T. Singleton), Eligible Gentleman (P. Sutherland), His Sweetheart (J. Hanniford), Dancing Master (G. Chryst), His Partner (B. Rodriguez), Dancing Couples (C. Messmer, P. Nearhoof, T. Fowler, P. Jerry) **CN** S. Kwak **PI** SB and M. Roark **WP** 21 Nov. 1932, Cologne, Germany, Ballets Jooss

PAVANE ON THE DEATH OF AN INFANTA

CH K. Jooss **ST** A. Markard **M** M. Ravel, "Pavane pour une Infante Défunte" **CO** R. Diffen, after Sigurd Leeder **L** JT **JP** 28 Jan. 1976, Hancher Auditorium, Univ. of Iowa, Iowa City **D** The Infanta (F. Corkle), Ladies and Gentlemen of the Court (I. Fraley, Rachel Ganteaume, Charlene Gehm, J. McCabe, Donna Ross, Roberto Medina, Dennis Poole, Craig Williams) **PI** SB **WP** Nov. 1929, Essen, Germany, Ballets Jooss

FACE DANCERS

CH M. Sappington **M** Michael Kamen (commissioned) **CO** W. Kim **L** TS **WP** 10 Feb. 1976, Auditorium Theatre, Chicago (under the title *Tactics*) **D** I. Darrell Barnett, G. Chryst, C. Holder, K. McKenzie, R. Sultzbach, R. Thomas, C. Gehm, J. Hanniford, D. Jackson, M. Kato, C. Messmer, B. Rodriguez, Sara Yarborough; II. 4 women, 5 men; III. R. Sultzbach, S. Yarborough, B. Rodriguez, C. Messmer, G. Chryst and Company

THE JOFFREY BALLET

ORPHEUS TIMES LIGHT

CH GA **AC** S. Barnard and J. Howell **M** José Serebrier **LI** J. Larson, poem "Orpheus Times Light" **CO** W. Kim **S** W. Kim **L** TS **WP** 21 Oct. 1976, CCT, N.Y.C. **D** Orpheus (D. Burke), Eurydice (I. Fraley), Pluto (C. Holder), Persephone (M. Kato), Angel (R. Thomas), Messengers (D. Barnett, R. Medina), Shades of Underworld (Cynthia Anderson, R. Ganteaume, C. Gehm, C. Messmer, Berissa Welles, Glenn Dufford, J. Hilding, P. Jerry, D. Poole, C. Williams) **CN** José Serebrier **Harpist** Nancy Allen **V** Linda Phillips

RODEO (OR, THE COURTING AT BURNT RANCH)

CH Agnes de Mille **ST** Vernon Lusby **M** Aaron Copland **CO** K. Love **S** Oliver Smith **L** TS **JP** 28 Oct. 76, CCT, N.Y.C. **D** Caller (R. Thomas), Head Wrangler (D. Burke), Champion Roper (R. Sultzbach), Cowgirl (B. Rodriguez), Ranch Owner's Daughter (J. Hanniford), Her Eastern Friends from Kansas City (K. Jurkowski, C. Messmer, Lisa Slagle), Cowhands (9 men), Womenfolk (6 women) **CN** S. Lipkin **RV** 25 Oct. 1983, CCT, N.Y.C. **ST** P. Sutherland **WP** 16 Oct. 1942, Metropolitan Opera House, N.Y.C., Ballet Russe de Monte Carlo

TCHAIKOVSKY PAS DE DEUX

CH G. Balanchine **ST** Sara Leland **M** P. I. Tchaikovsky (from *Swan Lake*, 1876) **CO** Karinska **L** JT **JP** 30 Oct. 1976, CCT, N.Y.C. **D** F. Corkle and D. Poole **CN** S. Lipkin **RV** 22 Oct. 1981, CCT, N.Y.C. **RV** 23 May 1996, Shubert Theatre, Chicago **ST** Victoria Simon **WP** 29 Mar. 1960, CCT, N.Y.C., New York City Ballet

Happily Ever After

CH T. Tharp **M** performed by "Snuffy" Jenkins, "Pappy" Sherrill and the Hired Hands with Harold Lucas and Kenny Meggs, add. music adapted by Richard Peaslee **CO** Santo Loquasto **L** JT **WP** 3 Nov. 1976, CCT, N.Y.C. **D** I. Tom Rawe,* Jennifer Way,* Shelley Washington,* C. Uchida,* ("Texas Quickstep," "Fifty Year Ago Waltz," "Rat Cheese Under the Hill," "Cacklin' Hen and Rooster Too," "Katy Did," "Took My Gal A-Walkin" [Charlie Poole and the North Carolina Ramblers], "Fresno Blues," "Alabama Jubilee") II. A. M. De Angelo ("Billy in the Low Ground") III. C. Anderson, C. Messmer, B. Rodriguez, R. Sultzbach ("I'm Sad and Blue," "A Corn Licker Still in Georgia" [The Skillet Lickers]); "Good Bye Little Bonnie," "Alabama Jubilee") 3 women and 1 man ("Lost Child"); 3 women and 1 man (Reprise); IV. R. M. Wright* with G. Chryst, R. Colton, J. Hilding, T. Rawe,* W. Whitener ("Cacklin' Hen and Rooster Too"). *Guest appearances through the courtesy of Twyla Tharp Dance Foundation

Cacklin' Hen (Revision of Happily Ever After)

CH T. Tharp **M** performed by "S." Jenkins, "P." Sherrill and the Hired Hands with H. Lucas and K. Meggs, add. music adapted by R. Peaslee **CO** S. Loquasto **L** JT **WP** 4 Feb. 1977, Auditorium Theatre, Chicago **D** I. "Billy in the Low Ground" [Traditional Country Music] (A. M. De Angelo); "Cacklin' Hen and Rooster Too" [By Skillet Lickers, adapted by R. Peaslee] (J. Hanniford with D. Barnett, G. Chryst, J. Hilding, R. Sultzbach, W. Whitener)

Touch Me

CH GA AC J. Howell **M** Rev. James Cleveland **CO** Geoffrey Holder **L** JT **WP** 1 June 1977, War Memorial Opera House, San Francisco **D** C. Holder **V** Rev. J. Cleveland and the Charles Fold Singers **RV** 10 Oct. 1989, Kennedy Center for the Performing Arts, Washington, D.C.

Pas de Deux Holberg

CH J. Cranko **ST** G. Tsinguirides **M** Edvard Grieg, "Suite in Old Style for String Orchestra," op. 40 **L** JT **JP** 3 June 1977, War Memorial Opera House, San Francisco **D** D. Jackson and K. McKenzie **CN** Allan Lewis **AL** I. Fraley and D. Poole **WP** 15 June 1969, Württemberg State Theater, Stuttgart, Germany, Stuttgart Ballet

La Vivandière Pas de Six

CH Arthur Saint-Léon, after Antonio Guerra, reconstructed by Ann Hutchinson Guest from research by Ivor Guest **ST** Maria Grandy **M** Jean-Baptiste Nadaud, based on themes by Daniel François Auber **L** P. Curry **JP** 18 Aug. 1977, Ravinia Festival, Highland Park, Ill. **D** A. M. De Angelo and K. McKenzie with Ursula Burke, C. Messmer, D. Ross, Ellen Troy **CN** A. Lewis **RV** 10 May 1981, Auditorium Theatre, Chicago **RV** 11 Apr. 1987, Opera House, Kennedy Center for the Performing Arts, Washington, D.C. **WP** 20 Oct. 1848, Théâtre de la Nation, Paris, Paris Opéra Ballet

JAZZ CALENDAR

CH F. Ashton ST F. Worth assisted by Michael Somes M Richard Rodney Bennett CO Derek Jarmon, supervised by R. Diffen S D. Jarmon, supervised by E. Burbridge L JT JP 31 Aug. 1977, Artpark, Lewiston, N.Y. D Monday (C. Anderson); Tuesday (A. M. De Angelo, Andrew Levinson, K. McKenzie); Wednesday (C. Gehm, T. Fowler, J. Hilding, Paul Shoemaker, R. Thomas); Thursday (G. Chryst, U. Burke, Amy Danis, C. Messmer, D. Ross, E. Troy, Carole Valleskey); Friday (I. Fraley, Tom van Cauwenbergh); Saturday (R. Estner, Darrell Barnett, G. Dufford, John Grensback, J. Hughes, P. Jerry, William Starrett, R. Sultzbach, W. Whitener); Sunday (R. Ganteaume) CN S. Lipkin WP 9 Jan. 1968, Royal Opera House, Covent Garden, London, Royal Ballet

ROMEO AND JULIET

CH Oscar Araiz AC Betty Baz M Sergei Prokofiev CO Renata Schussheim, supervised by Mabel Astarloa L JT JP 12 Oct. 1977, CCT, N.Y.C. D Juliet (L. Slagle, I. Fraley, D. Jackson), Romeo (K. McKenzie), Lady Capulet (B. Rodriguez), Lord Capulet (R. Estner), Paris (P. Jerry), Tybalt (G. Chryst), Mercutio (R. Sultzbach), Nurse (A. Danis), Mandolin Pas de Deux (A. M. De Angelo, J. Hughes), Lament [Prologue] (C. Anderson, J. Hanniford, C. Messmer), Young Girl (C. Messmer), Dancers, Characters in the Ball and Folk Dances, The Dead, The Lovers (13 women, 11 men) CN S. Lipkin WP 15 Sept. 1970, Buenos Aires, Argentina, Ballet Teatro San Martin

TARANTELLA

CH G. Balanchine ST S. Leland M L. M. Gottschalk, reconstructed and orch. by H. Kay CO Karinska L P. Curry JP 30 Oct. 1977, CCT, N.Y.C. D F. Corkle and W. Whitener CN S. Lipkin PI SB RV 26 Feb. 1991, New York State Theater, Lincoln Center, N.Y.C. WP 7 Jan. 1964, CCT, N.Y.C., New York City Ballet

LES PATINEURS

CH F. Ashton ST Brian Shaw M Giacomo Meyerbeer, from "Le Prophète" and "L'étoile du Nord," arr. by Constant Lambert CO William Chappell, supervised by R. Diffen S W. Chappell, supervised by E. Burbridge L JT JP 2 Nov. 1977, CCT, N.Y.C. D Entrée (F. Corkle, A. M. De Angelo); Pas des Patineurs (D. Ross, Gregory King, C. Valleskey, J. Hughes, U. Burke, Laurence Blake, C. Messmer, J. Grensback); Variation (Mark Goldweber); Pas de Deux (D. Jackson, G. Huffman); Ensemble (F. Corkle, A. M. De Angelo, M. Goldweber and Pas des Patineurs); Pas de Trois (F. Corkle, A. M. De Angelo, M. Goldweber); Pas de Deux (C. Anderson, Patricia Miller); Ensemble (2 women, 4 men); Finale (Ensemble) CN Terence Kern RV 12 Apr. 1994, New York State Theater, Lincoln Center, N.Y.C. WP 16 Feb. 1937, Sadler's Wells Theatre, London, Vic-Wells Ballet

L'AIR D'ESPRIT (A TRIBUTE TO OLGA SPESSIVTZEVA)

CH GA M Adolphe Adam CO A. C. Giannini L JT WP 9 Feb. 1978, Auditorium Theatre, Chicago D F. Corkle and Glenn White CN A. Lewis RV 9 Oct. 1987, Dorothy Chandler Pavilion, Los Angeles

MIRAGE

CH M. Sappington M M. Kamen (commissioned) CO W. Kim L TS WP 23 Feb. 1978, Henry and Edsel Ford Auditorium, Detroit, under *Pas De Deux (Untitled)*, extracted from *Face Dancers* D J. Hanniford and D. Barnett CN A. Lewis

BROUILLARDS

CH J. Cranko ST G. Tsinguirides M C. Debussy, selected Preludes for Piano ("Brouillards," "La Puerto del Vino," "Voiles," "General Lavine — Eccentric," "Bruyère," "Les fées sont d'exquises danseuses," "Feuilles mortes," "Hommage à S. Pickwick, Esq. P. P. M. D. C.," "Des pas sur la neige") and "The Girl with Flaxen Hair" L JT JP 5 Apr. 1978, CCT, N.Y.C. D Brouillards (Ensemble); La Puerto del Vino (Susan Frazer, L. Blake, T. Fowler, P. Shoemaker); Voiles (F. Corkle, R. Sultzbach); General Lavine — Eccentric [Cakewalk]- (Carl Corry, G. Dufford, W. Starrett); Bruyère (B. Taylor); Les fées sont d'exquises danseuses (C. Anderson, C. Gehm); Feuilles mortes (I. Fraley, G. Huffman); Hommage à S. Pickwick, Esq. P. P. M. D. C. (G. Chryst, L. Blake, C. Corry, G. Dufford, T. Fowler, P. Shoemaker, W. Starrett); Des pas sur la neige (D. Jackson, J. Hilding, C. Holder); Brouillards (Ensemble) PI SB WP 8 Mar. 1970, Württemberg State Theater, Stuttgart, Germany, Stuttgart Ballet

HEPTAGON

CH O. Araiz M F. Poulenc, Concerto in G Minor for Organ, Timpani and Strings CO S. Loquasto L JT WP 12 Apr. 1978, CCT, N.Y.C. D Master (C. Holder), Acolytes (G. Dufford, M. Goldweber, J. Hilding, G. Huffman, P. Jerry, A. Levinson) CN S. Lipkin **Organ Soloist** Leonard Raver

SUITE SAINT-SAËNS

CH GA AC S. Barnard and G. White M Camille Saint-Saëns, Caprice Valse from "Wedding Cake," op. 76; Serenade from "Serenade for Flute and Cello," op. 15; Minuet from Septet, op. 65; Pas Redoublé from "Pas Redoublé for Piano Duet," op. 86; arr. with introduction by E. Kaplan CO A. C. Giannini L TS WP 19 Apr. 1978, CCT, N.Y.C. D Caprice Valse (C. Anderson and C. Gehm, L. Slagle, Lisa Headley, T. Fowler, G. Huffman, G. White with C. Messmer, P. Miller, T. Singleton, Susan Stewart, E. Troy, C. Valleskey, L. Blake, G. Dufford, M. Goldweber, J. Hilding, J. Hughes, P. Jerry, Gregory King, A. Levinson); Serenade (L. Blake, C. Gehm, T. Singleton and company); Minuet (L. Headley, P. Miller, G. White, G. Huffman); Pas Redoublé (Entire company) CN A. Lewis PI SB RV 5 Nov. 1988, CCT, N.Y.C.

CHOPIN PRELUDES

CH O. Araiz AC B. Baz M Frédéric Chopin, Preludes for Piano, op. 28, nos. 1-6, 10-12, 14, 16-18, 20-23 CO O. Araiz, supervised by R. Diffen L JT JP 16 Aug. 1978, Ravinia Festival, Highland Park, Ill. D C. Anderson, S. Frazer, C. Gehm, J. Hanniford, D. Jackson, L. Slagle, G. Chryst, G. Dufford, G. Huffman, R. Sultzbach PI SB WP 15 Dec. 1977, Teatro Municipal, São Paulo, Brazil, Ballet of the Teatro Municipal

A WEDDING BOUQUET

CH F. Ashton ST Christopher Newton M Lord Berners, with words by Gertrude Stein CO L. Berners, supervised by Linda Fisher S L. Berners, supervised by E. Burbridge L JT JP 18 Oct. 1978, CCT, N.Y.C. D Webster (Bonnie Wyckoff); Two Peasant Girls (Cameron Basden, Lynne Chervony); Two Peasant Boys (C. Corry, W. Starrett); Josephine (J. Hanniford); Paul (D. Barnett); John (J. Hilding); Violet (S. Frazer); Ernest (G. Dufford); Thérèse (A. Danis); Julia (B. Rodriguez); Bridegroom (G. Chryst); Pépé, Julia's dog (L. Slagle); Arthur (R. Estner); Guy (B. Taylor); Four Guests (U. Burke, Elizabeth Corbett, C. Gehm, P. Miller); Two Gendarmes (Michael Bjerknes, Mike Michaels); Bride (Lynn Glauber); Bridesmaids (L. Headley, S. Stewart); Narrator (Anthony Dowell) CN Terence Kern RV 23 Jan. 1985, Dorothy Chandler Pavilion, Los Angeles WP 27 Apr. 1937, Sadler's Wells Theatre, London, Vic-Wells Ballet

A BRIDEGROOM CALLED DEATH

CH A. de Mille AC Gemze de Lappe, D. Orio, and P. Sutherland M Franz Schubert (Auf den Wasser zu singen"; "Das Lied im Grünen"; "Das Wandern"; "An die Freunde"; "Fischerlied"; "Ins Stille Land"; " Das Grab"; "Der Schiffer"; "Pause"; Waltzes from op. 9a. 18a, 33, 50, 67, 77; "Du bist die Ruh"; "Der Tod und das Mädchen" CO S. Simmons L TS JP 1 Nov. 1978, CCT, N.Y.C. D Maiden (D. Jackson); Bridegroom (G. Huffman); Other Bridegroom, Death (B. Taylor); Turning Girl (L. Glauber); Jumping Boy (C. Corry); Friends (E. Corbett, A. Danis, S. Frazer, C. Gehm, J. Hanniford, L. Headley, P. Miller, S. Stewart, C. Valleskey, M. Bjerknes, G. Dufford, P. Jerry. A. Levinson. G. King) PI SB V Arthur Burrows WP 11 Apr. 1975, Music Hall, Boston, Boston Ballet (under the title *Summer*)

CON AMOR

CH Dalal Achcar M A. Adam, excerpts from "Le Diable à Quatre," arr. by J. Lanchbery CO Maria Rocha L P. Curry JP 9 Nov. 1978, CCT, N.Y.C. D A. M. De Angelo and B. Taylor CN S. Lipkin WP Aug. 1975, Teatro Municipal, Rio de Janeiro, Brazil, with Merle Park and David Wall from the Royal Ballet

CHOURA (A TRIBUTE TO ALEXANDRA DANILOVA)

CH GA M Riccardo Drigo, arr. Stephen Douglas Burton CO A. C. Giannini Tutus Edrie Anne Blackwelder L TS WP 15 Nov. 1978, CCT, N.Y.C. D L. Headley, S. Danias, A. M. De Angelo, L. Blake, G. White, A. Levinson CN T. Kern

LE SPECTRE DE LA ROSE

CH M. Fokine ST Nicholas Beriozoff LI Jean-Louis Vaudoyer, adapted from a poem by Théophile Gautier M Carl Maria von Weber, *L'Invitation à la Valse* CO Geoffrey Guy, after Léon Bakst (Young Girl); Toer van Schayk (Spirit of the Rose) S G. Guy, after L. Bakst L David Mohr, adapted by TS JP 6 Mar. 1979, Mark Hellinger Theater, N.Y.C. D Young Girl (D. Jackson); Spirit of the Rose (Rudolf Nureyev) CN S. Lipkin WP 19 Apr. 1911, Théâtre de Monte Carlo, Monte Carlo, Diaghilev's Ballets Russes. [Production on loan to Joffrey Ballet from London Festival Ballet]

L'APRÈS-MIDI D'UN FAUNE

CH Vaslav Nijinsky, reconstructed by Elizabeth Schooling and W. Chappell **M** C. Debussy, "Prélude à L'après-midi d'un faune" **CO** Léon Bakst, reproduced by R. Ter-Arutunian **S** L. Bakst, reproduced by R. Ter-Arutunian **LI** V. Nijinsky **L** TS **JP** 6 Mar. 1979, Mark Hellinger Theater, N.Y.C. **D** Faun (R. Nureyev); Leader of the Nymphs (C. Gehm); Nymphs (U. Burke, R. Ganteaume, L. Headley, P. Miller, T. Singleton, B. Wyckoff) **CN** S. Lipkin **RV** 29 Dec. 1982, CCT, N.Y.C. **RV** 17 Mar. 1987, Civic Opera House, Chicago **WP** 29 May 1912, Théâtre du Châtelet, Paris, Diaghilev's Ballets Russes

EPODE (A TRIBUTE TO FELIA DOUBROVSKA)

CH GA M D. Shostakovich, Ballet Suite No. 2 (Adagio) **CO** supervised by Betty Williams — Studio One and John Allen **L** TS **WP** 25 May 1979, Lila Cockrell Theatre, San Antonio **D** P. Miller, G. White and M. Bjerknes, L. Blake, A. Levinson **CN** S. Lipkin

ILLUMINATIONS

CH F. Ashton **ST** John Taras **M** B. Britten, "Les Illuminations," for Soprano or Tenor and String Orchestra, op. 18; words from Arthur Rimbaud, "Les Illuminations" **CO** Cecil Beaton **S** C. Beaton **L** JT **JP** 13 May 1980, Auditorium Theatre, Chicago **D** Poet (G. Huffman); Sacred Love (P. Miller); Profane Love (B. Rodriguez); Dandy (G. Dufford); Birdcage Woman (Leslie Carothers); Postman (C. Valleskey); Waiter (Denise Dabrowski); Street Cleaner (Valmai Roberts); Chef (K. Jurkowski); Painter and Poster Sticker Assistants (U. Burke, Celeste Jabczenski); Chimney Sweep (Madelyn Berdes); Kiosk Lovers (C. Anderson, Tom Mossbrucker); Soldiers (A. Levinson, P. Shoemaker); King and Queen (M. Bjerknes, P. Miller); Train Bearers (C. Basden, S. Stewart); Acolytes (L. Headley, L. Glauber); Drummer (G. Dufford); Herald (J. Grensback); Bishop (P. Jerry); Coachmen (Glenn Edgerton, C. Corry); Being Beauteous (P. Miller and L. Blake, M. Bjerknes, P. Jerry, Wesley Robinson) **CN** T. Kern **V** Rodney Miller, tenor **RV** 6 Jan. 1983, CCT, N.Y.C. **WP** 2 Mar. 1950, CCT, N.Y.C., New York City Ballet

MOMENTUM

CH Choo San Goh **M** S. Prokofiev, Piano Concerto No. 1 in D-flat, op. 10 **CO** Carol Vollet Garner, supervised by Andrew Marley **L** JT **JP** 14 May 1980, Auditorium Theatre, Chicago **D** M. Berdes, C. Basden, James Canfield, C. Corry and C. Jabczenski, C. Gehm, L. Carothers, G. Edgerton, T. Mossbrucker, W. Robinson **CN** A. Lewis **PI** SB **WP** 19 Jan. 1979, Walt Whitman Auditorium, Brooklyn Center for the Performing Arts, Brooklyn College, N.Y., Joffrey II Dancers

MYTHICAL HUNTERS

CH G. Tetley **AC** Mary Hinkson **M** Oedoen Partos, "Hezionot" **CO** C. V. Garner **L** JT **JP** 15 May 1980, Auditorium Theatre, Chicago. **D** B. Rodriguez, C. Anderson, L. Carothers, L. Blake, P. Jerry, U. Burke, L. Glauber, C. Valleskey, M. Bjerknes, J. Hilding, A. Levinson, W. Robinson **CN** A. Lewis **WP** 25 Nov. 1965, Tel Aviv, Israel, Batsheva Dance Co.

Celebration

CH GA **M** D. Shostakovich, arr. by E. Kaplan **CO** S. Loquasto **L** TS **WP** 15 May 1980, Auditorium Theatre, Chicago **D** C. Basden, U. Burke, L. Headley, D. Jackson, C. Valleskey, L. Blake, J. Hilding, A. Levinson, W. Robinson, G. White **CN** A. Lewis

Random Dances

CH Marjorie Mussman **M** Jonathan Hancock, "Variations on a Secret Theme" **CO** Mimi Maxmen **L** JT **JP** 16 May 1980, Auditorium Theatre, Chicago **D** L. Carothers, G. Edgerton, M. Berdes, T. Mossbrucker, P. Jerry, D. Dabrowski, C. Jabczenski **PI** SB **WP** 9 Nov. 1979, Walt Whitman Auditorium, Brooklyn Center for the Performing Arts, Brooklyn College, N.Y., Joffrey II Dancers

Postcards

CH RJ **M** E. Satie, café songs and compositions (I. "Le Piège de Méduse:" Quadrille, Valse, Pas vite, Mazurka, Un peu vif, Polka, Quadrille); II. "Rêverie du Pauvre"; III. "Choses vues à droite et à gauche"; "Fugue à tâtons, fantaisie musculaire"; IV. "Le Picadilly"; V. "Je te veux"; VI. "Dapheneo"; VII. "La Diva de L'Empire"; VII. "Les Pantins dansent"; IX. "Tendrement"; X. Trois petites montées: marche de Cocagne, jeux de Gargantua"; XI. "Poudre d'Or") **CO** John David Ridge **S** Joe Brainard (show curtain) and Herbert Migdoll (backdrop), supervised by Linda Conaway **L** JT **WP** 12 June 1980, Opera House, Seattle, Wash. **D** L. Fuente, D. Jackson, C. Anderson, Ross Stretton, M. Bjerknes, P. Miller, M. Berdes, L. Carothers, J. Canfield, L. Blake, T. Mossbrucker, C. Basden, D. Dabrowski, Mary Linn Durbin, L. Glauber and C. Corry, G. Edgerton, M. Goldweber, J. Grensback **CN** T. Kern **PI** Janis Fransen **V** B. Quilling **RV** 1991 season **ST** S. Barnard **L** Craig Miller

Diverdissemente

CH GA **M** Giuseppe Verdi, ballet music for *Jerusalemme,* the 1847 Paris version of *I Lombardi,* reconstructed by E. Kaplan **CO** A. C. Giannini **WP** 19 June 1980, War Memorial Opera House, San Francisco **D** A. M. De Angelo and C. Basden, M. L. Durbin, L. Headley, S. Stewart **CN** T. Kern

Night

CH Laura Dean **M** L. Dean, "Night" (for two pianos) **CO** Mark Ginsburg, supervised by Zack Brown **L** JT **WP** 29 Oct. 1980, CCT, N.Y.C. **D** C. Basden, U. Burke, L. Chervony, V. Roberts, M. Goldweber, T. Mossbrucker, Luis Perez, G. Edgerton **PI** Paul Epstein and Patricia Graf

Helena

CH C. San Goh **M** Alberto Ginastera, Piano Concerto No. 1, op. 28 **CO** C. V. Garner, supervised by William Schroder **L** JT **WP** 6 Nov. 1980, CCT, N.Y.C. **D** B. Rodriguez, G. Huffman, M. Berdes, DeAnn Duteil, V. Roberts, S. Stewart, M. Bjerknes, J. Canfield, Eric Dirk, G. Edgerton, M. Goldweber, P. Jerry, T. Mossbrucker, L. Perez **CN** T. Kern **PI** SB

RELÂCHE (BALLET INSTANTANÉISTE)

CH Moses Pendleton **AC** Philip Holland **LI** Francis Picabia **M** E. Satie **CO** F. Picabia, supervised by S. Loquasto **S** F. Picabia, supervised by L. Conaway **Film** René Clair; **Director of Still Photography and Papparazzi** H. Migdoll; **Additional Papparazzi** Dave Archer, Linda Alaniz, Michael Lawrence, Jack Stone **L** JT **JP** 13 Nov. 1980, CCT, N.Y.C. **D** Woman (S. Danias); Man (G. Huffman); Fireman (M. Bjerknes); Men (12 men) **CN** S. Lipkin **PI** SB **WP** 9 May 1979, Salle Favart, Opéra Comique, with members of Paris Opéra Ballet; Ballets Suedois production of Relâche premiered 4 Dec. 1924, Théâtre des Champs-Elysées, Paris **CH** Jean Börlin

RETURN TO THE STRANGE LAND

CH Jiří Kylián **M** Leos Janacek, Sonata, 1905 (I, IV); "On an Overgrown Path," "Supplement," No. 2 (II); "In the Mist," No. 1 (III) **CO** J. Kylián **L** JT **JP** 19 Nov. 1980, CCT, N.Y.C. **D** I. B. Rodriguez, G. Huffman, G. Edgerton; II. C. Anderson, M. Bjerknes; III. B. Rodriguez, G. Huffman; IV. C. Anderson, M. Bjerknes, R. Stretton **PI** SB **RV** 6 Apr. 1994, New York State Theater, Lincoln Center, N.Y.C. **CO** J. Kylián rebuilt by Rosemarie Worton **L** Susan A. White **WP** 17 May 1975, Württemberg State Theater, Stuttgart, Germany, Stuttgart Ballet

UNFOLDING

CH Gray Veredon **M** Bohuslav Martinů, Concerto for Piano Trio and String Orchestra; "Toccata e Due Canzoni" **CO** Lynn Hoffman **L** Gail Dahl **JP** 14 May 1981, Auditorium Theatre, Chicago **D** M. Berdes, C. Gehm, C. Jabczenski, P. Miller, J. Canfield, T. Mossbrucker, J. Hilding, P. Jerry **CN** A. Lewis **PI** SB **Violinist** Arthur Tabachnik **Cellist** Barbara Haffner **WP** 12 Dec. 1980, Aaron Davis Hall, City College of New York, N.Y.C., Joffrey II Dancers

TRANSFIGURED NIGHT

CH J. Kylián **ST** Hans Knill **M** A. Schoenberg, "Verklärte Nacht" **CO** Joop Stokvis **S** J. Kylián, supervised by L. Conaway **L** JT **JP** 22 Oct. 1981, CCT, N.Y.C. **D** D. Jackson, C. Jabczenski, G. Huffman, J. Hilding, P. Jerry, G. Edgerton **CN** T. Kern **WP** 21 Oct. 1975, The Hague, Netherlands, Nederlands Dans Theater

THE TAMING OF THE SHREW

CH J. Cranko **ST** G. Tsinguirides **LI** after William Shakespeare **M** Kurt-Heinz Stolze, after Domenico Scarlatti **CO** Elisabeth Dalton **S** E. Dalton, supervised by L. Conaway **L** JT **JP** 23 Oct. 1981, CCT, N.Y.C. **D** Katherine (Marcia Haydée);* Petruchio (Richard Cragun); Bianca (P. Miller); Lucentio (Jay Jolley); Baptista (Jerry Kokich); Gremio (M. Bjerknes); Hortensio (A. Levinson); Whores (C. Gehm, C. Jabczenski); Innkeeper (P. Shoemaker); Priest (P. Shoemaker); Servants to Petruchio (M. Goldweber, C. Corry, E. Dirk, Julian Montaner); Pas de Six, Act II (C. Anderson, L. Carothers, D. Duteil, Daniel Baudendistel, J. Canfield, P. Jerry); Corps de Ballet (13 women, 12 men) **CN** T. Kern **RV** 5 Oct. 1985, Dorothy Chandler Pavilion, Los Angeles **WP** 16 Mar. 1969, Württemberg State Theater, Stuttgart, Germany, Stuttgart Ballet *Guest Artists, Stuttgart Ballet

LIGHT RAIN

CH GA AC S. Barnard M Douglas Adams and Russ Gautier, "Dream Dancer" CO A. C. Giannini L TS WP 4 Nov. 1981, CCT, N.Y.C. D C. Jabczenski and J. Canfield with C. Basden, M. Berdes, L. Carothers, L. Chervony, C. Corry, E. Dirk, D. Duteil, G. Edgerton, M. Goldweber, J. Hilding, T. Mossbrucker, C. Valleskey

FIRE

CH L. Dean M L. Dean CO Michael Graves S M. Graves, supervised by Tom Cariello L JT WP 30 Dec. 1982, CCT, N Y.C. D C. Basden, Patricia Brown, L. Chervony, D. Duteil, Julie Janus, V. Roberts, E. Dirk, G. Edgerton, D. Baudendistel, J. Montaner, T. Mossbrucker, L. Perez; Duet No. 1 (P. Brown, L. Perez); Duet No. 2 (V. Roberts, E. Dirk); Duet No. 3 (D. Duteil, T. Mossbrucker)

ROUND OF ANGELS

CH GA M Gustav Mahler, Adagietto, Symphony No. 5 in C-sharp Minor, op. 47 CO A. C. Giannini L TS WP 5 Jan. 1983, CCT, N.Y.C., under *New Ballet (untitled)* D P. Miller and J. Canfield with G. Edgerton, T. Mossbrucker, D. Baudendistel, J. Kokich, Ron Reagan CN A. Lewis

FIVE BRAHMS WALTZES IN THE MANNER OF ISADORA DUNCAN

CH F. Ashton ST Lynn Seymour M Johannes Brahms, Waltzes, op. 39, nos. 1, 2, 8, 10, 13, 15 CO David Dean L P. Curry JP 11 May 1983, Dorothy Chandler Pavilion, Los Angeles D Isadora (Jodie Gates) WP 16 June 1976, Sadler's Wells Theatre, London, (complete version performed by L. Seymour)

LOVE SONGS

CH William Forsythe AC Ronald Thornhill M recordings by Aretha Franklin ("If You Gotta Make a Fool of Somebody," "Baby I Love You") and Dionne Warwick ("Make It Easy on Yourself," "Going Out of My Head," "I Got Love," "There Is Always Something There to Remind You," "You're All I Need To Get By") CO Eileen Brady L P. Curry JP 30 Apr. 1983, Dorothy Chandler Pavilion, Los Angeles D Lauren Rouse, L. Carothers, C. Gehm, J. Gates, B. Rodriguez, J. Canfield, P. Jerry, A. Levinson WP 5 May 1979, National Theater, Munich, Germany, Stuttgart Ballet

DREAM DANCES

CH J. Kylián ST Susan McKee M Luciano Berio, "Folk Songs" (orchestral version) CO W. Kim S Walter Nobbe, supervised by Speed Hopkins L JT JP 18 Oct. 1983, CCT, N.Y.C. D "Black Is the Color" [U. S. A.] (C. Gehm, J. Hilding); "I Wonder as I Wander" [U. S. A.] (Dominique Angel, P. Brown), J. Canfield); "Loosin Yelav" [Armenia] (Dawn Caccamo, D. Duteil, G. Edgerton, T. Mossbrucker); "Rossignolet du Bois" [France] (C. Valleskey, P. Jerry); "A la Feminisca" [Sicily] (E. Dirk, Kevin O'Day); "La Donna Ideale" [Italy] (D. Angel, P. Miller, D. Jackson, C. Valleskey); "Ballo" [Italy] (D. Caccamo, G. Edgerton);

"Mottettu de Tristura" [Sardinia] (C. Gehm, P. Jerry, K. O'Day); "Malurous Qu'o Uno Fenno" [Auvergne] (E. Dirk); "Lo Fiolaire" [Auvergne] (D. Duteil, J. Hilding, J. Canfield); "Azerbaijan Love Song" [Azerbaijan] (D. Jackson, T. Mossbrucker) **CN** A. Lewis **Vocalist** Shirley Close, mezzo-soprano **WP** 7 Dec. 1979, The Hague, Netherlands, Nederlands Dans Theater

CLOVEN KINGDOM

CH Paul Taylor, reconstructed by Linda Kent **M** Arcangelo Corelli, selections from Concerti Grossi; Henry Cowell, excerpts from "Ostinato Pianissimo"; Malloy Miller, excerpts from "Prelude for Percussion"; combined by John Herbert McDowell **CO** S. Barrie (women's); headpieces by John Rawlings **L JT JP** 18 Oct. 1983, CCT, N.Y.C. **D** D. Angel, C. Basden, P. Brown, D. Caccamo, Jill Davidson, D. Duteil, L. Rouse, C. Valleskey, E. Dirk, T. Mossbrucker, K. O'Day, L. Perez **CN** A. Lewis **WP** 9 June 1976, Billy Rose Theatre, N.Y.C., Paul Taylor Dance Company

QUARTER TONES FOR MR. B (A TRIBUTE TO GEORGE BALANCHINE)

CH GA M T. Macero, "One-Three Quarters" **CO** Dancewear by Capezio Dance Theatre Shop of New York **L TS WP** 22 Oct. 1983, CCT, N.Y.C. **D** P. Miller, J. Janus, Elizabeth Molak, J. Canfield, M. Goldweber, T. Mossbrucker **CN** A. Lewis

ITALIAN SUITE

CH GA M Ermanno Wolf-Ferrari, *La Dama Boba* excerpts from the Overture (I); "The School for Fathers," Prelude (II) and Intermezzo (IV), *The Jewels of the Madonna*, Serenade and Intermezzo (III); *Il Campiello*, "Ritornello," Act III (V); *The Secret of Suzanne*, Overture (VI) **CO** C. V. Garner **L TS WP** 26 Oct. 1983, CCT, N.Y.C. **D** I. D. Angel, C. Basden, P. Brown, D. Caccamo, J. Janus, P. Miller, E. Molak, J. Canfield, C. Corry, E. Dirk, G. Edgerton, Kirby Hade, T. Mossbrucker, K. O'Day; II. D. Angel, C. Basden, Annette Bressie, P. Brown, D. Caccamo, J. Davidson, J. Janus, Kim Sagami; III. P. Miller, J. Canfield; IV. E. Molak; V. P. Miller, J. Canfield, J. Janus; VI. 9 women, 6 men **CN** Jonathan McPhee **RV** 3 Nov. 1989, CCT, N.Y.C. **RV** 6 Apr. 1994, New York State Theater, Lincoln Center, N.Y.C.

SQUARE DEAL

Composition and Visual Effects W. Forsythe **AC** R. Thornhill **M** W. Forsythe and Thomas Jahn (excerpts from "Gaenge, Part II"), taped; "Arrangement for Prepared Piano and Trombone," T. Jahn **CO** Douglas Furgusan, supervised by Alfred Kahout **S** supervised by S. Hopkins **Slide Graphics** Arthur Brady **L JT WP** 2 Nov. 1983, CCT, N.Y.C. **D** L. Carothers and C. Gehm, J. Hilding, D. Jackson, P. Jerry, P. Miller, L. Perez and D. Duteil, L. Rouse

JAMBOREE

CH GA AC S. Barnard **M** T. Macero, with add. orch. by Luther Henderson **CO** W. Kim **Front Curtain** Brad Braune **S** supervision S. Hopkins **L TS WP** 20 June 1984, Lila Cockrell Theatre, San Antonio **D** Lone Star Gent (Edward Morgan); Prairie Psalm (P. Miller, J.

Canfield); Split Rail (T. Mossbrucker, David Palmer); Retablo de Guadalupe (Madonna: C. Gehm; Attendants to Madonna: J. Kokich, Mark Baird; Young Man: L. Perez; Village Women: 8 women); Riverwalk (J. Gates, G. Edgerton); Jamboree (E. Morgan with 8 women, 10 men) **CN** A. Lewis

ROMEO AND JULIET

CH J. Cranko **ST** G. Tsinguirides **M** S. Prokofiev **CO** Jürgen Rose **S** J. Rose, supervised by S. Hopkins **L** JT **JP** 12 Dec. 1984, Kennedy Center for the Performing Arts, Washington, D.C. **D** Lord Capulet (J. Kokich); Lady Capulet (C. Gehm); Juliet (P. Miller); Tybalt (J. Hilding); Paris (T. Mossbrucker); Juliet's Nurse (C. Basden); Lord Montague (R. Thomas); Lady Montague (Elizabeth Parkinson); Romeo (J. Canfield); Mercutio (L. Perez); Benvolio (D. Palmer); Duke of Verona (P. Shoemaker); Friar Laurence (P. Shoemaker); Rosalind (Deborah Dawn); Gypsies (L. Carothers, J. Janus, C. Valleskey); King of the Carnival (E. Morgan); Two Carnival Couples (D. Angel, Tina LeBlanc, C. Corry, M. Goldweber); Nobles and Townfolk of Verona (13 women, 12 men) **CN** A. Lewis **RV** 20 Apr. 1990, Festival Hall, Tampa Bay Performing Arts Center, Tampa, Florida **ST** supervised by Reid Anderson **CO** supervised by Sally Ann Parsons **WP** 2 Dec. 1962, Württemberg State Theater, Stuttgart, Germany, Stuttgart Ballet. (An extensively revised version of the production staged by Cranko for the ballet of La Scala, Milan, Teatro Verde, Venice, 26 July 1958.)

HEXAMERON

CH Philip Jerry **M** "Hexameron, Grandes variations sur la marche des Puritains de Bellini," arr. for Solo Piano and Orchestra by Franz Liszt (Introduction and Theme; Variation 2; Variation 3; "Ritornello"; Interlude; Variation 6: "Interlude"; Finale), Sigismond Thalberg (Variation 1); Johann Peter Pixis (Variation 3); Henri Herz (Variation 4); Carl Czerny (Variation 5); Frédéric Chopin (Variation 6) **CO** Christian Holder **L** TS **WP** 25 Jan. 1985, Dorothy Chandler Pavilion, Los Angeles **D** Introduction and Theme (D. Jackson and J. Canfield with 6 women, 6 men); Variation 1 (3 women, 3 men); Variation 2 (3 women, 6 men); Variation 3 (4 women); Variation 4 (J. Gates, T. Mossbrucker); Variation 5 (5 men); Interlude (6 women, 1 man); Variation 6 (D. Jackson, J. Canfield); Finale (Full Company) **CN** A. Lewis **PI** SB

ARDEN COURT

CH P. Taylor **Restaged** L. Kent **M** William Boyce, from Symphonies nos. 1, 3, 5, 7, 8 **CO** Gene Moore **S** G. Moore **L** JT **JP** 22 Sept. 1985, Dorothy Chandler Pavilion, Los Angeles **D** D. Angel, J. Gates, Victoria Pasquale, Patrick Corbin, M. Goldweber, Douglas Martin, Peter Narbutas, D. Palmer, Ashley Wheater **CN** J. McPhee **WP** 15 Apr. 1981, CCT, N.Y.C. Paul Taylor Dance Company

UNTITLED

CH Robby Barnett, Alison Chase, Martha Clarke, M. Pendleton, Michael Tracy, Jonathan Wolken **M** Robert Dennis **CO** Malcolm McCormick **L** TS **JP** 26 Sept. 1985, Dorothy Chandler Pavilion, Los Angeles **D** J. Davidson, B. Rodriguez, P. Corbin, J. Hilding, P. Jerry, Raymond Perrin **WP** 1 Aug. 1975, Palmer Auditorium, Connecticut College, New London, Connecticut, Pilobolus

FORGOTTEN LAND

CH J. Kylián ST Roslyn Anderson M B. Britten, "Sinfonia da Requiem," op. 20 CO John Macfarlane, supervised by S. A. Parsons S J. Macfarlane, supervised by S. Hopkins L Joop Caboort JP 2 Oct. 1985, Dorothy Chandler Pavilion, Los Angeles D First Movement (B. Rodriguez, J. Janus, D. Caccamo, K. Sagami, D. Palmer, M. Goldweber, P. Jerry, A. Wheater, E. Parkinson, Linda Bechtold, G. Edgerton, Patric Parsons); Second Movement (5 women, 5 men); Third Movement (6 women, 6 men) CN A. Lewis WP 12 Apr. 1981, Württemberg State Theater, Stuttgart, Germany, Stuttgart Ballet

PASSAGE

CH James Kudelka ST Jeremy Blanton M Thomas Tallis, "Spem in Alium" CO Gretchen Warren L TS JP 24 Feb. 1986, Hancher Auditorium, Univ. of Iowa, Iowa City D D. Palmer and M. Goldweber, D. Jackson, P. Jerry, B. Rodriguez, C. Valleskey WP 16 Feb. 1982, Tampa, Florida, American Ballet Theatre II

THE HEART OF THE MATTER

CH J. Kudelka M S. Prokofiev, Piano Concerto No. 2 in G Minor CO S. Loquasto L TS WP 25 Feb. 1986, Hancher Auditorium, Univ. of Iowa, Iowa City D D. Caccamo and G. Edgerton with D. Angel, Beth Bartholomew, L. Carothers, D. Dawn, J. Gates, C. Gehm, J. Janus, L. Rouse, C. Valleskey, C. Corry, M. Goldweber, Randall Graham, K. Hade, D. Martin, T. Mossbrucker, P. Narbutas, P. Parsons, R. Perrin CN A. Lewis PI SB

FORCE FIELD

CH L. Dean M Steve Reich, "Six Pianos" CO S. A. Parsons, after L. Dean L TS WP 26 Feb. 1986, Hancher Auditorium, Univ. of Iowa, Iowa City D B. Rodriguez, P. Jerry and D. Angel, C. Basden, L. Carothers, P. Corbin, C. Corry, J. Gates, C. Gehm, M. Goldweber, R. Graham, J. Janus, T. LeBlanc, D. Martin, T. Mossbrucker, P. Narbutas, P. Parsons, R. Perrin, L. Rouse, C. Valleskey

BIRTHDAY VARIATIONS

CH GA AC S. Barnard and G. White M G. Verdi, from *I Lombardi* and *I Vespri Siciliani,* arr. and adapted by J. McPhee CO S. Simmons L TS WP 6 Mar. 1986, Civic Opera House, Civic Center for the Performing Arts, Chicago D D. Caccamo and G. Edgerton with C. Basden, J. Gates, V. Pasquale, T. LeBlanc CN J. McPhee RV 6 Mar. 1992, Northrop Auditorium, Univ. of Minnesota, Minneapolis RV 24 Jan. 1995, Auditorium Theatre, Chicago

ANNIVERSARY PAS DE DEUX (PIÈCE D'OCCASION)

CH GA AC S. Barnard and G. White M Victor Herbert, "Kiss Me Again" from *Mademoiselle Modiste* Lyrics Henry Blossom CO S. Simmons Headdresses Woody Shelp Hair Design Dale Brownell WP 1 Apr. 1986, New York State Theater, Lincoln Center, N.Y.C. D L. Carothers and A. Wheater with P. Corbin, D. Martin, T. Mossbrucker, D. Palmer PI Wally Harper V Barbara Cook, soprano

LA FILLE MAL GARDÉE

CH F. Ashton, after J. Dauberval **Reconstructed by** F. Worth and supervised by A. Grant **M** Ferdinand Hérold, adapted and arr. by J. Lanchbery **CO** O. Lancaster, re-created by J. D. Ridge **S** O. Lancaster, supervised by S. Hopkins **L** JT **JP** 11 Sept. 1986, Dorothy Chandler Pavilion, Los Angeles **D** Widow Simone (Stanley Holden); Lise (T. LeBlanc); Colas (D. Palmer); Thomas (P. Shoemaker); Alain (Edward Stierle); Village Notary (Richard Englund); Notary's Clerk (P. Corbin); Cockerel and Hens (P. Corbin, D. Angel, Mary Barton, Jennifer Demko, Nicole Duffy); Lise's Friends (8 women); Colas's Friends (6 men); Villagers (13 women, 5 men); Grooms (Mark Wuest, Cary Zateslo) **CN** A. Lewis **WP** 28 Jan. 1960, Royal Opera House, Covent Garden, London, Royal Ballet

THE GARDENS OF BOBOLI

CH Mark Haim **M** Tomaso Albinoni, excerpts from "Concerti a Cinque," op. 5, no. 1, 3rd movement [Overture]; op 9, no. 8, 2nd movement [First Section]; op. 9, no. 11, 3rd movement [Second Section]; op. 9, no. 5, 2nd movement [Third Section]; op. 9, no. 2, 2nd movement [Fourth Section]; op. 5, no. 9, 3rd movement [Fifth Section]; op. 9, no. 8, 3rd movement [Sixth Section] **CO** S. A. Parsons **L** P. Curry **JP** 17 Sept. 1986, Dorothy Chandler Pavilion, Los Angeles **D** L. Carothers, Jennifer Habig, E. Parkinson, V. Pasquale, L. Rouse, Parrish Maynard, P. Narbutas, Roger Plaut, Tyler Walters **CN** J. McPhee **WP** 5 Sept. 1986, Ogunquit, Maine, Joffrey II Dancers

ESTEEMED GUESTS

CH Mark Morris **AC** Keith Sabado **M** Carl Philipp Emanuel Bach, Concerto in A Major for Violincello and String Orchestra **CO** S. Loquasto **L** Phil Sandström **WP** 24 Sept. 1986, Dorothy Chandler Pavilion, Los Angeles **D** Allegro (J. Habig, B. Rodriguez); Largo (J. Janus, J. Habig, B. Rodriguez, J. Hilding, T. Mossbrucker); Allegro Assai (J. Hilding, T. Mossbrucker); Ensemble (5 women, 4 men) **CN** A. Lewis **Cellist** Stephen Erdody

THREE PRELUDES

CH Ben Stevenson **M** S. Rachmaninoff, Preludes for Piano, No. 10 in B Minor, op. 32; No. 1 in F# Minor, op. 23; No. 9 in A Major, op. 32 **L** P. Curry **JP** 17 Mar. 1987, Civic Opera House, Civic Center for the Performing Arts, Chicago **D** L. Carothers and P. Jerry **PI** SB **WP** 3 Sept. 1969, Delacorte Theatre, Central Park, N.Y.C., Harkness Youth Dancers

ALTERED STATES

CH Gail Kachadurian **M** John Corigliano, from the score for the film "Altered States" **CO** Natalie Garfinkle **L** TS **WP** 16 Apr. 1987, Opera House, Kennedy Center for the Performing Arts, Washington, D.C. **D** D. Caccamo and G. Edgerton **CN** A. Lewis

LE SACRE DU PRINTEMPS (PICTURES OF PAGAN RUSSIA IN TWO ACTS)

CH V. Nijinsky **ST and reconstructed by** Millicent Hodson **LI** I. Stravinsky and Nicholas Roerich **M** I. Stravinsky **CO** N. Roerich, supervised by S. A. Parsons **S** N. Roerich, super-

428

vised by Robert Perdziola **Design Consultant** Kenneth Archer, for reconstruction of Roerich designs L TS **Artistic Supervision** RJ, for reconstruction JP 30 Sept. 1987, Dorothy Chandler Pavilion, Los Angeles D Act I: Young Maidens (10 women); Women (10 women); Old Woman, 300 Years Old (C. Valleskey); Old Sage (P. Shoemaker); The Elders (7 men); Young People (5 men); Youths (6 men); Young Men (5 men). Act II: Chosen Virgin (B. Rodriguez); Young Maidens (12 women); Ancestors (20 men) CN A. Lewis WP 29 May 1913, Théâtre des Champs-Elysées, Paris, Diaghilev's Ballets Russes

THE NUTCRACKER

CH production after Alexandra Fedorova, based on original by M. Petipa and Lev Ivanov; GA, for "Waltz of the Snowflakes" and "Waltz of the Flowers"; ST George Verdak and S. Barnard LI based on E. T. A. Hoffmann's *The Nutcracker and the Mouse King* (1816) M P. I. Tchaikovsky CO J. D. Ridge; creative design for Mice, Mother Ginger, and Clara's Horse by K. Love S O. Smith L TS JP 10 Dec. 1987, Hancher Auditorium, Univ. of Iowa, Iowa City D Act I, Scene I: Dr. Drosselmeyer (Alexander Grant); His Nephew [The Nutcracker Prince] (G. Edgerton); Clara (M. Barton); Fritz (E. Stierle); Mayor Stahlbaum (A. Wheater); and Mrs. Stahlbaum (L. Carothers); Grandmother (Bonnie Fields); Grandfather (P. Shoemaker); Maiden Aunts (Kathryn Ginden, J. Habig); Governess (C. Basden); Guests (7 women, 7 men); Their Children (8 girls, 8 boys); Servants (D. Martin, Mark Wuest); Maids (B. Bartholomew, L. Bechtold); Mechanical Dolls: Columbine (Meg Gurin); Harlequin (J. Hilding); Vivandière (Cynthia Giannini); Soldier (P. Corbin). Scene 2: Nutcracker Doll (M. Goldweber); Nutcracker Prince (G. Edgerton); King of Mice (P. Maynard); First Battalion of Mice (7 men); Second Battalion of Mice (8 children); Cavalry Mice (4 children); Officers (5 men); Soldiers (12 children); Dolls under the Tree (8 children). Scene 3: Snow Queen (L. Carothers); Snow King (A. Wheater); Snow Prince (E. Stierle); Snowflakes (12 women); Snow Winds (6 men); Snow Trees (12 children). Act II: Sugar Plum Fairy (L. Carothers); Nutcracker Prince (A. Wheater). Divertissements: Chocolate from Spain (J. Gates); Coffee from Arabia (J. Janus, T. Mossbrucker); Tea from China (C. Giannini, E. Stierle); Nougat from Russia (L. Bechtold, P. Corbin, C. Corry, R. Perrin); Marzipan Shepherdesses (D. Caccamo, C. Basden, M. Gurin); Mother Ginger (Francis Kane) and Her Polichinelles (8 girls); Waltz of the Flowers: Pansy (D. Dawn); Rose (K. Sagami); Dahlia (V. Pasquale); Rhododendron (Valerie Madonia); Blue Bell (B. Bartholomew); Carnation (E. Parkinson); Clematis (K. Ginden); Columbine (J. Davidson); Cornflower (J. Habig); Iris (Johanna Snyder); Morning Glory (Amanda Smith); Peony (Jennifer Mattingly); Cavaliers (D. Martin, P. Maynard, John Sheaffer, T. Walters); Grand Pas de Deux: Sugar Plum Fairy (D. Caccamo) and Nutcracker Prince (G. Edgerton); Finale (Entire cast) CN A. Lewis WP 17 Dec. 1892, Maryinsky Theater, St. Petersburg, Russia, Imperial Ballet of the Maryinsky Theater; 17 Oct. 1940, 51st Street Theater, N.Y.C., staged by A. Fedorova, Ballet Russe de Monte Carlo

CONCERTO GROSSO

CH J. Kudelka M Jean Papineau-Couture, Concerto Grosso (rev.) CO Sylvain Labelle, supervised by S. A. Parsons L TS WP 3 Feb. 1988, Southern Alberta Jubilee Auditorium, Calgary, Alberta, Canada D L. Carothers, A. Wheater, T. LeBlanc, G. Edgerton, D. Dawn, T. Mossbrucker, C. Basden, J. Hilding, J. Gates, P. Narbutas, J. Janus, D. Martin, B. Rodriguez, T. Walters, J. Habig, R. Plaut, C. Valleskey, M. Wuest CN A. Lewis

COTILLON

CH G. Balanchine ST and reconstructed by M. Hodson M E. Chabrier, piano pieces "Scherzo-Valse," "Idylle," "Danse Villageoise," orch. by composer; "Menuet pompeux," "Tourbillon," "Mauresque," "Valse Romantique No. 3," orch. by V. Rieti LI Boris Kochno CO C. Bérard, re-created by J. D. Ridge S C. Bérard, supervised by Campbell Baird Design Consultant K. Archer, reconstruction for set and costumes L TS JP 26 Oct. 1988, CCT, N.Y.C. D Young Girl (T. LeBlanc); Young Man (E. Stierle); Mistress of Ceremonies (L. Carothers); Master of Ceremonies (J. Hilding); Hand of Fate (B. Rodriguez); Cavalier (G. Edgerton); Friend of Young Girl (C. Valleskey); Corps de Ballet (12 women, 6 men) CN A. Lewis WP 12 Apr. 1932, Théâtre de Monte Carlo, Monte Carlo, Monaco, Ballets Russes de Monte Carlo

BILLY THE KID (CHARACTER BALLET IN ONE ACT)

CH E. Loring ST Patrice L. Whiteside and Virginia Doris M A. Copland LI Lincoln Kirstein CO R. Fletcher, after original by Jared French, supervised by S. A. Parsons S R. Fletcher, after original by J. French L TS JP 2 Nov. 1988, CCT, N.Y.C. D Billy (J. Hilding); Pat Garrett (D. Martin); Alias (A. Wheater); Mother/Sweetheart (B. Rodriguez); Cowboy in Red (E. Stierle); Prospector (P. Narbutas); Dispatch Officer (P. Corbin); Dance Hall Girls, Mexican Girls, Gun Girls in Gray, Gun Girls in Tan, Housewives, Ranchers' Wives (15 women); Cowboys (6 men) CN John Miner WP 16 Oct. 1938, Chicago Civic Theatre, Chicago, Ballet Caravan

LES NOCES (RUSSIAN CHOREOGRAPHIC SCENES IN FOUR TABLEAUX, WITHOUT INTERRUPTION)

CH Bronislava Nijinska ST Irina Nijinska and Howard Sayette M I. Stravinsky T I. Stravinsky CO Nathalie Goncharova, supervised by J. D. Ridge, coordinated by John C. Gilkerson S N. Goncharova, supervised by C. Baird, coordinated by J. C. Gilkerson L C. Miller JP 6 Oct. 1989, Kennedy Center for the Performing Arts, Washington, D.C. D Bride (J. Janus); Bride's Parents (E. Parkinson, D. Martin); Bride's Friends (8 women); Bridegroom (D. Baudendistel); Bridegroom's Parents (C. Gehm, T. Walters); Bridegroom's Friends (12 men); Bride's Friend (D. Dawn); Bridegroom's Friend (Joseph Schnell); Entire Cast with L. Bechtold, A. Smith, J. Snyder, C. Valleskey, J. Gates, T. LeBlanc, C. Corry, E. Stierle CN A. Lewis V Janice Kestler, soprano; Bonnie Bradley, mezzo-soprano; Robert Baker, tenor; David Brundage, bass Choristers Washington Singers, directed by Paul Hill PI SB, James Holloway, Eileen Cornett, and Lisa Logan WP 14 June 1923, Théâtre Gaîté-Lyrique, Paris, Diaghilev's Ballets Russes

THE PANTAGES AND THE PALACE PRESENT "TWO-A-DAY"

CH GA; Louis Johnson for Charleston finale ST S. Barnard AC G. White M R. Harkness and E. Kaplan, arr. by E. Kaplan CO J. D. Ridge S Tony Straiges Hair Design Paul Huntley L TS WP 10 Oct. 1989, Opera House, Kennedy Center for the Performing Arts, Washington, D.C. D Voice (Tony Randall); 1. "Les Plumes de la Nuit": Adagio Team (J. Gates, D. Martin); Butterfly (C. Valleskey); Peacock (C. Gehm and 12 women); 2. "The Seven Society Swells" (E. Parkinson and 6 men); 3. "The Newport Beauties" (P. Narbutas and 8 women) 4. Miss Sunny and Her Polo Beaux (T. LeBlanc and 8 men) 5. "Omar and Farrah" (J. Janus and T. Mossbrucker) 6. "The Flames of Spain" (B. Rodriguez, T. Walters, E.

Stierle with 5 women, 4 men) 7. "La Loïe" (K. Ginden) 8. "Whiz Bang" (14 women, 14 men) CN A. Lewis

LACRYMOSA

CH Edward Stierle M W. A. Mozart, excerpts from Requiem, K.626: Introitus Requiem; Hostias (from Offertorium); Recordare, Confutatis, Lacrymosa (from Sequentia); Agnus Dei; Kyrie CO R. Worton, after Jennifer Irwin L TS JP 9 Mar. 1990, Lied Center for the Performing Arts, Univ. of Nebraska, Lincoln D E. Stierle, J. Gates, D. Baudendistel and L. Bechtold, M. Gurin, J. Habig, K. Sagami, Lissette Salgado, P. Narbutas, Brent Phillips, J. Schnell, Adam Sklute, M. Wuest WP 14 Oct. 1988, Aurora, Ill., Joffrey II Dancers

LILA

CH Alonzo King M Donald Ivan Fontowitz CO Sandra Woodall L C. Miller JP 1 Mar. 1991, New York State Theater, Lincoln Center, N.Y.C. D V. Madonia and B. Rodriguez, B. Phillips, J. Gates, K. Sagami, Jenny Sandler, A. Smith, Philip Gardner WP 3 Nov. 1989, Theater Artaud, San Francisco, LINES Dance Co.

RUNAWAY TRAIN

CH Christopher d'Amboise M B. Bartók, "Dance Suite" CO Holly Hynes L Mark Stanley WP 5 Mar. 1991, New York State Theater, Lincoln Center, N.Y.C. D T. LeBlanc and T. Walters with N. Duffy, K. Ginden, J. Sandler, A. Smith, Kyle Ahmed, Pascal Benichou, P. Gardner, Glen Harris CN A. Lewis

EMPYREAN DANCES

CH E. Stierle M Howard Hanson, Piano Concerto in G Major CO J. D. Ridge S C. Baird L TS WP 5 Mar. 1991, New York State Theater, Lincoln Center, N.Y.C. D D. Dawn, D. Baudendistel, J. Gates, T. Mossbrucker, K. Sagami, Pierre Lockett, L. Salgado, A. Sklute, M. Barton, L. Bechtold, C. Giannini, J. Janus, J. Snyder, Alexander Brady, B. Phillips, R. Plaut, Gregory Taylor, M. Wuest CN A. Lewis PI SB

PANORAMAGRAM

CH Charles Moulton M Bill Obrecht (commissioned) CO Frank Moore, supervised by J. D. Ridge S C. Baird L Debra Dumas WP 5 Mar. 1991, New York State Theater, Lincoln Center, N.Y.C. D B. Rodriguez, P. Benichou, B. Phillips, J. Gates, J. Schnell, V. Madonia and 10 women, 8 men

MOON OF THE FALLING LEAVES

CH Peter Pucci M Brent Michael Davids, "Pĕniṗimâkat-Ki'sox" (commissioned) CO Christine Joly L Howell Binkley WP 6 Mar. 1992, Northrop Auditorium, Minneapolis D Miguel Aviles,* Daniel Otevrel, Peter Pucci,* G. Taylor Musician B. M. Davids *Guest Artist

STRUCTURE AND LIGHT FIELD

CH L. Dean **M** Glenn Branca, "Structure" and "Light Field" **CO** R. Worton, after L. Dean **L** C. Miller **WP** 6 Mar. 1992, Northrop Auditorium, Minneapolis **D** *Structure* (B. Rodriguez, P. Lockett); *Light Field* (Cheryl Madeux, J. Snyder, N. Duffy, Maia Wilkins, P. Gardner, D. Otevrel, G. Taylor, K. Ahmed)

PRAYER

CH A. King **M** traditional Muslim chants **CO** S. Woodall **L** C. Miller **JP** 1 May 1992, Auditorium Theatre, Chicago **D** P. Benichou **WP** 22 May 1986, New Performance Gallery, San Francisco, LINES Dance Co.

GARDEN OF VILLANDRY

CH M. Clarke, Felix Blaska, R. Barnett **M** F. Schubert, Piano Trio in B-flat, op. 99 (Andante) **CO** Jane Greenwood **L** C. Miller **JP** 1 May 1992, Auditorium Theatre, Chicago **D** B. Rodriguez, P. Gardner, T. Walters **WP** 10 Apr. 1979, L'Espace Cardin, Paris, Crowsnest

LES PRÉSAGES

CH L. Massine **ST** Tatiana Leskova, assisted by Nelly Laport **M** P. I. Tchaikovsky, Symphony No. 5 in E Minor **LI** L. Massine **CO** André Masson, re-created by J. D. Ridge **S** A. Masson, re-created by C. Baird **L** **TS** **JP** 8 July 1992, War Memorial Opera House, San Francisco **D** Part I: Action (B. Rodriguez); Temptation (D. Dawn, J. Janus, C. Corry); Movement (10 women, 9 men). Part II: Passion (V. Madonia, D. Baudendistel); Fate (Harald Uwe Kern); Destinies (8 women, 5 men). Part III: Frivolity (T. LeBlanc); Variation (16 women). Part IV: Passion (V. Madonia); Frivolity (T. LeBlanc); Action (B. Rodriguez); Fate (H. U. Kern); Hero (D. Baudendistel); Destinies (12 women, 12 men) **CN** A. Lewis, with members of San Francisco Symphony **WP** 13 Apr. 1933, Théâtre de Monte Carlo, Monte Carlo, Monaco, Col. de Basil's Ballets Russes de Monte Carlo

BILLBOARDS

CH L. Dean, C. Moulton, M. Sappington, P. Pucci; **Conceived, Directed and Produced by** G. Arpino **Artistic Supervisor** S. Barnard **M** Prince Rogers Nelson: "Sometimes It Snows in April," "Trust," "Baby I'm a Star," "Thunder" [extended version, commissioned], "I Wanna Melt With U," "Computer Blue," "Purple Rain," "The Beautiful Ones," "Release It," "For You," "The Question of U," "It," "Willing and Able," "Gett off" **CO** R. Worton, after L. Dean; Charles Atlas; George Ramos; C. Joly assisted by David Brooks **Billboard Designs** H. Migdoll **S** C. Baird, for *Slide* and supervision for production **L** H. Binkley, supervised by S. A. White **WP** 27 Jan. 1993, Hancher Auditorium, Univ. of Iowa, Iowa City **D** *Billboard 1.* L. Dean: *Sometimes It Snows in April* (C. Madeux, P. Gardner, M. Wilkins, K. Ahmed, N. Duffy, G. Taylor, J. Snyder, R. Plaut, J. Sandler, J. Schnell, Rita Martinez, A. Brady, Fern Miller, Lin Zhen, K. Sagami, Calvin Kitten, Suzanne Lopez, B. Phillips); *Billboard 2.* C. Moulton: *Thunder* (V. Madonia and 4 women, 7 men) and *Purple Rain* (E. Parkinson and 4 women, 6 men); *Billboard 3.* M. Sappington: *Slide* (V. Madonia, B. Rodriguez, L. Salgado and 8 men), *Computer Blue* (B. Rodriguez, V. Madonia and ensemble), *The Beautiful Ones* (T. Mossbrucker and ensemble), *Release It* (T. Walters and ensemble); *Billboard 4.* P. Pucci: *Willing and Able* (J. Gates, P. Gardner with 9 women, 4 men)

SPRING WATERS

CH Asaf Messerer **ST** J. Blanton **M** S. Rachmaninoff, orch. version of the song "Spring Waters," op. 14, no. 11 **CO** A. C. Giannini **L** S. A. White **JP** 9 July 1993, War Memorial Opera House, San Francisco **D** L. Salgado and P. Lockett **CN** A. Lewis **Bolshoi premiere** in the West Croydon, Great Britain, 1956

A TRI-FLING

CH Randy Duncan **M** Tommy Mother (commissioned) **CO** J. Kevin Draves **L** H. Binkley **WP** 12 Apr. 1994, New York State Theater, Lincoln Center, N.Y.C. **D** M. Gurin, David Paul Kierce, P. Lockett

THE JOFFREY BALLET OF CHICAGO

INNER SPACE

CH Mehmet Sander **S** M. Sander, constructed by Xane Evans/Acryli Craft, Inc. and Alan Panovich **L** H. Binkley **JP** 9 May 1996, Northrop Auditorium, Minneapolis **D** Todd Stickney, K. Sagami, J. Sheaffer **WP** May 1992, Los Angeles Contemporary Exhibitions (LACE)

NUESTROS VALSES

CH Vicente Nebrada **ST** Zane Wilson and Steven Hoff **M** Teresa Carreño **CO** A. C. Giannini **L** H. Binkley **JP** 10 May 1996, Northrop Auditorium, Minneapolis **D** Meredith Benson, J. Janus, M. Wilkins, Lorena Feijoo, Jennifer Goodman, A. Sklute, T. Walters, J. Sheaffer, D. P. Kierce, C. Kitten **PI** May Sofge **WP** 1976, Bogatá, Colombia

LEGENDS

CH Ann Marie De Angelo, Sherry Zunker Dow, Joanna Haigood, Ann Reinking, M. Sappington; **Produced by** GA **M** recordings of Ella Fitzgerald, Judy Garland, Lena Horne, Bette Midler, Edith Piaf, Barbra Streisand, assembled by Ira Antelis, who composed overture **Backdrop** H. Migdoll **L** H. Binkley **WP** of production as one work and, in particular, sections by Reinking and Sappington, 10 May 1996, Northrop Auditorium, Minneapolis **D** J. Haigood: *Dance for Yal* [Feb. 1985, Bolinas, Calif.], vocals by Piaf, music and lyrics by Pierre Brasseur and Michel Emer ("Et Pourtant"), costumes by J. Haigood, dancer (M. Wilkins); A. Reinking: *My Heart Belongs to Me,* vocals by Streisand, music and lyrics by Alan Gordon, costumes by Virgil Sanner, dancers (K. Sagami, M. Benson, L. Feijoo, C. Kitten, Michael Anderson); A. M. De Angelo: *Stay With Me* [1983, Munich, Germany], vocals by Midler, music and lyrics by Jerry Ragovoy and George David Weiss, costumes by V. Sanner, dancers (Taryn Kaschock, G. Russell); M. Sappington: *Lena Goes Latin & Sings Your Requests,* vocals by Horne, music and lyrics by Lorenz Hart and Richard Rodgers ("The Lady Is a Tramp") and Howard Dietz and Arthur Schwartz ("By Myself"), costumes by V. Sanner, dancers (Tomi Paasonen, Patrick Simonello, C. Giannini, S. Lopez, J. Sandler); S. Z. Dow: *The Man That Got Away* [Aug. 1990, Evanston, Ill.] vocals by Garland, music and lyrics by Harold Arlen and Ira Gershwin, costumes by Jordan Ross, dancers (J. Janus, J. Sheaffer); A. Reinking: *Sentimental Journey,* vocals by Fitzgerald, music and lyrics by Bud Green, Les Brown and Ben Homer, dancers (M. Benson, N. Duffy, L. Feijoo, T. Kaschock, Alessandra Lange, R. Martinez, K. Sagami, Andrew Allagree, Steve Beirens, C. Kitten, Guillermo Leyva, P. Lockett, G. Russell, P. Simonello, Guoping Wang)

COPLAND MOTETS

CH R. Duncan **M** A. Copland "Four Motets" **CO** V. Sanner **L** Catherine Young **JP** 23 May 1996, Shubert Theatre, Chicago **D** T. Paasonen, J. Janus, P. Simonello **V** The Oriana Singers **WP** 9 May 1991, Auditorium Theatre, Chicago, Joseph Holmes Chicago Dance Theatre

INITIATION

CH R. Duncan **M** T. Mother **CO** V. Sanner **L** C. Young **JP** 31 May 1996, Shubert Theatre, Chicago **D** T. Paasonen, M. Anderson, T. Stickney, S. Beirens, P. Simonello **WP** 21 Oct. 1992, New Regal Theatre, Chicago, Joseph Holmes Chicago Dance Theatre

MUSICALS, TELEVISION SHOWS, OPERAS, AND OTHER DANCES BY ROBERT JOFFREY

APRIL IN PARIS BALL (A GALA DINNER AND DIVERTISSEMENTS)

"Les Plaisirs de Paris" in 10 Tableaux and Grand Finale **AC** Roberta Bernard **WP** 20 Apr. 1954, Grand Ballroom, Waldorf-Astoria Hotel, N.Y.C. **D** R. Bernard, Jacqueline Cecil, Marie Edith Cornelius, Diana Dear, Barbara Ann Gray, Sylvia Greenwald, Kathrine Gross, Phyllis Loring, Lila Meredith, Sandra Nikolas, Helen Petroff, Dana Sosa, Marty Trent, G. Arpino, Joseph Edwards, Bruce Holz, Charles Taboas, Jonathan Watts

MAIDENFORM'S 1954 DREAM SHOW

AC R. Bernard **ST** Lester Gaba **M** Norman Paris Trio **WP** 14 June 1954, Grand Ballroom, Waldorf Astoria Hotel, N.Y.C. **D** Renée Jeanmaire and Joffrey's dancers (unlisted)

OKLAHOMA!

M Richard Rodgers **LI and Lyrics** Oscar Hammerstein II **Director** Gustave Stern **Premiere** 16 July 1954, Green Lake Aqua Theatre, Seattle, Wash. **D** Laurey (Coby Larsen); Curly, (G. Arpino); Jud Fry (Darrell Henline); Ensemble (Bonnie Forrest, C. Larsen, Diane Lembo, Mary Nichols, Sandra Northrop, Carolyn Okada, Nedra Polk, Shirley Towers, G. Arpino, Martin Buckner, James De Bolt, William Guske, D. Henline, Michael Sears)

THE STUDENT PRINCE

M Sigmund Romberg **LI and Lyrics** Dorothy Donnelly **Director** G. Stern **Premiere** 23 July 1954, Green Lake Aqua Theatre, Seattle, Wash. **D** Waltz Soloists (C. Larsen and G. Arpino); Ensemble (B. Forrest, C. Larsen, D. Lembo, M. Nichols, S. Northrop, C. Okada, N. Polk, S. Towers, G. Arpino, M. Buckner, J. De Bolt, W. Guske, D. Henline, M. Sears)

CAROUSEL

M R. Rodgers **LI and Lyrics** O. Hammerstein II **Director** G. Stern **Premiere** 20 Aug. 1954, Green Lake Aqua Theatre, Seattle, Wash. **D** Hannah (C. Larsen); Boatswain (G. Arpino); Louise (D. Lembo); Carnival Boy (G. Arpino); Carnival Girl (C. Larsen); Ensemble (G. Arpino, M. Buckner, J. De Bolt, Art Gunner, W. Guske, D. Henline, Fran Wilcox)

APRIL IN PARIS BALL (A GALA DINNER AND DIVERTISSEMENTS)

AC R. Bernard **WP** 15 Apr. 1955, Grand Ballroom, Waldorf-Astoria Hotel, N.Y.C. No program available, but R. Bernard and Françoise Martinet were among the dancers. "After their entrance [Lafayette and his aides] there was a brilliant and colorful scene within Mount Vernon presented on the stage. There in a Colonial ballroom setting were gathered many noted persons of that era by well-known men and women of the present day." (*New York Times,* 16 Apr. 1955, p. 17)

HIGH BUTTON SHOES

M Jule Styne **LI** Stephen Longstreet **Lyrics** Sammy Cahn **Directors** G. Stern and Ralph Rosinbum **Premiere** 22 July 1955, Green Lake Aqua Theatre, Seattle, Wash. **D** G. Arpino, Gail Boden, M. Buckner, Robert Bull, Jerry Cole, J. De Bolt, D. Henline, C. Larsen, D. Lembo, Joan Maynard, Cicely Nichols, S. Northrop, Paul Owsley, M. Sears, Robert Vickrey, Carolyn Watanabe

GRIFFELKIN

CH and **ST** RJ **AC** R. Bernard **M** Lukas Foss **LI** Alastair Reid **CO** Rouben Ter-Arutunian **S** R. Ter-Arutunian **Director** Kirk Browning **Producer** Samuel Chotzinoff **WP** 6 Nov. 1955, NBC-TV, NBC Opera **D** Devil Mailbox (G. Arpino); Devil Lion (John Wilson); Dancers (R. Bernard, Robert Brett, Jerry Burr, J. Cecil, Nancy Demmler, J. Edwards, Gerald Gardiner, Margery Gray, Janet Greschler, W. Guske, Judith Janaro, D. Lembo, Eda Lioy, Bill Milie, Anthony Mordente, F. Martinet, Marcia Olsson, Nana Prudente, S. Northrop, Brunilda Ruiz, Tom Scott, M. Sears, Marilyn Smith, Beatrice Tompkins) **CN** Peter Herman Adler

SWISS CHRISTMAS ICE-TRAVAGANZA

CH and **ST** RJ **AC** R. Bernard **S** Don Gordon **Producer** Audrey Leeds Assoc., sponsored by the Exporters Assoc. of the Swiss Clothing Industry, Zurich; The Swiss National Travel Office **WP** 20 December 1955, Rockefeller Center Skating Pond, N.Y.C. **D** Soloists (G. Arpino and A. Mordente), Ensemble (R. Bernard, J. Cecil, Dianne Consoer, F. Martinet, B. Ruiz, Dorothy Virden, R. Brett, J. Edwards, M. Sears, J. Wilson)

CALL ME MADAM

M Irving Berlin **LI** Howard Lindsay and Russel Crouse **Lyrics** I. Berlin **Premiere** 10 July 1956, Green Lake Aqua Theatre, Seattle, Wash. **D** G. Arpino, C. Larsen, D. Lembo, G. Boden, J. Cecil, Nancee Charles, D. Consoer, Barbara Culbertson, S. Northrop, C. Okada, M. Smith, Richard Beaty, R. Brett, M. Buckner, J. De Bolt, D. Henline, M. Sears

THE KING AND I

M R. Rodgers **LI** O. Hammerstein II **Lyrics** O. Hammerstein II **Premiere** 17 July 1956, Green Lake Aqua Theatre, Seattle, Wash. **D** G. Boden, J. Cecil, N. Charles, D. Consoer, B. Culbertson, C. Larsen, D. Lembo, F. Martinet, C. Okada, M. Smith, G. Arpino, R. Beaty, R. Brett, M. Buckner, J. De Bolt, D. Henline, M. Sears, J. Watts

JOHNNY JOHNSON (A TWO-ACT MUSICAL PLAY)

ST Stella Adler **LI** Paul Green and Kurt Weill **CO** Betty Coe Armstrong **S** Wolfgang Roth **L** W. Roth **RV** premiere 21 Oct. 1956, Carnegie Hall Playhouse, N.Y.C. **CN** Samuel Matlowsky

LA TRAVIATA

M Giuseppe Verdi **Director** K. Browning **WP** 21 Apr. 1957, NBC-TV, NBC Opera, N.Y.C. **D** E. Lioy and J. Watts (Act III) **CN** Herbert Grossman

A MAN'S GAME (A TELEVISION MUSICAL)

M Maddy Russell and Jack Segal **LI** David Shaw **Lyrics** M. Russell and J. Segal **Producers** David Susskind and Alfred Levy **M** director Don Walker, arr. score director Paul Lammers **WP** 23 Apr. 1957, NBC-TV, Kaiser Aluminum Hour **D** Nanette Fabray, Gene Nelson, Paul Ford, Lew Parker, Leo Durocher

NEW YORK CITY OPERA (FALL 1957 SEASON, CITY CENTER THEATER)

General Director Julius Rudel **Ballet Director** RJ **Repertory** *Turandot* by Giacomo Puccini (9 Oct.); *Susannah* by Carlisle Floyd (10 Oct.); *La Traviata* by G. Verdi (11 Oct.); *Die Fledermaus* by J. Strauss (13 Oct. matinee); *Carmen* by Georges Bizet, solo dancers: D. Consoer and G. Arpino (13 Oct. evening); *Faust* by Charles Gounod (18 Oct.); *Macbeth* by G. Verdi, solo dancer: B. Tompkins (24 Oct.); *The Merry Widow* by Franz Lehar, solo dancers: B. Tompkins, D. Consoer, G. Arpino (27 Oct.) **D** New York City Opera Ballet (G. Arpino, R. Brett, Gage Bush, Alfonso Catá, D. Consoer, F. Martinet, Marie Paquet, B. Tompkins, Gayle Young, J. Watts*) *Courtesy of New York City Ballet

RIGOLETTO

M G. Verdi **Producer** S. Chotzinoff **Director** K. Browning **M and Artistic Director** P. H. Adler **S** Otis Riggs **CN** Jean Morel **Premiere** 16 Feb. 1958, NBC-TV, NBC Opera, N.Y.C.

NEW YORK CITY OPERA (SPRING 1958 SEASON, CITY CENTER THEATER)

General Director J. Rudel **Ballet Director** RJ **Repertory** *Regina* by Marc Blitzstein, solo dancers: D. Consoer, M. Paquet, F. Martinet, G. Arpino, N. Jorgensen, V. Nebrada (17 Apr.); *The Good Soldier Schweik* by Robert Kurka, solo dancers: D. Consoer, M. Paquet, F. Martinet, B. Ruiz, G. Arpino, N. Jorgensen, V. Nebrada, J. Neff (23 Apr.) **D** New York City Opera Ballet (D. Consoer, Gloria Gustafson, F. Martinet, M. Paquet, B. Ruiz, G. Arpino, Nels Jorgensen, Vicente Nebrada, John Neff)

VOYAGE TO THE MOON

ST Sarah Caldwell **M** J. Offenbach **LI** Vanloo, Leterrier and Mortier; English translation by Lindsay Cooke, adapted by Sarah Caldwell, Clyde Grisby and Eugene Haun **CO** Robert Fletcher **S** R. Fletcher **L** Pema **Premiere** 18 July 1958, Boston Public Garden, 7th Boston Arts Festival, The Opera Group **D** Moon Psychiatrists (G. Arpino, N. Jorgensen, B. Tompkins); Wonders of the Moon Ballet: Moon Fly (F. Martinet), Moon Moths (N. Jorgensen, V. Nebrada), King of the Moon Moths (G. Arpino), Queen of the Magic Moon Flowers (B. Tompkins), Princesses Moon Flowers (Oldyna Dynowska, M. Paquet), Moon Flowers-in-Waiting (G. Gustafson, Barbara Johnson, Denise Winsten). Ballet of the Frozen Kingdom: Princess Snowflake (B. Tompkins), Prince Icicle (G. Arpino), Snowflakes (F. Martinet, M. Paquet, O. Dynowska and G. Gustafson, B. Johnson, D. Winsten), Icicles (N. Jorgensen, V. Nebrada) **CN** S. Caldwell

NEW YORK CITY OPERA (FALL 1958 SEASON, CITY CENTER THEATER)

General Director J. Rudel **Ballet Director** RJ **Repertory** *Le Cenerentola* by G. Rossini (19 Oct.); *Ballet of the Four Seasons* by B. Britten, after Rossini, solo dancers: Spring (Rochelle Zide, G. Arpino), Summer (B. Ruiz, V. Nebrada), Autumn (M. Paquet, Paul Sutherland), Winter (F. Martinet, N. Jorgensen), Fairy Godmother [added to program 1 Nov.] (O. Dynowska) **D** New York City Opera Ballet (D. Consoer, M. Paquet, B. Ruiz, B. Tompkins, R. Zide, N. Jorgensen, V. Nebrada, P. Sutherland, J. Watts. Solo dancers: F. Martinet, G. Arpino)

NEW YORK CITY OPERA (SPRING 1959 SEASON, CITY CENTER THEATER)

General Director J. Rudel **Ballet Director** RJ **Repertory** *Street Scene* by Kurt Weill **CH** Richard Tone and Herbert Machiz; children's number **ST** RJ (2 Apr.); *The Devil and Daniel Webster* by Douglas Moore (5 Apr.); *Wuthering Heights* by C. Floyd (9 Apr.) **D** New York City Opera Ballet (G. Arpino, N. Jorgensen, F. Martinet, M. Paquet, P. Sutherland, R. Zide)

THE BARTERED BRIDE

M Bedřich Smetana **ST** Carlton Gauld **CN** James Sample **Premiere** 14 Aug. 1959, Norton Memorial Hall, Chautauqua, New York **D** Robert Joffrey Theatre Ballet (F. Martinet, M. Paquet, R. Zide, Mary Ellen Jackson, Suzanne Hammons, G. Arpino, N. Jorgensen, P. Sutherland, V. Nebrada, R. Beaty, J. De Bolt)

CAROUSEL

ST J. D. Howell **M** R. Rodgers **LI and Lyrics** O. Hammerstein II **CN** Henry Janiec **Premiere** 19 Aug. 1960, Norton Memorial Hall, Chautauqua, New York **D** Beauties of Europe (Carolyn Borys, S. Hammons, B. Ruiz); Clown (Richard Zelens); Ballerina (Annette Roman); Bear (Jeremy Blanton); Barker (N. Jorgensen); Sailor (J. De Bolt); Juggler (V. Nebrada); June Girl (B. Ruiz); Hannah (D. Lembo); Boatswain (G. Arpino); Louise (Rita [Lisa] Bradley); Ruffians (G. Arpino, V. Nebrada); Carnival Boy (J. Watts); Miss Snow (R. Zide); Enoch Snow, Jr. (J. De Bolt)

BRIGADOON

ST John Daggett Howell **M** Frederick Loewe **LI** Alan Jay Lerner **Lyrics** A. J. Lerner **CN** J. Rudel **Premiere** 21 Aug. 1959, Norton Memorial Hall, Chautauqua, New York **D** Harry Beaton (G. Arpino); Fishmonger (R. Zide); Jean MacLaren (M. Paquet); Maggie Anderson (F. Martinet); Sword Dancers (N. Jorgensen, P. Sutherland); Dancers (S. Hammons, M. E. Jackson, Maria Grandy, R. Beaty, J. De Bolt, V. Nebrada)

NEW YORK CITY OPERA (FALL 1960 SEASON, CITY CENTER THEATER)

General Director J. Rudel **Repertory** *Orfeo* by Claudio Monteverdi, dancers [F. Martinet, C. Borys, B. Ruiz, J. Watts] (29 Sept.); *Rigoletto* by G. Verdi (30 Oct.) **D** Soloists: F. Martinet, B. Ruiz, G. Arpino, J. Watts with Diana Cartier, J. De Bolt, Richard Gibson, S. Hammons, N. Jorgensen, V. Nebrada, A. Roman, J. Wilson, R. Zide (dancers are no longer designated as New York City Opera Ballet)

NEW YORK CITY OPERA (FALL 1961 SEASON, CITY CENTER THEATER)

General Director J. Rudel **Ballet Director** RJ **Repertory** *Aïda* by G. Verdi, dancers [F. Martinet, R. Zide, M. E. Jackson, Lawrence Rhodes, G. Arpino] (8 Oct.); *Wings of the Dove* by D. Moore, dancers [G. Arpino, P. Sutherland, F. Martinet, L. Bradley, M. E. Jackson, B. Ruiz, S. Hammons, M. Paquet, J. De Bolt, James Howell, N. Jorgensen, L. Rhodes, J. Wilson (12 Oct.); *The Marriage of Figaro* by W. A. Mozart (18 Oct.) **D** New York City Opera Ballet (all dancers listed above)

AÏDA

ST Harry Horner **M** G. Verdi **CO** H. Horner **S** H. Horner **CN** Milton Katims **Premiere** 7 June 1962, Opera House, Seattle, Wash. **D** F. Martinet, B. Ruiz, S. Hammons, L. Bradley, B. Culbertson, D. Lembo Talley, Noël Mason, J. Howell, Marshall Damon, Michael Falotico, Lee Fuller, Madeline Meyer, Claudia Bennett, Susan Cedarwall, Marilyn Gyorfi, Joan De Vere, Janet Keating, Dana Lord, Holly Savage, Francesca Corkle, N. Jorgensen, V. Nebrada, Helgi Tomasson, Finis Jhung, Warren Ruud

CHRONOLOGY OF WORKS

LOVE'S LABOUR'S LOST (BY WILLIAM SHAKESPEARE)

M John Morris **Director** Gerald Freedman **CO** Theoni V. Aldredge **S** M. Cho Lee **L** Martin Aronstein **Premiere** 9 June 1965, Delacorte Theater, Central Park, N.Y.C., New York Shakespeare Festival **D** Gerald Teijelo

NEW YORK CITY OPERA (SPRING 1968 SEASON, NEW YORK STATE THEATER)

General Director J. Rudel **Repertory** *La Traviata* by G. Verdi, solo dancer [Luis Fuente] (25 Feb. matinée); *The Marriage of Figaro* by W. A. Mozart (2 Mar. matinée); *Manon* by Jules Massenet, solo dancers [L. Bradley, Michael Uthoff, Maximiliano Zomosa, F. Corkle] (21 Mar.) **D** New York City Opera Dancers (L. Bradley, L. Fuente, M. Uthoff, M. Zomosa with Juliet Arenal, Hugh Appet, Gary Chryst, F. Corkle, Michelle Farr, Wesley Fata, Bill George, Phyllis Gutelius, Lynn Kothera, Michelle McKnight, Philip Maxwell, Seamus Murphy, Jr., Ernest Pagano, Kenny Pearl, Robert Peterson, Nicole Sowinska, Betteanne Terrell, Margot Travers, Christina Varjan, Gay Wallstrom, Marguerite Wesley, Glenn White)

NEW YORK CITY OPERA (FALL 1968 SEASON, NEW YORK STATE THEATER)

General Director J. Rudel **Repertory** Faust by C. Gounod (17 Oct.) **D** New York City Opera Dancers (L. Bradley, F. Corkle, Carmen de Lavallade, L. Fuente, N. Jorgensen, Buzz Miller, Charles Moore, Robert Powell, M. Uthoff)

NEW YORK CITY OPERA (SPRING 1969 SEASON, NEW YORK STATE THEATER)

General Director J. Rudel **Repertory** *Rigoletto* by G. Verdi (20 Mar.), no dancers listed

NEW YORK CITY OPERA (FALL 1969 SEASON, NEW YORK STATE THEATER)

General Director J. Rudel **Repertory** *Mefistofele* by Arrigo Boito (21 Sept.); *Capriccio* by Richard Strauss, solo dancer [Sally Brayley] (25 Sept.); *Lucia di Lammermoor* by G. Donizetti (9 Oct.) **D** no company listed

Acknowledgments

I can never adequately thank the people who have helped me in the past six years, who have talked and written to me about Robert Joffrey, his life, art, and company; who were participants in the history and have given me letters, diaries, books, photographs, and programs; who have opened up their archives; who have done research and assisted me with organization; who have read and criticized the manuscript in parts or whole; who have offered me a place to stay in distant cities; who have watched over my children; who have remained supportive, enthusiastic, and curious. I hope they will understand that I list their names in alphabetical order and omit their titles. I offer each my deepest gratitude. The institutions to which I am genuinely indebted for making available their collections are also included.

Pegeen H. Albig; Philip Allen; Laila Al-Marayati; Carol Ann Anawalt; Frank Andersen; Kenneth Archer; Gerald Arpino; Jean Arpino; Ballet Rambert Archives; Ninette Arpino Bandini; Clive Barnes; Ann Barzel; Janice Berman; Steve Boldt; Stephen Burr; Lorene Cary; Jennifer T. Chen; Charles P. Coldwell; David Colker; Gardner Compton; Rima Corben; Francesca Corkle; Richard J. Cross; Virginia Cross; Francis Cunningham; Kitty Cunningham; Edith D'Addario; Dance Collection, New York Public Library for the Performing Arts; Daniel Darst; Katharine Cunningham Darst; Ann Marie De Angelo; George Dorris; Clem Egan; Alex Ewing; Craig Fisher; Gloria Fokine; Denyce Freeman; Bill Goldstein; Beryl Goldwyn; Jonnie Greene; Robert Greskovic; Bruce Handler; Kalindi Akolekar Handler; Clark Hansen; Julie H. Hansen; Harkness Foundations for Dance; Jack Harpman; Diana Haskell; Millicent Hodson; Christian Holder; Rosa Elena Huezo; Karen Irvin; George Jackson; Jacob's Pillow Dance Festival; Veronica Jordan; Kabul University; Harvey Kaslow; Claudia Keene; Deno Kiddé; Tom Kiddé; Lisa Klinck; Leslie Kopp; Coby Larsen; Lileen Lay; Thaïs Leavitt; Dianne Consoer Leech; Roy Leeper; William Leighton; Omar K. Lerman; Herbert Lindenberger; Lili Cockerille Livingston; Mark Locher; Midge Mackenzie; P. W. Manchester; Donna Marberger; Françoise Martinet; Noël Mason; Alicia McDonough; Jan B. McGrath; Herbert Migdoll; Roberta Bernard Mitchell; Marcia Pinto Moe; Richard D. Moe; Robert A. L. Mortvedt Library, Pacific Lutheran University; Monica Moseley; Tom Mulvihill; Muslim Women's League; Marie Paquet Nesson; Newberry Library, Chicago Dance Archive; Madeleine Nichols; 92nd Street YM–YWHA Library; Martha Nishitani; Judy Nollar; May O'Donnell; Norton Owen; Barbara Palfy; Margaret Powell; Jane Pritchard; Shields Remine; Renée Renouf; Barbara C. Roberts; Gary Roberts; Garth Rogers; Richard Rouilard; Brunilda Ruiz Sutherland; San Francisco Performing Arts Library and Museum; Margo Sappington; Eugénie Schlueter; Tom Schoff; Seattle Public Library; Seattle Public Schools Archives; Naim Shah; Pakhtun Shah; Steven Siegel; Theodosia Skowronek-Nassar; Robert C. Smith; Alice B. Spalding; Hobart A. Spalding; Zaman S. Stanizai; Diane Lembo Talley; Kyle Taylor; Alfred S. Terlizzi; Glen Tetley; Thirteen/WNET, *Dance in America*; Eleanor H. Toews; Buddy Treviño; Susan Treviño; Marie Denunzio Turner; Richard Turner; Jack Viertel; Jonathan Watts; Lillian Wellein; William Weslow; Glenn White;

441

Acknowledgments

Laura Wise; Amnon Yariv; Bill Yeomans; Suzie Yeomans; Henry Young; Bertha Zamalloa; Rochelle Zide-Booth; Elizabeth Zimmer.

Richard N. Philp, editor of *Dance Magazine,* turned over to me his life's work on Robert Joffrey. His graciousness went beyond bounds. I am inestimably grateful to him. I also thank Lois Draegin for giving me her unpublished interviews (1984–85) with Joffrey and members of his company. Joffrey's words, thoughts, and stories are present in this book largely through the efforts of Philp and Draegin. Their contribution is major. I interviewed many, many people who are not directly quoted in this book. Their stories informed the shape and content of the finished manuscript. I hope these men and women will understand that I cannot thank them all, but my appreciation for their time and knowledge is great.

Doris Hering was my editorial dance consultant. For her invaluable guidance, unstinting commitment, and generosity with all that she knows and has seen, I thank her. Hamilton Cain at Scribner edited and shepherded this history through development with a skill and grace for which I am grateful. Alexandra Tomalonis was the sounding board for many of my formative ideas about Robert Joffrey and his company; I owe her a debt for reading the manuscript from its inception. Jacqueline Maskey's joyous dedication to dance and her perfectionism were my buoy. I thank the members of my writers group for their encouragement, humor, and insight: Emily S. Adelsohn, Rudd Brown, Blossom Elfman, Bettyann Kevles, Will Whittle, and Fran Pokras Yariv.

My appreciation for Jane Dystel, my conscientious literary agent, is unbounded. I also thank the Capezio/Ballet Makers Dance Foundation, Inc. for its magnanimous grant. Finally, for wonderful Barbara Dahn, who provided me with a studio beneath the eucalyptus trees in her backyard where I could write alone.

As for my husband, Bill, his many sacrifices, integrity, support, and love made this endeavor possible.

Index

Abyss (Hodes), 408
Acocella, Joan, 340–41, 346
Adams, Lawrence, 150n, 154
After Eden (Butler), 302, 410
Afternoon of a Faun (Robbins), 138n, 238
Aïda, 148, 269, 438
AIDS, 327, 333–34, 346, 350, 352, 361, 362
Aiello, Salvatore, 179
Ailey, Alvin, 147, 149, 187, 196
   company, 302–303
   Feast of Ashes, 150, 156, 173, 179, 181, 275n
   Mingus Dances, The, 278
Air d'Esprit, L' (Arpino), 418
A la Gershwin, 121, 122, 127
Albertieri, Luigi, 43
Alcina, 134
Alexander, Dorothy, 65, 104, 201, 206
Allegro Brillante (Balanchine), 135, 146, 396
Allen, Ivan, 109
Alonso, Alicia, 46, 116, 361
Altered States (Kachadurian), 428
Alvin Theatre, New York, 74
Amant, Saint, 65
Amaya, Carmen, 50
American Ballet Center/Joffrey Ballet
   School, 75–76, 97, 113–14, 123–24,
    126, 130, 132, 136–37, 139, 142,
    146, 165–66, 167, 189, 191, 195,
    203–5, 206, 236, 267, 318, 330, 347,
    350, 362
   apprentices, 205, 210, 219, 227–28, 229,
    234, 239, 252, 255–56, 260
   and Ford Foundation, 167, 187, 202,
    205
American Ballet Center Company, 124–35,
   395–96
   reviews, 129, 131
   tour, 124, 128–31
American ballet and dance, 39, 42, 45, 47,
   49, 51, 65, 72, 87, 90, 102–3, 127,
   129–30, 134, 139, 144, 165, 184,
   200, 206, 210, 215, 232, 238, 243,
   249, 280, 302, 310, 312, 335, 355
   and Joffrey, 199–201, 205, 317
American Ballet Theatre, 44n, 65, 132, 134,
   147, 165, 172, 179, 187–88, 190,
   200, 201–2, 209, 211, 212n, 219,
   220, 227, 231, 232, 233, 239, 269,
   271, 273, 281, 284n, 286–87, 299,
   302, 304–5, 314–15, 323–24, 360
   ABT II, 256n, 323, 336, 362
   and National Endowment for the Arts,
    206–7
   school, 115, 116
   See also Ballet Theatre
American Dance Festival, 74
American Festival Ballet, 144
American Guild of Musical Artists (AGMA),
   76, 191n, 274
American National Theater and Academy
   (ANTA), 152
Amory, Alice, 122
Anderson, Jack, 300
Andrew, Thomas, 131, 183
Animus (Arpino), 406
Annie Get Your Gun, 62, 63, 87
Anniversary Pas de Deux (Arpino), 427
Apollo (Balanchine), 136
L'Après-midi d'un faune (Nijinsky), 30, 123,
   318–20, 342, 345, 421
April in Paris Ball, Waldorf-Astoria Hotel,
   76, 434, 435
Araiz, Oscar, 305, 314
Archer, Kenneth, 335, 339, 343, 345, 351,
   360
Architectural Digest, 334
Arcs and Angels (Arpino), 402
Arden Court (P. Taylor), 426
Ardolino, Emile, 309–10

Arenal, Electa, 61–62, 64, 255
Argonaut, 119
Arnault, Ron, 358
Arova, Sonia, 92n, 115
Arpino, Anna Santanastasio, 35, 36, 55, 63, 64
Arpino, Gerald (Jerry), 10, 22, 24, 25
  as assistant director, 189, 204, 214, 304, 315
  birth, 34
  and Bliss, 270, 333, 351–52, 356–59
  as chief choreographer, 220, 251–52, 267, 281
  childhood, 35
  as choreographer, 50, 87, 105, 136–39, 141–42, 147–49, 151, 159, 166, 169, 175, 184, 186, 201, 206, 210–12, 216, 225, 242–44, 270-71, 326, 344, 348, 361
  and collaboration, 159, 175, 220–21, 226, 251–53, 260, 360
  and critics, 252
  as dancer, 50, 52, 57, 59, 62–64, 66, 68–69, 73–74, 89, 100–101, 105, 109, 118, 120-22, 125, 129, 130–31, 135, 146–48, 149, 184, 189, 216, 225
  dance training, 37, 38–53, 57–59, 63
  described, 34, 59, 101
  education, 35, 68
  family, 34–35, 55–56, 63
  finances, 116, 142, 360
  first exposure to ballet, 36–37
  Gerald Arpino and Company, 136
  and Harkness, 147–49, 151, 159, 167, 169–70, 173, 181–82, 188–89, 199
  health-food store, 116
  and Howell (*see* James Howell)
  influence, 252–361
  injury, 148, 234
  as Joffrey's lover, 22, 37–62
  as Joffrey's partner, 62 et seq.
  as Joffrey's successor, 349-50, 351-52, 355–64
  and Kennedy children, 175–76
  and musicals, 62, 87, 89
  and New Age, 264–65
  nickname, 100
  as nurturer, 63
  original name, 34
  personality, 56, 100–101, 149, 201, 220, 225
  religion, 35, 36, 48
  resignation, 358–59
  reviews, 87, 211, 212, 216, 242–43, 250, 281, 310
  in Seattle, 22, 36–53, 79, 87, 91, 148
  and Sokolow, 171
  as teacher, 59n, 75–76
  on television, 310
  and Wells, 41, 45, 50
  and World War II, 34, 35–37, 41, 49, 55, 101n
Arpino, Gerald, ballets
  Berkeley, 264–65
  costumes for, 136, 138, 176, 226, 254, 265
  lighting for, 49, 138, 264
  makeup, 254
  misfits in, 105, 225
  music for, 136–37, 138, 148, 151, 212, 213, 219, 226, 254, 260, 326, 360
  reviewed, 136, 137, 146, 242–43, 249, 255, 266, 276
  sets for, 137, 213, 226, 253, 276, 361
Arpino, Jean (Jeannie), 35, 36, 56, 63, 248
Arpino, Luigi, 34–35
Arpino, Ninette, 36, 56, 63
Arthur, Charthel, 204, 210, 231, 296, 304, 362
Ashton, Frederick, 82, 84, 164, 215, 216, 242, 243–44, 267, 268, 271, 298, 300, 303
  ballets, 84, 243, 267, 272, 276, 297–98, 299, 300–301, 325, 336, 338, 340
Astaire, Fred, 25, 27, 53
  and Ginger Rogers, 26
Astarte (Joffrey), 11–13, 79, 160, 244–51, 252, 253, 256–57, 260, 266, 293, 302, 309, 310, 403
As Time Goes By (Tharp), 281, 413
Atlanta Civic Ballet, 104, 206
At the Dawn of Humanity. See Time Out of Mind
Auden, W. H., 9, 10
audiences, 11, 77, 79, 86, 89, 101–2, 104–5, 111, 115, 117–21, 129–30, 143, 151, 156–57, 164, 172, 173, 179, 210, 211, 213, 217, 231, 239, 241–43, 247, 249–50, 252, 255, 265-67, 270–71, 275, 277, 278, 280, 284, 296, 301–2, 309, 311, 316–17, 348
Avant Garde Film Festival, 244
Axtmann, Ann, 228
Azad Pakhtunistan Association of America, 20

Babin, Stanley, 344, 361
Bachrach, Dr. Richard M., 232–35
Bagatelles (Contreras), 139, 141
Bal, Le, 92, 105, 108, 109, 110, 116, 393
Balanchine, George, 51, 70, 71, 73, 76, 102,
125–27, 131–32, 179, 213, 216, 220,
244, 271, 284, 336, 351
and critics, 215, 232, 241–43
death, 328n
and Joffrey, 80, 82, 127, 184–85, 191,
193, 220, 226, 241
and Rebekah Harkness, 164–66, 167,
182–83
as teacher, 57, 187–88
Ball, John F., 202
Ballet Chicago, 360
Ballard, Guy W., 48
Ballet Caravan, 102–3
Ballet News, 252, 331
Ballet Review, 218, 242–43, 250
Ballet Russe Company (Petroff and Gollner),
63
Ballet Russe de Monte Carlo, 27, 28–30,
33–34, 44n, 58, 59, 65, 93, 103–4,
107, 115–16, 127, 129, 134–35, 142,
147, 267, 268, 284, 312
Ballets de Paris, Les, 59–61, 62
Ballets Intimes, Les, 43
Ballets Jooss, 28, 235
Ballet Society, Inc., 138, 213
Ballets Russes, Diaghilev, 30, 43, 51, 58, 83,
216, 281, 286, 318, 341, 344–45
Ballets: U.S.A., 144, 232, 238
Ballet Theatre, 44n, 51, 59–60, 61, 69, 76,
78, 92n, 93, 97, 102, 104, 111, 113,
129, 283
Ballet Theatre Foundation, 93
Ballet Theatre Workshop, 76, 91n–92n,
93
See also American Ballet Theatre
Ball in Old Vienna, A (Jooss), 311, 415
Bal Masqué, Le (Joffrey), 78–79, 80, 81, 392
Barber, Samuel, 147, 164, 214
Bardyguine, George, 154, 179
Barghoorn, Frederick Charles, 185
Barnard, Scott, 252, 269, 293, 349
as assistant artistic director, 356
as ballet master, 253, 261, 295, 303–4,
328, 344, 348, 355
health, 295
Barn Dance (Littlefield), 71
Barnes, Clive, 12, 75n, 82, 87, 200, 214–15,
218, 223, 231–32, 239, 241, 249,

266, 277n, 280, 296, 304, 315, 317,
359
on Joffrey, 268
Barnes, Patricia, 280
Barnett, Robert, 201
Barr, Howard, 116
Bartered Bride, The, 134, 437
Bartwink, Theodore S., 195n
Baryshnikov, Mikhail, 256n, 281, 323, 328,
341
Barzel, Ann, 107–8, 136, 146, 170–71, 201
Basden, Cameron, 297, 326
as ballet mistress, 361
Baudendistel, Daniel, 361
Baum, Morton, 115, 213–14, 217, 220, 226,
244, 273
Bayadère, La, 269
Baylis, Meredith, 228, 330
Bays, Frank, 204, 219
Beaton, Cecil, 285
Beaty, Richard, 121
Beau Danube, Le (Massine), 283, 285,
288–89, 410
Beaumont, Cyril, 86
Beauty and the Beast, 259n
Becker, Lee, 139, 141
Bekefi, Maria, 51n
Bellevue Fine Arts series, 211
Bennett, Isadora, 67, 193, 205, 217, 219,
223–24, 269
Bennington College School of the Dance,
Vermont, 44–45, 47
Berdes, Madelyn, 325
Berg, Henry, 269
Bernard, Roberta, 64, 65, 70, 85, 361
Bethsabee de Rothschild Foundation, 74
Bettis, Valerie, 62, 77
Bickmore, Rex, 219, 231, 268
Biddle, Livingston, 207, 322
Big City (Jooss), 311, 414
Billboards, 326, 360, 361, 432
Billy the Kid (Loring), 71, 351, 360, 430
Bingham, Alice M., 82, 201
Birthday Variations (Arpino), 427
Bjerknes, Michael, 297
Bjørnsson, Fredbjørn, 146
Blair, David, 267, 287
Blanken, William J., Jr., 142, 256n
Blankshine, Robert, 9, 203–4, 210, 227,
254, 259, 260, 353
roles, 211–12, 236, 253–55
Blanton, Jeremy, 128, 363n
Bless You All, 62

Bliss, Anthony A. (Tony), 165–66, 270,
277n, 303–5, 311, 314–15, 322–24,
332–33, 343, 351–52, 355–56, 362
and Arpino, 270, 333, 351–52, 356–59
Bliss, Sally Brayley, 256, 270, 304, 315, 324,
325, 330–31, 336, 341, 349, 351–52,
356–57, 362
Blum, Anthony, 239
Bolender, Todd, 116
Whirligig, 116–17
Bolm, Adolph, 43, 179
Bolshoi Ballet, 65, 179, 184, 186, 211n
Borger, Irene, 327
Boris, Ruthanna, 226, 227
Cakewalk, 220–226, 227, 232, 236, 237
Borys, Carolyn, 135
Borzoi Book of Ballets, The, 46, 267
Boston Ballet, 342
Boston Opera, 98
Bostwick, Ronald, 204
Botka, Lola, 28n, 235–36
Bournonville, August
ballets, 146, 179–80, 184, 237, 243, 336
Bourrée Fantasque (Balanchine), 105
Boxes (M. Wilde), 404
Bradley, Lisa (Rita), 9, 80, 132–33, 146, 177,
184, 191n, 195, 199, 210, 239, 246,
259, 260
accidents, 184
health, 259
roles, 133–34, 135, 136, 138, 148–51,
154, 183–84, 186, 211, 219, 224,
226, 232, 236, 246
and Ulanova, 186
Brassell, Robert, 204, 210
Bremen, Arnold N., 361
Brenaa, Hans, 243
Briansky, Oleg, 172
Bridegroom Called Death, A (de Mille), 420
Brigadoon, 134, 438
Brockway, Merrill, 206, 219, 309
Brooklyn Academy of Music, 118, 119, 211,
361
Brooklyn High School for Homemaking, 73
Brooklyn Museum, 69
Brouillards (Cranko), 419
Brown, Vida, 127
Browne, Leslie, 328
Browne, Richard, 228, 239, 268
Browning, Kirk, 88, 118n
Bruhn, Erik, 58, 61, 92n, 93, 101, 113, 115,
145, 166, 168, 188, 318
and Rebekah Harkness, 183

Brunson, Perry, 228, 260
Buckle, Richard, 86
Bugaku (Balanchine), 213
Burbridge, Edward, 283
Burke, Dermot, 219, 228n, 239
health, 247, 261
roles, 239, 247, 261, 266, 310
as union representative, 274n–275n
Burlington Mills industrial show, 206
Burmann, Wilhelm, 204
Bush, Gage, 128, 256n, 323, 336, 351–52,
362
Bush, President George, 356
business and arts, 203, 331–32, 360
Bussey, Raymond, 204, 239
Bustillo, Zelma, 204, 210, 231, 362
Butler, John, 75, 106, 233, 302
Butt, Dan, 128

Caccamo, Dawn, 325
Cacklin' Hen (Tharp), 417
Cage, Betty, 80
Cakewalk (Boris), 220, 226, 227, 232, 236,
237, 400
Caldwell, Sarah, 98
Call Me Madam, 91, 436
Camera Three, 219
Canfield, James, 325, 326
Cansino, Elisa, 47–48
Caprices (Macdonald), 171, 399
Capezio, Inc., 82, 265, 334
award, 302
Carmen (Petit), 60
Carnegie Hall, New York, 144, 254
Playhouse, 98
Carothers, Leslie, 325, 326, 350
Carousel, 79, 134, 435, 438
Carroll, Elisabeth, 150, 154, 195
Carter, President Jimmy, 317–18
Cartier, Diana, 134, 204, 210, 321, 363n
Casalini, Angelo, 224
Cassidy, Claudia, 107n, 135
Catá, Alfonso, 116, 195, 204
Caton, Edward, 205
CBS-TV, 206, 219
Cecchetti, Enrico, 43, 50, 58, 83
Cecil, Jacqueline, 64
Celebration (Arpino), 422
Cello Concerto (Arpino), 402
Cerrone, Jean B. (Jeannot), 29, 147, 151,
171, 177, 179, 188, 189, 194
Chabriesque (Arpino), 410
Chapman, Rachel, 147

Chautauqua, New York, 134
Chazin, Judith, 64
Chervony, Lynne, 297, 325
Chicago American, 136, 146
Chicago Opera Ballet, 102, 104
Chicago Sun-Times, 107
Charivari (Goslar), 213, 254, 399
Chase, Lucia, 56, 76, 92n, 93, 102, 165,
    187, 190, 212n, 220, 241, 256n, 281,
    312
Chicago Tribune, 135
Chilean National Ballet, 235, 237
Chopin Preludes (Araiz), 419
Choreographers' Workshop, 65, 71, 72, 114,
    340
Choura (Arpino), 420
Christensen, Lew, 187
    William, 65
Christian Science Monitor, 345
Chronicle, San Francisco, 121
Chryst, Gary, 9, 228n, 261, 321, 325, 363n
    and Joffrey, 261–62, 287–89
    and Massine, 261–62, 289
    and politics, 263
    and race, 263
    roles, 254n, 255, 261, 263, 266, 287–89,
        310, 320
Chujoy, Anatole, 201, 211
Cinderella (Ashton), 299
Cinderella (Joffrey), 320–21
Cine-Teatro Tivoli, Lisbon, 154
City Center Joffrey Ballet, 220–311
    finances, 220, 231, 236, 238, 245, 248,
        259n, 269, 271, 272–75, 297, 299,
        303–6, 400–16
    meeting of dancers, 228-30
    reviews, 231–32, 239, 242–43, 249–50,
        268, 272, 280–81, 300, 311
    tours, 247, 306
    to Soviet Union, 302
City Center of Music and Drama, New York,
    11, 80, 114–15, 213–14, 216–20,
    223–24, 231, 238–40, 241, 242, 244,
    246, 269–70, 272–76, 280, 295, 297,
    301, 302–3, 309, 311n, 320, 340,
    360
City magazine, 282
Clarissa (Andrew), 131, 396
Clarke, Mary, 86
Clear, Ivy, 204, 210, 219, 231, 268
    roles, 232
Cloven Kingdom (P. Taylor), 425
Clowns, The (Arpino), 225, 252–55, 404

Clytemnestra (Graham), 244
Coburn, Kip, 253
Cockerille, Lili, 260–61
Cocteau, Jean, 281
Coe, Robert, 309
Colgrass, Michael, 219
Coliseum, London, 255
Collier, James Lincoln, 196
Colton, Richard, 256
Columbia Artists Management, Inc., 88–89,
    92, 97, 101, 102, 106, 108–109, 114,
    116, 120, 124, 128, 129, 142, 178,
    189, 191
Communism, 48, 75, 76, 86, 143, 178,
    180–81, 185–86
Community Concerts Series. *See* Columbia
    Artists Management
Compton, Gardner (James Gardner),
    244–48, 253, 309
Con Amor (Achcar), 420
Con Amore (L. Christensen), 135, 396
Concert Associates. *See* Columbia Artists
    Management
Concerto Grosso (Kudelka), 351, 429
Confetti (Arpino), 251, 406
Connecticut College School of the Dance, 137
Conrad, Karen, 201
Consoer, Dianne, 90, 92, 99, 100, 118, 121,
    128, 150n, 154, 168, 255n
Contrasts (Walker), 210, 213, 399
Contreras, Gloria, 139, 226
    Bagatelles, 139, 141
    Moncayo I, 226, 232
    Vitalitas, 226, 232
Contretemps (Job Sanders), 116–17, 394
"Conversations on the Dance," 313
Cook, Beth, 129
Copland Motets (R. Duncan), 434
Coppélia, 299
Corben, Rima, 10, 160, 253, 269, 282n,
    304, 338, 350, 352, 361
Corben, Roberta, 338, 350n
Corkle, Francesca, 9, 148, 228n, 269,
    293–96, 299, 304, 310, 347, 362
Cornish, Nellie, 43
    Cornish School of Music, 43, 45, 57, 88,
        91
Corry, Carl, 359
Cotillon (Balanchine), 351, 360, 430
Coton, A. V., 86
Courier-Express, 135
Cowen, Donna, 252, 261, 269, 276, 299
Craft, Robert, 342

Cranko, John, 141, 306, 325
Crawford, William, 272, 277n, 306
Creel, Eric, 64
Cristofori, John, 210, 268
  roles, 218, 236
Critics, 71–72, 118, 120, 131–32, 151–52,
  170–71, 174, 241–44, 250, 255, 270,
  281, 285, 345
Croce, Arlene, 242, 250, 276, 277, 280–81,
  310, 314–15
Crome Syrcus, 11, 246, 247
Cullberg Ballet, 240
Cunningham, Imogen, 50
Cunningham, Merce, 75, 77, 120, 132, 187,
  242, 253n, 303
  as teacher, 57
Curry, Penelope, 306, 333, 343, 349, 350,
  352, 356, 362
  as executive director, 343, 355–59

Dabin, Joel, 239
D'Addario, Edith, 10, 145, 217, 229–30,
  261, 330, 349–50, 362
Daily News, Chicago, 216n
Dale, Ted, 128, 154
Dallas Civic Opera Company, 134
d'Amboise, Jacques, 124, 239
Dance and Dancers, 82, 87, 172, 280
Dance Chronicle, 126n
Dance in America, 297, 309–11, 351
Dance Laboratory, 68
Dance Magazine, 46, 62, 67, 69, 76, 78,
  92n, 113, 119, 126, 131, 152, 172,
  187, 189, 193, 203, 218, 223, 247,
  250, 254, 257, 265, 267, 277, 288,
  306, 318, 340, 342, 347, 357, 358
  Awards, 163, 196, 262
Dance News, 53, 60, 68, 69, 79, 120, 131,
  152, 186, 211, 272
Dance Notation Bureau, 113
Dance Observer, 73
dancers, 18, 86–87, 139, 200, 209, 255–56,
  317
  as artists, 150–51, 169, 192, 251
Dancers, 297
Dances at a Gathering (Robbins), 271
Dance Sonata (O'Donnell), 68
Dance Theatre of Harlem, 61, 303
dance wear, 265
Dancing Times, The, 67–68, 136, 137, 184
Danias, Starr, 261, 266, 269, 299
Daniel, Clifton, 194, 215
Danieli, Fred, 132

Danilova, Alexandra, 28, 29, 33–34, 51, 65,
  91, 123, 126, 179, 288
Danto, Joanne, 204
D'Antuono, Eleanor, 134, 146, 362
Davis, Robert, 135
Dawn, Deborah, 325
Dean, Laura, 305, 326, 360
De Angelo, Ann Marie, 256, 269, 281, 286
  as associate director, 361
Dear, Diana, 64
De Bolt, James, 121, 136
Delacorte Theatre, New York, 172, 211–13,
  223, 240, 278, 295
de Mille, Agnes, 77, 264, 312–13
Denby, Edwin, 131–32, 223, 287
Deng Xiaoping, 318
Denham, Sergei, 34, 116, 284
Depression, the. *See* Great Depression
Detloff, Helen. *See* Devon, Helenka
Deuce Coupe (Tharp), 121, 272, 276,
  278–83, 335, 411, 414
  and *Parade,* 282–83
Deutsch, Armand, 329
de Valois, Ninette, 72
Devon, Helenka (Helen Detloff), 107n, 109,
  116
Diaghilev, Serge, 30, 56, 70, 83, 84, 125,
  227, 238, 268, 282–83, 318–19, 339,
  342
Diario Ilustrado, 156
Differences (Charlip), 404
Diggins, Peter S., 311
Dillingham, Charles, 323–24
Dim Lustre (Tudor), 51
Dingman, Edwina, 204, 210
Dirk, Erik, 325
Distractions (L. Christensen), 404
Diverdissemente (Arpino), 422
Dollar, William, 115
Donaldson, William H., 202
Donizetti Variations (Balanchine), 220, 226,
  232, 241, 401
Dorfman, Dan, 306
Dorothy Chandler Pavilion, Los Angeles. *See*
  Music Center of Los Angeles
Dorothy Culper's Dancing School, Seattle,
  26
Double Exposure (Layton), 409
Douglas, Helyn, 228, 239
Douglas, Scott, 101, 115, 205
Dow, Sherry Zunker, 361n
Draegin, Lois, 325, 332, 334–35, 338, 341
Draper, Paul, 77

Dream, The (Ashton), 243, 272, 276, 297–301, 338–39, 412
Dream Dances (Kylián), 424
Dreams of Glory (Saddler), 151, 153–56, 157, 158–60, 398
Druckman, Jacob, 276
drug and alcohol use, 233–35, 275n
Drums, Dreams, and Banjos (Arpino), 281, 415
Duell, Daniel and Joseph, 206
Duffy, Raymond, 98, 106–7
Dukes, Ashley, 81
Duncan, Isadora, 43, 47
Duncan, Randy, 361n
Dunham, Katherine, 50
Dunne, James, 261, 266, 269
Dunning, Jennifer, 359
Duteil, DeAnn, 297, 325

Eagle, Arnold, 224
economy, the, 76, 102–3, 165, 196, 270, 274–75, 314
Edgerton, Glenn, 297, 325
Edwards, Joseph, 64
Eglevsky, André, 27
Eighth Street Theatre, Chicago, 107
Electric Circus, New York, 245
Elegy (Arpino), 256–57, 403
Empyrean Dances (Stierle), 361, 431
Englund, Gage Bush. *See* Bush, Gage
Englund, Richard Bernard, 23, 29, 37, 38, 44n, 63, 71, 201, 256n, 323, 336, 340, 348, 349, 351–52, 355, 362
Epitaphs for a Circus, 252
Epode (Arpino), 297n, 421
Esteemed Guests (Morris), 341, 428
Estner, Robert, 261, 269, 321, 362
Eurythmics. *See* Jaques-Dalcroze
Evening Dialogues (Watts), 413
"Evening of Original Ballets," 80–81, 82
Everett, Marjorie L., 330
Ewing, Alexander, 68, 93–94, 114, 121, 132, 135, 138, 142, 144, 160, 167–68, 176, 178–79, 189–91, 195–96, 201–5, 214–17, 220, 238–39, 244–45, 248, 258–59, 266, 269–71, 273, 275, 305, 311, 353, 362
    wife's death, 270
Expressionism, German, 28

Façade (Ashton), 84, 243, 267, 297, 405
Face Dancers (Sappington), 416
Fallis, Barbara, 183n, 189

Fall River Legend (de Mille), 105
Fanfarita (Arpino), 405
Fashion Institute of Technology, New York, 151
Father Tobin, 55
Fatt, Amelia, 254, 267
Feast of Ashes (Ailey), 150, 156, 173, 179, 181, 275n, 398
Fedorova, Alexandra, 58, 60, 123
Fehl, Fred, 224
Feld, Eliot, 271, 276
    company, 277n, 302
    Jive, 276, 280
    Meadowlark, 276
Fenster, Nancy, 166, 195
Festival Ballet, London, 286, 318
Festival of Two Worlds, Spoleto, Italy, 144, 147
Field, John, 78, 99, 339
55th Street Dance Theater Foundation, 303, 311n
Fille mal gardée, La (Ashton), 300, 325, 338–40, 428
Fille mal gardée, La (Nijinska/Nault), 129, 134, 135, 157, 158, 219, 339, 395
Film, 11-13, 218, 244, 246, 309
Fire (Dean), 326, 424
Fitzgerald, Ella, 164
Five Brahms Waltzes in the Manner of Isadora Duncan (Ashton), 300, 424
Five Dances (Holder), 415
Flower Festival in Genzano pas de deux (Bournonville), 146, 179–80, 184, 237, 397
Fokine:
    Alexander, 58
    Gloria, 147
    Léon, 58, 147
Fokine, Michel, 58, 179, 285
    ballets, 27–28, 59, 84, 268, 284, 286–88, 345
Fonteyn, Margot, 46, 60, 164, 267
Force Field (Dean), 326, 427
Ford Foundation, 166, 167, 187–88, 191, 201–2, 205, 269, 275, 311–12, 316, 322
Forgotten Land (Kylián), 427
Forsythe, William, 305–6, 326
Foundation for American Dance, 202–3, 270, 305, 315, 349, 355-59
Frankie and Johnnie (Page), 71
Franklin, Frederic, 28, 30, 33–34, 51n, 135, 288, 312

Friedan, Betty
  The Feminine Mystique, 207
Frishman, Carol, 64
Frosch, Aaron, 177–78, 182, 188, 191, 194
Fuente, Luis, 204, 212, 325
  as ballet master, 286, 361
  and Joffrey, 285–86
  and National Ballet of Spain, 286
  roles, 211, 218, 236, 285, 286

Gain, Richard, 189, 191n, 195, 210, 216, 240
  and Arpino, 228, 251
  on Joffrey, 204
  roles, 281, 219, 236
Galbraith, John Kenneth, 159
Gallette, Marie. *See* Joffrey, Mary
Galveston Art Center, 296–97
Gamelan (Joffrey), 80, 148, 149–50, 156, 179, 181, 183, 189, 211n, 213, 226, 227, 228–30, 232, 250, 398
Game of Noah, The (Tetley), 210, 212n, 213, 399
Gandhi, Indira, 159
García-Márquez, Vicente, 284
Garbo, Greta, 25, 99
Garden of Villandry (Clarke, Blaska, Barnett), 432
Garden State Ballet, 132
Gardens of Boboli, The (Haim), 428
Gershunoff, Maxim, 128
Ghaffar Khan, Abdul, 19–20, 49
Gibson, Richard, 135
Gide, André, 66
Giselle, 200
  Peasant Pas de Deux, 121, 122, 395
Glass Heart, The (M. Wilde), 405
Goldman, Eric F., 143
Goldner, Nancy, 280, 311, 319
Goldweber, Mark, 361
Goldwyn, Beryl, 83
Golovitser, Val, 347, 349, 350–51, 352
Goodman, Erika, 228, 239, 254, 276, 281, 299
Gordon, Jean, 193
Goslar, Lotte, 205, 212n, 254
  Charivari!, 213, 254
Goth, Trudy, 65–66, 70, 72, 109, 114, 340
Gould, Morton, 276
government and arts, 143, 152, 153, 156, 165, 172, 176–77, 186, 196, 206–7, 245n, 313, 314, 328
Graham, Martha, 42, 44, 45, 47, 57, 67, 70,

72, 77, 86, 111, 137, 152, 187, 205, 209, 218, 226, 244
  Clytemnestra, 244
  School, 228
Gramercy School of Music and Dance, New York, 59n
Grand Pas Espagnol (Harkarvy), 411
Grandy, Maria, 116, 228, 325, 363n
Grant, Alexander, 267, 297, 338–39, 340, 350n, 351
Grauer, Rhoda, 322
Graves, Morris, 50
Graves, Roy, 68
Gray, Barbara Ann, 64, 78
Gray, Maxine Cushing, 53, 79
Great Depression, 23, 31, 35, 142
Greenfield, Meg, 32
Green Lake Aqua Theater, 79, 86, 87–88, 91, 116
Green, Ray, 61
Green Table, The, 28, 235–37, 239, 241, 243, 257, 260, 263, 268, 277, 310, 311, 339, 402
Gregory, Jacquelyn, 135
Greschler, Janet, 64
Gribler, Jeffrey, 206
Griffelkin (Joffrey), 88, 118n, 435
Grigorovich, Yuri, 297
Gustafson, Gloria, 92, 142
  Nina, 92, 97

Haigood, Joanna, 361n
Hamburg Ballet, 342
Hamilton, Gordon, 60
Hammons, Suzanne, 121, 148, 184, 195, 232, 236
Hanniford, Jan, 277, 293, 296, 310, 321
Happily Ever After (Tharp), 417
Harkness Ballet, 145n, 182–83, 188–95, 213, 215–16, 269, 299, 306, 362
Harkness Foundations for Dance, 360
Harkness Kean, Rebekah W., 143–44, 153–54, 157, 160–61, 165, 181, 211, 240, 245
  Blue Blood, 155
  and children, 163–64
  and company, 168, 170–71, 177–78, 182–83, 188–95, 306, 362
  as composer, 143–44, 151, 159, 163–64, 169, 175, 181
  and dancers, 150–51, 152, 153
  death, 155, 195n, 362
  and Internal Revenue Service, 178

and Joffrey, 147–96, 199, 214, 267
and the press, 192, 194
Rebekah W. Harkness Foundation, 144, 147, 152, 158, 171, 178–79, 192–95, 202, 205
and School of Ballet, 182, 270
and Theater, 182–83
William Hale Harkness Foundation, 192, 195
See also Harkness Ballet; Harkness Foundations for Dance; Watch Hill; Westbury Hotel
Harper Theater Dance Festival, Chicago, 214–15, 362
Harpman, Jack, 107, 108–9, 110–11, 117–18, 142, 154, 179, 195
Harpsichord Concerto in B Minor (Joffrey), 80, 81, 88, 393
Harris, Dale, 280
Harris, Louis, poll, 301
Hart, John, 267, 298
Haubert, Alaine, 268, 269, 285, 363n
Hawkins, Erick, 187
Heart of the Matter, The (Kudelka), 427
Heitzig, Rupert, 154, 158
Helena (Goh), 422
Henahan, Donal, 216n
Hennessy, Christine, 219
Heptagon (Araiz), 419
Hering, Doris, 67, 78, 79, 81, 119, 201, 210, 250
Hermann, Jane, 306
Herr, Sharon, 204
Hesse, Robert, 323, 329
Hexameron (Jerry), 337, 426
Hide and Seek (Joffrey), 61–62, 391
High Button Shoes, 82, 87, 435
High School of Performing Arts, New York, 61–63, 64, 66, 69–70, 71, 73, 97, 100, 139, 228, 261
Hightower, John, 239
Hilding, Jerel, 325, 363n
Hinkson, Mary, 205
Hodsoll, Frank, 331
Hodson, Millicent, 282–83, 335, 339, 342–46, 351, 360
Hoiby, Lee, 165
Holden, Stanley, 340
Holder, Christian, 9, 228, 229, 239, 263–64, 265, 285, 288, 316, 321–22, 325, 337
and Arpino, 251
and Joffrey, 262
on Massine, 287

roles, 251, 257, 261, 266, 277, 289, 310
and Zomosa, 257–58
Holdridge, Lee, 260
Holiday, 196
Holm, Hanya, 44n, 90
"Homage to Diaghilev," 318–21, 322
homosexuality, homoeroticism, and homophobia, 25, 37, 207–8, 217–18, 281, 329, 332, 337
Horst, Louis, 47, 72–73, 75
Horvath, Ian (Ernest), 204, 210, 218
to ABT, 240
and Cleveland/San José Ballet, 240
death, 327
Hotel Astoria, St. Petersburg, 180–81
House and Garden, 291
House of Sorrows. See Feast of Ashes
Howard, David, 201
Howell, James, 180, 276
as Arpino's assistant, 136–37, 148, 170, 201, 230, 251–52, 260, 261, 264, 326
as dancer, 166, 168–69, 195, 210, 230
death, 327
Hudson Review, 131, 345
Huffman, Gregory, 256, 310, 327
Hughes, Allen, 172, 192–94, 211, 213, 215
Humphrey, Doris, 75, 76–77, 209
Humphrey–Weidman Studio Theatre, New York, 66
Hurok, Sol, 107, 166, 179, 188, 190, 213, 215
Hutchinson, Ann, 61, 113, 238n

I AM religion, 48-49, 55, 74, 160, 294
Ichino, Nancy, 256
Illuminations (Ashton), 300, 421
Incubus (Arpino), 148–49, 156, 173–74, 176, 210, 211, 213, 225, 237, 397
Initiation (R. Duncan), 434
injuries to dancers, 109–11, 148, 213, 229, 230, 232–33, 239
Inner Space (Sander), 433
International Ballet, Marquis de Cuevas, 143
International Ballet Competition, Jackson, Miss., 297, 317, 339
International Theater Institute (I.T.I.), 297
Interplay (Robbins), 238, 276, 280, 411
Invitations (Andrew), 135, 396
Isaksen, Lone, 80, 145–46, 184, 191n, 245
and Harkness Ballet, 195, 240, 299
roles, 149–50
Italian Suite (Arpino), 425

Jabczenski, Celeste, 325, 326
Jackpot (Arpino), 276, 411
Jackson, Denise, 261, 269, 295, 300, 304,
    320, 325
Jackson, Mary Ellen, 121
Jacob's Pillow Dance Festival, 71, 76, 131,
    196, 209, 211, 216, 217, 240, 256,
    273, 317, 340
Jaenn, Esther, 204
Jaffa Khan, Dollha Anver Bey Doulat. See
    Joffrey, Joseph
Jamboree (Arpino), 297n, 425
Janus, Julie, 297
Jaques-Dalcroze, Emile
    Eurhythmics, 42, 83
Jazz Calendar (Ashton), 243, 300, 418
Jeanmaire, Renée "Zizi," 60
Jerome Robbins Film Archive, 309
Jerry, Philip, 256, 321, 325, 337, 363n
Jeu de Cartes (Cranko), 306, 414
Jhung, Finis, 148, 154, 195, 214n, 299
Jillana, 115, 123, 124
Jinx (L. Christensen), 404
Jive (Feld), 276, 280, 411
Joel, Lydia, 187
Joffrey, Joseph (Dollha Anver Bey Jaffa
    Khan, Doulat Khan) (father), 17–26,
    37, 43, 46, 48, 56, 119, 124, 128,
    142, 160, 170n, 190, 291–92
    Americanization, 20–21
    birth, 18
    death, 282n, 291
    emigration, 19–20
    ethnicity, 19, 21
    family, 19–20
    marriage, 21
    as Muslim, 17, 19, 20–21
    restaurant, 20, 21, 23, 26, 48, 170n
Joffrey, Marcus (Marcus Khan) (uncle),
    25–26, 27, 50, 119, 235
Joffrey, Mary (Marie Gallette) (mother), 17,
    21–23, 25, 36, 37, 52, 69, 119, 160,
    292–93, 353
    death, 334
    religion, 21–22
    as violinist, 21, 22, 36
Joffrey, Robert
    aloofness, 111, 145, 168–69, 183,
        188–93, 199, 228–30, 234, 245,
        275n, 305, 321–22, 343
    and American Ballet Center Company,
        124–35
    as Arpino's adversary, 141, 220
    and Arpino family, 56, 63
    as artistic director, 18, 52–53, 64–66,
        76–79, 84, 91, 114, 117, 120, 130,
        135, 155–56, 159–60, 173, 183, 189,
        214–16, 223–30, 238, 244, 268,
        272–75, 282, 293, 298–99, 345–46
    asthma, 23–24, 52–53, 61, 78, 92, 234,
        245, 338, 344
    awards and prizes, 26, 196, 291, 302
    background, 17, 23–24, 126, 160, 193,
        291–92
    and Balanchine, 57, 71, 73, 80, 82, 125,
        127
    and ballet competitions, 297
    and Ballets de Paris, 60–61
    birth, 17, 22
    and books, 29, 46, 68
    and celebrities, 175, 262
    childhood, 17, 23–30
    as choreographer, 11, 26, 52–53, 61–62,
        64–70, 73, 76–82, 85–87, 91, 98,
        108, 114–15, 118, 148, 166, 186,
        226, 244, 251, 268, 291, 293 (*see
        also* titles of individual works)
    and City Center Joffrey Ballet, 220–311
    and collaboration, 70, 128, 220–21, 223,
        227, 238, 246, 282, 343
    contracts AIDS, 333–34, 337–38, 340,
        345–53
    as dancer, 26–28, 31–33, 41–53, 57–64,
        68–69, 74, 261, 268, 349
    dance training, 24–27, 34, 38–53, 57–61
    death, 49, 155, 160, 188, 289, 327, 333,
        338, 352–53
    and Diaghilev, 30, 56, 70, 125
    eclecticism, 52, 66, 71, 77–79, 82, 101,
        127, 139, 173, 206, 227
    education, 23, 25–26, 31–32, 41, 45–46,
        56–57, 60, 68, 71
    and establishing a company, 26, 27, 39,
        42, 45, 49, 61, 64–66, 71, 74, 84, 86,
        88, 91, 152
    esthetic, 18, 29, 39, 42, 45, 65, 67,
        77–79, 99, 101, 120, 125–28, 136,
        144, 209, 226–27, 241, 250, 282,
        303, 341
    family, 19–20, 24–25, 37, 49–50, 282n,
        291–93
    and father, 18–26, 37, 56, 124, 128, 142,
        170n, 190, 291–92
    finances, 37, 60, 64, 80, 82, 92, 97,
        113–14, 116, 124, 139, 165–68, 190,
        200

first exposure to ballet, 25, 27–30

first solo concert, 52–53, 391

friends, 17, 23, 29, 32, 37, 45, 88

funeral, 353

and Gerald Arpino, 36 et seq.

and Harkness, 143–44, 147–96, 214, 267, 332 (breakup, 155, 157, 187–96, 199, 340)

homes, 22, 26, 45, 49, 56, 62, 75, 130, 265, 334–35, 347

homosexuality, 37–38, 50, 62, 126, 292

influence, 240

injury, 74

and International Theater Institute, 297

and Jacob's Pillow, 71, 76, 196, 209, 317, 340

jobs, 26, 27, 59–60, 61

legacy, 363–64

in London, 81–86

lovers, 62, 72, 73, 80, 247, 293, 310n

and meditation, 160, 296

and Moore, 71–72

and mother, 17, 21–23, 37, 52, 69, 160, 292–93, 353

and movies, 25, 53

and musicals, 79, 87–88, 89, 91, 297, 434–38

NEA member, 297

and Nijinsky, 29–30, 58, 73

as nurturer, 63, 100

and opera, 88, 114–15, 118, 134, 148, 435–39

original name, 22, 126

parents, 17, 18–25, 37, 49, 52, 55

parties, 64, 82, 93, 335, 353

perfectionism, 58, 69, 72, 135, 183

personality, 18, 24, 38, 56, 125–27, 247–48, 262, 268, 296, 353

physique, 24–25, 30, 42, 58, 65

praise, chary with, 110n, 141, 199

and predestination, 17, 22

privacy, 17–18, 31, 38, 49, 70, 126n, 221, 226, 296, 334, 337

and Rambert, 81–87, 125

and religion, 48, 160

reviews, 53, 71, 73

revivals of classics, 84, 123, 237–38, 243–44, 277, 282–89, 310, 341–46, 351

and Robert Joffrey Ballet, 76–81, 135–220

and Robert Joffrey Theatre Dancers, 88–91

school, 74–76, 97, 113–14, 118, 123–24, 126, 130, 142, 145, 165, 167, 200, 203–6, 216, 227, 349–50

in Seattle, 17–18, 22–53, 79, 87–88, 91, 119, 148, 247, 334, 353

self-perception, 17, 38, 91, 126–27

and Shawn, 71, 131, 193, 209, 217, 273

and Sokolow, 170–71

studios, 64, 66, 69, 75, 206

as teacher, 32–33, 41, 59–60, 61, 65, 73–76, 81, 83, 91, 97, 113, 115–16, 132–34, 147, 160–61, 200–201, 207, 216, 260, 296, 303

and television, 88, 89, 297, 309–10, 434–36

tours, 88-89, 92, 109, 111, 117, 135, 152–63, 178–86, 301–2

and Uncle Marcus, 25–26, 27

and Watts, 62, 75, 80, 255–56, 295, 346

and Wells, 38–53, 57–59, 64, 291–92

will, 343, 349, 351, 355

and writers, 71–72, 118, 120, 131–32, 174, 192–95, 352

and youth, 90, 91n, 92, 99, 101, 146n, 169, 177, 201, 204, 210–11, 296

Joffrey Ballet, 416–33

alumni, 361, 363

American, 45, 49, 65, 90, 102–3, 119, 146n, 172, 181–82, 184, 201, 210, 227, 335

cancellation of seasons, 314, 321, 360

and celebrities, 262

in Chicago, 107n, 214–15, 360–63

and classicism, 125, 136, 179, 184, 210, 212, 229, 259–60, 267, 281, 298–99, 303, 328, 336

dancers, 70, 89–90, 99–101, 111–12, 125–30, 134, 139, 149, 156, 168–69, 180–81, 183, 189–92, 195, 210–11, 231–35, 239–40, 251, 255–56, 259–60, 271, 277–79, 297–300, 316, 321, 325, 328–31, 240, 350, 359

eclecticism, 101, 106, 117, 227, 267–69, 270–72, 278, 315

energy of, 65, 105, 107, 130, 136, 185, 210, 231, 241, 261

esthetic, 101, 120, 144, 172, 226–27, 229, 241, 305, 360

finances, 311–12, 314–17, 318, 321–22, 237, 330–32, 336, 343, 348, 356–60, 363

home cities, 238, 245, 297, 322–23, 360

image, 129, 199, 201, 218, 223–30, 305

Joffrey Ballet (*cont.*)
 individuality of dancers, 105, 225, 231, 325, 328, 341,
 lecture-demonstrations, 156, 158, 183
 and male dancers, 29–30, 32, 57, 71, 73–74, 103, 113, 135, 158
 merger with ABT, 304–5, 314–15, 323, 360
 mutiny of dancers, 229–30
 origins, 64, 76, 124, 209, 216
 and paired couples, 325, 341
 photographs of, 224–25
 and popularizing, 89, 101, 106, 225, 248–49, 252, 277n, 299, 310
 regional, 89, 104
 residencies, 191, 238–39, 244, 247, 269, 297, 327–33, 340, 344
 reviews, 319–20, 325, 244–46
 revivals of classics, 84, 123, 237–38, 243–44, 268, 281–89, 277, 282–89, 295, 341–46, 360–61
 and sex ballets, 172, 212–13, 218, 247, 276, 281, 302, 332
 supporters, 92, 102, 114, 139, 142, 145, 147–52, 153, 155–56, 165, 192
 trendiness, 102, 248–50, 264–65
 and youth, 90, 91n, 92, 99, 101, 146n, 169, 177, 210–11, 225, 361
 See also American Ballet Center Company; City Center Joffrey Ballet; Joffrey II; Robert Joffrey Ballet; Robert Joffrey Ballet America; Robert Joffrey Theatre Ballet; Robert Joffrey Theatre Dancers
Joffrey, Robert, ballets, 52–53, 391–93
 costumes for, 81, 92, 105, 117, 118, 152, 206, 247, 295, 339
 lighting for, 12, 98, 119, 128, 152
 multimedia, 244–50
 music for, 11, 13, 52–53, 61, 66, 70, 73, 78, 85, 88, 91n, 105, 149, 216, 246, 294–96
 reviewed, 67–68, 71, 73, 78–79, 81, 86, 107–8, 131, 250, 295–96
 satire in, 105
 sets for, 12, 85–86, 123, 152, 247, 347
 on television, 88
 themes, 291
 use of film in, 11–13, 244–50
 use of voice in, 78–79, 88, 92, 105, 122, 296
Joffrey Ballet of Chicago, 360–63, 433–34
Joffrey II, 44n, 248n, 255–56, 297, 301,
 305, 318, 325, 330, 336, 341, 343, 355, 362
 tours, 255, 330
Johnny Johnson, 98, 436
Johns, Jasper, 155
Johnson, Barbara, 121
Johnson, Louis, 356
 Moods IV, 213
Johnson, President Lyndon, 185, 206, 269
Johnson, Pamela, 228, 239
Jones, John, 204, 210, 240
 roles, 218
Jooss, Kurt, 28, 120, 235–36, 268, 310–11
Jorgensen, Nels, 116, 121, 125, 135, 142, 184, 195, 210
 injury, 239
 roles, 118, 120, 148, 149, 158, 219, 239
Jowitt, Deborah, 81, 212, 280, 326
Judd, William, 89, 90, 109
Juilliard School of Music, 71, 163, 170, 183
Jurkowski, Krystyna, 256

Kai, Una, 126, 127, 135, 141, 147, 239
Kaleidoscope (Joffrey), 79, 92, 105–6, 117, 394. *See also A la Gershwin*
Kamin Dance Book Shop and Gallery, New York, 68
Karsavina, Tamara, 179
 Theatre Street, 46
Kay, Hershy, 254
Kaye, Nora, 58, 115
Kean, Dr. Benjamin H., 143, 153–54, 157, 163, 166, 167, 169–70, 175, 181, 183, 190, 194
Kean, Rebekah Harkness. *See* Harkness Kean, R.
Kelly, Gene, 25, 53
Kennedy, Jacqueline, 175–77
Kennedy, President John F., 143, 151, 154, 172, 175, 176–77, 181, 257
 assassination, 185, 186
Kennedy, Rose, 177
Kent, Allegra, 122, 123
Kettentanz (Arpino), 251, 255, 265n, 275n, 326, 409
Khrushchev, Nikita, 180
Kieth, Jacquetta, 64, 78
Kilby, Muriel, 121
Kim, Willa, 152, 226, 283, 295
King, A. Forest and Mary Ann Wells, 43, 45, 50, 292, 294
King, Alonzo, 361n

King and I, The, 91, 128, 436
Kingsley, Gershon, 135
Kipper, Barbara Levy, 356, 362
Kipper, David A., 362
Kirberger, Beuhal, 29, 33
Kirkland, Gelsey
    Dancing on My Grave, 275n
Kirov
    Ballet, 179, 182, 229
    School, 183
    Theatre, 180, 181
Kirstein, Lincoln, 51, 80, 102, 121, 131–32,
    142, 165, 190–91, 215, 220, 223,
    232, 241–42, 256n, 284, 287
    "Blast at Ballet," 103
Kiss, The (Arpino), 361
Kisselgoff, Anna, 283, 299, 319, 320–21,
    325, 346
Kitchell, Iva, 77
Kokich, Jerry, 297
Kolin, Marie, 64
Koner, Pauline, 90
Konservatoriet (Bournonville), 243, 406
Korean War, 102
Kovach, Betty, 136
Krasnopolsky, Yuri, 179
Krassovska, Nathalie, 29
Kriegsman, Alan M., 231, 344
Kudelka, James, 326, 351
Kylián, Jiří, 326

Lacrymosa (Stierle), 361, 431
Laine, Barry, 252
Laing, Hugh, 51
Lang, Nancy, 68–69
Laport, Nelly, 360
Larkin, Moscelyne, 201
Larsen, Coby, 42, 44n
Lassalle, Nancy, 138, 213
Layton, Joe
    Double Exposure, 278
Lazowski, Yurek, 268, 286–87
LeBlanc, Tina, 130, 325, 340–41
Leddick, David, 126n
Lee, Stephania, 232
Leeper, Dr. Roy, 327, 334
Legends, 360, 361, 433
Leighton, William (Bill), 262, 269, 296, 297,
    305, 353
Leland, Sara, 128
Lembo, Diane, 45, 88. *See also* Talley, Diane
    Lembo
Len-Soviet Theater, 182

Lerman, Omar K., 255, 269, 277n, 304
Leskova, Tatiana, 289, 360
Lesson, The (Flindt), 405
Lewis, Allan, 350n, 351
Leslie, Charles, 137
Life, 172, 244, 250
Light Fantastic, A (Arpino), 405
Light Field (Dean), 432
Light Rain (Arpino), 264, 326, 424
Lila (King), 431
Lilac Garden (Tudor), 105
Limón, José, 77, 187, 235, 276, 277n
    Moor's Pavane, The, 277–78
Lincoln Center, New York, 80, 166, 167,
    169, 171, 182–83, 188, 190, 220n
    New York State Theater, 182, 220n, 235,
    242, 302, 320
Linero, Mary, 64
Lipkin, Seymour, 232, 236n, 321
Littlefield, Catherine, 65
Lland, Michael, 64, 78n, 115, 124
Llupina, Anna, 186
Lobb, Vernon, 253
Longtin, Anna Marie, 146
Loring, Eugene, 191, 226, 244
    ballets, 226, 227, 351, 360
Los Angeles Ballet, 327–28
Los Angeles Herald Examiner, 9 (Preface)
Louis, Murray, 303
Love, Kermit, 283, 312
Love's Labour's Lost, 439
Love Song (Forsythe), 424
Lowell, Robert, 206
Lowry, W. McNeil, 166, 167, 187, 191,
    201–2, 275
Loyd, Sue, 241, 261, 269, 293–94, 327
    health, 294
Lucchi, Barbara, 65
Lurie, Samuel, 59
Lusby, Vernon, 312
Lynne, Gillian, 342

Macdonald, Brian, 147, 149, 166, 181
    Caprices, 171, 179
    Time Out of Mind, 150, 172, 179, 181,
    184
Mackenzie, Midge, 244–46, 247–48
MacMillan, Kenneth, 166, 168
    Laiderette, 86
Macero, Teo, 170, 213
Madonia, Valerie, 361
Magic Swan, The. See Swan Lake
Magno, Susan, 204, 210, 268

Mahon, George, 207
Maidenform's 1954 Dream Show, 434
Makaroff, Tania, 65
Malagueña (Wells), 53
male dancers, 29–30, 32, 57, 71, 73–74,
    103, 113, 135, 166, 200, 207, 209,
    217–18, 223, 239, 326
Manchester, P. W., 68, 69, 71–72, 78, 81, 82,
    87, 120, 121, 131, 152, 199, 201,
    212, 256n, 284
    Vic-Wells: A Ballet Progress, 72
Mannequins, The (M. Wilde), 403
Man's Game, A, 436
Maracci, Carmelita, 50, 51n, 77
Marberger, A. Aladar, 293, 297, 310n, 338,
    350, 353, 362
    contracts AIDS, 333–34
    death, 362
Marberger, Donna, 334
Marchand, Colette, 60
Marie Jeanne, 132
Mark Hellinger Theater, New York, 318, 320
Markova, Alicia, 27, 165–66, 270
Marks, Bruce, 342
Marquis, Alice Goldfarb: *Art Lessons,* 331
Martin, John, 69, 72, 119, 172
Martinet, Françoise, 65, 109–10, 111, 116,
    121, 125, 132, 135, 147, 156, 168,
    296
    and Joffrey, 119, 189
    and Mary Ann Wells, 44n, 45, 109
    on Rebekah Harkness, 152, 154
    roles, 110, 118–19, 129, 148, 150
    teaching, 195, 205, 362
Marx, Louis, Jr., 202
Maskey, Jacqueline, 172
Mason, Noël, 148, 166, 169, 177, 195, 210,
    227, 240, 253, 260, 363n
    on Harkness Ballet, 213
    health, 257
    on Joffrey, 205
    roles, 213, 219, 239
    and Zomosa, 237, 256–59
Massine, Léonide, 27, 29, 30, 84, 125,
    243–44, 261, 268, 271, 283–89, 310
    ballets, 243, 272, 276, 281–85, 288–89,
    345, 360
    death, 289
Massine Weinbaum, Tatiana, 27, 261–62,
    268, 284n, 285, 287
Maule, Michael, 131
Maynard, Olga, 265
McCarthy, Senator Joseph, 48

McDonagh, Don, 242
McDowell, Yvonne, 204
McKenzie, Kevin, 300, 363
McRae, Edna, 205
Meadowlark (Feld), 276, 410
Menotti, Gian Carlo, 90, 143, 144, 147,
    188, 214
Mercier, Margaret, 166, 172, 184, 195, 295,
    363n
Metropolitan Opera House, New York, 60,
    163, 165, 220, 270, 304, 324
Meykar, Roena, 38, 44n
Mid-America Arts Alliance, 301
Migdoll, Herbert, 223–25, 245, 246, 249,
    262, 335, 338, 347, 348, 350, 352,
    361
    on Joffrey, 224
Miller, Hubbard, 114, 246
Miller, Mayne, 147
Miller, Patricia, 325
Ming Cho Lee, 184, 226
Mingus Dances, The (Ailey), 278, 409
Minkus *Pas de Trois,* 241, 403
Mirage (Sappington), 419
Mitchell, Arthur, 61
Mitchell, Janet, 150n, 203
Mitchell, Roberta Bernard. *See* Bernard,
    Roberta
Modesto Bee, 129
Momentum (Goh), 421
Moncayo I (Contreras), 226, 232, 401
Moncion, Francisco, 122
    Pastorale, 121–22, 179, 184, 225, 227
Mondale, Joan, 313
Monotones I, II (Ashton), 243, 251,
    300–301, 414
Montalbano, George, 228, 239, 268
Moods IV (Johnson), 213
Moon of the Falling Leaves (Pucci), 431
Moore, Lillian, 61, 71–72, 76, 78, 82, 113,
    121, 123, 136, 137, 177, 205, 228,
    237–38
    Artists of the Dance, 29
    death, 245n, 255
Moore Theatre, Seattle, 27, 28
Moor's Pavane, The (Limón), 277–78, 412
Morales, Hilda, 204
Mordente, Anthony, 65, 73, 74
Morgan, Edward, 297, 362
Morison, Bradley G. and Julie Gordon Dal-
    gleish, 102
Morris, Mark, 341
Mossbrucker, Tom, 325

Moulton, Charles, 360
Moves (Robbins), 238, 241, 276–77, 403
Multimedia ballet, 244–50, 282
Murdock, David H., 329, 332–33, 356–60
Murdock, Gabriele, 329
Music Center of Los Angeles, 322–23,
        327–33, 335, 338, 340, 358–60
    Dorothy Chandler Pavilion, 328, 333, 344
Mussman, Marjorie, 210, 236, 268, 363n
Mythical Hunters (Tetley), 421

Nahat, Dennis, 204, 210, 219, 240, 261, 363
    to ABT, 229
    and Cleveland/San José Ballet, 240
    injury, 229
    and Joffrey, 228–30
    teaching, 229
Napoleon, 56, 130, 204, 268
Nation, 131, 280, 311, 319
National Ballet of Canada, 44n, 268, 277,
        297
National Council on the Arts, 176, 206, 317
National Endowment for the Arts (NEA),
        165, 196, 206–7, 259n, 269, 273,
        275, 301, 306, 311, 313, 318, 322,
        331, 358, 360
    touring program, 362
National Foundation on the Arts and the
        Humanities, 206
National Medal of the Arts, 331
Nault, Fernand, 113, 116, 129, 147, 149
    Roundabout, 151
NBC-TV Opera Theater, 88, 118, 309
Nearhoof, Pamela, 299
Nebrada, Vicente, 116, 121, 146, 148, 363
Nederlander, James, 318, 320
Neger, Shirley, 65
Nehru, Prime Minister Jawaharlal, 159
Nelson, Joseph, 146, 150n
Nelson, Ted, 281
Neoclassicism, 51, 127, 184
Neumeier, John, 342
New England Conservatory of Music,
        Boston, 63
News-Review, 118
Newsweek, 32, 187, 219–20, 328–29
Newton, Michael, 329, 332–33
New York, 301, 306
New York City Ballet, 41, 44n, 51, 57, 61,
        65, 76, 80, 93, 102, 103, 115, 116,
        121, 122, 127, 131, 138, 141, 145n,
        152, 165, 191, 200, 209, 216, 220n,
        231–32, 239, 272–73, 299, 302

    audiences, 217
    and critics, 215, 241–42
    first Russian tour, 153–54, 166, 172,
        179, 184–85
    and Ford Foundation, 187, 243
    strike by dancers, 274
New York City Opera, 114–15, 142, 188,
        248n, 272, 302, 436–39
    ballet company, 115
New Yorker, 277, 280, 314, 345
N.Y. Export: Opus Jazz (Robbins), 238, 413
New York Herald Tribune, 27, 71–72, 78,
        131, 134, 136, 152, 195, 210, 219
New York Post, 87, 359
New York Public Library for the Performing
        Arts, 87
    Dance Collection, 34, 155, 218, 241
New York Shakespeare Festival, 167, 171,
        196, 211, 273
New York State Council on the Arts, 236,
        239, 311
New York Times, 12, 69, 72, 87, 88, 119,
        172, 185–86, 192–94, 211, 213,
        214–15, 218, 219, 231, 232, 241,
        266, 274, 277n, 283, 285, 299, 309,
        310, 319–20, 325, 346, 357, 359
    Magazine, 335
Night (Dean), 326, 422
Nightwings (Arpino), 225, 226, 232, 237,
        253, 400
Nijinska, Bronislava, 360
Nijinsky, Vaslav, 29–30, 58, 73, 81, 83, 84,
        85, 100, 179, 182, 282, 286–88,
        318–20, 335, 341–42, 345
    Sacre du printemps, Le, 282, 306, 335,
        338–40, 341–46
Nikolais, Alwin, 303
1950s, the, 102–4
1960s, the, 143, 165, 235, 244–45, 256, 264
1970s, the, 263–64, 280, 283, 306
92nd Street YM-YWHA, New York, 68,
        76–77, 88, 109, 142, 256, 260
    Theresa L. Kaufmann Auditorium, 66,
        76–77, 81, 136
Nishitani, Martha, 137
Noces, Les (Nijinska), 360, 430
North Carolina School of the Arts, 362
Notation, 238, 277, 298
Novikoff, Ivan, 27, 28, 29, 31, 32–33,
        36–38, 119, 200, 238, 285, 336, 349
    Novikoff Festival Ballet, 33
    School of Russian American Ballet, 33
Nuestros Valses (Nebrada), 433

Nureyev, Rudolf, 164, 179, 318–20, 322
Nutcracker, The (Ivanov), 33, 179, 269
Nutcracker, The (Fedorova), 28, 58, 59
Nutcracker, The (Joffrey production), 33n,
    298, 306, 325, 335–36, 338, 339–40,
    341, 344, 347–50, 361, 429
Nutcracker, The Grand Pas de Deux (Balan-
    chine), 116–17, 394

Oboukhoff, Anatole, 57
O'Connor, John J., 271
O'Donnell, May, 42, 44, 51, 59–60, 61,
    68–69, 74, 77, 218, 285
    Dance Sonata, 68, 74
O'Donnell, May (*cont.*)
    May O'Donnell and Company, 59, 61,
    62, 63, 64, 68–69, 74
Oeuf à la coque, L' (Petit), 60
Offenbach in the Underworld (Tudor), 415
Oh, Calcutta!, 240
Oklahoma!, 44n, 79, 312, 434
Olaf, King of Norway, 269
Olympics (Arpino), 201, 210, 212n, 213,
    217–19, 223, 225, 226, 227, 237,
    249, 310, 361, 400
    film of, 218
Opus 1 (Cranko), 306, 415
Opus '65 (Sokolow), 212–13, 241, 400
Original Ballet Russe, 63, 286
Orio, Diane, 261, 269, 296
Orpheus (Balanchine), 67, 81, 85n
Orpheus Times Light (Arpino), 416
Owen, Norton, 217, 340
Owens, Haynes, 228, 239

Pacific Lutheran University, 238, 245, 269,
    291
    Eastvold Auditorium, 245
Pacific Northwest Ballet, 269
    Pacific Northwest Association, 245n, 269
Page, Ruth, 65, 102
Palace, The (Arpino), 159, 166, 169–70, 171,
    175–77, 179–80, 181–82, 356, 398
Palmer, David, 340, 363n
Panoramagram (Moulton), 431
*Pantages and the Palace Present "TWO-A-
    DAY," The* (Arpino), 356, 430. *See
    also Palace, The*
Paper Mill Playhouse, Millburn, New Jersey,
    62
Papp, Joseph, 171, 193, 196, 211, 214, 273,
    359
Paquet, Marie, 116, 118, 135, 180, 184, 363n

Paquita pas de deux (Petipa/Fedorova), 58
Parade (Massine), 272, 276, 281–85, 289,
    310, 318, 335, 345, 412
    and *Deuce Coupe,* 282–83
    makeup for, 289, 310
Paris Opéra Ballet, 52, 190
Parkinson, Elizabeth, 297
Parrott, Lalan, 121
Partita for 4 (Arpino), 136–37, 141, 146,
    172, 175, 396
Pas de Deux Holberg (Cranko), 417
Pas de Dix/Raymonda Variations (Balan-
    chine), 127, 128–29, 131, 135, 146,
    241, 395
Pas de Quatre (Perrot/Dolin, Lester), 78, 81
Pas des Déesses (Joffrey), 77–78, 79, 81,
    89–90, 92n, 98, 99, 101, 105, 110,
    116, 118, 120, 121, 128, 135, 157,
    158, 210, 213, 219, 224, 229, 304,
    339, 392
    in Ballet Rambert repertoire, 86, 214
    in Ballet Theatre repertoire, 92n, 120
Passage (Kudelka), 427
Pastorale (Monicon), 121–22, 128, 131,
    135, 179, 184, 225, 227, 395
Patineurs, Les (Ashton), 300–301, 418
Patterns (Williams), 171, 179, 399
Pavane on the Death of an Infanta (Jooss),
    311, 416
Pavillon d'Armide, Le pas de trois (Fokine),
    58
Pavlova, Anna, 29, 43, 57, 58, 76, 103, 179,
    320, 335
Paxton, Steve
    Music for Word Words, 253n
Pendleton, Moses, 326
People, 333
Peress, Maurice, 138, 213, 219
Perez, Luis, 325
Perrin, Patricia, 236n
Perrot, Jules
    The Judgment of Paris, 77
    Pas de Quatre, 78
Persephone (Joffrey), 66–68, 70–71, 81,
    85–86, 209, 214, 227, 392
Perspectives (Sokolow), 170–71, 173
Petit, Roland, 60, 81, 120, 125, 271
Petrouchka (Fokine), 27–28, 59, 84, 268,
    286–88, 292, 318–19, 320, 345, 407
Philadelphia Inquirer, 216n
Philip Morris Companies, 331–32, 360
Philp, Richard N., 188, 247, 277, 288, 339,
    347–48

Phoenix Theatre, New York, 91n, 93, 144, 147
Picasso, Claude, 283
Picasso, Pablo, 30, 159, 268, 282, 283, 285
Pierrot Lunaire (Joffrey), 79, 80–81, 88, 393
Pietra, Susi della, 283
Pineapple Poll (Cranko), 407
Piro, Lillian, 358
Pitkin, William, 128, 232
Playbill, 224, 248, 276
Playboy, 244
Pokotilow, David, 128
Poppet, The (Arpino), 406
popularization, 89, 101, 106, 225, 248–49, 282, 310
Postcards (Joffrey), 79, 286, 304, 339, 422
Pratt Institute, Brooklyn, 56–57
Prayer (King), 432
Présages, Les (Massine), 289, 360, 432
Primus, Pearl, 144
Prinz, John, 203, 239
Providence Sunday Journal, 250
Pucci, Peter, 360
Pulcinella (Massine), 289, 413
Punch (Joffrey), 52
Push Comes to Shove (Tharp), 281

Quarter Tones for Mr. B (Arpino), 425
Quartet (M. Uthoff), 404
Queen Elziabeth, 82
Quintana, Regina, 232

Radosevic, Ani, 134
Rainforest (Cunningham), 253n
Raiss, Renzo, 144
Rambert, Marie, 72, 81–87, 91, 125
    Ballet Rambert, 72, 81, 83, 87, 89, 91, 111, 214, 271, 361
Ramos, George, 204, 210, 240
Random Dances (Mussman), 422
Raph, Alan, 260
Ravel, Maurice, 138, 141, 151, 219
Ravinia Festival, 274n–275n, 321
Ray, Sandra, 146
Raymonda (Petipa/Balanchine, Danilova), 127
Raymonda Variations. See Pas de Dix
Reagan, Nancy, 328–30, 332
Reagan, President Ronald, 328–30
Reagan, Ronald Prescott, 318, 328–31
Record-Searchlight, 118
Red Shoes, The (film), 60, 104, 283
Reflections (Arpino), 265n, 408

Regional ballet, 104, 187, 200–201, 210n, 211, 274
Reinking, Ann, 361n
Relâche (Börlin/Pendleton), 326, 423
Relativity of Icarus, The (Arpino), 281, 414
Remembrances (Joffrey), 79, 272, 276, 291–96, 298, 310, 412
Remington, Barbara, 232, 239, 285
Rendez-vous, Le (Petit), 60
Reporter, 231
Return to the Strange Land (Kylián), 423
Reynolds, Nancy, 287
Reza Shah Pahlavi, Mohammed, 157
Rhodes, Lawrence, 80, 134, 145, 184, 191n, 229, 363
    Harkness Ballet, 195, 215n, 240, 299
    on Joffrey, 168–69, 183
    roles, 136–37, 146, 149–51, 154, 172, 211n
Richard, Don, 219, 235
Ridge, John David, 339, 346, 349
Rieger, Karina, 154, 195
Riera, Rodrigo, 212, 213
Rigoletto, 118, 436
Rizzo, Marlene, 150n, 154, 195
Roark, Mary, 128, 236n
Robbins, Jerome, 66, 82, 139, 144, 164, 216, 227, 238, 244, 271, 276–77, 280
Robert Joffrey Ballet, 76–81, 135–220, 396–400
    in Afghanistan, 157–58
    at City Center, 216–20
    finances, 142, 144, 146, 147, 149, 152, 153, 165–68, 178, 192, 201–3, 205, 206, 217
    and Ford Foundation, 167, 187–88, 191, 205
    Foundaton for American Dance, 202–3
    internal politics, 153
    morale, 168–69
    and New York City, 120, 166, 167, 171, 188–89, 211
    and Rebekah Harkness, 143–96, 199, 214
    reviews, 135–36, 152, 153, 156, 172, 184–85, 211, 212–13, 215–16, 218
    to Soviet Union, 159, 166, 172–73, 178–86, 191n
    tours, 135, 142, 145, 152–63, 178, 189, 191, 201, 214
    and unions, 149, 152, 191n–92
    workshops, 139, 141, 147, 149–52, 168–71, 226
    See also "Evening of Original Ballets"

Robert Joffrey Ballet America, 191, 195
Robert Joffrey Theatre Ballet, 113, 116
 reviews, 117, 118–21
 tour, 117–21
 and unions, 119
Robert Joffrey Theatre Dancers, 88–91, 103,
 104, 112, 226, 393–94
 finances, 102, 106, 109
 nickname, 107n
 reviews, 107–8, 111
 and social issues, 106
 tours, 97–112
Robinson, Nancy, 269
Rockefeller Foundation, 200, 274
Rockwell, Elizabeth Goode, 61
Rodeo (de Mille), 71, 312–13, 318, 416
Rodriguez, Beatriz, 256, 269, 277, 312–13,
 325
 in *Sacre du printemps,* 344
Roerich, Nicholas, 30, 81, 339, 341, 342,
 344–45
Rogers, Garth, 38, 353
Roll, Donna, 296
Romanoff, Dimitri, 286n
Romantic ballet, 77–78, 335
Romeo and Juliet (Araiz), 305, 314, 418
Romeo and Juliet (Cranko), 325, 335, 336,
 338, 426
Romero, Rafael, 228, 239
Romett, Zena, 128
Rooms (Sokolow), 402
Roosevelt, President Franklin Delano, 31
Ropes (Arpino), 136–38, 141, 146, 147,
 151, 179–80, 184, 214, 225, 237,
 396
Rosenthal, Jean, 152
Roslavleva, Natalia, 184–85
Ross, Harriet G., 362
Roundabout (Nault), 151, 398
Round of Angels (Arpino), 326–27, 424
Royal Ballet, 72, 84, 163–64, 166, 216, 251,
 267, 286, 297, 300, 303, 339
Royal Danish Ballet, 65, 104, 123, 146, 286
Royal Winnipeg Ballet, 44n, 277
Rudel, Julius, 114–15, 134
Rudko, Lionel, 254
Ruiz, Brunilda, 65, 80, 99–100, 116, 119,
 121, 125, 135, 147, 184, 191n, 362
 accidents, 106, 137–38
 and Harkness Ballet, 195, 299
 on Joffrey, 74, 192
 roles, 90, 105, 122, 129, 137–38, 146,
 148, 158

Rumpelstiltskin (Wells), 39
Runaway Train (C. d'Amboise), 431
Russell, Francia, 239

Sacre du printemps, Le (Nijinsky), 81, 85,
 282, 306, 335, 338–40, 341–46, 351,
 428
 and earthquake, 344
Sacred Grove on Mount Tamalpais (Arpino),
 265n, 411
Saddler, Donald, 147, 149, 151, 154–55,
 159–60, 171, 183
 Dreams of Glory, 151, 153–56, 157,
 158–60
Sadler's Wells Ballet, 60, 72
Sadler's Wells Theatre, 86
Sadler's Wells Theatre Ballet, 65
Sagan, Bruce, 214–15, 362
Sagan, Judith, 214–15
St. Denis, Ruth, 103, 209
San Antonio workshops, 296–97, 340, 362
Sander, Mehmet, 361n
Sanders, Dirk, 120, 124
 Yesterday's Papers, 120–22, 225, 227
Sanders, Job, 115
 Contretemps, 116–17
San Francisco Ballet, 145n, 187
San Miguel, Lolita, 65
Sappington, Margo, 206, 219, 227, 363
 as choreographer, 240, 302, 360
 injury, 233
 and *Oh, Calcutta!,* 240
 roles, 212, 227
Sarry, Christine, 166, 191n, 195
Satie, Erik, 30, 282
Saturday Review, 131, 244, 280, 317
Scanlon, Jennifer, 277
Scaramouche (Joffrey), 72, 76, 392
Scarlet Scissors, The (Ashton), 84
Schéhérazade (Fokine), 28, 29
Schlein, Judy, 65, 70
Schofer, Marvin, 66, 68, 77, 89
Schoof, Leslie E., 337
School of American Ballet (SAB), 51, 53,
 56–57, 61, 73, 139, 145, 166, 187
Schuman, William, 166, 167, 169, 171,
 182–83
Schwartz, Barbara, 293, 334
Schwarz
 Hermene, 65, 206
 Josephine, 201, 206
Scotch Symphony (Balanchine), 239, 241, 401
Searles, Baird, 65

Sears, Michael, 65
Sea Shadow (Arpino), 138–39, 141, 151, 155, 157, 172, 179, 184, 199, 206, 210, 213, 219, 226, 238, 239, 397
Seattle Opera House, 148
Seattle Post-Intelligencer, 87
    Seattle World's Fair, 148
Sebastian, Stuart, 206
Secret Places (Arpino), 276, 403
Segarra, Ramon, 204
Seguin, Manet, 116, 154
Selassie, Haile, 173, 176, 177
Seravalli, Rosana, 154
Sergeyev, Konstantin, 182
Shah, Aurang, 19, 20, 43, 282n, 291
Shah, Naim, 20, 24, 25, 37, 221
Shankar, Ravi, 160
Sharp, Hazel, 43
Shashkine, Sergei, 173, 180
Shawn, Ted, 71, 131, 193, 196, 201, 209, 213, 214, 217, 273, 340
    death, 317n
    Men Dancers, 71, 103, 209
    Olympiad, 213, 217
Shearer, Moira, 60
Shollar, Ludmila, 109
Shuler, Arlene, 204, 239
Shurr, Gertrude, 42, 51, 59, 61, 62, 64, 77, 209, 218, 285
Siegel, James E., 311, 314
Siegel, Marcia B., 225, 250, 266, 280, 296, 345
Silva, Donna, 204, 219
Singer, Norman, 273
Singleton, Trinette, 12, 204, 210, 212n, 239, 247, 268, 328, 362
Skaggs Foundation, 343
Skelton, Thomas, 98n, 128, 179, 195, 213, 247–48
Skibine, George, 190–91, 192, 194, 195, 196
Slade School of Art, London, 85
Slaughter on Tenth Avenue (Balanchine), 102
Slavonic Folk Dance (Joffrey), 53
Sleeping Beauty, The (Petipa), 46, 60, 173, 179, 205, 267, 299, 336
    Rose Adagio, 105
    Vision scene pas de deux, 109, 117, 394
Smith, Felix, 150n, 154, 195
Smith, Oliver, 102, 281, 312, 347
Soederbaum, Ulla, 238n
Soirée Musicale (Tudor), 121, 122–23, 227, 237, 395

Sokolow, Anna, 163, 166, 170–71, 175, 213
    and Rebekah Harkness, 170
    works, 170–71, 173, 175, 212–13
Solarwind (Arpino), 251, 407
Solway, Diane, 350
Sommers, Ben, 82, 201, 334
Sommers, Estelle, 265, 334
Sorell, Walter, 170–71, 250
Sosa, Dana, 65
Soto, Helio de, 116
Southeastern Regional Ballet Festival, The, 104
Spectre de la rose, Le (Fokine), 29, 58, 318–20, 420
Spedden, Catherine, 31–32
Spring Waters (Messerer), 433
Squadron, Howard M., 202, 303
Square Dance (Balanchine), 146, 158, 241, 295, 397
Square Deal (Forsythe), 425
Stanford
    Festival of the Arts, 238
    University, 245
State Teachers College, Frostburg, Maryland, 97
    Compton Auditorium, 104
Stephen, Edith, 75
Stevens, Roger, 206–7
Stevenson, Adlai E., 152, 153, 155
Stierle, Edward, 325, 327, 340–41, 350, 361
Still Point, The (Bolender), 407
Stone, Bentley, 65, 82
Stone, Deidre, 65, 66
Strauss, John, 70, 73
Stravinsky, Igor, 30, 51, 81, 85, 287, 339, 341–43, 344
Stretton, Ross, 320
Structure (Dean), 432
Stuart, Virginia, 179
    roles, 181
Student Prince, The 79, 435
Stuttgart Ballet, 216
Suite of Waltzes (Joffrey), 52
Suite Saint-Saëns (Arpino), 264, 297n, 326, 419
Sultzbach, Russell, 256, 281, 310, 312
supporters of ballet, 92–93, 102, 114, 139, 142, 145, 153, 155–56, 165, 171–72, 179, 187–88, 193, 196, 203, 236, 248, 256n, 272–73, 275, 297n, 304, 314, 322, 330–32, 336, 343, 357, 359–60, 362. *See also* Harkness Kean, Rebekah

Sutherland, Joan, 134
Sutherland, Paul, 80, 121, 135, 180, 184, 239, 295, 362
  on Arpino, 138
  on Joffrey, 155, 158, 168–69
  on Rebekah Harkness, 169
  roles, 136–38, 149–41, 154, 183–84, 310
Swan Lake, 90, 179, 205, 269, 299
  act 3 (Petipa/Fedorova), 58
  pas de deux, 89
Sweet Charity, 240
Swiss Christmas Ice-Travaganza, 435
Les Sylphides (Fokine), 29, 89, 336
Syse, Glenna, 107

Tallchief, Maria, 131, 188
Tallchief, Marjorie, 190
Talley, Diane Lembo, 292, 335, 338, 347, 349, 350, 353
  as executive assistant, 338, 344
  See also Lembo, Diane
Talmage, Robert, 228, 261, 262, 269
Taming of the Shrew (Cranko), 325, 327, 423
Tarantella (Balanchine), 418
Tarpy, William, 179
Tass, 184, 193
Taub, Eric, 331
Taylor, Burton, 166, 269, 277, 298, 299, 304, 321, 327
Taylor, Paul, 187, 242, 303
Tchaikovsky Pas de Deux (Balanchine), 416
Teenage Scaramouche (Joffrey), 69–70
  T S (Wells), 69–70
  See also Scaramouche
Television, 88, 102, 104, 118, 206, 277n, 297, 309–10, 313, 351
Ter-Arutunian, Rouben, 152, 172
Terry, Walter, 27, 68, 71–72, 78, 79, 131, 136, 151, 152, 155, 160, 170–71, 175, 210, 232, 239, 317
  and Rebekah Harkness, 174, 183, 194–95, 211, 215n
Tetley, Glen, 90–91, 92n, 99, 101, 105, 106, 110, 116, 205, 212n
  The Game of Noah, 210, 212n, 213
  Mythical Hunters, 421
Tharp, Twyla, 278, 326, 362
  ballets, 272, 276, 278–83
  and Joffrey, 279
Theater ander Wien, 255
These Three (Loring), 226, 227, 232, 401
Thomas, Richard, 179, 183, 189, 195

Thomas, Robert, 261, 266, 269
Thompson, Basil, 260, 285–86, 303
Three Preludes (Stevenson), 428
Time, 13, 172, 218, 219, 244, 248, 249–50, 334
Time Cycle (Bolender), 408
Time Out of Mind (Macdonald), 150, 172, 184, 295, 397
Times, Raleigh, 136
Tipton, Jennifer, 269, 343
Tobey, Marc, 51
Tobias, Roy, 80, 122, 131
Tobias, Tobi, 301
Todd, Arthur, 172, 239
Todd, Carol, 204
Tomasson, Helgi, 150–51, 191n, 229, 299, 363
  and Harkness Ballet, 195, 215n, 299
  and Joffrey, 145–46, 169
  roles, 146, 148, 154
Tompkins, Beatrice, 65, 76, 79, 90–91, 98–99, 105, 106, 117, 118, 121, 125–26, 132, 255
  injury, 109–11
  as teacher, 126, 205
Touch Me (Arpino), 251, 417
Touring
  conditions, 98–99, 108–9, 111, 117
  itineraries, 108, 117, 189
Transfigured Night (Kylián), 423
Traviata, La, 118n, 436
Treviño, Buddy and Susan, 296, 362
Tribune-Herald, 118
Tricorne, Le (Massine), 243, 268, 283, 285, 406
Tri-Fling, A (R. Duncan), 433
Trinity (Arpino), 252, 260–61, 263–66, 270–71, 275n, 302, 310, 321, 407
  title, 264
Trisler, Joyce, 136, 203
Tudor, Antony, 51, 82, 122, 216, 299, 362
  ballets, 82, 121–23, 227, 237
  Tudor Trust, 362
Turney, Matt, 203
Turning Point, The (film), 328–29
24 Hour Liberty (Joffrey), 53
Two Studies: Obsession and Dedication (Joffrey), 52

Uchida, Christine, 256
Ulanova, Galina, 46, 186
Umpateedle (Joffrey), 73, 76, 392
Unfolding (Veredon), 423
Unger, Craig, *Blue Blood,* 155

unions, 76, 149, 152, 191–92, 274, 317
United Nations, 152, 154
U.S. Department of State
  Fulbright grants, 236
  as tour sponsor, 152–63, 178–86, 302
University of California
  Berkeley, 264–65, 269, 342
  Los Angeles, 189
University of Iowa, Hancher Auditorium, 101n, 344, 347
Untitled (Pilobolus), 426
Uthoff, Ernst, 28n, 235–36, 237
Uthoff, Michael, 210, 232n, 235, 259, 260, 363
  and Hartford Ballet, 259
  injury, 239
  on Joffrey, 228, 229, 234
  roles, 218, 226, 232, 236
  and Zomosa, 258

Vaala, Martha, 228
Vaganova, Agrippina, 50, 123, 179
Valentine (Arpino), 408
Valleskey, Carole, 359, 363n
Valse, La (Balanchine), 105
van Hamel, Martine, 268–69, 271
Vanity Fair, 334
van Praagh, Peggy, 122, 237
Variety, 231
Vaughan, David, 82, 318
Ventana, La (Bournonville), 237
Venza, Jac, 152, 309
Verdak, George, 348
Verdy, Violette, 61, 123, 172, 205
Verso, Edward, 268, 269, 285
Vestris, Auguste, 52
Vestris Suite (Joffrey), 52
Vickrey, Robert, 166
Vienna Festival, 255
Vietnam War, 146n, 235, 263
Village Voice, 81, 280, 326
Villella, Edward, 57–58, 61–62, 74, 123, 124, 172, 203, 239
Vilzak, Anatole, 109
Virginian-Pilot, 135
Visualization, 42, 48–49, 58
Vitalitas (Contreras), 226, 232, 401
Vivandière, La, pas de six (Saint-Léon), 417
Viva Vivaldi! (Arpino), 206, 210, 211–12, 213, 223, 225, 226, 237, 242–43, 361, 400
Vladimiroff, Pierre, 57, 121
Volkova, Vera, 123, 145, 147

Voorhees, John, 87
Voyage to the Moon, 437

Wagner, Richard, 150n
Wagner, Richard (composer), 294
Wagoner, Dan, 203
Walker, Norman, 205, 212n, 261, 317
  Contrasts, 210, 213
Wallberg, Betty Jo, 61
Wall Street Journal, 271, 327, 332
Wallstrom, Gay, 252, 269
Washington Post, 344
Watch Hill, Rhode Island, 147–51, 154, 160, 166, 168–71, 196, 245, 252
  Holiday House, 149, 170
Watts, Jonathan (John Leech), 61, 65, 81, 100, 121, 150n, 154, 296, 297, 335
  and Joffrey, 62–63, 70, 73–74, 75, 91, 168, 295, 346
  and Joffrey II, 255–56
  in New York City Ballet, 61, 80, 116, 121, 127, 154, 255, 295
  roles, 68, 70, 80–81, 118n, 127, 146, 149, 295–96
  teaching, 195, 362
Wayne, Dennis, 269, 276, 363n
Weber, Jack, 137
Webster, Daniel, 216n
Wedding Bouquet, A (Ashton), 300–301, 420
Weewis (Sappington), 302, 409
Wellein, Lillian, 63–64, 65, 66, 78, 255
Wells, Mary Ann, 34, 38–53, 57, 58, 59, 64, 69–70, 91, 109, 119, 133, 160, 200, 206, 218, 232, 234, 246, 281, 285, 294, 335, 336, 347, 353
  death, 291
  School of Dance, 38, 44
Weslow, William, 41, 44n
Westbury Hotel, New York, 163, 164, 189
Wetzel, Harry, 329
Whirligig (Bolender), 116–17, 394
White, Glenn, 234–35, 252, 260, 261, 264, 269, 276, 296, 309, 326, 327
White House, the, 172–73, 175–77, 185, 269, 317
  Festival of the Arts, 206
Whitener, William, 269
Wilde, Patricia, 172
Williams, E. Virginia, 166, 174, 201
  Patterns, 171, 179
Williams, Henrietta, 23
Williams, Stanley, 166, 168, 173

Williamson, Karen, 228, 239
William Tell Variations (Bournonville), 406
Wilson, John, 59, 65, 69, 78, 90, 99, 100,
	105, 110n, 116, 121, 122, 125, 127n,
	136, 146, 154, 158, 174, 181, 185,
	327, 339
Wilson, June, 154
Winter Garden Theater, New York, 60, 61
Witch, The (Cranko), 141
Within Four Walls (Joffrey), 79, 89, 92, 105,
	107, 117, 225, 393
Wolf, Mr., 173
Wolf Trap Farm, Virginia, 298
Woman's Century Club Theatre, Seattle, 52
Wood, Donna, 206
Wood, Richard, 239
Woodsum, Harold E., Jr., 202
Workout (Joffrey), 91n–92n, 393
World Journal Tribune, 232, 239
World War II, 31, 90, 99, 102, 196
Worth, Faith, 298, 340
Wright, Rebecca, 9, 206, 228, 239, 263,
	279–80, 296, 299–300, 363n
	to ABT, 299
	roles, 251, 261, 298

Yahiro, Arthur, 68
Yesterday's Papers (Dirk Sanders), 120–22,
	225, 227, 253n, 394

Yon, Violetta, 65
Young, Gayle, 116
Young, Henry A., 315–16, 322
Youskevitch, Igor, 28, 30

Zaraspe, Hector, 205, 212, 227–28, 260,
	318
Zelens, Richard, 128
Zellerbach Hall, Berkeley, 265
Zide, Rochelle, 10, 115–16, 123–24, 133,
	135, 363n
	and Arpino, 136, 220, 225
	as ballet mistress, 220, 227
	in Ballet Russe de Monte Carlo, 115–16,
	129
	injury, 154n
	and Joffrey, 115–16, 125–26, 129–30,
	220
	roles, 120–21, 123, 129, 131, 146
Zodiac, The, 166, 174
Zomosa, Maximiliano, 9, 231, 232, 235–37,
	247, 266
	in *Astarte,* 12–13, 256, 260
	in *Green Table,* 236–37, 239, 260
	injuries, 257
	and Noël Mason, 256–59
	other roles, 236, 237, 247, 256, 259n
	suicide, 258, 260
Zoritch, George, 30

DATE DUE

AUG 2 4 1998			
FEB 0 1 2012			

#47-0108 Peel Off Pressure Sensitive